DISCOURSE STUDIES

 [ ] :

A MULTIDISCIPLINARY INTRODUCTION

SAGE has been part of the global academic community since 1965, supporting high quality research and learning that transforms society and our understanding of individuals, groups, and cultures. SAGE is the independent, innovative, natural home for authors, editors and societies who share our commitment and passion for the social sciences.

Find out more at: **www.sagepublications.com**

DISCOURSE STUDIES

A MULTIDISCIPLINARY INTRODUCTION

SECOND EDITION

EDITED BY **TEUN A. VAN DIJK**

Los Angeles | London | New Delhi
Singapore | Washington DC

First published Vol 1 – 2006 (x2)
Vol 2 – 2003, 2004, 2005, 2007 (x2), 2008, 2009

SAGE Publications Ltd
1 Oliver's Yard
55 City Road
London EC1Y 1SP

SAGE Publications Inc.
2455 Teller Road
Thousand Oaks, California 91320

SAGE Publications India Pvt Ltd
B 1/I 1 Mohan Cooperative Industrial Area
Mathura Road
New Delhi 110 044

SAGE Publications Asia-Pacific Pte Ltd
33 Pekin Street #02-01
Far East Square
Singapore 048763

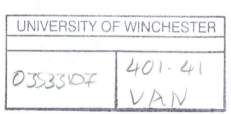

Library of Congress Control Number: 2010934661

British Library Cataloguing in Publication data

A catalogue record for this book is available from the British Library

ISBN 978-1-84860-648-7
ISBN 978-1-84860-649-4 (pbk)

Typeset by C&M Digitals (P) Ltd, Chennai, India
Printed and bound in Great Britain by TJ International Ltd, Padstow, Cornwall
Printed on paper from sustainable resources

Contents

Contributor Biographies   vii

Preface   xv

1 Introduction: The Study of Discourse   1
Teun A. van Dijk

2 Discourse, Grammar and Interaction   8
Susanna Cumming, Tsuyoshi Ono and Ritva Laury

3 Discourse Semantics   37
Russell S. Tomlin, Linda Forrest, Ming Ming Pu and Myung Hee Kim

4 Narrative in Everyday Life   64
Elinor Ochs

5 Argumentation   85
Frans H. van Eemeren, Sally Jackson and Scott Jacobs

6 Discourse Semiotics   107
Theo van Leeuwen and Gunther Kress

7 Discourse and Cognition   126
Arthur C. Graesser and Keith Millis

8 Discourse Pragmatics   143
Shoshana Blum-Kulka and Michal Hamo

9 Conversation Analysis: An Approach to the Analysis
    of Social Interaction   165
Anita Pomerantz and B.J. Fehr

10 Dialogue in Institutional Interactions   191
Paul Drew and Marja-Leena Sorjonen

11 Gender and Power in Discourse   217
    Michelle M. Lazar and Cheris Kramarae

12 Discourse, Ethnicity and Racism   241
    Yasmin Jiwani and John E. Richardson

13 Discourse and Identity   263
    Anna De Fina

14 Organizational Discourse   283
    Dennis K. Mumby and Jennifer Mease

15 Discourse and Politics   303
    Paul Chilton and Christina Schäffner

16 Discourse and Culture   331
    Elizabeth Keating and Alessandro Duranti

17 Critical Discourse Analysis   357
    Norman Fairclough, Jane Mulderrig and Ruth Wodak

18 Discourse and Ideology   379
    Teun A. van Dijk

Index   408

Contributor Biographies

Shoshana Blum-Kulka is Professor Emerita in the Department of Communication and School of Education at the Hebrew University. Her research focuses on media discourse, political discourse, cross-cultural pragmatics, pragmatic development in first and second language and family discourse. She has served on the editorial board of *Narrative Inquiry*, *Journal of Pragmatics*, *Journal of Sociolinguistics*, *Research on Language and Social Interaction* and *Discourse Studies*. Her books include *Dinner Talk* (1997) and *Talking to Adults* (2002), (with Catherine Snow). She is currently involved in research on the pragmatic development of Hebrew speaking Israeli children as a first and as a second language. Address: Department of Communication, Hebrew University, Jerusalem, Israel. E-mail: mskcusb@mscc.huji.ac.il

Paul Chilton is a cognitive linguist and discourse analyst working in an inter-disciplinary and inter-cultural context. He obtained his first degree and doctorate at Oxford University. He has held posts at Nottingham, Warwick, Aston and the University of East Anglia. Currently, he is a professor of linguistics in the Department of Linguistics and English Language at Lancaster University. In the field of cognitive linguistics he has published books and articles on metaphor and spatial conceptualisation and has developed a model of discourse on geometrical principles. In discourse analysis he has investigated numerous aspects of political discourse and critically examined the methods of CDA. He is also principal coordinator of the Leverhulme-funded project New Discourses in Contemporary China. Amongst his publications are *Security Metaphors*, which uses a cognitive-linguistic approach to the metaphor in international discourse, and *Analysing Political Discourse*, which combines a variety of approaches from CDA and from cognitive linguistics. His earlier work included the study of Catholic poetry in the cultural and political context of early modern France. E-mail: p.chilton@lancaster.ac.uk

Susanna Cumming is a linguist specializing in discourse and grammar and related issues, including syntactic change, the lexicon in discourse, and computer text generation. Her primary language area is Malay/Indonesian; she has written a book on constituent order change (*Functional Change: the Case of Malay Constituent Order*, 1991). She has been a faculty member at the University of Colorado, Boulder and the University of California, Santa Barbara.

Anna De Fina is Associate Professor of Italian Language and Linguistics in the Italian Department at Georgetown University. Her interests and publications focus on discourse and migration, code-switching, identity and narrative. Her books include *Identity in Narrative: A Study of Immigrant Discourse* (2003, John Benjamins) and the co-edited volumes *Italiano e italiani fuori d' Italia* (2003, Guerra, with F. Bizzoni), *Dislocations, Relocations, Narratives of Migration* (2005, St. Jerome Publishing, with M. Baynham), *Discourse and Identity* (2006, Cambridge University Press, with Deborah Schiffrin and Michael Bamberg), *Selves and Identities in Narrative and Discourse* (2007, John Benjamins, with Michael Bamberg and Deborah Schiffrin). E-mail: definaa@georgetown.edu

Paul Drew teaches in the Sociology Department at the University of York, and is also Director of the newly-established Centre for Advanced Studies in Language & Communication. He has researched extensively on some of the basic practices and processes of ordinary social interaction, as well as those in institutional interactions – especially in legal and medical settings. His most recent and current research focuses on the construction of social actions in talk (e.g. requests, offers, complaints), which represents something of a return to 'speech acts' and how they are conducted in interaction. He has also done applied research, most recently for the (UK) Department of Work and Pensions, on interviews between advisers and benefits claimants (unemployed people) in Job Centres. E-mail: wpd1@york.ac.uk

Alessandro Duranti is Professor of Anthropology and Dean of Social Sciences at the University of California, Los Angeles. He has carried out fieldwork in (Western) Samoa and in the United States, where he studied political discourse, verbal performance, and everyday routine interactions (e.g., greetings). He has written on intentionality, agency, linguistic relativity, and, more recently, the role of improvisation in musical and verbal interactions. He is a Fellow of the American Academy of Arts and Sciences and past President of the Society for Linguistic Anthropology. E-mail: aduranti@anthro.ucla.edu

Norman Fairclough was formerly Professor of Language in Social Life at Lancaster University, and is now Emeritus Professor. He has published widely on critical discourse analysis, including the books *Language and Power* (1989), *Discourse and Social Change* (1992), *Discourse in Late Modernity* (1999, with Lilie Chouliaraki), *New Labour, New Language?* (2000), *Analyzing Discourse* (2003), *Language and Globalization* (2003) and *Critical Discourse Analysis* (2nd edition 2010). He is now working with Isabela Ietcu-Fairclough on a book for Routledge on political discourse. E-mail: eianlf@exchange.lancs.ac.uk

B.J. Fehr is a visiting assistant professor in the Communication Department at the University at Albany, SUNY, USA. Her research is focused on the social organization of everyday human interaction from the perspective of ethnomethodology and conversation analysis. E-mail: bfehr@albany.edu

Arthur Graesser is a full professor in the Department of Psychology, an adjunct professor in Computer Science, and co-director of the Institute for Intelligent Systems at the University of Memphis. He is the editor of *Journal of Educational Psychology* and has published over 400 articles in journals, books, and conference proceedings, written two books and edited nine books (one being the *Handbook of Discourse Processes*). He has designed, developed, and tested cutting-edge software in learning, language, and discourse technologies, including AutoTutor, Coh-Metrix, HURA Advisor, SEEK Web Tutor, MetaTutor, Operation ARIES, Question Understanding Aid (QUAID), QUEST, and Point&Query. E-mail: a-graesser@memphis.edu

Michal Hamo (PhD, Department of Communication and Journalism, The Hebrew University of Jerusalem, 2005) is a lecturer at Netanya Academic College, Israel. Her research interests include discourse analysis, media and broadcast talk analysis, and the relations between popular television and its cultural, social and institutional contexts. Email: michal.hamo@gmail.com

Sally Jackson is Professor of Communication at the University of Illinois, Urbana-Champaign. She is currently on leave from the faculty, serving as Chief Information Officer and Associate Provost, overseeing the university's computing and communications infra-structure. Her work in argumentation has received awards from the National Communication Association (USA), the International Society for the Study of Argumentation, and other scholarly associations. E-mail: sallyj@illinois.edu

Scott Jacobs (Ph.D., University of Illinois, 1982) is Professor of Communication at the University of Illinois at Urbana-Champaign. Previous appointments include the University of Nebraska, Michigan State University, the University of Oklahoma, and the University of Arizona. He has published on argumentation, discourse pragmatics, and research methods in *Argumentation, Argumentation & Advocacy*, *Communication Monographs*, *Communication Yearbook*, *Conflict Resolution Quarterly*, *Human Communication Research*, *Informal Logic*, *Journal of Pragmatics*, and *Quarterly Journal of Speech*. He is a co-author of *Reconstructing Argumentative Discourse*, a co-editor of *Argumentation*, former editor of *Communication Theory*, and recent director of the bi-annual NCA/AFA Summer Conference on Argumentation. E-mail: curtisscottjacobs@gmail.com

Yasmin Jiwani is an associate professor in the Department of Communication Studies at Concordia University, Montreal. Her publications include *Discourses of Denial: Mediations of Race, Gender and Violence*, as well as a co-edited collection titled *Girlhood, Redefining the Limits*. Yasmin is also a co-founder of RACE, Researchers and Academics of Colour for Equity, a Canadian based organization. Her work has appeared in various journals and anthologies. Her research interests include mediations of race, gender and violence in the context of war stories, femicide reporting in the press and representations of women of colour in popular television. Email: yasmin.jiwani@gmail.com. Webpage: http://coms.concordia.ca/faculty/jiwani.html

Elizabeth Keating is Professor of Anthropology at the University of Texas at Austin. Her research interests include social impacts of new communication technologies, the role of language in social stratification, language and space (including computer gaming space), multimodality, sign language, and cross-cultural engineering design collaborations. She has conducted fieldwork in Micronesia, the U.S., Romania, India, Brazil, and Germany. She is the author of *Power Sharing: Language, Gender, Rank and Social Space in Pohnpei, Micronesia* (Oxford University Press), as well as numerous journal articles and book chapters. She is a past editor of the *Journal of Linguistic Anthropology*. E-mail: ekeating@mail.utexas.edu

Myung-Hee Kim is Professor of English Language and Culture at Hanyang University, ERICA Campus, Korea. Her research interests include discourse analysis, conversation analysis, corpus linguistics, language teaching, and the relationship between language and culture.

Cheris Kramarae is a research associate at the Center for the Study of Women in Society, University of Oregon, USA, where she also served as director. She was a director of women's studies at the University of Illinois at Urbana-Champaign, USA, and an international dean at the International Women's University, in Germany. Her research areas include gender and new media, technology, education, and communication. She and Dale Spender are the editors of the 4 vol. *Routledge International Encyclopedia of Women: Global Women's Issues and Knowledge*. E-mail: cheris@uoregon.edu

Gunther Kress is Professor of Semiotics and Education at the Institute of Education, University of London. His interests are in meaning-making and communication in contemporary environments; with an interest in developing a social semiotic theory of multimodal communication. Among his (more recent) books are *Social Semiotics* (1988, with R Hodge); *Before Writing: Rethinking the Paths to Literacy* (1996); *Reading Images: The Grammar of Graphic Design* (1996/2006); *Multimodal Discourse: The Modes and Media of Contemporary Communication* (2002) both with Theo van Leeuwen; *Literacy in the New Media Age* (2003); *Multimodality: A Social Semiotic Approach to Contemporary Communication* (2010). E-mail: G.Kress@ioe.ac.uk

Ritva Laury is Professor of Finnish at the University of Helsinki. She received her Ph.D. in linguistics from the University of California, Santa Barbara in 1995. Most of her research has focused on the emergence of grammar from patterns of language use. She is the author of *Demonstratives in Interaction: The Emergence of a Definite Article in Finnish* (Benjamins, 1997) and the editor of *Minimal Reference: The Use of Pronouns in Finnish and Estonian* (Finnish Literature Society, 2005) and *Crosslinguistic Studies of Clause Combining: The Multifunctionality of Conjunctions* (Benjamins, 2008). E-mail: ritva.laury@helsinki.fi

Michelle M. Lazar is Associate Professor in the Department of English Language and Literature at the National University of Singapore. She is Assistant Dean in the Faculty of Arts and Social Sciences and Academic Convenor of the Gender Studies Minor Programme at the university. Her research interests are in critical discourse analysis, feminist and gender studies, media and political discourse, and multimodal discourse analysis. She is an elected member of the International Gender and Language Advisory Council and is the founding editor of the Routledge Critical Studies in Discourse monograph series. E-mail: ellmml@nus.edu.sg

Jennifer J. Mease (Ph.D. University of North Carolina) is an assistant professor in the Department of Communication at Texas A&M University. Her research addresses how social bias is built into organizational processes and how people organize to interrupt those processes. Her work with diversity consultants focuses on how organizational actors who are motivated by social justice develop strategies to pursue social change when working with capital based organizations . E-mail: jmease@tamu.edu

Keith Millis is a full professor in the Psychology Department at Northern Illinois University. He completed a post-doc at Carnegie Mellon University after receiving his Ph.D. in 1989. He has authored several articles and book chapters on discourse comprehension and inference generation. He is the project director of Operation ARIES!, a serious game designed to teach aspects of scientific inquiry. E-mail: kmillis@niu.edu

Jane Mulderrig (PhD, Lancaster University) is a lecturer in Applied Linguistics at Sheffield University. She is on the editorial boards of *Glossa, Discourse, and Journal of Critical Education Policy Studies*. Her main research interests are in applying corpus-based critical discourse analysis to investigate questions of identity, power and personality in a range of discourse contexts. Her publications use this approach to investigate New Labour 'spin', discourses of the knowledge economy in UK education policy, and most recently to develop a linguistic approach to the analysis of 'soft power' in contemporary governance. Jane has also published in the area of disability and gender policies, and equality and human rights. She is currently investigating public discourses of ageing. For details of other activities and to download publications see: http://sheffield.academia.edu/JaneMulderrig; http://www.shef.ac.uk/english/staff/mulderrig.html. E-mail: j.mulderrig@sheffield.ac.uk

Dennis K. Mumby (Ph.D., Southern Illinois University, Carbondale) is Professor and Chair in the Department of Communication Studies at the University of North Carolina at Chapel Hill. His research examines the relationships among discourse, power, and identity in work settings. He has published several books, including *Communication and Power in Organizations* (Ablex, 1988), *Reworking Gender* (Sage, 2004, with Karen Ashcraft), *Engaging Organizational Communication Theory and Research* (Sage, 2005, with Steve May), and *Reframing Difference in Organizational Communication Studies* (Sage, 2010). He is past chair of the Organizational Communication Division of the International Communication Association. E-mail: mumby@email.unc.edu

Elinor Ochs is UCLA Distinguished Professor of Anthropology and Applied Linguistics. Drawing upon fieldwork in Madagascar, Samoa, and the U.S., Ochs co-pioneered the field of language socialization, which analyzes how novices are apprenticed through and into socio-culturally organized communicative practices. Ochs analyzes how family co-narration involves children in problem-solving about life experiences and promote or hinder typical and neurodevelopmentally impaired children's development. Selected books include Capps, L. and Ochs, E. (1995) *Constructing Panic*; Ochs, E. and Capps, L. (2001) *Living Narrative*, and Ochs, E. (2006) *Linguaggio e Cultura: Lo Sviluppo delle Competenze Communicative*. Honors include: MacArthur Fellow, American Academy of Arts and Sciences Fellow; Guggenheim Fellow; Distinguished Lewis Henry Morgan Lecturer; Honorary Doctorate (Linköping University). E-mail: eochs@anthro.ucla.edu

Tsuyoshi Ono is an associate professor at the University of Alberta, Canada, where he directs the Spoken Discourse Research Studio. His main area of research lies in the study of grammatical structure based on the examination of conversation data in which he and his collaborators have published widely. He is currently engaged in two large-scale projects with researchers both in Japan and the U.S.: a corpus of everyday spoken Japanese and a documentation of the Ikema dialect of Miyako, an endangered language spoken on remote Japanese islands near Taiwan. E-mail: tsuyoshi.ono@ualberta.ca

Anita Pomerantz is O'Leary Professor in the Department of Communication at the University at Albany, SUNY. Using audio and videotapes of interaction, she analyzes preference rules and practices for agreeing and disagreeing, seeking information, and negotiating responsibility for blameworthy and praiseworthy deeds. She studies provider-patient roles, patients' methods for actualizing their agendas, and the work of supervising physicians in ambulatory clinics. She has served as Chair of the Language and Social Interaction Division of the National Communication Association and the International Communication Association and currently serves on a number of editorial boards of language-oriented journals .E-mail: apom@albany.edu

Ming-Ming Pu is Professor of Linguistics at University of Maine, Farmington, obtained her Ph.D in psycholinguistics from University of Alberta, Canada. Her research interests include cognitive linguistics, discourse studies, and comparative studies of structure and function between Chinese and English. E-mail: mingpu@maine.edu

John E. Richardson is a senior lecturer in the School of Arts and Culture, Newcastle University. He is on the editorial boards of *Discourse and Society*, *Social Semiotics* and the *Journal of Language and Politics*, and is Special Issues Editor for *Critical Discourse*

Studies. His research interests include structured social inequalities, British fascism, racism in journalism, critical discourse studies and argumentation. His recent books include *Language and Journalism* (2009) and *Analysing Journalism: An Approach from Critical Discourse Analysis* (2007), and he is currently writing a book, contextualising and analysing the multimedia discourses of the British National Party (Bloomsbury Academic, 2012).

Christina Schäffner is Professor of Translation Studies at Aston University, Birmingham. She received her PhD in English philology from Leipzig University, Germany. Her main research interests are translation and politics, political discourse analysis, metaphor research (especially metaphors in political texts and from a translational perspective), and translation didactics. She has published widely in these fields. She is a past Secretary General of the European Society for Translation Studies (EST, 1998-2004). E-mail: c.schaeffner@aston.ac.uk

Marja-Leena Sorjonen is Professor of Finnish language at the University of Helsinki. She specializes in the interplay between interaction and grammar, and in linguistic variation. She has worked widely on different types of institutional interactions. Her publications in English include *Responding in Conversation. A Study of Response Particles in Finnish*, chapters in edited volumes and articles in journals such as *Discourse Studies*, *Journal of Pragmatics*, *Language in Society* and *Research on Language and Social Interaction*. E-mail: marja-leena.sorjonen@helsinki.fi

Russell S. Tomlin is Professor of Linguistics at the University of Oregon. He works in the area of language and cognition with an emphasis in the roles of attention and memory in language production. E-mail: tomlin@uoregon.edu

Teun A. van Dijk retired as professor of discourse studies of the University of Amstedam in 2004. Since 1999 he is visiting professor at Pompeu Fabra University, Barcelona. After earlier work in literary theory, text grammar, discourse pragmatics and the psychology of text processing, his research since the early 1980s has mainly focused on the critical study of racism and discourse, news in the press, ideology and context. His current research is about discourse and knowledge. He published extensively on these topics, and has lectured widely, especially in Latin America. He was founding Editor of *Poetics*, and of *Text* (now *Text & Talk*) and at present he is founding Editor of the international journals *Discourse & Society*, *Discourse Studies*, *Discourse and Communication* and the on-line journal *Discurso & Sociedad* (www.disssoc.org). His last books are *Discourse and Context* and *Society and Discourse* (published by Cambridge University Press, in 2008 and 2009) and (Ed.) *Racism and Discourse in Latin America* (Lexington Books, 2009). E-mail: vandijk@discourses.org. Internet: www.discourses.org

Frans H. van Eemeren is Professor of Argumentation Theory at the University of Amsterdam, President of the International Society for the Study of Argumentation, Editor of the journal *Argumentation* and the book series Argumentation Library and Argumentation in Context. Besides Distinguished Scholar of the American National Communication Association he is Doctor honoris causa of the University of Lugano. Among his book publications are *Speech Acts in Argumentative Discussions*, *Argumentation, Communication, and Fallacies*, *Reconstructing Argumentative Discourse*, *Fundamentals of Argumentation Theory*, *A Systematic Theory of Argumentation*, *Argumentative Indicators in Discourse*, *Fallacies and Judgments of Reasonableness*, and *Strategic Maneuvering in Argumentative Discourse*. E-mail: F.H.vanEemeren@uva.nl

Theo van Leeuwen is Professor of Media and Communication and Dean of the Faculty of Arts and Social Sciences at the University of Technology, Sydney. He has published widely in the areas of social semiotics, critical discourse analysis and multimodality. His books include *Reading Images: The Grammar of Visual Design* (with Gunther Kress); *Speech, Music, Sound*; *Introducing Social Semiotics*; *Global Media Discourse* (with David Machin); *Discourse and Practice: New Tools for Critical Discourse Analysis*; and *The Language of Colour*. He is a founding editor of the international journal *Visual Communication*. Email: Theo.vanleeuwen@uts.edu.au

Ruth Wodak is Distinguished Professor of Discourse Studies at Lancaster University since 2004 and has remained affiliated to the University of Vienna where she became full professor of Applied Linguistics in 1991. Besides various other prizes, she was awarded the Wittgenstein Prize for Elite Researchers in 1996. She is currently President elect of the Societas Linguistica Europea. Recently, she was also awarded an honorary doctorate by Örebro University, Sweden. Her research interests focus on discourse studies; gender studies; language and/in politics; prejudice and discrimination; and on ethnographic methods of linguistic field work. She is member of the editorial board of a range of linguistic journals and co-editor of the journals *Discourse and Society*, *Critical Discourse Studies*, and *Language and Politics*, and co-editor of the book series Discourse Approaches to Politics, Society and Culture (DAPSAC). She has held visiting professorships in Uppsala, Stanford University, University Minnesota, University of East Anglia, and Georgetown University, and is corresponding member of the Austrian Academy of Sciences. 2008/09, she held the Kerstin Hesselgren Chair of the Swedish Parliament (at University Örebrö). Recent book publications include *Ist Österreich ein 'deutsches' Land?* (with R. de Cillia, 2006); *Qualitative Discourse Analysis in the Social Sciences* (with M. Krzyżanowski, 2008); *Migration, Identity and Belonging* (with G. Delanty, P. Jones, 2008); *The Discursive Construction of History: Remembering the Wehrmacht's War of Annihilation* (with H. Heer, W. Manoschek, A. Pollak, 2008); *The Politics of Exclusion* (with M. Krzyżanowski, 2009); *Gedenken im Gedankenjahr* (with R. de Cillia, 2009); and *The Discourse of Politics in Action: 'Politics as Usual'* (2009). E-mail: r.wodak@lancaster.ac.uk. Internet: http://www.ling.lancs.ac.uk/profiles/265

Preface

After more than a decade the time has come to issue the second edition of *Discourse Studies: A Multidisciplinary Introduction*, which was first published in 1997. For obvious practical reasons this time the book appears as one volume, with the regrettable but unavoidable consequence of a slight reduction of size.

The new cross-discipline of Discourse Studies has developed just as impressively since the end of the 1990s as it already had in the three decades since its beginnings in the mid-1960s in Anthropology, Linguistics, Literary Studies, Sociology, Cognitive and Social Psychology, Communication Studies and Political Science, respectively, and roughly in this order. Several universities now have special Master's programmes in the subject and there are now more than half a dozen specialized journals in the field. Congresses and symposia of discourse and conversation analysis have become as regular as those in the original mother disciplines in the humanities, social sciences and cognitive sciences that feature sections specialized in discourse, text or conversation. In the summer of 2010, the ISI Web of Knowledge featured 43,379 articles with the term 'discourse' in their topic or title, and explicitly 'discourse analysis' as the topic of 3210 articles. As of today (1 August 2010) the Library of Congress lists 5319 books on discourse analysis in its catalogue. In other words, what was a fledgling but contemporary movement in the social sciences and linguistics around the 1970s, has grown four decades later to have become a discipline of its own, despite the fact that the conservative nature of academic institutionalization does not yet acknowledge independent departments of Discourse Studies.

This spectacular growth in the study of text and talk is not limited to this formal organization of the field. New theories, methods, descriptive, ethnographic, experimental, automated and formal studies, and hitherto unexplored areas and sub-disciplines have proliferated both within the original disciplines as well as autonomously as new directions in the field of Discourse Studies. The updated chapters of this book bear witness to these developments, as do several new chapters.

Of these new trends in the field, we may first mention the now generally recognized multimodal nature of discourse, reflected in at least a dozen monographs and hundreds of articles on this broader 'semiotic' approach to text and talk, so obviously necessary owing to the ubiquitous presence of discourse on the internet and other new media. This interest in the multimodal nature of discourse now also extends to the much more broadly conceived 'embodied' nature of language and communication.

Secondly, also spurned by the presence of computers in virtually every academic context, the number of corpus-based studies has provided a quantitative precision where earlier impressionistic assessment of frequencies were rife.

Thirdly, and for the same reason, Artificial Intelligence now routinely presents formal simulations of text production and comprehension within the growing field of Natural Language Processing, which more adequately might be called the field of Discourse Processing, because these studies are seldom limited to the simulation of isolated sentences.

Within the cross-discipline of Cognitive Science, also hugely successful in the last decades, these more formal approaches are being joined by a steadily growing number of experimental studies on the production and comprehension of discourse, which today increasingly possess a neuroscientific grounding in the complex, multimodal structures of the brain. Even more profoundly such a development touches upon the biological make-up and genetic heritage of humans as the only species that have developed not only natural languages, but also and especially the ability to interact and communicate by complex discourse – that is, beyond simple bodily signs and signals.

Obviously, most of this new sub-discipline still needs to be explored. As yet we have no idea how the many genres of human communication and discourse have accompanied the phylogenetic development of language and as an adaptation to the environments of everyday life in various cultures. Whereas conversation and storytelling about past experiences are no doubt universal and hence deeply programmed into our language and communication faculties (and their multimodal extensions), obviously news reports in the press, scholarly articles, and formal indictments in court or websites are professional and institutional developments of a much more recent nature.

These new developments, partly giving rise to new cross-disciplines and sub-disciplines, also show up in the increasing variation of topics studied in the field – which originally started with the analysis of such classic topics as the organization of communicative events, cohesion and coherence, turn taking, the functional moves of different genres, scripts in memory for stories, narrative and argumentation structures, among others.

Today such a list is vastly more varied and ambitious, showing how discourse and its structural and functional properties are fundamentally involved in the everyday lives of language users as communicators and members of organizations, social groups and cultural communities. Conversation analysis has gone far beyond the study of everyday talk, and now as a matter of course examines professional interaction and talk in institutional settings, for instance news and political interviews, among many other genres. The notions of *identity*, *ideology* and *power* are now common in hundreds of discourse studies in the social and political sciences, as are studies of the discursive manifestations of gender and ethnicity. Beyond these largely descriptive analyses of text and talk in their social contexts, the applied studies of discourse have also gone beyond the obvious fields of first and second language learning, literacy and education, and in addition currently deal with the discourse of autistic children or people with Alzheimer's disease, thus providing diagnostic instruments that hitherto were limited to the lexicon or simple sentence grammar.

We can thus witness that the cross-discipline of Discourse Studies has gained a breadth and theoretical and methodological depth during the last decade. It is indeed now formally established as a field with its many book publications, introductions and handbooks, as well as its own journals and university programmes and congresses. The multiple methods of discourse and conversation analysis are becoming increasingly common in all the humanities, social and cognitive sciences. The variety of topics studied is as great as the variety of functions of text and talk in everyday informal, organizational and institutional life and interaction, with numerous applications now also extending into the clinical field. The very definition of discourse has also extended to multimodal and embodied communication, and explorations of the cognitive aspects of discourse processing are increasingly being grounded in neuropsychological studies of the brain.

Discourse is no longer just conceived of as verbal text and talk, but also encompasses the nature of contexts as models of communicative events pragmatically controlling such discourse, and its appropriateness is now being investigated, obviously in a multidisciplinary paradigm. The success of Critical Discourse Studies shows the fundamental importance of the role of text and talk in the reproduction of power and domination in society, as well as in the discursive challenge of dissent.

Despite these successes in new fields, theories, methods and topics of Discourse Studies, this fledgling cross-discipline and its history of barely half a century is still young when compared with its mother disciplines – if, that is, we ignore the rich tradition of two millennia of classical rhetoric. There are still vast areas and a myriad of topics to be explored. We have just entered the field of the neuroscientific study of discourse and its important applications, and as yet we can barely grasp the fundamental role of knowledge in the production, management and understanding of discourse, and, vice versa, the role of discourse in the sociocultural reproduction of knowledge. We know that the talk and text of group members may be ideologically framed, but as yet we have no standard method to analyse ideological discourse in general, or sexist and racist discourse in particular. The topic of the important links between discourse and social class is still waiting to be explored in sophisticated detail – no doubt also because most discourse analysts don't have the daily experience of grinding poverty. Computers have been programmed to produce and understand discourse, but as yet are unable either to conduct a natural conversation with human language users, or produce a news report on the basis of course texts, interviews or eyewitness testimonies, as well as most other genres of text or talk. Indeed, dozens of genres have been systematically analysed for their overall organization, their moves, style, lexicon and social functions, but there are many hundreds if not thousands of genres, in many different cultures, still waiting for such systematic description. In sum, most linguistic, semiotic, cognitive, neurological, social, political and cultural aspects of discourse will remain on the agenda for decades to come.

This multidisciplinary introduction to the fascinating cross-discipline of Discourse Studies offers the theories, methods and data that represent the state of the art in the field and the first steps of these future developments. Besides offering a first, pedagogically

ONE

Introduction: The Study of Discourse

Teun A. van Dijk

THE DEVELOPMENT OF THE CROSS-DISCIPLINE OF DISCOURSE STUDIES

Although the roots of the cross-discipline of Discourse Studies go back to classical rhetoric as the study of 'speaking well' (*bene dicendi*) in public discourse, its contemporary emergence must be sought in remarkably parallel developments in the humanities and social sciences between 1964 and 1974.

- After its structural studies of folktales, **anthropology** extended its ethnographic research to include the study of *communicative events* in general.
- Similarly, **sociology** turned towards the detailed analysis of *interaction*, in general, and to everyday *conversation*, in particular, and thus aimed to reconstruct the basis of a social order that hitherto had been accounted for in terms of the abstract *structure* of groups, organizations and institutions.
- Scholars in **linguistics**, **psycholinguistics** and **sociolinguistics** recognized that the study of actual language use should not be limited to the grammatical analysis of isolated sentences, and advocated a focus on the structures, strategies and processes of the cognitively and socially *situated text and talk of real language users*.
- **Cognitive psychology**, just having liberated itself from its behaviourist shackles, rediscovered the mind and memory, and hence the role of knowledge and other mental representations in its study of the processes of language production and comprehension, at the same time amplifying the scope from sentences to cover *discourse*.
- Somewhat later, in the 1980s, at least some scholars in **social psychology** emphasized that instead of laboratory studies of 'behaviour,' attitudes or attribution, among many other phenomena, psychologists should focus on *discourse and interaction* and the way these 'construe' reality as well as the mind.
- Finally, the **study of communication** has always been interested in the analysis of 'messages' – for instance, in the mass media, political communication, interpersonal communication and health communication, as well as in their production and 'effects' on recipients and society as a whole. Earlier approaches, such as Content Analysis, have gradually been complemented with more detailed qualitative, discourse analytical and conversational analytical analyses.

Today, these originally separate and largely independent developments towards the study of the structures and strategies of real language use by real language users are increasingly overlapping and merging, at the same time influenced by, and also influencing, their respective mother-disciplines. Research into discourse today thus combines the study of language use, verbal interaction, conversation, texts, multimodal messages and communicative events. Methodologically, it may range from formal analyses of abstract sentence, conversation or argumentation structures, on the one hand, to laboratory studies of cognitive processes or mental representations, as well as ethnographic observations of socially situated talk and interaction (among many other methods) on the other hand.

RELATED CROSS-DISCIPLINES

These parallel developments did not emerge on their own. The 1960s had also witnessed the cross-disciplinary emergence of **semiotics**, especially in the humanities, which introduced the integrated analysis of narrative, pictures, film, gestures and paintings and other forms of non-verbal 'texts' and communication that went beyond traditional literary studies or art history. Semiotics at the same time influenced the sister cross-disciplines of Discourse Studies and Communication Studies by emphasizing that text and talk, especially in the age of the internet, were more than just written or spoken language, but should be studied in their entire multimodal complexity.

Whereas virtually all disciplines studying language until the 1970s limited their analysis to include expressions (sounds, syntax, lexicon) and – later – to meaning, the philosophy of language paralleled sociology by stressing the fundamental relevance of a third major dimension of human communication: *action*. Speech acts, conversational postulates, politeness, indexicality and related phenomena thus became the seemingly heterogeneous objects of research in what was soon to be called **pragmatics**. This new, *context-oriented*, cross-discipline of the humanities and the social sciences is now increasingly overlapping and even merging with discourse studies, conversation analysis and sociolinguistics.

At the other end of the broad range of discourse studies, the more formal analysis of discourse in linguistics, logic, philosophy and computer science joined cognitive psychology and, more generally, **cognitive science** within the study of **Artificial Intelligence**, for instance in the design of programs of automatic translation, human–machine interaction, expert systems, and other developments that require the explicit formulation of rules as well as implementation of the fundamental role of knowledge in discourse production and comprehension. Contemporary interest in **corpus linguistics** and its application in the study of discourse may be fruitfully integrated into this development of the automated analysis or simulation of text or talk.

Finally, the last decade has also broadened and deepened the empirical study of the mental representations and processes involved in discourse production and comprehension by exploring their neural infrastructures in the brain in the new cross-discipline of **neuroscience**. Although still in its infancy, and as yet far removed from a sophisticated neurological account of the details of discourse processing, it is hoped that at least some of the mysteries of the relations between socially situated discourse, knowledge and interaction may in the future be resolved with its help.

After nearly half a century, the cross-disciplinary study of discourse has come of age and has also established itself as a vibrant cross-discipline in virtually all areas of the humanities and social sciences, as well as in history, literature and – surprisingly quite modestly as yet – in political science. Thousands of articles, hundreds of monographs, dozens of handbooks and introductions, half a dozen specialized journals, annual national and international congresses and new university programmes bear witness to its academic success and embeddedness.

Today, also in the original mother-disciplines, the study of language use is no longer limited to an analysis of abstract structures of words, clauses, sentences or propositions, but is part of an integrated account of a socially and culturally situated and cognitively based multimodal discourse as interaction and human communication. Not surprisingly, this development also emphasizes that whereas various forms of communication are widespread among other species, the uniquely human forms of the use of natural languages take the shape of coherent and contextually appropriate text and talk.

PROPERTIES OF DISCOURSE

The various chapters in this book provide a systematic introduction to the structural, cognitive and social properties of discourse. By way of an introduction to these introductions, the novice may especially need a brief summary of the fundamental properties of text and talk. Although definitions of such complex notions as society, culture, mind and language are usually a rather pointless enterprise, and while whole disciplines have developed to provide insight into such phenomena, teachers of Discourse Studies are regularly confronted with requests regarding a definition of the very notion of discourse. In order to partially comply with such requests, we must at least enumerate the following major properties that have been highlighted within decades of research in various areas of the field:

1 **Discourse as social interaction** Perhaps most fundamentally, discourse is defined as a form of *social interaction among human participants* (by extension, including human–machine interaction). Besides speaking (writing or signing) and meaning, language users engaged in talk or text will accomplish social acts of many kinds and will do so by jointly and mutually coordinating their action, as a meaningful and socially appropriate interaction. It is this fundamental interactional dimension of discourse that defines the basis of the **social order** of human societies. This dimension is especially focused on **pragmatics** and (various kinds of) **Conversation Analysis**.

2 **Discourse as power and domination** As one of the fundamental aspects of the social order construed and reproduced by discourse, *power* and *power abuse* (domination) may be defined in terms of a preferential *access* to, and *control* over, public discourse by social groups or organizations. This property of public discourse as a scarce symbolic

power resource is especially focused on more **critical, sociopolitical approaches to discourse**, for instance in the study of domination based on gender, class, ethnicity or sexuality. By a complex process of controlling the minds (knowledge, attitudes, ideologies, norms, values, intentions) of language users, and indirectly the actions based on these mental representations, discourse may on the one hand be an important condition of social inequality, and on the other a prominent tool of resistance and dissent as forms of counter-power. Here we are dealing with the crucial role of discourse in the **political order** of society.

3   **Discourse as communication**   One of the many goals of interaction by text and talk is the *expression and communication of beliefs among language users*. It is in this way that we come to know about the knowledge, intentions, goals, opinions and emotions of others, about how we acquire and update socially *shared and distributed* knowledge and thus the very conditions of coordinated interaction. This dimension defines the no less fundamental **cognitive order** of human societies. Interaction and cognition mutually presuppose each other, and no account of discourse is complete without a theoretical and empirical study of both dimensions. Unfortunately, in most current research, the cleft between cognition and interaction remains one of the major divisions of the field. This aspect of discourse is especially studied in **cognitive psychology** and in the **cognitive sciences** more generally, as well as in the field of **communication studies**, dealing with the effects and influences of messages on the minds of audiences.

4   **Discourse as contextually situated**   Discourse as interaction and communication does not occur in a vacuum, but is instead part of a social *situation* in people's everyday lives, and as an experience among others. Participants represent the for-them-relevant parameters of this situation (such as Setting, Participant Identities and Relations, Goals, Current Action and Knowledge) in a subjective mental model that defines the context and allows language users to engage in text or talk that is *appropriate* to the current communicative situation. The conditions and rules for such contextually-based appropriateness are especially studied in **pragmatics**, whereas the influence of social class, gender, age and ethnicity are specifically examined in **sociolinguistics**, and the contextual variation of expressions (e.g., formal *vs.* informal language use) in **stylistics**. Since contexts will typically vary across cultures, such an account also provides the basis for a (cross) *cultural study* of discourse in **linguistic anthropology**. A special case of contextual situatedness is the *intertextual* relation with other text and talk in the same or other situations. If these are situations of previous ages, such intertextual analysis also provides a basis for a **historical approach** to discourse.

5   **Discourse as social semiosis**   Text and talk are not limited to the use of natural human languages but more broadly implement other semiotic systems of sounds, visuals, gestures and other embodied meaningful social activity within multimodal discourse – advocated especially in what today is called **social semiotics**, after earlier semiotic studies of literature, film, dance and other forms of symbolic expression, interaction and communication.

6   **Discourse as natural language use**   Despite the emphasis placed, in the research of previous decades, on the interactional, cognitive, situated and semiotic properties, conditions and consequences of discourse, its core property is undoubtedly the use of natural language as the unique humane ability to produce and understand well-formed, meaningful and appropriate combinations of words, sentences or other units of rule-based language use. Hence the central relevance of **linguistics** and its sister-disciplines for the study of discourse.

7   **Discourse as complex, layered construct**   Discourse analysis defines discourse as a complex, layered, multidimensional object or phenomenon integrating the three major dimensions of natural languages: *Form or Expression* (sounds, visuals, words, phrases, etc.), *Meaning* and *Action*. Each of these levels or dimensions is then further analysed in terms of more specific phonological, semiotic, syntactic, lexical, semantic, schematic, pragmatic and interactional theories. Beyond the *local structures* (sequences) of sentences, turns or moves, discourse analysis also pays attention to more *global structures*, such as the organizational schemata (*superstructures*) of conversations, news reports or scholarly articles. Similarly, meaning and action are not only described at the local level of propositions or actions expressed or performed by the utterance of sentences, but also in terms of global meanings (*macrostructures,* topics, gist) and global actions, for instance in **discourse grammars** and **Conversation Analysis**. Finally, across these levels, **rhetoric** – among other things – examines the special structures or operations (such as repetitions, hyperboles and euphemisms) that emphasize or de-emphasize the local meanings of discourse. What is important here is that the different levels or dimensions are not studied in isolation, but precisely as mutually related: well-formed discourse expressions are interpreted as meaningful and performed as appropriate social actions.

8 **Sequences and hierarchies** One of the crucial structural properties of text and talk is their *sequentiality*. At each of the levels mentioned above, discourse features structures consisting of sequences of sounds, words, sentences, propositions, moves or actions, according to the temporal order of discourse production and comprehension. This means that, in general, units at each level are conditioned by or interpreted with respect to previous ones, and as preparing next ones, thus defining the formal *cohesion* and semantic and pragmatic *coherence* of text and talk. At the same time, as we have seen, local sequences may be combined to form higher level units in complex *hierarchical structures* (e.g., sentences into paragraphs into sections, chapters, etc. in written texts, or sequences of turns at talk into the introduction or conclusion of a lecture). Finally, in addition to these 'horizontal' and 'vertical' axes of discourse structures, we may distinguish a third one, characterized by such notions as foregrounding, emphasis, focus, highlighting, etc. as against backgrounding, mitigation, and so on. These three major orientations in the study of discourse structure may be metaphorically visualized and conceived of as forming a cube: Left *vs.* Right, Top *vs.* Bottom and Front *vs.* Back, respectively. Sequentiality, hierarchy and grounding are properties of text and talk that are examined in virtually all areas of the study of discourse, especially in **discourse grammar** and **Conversation Analysis**, as well as **narrative and argumentation studies**.

9 **Abstract structures *vs.* dynamic strategies** Discourse may alternatively or complementarily be studied as an object consisting of abstract structures, or as a dynamic, changing sequence of events, or as the strategically oriented mental operations or moves of social action. Thus, syntactic structures or overall schematic formats will tend to be analysed in terms of abstract structures, whereas conversations or more generally talk in interaction will be examined in more dynamic terms, as an ongoing performance or accomplishment – as is also the case for **cognitive approaches to discourse production and comprehension**.

10 **Types or genres** Discourse comes in various types, sorts or genres, such as everyday conversations, parliamentary debates, news reports in the press, scholarly articles or advertisements, among many others. These different genres may be partly characterized by the set of their typical structures, or *register*, such as by the inclusion of passive verbs, first person pronouns and narrative schemas in everyday storytelling, or by argumentative schemas in editorials or scholarly articles. However, when characterized as types of *activities*, as is the case for parliamentary debates, discourse genres should rather be defined in terms of the parameters of the *context* as defined above. It is this aspect of discourse that is especially focused on **genre studies**.

RESEARCH ON DISCOURSE

Several of these basic properties of discourse may be studied in combination, for instance in multidisciplinary research on the contextual constraints of parliamentary speeches and their influence on semantic topics, implications or argumentative fallacies, which in turn may condition the political opinions of recipients and the ways in which politicians may thus manipulate the citizen vote. On the other hand, other research may simply focus on the way shared knowledge ('common ground') of participants can influence the syntactic and semantic structures of sentences in conversation, or how everyday storytelling may vary across cultures, among myriad other research topics.

Whereas earlier research typically focused on the structural details of just one level of text or talk (for instance, the semantics of coherence, turn-taking in conversation or narrative structures), we have come to realize that such structures are often dependent on structures or constraints at other levels or dimensions of discourse, such as those of context, social interaction and cognition. Thus if the chapters in this book intentionally focus on just one aspect of discourse, this does not mean that such structures cannot or have not been studied in a broader, multi-level or multidisciplinary framework, but only that a single chapter cannot deal with all the relevant aspects of text or talk.

What (not) to study?

A key problem (not only beginning) students of discourse often struggle with is deciding which structures, levels, units or properties of a specific discourse genre they should study for a paper or a thesis. As is the case for all discourse, such scholarly discourse will also depend on its context, and especially on the goals, the time available, relevant resources, and the activity or genre studied, as well as the current interests, previous knowledge and expertise of a researcher. Obviously, one cannot possibly study the detailed syntactic structures of a thousand news reports in the press within a few weeks or months. Such an objective would be quite unrealistic if it were even relevant at all. Nor, in fact, could this be applied to the argumentative structures of even a mere dozen news reports, simply because that unlike editorials, these do not typically feature argumentative schemas. To study pronouns one needs to know about grammar and coherence in discourse, and in order to run a psychological experiment on memory and television news one needs special laboratory resources and a knowledge of experimental methods. In addition, within a throng of experts with decades of experience, no one person can study, in any detail, all the properties of discourse that are mentioned above even if limiting the project to one specific genre, such as news interviews, scholarly articles or television advertising – hence the need to make choices within the constraints of the context of a project.

Discourse analytical research is as varied as the structures, dimensions and properties of text and talk and their functions in interaction, communication and society, as briefly summarized above. Projects may usefully focus on just one of the many unexplored details of *discourse structure* at the levels described previously, for instance interruptions in television debates, functional moves in news reports, or assignments in textbooks. They may do so with a more or less formal, qualitative *vs.* quantitative, descriptive, experimental, ethnographic and/or critical research method. No doubt this lies at the very core of all discourse research.

Besides such *discourse-centered research*, more *problem-oriented research*, especially in the social sciences, may focus on a *social or political problem or issue*, such as the learning problems of adolescents in a specific school or subject, the proliferation of ethnic prejudice in society, or how then Prime Minister Tony Blair manipulated parliament into accepting his motion to go to war in Iraq – among a vast number of other problems that can be fruitfully studied in a discourse-analytical perspective.

It should finally be stressed that, contrary to what is often assumed outside of the field, *Discourse Analysis is not a method of research, but a (cross) discipline*. Hence, we prefer to speak about the discipline of Discourse Studies, as the title of this book shows. In Discourse Studies, researchers may make use of a large number of formal, descriptive, ethnographic, experimental and other methods. It is true that, unlike the method of Content Analysis as used in the social sciences, the methods of Discourse Analysis usually tend to be qualitative rather than quantitative. However, qualitative descriptions of specific discourse structures may be perfectly well combined with a quantitative account, as is the case for corpus-based approaches and most experimental studies.

CONCLUSION

Although Discourse Studies has indeed come of age, it remains a young discipline. There are a vast number of genres and properties of text and talk that remain unexplored. The different levels and dimensions of discourse still need to be interrelated. We are still a long way from being able to program computers to understand discourse as human beings do – and we are only just beginning to understand how it is that language users are mentally able to manage the complex structures of meaningful and appropriate text and talk in real time. There are countless social problems that may also need a discourse analytical approach. It is no secret that scholars from different disciplines and approaches may sometimes show little enthusiasm for learning about each others' research, even when a broader orientation would be very relevant for their own research project. Despite its multidisciplinary origins, Discourse Studies also acknowledges that many research projects and groups will focus on only one property of discourse, thereby ignoring its constraints on other levels. In sum, as is the case for any discipline, Discourse Studies is only human too and hence shows all the limitations of human conduct.

This book provides a multidisciplinary introduction to the impressive advances of half a century of Discourse Studies as reported in a great many publications. Yet not only the obvious limitations of an introductory book but also those more generally of a young discipline should stimulate students to further explore the large number of properties and problems of text and talk that have not been addressed in this volume.

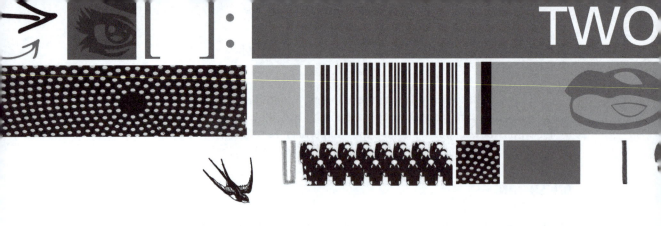

TWO

Discourse, Grammar and Interaction

Susanna Cumming,
Tsuyoshi Ono and Ritva Laury[1]

This chapter deals with the relation of discourse to grammar, setting forth what we will call a 'discourse-functional approach' to grammatical phenomena. Discourse-functional grammarians view discourse – that is, the spoken, signed or written language used by people to communicate and interact in natural settings – as the primary locus for the grammars of the world's languages, not only as the place where grammar is manifested in use, but also as the source from which grammar is formed or 'emerges' (Hopper, 1988). In this view, grammar originates in recurrent patterns in discourse, and these patterns continually shape it. This approach to grammar is distinct from what might be called the 'autonomist' approach, which views grammar as having an existence that is entirely independent of its communicative uses.

Discourse-functional approaches to grammar have two goals. The first goal is a descriptive one: are traditional grammatical categories, identified mostly based on the examination of constructed examples (categories that have been taken for granted, such as phrases, clauses, sentences and parts of speech) found in actual discourse, and if so, how are these shaped and used? For instance, a more specific question would be (having found full NPs and pronouns to express the 'same' content in the discourse) in which contexts is each of these forms used? The second goal here is explanatory: why do languages have the particular

---

[1]This chapter was originally written by Cumming and Ono for the first edition of the present volume and has been substantially updated by Ono and Laury for this current edition.

resources they have? That is, why are specific grammatical resources, such as pronouns, available in many or all languages, and why are certain functions typically realized by certain kinds of forms? Because both of these concerns have consequences for language universals and typology, we pose the following questions: 1) are there categories and patterns that are shared cross-linguistically, and 2) if so, are these motivated by the same factors? For instance, the universal tendency for subjects to precede objects can be explained by the fact that subjects will typically have referents that are related to the discourse topic, and that cross-linguistically topical information will tend to occur early on in the clause.

Discourse linguists who are interested in grammar have tended to focus on three general kinds of explanations. Cognitive explanations appeal to the cognitive resources and processes used by interactants in producing and understanding language. Social or interactional explanations appeal to the dynamics of the interactional situations in which language (especially spoken language) is used, and to the social and/or cultural norms, resources, and goals of interactants. Finally, diachronic explanations focus on the relationship between discourse-functional pressures on grammars and grammatical change; this type of explanation is often called 'grammaticalization'.

These three sources of explanation are not, of course, mutually exclusive; indeed they are interrelated in many complex ways. Discourse linguists believe that the great variety of formal repertoires among the world's languages has come about through the interaction of different functional pressures which will sometimes compete – forcing speech communities to 'choose' between two or more well-motivated outcomes – and sometimes converge, leading to very general or even universal patterns of language structure (see Du Bois, 1985).

HISTORICAL OVERVIEW

The school of linguistics characterized above emerged in its present form in the mid-1970s, when 'functional' linguists in the USA began to distinguish themselves from 'formal' (autonomist) linguists. This new school of linguistics owed much to older European social and communicative approaches, especially the Firthian approach as extended by Halliday (see, for example, Halliday, 1967–8 and other works summarized in Halliday, 1985), and the Prague School tradition developed under the 'functional sentence perspective' promoted by Firbas (1966), Daneš (1974), Mathesius (1975) and others. These approaches viewed the social setting of language, its communicative function, and especially the management of information in discourse as being central to any understanding of grammar.

A group of American linguists were also working on discourse at this time. Dwight Bolinger contributed a long series of studies (e.g., Bolinger, 1952; 1986; 1989) which demonstrated the importance of understanding language in use; moreover, he was a pioneer in understanding the special characteristics of spoken language, especially intonation. Pike (1954), Longacre (1972) and Grimes (1975) also represented an approach to linguistics which always saw discourse as central to understanding language.

Another thread that was centrally important to the nascent discourse functionalism of the mid-1970s was the typological school of linguistics inspired by the seminal work of Greenberg (1966) and others, which focused attention on the universal properties of human languages for the first time. Greenberg and his followers included observations about statistical tendencies in the languages of the world, as well as correlations between the characteristics of different syntactic subsystems – such as word order in the noun phrase and the clause. These new observations demanded explanations, which discourse-functional approaches were in a good position to provide.

The mid-1970s also saw the inception of several other streams in related disciplines which have continued to influence and be influenced by the discourse-functional approach to grammar in the years since. Since one aspect of the discourse-functionalist approach centrally involves cognitive factors, results in psycholinguistics and, more recently, cognitive science have continued to be brought to bear on problems of grammar in discourse. Yet another important pair of influences on the discourse-functional approach comes from the fields of anthropology on the one hand and sociology on the other. Since the contributions from other disciplines are covered extensively elsewhere in this volume, we will not consider them further here.[2]

In what follows, we will discuss foundational work in discourse and grammar from the mid-70s onwards, when scholars increasingly started working on discourse data. In particular, we will highlight the area often called discourse-functional linguistics which became active starting in the 1980s (e.g., Chafe, 1980; Hopper and Thompson, 1980; 1984; Givón, 1983). Through the examination of actual discourse data, much of this research focuses on the connection between linguistic structures and cognitive and discourse factors and shows that language structure is motivated, which is often supported by quantitative and distributional evidence and by the way language changes. This research also began to reveal the nature of linguistic categories in actual use, which is in clear contrast with the categories that were established which were based on constructed data. We will also discuss work undertaken in a new research framework called Interactional Linguistics (e.g., Ochs, Schegloff and Thompson, 1996; Selting and Couper-Kuhlen, 2001) which, by utilizing the methodology of an area in sociology called Conversation Analysis (Sacks, Schegloff and Jefferson, 1974), combined with discourse-functional linguistics and linguistic anthropology, examines grammar and interaction in conversation – the fundamental form of language. Studies in this area are uncovering how grammatical resources are exploited by speakers and how they are coordinated with interactional factors. A number have found that the actual production of grammar is locally managed – that is, transpiring in real time, second-by-second, and always contingent on negotiations with the other participants in the

---

[2]Another related and contemporaneous area of investigation, from within the field of linguistics, focuses on the connection between structure and meaning, represented particularly by the framework of Cognitive Linguistics (e.g., Langacker 1987; 1991). Practitioners of this approach have coined the term 'usage-based linguistics', which, though their actual research is often practised based on the examination of constructed data, very aptly captures what the approach described in this chapter is trying to do.

speech event. Moreover, grammatical patterns resulting from this process may often be those that are considered 'syntactically ill-formed' in traditional accounts, yet they are what interactants will primarily operate with in actual interaction. This line of research has therefore been uncovering the nature and workings of grammatical resources in actual interactional contexts and reshaping our understanding of the fundamental categories of linguistic analysis. A large amount of concentrated research is currently being done within this framework in North America, Europe and East Asia.

METHODOLOGY AND DATA

As suggested above, a discourse-functional linguist builds on the idea that the use of language to communicate in natural settings is fundamental to the organization of languages. The primacy of grammar in discourse both as an object of description and as a source of explanations has had important methodological consequences for discourse grammarians.

Most importantly, unlike 'autonomist' grammarians, discourse grammarians have increasingly restricted their attention over the last three decades to naturally occurring data, as opposed to invented examples. Increasingly also, discourse-functional linguists have attempted as much as possible to include in their database the context within which the discourse occurs – not just the linguistic context, but also the ethnographic and extralinguistic context, including both its social and its physical aspects. This is because context can often provide clues to locally relevant functional pressures that are not detectable from the linguistic signal alone. Awareness of the importance of context in shaping linguistic structure has led to increasing interest in the nature of 'context' as an object of study in itself. Many discourse linguists have come to the realization that we have to understand discourse and its context as mutually creating and constraining, rather than seeing this simply as a unidirectional process.

Another concomitant of the discourse-functional perspective has to do with the issue of text frequency. Many discourse grammarians feel that text frequency is vital to understanding the discourse motivations for particular grammatical constructions. This is because they have started to acknowledge that those functional pressures that have the most opportunity to affect communicators are also those most likely to affect language form: in the words of Du Bois (1985), 'grammars code best what speakers do most'. This observation has had two significant consequences for the methodology of discourse approaches to grammar. First, many discourse grammarians have adopted a quantitative methodology and been very concerned with statistical correlations between particular grammatical forms and aspects of the linguistic and non-linguistic context.[3] Second,

---

[3]Discourse-functional linguistics, however, has tended not to go along with the recent developments in another area called Corpus Linguistics because, while the latter involves statistical analyses of large amounts of written data and/or transcripts of spoken data, it does not examine the actual workings of grammar in interaction, which can only be studied by closely examining original recordings.

many discourse grammarians have recently begun to focus increasingly on the form of language which occupies most language users' time and attention everywhere in the world: everyday 'talk in interaction'. While other discourse genres and styles, produced under different kinds of functional constraints and pressures, are still considered relevant, talk in interaction is seen as having a privileged position as a source of explanation for language structure and change. This is motivated by the ultimate goal of linguistic research shared by many researchers, which is to gain an understanding of the fundamental linguistic behaviour – spoken language.

Because of the focus on natural data and full context, discourse linguists find themselves using increasingly advanced technologies for collecting and analysing data. The first step here was a move away from the analysis of written discourse towards an analysis of spoken discourse with audio recordings and transcripts, using increasingly sophisticated audio equipment and richer and richer transcription systems (Edwards and Lampert, 1993). This methodology is now supplemented by a trend towards utilizing video cameras, which can provide information about non-linguistic as well as linguistic contexts. Moreover, the use of transcripts as the primary basis for analysis is supplemented by working with the original audio or video recording directly, since transcription, no matter how rich, will always sacrifice much of the information available to interactants in the context. Emerging multimedia technologies such as the digitization of sound and video are being exploited to facilitate this process: digitized audio and video data can be played back endlessly without any degradation of the signal and also stored in databases and accessed in any order, while particular segments in the recording can be easily accessed and kept track of.

These factors are responsible for the distinctive methodological characteristics associated with studies in the discourse-functional mold: an insistence on carefully recorded natural data and an interest in quantitative and distributional information about grammatical patterns.

THE NATURE OF ANALYTICAL CATEGORIES

One of the most fundamental ways in which discourse-functional linguistics has divided itself off from autonomist linguistics has been in its treatment of the basic categories of analysis. Discourse-functional linguists have explicitly rejected the idea that the categories of grammar are Aristotelian – that is, that they are structured such that a given item either is or is not a member of a category, and tests should be discoverable to determine which is the case (see, for example, Givón, 1989, for arguments against this view). Rather, they have proposed a number of other models of category structure, using a variety of terms including hierarchies, scales, continua, and prototypes. These proposals all have in common the view that category membership can be a matter of degree.

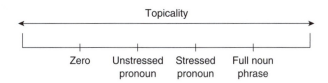

Figure 2.1   A scalar category

The simplest type of a non-Aristotelian category views category membership as scalar, where its different degrees can be plotted along a single dimension. For instance, Givón (1983) proposes that the category 'topic' is scalar. He suggests that topicality itself is continuous (a referent at a particular point in discourse may be more or less topical), but that a given language will divide up the continuum according to its inventory of linguistic forms. For instance, a language which contrasts 'zero anaphora', a set of unstressed pronouns, a set of stressed pronouns, and full noun phrases will divide up the topicality continuum as in Figure 2.1. As shown in this figure, phonologically 'lighter' material falls closer to the left end of the scale, while phonologically 'heavier' material falls closer to the right end.

Some types of linguistic categories will not fit the 'scale' model well, because they can be viewed as varying along more than one dimension. An alternative model is the prototype structure suggested by Rosch (1978), in which a 'central' member of a category has a collection of related characteristics, but non-central members can diverge in various ways according to how many and which of these characteristics are lacking. In the next two sections we will present two analyses of this type, which will then be followed by a brief discussion of on-going language change as part of the reason why categories of grammar are not Aristotelian, and of more recent, conversation-based work in discourse-functional linguistics, which has been shedding more light on the actual nature of linguistic categories.

Transitivity

One example of a category distinction which is traditionally viewed as Aristotelian is the distinction between transitive and intransitive verbs. This distinction is addressed in an influential paper by Hopper and Thompson (1980). They propose that the distinction between 'transitive' and 'intransitive' verbs – in traditional grammars, simply a matter of whether the verb takes an object – needs to be broken down into distinct factors, in order to explain various cross-linguistic correlations between the argument structure of a verb and a number of grammatical characteristics. The factors cited by Hopper and Thompson include matters relating to the agent (such as volitionality), the verb (such as telicity, having an endpoint), and the patient (such as affectedness), as well as the overall argument structure of the clause. These factors (which, taken together, are characterized as 'discourse transitivity')

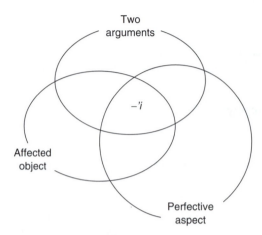

Figure 2.2   Transitivity as a prototype category

are shown to correlate with each other in a sample of languages. In Tongan, for instance, there is a 'transitive' marker - *'i* which is used when the object is totally affected by the action of the verb, and also used as a marker of the perfective aspect:[4]

(1) (a) Na'e   taipe 'e   he   tangata'a   e   topi.
        PAST type   ERG DEF man   ABS   DEF   letter
        'The man is typing the letter.'

    (b) Na'e   tanu-**'i**   'e   he   tangata 'a   e   ika.
        PAST bury-TRANS ERG DEF man   ABS   DEF fish
        'The man buried the fish.'

This example illustrates the convergence of various aspects of transitivity which are in principle independent. This convergence is illustrated in Figure 2.2. That these three factors might be coded by separate linguistic devices (as they are in many languages) is represented in the diagram by the fact that there are non-overlapping sections of the circles; that these will often tend to converge is represented by the overlapping section in the middle.

Given this understanding of the way in which a multi-functionality of the linguistic forms of the world's languages supports a common notion of discourse transitivity, it is easy to see how a clause in discourse can be understood as more or less 'discourse-transitive' even in a language which doesn't have multi-functional forms of the type illustrated by Tongan. Even in English, for instance, a clause which has two arguments, the perfective aspect, and a completely affected object can be thought of as 'more transitive' than one which is missing one or more of these characteristics. Hopper and Thompson go on to demonstrate that

---

[4]The following glossing abbreviations are used in these examples: PAST = past; ERG = ergative; DEF = definiteness; ABS = absolutive; TRANS = transitive.

clauses which have many attributes associated with high transitivity share a common discourse function – that of marking the 'foreground' or event line of a narrative – whereas clauses that have fewer transitivity attributes tend to be off the event line, occurring for instance in descriptive passages. This contrast is argued to constitute the 'discourse basis' for the typological correlation among the transitivity parameters.[5]

Lexical classes

Another set of categories which are traditionally viewed as Aristotelian is the set of word classes or 'parts of speech' in the lexicon. Hopper and Thompson (1984) propose a proto-type view of one word-class contrast, that between nouns and verbs. They argue that the primary motivation for the lexical categories 'noun' and 'verb' has to do with speakers' need on the one hand to establish time-stable referents and track them through discourse – the function primarily associated with nouns – and on the other hand to move events in the discourse forward through time – the function primarily associated with verbs. They also argue that the morphological properties associated with these two categories (such as number and noun class for nouns, and tense and aspect for verbs) are motivated by these distinct discourse functions. Consequently, when nouns and verbs are associated with discourse functions other than the 'central' or 'prototypical' ones described above, these distinctive morphological markers will tend to be lost.

For instance, consider the first occurrence of the word *paper* in the following example, taken from a conversation about work in a paper recycling mill (*mayate* is a Mexican Spanish term for an African-American).[6]

(2) 21   G: .. But the mayate,
     22   ... apparently,
     23   .. it seems like he's,
     24   ... worked in a —
→ 25   D: ... paper company before.
     26   G: Yeah.
     27   He knows about paper.

---

[5]In a more recent paper, Thompson and Hopper (2001) show that transitivity is generally very low in everyday face-to-face conversation and suggest genre as the factor which accounts for their findings.

[6]This and the following example are from English conversational data collected and transcribed by Danae Paolino. The following transcription conventions are used:

1   Line breaks represent intonation units.
2   Line-final punctuation reflects intonation contours.
3   Two dots represent a short pause; three dots represent a longer pause.
4   Brackets [ ] indicate overlap between speakers.

Since there are many different systems of discourse transcription in use in the material we have drawn our examples from, with different kinds of information being notated in each system, we have simplified many of the examples by omitting notations such as timing and breath when these are not relevant to the discussion.

The word *paper* in line 25 is non-referential: no specific paper is being mentioned. The fact that *paper* is not being used to track a time-stable referent in the discourse is indicated by the fact that the mention of paper in G's turn isn't a pronoun (he doesn't say 'he knows about *it*' even though both nouns arguably have the same generic referent: paper in general). Consequently, the normal morphological and syntactic attributes that are associated with nouns are lost in this context: the noun can't take articles or modifiers and can't be pronominalized.

A similar point can be made for verbs. Consider the verb *stock boost* in line 4 of the following, taken from the same conversation as (2):

    (3) 1   G: .. Can you imagine man?
         2   ... They hired summer help,
         3   .. They're paying seven fifty,
       →4   to stock boost,

This is a purpose clause, and as such it doesn't refer to a real event that is asserted to have occurred. Because of this it is restricted to a 'stripped down' form that doesn't allow for the normal morphological and syntactic trappings of verbs, such as tense marking, person agreement, and the expression of the subject.

Hopper and Thompson propose the term 'categoriality' for the property of being prototypical in function and having the full morphological and syntactic 'trappings' of a category. For instance, non-referential nouns or verbs in purpose clauses can be said to be low in categoriality. The categories 'noun' and 'verb' are said to be appropriately described by a prototype structure rather than a scale, because there are different ways in which an expression can diverge from the central function of each category. A verb, for instance, can fail to move the event line forward by referring to a non-actual situation, as in the purpose clause example above, or by referring to a state rather than an event, or by being presupposed rather than asserted. These are all different ways of being low in categoriality, and they cannot be arranged along a single dimension.

Categories in everyday talk

As the above discussion shows, discourse-functional linguists have used evidence from discourse variation and from typology to challenge the nature of 'grammatical category', which is at the heart of traditional approaches to grammar but has simply been assumed without having been tested against language use. More recently, this line of research has extended into the exploration of everyday talk, the primary form of human language. Ono and Thompson (2009) have thus shown that the use of Japanese adjectives in everyday talk is actually largely restricted to certain formulaic expressions, and Englebretson (2003; 2008) has also shown that grammatical categories which have been assumed for Indonesian by approaches influenced by Western languages either do not exist or are considerably different from the standard description.[7] Along the same lines, Tao (2003) has shown that the argument structure of the common English verbs *remember* and *forget* in everyday conversation is quite different from what had been earlier assumed. Earlier, *remember* was suggested to be a transitive verb which takes either a noun phrase (*I remember that story*), a clause (*I remember that I turned off the lights*) or a non-finite form such as a gerund (*I remember doing that*) as its object. However, Tao found that in actual use, both *remember* and *forget* occur frequently without any object at all (as in *The chapter is becoming two chapters. Remember?*: Tao, 2003: 87) and that, counter to previous assumptions, both verbs are quite unlikely to take clauses as their objects in spoken language.

All these studies show that our assumptions about the grammatical behaviour of actual linguistic items and general categories can be considerably enriched by studying their actual use. In addition, they suggest that grammatical categories in everyday talk will differ from traditional accounts, partly owing to the very nature of human language as a constantly changing phenomenon. Any piece of live discourse data represents a temporal outcome of the ongoing change involving variations, some specific examples of which we will observe in the rest of the chapter. This then asks discourse functionalists for more innovative ways of conceptualizing grammar in interaction, which Hopper (1988; 1998) and Du Bois (2003) have begun to capture.

EXPLANATORY THEMES

There are a number of explanatory themes, or functional dimensions, which have been especially important in discourse-functional work and have tended to recur. In the following sections we will outline the themes that have emerged as being most central. For each theme, we will give examples of grammatical phenomena that have been usefully addressed in terms of each theme.

One large body of research in studies of discourse and grammar is related to the theme of 'information flow', which has to do with the way information is distributed within and across clauses.

While information flow can be seen as primarily relating to the discourse context of an utterance, other kinds of contextual factors are relevant too. In this chapter we also discuss the speaker's attitude towards a referent or a proposition, and factors having to do with the interaction, which relate not just to the speaker or the hearer, but also to the actual second-by-second interaction between them. Examining these factors is a central focus in Interactional Linguistics, which has resulted in a large amount of concentrated research (Couper-Kuhlen

---

[7]Recently, typologists, who mostly work with dictionaries/grammars and constructed data, have also pointed out that certain grammatical categories such as 'passive' or 'direct object' might not be cross-linguistically valid (Dryer, 1997; Croft, 2001; 2007).

and Selting, 1996; Ochs, Schegloff and Thompson, 1996; Selting and Couper-Kuhlen, 2001; Ford, Fox and Thompson, 2002a; 2002b; Couper-Kuhlen and Ford, 2004).

Finally, we provide our view of the future of discourse-functional approaches to linguistics and list some outstanding research questions.

INFORMATION FLOW

'Information flow' is perhaps the best-known and most widely exploited of the conceptual tools employed by discourse-functional grammarians, and one which produced focused and influential research in the early stages of the development of discourse-functional linguistics. More or less the same range of phenomena appears in the literature under a variety of names; the terminology we adopt here is that of Chafe (1994), but other widely used terms include 'communicative dynamism', 'givenness', 'topicality', 'thematicity', and 'focus'. The idea underlying information flow is that a primary function of language is to convey information from the speaker to the addressee. Information differs in how accessible it is, or how easy it is to process, from either the speaker's or the addressee's point of view. From the speaker's point of view, we can think in terms of information which is in or out of attention or the focus of 'consciousness' (to use Chafe's term). From the addressee's point of view, we can think in terms of information which is more or less expected or predictable given the setting and the previous discourse (Prince, 1981; Givón, 1983). We expect information which is relatively accessible or predictable to be coded with less linguistic work; conversely, information which is relatively inaccessible or surprising should be coded with special, heavy or 'marked' linguistic mechanisms. Moreover, predictability may have several different sources, which can be distinguished by linguistic coding devices (as the discussion of the difference between pronouns and definite articles given below shows).

Information flow is generally taken to be a cognitive matter, to be understood in terms of the dynamic mental states of the speaker and addressee during discourse production and consumption. Since it is speakers who make linguistic decisions, discourse grammarians are primarily interested in their mental states. On the other hand, since speakers take addressees' needs (as assessed through discourse history, observation, and general expectations) into account when producing discourse, the mental state of the addressee – or, more accurately, the speaker's model of the mental state of the addressee – must also be taken into account. These relationships are shown in Figure 2.3.

What is misleading about this figure is that it suggests that the 'same' information is present in the mind of the speaker, in the linguistic signal, and in the mind of the addressee – and moreover that the speaker's representation of the addressee is exact. This is of course unlikely to be the case. However, it may correspond to the folk model that interactants have about communication. For this reason it is a relevant view and a convenient one to adopt as a first approximation.

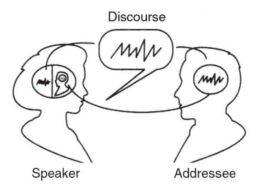

Figure 2.3   A simplified model of information in discourse

Since access to the mental representations constructed by speakers and hearers in natural settings is difficult to obtain, discourse-functional linguists will often operationalize aspects of these representations in terms of characteristics of the discourse itself. For instance, 'less accessible/predictable' may be operationalized as 'not recently mentioned' or 'distant in the text'. Alternatively, using experimental means, researchers may manipulate speakers' representations. For instance, they may provide material to verbalize by showing subjects a film and asking them to describe what happened, as in work by Chafe (1980) and Tomlin (1987).

Information flow factors have been cited in relation to a very wide range of grammatical phenomena. Perhaps the most fundamental are matters relating to the quantity of information in a unit (especially with regard to the noun phrase form) and its arrangement (as realized in the order of elements and their roles in argument structure). The following sections discuss information flow in relation to noun phrase form, constituent order, and argument structure; for additional topics, see the recommended reading at the end of the chapter.

Noun phrase form

One of the more well-studied areas of investigation by discourse-functional linguists is the choice – traditionally characterized as 'optional' – among different referential forms such as full noun phrases, pronouns, and 'zero anaphora' (simple omission), and also the use of articles (such as in English *the* and *a*) and other determiners. The major finding here has been that the degree of explicitness of a referential form correlates with how accessible the speaker judges the referent to be in the hearer's mind (Chafe, 1976; 1987; 1994). Full noun phrases are associated with referents which the speaker judges are not active in the hearer's consciousness, while pronouns are associated with active concepts. Articles, on the other hand, are associated with an information status factor that Chafe (1976) characterized as 'identifiability': the speaker's assumption that a hearer can identify a referent based either on a prior mention in discourse or on knowledge obtained from other sources. Definite marking *the* is associated with identifiable referents, while indefinite marking *a* is associated with non-identifiable ones.

Consider the following example, which includes both of the examples (2) and (3) that we considered above:

(4)	1	G:	... Can you imagine man?
	2		... They hired summer help,
	3		.. They're paying seven fifty,
	4		to stock boost,
	5		three machines man.
	6		... Two dudes.
	7		.. A mayate,
	8		.. and a white dude.
	9	D:	Nobody in finishing?
	10		... Just two guys they hired?
	11	G:	... Uh,
	12		... and one more,
	13		.. on the tables.
	14		... Uh,
	15		... Zamorra's uh .. brother-in-law.
	16	D:	.. Is that right?
	17	G:	... Yeah.
	18	D:	... Wow.
	19	G:	... So they got three new guys.
	20		... But they're summer help.
	21		.. But the mayate,
	22		... apparently,
	23		.. it seems like he's,
	24		... worked in a —
	25	D:	... paper company before.
	26	G:	Yeah.
	27		He knows about paper.

In this example, speaker G is attempting to establish a referent for speaker D. The first mention of the referent, *a mayate* (line 7), is accomplished with a noun phrase marked with an indefinite article. The next reference, which doesn't occur until several lines further down (line 21), is accomplished with a noun phrase marked with *the*. By this time, the referent is identifiable (by virtue of prior reference), but it has not been mentioned recently enough to be considered active in the hearer's consciousness. The third and fourth references, occurring directly afterwards (lines 23 and 27), are each accomplished with a personal pronoun *he*; this reflects the fact that the referent was mentioned in the immediately previous context, and thus the speaker can assume that the referent is active in the mind of the hearer.

This illustrates the following general pattern: when a referent is not active in the hearer's consciousness at the time of mention, it is likely to be expressed with an indefinite noun phrase. When it is identifiable but not fully active (for instance, it has been introduced but not mentioned recently), a definite noun phrase will be used. Finally, when it is fully active (for instance, because it has just been mentioned), a pronoun will be used.

Another factor relevant to the choice of the full noun phrase *the mayate* in line 21 is the fact that the immediately preceding line contains a reference to a set of which the *mayate* is a member (the 'three new guys'). Thus, there are three human referents available in the context. It is generally the case that environments which contain more than one semantically compatible referent will give rise to the use of full noun phrases rather than pronouns (Clancy, 1980; Givón, 1983; Fox, 1987); Givón calls this situation 'potential interference'.

As suggested above, there are other sources of identifiability besides a prior mention in the text. In line 13 of example (4), the noun phrase *the tables* is definite because G and D have worked in the same environment, and therefore G can assume that D is able to identify the tables he means.

Though it is generally accepted that information flow factors are the primary factors involved in selecting noun phrase form, various other factors have also been shown to be relevant; some of these will be discussed below.

Constituent order

Constituent order – the order of elements in the clause, especially the relative positions of the verb, subject and object – is another area where information status has long been recognized as playing a crucial role. Prague School linguists observed that, especially in languages with a relatively flexible constituent order, given information tends to come earlier in the clause than new information. In Indonesian, for instance, the subject of the existential/locative verb *ada* 'be (at)' precedes the verb when it is given information, but follows it when it is new information. This is illustrated in examples (5) and (6) respectively.[8]

(5) katakan saja yang map hitam itu,
     Say just REL folder black that
     ... Map hitamnya,
     ... folder black:the
     S V
→ **dia** ada di lemari sini.
     they be at cupboard here

     'Say for instance the black folders ... the black folders, they're in the cupboard here.'

(6) ... Tapi,
     ... But
     ada s- —
     be —

---

[8]The examples in this section are taken from a transcript by Michael Ewing of an office conversation collected by Susanna Cumming. The labels above the Indonesian show the relative position of the various grammatical elements in the clause: V = verb; S = intransitive subject. The following glossing abbreviations are used in the Indonesian and Malay examples: PL = plural; REL = relative clause marker.

>   V   S
> →   ada **dua hal   yang mau   saya kasih   tahu**,
>   be   two thing REL want I   give know
>   sama anda-anda ya?
>   to you:PL   yes
>
>   'But, there's o- there are two things I want to tell you, OK?'

While English is a relatively fixed word-order language, it also has a tendency to arrange given and new information in this way, as reflected in the glosses of the above examples: ***they*** *are in the cupboard* versus *there* *are* ***two things I want to tell you***. In the latter sentence, the 'fixedness' of English word order is respected by the presence of the 'dummy subject' *there*, but the understood subject of the sentence is *two things I want to tell you*, which comes clause-finally.

While the pattern illustrated here (old information first, new information last) is widespread, there is a competing pattern in many languages which favours the initial position for certain kinds of unexpected information, especially information which is contrastive or 'resumptive' (that is, it has been mentioned before but not for some time). This pattern is commonly found, for instance, in Classical Malay, a language which is a precursor of Modern Indonesian but which exhibits significantly different constituent order patterns (see Cumming, 1991). The function of the clause-initial position has been termed 'newsworthiness' which includes new and contrastive information, and is discussed with relation to polysynthetic languages in Mithun (1987).

Preferred argument structure

Another area where information flow factors have been shown to be crucially relevant to linguistic coding is that of 'argument structure', a term which refers to the syntactic and semantic roles of the noun phrases in a clause. It has been noted for some time, for instance, that subjects strongly tend to have a given referent (Li, 1976). This is usually held to derive from the fact that subjects – especially of transitive verbs – tend to be agents, agents tend to be human, and humans tend to be discourse topics; thus they are likely to be given. Du Bois (1985; 1987) has extended this analysis, showing that new information also has preferences: new referents are much more likely to be introduced as objects of transitive verbs or as subjects of intransitive verbs in many different languages. Example (6) above showed the use of an intransitive verb to introduce a referent (existential and locative verbs are particularly suited for this function); the following example, excerpted from example (4), shows how a transitive verb is used to introduce new information in the object position. (Note that the subject of the verb is a pronoun, in accordance with the tendency for transitive subjects to be given.)

(7) … So they got three new guys.

Thus, the objects of transitive verbs tend to contain new information and the subjects of transitive verbs tend to contain given information, while intransitive subjects are sometimes given (like transitive subjects) and sometimes new (like transitive objects). Du Bois argues that this observation explains the fact that most languages in the world will exhibit one of two major case-marking patterns: one in which subjects of intransitives have the same case marking as subjects of transitives (the so-called 'nominative-accusative' pattern, found in Indo-European languages and elsewhere), and another in which the subjects of intransitives have the same case marking as the objects of transitives (the so-called 'ergative' pattern, found in many Native American, Australian, and Pacific languages as well as elsewhere).

SUBJECTIVITY AND INTERSUBJECTIVITY

The range of phenomena associated in the literature with 'subjectivity/intersubjectivity', also called 'stance', 'speaker attitude', 'perspective', 'empathy', 'interpersonal metafunction', and simply 'subjectivity', has been held to influence a wide range of aspects of linguistic form. Unlike information flow factors, attitude factors reflect neither the content of an utterance nor its informational aspects, but rather how the states of affairs being discussed are viewed or assessed. Here, we will discuss the influence of stance on the noun phrase form and argument structure as well as the clausal structure.

Noun phrase form

There have been studies which suggested that referential choice was determined by stance. Several show that in some languages the explicitness of referential forms correlates with the degree of empathy (Clancy, 1980; Duranti, 1984): the more empathy the speaker feels towards the referent, the less explicit the form used (for example, zero anaphora and pronoun).

The converse can also be true: sometimes a fuller form will be used to indicate a lack of empathy. Mayes and Ono (1991) also suggest that a particular set of explicit forms (anaphoric demonstrative plus noun) in Japanese is used to indicate a certain social distance between the speaker and the referent, regardless of the degree of accessibility of the referent in the hearer's mind. Consider the following example.[9]

(8) H:　iwayuru furui taipu no eigyoo- moo
　　　　so-called old type of sales:person EMPH
　　　　'Because (he) is an old world sales-'

　　 T:　ne.
　　　　PRT
　　　　'Yeah.'

---

[9]Example from Mayes and Ono (1991). Abbreviations: EMPH = emphasis; PRT = particle.

H: tenkeitekina eigyooman da kara **ano hito**.
    typical sales:person be because that person
    'typical sales person, that person.'

T: honto yan nacchau **ano hito**.
    really disgusted become that person
    '(I'm) really tired of that person.'

The use of the more explicit *ano hito* in the last two lines can be explained by the speaker's stance toward the referent. In the context of the conversation, the participants were complaining about a co-worker. The use of *ano hito* clearly indicates a certain social/emotional distance and thus a lack of empathy between the speaker and the referent. The unusual constituent order of the final clause in this example is probably also stance-related: Ono and Suzuki (1992) and Ono (2006) report some instances where predicates indicating strong emotion are expressed before their arguments in Japanese, which is otherwise known for its rigid predicate-final order.

Demonstratives appear to be powerful devices for the expression of social distinctions crosslinguistically. In Mayan, for example, demonstratives can be used to show that the person referred to, even though she or he is a participant in the conversation, is being excluded from the currently unfolding interaction, or, in other words, is not a recipient for the current turn at talk (Hanks, 1990); in Finnish, conversely, a demonstrative can be used to indicate that a copresent person is being included in the interaction (Seppänen, 2003). This is particularly interesting in that third person forms (such as demonstratives, personal pronouns such as *she*, and noun phrases such as *that guy*) have previously been assumed to be used for persons who are not participants in the conversation.

Argument structure

Several researchers have suggested that there is a direct relationship between the stance taken by a speaker and the mapping of event participants onto case roles in discourse. In such accounts, agents or subjects are generally held to have a special syntactic status, either because the speaker takes their 'point of view' (as suggested in, for example, Chafe, 1994), or because they are held socially 'responsible' for the event (the account preferred in, for example, Duranti and Ochs, 1990; see also Duranti, 1994). Consider the following example from a traditional Samoan village council meeting (Duranti, 1994: 132). Tafili reveals a rumour that has forced her brother Savea to file a suit against Igu. First, Tafili says:[10]

(9) e (le)aga 'o 'upu gei ou ke kaukala iai,
     'because these words I am going to talk about,'

---

[10]Example from Duranti (1994). Abbreviations: ART = article; EMP = emphasis; ERG = ergative marker; NEG = negative; PRED = predicate marker; PRO = pronoun; PST = past; TA = tense/aspect marker.

→ "'ua fa'akau　　Savea　　**e**　**Igu**　i　　kupe."...
　PST buy　　　Savea　　ERG Igu　with　monies
　'"Savea has been bought by Igu with money."...'

ia 'ua kakau ai lā ga kulāfogo 'upu gā,
'so it has been necessary to try in court those words,'

In this quote reporting the rumour, *Igu* is marked by *e* (an 'ergative' marker, which makes it explicit that Igu is the agent of a transitive clause). Duranti suggests that this case marker is associated with attributed responsibility – which is relevant here, because this is an accusation of wrongdoing. However, later in the same meeting, Savea says:

(10) → e leai ā se kupe **a Igu** o maimau
　　　　 TA NEG EMP ART money of Igu PRED wasted
　　　　 'there is no money of Igu's wasted'

　　　　 e kokogi ai sa'u fāsefulu kālā ...
　　　　 TA pay PRO my forty dollars
　　　　 'to pay my forty dollars ...' (or 'to pay forty dollars for me')

Here, the same event is described, but this time *Igu* is marked by the genitive marker *a*. Apparently, in this scene, Savea is reframing the event in a way which minimizes Igu's responsibility.

　　More generally, since human referents are ordinarily taken to be responsible for actions, and speakers tend to take their point of view, much crosslinguistic work has shown that human mentions strongly tend to be made in core grammatical roles, especially as subjects (e.g., Du Bois, 1987; Thompson, 1997; Nakayama and Ichihashi-Nakayama, 1997; Helasvuo, 2001a, 2001b).

LEXICALIZED CLAUSES AS EPISTEMIC/EVIDENTIAL/EVALUATIVE FRAGMENTS

An important body of work has centred on subject–verb combinations such as the English *I think* and *I guess*. It has been argued that, unlike what was traditionally assumed, the main function of these expressions is not the reporting of a speaker's internal mental states, but that they rather serve as devices used in discourse to index subjectivity and stance (Kärkkäinen, 2003). Consider the following example (taken from Du Bois, Chafe, Meyer and Thompson, 2000), in which a lawyer is preparing a client for trial.[11]

(11)　REBECCA:　[Becau]se,
　　　　RICKIE:　　[2(SNIFF)2]
　　　　REBECCA:　[2(H)2] number one they pick out,
　　　　　　　　　.. I think .. more vulnerable peo[ple.

---

[11]Abbreviations: (SNIFF) = sniff; (H) = inhalation.

In this example, *I think*, rather than simply reporting Rebecca's thoughts, is used to frame a certain kind of a stance; in the context, without the *I think*, Rebecca could be heard as indicating that her addressee, Rickie, is vulnerable; in a previous discussion, Rickie has acted in ways that might be interpreted as being vulnerable (she has been crying and can still be heard sniffing through this excerpt); the use of *I think* appears to mitigate this potentially face-threatening utterance (see Kärkkäinen, 2003: 119 for an analysis of this example).

In recent research, it has also been stressed that the marking of stance in discourse is not an individual activity. Instead, it has been argued that stance taking should be seen as inherently dialogic and intersubjective, an activity that discourse participants engage in together. Stance building has been shown to involve the alignment of participants with the stances already being displayed by others. In other words, people do not express their stances out of the blue, prompted by their own internal feelings, but rather they shape their stances in response to what the other people they are talking with have expressed. For example, it is very common for participants in conversation to acknowledge the stances taken by others by conceding to them prior to expressing a differing stance (see, for example, Du Bois, 2007; for other papers see Englebretson, 2007; for concession, see Couper-Kuhlen and Thompson, 2000). In the example above, the stance Rebecca takes can be understood to relate to Rickie's emotional stance, and in a subsequent interaction (not shown here) she can be seen to align with or respond to the stance taken by Rebecca.

There has also been a great interest in the display of affect or emotion in conversation. In this work, researchers have investigated the division of labour between vocal and gestural expressions as markers of stance, affect and affiliation (e.g., Goodwin and Goodwin, 2000; Stivers, 2008; Couper-Kuhlen, 2009).

We have seen in this section that many of the factors usually associated with information flow considerations – including pronoun use, constituent order, and case marking, as well as clausal structures – may also be associated with factors relating to the speaker's attitude. In the next section, we explore additional social factors in relation to the shaping of grammar.

INTERACTIONAL FACTORS

Recently, many researchers have focused on the contingent nature of grammatical structure in conversation. Ford (2004) has shown that syntactic units in conversation, far from being first fully planned in the mind of the speaker and then spoken out loud, in fact emerge in response to what happens in an interaction and are always subject to revisions and additions. In addition, pressures from the demands of conversational interaction have been associated with the use of a wide range of grammatical constructions. Various aspects of syntax can be understood as being motivated by the goals that arise for interactants out of the turn-taking system of conversation (described by Pomerantz and Fehr in Chapter 9 of this book). Here, we will focus on the effects of interactional pressures on several areas of syntax which relate to motivations for presenting information in a particular sequence.

Left-dislocation

'Left-dislocation' is the construction found in sentences such as *Sandy, she likes garlic.* According to traditional accounts, this construction involves 'fronting' a noun phrase and replacing it with a 'pronoun copy'; it is viewed as a simple, monoclausal construction. However, both Keenan and Schieffelin (1976) and Geluykens (1992) have shown that this construction is likely to be interactionally complex, involving contributions from more than one interactant, and that it is designed to fulfil interactional goals. For example, Geluykens (1992: 36) presents such examples as the following:

(12) A: well **Sir Garnet Wolseley**
       B: yes ((sure oh oh))
       A: he was the one who did all the army reforms in the eighteen eighties

Here, speaker A introduces a referent in the discourse with a noun phrase, and only after the introduction has been confirmed by speaker B does A come back and say something about the referent. Thus, the left-dislocation construction is distributed across three turns by two speakers, and involves a negotiation between them as to the identifiability of the referent. So the examination of left-dislocation in discourse shows that its use involves heavy interactional work, and this further suggests that the existence and characteristics of the construction itself may be interactionally motivated.

In more recent work on left-dislocations, scholars have focused on the ways that participants in a conversation will use the construction as a resource for organizing their temporally unfolding actions. It has been noted that they are used not only for the negotiation of reference, but also for displaying stance (either in terms of agreement or disagreement), and for repairing utterances already produced (Pekarek Doehler, forthcoming).

Final adverbial clauses and increments

Adverbial clauses are those which are subordinate to a main clause and which may be placed either before or after the clause they modify. In English, they are usually introduced with 'subordinating conjunctions' such as *before*, *because*, or *although*. Since they can occur in more than one position, it is then relevant to examine the factors which will determine where they do actually occur. A comparison of a number of studies, including Chafe (1984) and Thompson (1987) on narrative, Matthiessen and Thompson (1988) on expository discourse, and Ford (1993) on conversation, reveals that initial adverbial clauses are most commonly associated with the function of creating and reflecting discourse structure by signalling shifts in time, place or orientation – as in *When I was living there for the couple of years* … (taken from Du Bois, Chafe, Meyer and Thompson, 2000). On the other hand, Ford (1993) has suggested that when an adverbial clause is produced in a final position, following a falling intonation contour in the conversation, it is motivated by interactional factors. For example, she finds examples such as the following in her conversational data:[12]

<pre>
(13) 1 A: Did you get ye=r your first pay check from it?
     3   .. at least?
     4 R: No= I won't get that for a couple weeks yet.
     5 A: Oh,
     7   .. W'l
     8 R: 'Cause it takes a long time.
     9 A: at least it's in the bank,
    10 R: ... Yeah it will be.
</pre>

In lines 1–3, A asks R a question. R's answer in line 4 is somewhat unexpected, as is shown by A's utterance *oh* in line 5 (Heritage, 1984). Ford suggests that the adverbial clause in line 8 is used in response to A's signal of interactional trouble, that is, as a clarification for the unexpected answer. Thus we can see that interaction motivates the use of final adverbial clauses in English.

It should be noted that this example also exhibits another interactionally motived grammatical phenomenon often called increment: a syntactically fitted re-completion of turns at talk which have already been brought to completion. For example, in line 1, A first produces a question *Did you get ye=r your first pay check from it?*, which is syntactically, prosodically, and pragmatically complete, creating a situation where R is expected to respond. Not receiving a proper uptake from R, as indicated by the pause in line 3, A produces an increment *at least?*, which is syntactically fitted with the first utterance, which creates another syntactic, prosodic, and pragmatic ending *Did you get ye=r your first pay check from it .. at least?*, giving R another chance to respond. Now, as seen in line 4, R produces a proper uptake by saying *No= I won't get that for a couple weeks yet*. Thus we can see another type of ordering element which is motivated by interaction, one which has been receiving substantial research attention in recent years (Auer, 1996; Schegloff, 1996; Ford, Fox and Thompson, 2002c; Couper-Kuhlen and Ono, 2007).

Biclausal and multiclausal constructions

Recently, many discourse grammarians have focused on the nature of biclausal and multiclausal constructions, that is, combinations of two or more clauses (roughly, a clause consists of a predicate and its associated arguments). One issue has to do with expressions such as *I think* and *I guess*, discussed above in connection with stance. While traditionally such expressions are assumed to function as the main clause found with their subordinate clause in constructed examples like *I think that I will have beer instead*, it has been pointed out

---

[12]Example from Ford (1993: 115). The transcription has been altered slightly to agree with earlier examples.

that, in frequent use in discourse, they have been routinized and reduced to such a degree that they can be said to function as 'epistemic/evidential/evaluative fragments' (e.g., Bybee and Scheibman, 1999; Scheibman, 2000; 2001; Thompson, 2002; Hopper and Thompson, 2008). This routinization has been coupled with increased use of the expression in various syntactic positions and not only in the initial position in a clause combination, where one could expect a regular main clause to be located in languages like English (see example (11) above, where *I think* is used in a syntactic position different from that occupied by main clauses). This has led researchers to conclude that expressions of this kind are no longer functioning as main clauses in a variety of languages (see, for example, Günthner and Imo, 2003, on German).

Even when such expressions occur in the beginning of an utterance, conversation data have shown that they are better analysed as projective devices (Auer, 2005; Hopper and Thompson, 2008), which indicate that more talk is on the way, thereby buying the speaker more time to formulate what s/he is going to say, as well as framing that talk as performing a specific type of action (such as a quote or an assessment). In addition, what participants seem to orient towards in subsequent talk is not the formulaic 'main' clause (such as *I think* or the French *je veux dire* 'I mean'), but rather the talk that follows. These facts would make it more difficult to analyse an expression containing such a formulaic expression as a biclausal construction (e.g., Thompson, 2002; Hopper and Thompson, 2008). Consider the next example, taken from a French conversation concerning bilingualism. The speaker is explaining that items in a bilingual's two languages are never exactly the same, even if they are translation equivalents of each other.

(14) 8   L: ouais c'est que c'est c-c'est basé sur des connotations,
               'yeah it's that it's it's based on connotations,'

    9   **je veux dire** euh: (1.4) des endroits de la maison la waschküche
               'I mean places in the house the laundry-room ((in German))'

   10   on disait la waschküche pour la buanderie,
               'we used to say the laundry-room ((in German)) for laundry-room,'

   11   par exemple ben c'était pas seulement n'importe quelle
               'for instance well it wasn't just whatever'

   12   buanderie c'était celle du bas.
               'laundry-room it was the one below.'

The expression *je veux dire* 'I mean' in line 9 is used by L to tie together a) the generalization in line 8 about how words that have the 'same' meaning are not equivalent, because their meanings are based on connotations (i.e., each word in each language has a specific connotation), and b) the example illustrating this generalization which L presents in lines 9–12: the German word *waschküche* that her family used only referred to the laundry room which they had downstairs. Notice that *je veux dire* 'I mean' is immediately followed by the hesitation *euh:* and a relatively long 1.4 second pause in line 9, which suggests that *je veux dire* is used to hold the floor: the speaker is going to continue, and therefore another speaker should not take a turn (Pekarek Doehler, forthcoming).

Another phenomenon having to do with clause combining involves the collaborative nature of conversational discourse. Clause combinations can be produced so that one participant will produce one part and another participant will produce another part (e.g., Helasvuo, 2003). In languages like Japanese, where main clauses normally occur after their subordinate clauses, a speaker or even another participant can 'subordinate' a clause after it has already been completed (Tanaka, 2001). A third issue analysts have focused on has to do with the tendency of conjunctions to be grammaticized into particles. In many languages, forms which in traditional grammars have been analysed as subordinate conjunctions will turn out to be used to initiate and end clauses for which a main clause is difficult or impossible to identify. Often, such use of a conjunction as a clause-final or clause-initial particle can be seen as a result of an on-going language change; for example, the English *but* appears to be currently in the process of becoming a final particle (Mulder and Thompson, 2008). The Finnish conjunction *että* 'that', on the other hand, has uses both as a subordinate conjunction and as an initial and final particle. However, the dividing line between the conjunction and the particle use is not always easy to draw, something that is typical of forms undergoing a category change (Laury and Seppänen, 2008). As previously mentioned, category overlap due to on-going change is an ever present quality of human languages.

CONCLUSION

In the preceding sections, we have shown that a number of linguistic phenomena must be understood in terms of their functions in discourse. By establishing the discourse basis of linguistic phenomena, discourse-functional grammarians have demonstrated the importance of using natural discourse data in linguistics. In this final section, we would like to discuss several directions taken by research which we feel are either the most promising or the most necessary for the future of discourse and grammar research to be both fruitful and exciting.

Large-scale audio/video corpora: First of all, the field still does not have sizable databases for most languages where not only the transcripts but also the original audio and video recording of everyday talk are available. This is particularly important in light of the new development in Interactional Linguistics where grammar is considered part of a multimodal system which includes nonverbal features such as gaze and body movement, making it mandatory for us to have the video recording in the analysis. Given this critical development in the field, in our attempt to understand human language, creating sizable databases representing everyday talk in transcripts and audio/video recording is the most urgent and exciting task in the field.

Multimodality: Second, as indicated above, multimodality appears to be the area where the majority of current research attention is being focused. It is interesting to see a great number of studies which have been showing that grammar, which was once given an independent status, can only be understood in connection with other modes of human behavior, underscoring the importance of trying to pin down what we know about and what we can do with language in actual human behaviour.

Other areas: Third, nearly all of the research described in this chapter is related primarily to issues of morphosyntax: much attention has been paid, for instance, to how a speaker chooses between various linguistic forms and the nature, shape and use of particular linguistic categories and constructions, but very little has concentrated on areas outside of morphosyntax. Though there have been some attempts to understand the nature of phonetic and phonological knowledge and skills by researchers such as Local, Couper-Kuhlen, Bybee and their associates (Local, Kelly and Wells, 1986; Couper-Kuhlen and Selting, 1996; Local, 1996; Bybee, 2001; Couper-Kuhlen and Ford, 2004) based on the study of discourse data, studies focusing on areas such as the lexicon and semantics in discourse data, particularly in everyday talk, are rather rare, and thus much needed.

Modelling: Finally, and related to the last point, we would also like to highlight that there has not been much effort among the discourse-functional linguists whose work is described above in trying to establish a coherent overall model of human language: a model which would clarify how functional factors which have been singly and independently suggested to motivate particular linguistic forms interact with each other, and in which those interacting functional factors are incorporated with structural aspects of language in order to model the processes involved in human communication. Needless to say, such a model should include not only components covered by the traditional areas of linguistics such as morphosyntax and semantics, but also components which deal with such cognitive and interactional factors as memory, attention, empathy, affect, and interaction. Moreover, it must also incorporate those components covered by such other areas of linguistics as phonetics and phonology which have been given relatively little attention by discourse-functional linguistics. Explicit modelling should be one of the eventual goals of discourse-functional linguistics, and we believe that having focused on actual language use for some time, the field is in a privileged position where the first steps toward this goal can be taken in a more concrete manner.

NOTE

The authors would like to thank Sandy Thompson, Mike Ewing and Robert Englebretson for their comments on a draft of this chapter. We would also like to thank Maggie Camp, Yuka Matsugu and Hiromi Aoki for their help in our preparation of the manuscript.

FURTHER READING

For those who wish to explore further this emerging area of linguistics, where actual usage is examined in order to theorize about human language, the following set of readings will be good starters.

Bybee, J. (2010) *Language, Usage and Cognition.* Cambridge: Cambridge University Press.
This is the most recent attempt by an innovative usage-based grammarian to model language use, change, and structure in an integrated manner.

Couper-Kuhlen, E. and Selting, M. (eds) (1996) *Prosody and Conversation.* Cambridge: Cambridge University Press.
A first and influential collection of articles in Interactional Linguistics focusing on how prosody is structured and used in conversation.

Ford, C.E., Fox, B.A. and Thompson S.A. (2003) 'Social interaction and grammar', in M. Tomasello (ed.), *The New Psychology of Language: Cognitive and Functional Approaches to Language Structure*, Vol. 2. Mahwah, NJ: Lawrence Erlbaum. pp. 119–143.
This is a good introductory article to Interactional Linguistics. It should perhaps be read before or in conjunction with Ochs, Schegloff, and Thompson (1996).

Hopper, P. (1998) 'Emergent grammar', in M. Tomasello (ed.), *The New Psychology of Language: Cognitive and Functional Approaches to Language Structure.* Mahwah, NJ: Lawrence Erlbaum. pp. 155–175.
This article is an approachable introduction to Hopper's influential theory of grammar.

Ochs, E., Schegloff, E.A. and Thompson, S.A. (eds) (1996) *Interaction and Grammar.* Cambridge: Cambridge University Press.
This volume contains some of the earliest research in Interactional Linguistics by functional grammarians, anthropological linguists and conversation analysts. The introduction to the volume by the three editors is a useful statement regarding the nature of the paradigm and the research traditions which influenced it.

ONLINE READING

The following articles are available at www.sagepub.co.uk/discoursestudies.

Fox, B.A. (2007) 'Principles shaping grammatical practices: an exploration', *Discourse Studies*, 9(3): 299–318.

Thompson, S.A. and Couper-Kuhlen, E. (2005) 'The clause as a locus of grammar and interaction', *Discourse Studies*, 7(4-5): 481–505.

REFERENCES

Auer, P. (1996) 'On the prosody and syntax of turn-taking'. In E. Couper-Kuhlen and M. Selting (eds), *Prosody and Conversation*. Cambridge: Cambridge University Press. pp. 57–100.
Auer, P. (2005) 'Projection in interaction and projection in grammar'. *Text*, 25 (1): 7–36.
Auer, P. and di Lurio, A. (eds) (1992) *The Contextualization of Language*. Amsterdam: Benjamins.
Bolinger, D. (1952) *Fonos of English*. Cambridge, MA: Harvard University Press.
Bolinger, D. (1986) *Intonation and its Parts*. Stanford, CA: Stanford University Press.
Bolinger, D. (1989) *Intonation and its Uses*. Stanford, CA: Stanford University Press.
Bybee, J. (2001) *Phonology and Language Use*. Cambridge: Cambridge University Press.
Bybee, J. and Scheibman, J. (1999) 'The effect of usage on degrees of constituency: the reduction of *don't* in English'. *Linguistics*, 37 (4): 575–96.
Chafe, W. (1976) 'Givenness, contrastiveness, definiteness, subject, topics, and point of view'. In C.N. Li (ed.), *Subject and Topic*. New York: Academic Press. pp. 25–55.
Chafe, W. (ed.) (1980) *The Pear Stories: Cognitive, Cultural, and Linguistic Aspects of Narrative Production*. Norwood, NJ: Ablex.

Chafe, W. (1984) 'How people use adverbial clauses'. In *Proceedings of the Tenth Annual Meeting of the Berkeley Linguistics Society*. Berkeley, CA: Berkeley Linguistics Society. pp. 437–49.

Chafe, W. (1987) 'Cognitive constraints on information flow'. In R.S. Tomlin (ed.), *Coherence and Grounding in Discourse*. Amsterdam: Benjamins. pp. 21–51.

Chafe, W. (1994) *Discourse, Consciousness, and Time*. Chicago, IL: University of Chicago Press.

Clancy, P. (1980) 'Referential choice in English and Japanese narrative discourse'. In W. Chafe (ed.), *The Pear Stories: Cognitive, Cultural, and Linguistic Aspects of Narrative Production*. Norwood, NJ: Ablex. pp. 127–202.

Couper-Kuhlen, E. (2009) 'A sequential approach to affect: the case of "disappointment"'. In M. Haakana, M. Laakso and J. Lindström (eds), *Talk in Interaction: Comparative Dimensions*. Helsinki: Suomalaisen Kirjallisuuden Seura. pp. 94–123.

Couper-Kuhlen, E. and Ford, C.E. (eds) (2004) *Sound Patterns in Interaction*. Amsterdam: Benjamins.

Couper-Kuhlen, E. and Ono, T. (2007) '"Incrementing" in conversation: a comparison of practices in English, German and Japanese'. *Pragmatics*, 17 (4): 513–52.

Couper-Kuhlen, E. and Selting, M. (eds) (1996) *Prosody and Conversation*. Cambridge: Cambridge University Press.

Couper-Kuhlen, E. and Thompson, S.A. (2000) 'Concessive patterns in conversation'. In E. Couper-Kuhlen and B. Kortmann (eds), *Cause, Condition, Concession, and Contrast: Cognitive and Discourse Perspectives*. Berlin: Mouton de Gruyter. pp. 381–410.

Croft, W. (2001) *Radical Construction Grammar: Syntactic Theory in Typological Perspective*. Oxford: Oxford University Press.

Croft, W. (2007) 'Beyond Aristotle and gradience: a reply to Aarts'. *Studies in Language*, 31: 409–30.

Cumming, S. (1991) *Functional Change: The Case of Malay Constituent Order*. Berlin: Mouton de Gruyter.

Daneš, F. (1974) 'Functional sentence perspective and the organization of the text'. In F. Daneš (ed.), *Papers on Functional Sentence Perspective*. Prague: Academia. pp. 106–28.

Dryer, M. (1997) 'Are grammatical categories universal?'. In J. Bybee, J. Haiman and S.A. Thompson (eds), *Essays on Language Function and Language Type: Dedicated to T. Givón*. Amsterdam: Benjamins. pp. 115–43.

Du Bois, J.W. (1985) 'Competing motivations'. In J. Haiman (ed.), *Iconicity in Syntax*. Amsterdam: Benjamins. pp. 343–65.

Du Bois, J.W. (1987) 'The discourse basis of ergativity'. *Language*, 63 (4): 805–55.

Du Bois, J.W. (2003) 'Argument structure: grammar in use'. In J.W. Du Bois, L.E. Kumpf and W.J. Ashby (eds), *Preferred Argument Structure: Grammar as Architecture for Function*. Amsterdam: Benjamins. pp. 10–60.

Du Bois, J.W. (2007) 'The stance triangle'. In R. Englebretson (ed.), *Stancetaking in Discourse: Subjectivity, Evaluation, Interaction*. Amsterdam: John Benjamins. pp. 139–82.

Du Bois, J.W., Chafe, W.L., Meyer, C. and Thompson, S.A. (2000) *Santa Barbara Corpus of Spoken American English, Part One*. Philadelphia, PA: Linguistic Data Consortium.

Du Bois, J.W., Kumpf, L.E. and Ashby, W.J. (eds) (2003) *Preferred Argument Structure: Grammar as Architecture for Function*. Amsterdam: Benjamins.

Duranti, A. (1984) 'The social meaning of subject pronouns in Italian conversation'. *Text*, 4 (4): 277–311.

Duranti, A. (1994) *From Grammar to Politics*. Berkeley, CA: University of California Press.

Duranti, A. and Goodwin, C. (eds) (1992) *Rethinking Context: Language as an Interactive Phenomenon*. Cambridge: Cambridge University Press.

Duranti, A. and Ochs, E. (1990) 'Genitive constructions and agency in Samoan discourse', *Studies in Language*, 14 (1): 1–23.

Edwards, J. and Lampert, M. (eds) (1993) *Talking Data: Transcription and Coding in Discourse Research*. Hillsdale, NJ: Erlbaum.

Englebretson, R. (2003) *Searching for Structure: the Problem of Complementation in Colloquial Indonesian Conversation*. Amsterdam: John Benjamins.

Englebretson, R. (ed.) (2007) *Stancetaking in Discourse: Subjectivity, Evaluation, Interaction*. Amsterdam: John Benjamins.

Englebretson, R. (2008) 'From subordinate clause to noun-phrase: yang constructions in colloquial Indonesian'. In R. Laury (ed.), *Crosslinguistic Studies of Clause Combining: the Multifunctionality of Conjunctions*. Amsterdam: Benjamins. pp. 1–34.

Firbas, J. (1966) 'On defining the theme in functional sentence perspective'. *Travaux Linguistiques de Prague*, 2: 267–80.

Ford, C.E. (1993) *Grammar in Interaction: Adverbial Clauses in American English Conversations*. Cambridge: Cambridge University Press.

Ford, C.E. (2004) 'Contingency and units in interaction'. *Discourse Studies*, 6 (1): 27–52.

Ford, C.E. and Fox, B. (1996) 'Interactional motivations for reference formulation: he had. this guy had, a beautiful, thirty-two O:lds'. In B. Fox (ed.), *Anaphora in Discourse*. Amsterdam: Benjamins. pp. 145–68.

Ford, C.E., Fox, B.A. and Thompson, S.A. (2002a) 'Social interaction and grammar'. In M. Tomasello (ed.), *The New Psychology of Language: Cognitive and Functional Approaches to Language Structure, Vol. 2*. Mahwah, NJ: Lawrence Erlbaum. pp. 119–43.

Ford, C.E., Fox, B.A. and Thompson, S.A. (eds) (2002b) *The Language of Turn and Sequence*. Oxford: Oxford University Press.

Ford, C.E., Fox, B.A. and Thompson, S.A. (2002c) 'Constituency and the grammar of turn increments'. In C. Ford, B.A. Fox, and S.A. Thompson (eds), *The Language of Turn and Sequence*. Oxford: Oxford University Press. pp. 14–38.

Fox, B. (1987) *Discourse Structure and Anaphora: Written and Conversational English*. Cambridge: Cambridge University Press.

Fox, B. and Hopper, P. (eds) (1994) *Voice: Form and Function*. Amsterdam: Benjamins.

Fox, B. and Jasperson, R. (1995) 'The syntactic organization of repair'. In P. Davis (ed.), *Descriptive and Theoretical Modes in the New Linguistics*. Amsterdam: Benjamins. pp. 77–134.

Fox, B. and Thompson, S.A. (1990) 'A discourse explanation of relative clauses in English conversation'. *Language*, 66 (2): 297–316.

Geluykens, R. (1992) *From Discourse Process to Grammatical Construction: On Left-Dislocation in English*. Amsterdam: Benjamins.

Givón, T. (ed.) (1983) *Topic Continuity in Discourse: a Quantitative Cross-Language Study*. Amsterdam: Benjamins.

Givón, T. (1989) *Mind, Code and Context Essays in Pragmatics*. Hillsdale, NJ: Erlbaum.

Givón, T. (1990) *Syntax: A Functional-Typological Introduction*. Amsterdam: Benjamins.

Goodwin, C. (1979) 'The interactive construction of a sentence in natural conversation'. In G. Psathas (ed.), *Everyday Language: Studies in Ethnomethodology*. New York: Irvington. pp. 97–121.

Goodwin, C. (1981) *Conversational Organization: Interaction between Speaker and Hearers*. New York, NY: Academic Press.

Goodwin, C. and Goodwin, M.H. (2000) 'Emotion within situated activity'. In N. Budwig, I.C. Uzgiris and J.V. Wertsch (eds), *Communication: An Arena of Development*. Stanford CT: Ablex. pp. 33–54.

Greenberg, J. (1966) *Language Universals*. The Hague: Mouton.

Grimes, J. (1975) *The Thread of Discourse*. The Hague: Mouton.

Gumperz, J. (1982) *Discourse Strategies*. Cambridge: Cambridge University Press.

Günthner, S. and Imo, W. (2003) 'Die reanalyse von matrixsätzen als diskursmarker: *ich mein*-konstruktionen im gesprochenen Deutsch'. In M. Orosz and A. Herzog (eds), *Jahrbuch der Ungarischen Germanistik 2003*. Budapest/Bonn: DAAD. pp. 181–216.

Haiman, J. (1985) *Natural Syntax*. Cambridge: Cambridge University Press.

Halliday, M.A.K. (1967–8) 'Notes on transitivity and theme in English, parts 1–3'. *Journal of Linguistics*, 3 (1): 37–81, 3 (2): 199–244, and 4 (2): 179–215.

Halliday, M.A.K. (1985) *An Introduction to Functional Grammar*. London: Edward Arnold.

Hanks, W. (1990) *Referential Practice: Language and Lived Space among the Maya*. Chicago, IL: University of Chicago Press.

Helasvuo, M-L. (2001a) *Syntax in the Making: the Emergence of Syntactic Units in Finnish Conversation*. Amsterdam: Benjamins.

Helasvuo, M-L. (2001b) 'Emerging syntax for interaction: noun phrases and clauses as a syntactic resource for interaction'. In M. Selting and E. Couper-Kuhlen (eds), *Studies in Interactional Linguistics*. Amsterdam: John Benjamins. pp. 25–50.

Helasvuo, M-L. (2003) 'Argument splits in Finnish grammar and discourse'. In J.W. Du Bois, L.E. Kumpf and W.J. Ashby (eds), *Preferred Argument Structure: Grammar as Architecture for Function*. Amsterdam: John Benjamins. pp. 247–72.

Heritage, J. (1984) 'A change-of-state token and aspects of its sequential placement'. In J.M. Atkinson and J. Heritage (eds), *Structures of Social Action: Studies in Conversation Analysis*. Cambridge: Cambridge University Press. pp. 299–345.

Hopper, P. (1988) 'Emergent grammar and the a-priori grammar postulate'. In D. Tannen (ed.), *Linguistics in Context: Connecting, Observation, and Understanding*. Norwood, NJ: Ablex. pp. 117–34.

Hopper, P. (1998) 'Emergent grammar'. In M. Tomasello (ed.), *The New Psychology of Language: Cognitive and Functional Approaches to Language Structure*. Mahwah, NJ: Lawrence Erlbaum. pp. 155–75.

Hopper, P. and Thompson, S.A. (1980) 'Transitivity in grammar and discourse', *Language*, 56 (2): 251–99.

Hopper, P. and Thompson, S.A. (1984) 'The discourse basis for lexical categories in universal grammar', *Language*, 60 (4): 703–52.

Hopper, P. and Thompson, S.A. (2008) 'Projectability and clause combining in interaction'. In R. Laury (ed.), *Crosslinguistic Studies of Clause Combining: the Multifunctionality of Conjunctions*. Amsterdam: John Benjamins. pp. 99–124.

Iwasaki, S. (1993) *Subjectivity in Grammar and Discourse: Theoretical Considerations and a Case Study of Japanese Spoken Discourse*. Amsterdam: Benjamins.

Kärkkäinen, E. (2003) *Epistemic Stance in English Conversation. A Description of its Interactional Functions, with a Focus on I Think*. Amsterdam: John Benjamins.

Keenan, E. and Schieffelin, B. (1976) 'Foregrounding referents: a reconsideration of left dislocation in discourse'. In *Proceedings of the 2nd Annual Meeting of the Berkeley Linguistics Society*. pp. 240–57.

Langacker, R.W. (1987) *Foundations of Cognitive Grammar, vol. 1, Theoretical Prerequisites*. Stanford, CA: Stanford University Press.

Langacker, R.W. (1991) *Foundations of Cognitive Grammar, vol. 2, Descriptive Application*. Stanford, CA: Stanford University Press.

Laury, R. and Seppänen, E.-L. (2008) 'Clause combining, interaction, evidentiality, participation structure and the conjunction-particle continuum: the Finnish että'. In R. Laury (ed.), *Crosslinguistic Studies of Clause Combining: the Multifunctionality of Conjunctions*. Amsterdam: Benjamins. pp. 153–78.

Li, C. (ed.) (1976) *Subject and Topic*. New York, NY: Academic Press.

Local, J. (1996) 'Conversational phonetics: some aspects of news receipts in everyday talk'. In E. Couper-Kuhlen and M. Selting (eds), *Prosody in Conversation: Ethnomethodological Studies*. Cambridge: Cambridge University Press. pp. 175–230.

Local, J., Kelly, J. and Wells, B. (1986) 'Towards a phonology of conversation: turn-taking in Tyneside English'. *Journal of Linguistics*, 22 (2): 411–37.

Longacre, R.E. (1972) *Hierarchy and Universality of Discourse Constituents in New Guinea Languages: Discussion*. Washington, DC: Georgetown University Press.

Longacre, R.E. (1976) *Anatomy of Speech Notions*. Liase: Peter de Ridder Press.

Mathesius, V. (1975) *A Functional Analysis of Present-Day English on a General Linguistic Basis* (trans. L. Duskova, ed. J. Vacek). Prague: Academia.

Matthiessen, C.M.I.M. and Thompson, S.A. (1988) 'The structure of discourse and "subordination"'. In J. Haiman and S.A. Thompson (eds), *Clause Combining in Grammar and Discourse*. Amsterdam: Benjamins. pp. 275–329.

Mayes, P. and Ono, T. (1991) 'Social factors influencing reference in Japanese: with special emphasis on *ano hito*'. *Santa Barbara Papers in Linguistics*, 3: 84–93.

Mithun, M. (1987) 'Is basic word order universal?'. In R.S. Tomlin (ed.), *Coherence and Grounding in Discourse*. Amsterdam: Benjamins. pp. 282–328.

Mulder, J. and Thompson, S.A. (2008) 'The grammaticization of *but* as a final particle in English conversation'. In R. Laury (ed.), *Crosslinguistic Studies of Clause Combining: the Multifunctionality of Conjunctions*. Amsterdam: John Benjamins. pp. 179–204.

Nakayama, T. and Ichihashi-Nakayama, K. (1997) 'Discourse perspective for core-oblique distinction in Japanese'. *Santa Barbara Papers in Linguistics*, 5: 158–77.

Ochs, E., Schegloff, E. and Thompson, S.A. (eds) (1996) *Grammar and Interaction*. Cambridge: Cambridge University Press.

Ono, T. (2006) 'An emotively motivated post-predicate constituent order in a "strict predicate final" language: emotion and grammar meet in Japanese everyday talk'. In S. Suzuki (ed.), *Emotive Communication*. Amsterdam: Benjamins. pp. 139–53.

Ono, T. and Suzuki, R. (1992) 'Word order variability in Japanese conversation: motivations and grammaticization'. *Text*, 12 (3): 429–45.

Ono, T. and Thompson, S.A. (2009) 'Fixedness in Japanese adjectives in conversation: toward a new understanding of a lexical (part-of-speech) category'. In R. Corrigan, R. Moravcsik, H. Ouali, and K. Wheatley (eds), *Formulaic Language*. Amsterdam: Benjamins. pp. 117–45.

Pekarek Doehler, S. (forthcoming) 'Emergent grammar for all practical purposes: the on-line formatting of left- and right dislocations in French conversation'. In P. Auer and S. Pfänder (eds), *Emergent Grammar*. Berlin: Mouton de Gruyter.

Pike, K. (1954) *Language in Relation to a Unified Theory of the Structure of Human Behavior*. The Hague: Mouton.

Prince, E.F. (1978) 'A comparison of WH-clefts and It-clefts in discourse'. *Language*, 54 (4): 883–906.

Prince, E.F. (1981) 'Toward a taxonomy of given – new information'. In P. Cole (ed.), *Radical Pragmatics*. New York: Academic Press. pp. 223–55.

Rosch, E. (1978) 'Principies of categorization'. In E. Rosch and B.B. Lloyd (eds), *Cognition and Categorization*. Hillsdale, Erlbaum. pp. 27–48.

Sacks, H., Schegloff, E.A. and Jefferson, G. (1974) 'A simplest systematics for the organization of turn-taking for conversation'. *Language*, 50 (4): 696–735.

Schegloff, E.A. (1996) 'Turn organization: one direction for inquiry into grammar and interaction'. In E. Ochs, E.A. Schegloff and S.A. Thompson (eds), *Interaction and Grammar*. Cambridge: Cambridge University Press. pp. 52–133.

Scheibman, J. (2000) 'I dunno … a usage-based account of the phonological reduction of don't in American English conversation'. *Journal of Pragmatics*, 32: 105–24.

Scheibman, J. (2001) 'Local patterns of subjectivity in person and verb type in American English conversation'. In J. Bybee and P. Hopper (eds), *Frequency and the Emergence of Linguistic Structure*. Amsterdam: John Benjamins. pp. 61–89.

Selting, M. and Couper-Kuhlen, E. (eds) (2001) *Studies in Interactional Linguistics*. Amsterdam: Benjamins.

Seppänen, E.-L. (2003) 'Demonstrative pronouns in addressing and referring in Finnish'. In I. Taavitsainen and A. Jucker (eds), *Diachronic Perspectives on Address Term Systems*. Amsterdam: Benjamins. pp. 375–99.

Shibatani, M. (ed.) (1988) *Passive and Voice*. Amsterdam: Benjamins.

Stivers, T. (2008) 'Stance, alignment and affiliation during story telling: when nodding is a token of preliminary affiliation'. *Research on Language in Social Interaction*, 41: 29–55.

Tanaka, H. (2001) 'The implementation of possible cognitive shifts in Japanese conversation: complementizers as pivotal devices'. In M. Selting and E. Couper-Kuhlen (eds), *Studies in Interactional Linguistics*. Amsterdam: Benjamins. pp. 81–111.

Tao, H. (2003) 'A usage-based approach to argument structure: "remember" and "forget" in spoken English'. *International Journal of Corpus Linguistics*, 8 (1): 75–95.

Thompson, S.A. (1987) '"Subordination" and narrative event structure'. In R.S. Tomlin (ed.), *Coherence and Grounding in Discourse*. Amsterdam: Benjamins. pp. 435–54.

Thompson, S.A. (1990) 'Information flow and "dative shift" in English'. In J. Edmondson, C. Feagin and P. Mühlhäusler (eds), *Development and Diversity: Linguistic Variation across Time and Space*. Dallas: Summer Institute of Linguistics and University of Texas at Arlington. pp. 239–54.

Thompson, S.A. (1997) 'Discourse motivations for the core-oblique distinction as a language universal'. In A. Kamio (ed.), *Directions in Functional Linguistics*. Amsterdam: Benjamins. pp. 59–82.

Thompson, S.A. (2002) 'Object complements' and conversation: towards a realistic account'. *Studies in Language*, 26 (1): 125–64.

Thompson, S.A. and Hopper, P.J. (2001) 'Transitivity, clause structure, and argument structure: evidence from conversation'. In J.L. Bybee and P.J. Hopper (eds), *Frequency and the Emergence of Linguistic Structure*. Amsterdam: Benjamins. pp. 27–60.

Tomlin, R.S. (1987) 'Linguistic reflections of cognitive events'. In R.S. Tomlin (ed.), *Coherence and Grounding in Discourse*. Amsterdam: Benjamins. pp. 455–79.

Discourse Semantics

Russell S. Tomlin, Linda Forrest,
Ming Ming Pu and Myung Hee Kim

THE PROBLEM OF MEANING

It is remarkable how well we communicate with one another. Whether we relate the common events of our day-to-day lives or argue passionately for our ideologies; whether we read a newspaper account of a world event or an academic paper on human language; whether we compose a simple thank-you note or a legal brief, our problems remain the same: how can we ensure that our comprehender gets the message we intend, and how do we derive the message intended from what we hear or read? Our problems as linguists also remain the same: for the comprehender, whether listening or reading, we must describe and account for how meaning is derived from any of these multiple sources; and, for the producer, whether speaker or writer, we must account for how meaning is conveyed. This problem of meaning, this problem of discourse semantics, is a complex one, involving interplay among a wide array of linguistic and non-linguistic processes.

Consider the text fragment in (1).

(1) Text fragment
    1   ... puck knocked away by Dale McCourt
        Ø picked up again by Steve Shutt/
        Now Shutt coming out, on the Detroit zone/
        He played it out in front/
    5   There's Lemaire with a shot.
        and it was blocked by Reed Larson/

This fragment is a short segment transcribed from the online description of an ice hockey game. The announcer alternates between active and passive voice (lines 4 vs lines 1, 2, and 6), between nominal and pronominal form, and between existential clause type (line 5) and simple clauses (line 3). What is it about the message the announcer conveys that leads to the selection of these alternative structures?

This chapter provides an introduction to the concepts and processes underlying our intuitions about how matters of emphasis and importance and prior knowledge contribute to the meaning one derives from text and discourse during comprehension, and how these contribute towards and shape decisions about the use of language structures in the service of larger meanings.

Metaphors of Discourse Interaction

The way one thinks of discourse has a strong effect on the kind of theory of discourse semantics one creates. The most naive metaphor can be called the *conduit metaphor* of discourse (Reddy, 1979). In this view, the speaker packages his intended meaning into a textual artifact. This artifact *contains* the meaning intended by the speaker. It is conducted to the listener in either spoken or written form. The text is then unpacked and its meaning extracted from the text artifact by the listener.

We will embrace an alternative metaphor here – the *blueprint metaphor* of discourse. In this view, the speaker holds a conceptual representation of events or ideas which he intends should be replicated in the mind of the listener. The listener is neither helpless nor passive in this endeavour but actively engages in constructing her own conceptual representation of the matters at hand. The speaker behaves as a sort of architect and his linguistic output, the text, can be viewed as a blueprint to aid the listener during the construction of a conceptual representation. Just as a true blueprint contains no actual building materials but depicts by convention how existing materials should be employed in constructing a given edifice, so the text itself contains little or no meaning per se but serves by convention to guide the listener in constructing a conceptual representation.

Building or interpreting text blueprints requires dealing with two fundamental problems. The first is integrating the semantic information provided in each utterance into a coherent whole. The speaker must select pertinent concepts and events from his experience and organize these in a way that is helpful to the listener. The listener must integrate any utterances heard into a coherent representation which permits her to access or construct concepts and events that are virtually identical to those held by the speaker. We can call this the problem of *knowledge integration*.

The second fundamental problem here is managing the flow of information between speaker and listener in a dynamic, real time interaction. The speaker helps the listener succeed in knowledge integration by directing the listener's efforts to process the information provided through the text. For example, the speaker will help the listener by exploiting information held in common as a prelude to or anchor for the information the speaker believes will be novel or unexpected for the listener. The coherence of the knowledge held by the listener will be affected by how cohesive the information is that the speaker offers. We call this the problem of *information management*.

Knowledge integration requires effective information management, but effective information management is not enough to account for knowledge integration.

KNOWLEDGE INTEGRATION IN DISCOURSE

To appreciate the complexity of discourse semantics in both production and comprehension, let us consider two examples. First, for the speaker, consider a simple line drawing, perhaps an illustration from a children's book.

There are a number of important matters one must deal with in developing a theory of discourse semantics. To begin with, the speaker must have in mind some sort of *conceptual representation* of the subject matter under discussion. It is this representation which is the fundamental 'meaning' the speaker works with in constructing a discourse. Most of the time as linguists we will think of the conceptual representation as a set of propositions, sometimes referred to as a text representation (Kintsch, 1974; van Dijk and Kintsch, 1983), but a conceptual representation need not be simply or only propositional. In the case of a simple line drawing the speaker will form some sort of *visual* representation for the picture, which he will access when speaking. For other kinds of experience there may well be other kinds of representation. For example, a conceptual representation for, say, tasting coffee may well be different from one for listening to music, which in turn may be distinct from one for shifting gears in a car. In addition, we must also remember that we can create conceptual representations as well as access them from memory or perceptual experience.

Added to this, conceptual representations are *dynamic*. While a line drawing is itself static, our viewing of it is not: our eyes will move from one element to another, pausing here and there, skipping here and there, forming smaller scale images and impressions. In the same vein, most conceptual representations are dynamic: we do not view pictures so much as we do scenes and other sorts of unfolding events. Even our abstract efforts are dynamic, as we leap from idea to idea.

The conceptual representation alone, though, is not the meaning of the discourse. Somehow the speaker must select information from the overall conceptual representation and build a text from that selected information. The speaker will select information he believes the listener needs, and that information will be presented to help the listener make sense of what is heard. How the speaker *manages* information plays a critical role in discourse. Discourse management involves four independent threads.

1   The speaker never *merely* outputs a conceptual representation via language. The speaker always has some *purpose* or *goal* in mind. Such goals constrain how conceptual representations are searched and the selection of information to convey. In general, goals are seen as part of the discourse context, and their analysis is more commonly pursued through the study of discourse pragmatics (van Dijk, 2008). The line drawing selected will yield different descriptions depending on whether the speaker is asked to 'describe what seems to be happening' or 'evaluate the quality of the drawing'. In each case the speaker will access a visual representation of the picture, but the information selected and ultimately incorporated into a verbal description will be different. We can think of these different goals in speaking as distinct *rhetorical goals* for discourse production, and the associated selection processes we will call *rhetorical management*.

2   Constrained by rhetorical goals, the speaker accesses the conceptual representation, dynamically selecting referents and propositions for the listener. The speaker makes real time decisions about which referents and propositions are more central to the developing discourse. Such *starting points* ultimately assist the listener in building her own conceptual representation. We can think of important *referents* or starting points as the *thematic organization* of discourse, and the associated pragmatic notions and processes we will call *thematic management*.

3   In parallel with thematic management, the speaker will also monitor dynamically which referents and propositions seem to be available to the listener already and which require an introduction or reintroduction. We can think of the interlocking pattern of referents and propositions held in common or not as the *referential organization* of discourse, and the associated pragmatic notions and cognitive processes we will call *referential management*.

4   The speaker will monitor dynamically which referents and propositions he wishes to ensure are brought to the attention of the listener. From time to time, the speaker may not be certain that the listener has the right referent in mind at the right time, or he may wish to somehow *highlight* a particular referent or proposition. We can think of efforts to draw the listener's attention to particular referents and propositions as the *focus organization* of discourse, and the associated pragmatic notions and cognitive processes we will call *focus management*.

These four arenas of discourse management define the central problems of information management in discourse. While there is an extensive literature dealing with each of these areas, there is at present no single, comprehensive model of how they fit together that will account for knowledge integration (but cf. Vallduvi, 1992; or Lambrecht, 1994; or Levelt, 1989).

Turning second to the listener, one can see that the listener's problem parallels the speaker's, but it is not simply its reversal. The listener will form a conceptual representation as discourse is encountered. She will use information extracted from the text in concert with information already at hand to construct a conceptual representation. Consider the discourse sample in (2) and imagine the scene created in your mind as you read it.

(2)   A boy with a pail on his head is trying to catch a frog who is falling off a tree stump and the boy has accidentally caught his dog with the net.

The listener encounters utterances one by one in real time. She creates a conceptual representation of the events the speaker blueprints via the text, and she does this by employing all of the information at her disposal to create some sort of *text representation*. This text representation is something like the gist of the text, a cohesive and complete general picture of the events or other subject matter discussed. Perhaps the best known model of text representation is that of Kintsch and van Dijk (1978). A text representation for them is a set of propositions, linked together through common referents and other features of events like time or place, and connected to a higher order discourse theme or *macroproposition*. Other models (Gernsbacher, 1990; Kintsch, 1988; Reinhart, 1981; Vallduvi, 1992) follow this general pattern. None of these models grapples with the larger problem of how the text is tied to developing the final conceptual representation which the text blueprints, for instance, the mental image resulting from comprehending (2).

In dealing with the text blueprint as it arrives in dynamic time, the listener employs at least three distinct kinds of knowledge to decode the text and integrate its information into a text representation. The listener exploits the *morpho-syntactic details* of her grammar as they code the flow of information in the text and discourse. She entertains *implicatures* derived from the pragmatic interpretation of the sentences in the text against the wider discourse context. And she also employs general processes of *inference* to help make wider connections between the current text and her larger store of knowledge.

It is important to see that all of these processes are involved in knowledge integration. But it is also important to see that these contributions are distinct. It is easy for the linguist to include facts about implicature and inference in descriptions of the function of linguistic forms in discourse. Yet the same is true for the psychologist or psycholinguist who concludes that his or her observations about language use are facts about the linguistic system when they might be due to non-linguistic processes of planning or inference. Two excellent resources to help guard against such confusions can be found in Levinson (1983) or Leech (1983).

There are two useful models of knowledge integration in comprehension: Gernsbacher's (1990) structure building model and Kintsch's (1988) construction-integration model. In Gernsbacher's *structure building model*, the listener's goal is to build a coherent mental representation or 'structure' of the information in the discourse. The listener uses many general cognitive processes and mechanisms to lay a foundation for the mental structure. Once the foundation has been laid, the listener develops her mental structure by *mapping* incoming information onto the previous structure. However, the new information can only be mapped onto a current structure if it coheres with the earlier information. If the new information is less coherent, listeners must *shift* to begin building a new structure.

Kintsch's (1988) *construction-integration model* also deals well with knowledge integration. Consider the sentence, *Mary baked a cake for Sally and burned her fingers.* In order to understand the utterance, the listener needs to know more than the words and phrases that were uttered by the speaker. She needs to have a good deal of general knowledge about how the world works, in this case, that baking entails that the object will be very hot for a period of time. She must also know how language works, for example, that the verb *bake* requires an agent and that this role is filled by Mary in this sentence. Further, the listener needs to know specific information about the situation in which the words were uttered. It is not clear from the words alone whether Mary baked the cake as a gift for Sally, or whether Sally was obligated to make a cake and Mary did it in her place.

Knowledge integration meshes real world knowledge and knowledge about one's language with the actual utterances in a discourse. The speaker employs nonlinguistic knowledge to observe and understand events in the world and their relevance to the listener. He then uses this knowledge and knowledge about his language to choose particular linguistic structures that will be informative to the listener. The listener, for her part, must interpret these linguistic structures using her own linguistic and nonlinguistic knowledge. This task is made easier if the speaker manages his task well of providing the listener with appropriate information. In the next four sections, we will explore how speakers manage the task of controlling information for their listeners.

THE RHETORICAL MANAGEMENT OF DISCOURSE

Speaking involves both information and action. Information includes the details of propositional content as well as pragmatic matters – emphasis, importance, presupposition – which will guide how the semantic content should be interpreted. Action includes the details of discourse planning, both global and local, which will help direct pragmatic matters for the speaker and also help constrain interpretation by the listener. Rhetorical management contributes to discourse semantics both through the pragmatics of content and context (van Dijk, 2008) and through the deployment of the particular organizational structures that will shape a narrative or argument.

The use of linguistic structures in discourse is related to linguistic actions taken by the speaker. At the sentence level, the linguistic action of, say, *issuing a command* can be carried out through a number of linguistic structures: an imperative (*Give me your money; Let me have your money*), an interrogative (*Could I have your money?*), or a declarative (*I want your money*). These examples demonstrate that the form of an utterance is separable from the action, in this case the *speech act*, which the utterance carries out.

Speech act theory (Levinson, 1983; Searle, 1969; 1979) recognizes that language is used to do things (Austin, 1962). Speech act analysis of discourse focuses on local matters affecting the clause or sentence type. But language as action is reflected in higher level aspects of discourse organization as well. For example, Swales (1981) examined some 48 introductions to scientific and technical articles. He identified four crucial component actions within each introduction. These actions, which Swales called *moves*, capture critical kinds of information selected by the speaker from his conceptual representation of the subject matter.

There are numerous threads of research which pursue work in this area. Probably the best known is the British tradition of discourse analysis associated with Coulthard and Sinclair (Coulthard, 1977; Coulthard and Montgomery, 1981; Sinclair and Coulthard, 1975). Their classic work (Sinclair and Coulthard, 1975) examined the structure of classroom discourse in British schools. Mehan (1979) has developed similar lines of research within education.

Researchers in Artificial Intelligence have examined the goal-oriented structure of discourse and its relation to the structure of the knowledge that the discourse is about. Grosz (1974) examined the language used in assembling a water pump, investigating connections between knowledge representations and referential form. Such task-based discourse work has been conducted by Cohen and Perrault (1979), Baggett (1982), McKeown (1985), Sidner (1983), and others.

Linguists have also examined the organization of discourse in this fashion. Early work by Propp (1958) investigated the organization of Russian fairy tales. Grimes (1975) developed an inventory of rhetorical predicates to capture the intentional structure of discourse. Levy (1979) examined the structure of informal interviews of students completing course schedules. Hinds (1979) looked at procedural discourse in Japanese. Mann and Thompson (1986) offered a rich system for describing the fine-grained details of rhetorical management in natural discourse. This Rhetorical Structure Theory (RST) has been applied to such diverse areas as discourse analysis, theoretical linguistics, computational linguistics, and Artificial Intelligence, and has seen considerable success especially in text and natural language generation, automatic phrase extraction and corpus text analysis (Taboada and Mann 2006a; 2006b).

All of these efforts propose an inventory of hierarchically organized actions of one kind or another. High-level structures can be decomposed into constrained sets of lower order units; lower order units combine in constrained ways to form higher levels of discourse organization. Thus Swales's introduction is decomposed into four moves and these four distinct move types combine to make a well-formed introduction.

Understanding rhetorical management is important for discourse semantics for two reasons: 1) the integration of information into the text is never merely a matter of processing individual utterances – the utterances are integrated with respect to higher order considerations, and these considerations are what is managed by the rhetorical component; and 2) there is an important role to be played by the syntax, morpho-syntactic coding, in signalling one or another information status as the discourse unfolds. The determination of which information is thematic or focused and so on is very much tied to the higher order rhetorical goals for which the discourse was initiated.

THE REFERENTIAL MANAGEMENT OF DISCOURSE

The key insight within referential management is that certain concepts seem to be held in common or shared by speaker and listener, while others are not. Information held in common makes up part of the conceptual scaffolding on which each depends for effective communication. The key questions are: 1) what does it mean to say that speaker and listener 'share' information, and (2) how is referential management tied to knowledge integration?

Virtually every theory of discourse structure draws a distinction between *given information* and *new information* (also referred to as *old vs new, known vs unknown*, or *shared vs new*). Each clause or utterance contains elements the speaker believes he holds in common with the listener and elements the speaker believes he does not. So in the discourse fragment in (3), the bold-faced NPs are generally taken to be given information and the italicized NPs new information.

(3) Text fragment from the popular novel *Sarum* by E. Rutherford (1988: 15):

   1 The next day **he** discovered *the lake*.
       It was *a small, low hill about five miles inland*
       that first attracted **his attention**.
       It looked like [*a place from*
   5 *which he could spy out the land and*
       where they could camp at least for the night].
       When **he** reached **the place**, however,
       he was surprised and delighted to find
       that hidden below **it** and in **his path**

10 lay *a shallow lake about half a mile across*.
    At **its eastern end**, *a small outlet* carried **its water** away towards **the sea**.
    Tracing round **the lake**
    he found that
    it was fed from **the north** and **the west** by *two small rivers*.
15 On **its northern side** was *a flat, empty marsh*.
    The water, sheltered by **the hill**, was very still;
    there was *a sweet smell of fern, mud and water reed*.
    Over **the surface of the lake**, *a heron* rose
    and *seagulls* cried.

The bold-faced NPs in 1, 4, 7, 8, 9, 12, 13, 14, 16 represent given information because they have been mentioned before in the text. The italicized NPs in 1, 2, 10, 11, 15, 17, 18, 19 represent new information, for they have just been introduced. Other cases are a bit less clear. The NPs in 3, 11, 14, 15, 18 are marked bold, and their putative status as given must be related to the knowledge shared by writer and reader about lakes and their environs. But lakes also include native birds, like herons and gulls, so one wonders why the NPs in 18 and 19 cannot count also as given.

Conceptual foundations for given and new information

There are two basic ideas about given and new information: 1) given information represents a referent shared in some way by speaker and listener; 2) given information is a cognitively activated referent.

Given information as shared information

Traditionally, referential management asserts that a given semantic argument also holds a pragmatic status like *old* or *given* or *known* information. Within the Prague School, Mathesius (1939) suggested that one portion of the utterance represents information that is assumed to be possessed by the listener from the preceding context or may be inferred by her from the context. Such information is *known* (*old*, *given*) information. It is contrasted with that portion of the utterance which the speaker presents as new (unknown) information and which is the content of the utterance. Mathesius examined how this status of information was signalled via strategies such as word order, intonation, and other constructions. These ideas were developed by other Prague School scholars, such as Danes and Firbas.

Halliday (1967a; 1967b) relates each unit of information in a given sentence to the preceding discourse. He draws a distinction between *given* and *new* information. New information represents information the speaker treats as not known to the listener. Given information represents information the speaker treats as known to the listener. Unlike the Prague School researchers, Halliday draws a further distinction between *known* and *unknown* information. For Halliday, information is known if the speaker assumes the listener can identify the referent, and is unknown if the speaker assumes the listener cannot identify the referent. DuBois (1980) also considers the importance of identifiability in referential management.

Prince (1981) finds these intuitively appealing notions too simplistic. She proposes a multi-way distinction in types of information. 1) A referent is *new* when it is introduced into the discourse for the first time. New referents may be *brand-new*, that is, newly created by the speaker, or simply *unused*, entities the listener is assumed to know about but which have not been mentioned previously in the discourse. 2) A referent is considered *evoked* if it is already part of the discourse. An evoked referent may be *textually evoked* if the listener had evoked it earlier on instructions from the speaker (as by the speaker's mention of the referent), or it may be *situationally evoked* if the listener knows to evoke it all by herself, such as 'you' referring to the listener. 3) A referent is *inferable* if the speaker assumes the listener could have inferred it, using knowledge and reasoning. A referent may be inferable either from the text or from the situation.

Given information as a degree of memorial activation

Chafe (1976; 1987; 1994) discusses information status in terms of what is activated in our consciousness. He proposes that a particular concept may be in any one of the three different activation states at a particular time of discourse processing: *active* (corresponding to the 'given'), *semi-active* (accessible), or *inactive* (corresponding to the 'new').

If the speaker assumes, prior to uttering an intonation unit, that a concept is already active in the listener's mind, he will verbalize that concept in an attenuated manner, most probably pronominalizing it. If he assumes that a concept is not presently activated in the listener's consciousness, he will verbalize that concept in a less attenuated manner, most probably nominalizing it.

Clark and Haviland (1974) relate these notions to memorial processes in their discussion of the 'given-new strategy'. Each sentence produced by a speaker contains some information that is old or given, and some that is new. The old information serves as an indication of where, in the listener's memory, she will find information related to that conveyed by the present sentence, and thus 'an instruction specifying where the new information is to be integrated into the previous knowledge' (1974: 105). Consequently, pronouns and definite noun phrases (NPs) are more likely to refer to old or given entities, and indefinite NPs to new information.

Givon (1983) also considers referential management in cognitive terms. He observes that the speaker estimates to what extent a given referent is mentally accessible to his listener. If this accessibility is high, the speaker will use an attenuated referential form to index the referent (ellipsis or pronominalization). If accessibility is lower, the speaker will use a longer form, perhaps a simple nominal NP or one with some modification. If accessibility is very low, the speaker may introduce a referent into the conceptual representation through an indefinite NP or some other device.

Ariel (1990; 1991; 1994; 1996) proposes and develops a cognitive approach to sentence and discourse anaphora which purports that referring expressions indicate the specific degree of accessibility of mental representations. She argues that a given anaphor signals a particular degree of cognitive accessibility to its potential intended referent, through which an antecedent is selected. In other words, antecedents are not given in advance but 'accessed' via the selected form of a particular anaphor together with its specific set of semantic properties as well as its pragmatic and contextual information. In this view, accessibility is a function of both the context in which an entity is mentioned and the cues used to access it.

REFERENTIAL MANAGEMENT AND KNOWLEDGE INTEGRATION

One important problem in reference management has been understanding how the speaker and listener can keep track of referents during discourse production and comprehension. Keeping track of these referents involves three related problems: 1) introducing referents to the discourse; 2) sustaining the reference once a referent has been introduced; and 3) reintroducing referents after a long hiatus. Virtually every approach at present employs some notion of managing a mental model or conceptual representation for this purpose. Speakers will use particular linguistic forms to introduce referents to the discourse, typically indefinite NPs or focal sentence intonation or word order. Such introductions can be thought of as moving a referent from off stage onto the stage, or from some long-term memory store into the current conceptual representation.

Speakers will also use other linguistic forms, most typically anaphoric forms, pronominalization or definite NPs, to signal referents which are already available to the listener. Such referents can be thought of as activated or emplaced within the conceptual representation. In addition speakers may reintroduce a referent after a long hiatus or some other interruption. Keeping track of referents over time involves an important interplay between the activation status of a referent and the granularity of discourse. Of the numerous linguistic and psycholinguistic approaches to reference management in discourse, the episode model (Fox, 1987; Marslen-Wilson et al., 1982; van Dijk and Kintsch, 1983) has been the most influential. It considers the use of *anaphora* to be a function of a particular discourse structure – the paragraph or *episode*. While texts may be produced in a linear fashion, they are nevertheless hierarchically organized and processed as episodes, i.e. semantic units dominated by higher level macropropositions (van Dijk and Kintsch, 1983).

The notion of episode as a semantic unit dominated by a macroproposition has been found to have psychological relevance in several studies. Black and Bower (1979), for example, demonstrated, in a psychological study of story processing the existence of episodes as chunks in narrative memory. Similarly, Guindon and Kintsch (1984) found that macrostructure formation appears to be a virtually automatic process. That is, people appear to form macrostructures during reading and derive relevant macropropositions for a passage as soon as possible. Their findings provided evidence for the episode and the *macrostructure* theories of Kintsch and van Dijk (1978) and Schank and Abelson (1977).

The cognitive basis of discourse organization helps us to further understand the relationship between discourse structure and anaphora. An episode, as a semantic unit subsumed under a macroproposition, is the textual manifestation of a memory chunk which represents sustained attentional effort and endures until an episode boundary is reached. Attention shifts when the processing of the episode is completed. In other words, 'the macroproposition remains in Short Term Memory for the rest of the interpretation of the same episode. As soon as propositions are interpreted that no longer fit that macroproposition, a new macroproposition is set up' (van Dijk, 1982: 191). At an episode boundary the encoding load is much heavier, the reference under concern is less accessible, and hence a more explicit anaphoric form is required to code the referent. Within an episode, when the macroproposition is maintained, the referent under consideration is more accessible, and hence a less explicit anaphoric form is sufficient to code the reference.

Indeed many studies on anaphora have reported the alternation between nominal and pronominal to be a function of the paragraph or episodic structure. Hinds (1979), for example, discusses how paragraph structure controls the choice of NPs and pronouns. He finds that noun phrases are used to convey 'semantically prominent' information in the peak sentences of a paragraph, while pronouns are used to indicate 'semantically subordinate' information in non-peak sentences. Fox (1987) demonstrated that structural factors of discourse establish the basic patterns of anaphora: NPs are generally used at the beginning of a 'development structure' to demarcate new narrative units, whereas pronominals are used within that structure. Marslen-Wilson et al. (1982) argue that a speaker's use of referential devices is governed by discourse structure and the context of speaking. The general pattern of anaphora is that NPs and proper names are used to establish an initial reference at an episode when a particular referent is in a state of low focus, whereas pronouns are used to maintain the reference within an action sequence when a particular referent is in a state of high focus.

While the episode model presupposes the importance of cognitive constraints and the hierarchical organization of discourse, it faces difficulties to the extent that structural units such as paragraph, episode, event and theme are not well defined theoretically. Many structural units are hard to identify in spoken and written texts, and are prone to misinterpretation.

Tomlin (1987a) attempts to solve the problem of prior studies by introducing the attention model, where he links the use of anaphora directly to the cognitive activities of attention and memory. He argues that an episode represents sustained attentional effort and this endures until that attention is diverted. In his study, each episode was represented by a slide picture; the shutter release cycle of the slide projector, which imposed a sufficiently strong perceptual disruption for the subject, served as the episode boundary. He demonstrated experimentally that NPs were used at the boundary of episodes when attention shifted, while pronominals were used within episodes when attention was sustained (see also Tomlin and Pu, 1991).

Another important model of referential management is the distance model proposed by Givon (1983), which argues for a correlation between anaphora and referential distance in discourse, such as number of clauses between a given anaphor and its antecedent.

The 'iconicity principle' underlying the model is that the longer the distance, the harder it is for the listener to identify the referent, and so a more explicit referential form (such as a full noun phrase) is required. The shorter the distance, the easier it is for the listener to identify the referent, and hence a less explicit referential form (a lexical pronoun or a zero anaphor) is required.

THE THEMATIC MANAGEMENT OF DISCOURSE

The key insight within thematic management is that certain concepts and propositions seem more central or important to the development of the discourse than others. Such central concepts and propositions provide the framework or scaffolding around which the details of the discourse are emplaced. The key questions here are: 1) What makes a concept or proposition more central? 2) How is that centrality tied to the developing discourse? 3) What does the speaker do to convey centrality to the listener? And 4) How does the listener know when to construe a concept or proposition as central?

Theme or topic: conceptual starting point

There are several quite excellent reviews of ideas and issues of clause level theme or topic (Gómez-González, 2001; Goodenough, 1983; Gundel, 1988b; Jones, 1977; Schlobinski and Schütze-Coburn, 1992). Each clause or utterance is theorized to contain one element which is more important or central to the discourse (more technically, which serves as the *starting point* of the utterance) or which serves as the element *about which* the predication is asserted.

To understand the idea of theme or topic requires that one deal with three interrelated matters. Firstly, there is the theoretical definition of theme or topic, which is generally articulated in terms of *starting point* or *aboutness*. Secondly, there is its manifestation through syntactic form, most generally discussed in terms of the constituent order (initial or preposed), or syntactic subject, or other morpho-syntactic cues (such as *wa* in Japanese: see Hinds et al., 1987). Thirdly, there is the interplay between these two areas and the extent to which the definitions of theme or topic include information about its syntactic manifestation.

In the paragraph fragment in (4), the bold-faced NPs are ostensibly clause level themes. In each case, the referent seems introspectively to satisfy requirements of importance, centrality, starting point, and aboutness.

(4) Text fragment from the popular novel *Sarum* by E. Rutherford (1988: 206)

1   Late in the winter, while the snow was still on the ground,
     a new figure of great significance arrived on the island.
     He was tall, middle aged, with a thin, kindly face and receding hair.

He had two peculiarities that Porteus observed:

5 **he** stooped when he spoke to people,

as though Ø concentrating intently on what they said;

but when Ø not involved in conversation

his eyes often seemed to grow distant

as though he were dreaming of some far off place.

10 **He** was Julius Classicianus, the new procurator and replacement for the disgraced Decianus Catus.

His responsibility included all the island's finances.

Under the Roman system of divided authority, **he** reported direct to the emperor.

From a global point of view, this paragraph introduces a new character to the novel, one Julius Classicianus, and provides his initial description. This paragraph illustrates well the basic ideas and issues surrounding clause level theme or topic. Firstly, several of the clauses exhibit prototypical cases of clause level theme (3, 4, 5, 10, 12). In each of these cases, the referent of the bold-faced NP is the central or most important character in this paragraph. It is also the referent about whom the predication is asserted. And it is also the referent from which the description proceeds. Though it cannot be a defining characteristic of theme, it is also not an accident that the relevant NP in each case is the subject of the clause. It is on such cases that the central theoretical ideas of theme and topic have been constructed.

Secondly, several of the clauses illustrate cases which remain problematic in discussions of theme and topic. To begin with, it is not clear how to treat the subject of clause 2, *a new figure of great significance*. Some would argue that this NP is *not* a theme because the information is referentially new, unlike the NPs in the prototypical cases. Others would say that this NP is thematic precisely because its referential status is in principle independent of its thematic status, and in this clause it is this NP which is the starting point of the utterance and about which a prediction is asserted.

Thirdly, it is not clear how to treat the subjects of clauses 8 and 11. Neither denotes the principal character of the paragraph, so it is difficult to sustain a view that the referent is somehow important. Yet for each clause itself, the bold-faced NP seems to be the starting point of the utterance and the NP about which the utterance is predicated.

Finally, there are a number of subordinate clauses, some of which are embedded, that have either explicit or elliptic subjects. It remains unclear exactly how the thematic status of key NPs in these clauses is to be treated.

With these observations in mind, we can now turn to explore more carefully major ideas about clause level theme and topic.

Conceptual foundations for theme and topic

Despite an individual variation in the formulation of definitions and the specific terms defined, there are essentially three basic ideas of what constitutes a clause level theme or topic: 1) the theme is what the sentence *is about*; 2) the theme is the *starting point* of the sentence; and 3) the theme is the *centre of attention* for the sentence.

Theme as aboutness

Classical scholarship on language and logic distinguished those portions of a sentence about which something is predicated and that which is predicated of it, classically the difference between *subject* and *predicate*. Contemporary research has developed this idea, leading to many formulations of clause level theme or topic in terms of aboutness. A particular referent counts as theme when it is this referent that the remainder of the sentence is about. One classic 'test' for aboutness comes from Gundel (1974; 1988b): in a given context, a particular NP will count as a topic if it can be included in a preposed adverbial with *As for*. Thus, the bold-faced NP in example (4), clause 8, counts as a topic because this referent felicitously fits into the following sentence:

> (5) As for his eyes, they seemed to grow distant ...

Theme or topic as *aboutness* dominates current research in this area. It begins with classical research from the Prague School, proceeds through Halliday (1967b; 1973; 1976) and Halliday and Fawcett (1987), and features prominently in much current research (Gundel, 1974; 1988b; Hajicova, 1984; Lambrecht, 1994; Reinhart, 1981; Vallduvi, 1992).

Theme as starting point

Theme is also conceptualized as the starting point of the utterance as a message. The starting point helps to frame the utterance, tying the predication to something already known and shared by the discourse participants. It is a common feature of this approach to require that theme be given or known information. This approach differs from *aboutness* largely in terms of its greater emphasis on the dynamic nature of discourse, and on its processing over time or its flow in time (Chafe, 1994). This approach is reflected in the early work of Weil (1887) and very early formulations of Prague School thinking (Mathesius, 1929). More recent work employing this view includes Chafe (1994) and MacWhinney (1977).

Theme as centre of attention

There is yet a third view of theme which ties the clause level theme or topic to some notion of attention. Early work in this area observed that certain concepts come to mind first in the production of utterances, and it is this coming-into-consciousness that defines the theme. Thus, van der Gabelenz (1868), discussed in Gundel, (1974: 24), distinguishes *psychological subject*, 'the idea which appears first in the consciousness of the speaker ... what makes him think and what he wants the hearer to think of', from *psychological predicate*, 'that which is joined to the psychological subject'. There is also important work in psycholinguistics which takes this view (Prentice, 1967; Sridhar, 1988; Tannenbaum and Williams, 1968). Some linguists have examined how cognitive theories of attention are tied to the classical notions of theme or topic (Tomlin, 1983; 1995; 1997).

Discourse level theme (global theme)

Generally, in a stretch of connected discourse, one referent will emerge as central, or the one that the propositions in the discourse are about. This global significance of one referent affects choices made at the clause level; that is, the clause level theme is in some way a local reflection of some higher level unit of discourse, something like a paragraph or episode. Given two competing referents at the clause level, it seems natural that the local theme would be related to the more general or higher order theme. That is, if a given paragraph or episode is about Mary (and not really about John), then clauses in that paragraph dealing with both Mary and John should tend to treat Mary as clause level theme because Mary contributes to a better coherence with the higher level episode or paragraph theme.

The term 'global theme' is also related to the notion of what the overall discourse is about. In this case, the global theme has the form of a proposition rather than a noun phrase (Jones, 1977; Keenan and Schieffelin, 1976; van Dijk, 1985). Although not as strong as the claims on local sentence level themes, there has been a recognition of the importance of global theme. As an illustration, consider the following passage (from van Dijk, 1985: 298):

(6) This morning I had a toothache. I went to the dentist. The dentist has a big car. The car was bought in New York. New York has had serious financial troubles.

Although each sentence is connected with the previous one by having a common referent, the passage as a whole lacks coherence, owing to the lack of a global theme.

Further, a well defined global theme facilitates text comprehension; it functions as an advance organizer (Frase, 1975), scaffolding (Anderson et al., 1978), or anchor point (Pichert and Anderson, 1977) by evoking a mental model (representation) in the comprehender. A well defined global theme can also evoke corresponding knowledge structures whether such an organizational structure is called a *schema* (Rumelhart, 1980), *frame* (Minsky, 1975), *script* (Schank and Abelson, 1977), or *scenario* (Sanford and Garrod, 1980). The fact that comprehenders construct discourse models as well as linguistic representations has been corroborated in a number of studies (see, for example, Bransford and Johnson 1972).

Lastly, how do sentence level theme and discourse level theme interact with each other? There has been widespread speculation that the assignment of lower level themes is a function of the higher level themes. Although this may be true, Kim's (1996; 2002) experimental studies which separated global theme from local theme showed that their influences on subject assignment in English and Korean are significant and also suggested that they, in fact, have separate functions in discourse production.

Foreground and background: propositional centrality

Like other central discourse notions, the idea of *foreground* versus *background* information in discourse arises from attempts to explain structural alternations in language for which no obvious semantic explanations are apparent. Consider, for example, the paragraph in (7):

(7)   Sample paragraph

> **It was a calm, peaceful day** *as the little fish took its daily swim throughout its home territory. Gracefully sliding up to the surface of the water,* **the little fish is startled by one of its feared enemies – the crab. They stare at each other surprisedly**, *though the little fish soon realized its danger. Before the little fish could escape unharmed,* **the crab began to attack frantically**, *its long claws snapping at any part of the fish. Without thinking twice about it,* **the fish dashed away from the crab**.

The italicized clauses are all dependent adverbial clauses; the bold-faced clauses are all straightforward independent clauses. The critical question is this: what determines whether a given proposition in this fragment shows up as a dependent clause or as an independent clause? The classical answer is simple enough: the more important ideas are found in the independent clauses, the less important and supporting ideas are found in the dependent clauses. And it is this classical idea that is captured and developed in the various treatments of the discourse notion of *foreground* versus *background information.*

The earliest work on foregrounding (Grimes, 1975; Longacre, 1968; 1976a; cf. also Labov and Waletzky, 1967) distinguished *backbone* information from *background* information and employed this distinction to account for syntactic alternations in a number of languages. For biblical Hebrew, Longacre (1976a) observed that the subset of clauses with the *waw*-predicate construction formed a coherent abstract of the overall narrative while the remaining clauses did not. Thus, it appeared that the *waw*-predicate construction was used to signal the importance of those clauses that formed the backbone of the narrative.

Later work by Hopper (1979) developed the original ideas of Longacre and Grimes. Foreground information in narrative discourse includes 'the parts of the narrative belonging to the skeletal structure of the discourse' (1979: 213). Background information is 'the language of supportive material which does not itself relate the main events' (1979: 213). Hopper (1979) claimed that foreground clauses correlate with both independent clauses and perfective aspect (see also Hopper and Thompson, 1980). Further, Hopper linked foreground information with the event line of narrative discourse (Hopper, 1979; Labov and Waletzky, 1967). The clauses which relate events falling on the main event line are foreground clauses, while those which do not fall on the main event line are the background ones. The role of verb tense-aspect and specific clause structure in foregrounding and backgrounding information in discourse has been examined in more recent studies (Carreiras, Carriedo, Alonso and Fernández, 1997; Depraetere, 1996; Glasbey, 1998; Youssef and Winford, 1999).

Most work on the foregound–background distinction has been directed at narrative discourse. Expository discourse requires a treatment of foregrounding which is not dependent on the notion of event line for its theoretical definition (Jones and Jones, 1979). Tomlin (1984; 1985; 1986) offers a treatment of foregrounding which alleviates the dependence on event line for both theoretical and empirical purposes. In this treatment, foregrounding is viewed as a thematic matter. The centrality of any given proposition in discourse arises from the intersection of the theme of the discourse at that point and the rhetorical goal of the discourse.

FOCUS MANAGEMENT

The central observation within focus management is that certain concepts and propositions seem to be more novel or unexpected from the listener's viewpoint. In fact, the novel concepts and propositions appear to be the target of the speaker's utterance, that is, what the speaker wishes the listener to specifically add to her mental representation. The key questions here are: 1) What makes a concept or proposition more novel? 2) How is the novel concept tied to the developing discourse? 3) What does the speaker do to convey the novelty to the listener? And 4) How does the listener know when to construe a concept or proposition as novel?

FOCUS AS PROMINENCE

The term 'focus' is used by linguists to refer to resources for packaging information in order to make some information stand out for the listener. Focus management is concerned with how the speaker lets the listener know what in particular she should notice about that central element.

All languages provide speakers with a variety of devices for making some information seem more prominent or significant than other information. In English (as in many other languages), some words can be said with extra stress. For example, consider these sentences:

(8)   I'M not mad at you.

(9)   I'm not mad at YOU.

In each case, the component words are identical, but by putting extra stress on different words, slightly different meanings are conveyed. Sentence (8) implies that while I'm not mad at anyone, someone else is, in fact, mad at you. On the other hand, (9) implies that I *am* mad at someone, but my anger is not directed towards you. By making one word stand out more than the others, the listener is invited both to infer why that particular piece of information is important and to contrast it with other possible situations. In these situations, the focused information is said to have a contrastive function.

Formulations of focus

These differences of importance between the elements of a sentence were first characterized by Weil (1887 [1844]). He proposed that the 'focus' of one sentence was related to the topic (or theme) of the next. His work was followed by Prague School scholars who were interested in the communicative dynamism of the elements of sentences (Firbas, 1974; Vachek, 1966). Halliday (1967a) elaborated on Prague School work, investigating what he called *information structure*. For Halliday, focus was the new information marked by pitch prominence, while theme was the element expressed in the first position of a sentence.

Following Halliday's work and later research by Chomsky (1970), the importance of topic and focus in determining the semantic representation of sentences was embraced by most linguists. It is often assumed that, in many European languages, focus is primarily in the last position. In this position, it need not be marked with stress. When a focused element occurs earlier in the sentence, it receives intonational stress and the NPs which follow it are theme. Other languages use variations of these strategies. For example, in Yagua (Payne, 1992), focused information occurs in the first position in the sentence and is also sometimes repeated in the last position.

An important contribution to the study of focus was Chafe's (1976) work on the statuses of referents, that is, the ideas that nouns within a sentence represent. One status is the 'speaker's assessment of how the addressee is able to process what he is saying against the background of a particular context' (1976: 27). Here, focus has to do with how the message is packaged, that is, how the speaker presents the message to the listener, rather than the content of the message per se. The speaker will package messages in different ways, depending on his assessment of the listener's mental state, namely what she is presently thinking about. Chafe investigated focus of contrast (or contrastiveness) as one packaging phenomenon. In English, this is conveyed by a high pitch and stress on one element of the sentence.

A very useful and detailed discussion of the different types of focus phenomena found in language has been presented by Dik (Dik et al., 1981; Dik, 1989). Dik tries to determine what different categories of focus there must be if we are to account for all the focus phenomena of different languages. Like others, Dik (1978; 1989) contrasts topic and focus. The topic presents the entity 'about' which the predication predicates something in the given setting. The focus represents what is relatively the most important or salient information in the given setting.

Like Chafe and Halliday, Lambrecht (1994) has been concerned with how information is structured. He seeks to understand how speakers manipulate the focus of an utterance to meet what they assume are the needs of the listener. For Lambrecht, the focus is that portion of the proposition which is asserted, what the listener is expected to know or take for granted as a result of hearing the sentence uttered. Asserted information is contrasted with presupposed information, what the speaker assumes the listener *already* knows or takes for granted. Lambrecht identifies three distinct types of focus: predicate focus, argument focus, and sentence focus. Each type occurs in distinctly different types of communicative situations.

Prince (1978) explores two different English focus constructions by studying their use in natural discourse. These constructions, known as clefts (or it-clefts) and pseudo-clefts (or WH-clefts), are shown in the following examples:

(10) (a) John lost his keys. (Neutral construction)
      (b) What John lost was his keys. (Pseudo-cleft)
      (c) It was his keys that John lost. (Cleft)

Although all three sentences convey the same basic information, they differ in the way they package the pieces of information. Specifically, they differ in terms of which information is focused and which is presupposed. Logically, both (b) and (c) presuppose that 'John lost something' while (a) does not. The information that is not presupposed in (b) and (c) is the identity of the 'something', namely, 'the keys', which is the focus. Since both (b) and (c) have the same presuppositions and the same focus, many linguists have considered them essentially synonymous (Bolinger, 1972; Chafe, 1976). Prince's work demonstrates that this is not the case.

Recently, Lee, Gordon and Büring (2007) present a collection of papers exploring the semantic and prosodic components of topic and focus from a broad typological perspective, demonstrating the scope of and constraints on the intonational realization of focus in various languages.

Overall, speakers will try to make some information more prominent or salient to their listeners. Depending on which language they are using, they have a number of devices at their disposal in order to achieve this goal of focusing information.

COGNITIVE APPROACHES TO DISCOURSE SEMANTICS

The long-term future of studies in discourse semantics lies in the development of cognitive models of discourse comprehension and production. It has been extremely difficult to develop definitions which are both theoretically satisfying and empirically manageable for basic notions in information management – theme, given/new, foregrounding, focus, etc. This has led a number of investigators to pursue a strategy in which discourse notions are operationalized in cognitive terms or in which traditional ideas are replaced outright by cognitive alternatives.

Within referential management, there has been considerable interest in recasting traditional notions of given and new in terms of memory or memorial activation. Chafe (1987) offers such a treatment, though he does not connect his theory directly with the cognitive literature. Others have incorporated ideas from the study of memory (see Cowan, 1988, for a review) into a model of referential management based on the experimental manipulation of episodic structure and memorial activation (Tomlin and Pu, 1991).

Within thematic management, there has been considerable interest in demonstrating a connection between theme and attention. There are several quite excellent summary articles available on this (Cowan, 1988; Posner and Raichle, 1994; Tomlin and Villa, 1994). Work by Tomlin and his students argues that the idea of theme itself can be reduced to cognitive terms, in particular to attention detection at the moment of utterance formulation detection (Forrest, 1992; Tomlin, 1995; 1997; Tomlin and Villa, 1994). In this view, the cognitive processes of attention are not merely the cognitive reflexes of linguistic theme or topic; rather the notion of theme or topic is treated as an artifact emerging from the employment of attention within a conceptual representation during discourse production. More recent work in this vein extends the theme or topic as an attention connection into other aspects of cognitive processing (Myachykov and Tomlin, 2008; Myachykov, Posner and Tomlin, 2007; Myachykov, Tomlin and Posner, 2005).

Within focus management, there are a number of important treatments of focus which appeal to cognition, notably Lambrecht (1994) and Vallduvi (1992). Some others have been looking at focus as another arena involving attention (Erteschik-Shir, 1986; Levelt, 1989). Under this treatment, focus is seen not as a status for NPs or arguments, but as the outcome of directing the listener's attention to a referent during discourse production and comprehension. One such treatment of interest is Erteschik-Shir's notion of dominance, in which a constituent is dominant if the speaker intends to direct the listener's attention towards a particular referent.

All of these efforts show more in common than just a desire to overcome the problems of developing adequate theoretical definitions within information management. These approaches are moving away from a conceptualization of text structure holding pragmatic statuses (for example, that NP is a topic; that argument is a focus) towards a conceptualization of discourse and grammars that is dynamic. In this view, morpho-syntactic cues reveal the memorial and attentional characteristics of the speaker's conceptual representation and direct those of the listener to conform to the speaker's conceptual representation. Attention and memory flow through conceptual representations in real time; there is every reason to believe, as Chafe (1974) observed early on, that information flows through discourse over time.

Models of knowledge integration

Researchers are also moving increasingly towards cognitive treatments of knowledge integration. Knowledge integration requires large-scale models of how individual propositions are incorporated into textual representations and then integrated to generate final conceptual representations in the listener.

The two models of particular importance in this area have already been discussed: Gernsbacher's structure building model and Kintsch's construction-integration model. However a more comprehensive model of knowledge integration in discourse is needed. Firstly, a more comprehensive model must deal more effectively with the role of morpho-syntax in aiding knowledge integration. Neither Gernsbacher nor Kintsch deals fully with how the form of an utterance (as opposed to its content) contributes to knowledge integration. Secondly, it must deal with how text representations – the set of connected propositions tied closely to the actual text blueprint – are to be related to deeper conceptual representations, in production as well as comprehension. Thirdly, it must also deal explicitly with the dynamic nature of language use and conceptualization. The temporal features of language use probably do not sit outside of discourse semantics but instead constrain the kinds of systems that ultimately operate as humans create discourse together.

CONCLUSION

In this chapter we have discussed the central issues and concepts of discourse semantics. This area involves two main problems. The first is the problem of knowledge integration: how the individual propositions in a text and discourse are integrated to reflect the speaker's conceptual representation well and to optimize the creation of an appropriate conceptual representation in the listener. The second is the problem of information management: how information is organized and distributed as the speaker and listener interact during the blueprint creation process. In this area we looked at four distinct arenas of information management: rhetorical management, referential management, thematic management, and focus management. Each contributes in a distinct way to increase the efficacy of knowledge integration as the discourse unfolds.

This effort has two serious limitations. Firstly, we have not looked at formal models of discourse semantics. This is an area better left to those more knowledgeable, although interested readers might wish to examine key work here such as that done by Kamp and Reyle (1993). Secondly, it is not possible to provide as detailed a look at the work of individual scholars as one might wish to do. We have settled on trying to extract for our readers the most central insights in each arena. Hopefully, this effort will lead some to a more careful examination of the original sources and related work.

FURTHER READING

Among the works of value to read with care are the following, which are related to the issues explored in this chapter.

Gernsbacher, M.A. (1990) *Language Comprehension as Structure Building*. Hillsdale, NJ: Lawrence Erlbaum.
This study proposes an important structure-building framework that regards the goal of language comprehension as the building of a coherent, mental representation of structure. It delineates, with empirical evidence, general cognitive processes and mechanisms underlying language comprehension and the role memory activation plays in the structure-building process.

Graesser, A.C. and Millis, K. (2010) 'Discourse and Cognition' (Chapter 7, this volume).
In this chapter, the authors provide a good general overview of recent research on discourse studies that take a cognitive approach, and discuss in detail the recent progress made in various fields, especially in computational linguistics, in constructing multilevel discourse models, which have important implications for discourse comprehension mechanisms.

Halliday, M.A.K. and Matthiessen, C. (1999) *Construing Experience Through Meaning: A Language-based Approach to Cognition*. New York: Cassell.
This book, based on Halliday's systemic-functional theory, offers a comprehensive view of semantics and its relationships to cognition as well as syntax, focusing on the construal of human experience as a semantic system. It represents an interesting alternative approach to the study of the relationship between language and cognition, i.e., '[i]nstead of explaining language by relation to cognitive processes, we explain cognition by relation to linguistic processes' (p. x).

Levelt, W.J.M. (1989) *Speaking*. Cambridge, MA: MIT Press.

This work not only provides a foundational discussion of language processing and production but also represents a critically important starting point for approaching the complexity of cognition and language overall and its interface with matters of discourse semantics.

van Dijk, T.A. (forthcoming) *Discourse and Knowledge*. Cambridge: Cambridge University Press.
van Dijk's forthcoming book, a continuation and expansion of his earlier work on discourse and cognition, is a comprehensive study of knowledge integration and conceptual representations in discourse processing. We would like to direct readers' attention specifically to the chapter of 'Discourse, knowledge and cognition', which explores and details the cognitive foundation for the theory of the relations between discourse processing and the knowledge system.

ONLINE READING

The following articles are available at www.sagepub.co.uk/discoursestudies.

Anderson, R.C., Spiro, R.J. and Anderson, M.C. (1978) 'Schemata as scaffolding for the representation of information in connected discourse', *American Educational Research Journal*, 15(3): 433–40.

Taboada, M. and Mann, W.C. (2006a) 'Rhetorical structure theory: Looking back and moving ahead', *Discourse Studies*, 8(3): 423–59.

Taboada, M. and Mann, W.C. (2006b) 'Applications of rhetorical structure theory', *Discourse Studies*, 8(4): 567–88.

REFERENCES

Anderson, R.C., Spiro, R.J. and Anderson, M.C. (1978) 'Schemata as scaffolding for the representation of information in connected discourse'. *American Educational Research Journal*, 15: 433–40.
Ariel, M. (1990) *Accessing Noun-phrase Antecedents*. London: Routledge/Croom Helm.
Ariel, M. (1991) 'The function of accessibility in a theory of grammar'. *Journal of Pragmatics*, 16 (5): 443–63.
Ariel, M. (1994) 'Interpreting anaphoric expressions: a cognitive versus a pragmatic approach'. *Journal of Linguistics*, 30: 3–42.
Ariel, M. (1996) 'Referring expressions and the +/- coreference distinction'. In T. Fretheim and J.K. Gundel (eds), *Reference and Referent Accessibility*. Amsterdam: John Benjamins. pp. 13–35.
Austin, J.L. (1962) *How To Do Things with Words*. Oxford: Clarendon Press.
Baggett, P. (1982) 'Information content equivalent movie and text stories'. *Discourse Processes*, 5: 73–99.
Black, J.B. and Bower, G.H. (1979) 'Episodes as chunks in narrative memory'. *Journal of Verbal Learning and Verbal Behavior*, 18: 309–18.
Bolinger, D. (1972) 'A look at equations and cleft sentences'. In E.S. Firchow, K. Grimstad, N. Hasselmo and W.A. O'Neil (eds), *Studies for Einar Haugen Presented by Friends and Colleagues*. The Hague: Mouton. pp. 96–114.
Bransford, J.D. and Johnson, M.K. (1972) 'Contextual prerequisites for understanding: some investigations of comprehension and recall'. *Journal of Verbal Learning and Verbal Behavior*, 11: 717–26.
Carreiras, M., Carriedo, N., Alonso, M. and Fernández, Á. (1997) 'The role of verb tense and verb aspect in the foregrounding of information during reading'. *Memory and Cognition*, 25: 438–46.
Chafe, W. (1974) 'Language and consciousness'. *Language*, 50: 111–33.
Chafe, W. (1976) 'Givenness, contrastiveness, definiteness, subjects, topics, and points of view'. In C.N. Li (ed.), *Subject and Topic*. New York: Academic Press. pp. 25–56.
Chafe, W. (1979) 'The flow of thought and the flow of language'. In T. Givon (ed.), *Discourse and Syntax*. New York: Academic Press. pp. 159–81.

Chafe, W. (1980a) 'The deployment of consciousness in the production of narrative'. In W. Chafe (ed.), *The Pear Stories: Cognitive, Cultural, and Linguistic Aspects of Narrative Production*. Norwood, NJ: Ablex. pp. 9–50.

Chafe, W. (ed.) (1980b) *The Pear Stories: Cognitive, Cultural, and Linguistic Aspects of Narrative Production*. Norwood, NJ: Ablex.

Chafe, W. (1987) 'Cognitive constraints on information flow'. In R. Tomlin (ed.), *Coherence and Grounding in Discourse*. Amsterdam: John Benjamins. pp. 21–51.

Chafe, W. (1994) *Discourse, Consciousness, and Time*. Chicago: University of Chicago Press.

Chomsky, N. (1970) 'Deep structure, surface structure, and semantic interpretation'. In R. Jacobson and S. Kawamoto (eds), *Studies in General and Oriental Linguistics: Presented to Shiro Hattori on the Occasion of his Sixtieth Birthday*. Tokyo: TEC Corp.

Clark, H.H. and Haviland, S.E. (1974) 'Psychological processes as linguistic explanation'. In D. Cohen (ed.), *Explaining Linguistic Phenomena*. Washington, DC: Hemisphere. pp. 91–124.

Cohen, P.R. and Perrault, C.R. (1979) 'Elements of a plan-based theory of speech acts'. *Cognitive Science: a Multidisciplinary Journal of Artificial Intelligence, Psychology, and Language*, 3: 177–212.

Coulthard, M. (1977) *An Introduction to Discourse Analysis*. London: Longman.

Coulthard, M. and Montgomery, M. (eds) (1981) *Studies in Discourse Analysis*. London: Routledge and Kegan Paul.

Cowan, N. (1988) 'Evolving conceptions of memory storage, selective attention, and their mutual constraints within the human information-processing system'. *Psychological Bulletin*, 104 (2): 163–91.

Depraetere, I. (1996) 'Foregrounding in English relative clauses'. *Linguistics*, 34: 699–731.

Dik, S. (1978) *Functional Grammar*. Amsterdam: North-Holland.

Dik, S. (1989) *The Theory of Functional Grammar*. Dordrecht: Foris.

Dik, S. (1997) *The Theory of Functional Grammar, Vol 2*. New York: Mouton de Gryuter.

Dik, S., Hoffmann, M.E., Jong, J.R.D., Djiang, S.I., Stroomer, H. and Vries, L.D. (1981) 'On the typology of focus phenomena'. In T. Hoekstra, H.V.D. Hulst, and M. Moortgat (eds), *Perspectives on Functional Grammar*. Dordrecht: Foris. pp. 41–74.

DuBois, J.W. (1980) 'Beyond definiteness: the trace of identity in discourse'. In W. Chafe (ed.), *The Pear Stories: Cognitive, Cultural and Linguistic Aspects of Narrative Production*. Norwood, NJ: Ablex. pp. 203–73.

Erteschik-Shir, N. (1986) 'Wh-questions and focus'. *Linguistics and Philosophy*, 9: 117–49.

Fawcett, R.P. (2000) *A Theory for Systemic Functional Linguistics*. Amsterdam: John Benjamins.

Firbas, J. (1964a) 'From comparative word-order studies (thoughts on V. Mathesius' conception of the word-order system in English compared with that in Czech)'. *Brno Studies in English*, 4: 111–28.

Firbas, J. (1964b) 'On defining the theme in functional sentence analysis'. *Travaux Linguistiques de Prague*, 1: 267–80.

Firbas, J. (1974) 'Some aspects of the Czechoslovak approach to problems of functional sentence perspective'. In F. Danes (ed.), *Papers on Functional Sentence Perspective*. The Hague: Mouton. pp. 11–37.

Firbas, J. (1987a) 'On the delimitation of theme in functional sentence perspective'. In R. Dirven and V. Fried (eds), *Functionalism in Linguistics*. Amsterdam: John Benjamins. pp. 137–56.

Firbas, J. (1987b) 'On two starting points of communication'. In R. Steele and T. Threadgold (eds), *Language Topics*. Amsterdam: John Benjamins. pp. 23–46.

Firbas, J. (1992) *Functional Sentence Perspective in Written and Spoken Communication*. Cambridge: Cambridge University Press.

Forrest, L.B. (1992) 'How grammar codes cognition: syntactic subject and focus of attention'. Unpublished MA thesis, University of Oregon.

Fox, B.A. (1987) *Discourse Structure and Anaphora in Written and Conversational English*. Cambridge: Cambridge University Press.

Frase, L.T. (1975) 'Prose processing'. In G.H. Bower (ed.), *The Psychology of Learning and Motivation: Advances in Research and Theory*. New York: Academic Press. pp. 1–47.

Gernsbacher, M.A. (1990) *Language Comprehension as Structure Building*. Hillsdale, NJ: Lawrence Erlbaum.

Givon, T. (ed.) (1983) *Topic Continuity in Discourse: A Quantitative Cross-Language Study*. Amsterdam: John Benjamins.

Givon, T. (1989) *Mind Code and Context: Essays in Pragmatics*. Hillsdale, NJ: Lawrence Erlbaum.

Givon, T. (1991) 'Serial verbs and the mental reality of "events": grammatical vs cognitive packaging'. In E. Traugott and B. Heine (eds), *Approaches to Grammaticalization, vol. 1*. Amsterdam: John Benjamins. pp. 81–127.

Glasbey, S. (1998) 'Progressives, states, and backgrounding'. In S. Rothstein (ed.), *Events and Grammar*. Dordrecht, the Netherlands: Kluwer. pp. 105–24.

Gómez-González, M.A. (2001) *The Theme-Topic Interface: Evidence from English*. Philadelphia: John Benjamins.

Goodenough, C. (1983) 'A psycholinguistic investigation of theme and information focus'. Unpublished PhD dissertation, University of Toronto.

Grimes, J. (1975) *The Thread of Discourse*. The Hague: Mouton.

Grosz, B. (1974) 'The structure of task oriented dialogue' (in German). In *IEEE Symposium on Speech Recognition: Contributed Papers*. Pittsburgh, PA: Carnegie Mellon University Computer Science Department. pp. 250–3.

Guindon, R. and Kintsch, W. (1984) 'Priming macroproposition: evidence for the primacy of macroproposition in the memory for text'. *Journal of Verbal Learning and Verbal Behavior*, 23 (4): 508–18.

Gundel, J. (1974) 'The role of topic and comment in linguistic theory'. PhD dissertation, University of Texas, Austin.

Gundel, J. (1988a) 'Universals of topic-comment structure'. In M. Hammond, E. Moravcsik and J. Wirth (eds), *Studies in Syntactic Typology*. Amsterdam: John Benjamins. pp. 209–39.

Gundel, J.K. (1988b) *The Role of Topic and Comment in Linguistic Theory*. New York: Garland.

Hajicova, E. (1984) 'Topic and focus'. In P. Sgall (ed.), *Contributions to Functional Syntax, Semantics, and Language Comprehension*. Amsterdam: John Benjamins. pp. 189–202.

Halliday, M.A.K. (1967a) 'Notes on transitivity and theme in English, Part 1'. *Journal of Linguistics*, 3: 37–81.

Halliday, M.A.K. (1967b) 'Notes on transitivity and theme in English, Part 2'. *Journal of Linguistics*, 3: 199–244.

Halliday, M.A.K. (1973) *Explorations in the Functions of Language*. London: Edward Arnold.

Halliday, M.A.K. (1976) 'Theme and information in the English clause'. In G. Kress (ed.), *Halliday: System and Function in Language*. London: Oxford University Press. pp. 174–88.

Halliday, M.A.K. (1985) *An Introduction to Functional Grammar*. London: Edward Arnold.

Halliday, M.A.K. and Fawcett, R.P. (eds) (1987) *New Developments in Systemic Grammar. Theory and Description*. London: Frances Pinter.

Halliday, M.A.K. and Matthiessen, C. (2004) *An Introduction to Functional Grammar, 3rd edn*. London: Edward Arnold.

Hawkinon, A.K. and Hyman, L.M. (1974) 'Hierarchies of natural topic in Shona'. *Studies in African Linguistics*, 5: 147–70.

Hinds, J. (1979) 'Organizational patterns in discourse'. In T. Givón (ed.), *Syntax and Semantics 12: Discourse and Syntax*. New York: Academic Press. pp. 135–57.

Hinds, J., Maynard, S.K. and Iwasaki, S. (eds) (1987) *Perspectives on Topicalization: The Case of Japanese 'wa'*. Amsterdam: John Benjamins.

Hopper, P. (1979) 'Aspect and foregrounding in discourse'. In T. Givon (ed.), *Discourse and Syntax*. New York: Academic Press. pp. 213–41.

Hopper, P. and Thompson, S. (1980) 'Transitivity in grammar and discourse'. *Language*, 56: 251–99.

Johnson-Laird, P.N. (1983) *Mental Models*. Cambridge, MA: Harvard University Press.

Jones, L.B. and Jones, L.K. (1979) 'Multiple levels of information in discourse'. In L. Jones and L. Jones (eds), *Discourse Studies in Mesoamerican Languages: Discussion*. Arlington, TX: Summer Institute of Linguistics. pp. 3–28.

Jones, L.K. (1977) *Theme in Expository English*. Lake Bluff, IL: Jupiter Press.

Kamp, H. and Reyle, U. (1993) *From Discourse to Logic*. Dordrecht: Reidel.

Keenan, E.L. (1976) 'Toward a universal definition of subject'. In C.N. Li (ed.), *Subject and Topic*. New York: Academic Press. pp. 305–33.

Keenan, E.O. and Schieffelin, B. (1976) 'Topic as a discourse notion'. In C.N. Li (ed.), *Subject and Topic*. New York: Academic Press. pp. 337–84.

Kim, M.H. (1996) 'Pragmatic determinants of syntactic subject in English'. *Journal of Pragmatics,* 25: 839–54.

Kim, M.H. (2002) 'Thematic management in Korean'. In M. Louwerse and W. van Peer (eds), *Thematics: Interdisciplinary Studies*. Amsterdam: John Benjamins. pp. 137–56.

Kintsch, W. (1974) *The Representation of Meaning in Memory*. Hillsdale, NJ: Lawrence Erlbaum.

Kintsch, W. (1988) 'The role of knowledge in discourse comprehension: a construction integration model'. *Psychological Review,* 95 (2): 163–82.

Kintsch, W. and van Dijk, T. (1978) 'Toward a model of text comprehension and production'. *Psychological Review*, 85: 363–94.

Labov, W. and Waletzky, J. (1967) 'Narrative analysis: oral version of personal experience'. In J. Helm (ed.), *Essays on the Verbal Arts*. Seattle: University of Washington Press.

Lambrecht, K. (1981) *Topic, Antitopic, and Verb Agreement in Non-Standard French*. Philadelphia: John Benjamins.

Lambrecht, K. (1987a) 'Aboutness as a cognitive category: the thetic categorical distinction revisited'. In J. Aske, N. Beery, L. Michaelis and H. Filip (eds), *Proceedings of the Thirteenth Annual Meeting of the Berkeley Linguistics Society*. pp. 366–82.

Lambrecht, K. (1987b) 'On the status of SVO sentences in French discourse'. In R. Tomlin (ed.), *Coherence and Grounding in Discourse*. Amsterdam: John Benjamins. pp. 217–61.

Lambrecht, K. (1994) *Information Structure and Sentence Form*. Cambridge: Cambridge University Press.

Lee, C., Gordon, M. and Büring, D. (eds) (2007) *Topic and Focus: Cross-Linguistic Perspectives on Meaning and Intonation*. Dordretcht, the Netherlands: Springer.

Leech, G.N. (1983) *Principles of Pragmatics*. London: Longman.

Levelt, W.J.M. (1989) *Speaking*. Cambridge, MA: MIT Press.

Levinson, S.C. (1983) *Pragmatics*. Cambridge: Cambridge University Press.

Levy, D.M. (1979) 'Communication goals and strategies: between discourse and syntax'. In T. Givon (ed.), *Syntax and Semantics: Discourse and Syntax*. New York: Academic Press. pp. 183–210.

Longacre, R.E. (1968) *Discourse, Paragraph, and Sentence Structure in Selected Philippine Languages*. Santa Ana, CA: Summer Institute of Linguistics.

Longacre, R.E. (1976a) 'The discourse structure of the Flood narrative'. In G. Macrae (ed.), *Society of Biblical Literature: 1976 Seminar Papers*. Missoula, MT: Scholars Press. pp. 235–62.

Longacre, R.E. (1976b) *An Anatomy of Speech Notions*. Lisse, the Netherlands: Peter de Ridder Press.

MacWhinney, B. (1977) 'Starting points'. *Language*, 53: 152–68.

Mann, W.C. and Thompson, S.A. (1986) 'Relational proposition in discourse'. *Discourse Processes*, 9: 57–90.

Marslen-Wilson, W., Levy, E. and Tyler, L. (1982) 'Producing interpretable discourse: the establishment and maintenance of refence'. In R.J. Jarvella and W. Klein (eds), *Speech, Place, and Action*. Chichester: Wiley. pp. 339–78.

Martin, J.R. and Rose, D. (2003) *Working with Discourse: Meaning Beyond the Clause*. London & New York: Continuum.

Mathesius, V. (1929) 'Zur Satzperspektive im modernen Englisch'. *Archiv fur das Studium den neuren Sprachen and Literaturen*, 155: 202–10.

Mathesius, V. (1939) 'O tak zvanem aktualnim clelneni vetnem [On the so-called actual bipartition of the sentence]'. *Slovo a Slovcesnost*, 5: 171–4.

Mathesius, V. (1975) 'On the information-bearing structure of the sentence'. In S. Kuno (ed.), *Harvard Studies in Syntax and Semantics*. Cambridge, MA: Harvard University Press. pp. 467–80.

McKeown, K.R. (1985) *Text Generation: Using Discourse Strategies and Focus Constraints to Generate Natural Language Text*. Cambridge: Cambridge University Press.

Mehan, H. (1979) *Learning Lessons*. Cambridge, MA: Harvard University Press.

Minsky, M. (1975) 'A framework for representing knowledge'. In P.H. Winston (ed.), *The Psychology of Computer Vision*. New York: McGraw-Hill.

Mithun, M. (1987) 'Is basic word order universal?'. In R.S. Tomlin (ed.), *Coherence and Grounding in Discourse*. Amsterdam: John Benjamins. pp. 281–328.

Myachykov, A. and Tomlin, R.S. (2008) 'Perceptual priming and structural choice in Russian sentence production'. *Journal of Cognitive Science*, 9 (1): 31–48.

Myachykov, A., Posner, M.I. and Tomlin, R.S. (2007) 'A parallel interface for language and cognition: theory, method, and empirical evidence'. *Linguistic Review*, 24: 457–74.

Myachykov, A., Tomlin, R.S. and Posner, M.I. (2005) 'Attention and empirical studies of grammar'. *Linguistic Review*, 22: 347–64.

Payne, D.L. (ed.) (1992) *Pragmatics of Word Order Flexibility*. Amsterdam: John Benjamins.

Pichert, J.W. and Anderson, R.C. (1977) 'Taking different perspectives on a story'. *Journal of Educational Psychology*, 69: 309–15.

Posner, M.I. and Raichle, M.E. (1994) *Images of Mind.* New York: Scientific American Library.

Prentice, J.L. (1967) 'Effects of cuing actor vs. cuing object on word order in sentence production'. *Psychonomic Science,* 8: 163–4.

Prince, E.F. (1978) 'A comparison of WH-clefts and it-clefts in discourse'. *Language,* 54: 883–907.

Prince, E.F. (1981) 'Towards a taxonomy of given-new information'. In P. Cole (ed.), *Radical – Pragmatics.* New York: Academic Press. pp. 223–56.

Prince, E.F. (1985) 'Topicalization and left-dislocation: functional analysis'. *Annals of the New York Academy of Sciences,* 433: 213–25.

Propp, V. (1958) *Morphology of the Folktale.* Bloomington, IN: Indiana University Research Center in Anthropology, Folklore, and Linguistics.

Reddy, M.J. (1979) 'The conduit metaphor: a case of frame conflict in our language about language'. In A. Ortony (ed.), *Metaphor and Thought.* Cambridge: Cambridge University Press. pp. 284–324.

Reinhart, T. (1981) 'Pragmatics and linguistics: an analysis of sentence topics'. *Philosophica,* 27 (1): 53–94.

Rochester, S.R. and Martin, J.R. (1977) 'The art of referring: the speaker's use of noun phrases to instruct the listener'. In R.O. Freedle (ed.), *Discourse Production and Comprehension: Advances in Discourse Processes.* Norwood, NJ: Ablex.

Rumelhart, D. (1980) 'Schemata: the building blocks of cognition'. In B. Spiro, B.C. Bruce and W.F. Brewer (eds), *Theoretical Issues in Reading Comprehension.* Hillsdale, NJ: Erlbaum.

Rutherford, E. (1988) *Sarum.* New York: Ivy Books.

Sanford, A.J. and Garrod, S. (1980) 'Memory and attention in text comprehension: the problem of reference'. In R. Nickerson (ed.), *Attention and Performance VIII.* Hillsdale, NJ: Lawrence Erlbaum.

Schank, R.C. and Abelson, R.P. (1977) *Scripts, Plans, Goals, and Understanding.* Hillsdale, NJ: Lawrence Erlbaum.

Schlobinski, P. and Schütze-Coburn, S. (1992). 'On the topic of topic and topic continuity'. *Linguistics,* 30 (1): 89–122.

Searle, J.R. (1969) *Speech Acts.* Cambridge: Cambridge University Press.

Searle, J.R. (1979) *Expression and Meaning: Studies in the Theory of Speech Acts.* Cambridge: Cambridge University Press.

Sidner, C.L. (1983) 'Focusing in the comprehension of definite anaphora'. In M. Brady and R.C. Berwick (eds), *Computational Models in Discourse.* Cambridge, MA: MIT Press. pp. 267–330.

Sinclair, J.M. and Coulthard, R.M. (1975) *Towards an Analysis of Discourse.* Oxford: Oxford University Press.

Sridhar, S.N. (1988) *Cognition and Sentence Production: Cross-Linguistic Study.* New York: Springer-Verlag.

Stout, G.F. (1896) *Analytic Psychology* (2 vols). London: Swan Sonnenschein & Co.

Swales, J. (1981) *Aspects of Article Introductions* (Aston ESP Research Report no. 1). The Language Studies Unit, University of Aston in Birmingham.

Taboada, M. and Mann, W.C. (2006a) 'Rhetorical Structure Theory: Looking back and moving ahead'. *Discourse Studies,* 8 (3): 423–59.

Taboada, M. and Mann, W.C. (2006b) 'Applications of Rhetorical Structure Theory'. *Discourse Studies,* 8 (4): 567–88.

Tannenbaum, P.H. and Williams, F. (1968) 'Generation of active and passive sentences as a function of subject and object focus'. *Journal of Verbal Learning and Verbal Behavior,* 7: 246–50.

Tomlin, R.S. (1983) 'On the interaction of syntactic subject, thematic information, and agent in English'. *Journal of Pragmatics,* 7: 411–32.

Tomlin, R.S. (1984) 'The treatment of foreground-background information in the on-line descriptive discourse of second language learners'. *Studies in Second Language Acquisition,* 6: 115–42.

Tomlin, R.S. (1985) 'Foreground-background information and the syntax of subordination'. *Text,* 5: 85–122.

Tomlin, R.S. (1986) 'The identification of foreground-background information in on-line descriptive discourse'. *Papers in Linguistics,* 19: 465–94.

Tomlin, R.S. (1987a) 'Linguistic reflections of cognitive events'. In R. Tomlin (ed.), *Coherence and Grounding in Discourse.* Amsterdam: John Benjamins. pp. 455–80.

Tomlin, R.S. (1987b) 'The problem of coding in functional grammars'. Paper presented at the UC Davis Conference on the Interaction of Form and Function in Language, Davis, California, April.

Tomlin, R.S. (1995) 'Focal attention, voice, and word order: an experimental, cross-linguistic study'. In P. Downing and M. Noonan (eds), *Word Order in Discourse*. Amsterdam: John Benjamins. pp. 517–54.

Tomlin, R.S. (1997) 'Mapping conceptual representation into linguistic representation: the role of attention in grammar'. In J. Nuyts and E. Pederson (eds), *With Language in Mind*. Cambridge: Cambridge University Press. pp. 162–89.

Tomlin, R.S. and Pu, M.M. (1991) 'The management of reference in Mandarin discourse'. *Cognitive Linguistics,* 2 (1): 65–95.

Tomlin, R.S. and Villa, V. (1994) 'Attention in cognitive science and SLA'. *Studies in Second Language Acquisition,* 16 (2): 183–204.

Vachek, J. (ed.) (1966) *The Linguistic School of Prague: An Introduction to its Theory and Practice*. Bloomington, IN: Indiana University Press.

Vallduvi, E. (1992) *The Informational Component*. New York: Garland.

van Dijk, T.A. (1977) 'Sentence topic and discourse topic'. In B.A. Stolz (ed.), *Papers in Slavic Philology I: In Honor of James Ferrell*. Ann Arbor, MI: Department of Slavic Languages and Literature, University of Michigan.

van Dijk, T.A. (1980) *Macrostructures*. Hillsdale, NJ: Lawrence Erlbaum.

van Dijk, T.A. (1982) 'Episodes as units of discourse'. In D. Tannen (ed.), *Analyzing Discourse: Text and Talk*. Washington, DC: Georgetown University Press. pp.177–95.

van Dijk, T.A. (ed.) (1985) *Handbook of Discourse Analysis*. London: Academic Press.

van Dijk, T.A. (2008) *Discourse Context*. Cambridge: Cambridge University Press.

van Dijk, T.A. and Kintsch, W. (1983) *Strategies of Discourse Comprehension*. New York: Academic Press.

van der Gabelenz, G. (1868) 'Ideen zur einer vergleichenden Syntax: Wort und Satzstellung'. *Zeitschrift für Völkerpsychologie und Sprachwissenschaft*, 6: 376–84.

Weil, H. (1887 [1844]) *The Order of Words in the Ancient Languages Compared with That of the Modern Languages* (trans. C. Super), 3rd edn. Boston: Ginn & Co.

Youssef, V. and Winford, J. (1999) 'Grounding via tense-aspect in Tobagonian Creole: discourse strategies across a Creole continuum'. *Linguistics*, 37 (4): 597–624.

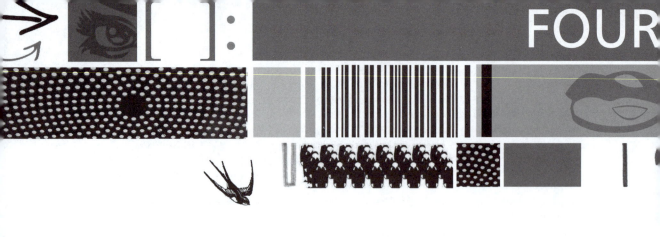

FOUR

Narrative in Everyday Life

Elinor Ochs

THE SCOPE OF NARRATIVE

In the search for what distinguishes the human species, the use of narrative to decipher human existence is significant. We might even say that humans display a narrative instinct, which motivates the flourishing of an array of narrative genres in each community. And why does narrative merit this status? James (1904) characterized subjective experience as a quasi-chaos, while Kundera (1995) despairingly compared the present moment to walking in a fog. Only *afterwards* do we grapple with the contours and meaning of an experience, with narrative as the universal yet imperfect medium to this end. The rub is that experience becomes linguistically and socio-culturally transformed through narrative *genres* and through the *activity* of recounting experiences for, to, and with particular interlocutors.

Imagine a world without narrative: going through life not telling others what happened to you or someone else, and not recounting what you read in a book or saw in a film. Not being able to hear or see or read dramas crafted by others. No access to conversations, printed texts, pictures, or films that are about events framed as actual or fictional. Imagine not even composing interior narratives, to and for yourself. No. Such a universe is unimaginable, for it would mean a world without history, myths or drama, and lives without reminiscence, revelation, and interpretive revision.

When we think about narrative, literary forms come to mind as narrative texts par excellence. At least since Aristotle's *Poetics* (1962), narrative genres such as tragedy and comedy have been the preoccupation of philosophers and critics. As a fundamental genre that organizes the ways in which we think and interact with one another, however, narrative encompasses an enormous range of discourse forms, including popular as well as artistic genres. The most basic and universal form of narrative may not be the product of a poetic muse but of ordinary conversation.

Our species is fortunate to have access to several communicative modalities that are available to create a narrative. Narratives can be produced through spoken, written, kines-thetic, pictorial, and musical modes of representation. Spoken and written narratives are commonplace. Dramatic enactments of events through body movements and facial expressions may be even more basic a narrative vehicle, given the historicity, ubiquity, and entice-ment of performance (Aristotle, 1962). Burke (1973: 103) harkens back to ritual drama 'as the Ur-form, the "hub", with all other aspect of *human* action treated as spokes radiating from this hub'. And every picture tells a story in the form of a more or less compressed nar-rative. Indeed the history of art is in part a history of narrative representation (Adorno, 1984; Berger, 1972; Marsack, 1991). In some cases, a narrative is communicated through a series of depictions, as in certain forms of cave art or some medieval illustrated manuscripts. In other cases, the sequence of events is compressed into a single representation, requiring the viewer to untangle the storyline from different elements in the scene. From one point of view, minimalist art places heavy demands on viewers by inviting them to create a narrative from highly abstract and elusive forms and juxtapositions. But from another point of view, minimalism liberates the viewer from having to discern a single, authoritative narrative scripted by artist or patron, so that the viewer is free to construe a range of possible narratives suggested or inspired by the visual forms.

The range of narrative interpretation that characterizes the paradigms of visual art also characterizes other narrative modes, particularly music. Instruments, tonality, and melodic leitmotifs may more or less explicitly, and more or less iconically, build characters and move them through emotional and actional realms (Feld and Fox, 1994). Feld (1982) describes how the Kaluli people of Papua New Guinea relate the melodic contours of bird songs to particular forms of human sentiment, activity, and states of being. Certain pitches, for example, will convey sadness and weeping, which in turn may evoke loss and aband-onment. The Kaluli reproduce these melodic contours in sung narrative performances to arouse strong feelings from those listening (Schieffelin, 1976).

While a narrative may be crafted through one communicative channel (e.g. speech or writing) narrators may draw upon a multiplicity of communicative resources. They may both orally recount an event and read from a book or newspaper about that event. Similarly, American children who engage in a narrative activity called 'Sharing Time' at school will tell a story using both words and displays of objects brought from home (Michaels, 1981). In courtroom narration, witnesses and lawyers may also piece together a plausible narrative, using objects and images that they will construct as evidence (Goodwin, 1994). Likewise, scientific narratives of the physical universe may also incorporate graphs, diagrams and other figures (Ochs, Jacoby and Gonzales, 1994). In the throes of working through a scien-tific problem, scientists may recount narratives in which they will assume the perspective of physical elements depicted in a graph, as illustrated in the following excerpt from a laboratory narrative:

[Cause you're telling me
[((*looks at board*))
[that [I go here and there's still a decay (present).
[((*points to 2 locations on graph*))
[But you're telling me that
[((*looks at board*))
[if I come in this way [(0.5) and [go he:re
[((*points to 2 different locations on graph*))
and [go he:re there's no decay.[1]
[((*moves finger to different location on graph*))

In this excerpt, the principal investigator of a physics project uses voice and gesture to narrate himself as a physical entity going through projected changes in physical states that are represented as symbolic points within a graph drawn on the board. Picture books also interweave images with linguistic text, inviting readers to pursue a narrative line across these two modalities. And theatrical drama can be enacted through a variety of modalities including pantomime, voice, written text, visual image, and musical instrumentation.

In the course of telling a narrative, speakers may engage in a wide range of other discourse genres (Ochs and Capps, 2001). For example, they might embed an argument within a narrative, as in the following exchange among family members narrating a story:

Mom: =We didn't laugh believe me.
Rhoda: [Yes you did – you st[arted to laugh.
Corky: [((*shaking head no*)) [hh
        ((*Mom looks to Corky for confirmation of memory*))
Mom: I don't think we did – I [had to go-
Rhoda: [YES YOU DI:D.[2]

In this example, Rhoda accuses her family of laughing at her during an embarrassing incident. When an interlocutor is the butt of a narrative, he or she will often dispute the account of events. Gossip – a form of narrative in which a breach in cultural norm is recounted – is characteristically contentious (Besnier, 2009; Brenneis, 1984; Goodwin, 1990; Haviland, 1977). The highly confrontative nature of gossip is captured in Goodwin's account (1990: 209) of this activity among African-American girls. These pre-adolescents will engage in complex, conflict-laden narratives called 'He-Said-She-Said', wherein one girl will tell another/others about what a third girl said about her/them (e.g. 'They say y'all say I wrote everything over there'). This reported accusation is refuted (e.g. '*UH*UH.= *THAT*WAS VINCENT SAID.'), in turn triggering lengthy public discussion.

---

[1]This excerpt is drawn from a corpus collected as part of two research projects on the problem-solving discourse of physicists supported by the Spencer Foundation: 'Socialization of Scientific Discourse' (1990–1993) and 'The Social Construction of Scientific Knowledge' (1994–1997): E. Ochs, Principal Investigator.

[2]This excerpt is drawn from a corpus collected as part of a research project on 'Discourse Processes in American Families', supported by the National Institute of Child Health and Development (1986–89): E. Ochs, T. Weisner, Co-Principal Investigators.

Not only can narrative house other language activities, it can itself also be incorporated into a larger genre or activity. For example, not only can a narrative house a dispute, it can also be housed within an ongoing dispute, as when someone launches a story to illustrate a point he or she is advocating. Narratives can also appear as part of a prayer. In the following example, a child begins to say grace at the dinner meal, but in the midst of a formulaic thanksgiving, she launches a narrative about events in her day:

Laurie:	=kay – Jesus? – plea:se – um – help us to love
	and .hh um – Thank you for letting it be a n:ice day
	and for taking a (fine/fun) nap?
	.hh – a:nd – for (letting) Mommy go bye
	and I'm glad that I cwied today?
	cuz I like cwying [.hh and
Annie?:	[((*snicker*))
Laurie:	I'[m glad (that anything/everything) happened today=
Roger?:	[((*snicker*))
Laurie:	=in Jesus name
	((*claps hands*)) A̲:-MEN![3]

In this example, Laurie's story about crying at school when 'Mommy go bye' is framed within her saying of grace. Grace, however, does not function simply as a set of bookends for Laurie's narrative, as visualized below:

Grace ½ Narrative ½ Grace

Rather, features of the genre of grace seep into the telling of the story:

G r N a ARRA c TIVE e

In particular, a defining feature of grace is an expressed sentiment of thankfulness. This sentiment organizes Laurie's narrative when she recounts 'I'm glad that I cwied today' and 'I like cwying'. Events like crying, which are normally associated with sadness, are imbued with a sensibility appropriate to the occasion of giving thanks for a meal. In this fashion, narratives become organized by the contexts in which they are constructed.

When we think about written narratives, many of us will envision them as different from Laurie's narrative. Delimited by titles and typographical spacing, perhaps even a book cover, written texts will appear to have defined boundaries. However, even written texts can be part of an ongoing communicative interaction – for example, a dispute or a supplication or a political agenda – that in subtle and profound ways will shape the narrative text. Burke (1973: 1) notes, 'Critical and imaginative works are answers to questions posed by the situation in which they arose. They are not merely answers, they are *strategic* answers,

---

[3]This excerpt is drawn from the corpus described in note 2 previously.

stylized answers.' Scholars ranging from Burke to Russian formalists (Bakhtin, 1981; Todorov, 1984) to proponents of cultural studies (Williams, 1982; 1983) have implored interpreters of narrative to embed such texts in the social and historical dialogues in which they participate.

Narratives are authored not only by those who introduce them but also by the many readers and interlocutors who influence the direction of the narrative (Bakhtin, 1981; 1986; Bauman, 1986; Goodwin, 1981). This co-authorship is most evident in conversational narratives, where interlocutors will ask questions, comment and otherwise overtly contribute to an evolving tale (Goodwin, 1984; 1990; Jefferson, 1978; Mandelbaum, 1987a; Sacks, 1978). The interactional production of narrative maintains and transforms persons and relationships (Matttingly and Garro, 2000). How we think about ourselves and others is influenced by both the message content of jointly told narratives and the experience of working together to construct a coherent narrative.

Given the variety of communicative channels and genres that realize narrative activity, it is an enormous task to consider how it is rooted in cultural systems of knowledge, beliefs, values, ideologies, action, emotion, and other dimensions of social order. Typically, cultural analyses of narrative will focus on a particular context of narrative activity, for example spoken or sung narrative performances (Bauman, 1986; Briggs, 1992; Feld, 1982), mythic tales (Hymes, 1971; Lévi-Strauss, 1955), conversational narratives of personal experience (Miller et al., 1990; Morgan, 1991; Ochs and Taylor, 1992b), reading storybooks (Heath, 1983), gossip (Besnier, 2009; Brenneis, 1984; Goodwin, 1990; Haviland, 1977), or classroom narrative performances (Michaels, 1981). Narrative in each of these contexts is rendered meaningful *vis-à-vis* some property of local ethos, e.g. an orientation towards autonomy or intervention, explicit moralizing, the sacredness of text, the facticity of text, imagined selves, social asymmetries, and so on. To date no study has examined narrative activity as it is variously construed across modes, settings, and participants within a single speech community. As such, we need to be cautious when positing broad generalizations that identify a culture with one narrative style.

NARRATIVE AND TIME

The term 'narrative' is used either in a narrow sense to specify the genre of a story or in a broad sense to cover a vast range of genres, including not only stories but also reports, sports and news broadcasts, plans, and agendas among others. What holds these diverse modes of narrative together? Regardless of the contexts in which they emerge, the modalities through which they are expressed, and the genres laminated within them, all narratives will *depict a temporal transition from one state of affairs to another.* This attribute does not uniquely define narrative. We may think of this temporal attribute as a necessary but not sufficient characterization of narrative. As will be discussed later, narratives depict far more than an ordering of events.

Ricoeur (1988) refers to the temporal property of narrative as the 'chronological dimension'. It is captured linguistically by a sequence of two or more clauses that are temporally ordered (Labov, 1972). This characterization encompasses narratives that are captivating as well as those that are dull. It includes accounts of enigmatic events as well as those that are predictable. A narrative can be a simple chronicle of events or an account that contextualizes events, by attempting to explain them and/or persuade others of their relevance.

Narratives may concern past, present, future, hypothetical, habitual, or other culturally relevant modes of reckoning time (Ochs and Capps, 2001). Narratives that are primarily concerned with *past events* include broad genres such as stories, histories, and reports concerning either professional or personal matters. Polanyi (1989: 17), for example, notes that 'stories and past time reports are specific, affirmative, past time narratives which tell about a series of events which took place at specific unique moments in a unique past time world'. Labov and Waletsky (1968: 287) refer to personal stories as 'narratives of personal experience' and characterize them linguistically as 'one method of recapitulating past experience by matching a verbal sequence of clauses to the sequence of events which (it is inferred) actually occurred'. Two of the narratives excerpted above, about Rhoda's embarrassment and Laurie's crying, are narratives of personal experience.

Narratives can also be primarily concerned with sequences of events taking place in *present* time, for example, sports broadcasts in which commentators will narrate actions, strategies, and the reactions of players and their audiences. Alternatively, narratives may focus on a projected *future*, as with event sequences such as agendas, prescriptions, advice, suggestions, instructions, forecasts, warnings, threats, and planning generally. The narrative recounted in the physics laboratory above, for example, projects changes in the physical universe that are hypothesized to transpire under certain conditions. Similarly, in the following excerpt, a young girl narrates a series of suggestions, forming a plan for her birthday party:

Sally: Mommy! I know what I'munna do for my birthday? –
          Could we paint our face for our birthday?
Mom: If you want,

          .
          .
Sally: ((*counting on her fingers as she speaks*)) Mommy, paint our face, number one –
          Okay, now. go to the park, number two,
          Daddy has to play monster, number three,
          U:m: – number !FOU:?:r! go to miniature golf
          And number five go to UCL pool –
          And number SIX? – kiss Mommy,
          Ha-ha I'm just kidding,[4]

While scientific narratives (e.g. experimental reports) reckon time primarily in terms of scientific units of measurement, autobiography and other genres of personal narrative reckon time in terms of a person's apprehension of time. Narrative time is *human* time, not clock time (Heidegger, 1962; Ricoeur, 1988). We experience ourselves in the present time

---

[4]This excerpt is drawn from the corpus described in note 2 previously.

world, but with a memory of the past, and an anxiety for the future. Narrative serves the important function of bringing the past into the present time consciousness, providing a sense of continuity to the self and society. But perhaps even more importantly, narrative accounts of past events can help us to manage our uncertain future. In Heidegger's framework, when we construct narratives about the past, we apprehend them in terms of what they imply for the present and future.

For these reasons, narratives that touch on past events are always about the present and future as well (Ochs, 1994). In some cases, narratives will provide new models and open up novel possibilities for the shape of our lives to come. Nowhere is this more poignant than in cases in which illness, accidents, or catastrophes require a person to recast their life towards a radically different future (Briggs and Mantini-Briggs, 2003; Mattingly, 1998; Shohet, 2007; White, 2007). Narratives about the past will often set off a concern about the present or future. For example, in the He-Said-She-Said narratives told by African-American girls, gossip about the past 'instigates' one of the interlocutors (the accused) to defend herself in the present and posit how she will redress the offence in the future (Goodwin, 1990: 271):

> Barbara: Well you *t*ell her to come say it in
> front of my fa:ce. (0.6) And *I'*ll *p*ut
> *her* somewhere.

In conversational narrative, a concern for the present and future may crop up at any point in the telling. Co-narrators will wander over the temporal map, focusing on the past, then relating it to the present and future, and then returning to another piece of the past. For example, after Laurie recounts (during grace) how she cried when her mother left her at school, the family returns to Laurie's predicament to help her face tomorrow (Ochs, 1994: 129):

> Mother: but honey? – I only work –
> this – it was only this week
> that I worked there all week?
> because it was the first week? of school
> Annie: [but – [she cried at three o'clock too
> (0.2)
> Mother: but after this? – it – I only work one day a week? there
> and that's Tuesday.

The family then ricochets from relevant bits of the past:

> Mother: Laurie? – you didn't take yer ((*shaking head no*)) –
> blanket to school either did you.
> Laurie: No I (for)got it ((*petulant*)).

to strategies for conquering the future:

Mother:	We'll hafta get it out of the closet –
	and put it over there with the <u>lunch</u> stuff.
	(2.0)
Jimmy:	yes – so you could – bring it (with/to) school.

What is the import of experienced time (human time) for understanding narrative? One implication is that stories and plans co-occur in the same narrative. Rather than asking, 'What genre of narrative is this text?', scholars now ask, 'How is this text organized simultaneously as a story, a plan, a broadcast, and/or a forecast?' The task of the narrators and scholars is to follow the different genres that run through a narrative text and analyse their interconnections.

For the remainder of this chapter, the discussion will focus on the characteristics of one narrative genre, namely stories. We will pursue the linguistic, psychological, and socio-logical structuring of such narratives.

NARRATIVE POINT OF VIEW AND PLOT STRUCTURE

While narratives can in principle recount utterly predictable events, usually stories will concern noteworthy events. Something has happened that the storyteller has found surprising, disturbing, interesting, or otherwise tellable (Labov and Waletsky, 1968). Stories normally have a point to make, which organizes the construction of the narrative itself. Often the point will be a moral evaluation of an occurrence, action, or psychological stance related to a set of events.

Stories are not so much depictions of facts as they are construals of happenings. Burke (1962) looked at stories as *selections* rather than as *reflections* of reality. And Goffman (1974: 504) notes,

> A tale or anecdote, that is, a replaying, is not merely any reporting of a past event. In the fullest sense, it is such a statement couched from the personal perspective of an actual or potential participant who is located so that some temporal, dramatic development of the reported event proceeds from that starting point. A replaying will therefore incidentally be something that listeners can empathetically insert them-selves into, vicariously re-experiencing what took place. A replaying, in brief, recounts a personal experi-ence, not merely reports on an event.

Aristotle introduced the term *mythos* or 'plot' to characterize how events and emotions are interwoven to form a coherent narrative. It is plot that distinguishes a list of events from a history or story (Bruner, 2003; Frye, 1957; Ricoeur, 1981; White, 1981). In creating a plot, historians and storytellers will give structure to events within a sense-making scheme. The plot knits together circumstantial elements such as scenes, agents, agency (instruments), acts, and purposes into a coherent scheme that revolves around an exceptional, usually troubling, event (Burke, 1962).

The plot can be seen as a theory of events in the sense that it provides an explanation of those events from a particular point of view (Feldman, 1989; Ochs, Taylor, Rudolph and

Smith, 1992). In this sense, stories are akin to scientific narratives. While scientific narratives de-emphasize agents and motives (Latour, 1987), they share with story narratives the property of recounting something out of the usual – an enigma, a discrepancy, an oddity, a challenge, an upset that disturbs the equilibrium. Furthermore, both scientific and personal narratives will try to shed light on that problem by placing it within a sequence of cause-effect events and circumstances.

The capacity to create and decipher plots is a quintessential faculty of the human species. Stories are cultural tools par excellence for understanding unusual and unexpected conduct or troubling concerns (Wilce, 1998). In so doing, they 'render the exceptional comprehensible' (Bruner, 1990: 52). Because stories recount events that depart from the expected, they also serve to articulate and sustain common understandings of what a culture deems ordinary. For this reason, narrative is a powerful means of socializing children into local notions of situational appropriateness. Co-narrators will often comment on how they would behave in the reported events and how others should have conducted themselves. As participants to these narrative interactions, children come to understand what is expected, normal, and appropriate.

BUILDING A NARRATIVE

How are story narratives constructed? How are they initiated and developed, and how do they come to completion? When we see a printed text, a title or other visible feature, we may initially identify the text as a possible story. While stories told in conversation do not have titles, they do often have *story prefaces* (Sacks, 1992). Instead of abruptly beginning a story, a teller transitions into it with the co-operation of other interlocutors. This activity is accomplished through story prefaces such as 'You want to hear a story?', wherein interlocutors will indicate their intention to tell a relevant story and elicit a go-ahead to do so from others. Tellers of stories in conversational interaction will often have an additional task: not only do they have to let others know that a story is coming up (which will occupy the floor for more than one utterance); they will also need to link their story at least vaguely to current talk. This goal may be accomplished through a repetition of some portion of the prior talk, as in the example below (Jefferson, 1978: 221):

Roger: Speakin about *forties*. I worked on a k-o:n Morganelli's
          Forty.

Sometimes story prefaces will be introduced by someone other than the person who will eventually initiate the story. For example, women will sometimes preface and forward a story for their husbands to tell (Goodwin, 1986; Mandelbaum, 1987b). In the excerpt below, Phyllis prefaces a story in a way that retains her husband Mike as its principal teller (Goodwin, 1986: 298):

Phyl: *M*like siz there wz a big fight down there las' night,
Curt: Oh rilly?
         (0.5)
Phyl: Wih *K*eegan en, what.
         Paul [de Wa::*ld*?]
Mike: Paul de *Wa*:l d. Guy out of…

Once a story has been launched, it assumes a particular structure. The elements that comprise a story have been analysed by philosophers, folklorists, literary critics, and discourse analysts at least since the days of Aristotle. He described in some detail the architecture of tragedy and comedy and characterized the former in terms of the principles of plot, character (moral habits), language, thought, spectacle (manner), and melody. For Aristotle, the soul of tragedy was the plot, and character was of secondary importance. A plot had to have a beginning, a middle, and an end, but this progression was not as obvious as it might first appear (Aristotle, 1962: 52):

> A beginning is that which does not come necessarily after something else, but after which it is natural for another thing to exist or come to be. An end, on the contrary, is that which naturally comes after something else, either as its necessary sequel or as its usual (and hence probable) sequel, but itself has nothing after it. A middle is that which both comes after something else and has another thing following it. A well-constructed plot, therefore, will neither begin at some chance point nor end at some chance point, but will observe the principles here stated.

Classic literary studies have drawn on these Aristotelian principles when analysing the structure of story narratives (Barthes, 1988; Frye, 1957; Propp, 1986; Ricoeur, 1988). Labov's linguistic analysis of oral narratives of personal experience in New York City also harks back to Aristotle's notion of the narrative essentials of a beginning, middle and end. Those narratives were produced in response to the question, 'Were you ever in a situation where you were in serious danger of being killed?' Labov comments that these were 'complete in the sense that they have a beginning, a middle, and an end', but some more fully formed narratives displayed the following features of personal experience narratives (1972: 363): 1) Abstract (e.g. 'My brother put a knife in my head'); 2) Orientation (e.g. 'This was just a few days after my father died'); 3) Complicating Action (e.g. 'I twisted his arm up behind him …'); 4) Evaluation (e.g. 'Ain't that a bitch?'); 5) Result or Resolution (e.g. 'After all that I gave the dude the cigarette, after all that'); and 6) Coda (e.g. 'And that was that.').

Cognitive psychologists will analyse stories as having 'story grammars' (Mandler and Johnson, 1977; Stein and Glenn, 1979; Stein and Policastro, 1984). In Stein and Glenn (1979), the major 'grammatical' constituents of stories include: 1) a setting; either 2) an initiating event or 3) an internal response; 4) an overt attempt; 5) a consequence. Stein and Policastro also add a sixth story component: a reaction to 3, 4, or 5. Mandler and Johnson include as well an 'ending' component, and make a further distinction between stories that are goal-oriented and those that are not. Those that are goal-oriented parallel the Stein and Glenn model. Stories that are not goal-oriented consist of 1) a setting; 2) a beginning; 3) a simple reaction (either an emotional response or an unplanned action); and 4) an ending. All constituents comprising a story episode, and with the exception of the setting, are seen as invariantly ordered.

The concept of *setting* is common to literary, linguistic, and psychological models of narrative. Story grammars and linguistic conceptualizations of setting define setting in terms of the physical, social, and temporal context of protagonists' conduct. Literary analyses of stories and cultural psychological approaches emphasize that setting goes beyond time and space and social circumstance to encompass the psychological climate that anticipates a beginning narrative event. The historical rise of the novel and other narrative genres is linked to greater attention being paid to what Bruner (1990) calls the 'mental landscape', including the emotional states, morality, perspectives, and motives of protagonists as they enter a crucial narrative event. It is the psychological climate that colours protagonists as tragic hero/heroines or comedic fools. Aristotle notes, for example, that a tragedy rests on establishing that the protagonist is of high moral fibre and is an unwitting victim of circumstances. This psychological context will be established in settings.

While pieces of a setting will appear at the start of stories, narrators may also delay revealing crucial aspects of the setting until much later in the story. There are many reasons for this. One is that the narrator may wish to slowly disclose vital elements of the context to build suspense. If the narrator were to reveal all the relevant background initially, the story loses its dramatic tension. Another reason is that narrators themselves are not always aware of important details of the story setting at the start of the storytelling. It is only when the story is underway that storytellers will make a connection between a prior circumstance and the troublesome event of concern in the narrative. In conversational storytelling, a narrator may be reminded of such circumstances by co-narrators participating in the interaction (Ochs, Smith and Taylor, 1989), and in therapeutic conversations, the psychotherapist will often be instrumental in evoking unmentioned states of mind, actions, or conditions that may render a narrative event more meaningful (Capps and Ochs, 1995).

Another reason for late revelations of settings is that narrators will at first try to present themselves in the best light as protagonists (Ochs, Smith and Taylor, 1989). They will build settings in such a way that their emotions and actions will seem reasonable and worthy of an interlocutor's empathy. Yet sometimes the best laid plans of mice and men will run amok, when other co-narrators bring out undisclosed pieces of the setting that will unravel this positive self-portrayal. Such dissembling occurs in the narrative excerpt below. The story opens with nine-year-old Lucy complaining about how her school principal inadequately punished a girl who pulled up her friend's dress in front of some boys (Ochs et al., 1992: 47):

Lucy: I don't think Mrs. um Andrew's being fair because um

　　.

　　.

　　When we were back at school um –
　　this girl? – she pulled um -Vicky's <u>dress</u> ((*puts hand to knee*))
　　up t'here ((*gestures with hand high on chest*)) in front of the boys

Mom: mhm?

Lucy: she only – all she did was get a <u>day</u> in de<u>ten</u>tion

After her family aligns with Lucy's perspective, her six-year-old brother Chuck introduces a piece of the setting unbeknownst to her parents: Lucy herself had been punished by the principal and for the same length of time (one day) as the girl who embarrassed her friend:

Chuck:	Lucy? – you only went to it <u>once</u> – right?=
Father:	=((*clears throat*))
	(0.1) ((*Lucy arches her back, eyes open wide, looks shocked, starts shaking her head no once, father looking at her*))
Mother:	(<u>You'</u> [ve been in it/<u>You</u> can tell us can't you?)
Father:	[(I'm lis?tening)
Lucy:	((*low to Chuck*)) (thanks)
	(0.4)
Lucy:	((*louder*)) [<u>yeah</u> – that – (was)
Mother:	[(She was in it) once?
	(0.6)
Lucy:	Once.

Lucy's plight is a common one in conversational storytelling. When we tell stories among intimates such as family members and friends, we are vulnerable to their knowledge of our lives. They can at any moment introduce background information that undermines the point we as narrators are trying to convey.

All characterizations of stories will specify *a key event that disrupts the equilibrium of ordinary, expected circumstances*. For example, the notions of 'complication' (Aristotle, 1962), 'trouble' (Burke, 1962), 'deviation from the ordinary' (Bruner, 1990), 'complicating action' (Labov, 1972), 'initiating event' (Stein and Glenn, 1979), and 'inciting event' (Sharff, 1982) all concern an unpredictable or unusual or problematic event on which a narrative episode focuses. In the story that Laurie tells while saying grace, for instance, she focuses on the problematic event of 'Mommy go bye'. In Lucy's story, the focus initially is on the problematic conduct of a schoolmate: 'this girl? – she pulled um – Vicky's <u>dress</u> up t'here in front of the boys'.

In many stories, the key troublesome event is seen as provoking *psychological responses* and *actions* that attempt to reinstate a sense of equilibrium. In Mandler and Johnson's (1977) framework, these are goal-directed stories. For example, in Laurie's story, 'Mommy go bye' is seen as inciting Laurie to cry. In Lucy's story, the schoolmate's transgression is seen as inciting the principal to punish the transgressor with a day's detention.

These psychological and actional responses in turn will have *outcomes*, which may then engender *further psychological responses and actions*. For example, in Lucy's story, she becomes upset when she discovers that the principal gave the schoolmate only one day's detention. She tells her family that the principal is not fair; and when her mother asks her, '<u>You</u> think she should have gotten suspended?', Lucy responds, 'At LEAST!'.

In a study of the narrative construction of agoraphobia, Capps and Ochs (1995) found that the narratives of a panic experience told by an agoraphobic woman consistently delineated a series of spiralling problematic events, wherein one problem would lead to another: For example, a traffic jam was seen as inciting heightened awareness. This realization in turn incited panic, which then incited the protagonist to initiate a series of attempts to mitigate that panic that failed, thus inciting further panic until eventually the protagonist communicated her distress and escaped the situation. In stacking each problem upon another problem, the narrator constructed a world in which she was helpless and driven by panic.

When storytellers recount that a problematic event incited psychological responses or actions, the story appears to be capped in past time. As discussed earlier, however, stories have a way of edging into the future, and storytellers will often frame an inciting event, a psychological response or an attempt to handle that event as *still* unresolved, *still* problematic at the time of its telling. For example, in Laurie's story, while she herself treats the problematic event of 'Mommy go bye' as finished business ('I'm glad (that anything/ everything) happened today in Jesus name A:-MEN!'), her mother does not. Laurie's mother treats both 'Mommy go bye' and Laurie's response as *current* problems, which provoke her to propose a set of future helpful actions. In the case of panic stories, agoraphobia sufferer consistently framed panic as not only a past problem but also as an ongoing problem with debilitating consequences. Indeed a hallmark of agoraphobia is the tendency to ruminate about the consequences of past panic episodes for future life experiences. The storied past becomes a rationale for the here-and-now and beyond (Capps and Ochs, 1995).

Many narratives will appear to be motivated by narrators' current dissatisfaction with how they or some other protagonist handled a situation, as in Lucy's complaint about the response of her school principal to a school problem. Indeed one motivation for narrators to initiate stories is to work through with other interlocutors how they currently feel or should feel about some element of a past situation. Havel notes in *Letters to Olga* (1989) that this motivation is part of an all-encompassing quest to relate our personal lives to a broader horizon of relationships, places, objects, ideologies, values, and other human concerns. Our experiences are full of enigmas, and we tell stories to probe with others these mysteries and frustrations. While the character of co-narration varies, the activity offers an opportunity and a potential for communal reflection not only on the meaning of particular experiences but also on the meaning of life on historical, cultural and cosmological planes.

In many communities, the activity of problem-solving through collaborative narration is emblematic of friendship, collegiality, or family membership. Members of these communities are not always able to enjoin familiars to narratively work through problems. Even in close physical proximity of family and friends, persons may feel awkward or incapable of presenting an unresolved narrative (Jackson, 2002). In the absence of informal problem-solving encounters of this sort, would-be narrators may bring their stories to community practitioners. In a number of societies, these practitioners are said to engage in 'disentangling' (Watson-Gegeo and White, 1990) and in others, in 'psychotherapy' (McLeod, 1997).

NARRATIVE IDENTITIES

Narrative is not only a genre, it is also a social activity involving different participant roles. Both Bakhtin (1981) and Goffman (1974) distinguish the narrative role of the author (or, in Goffman's words, the principal) from that of the narrator (or, in Goffman's words, the animator). As noted earlier, Bakhtin also inspired the perspective that the narrative audience plays a key role in the construction of narrative. The audience is a co-author of narrative form and meaning.

Mandelbaum (1987a) suggests that audience involvement varies in storytelling, distinguishing between teller-driven and recipient-driven stories. Teller-driven stories resemble Goffman's depiction of a story (1974: 509): 'Sometimes [the participant] will sustain his story across several consecutive turns, the interposing talk of others largely taking the form of encouragement, demonstrations of attentiveness and other "back channel" effects.' In recipient-driven storytelling, recipients will take a more active role (Mandelbaum, 1987: 238): 'teller and recipient together work out what a storytelling is "about" and how it is to be understood.' Recipient-driven storytelling characterizes those situations in which the recipient is also a story protagonist, especially when the recipient is the butt of a story. This observation resonates with Goodwin's (1990) study of He-Said-She-Said interactions, where the primary story recipient is both the object of an accusation and highly active in structuring the ensuing story.

Story recipients will vary in their knowledge and expertise concerning story details (Goodwin, 1986). In storytelling interactions among adult Americans, recipients who are more knowledgeable about events being recounted will tend to contribute more to the ongoing telling. Knowledge is not always a basis for narrative rights, however. Children, for example, will often not get to recount stories about themselves but rather are expected to listen as one or both parents assume this right (Taylor, 1995). Similarly, Sampson (1982) notes that persons who have been sick or injured in Australian Aborigine communities do not have the right to tell the story of their illness. The sick are thought to be not themselves in this condition and therefore unable to portray events. Instead those persons who cared for the sick person will retain this right.

The assignment of the roles of teller and audience breaks down in conversational storytelling in which many participants will construct the story. Particularly where storytelling includes close friends and family members, this telling can be widely shared. In examining family storytelling, Ochs, Taylor, et al. (1992) found it useful to consider all family members present as co-tellers, in that the telling routinely shifted from one family member to another in the course of a story. They distinguished an *initial teller* (someone who introduces a story) from *other tellers* (those who contribute to the telling of a story once introduced). Rather than assuming a minor role, family members as other tellers contributed substantially to the story construction, including supplying pieces of the setting, positing psychological responses and attempting to resolve the central story problem. For example, after Lucy as the initial teller introduced the story about the schoolmate who received only one day of detention, her mother continued the story by suggesting Lucy's psychological response to the schoolmate's offensive actions:

```
Lucy:      she only – all she did was get a day in detention
Mother:    mhm? – you think she should have gotten suspended?
           (0.6)
Lucy:      at LEAST

               .
               .
Mother:    (cuz Lucy) was really embarrassed
           ((nodding yes, talking while eating))
           (1.6)
Mother:    (I mean you/Lucy really) would have liked to kill the – the girl – huh?
Lucy:      ((nods yes slowly, as she chews, fork in mouth))
           [
Mother:    (cuz) you were upset with her –
           ((speaking very fast)) but you were held back
           because you (thought) your school was goin' to do it
           and the school didn't do it and you feel upset
```

Other family members then chimed in as well as co-tellers. Lucy's younger brother Chuck, for example, suggested that he would give more detention as punishment:

```
Chuck:     I think? she should – be: in there for a h- whole MONTH? or so =
?:         =(well maybe)
           (0.6)
Chuck:     each day she('d) hafta go there – each day each day each day
           even if? ...
```

And as noted earlier, it is Chuck who takes the story in a radically different direction when he discloses that Lucy herself received detention.

NARRATING LIVES

When those involved in narrative interactions actively participate as both tellers and recipients, they exercise their entitlement to co-author a narrative. When that narrative concerns a lived experience, co-authors will impact the understanding of that experience. It is not only a narrative but also a life or a history that is collaboratively constructed. Given that narrative is a sense-making activity and a primary vehicle for retaining experiences in memory, the entitlement to co-tell a narrative is a powerful right, encompassing past, present, future, as well as imagined worlds.

As co-tellers construct a story, they may determine what happened, discerning the *truth* status of events and cementing them as such in memory, as in the following narrative recounted by a mother and child (Fivush and Reese, 1992: 7):

MOTHER:	Do you remember last Easter?
CHILD:	Yeah
MOTHER:	What did we do at Easter?
CHILD:	What?
MOTHER:	What did we do at Easter?
CHILD:	Yeah
MOTHER:	Can't remember?
CHILD:	Yeah
MOTHER:	We dyed Easter eggs
CHILD:	Yeah
MOTHER:	Who helped us dye Easter eggs?
CHILD:	What?
MOTHER:	Do you remember who helped us dye Easter eggs?
CHILD:	Yeah
MOTHER:	Who?
CHILD:	(no response)
MOTHER:	Grandma Shirley

Co-tellers may also determine what *could* have happened in the past or what could happen in the future, a phenomenon referred to as side-shadowing (Morson, 1994). Side-shadowing creates non-linear stories in that storylines are cast as having gone or as about to go in more than one possible direction. These stories entertain different perspectives on events, in much the same way that scientists will pose alternative trajectories for the physical events they are observing in their laboratories. Side-shadowing can cast doubts about past or future events. When applied to one's own experience, side-shadowing may have ramifications for how a narrator casts the direction that his or her life has taken. For example, Shohet (2007) found that side-shadowing characterized the life stories of young women struggling to recover from anorexia, while women who perceived themselves as fully recovered recounted more linear narratives, with an anorexic past superseded by a healthy present.

Co-tellers also may recount what *should* have happened, thereby evaluating the *moral* status of protagonists (Duranti, 1994; Ochs and Capps, 2001). Often narrators will cast the actions of protagonists as morally dispreferred, and then recount what anyone with common sense would have done in the same situation. All of the narratives illustrated in this chapter communicate strong moral messages about lives, but perhaps the most striking is the story of Lucy and the girl who was given only one day's detention in school. In this narrative, family members criticized the principal's light punishment of the girl and supported Lucy's judgment that the girl should have received at least three days of detention. Stories like this that present differentially valenced moral ways of acting, thinking and feeling are vehicles for affirming or creating family and community values.

Yet, in other situations, co-tellers will challenge one another's explanations of emotions, actions, and circumstances. This often happens when stories are narrated among those who share a history with one another and with the protagonists in a story narrative. In societies such as that of the mainstream United States, those who are privy to background information that is relevant to an unfolding story may introduce elements that will radically alter the storyline. For example, in the story about school detention, Lucy's younger brother's revelation of her detention experience undermines Lucy's explanation of why the school principal is not fair. Whereas Lucy had based her sense of injustice on the gravity of the schoolmate's transgression, her brother provides an alternative basis for Lucy's judgement: the principal was not fair to give Lucy and the schoolmate equal amounts of detention. Here alignment gives way to a potentially adverse disclosure.

Co-narration that involves challenging and redrafting storylines is akin to an academic and legal challenging and revision of explanations for events. In both cases, challenges will recast a narrative account as a *version* of experience rather than as fact. As such, a collaborative storytelling of personal experiences can be a provenance for socializing the intellectual skills demanded in professional worlds. As with all human actions, challenging how someone else is telling a story is socially organized, and there are expectations concerning which stories are challengeable. For example, the White working families in Heath's (1983) study discouraged children from disagreeing with written narratives. Similarly, families, institutions and communities may vary in their expectations concerning who will assume the role of challenger. In many communities, for example, adults more than children and husbands more than wives are given this entitlement (Fader, 2009; Goody, 1978; Heath, 1983; Ochs and Taylor, 1992b). In the White middle-class American families studied by Ochs and Taylor, mothers challenged more than twice as often and fathers more than three times as often as did children in collaborative narrative interactions. Because narrative activity is ubiquitous in these households, the recurrent narrative roles of family members help to constitute their social positions. The predilection for American middle-class parents, especially fathers, to challenge narrative accounts is well understood by young children, who in turn will display a predilection to sabotage or only minimally comply with parental efforts to elicit their stories. Familiar to these households are exchanges of the type: 'What did you do at school today?'–'Nothing.' Children in these families are loath to have their stories critiqued by parental co-narrators.

CONCLUSION

Narrative activity in these ways is at once a discursive medium for reinforcing moral paradigms, probing the contours and meaning of events, and instantiating identities and positions. Narrative activity allows members of communities to reflect upon events, thoughts and emotions, but this opportunity may be asymmetrically allocated, granting reflective rights to some more than others. Crucial to the construction of self, other, and society, co-narration crafts biographies and histories. Yet the meaning of existence – what is possible, actual, reasonable, desirable – tends to be defined by some more than others. To these ends, narrative has the capacity to limit or transform the human psyche.

FURTHER READING

The following readings cover the spectrum of narrative practices in everyday life and their consequences for individuals, institutions, the fabric of social relationships, and the human condition.

Bruner, Jerome (2003) *Making Stories: Law, Literature, Life*. Cambridge: Harvard University Press.
This book presents the idea that narrative is critical to understanding experience, in that it imposes a plot structure onto life events, complete with protagonists, troubles-telling, and attempts at resolution, all laced with moral valences that support tellers' points of view.

Mattingly, Cheryl and Garro, Linda C. (2000) *Narrative and the Cultural Construction of Illness and Healing*. Berkeley, CA: University of California Press.
This edited volume comprises an array of studies on the role of narrative in medical sense-making and healing across societies. The Introduction provides a comprehensive and acute view of how narrative helps those with medical conditions to reconfigure their identities and futures.

Ochs, Elinor and Capps, Lisa (2001) *Living Narrative: Creating Lives in Everyday Storytelling*. Cambridge, MA: Harvard University Press.
This book argues that when people recount narratives, they are pulled by two opposing tendencies – to use canonical plots to make sense out of their experiences ('the drive for coherence') and to search for alternative explanations for life events that transpired ('the drive for authenticity'). The book considers these two orientations in relation to narrative structure, children's development, disability, illness, and the construction of personhood and self.

ONLINE READING

The following articles are available at www.sagepub.co.uk/discoursestudies.

Laura A. Sterponi (2003) 'Account episodes in family discourse: the making of morality in everyday interaction', Discourse Studies, 5(1): 79–100.

Jan Blommaert (2001) 'Investigating narrative inequality: African asylum seekers' stories in Belgium', Discourse & Society, 12(4): 413–49.

Betsy Rymes (1995) 'The construction of moral agency in the narratives of high-school drop-outs', Discourse & Society, 6(4): 495–516.

REFERENCES

Adorno, T. (1984) *Aesthetic Theory*. London: Routledge & Kegan Paul.
Aristotle (1962) *Poetics*. New York: Norton.
Bakhtin, M.M. (1981) *The Dialogic Imagination: Four Essays* (ed. by M. Holquist, translated by C. Emerson and M. Holquist). Austin, TX: University of Texas Press.
Bakhtin, M.M. (1986) *Speech Genres and Other Late Essays*. Austin, TX: University of Texas Press.
Barthes, R. (1988) *The Semiotic Challenge*. New York: Hill and Wang.
Bauman, R. (1986) *Story, Performance, and Event*. Cambridge: Cambridge University Press.
Berger, J. (1972) *Ways of Seeing*. London: BBC and Penguin Books.
Besnier, N. (2009) *Gossip and the Everyday Production of Politics*. Honolulu: University of Hawaii Press.

Brenneis, D. (1984) Grog and gossip in Bhatgaon: style and substance in Fijian Indian conversation. *American Ethnologist*, 11: 487–506.

Briggs, C.L. (1992) '"Since I am a Woman, I will Chastize my Relatives": gender, reported speech, and the (re)production of social relations in Warao ritual wailing'. *American Ethnologist*, 19: 337–61.

Briggs, C. and Mantini-Briggs, C. (2003) *Stories in the Time of Cholera: Racial Profiling during a Medical Nightmare*. Berkeley: University of California Press.

Bruner, J. (1990) *Acts of Meaning*. Cambridge: Harvard University Press.

Bruner, J. (1991) The Narrative Construction of Reality. *Critical Inquiry*, 18: 1–21.

Bruner, J. (2003) *Making Stories: Law, Literature, Life*. Cambridge: Harvard University Press.

Burke, K. (1962) *A Grammar of Motives and a Rhetoric of Motives*. Cleveland and New York: Meridian Books.

Burke, K. (1973) *The Philosophy of Literary Form*. Berkeley, CA: University of California Press.

Capps, L. and Ochs, E. (1995) *Constructing Panic*. Cambridge: Harvard University Press.

Capps, L., Bjork, R. and Siegel, D. (1993) The Meaning of memories. *UCLA Magazine*, 4(4): 8–10.

Duranti, A. (1986) 'The audience as co-author: an introduction'. *Text*, 6–3: 239–47.

Duranti, A. (1994) *From Grammar to Politics: Linguistic Anthropology in a Western Samoan Village*. Berkeley and Los Angeles: University of California Press.

Fader, A. (2009) *Mitzvah Girls: Bringing up the Next Generation of Hasidic Jews in Brooklyn*. Princeton: Princeton University Press.

Feld, S. (1982) *Sound and Sentiment: Birds, Weeping, Poetics, and Song in Kaluli Expression*. Philadelphia: University of Pennsylvania Press.

Feld, S. and Fox, A.A. (1994) 'Music and language'. *Annual Review of Anthropology*, 23: 25–53.

Feldman, C. (1989) 'Monologue as problem-solving narrative'. In K. Nelson (ed.), *Narratives from the Crib*. Cambridge, MA: Harvard University Press.

Fivush, R. and Reese, E. (1992) 'The social construction of autobiographical memory'. In M.A. Conway, H. Spinnler, D.C. Rubin and W. Wagenaar (eds), *Theoretical Perspectives on Autobiographical Memory*. Netherlands: Kluwer. pp. 1–28.

Frye, N. (1957) *The Anatomy of Criticism*. Princeton, NJ: Princeton University Press.

Goffman, E. (1974) *Frame Analysis: An Essay on the Organization of Experience*. New York: Harper and Row.

Goodwin, C. (1981) *Conversational Organization: Interaction Between Speakers and Hearers*. New York: Academic.

Goodwin, C. (1984) 'Notes on story structure and the organization of participation'. In M. Atkinson and J. Heritage (eds), *Structures of Social Action*. Cambridge: Cambridge University Press. pp. 225–46.

Goodwin, C. (1986) 'Audience diversity, participation and interpretation'. *Text*, 6(3): 283–316.

Goodwin, C. (1994) 'Professional vision'. *American Anthropologist*, 96(3): 606–33.

Goodwin, M. (1990) *He-Said-She-Said: Talk as Social Organization among Black Children*. Bloomington, IN: Indiana University Press.

Goody, E. (1978) *Questions and Politeness: Strategies in Social Interaction*. Cambridge: Cambridge University Press.

Havel, V. (1989) *Letters to Olga*. New York: Holt.

Haviland, J. (1977) *Gossip, Reputation, and Knowledge in Zinacantan*. Chicago: University of Chicago Press.

Heath, S. (1983) *Ways with Words: Language, Life and Work in Communities and Classrooms*. Cambridge: Cambridge University Press.

Heidegger, M. (1962) *Being and Time*. New York: Harper & Row.

Hymes, D. (1971) 'The "wife" who "goes out" like a man: re-interpretations of a Clackamas Chinook myth'. In P. Maranda and E.K. Maranda (eds), *Structural Analyses of Oral Traditions*. Philadelphia: University of Pennsylvania Press.

James, W. (1904) 'Does "consciousness" exist?' *Journal of Philosophy, Psychology and Scientific Methods*, 1(18): 477–91.

Jefferson, G. (1978) 'Sequential aspects of storytelling in conversation'. In J. Schenkein (ed.), *Studies in the Organization of Conversational Interaction*. New York: Academic. pp. 219–48.

Kundera, M. (1995) *La Lenteur*. Paris: Editions Gallimard.

Labov, W. (1972) *Language in the Inner City: Studies in the Black English Vernacular*. Philadelphia: University of Pennsylvania Press.

Labov, W. and Waletzky, J. (1968) 'Narrative analysis'. In W. Labov et al. (eds), *A Study of the Non-Standard English of Negro and Puerto Rican Speakers in New York City*. New York: Columbia University. pp. 286–338.

Latour, B. (1987) *Science in Action*. Cambridge, MA: Harvard University Press.

Lévi-Strauss, C. (1955) *Tristes Tropiques*. Paris: Plon.

McLeod, J. (1997) *Narrative and Psychotherapy*. London: Sage.

Mandelbaum, J. (1987a) *Recipient-driven Storytelling in Conversation*. Unpublished PhD dissertation, University of Texas at Austin.

Mandelbaum, J. (1987b) 'Couples sharing stories'. *Communication Quarterly,* 35: 144–170.

Mandler, J. and Johnson, N.S. (1977) 'Remembrance of things parsed: story structure and recall'. *Cognitive Psychology*, 9: 111–51.

Marsack, A. (1991) *The Roots of Civilization*. Mount Kisco, NY: Moyer Bell.

Mattingly, C. (1998) *Healing Dramas and Clinical Plots: The Narrative Structure of Experience*. Cambridge: Cambridge University Press.

Mattingly, C. and Garro, L. (2000) *Narrative and the Cultural Construction of Illness and Healing*. Berkeley, CA: University of California Press.

Michaels, S. (1981) '"Sharing Time": children's narrative styles and differential accesss to literacy'. *Language in Society*, 10: 423–42.

Miller, P., Potts, R., Fung, H., Hoogstra, L. and Mintz, J. (1990) 'Narrative practices and the social construction of self in childhood'. *American Ethnologist,* 17(2): 292–311.

Morgan, M. (1991) 'Indirectness and interpretation in African American women's discourse'. *Pragmatics*, 1(4): 421–51.

Morson, G. (1994) *Narrative and Freedom: The Shadows of Time*. New Haven and London: Yale University Press.

Ochs, E. (1994) 'Stories that step into the future'. In D. Biber and E. Finegan (eds), *Perspectives on Register: Situating Language Variation in Sociolinguistics*. Oxford: Oxford University Press. pp. 106–35.

Ochs, E. and Capps, L. (2001) *Living Narrative: Creating Lives in Everyday Storytelling*. Cambridge, MA: Harvard University Press.

Ochs, E. and Taylor, C. (1992a) 'Science at dinner'. In C. Kramsch (ed.), *Text and Context: Cross-disciplinary Perspectives on Language Study*. Lexington, MA: D.C. Heath.

Ochs, E. and Taylor, C. (1992b) 'Family narrative as political activity'. *Discourse and Society*, 3(3): 301–40.

Ochs, E. and Taylor, C. (1994) 'Mothers' role in the everday reconstruction of "Father Knows Best"'. In K. Hall (ed.), *Locating Power: Proceedings of the 1992 Berkeley Women and Language Conference*. Berkeley, CA: University of California.

Ochs, E., Jacoby, S. and Gonzales, P. (1994) 'Interpretive journeys: how physicists talk and gesture through graphic space'. *Configurations* (Special Issue: *Located Knowledges: Intersections between Cultural, Gender, and Science Studies*, edited by M. Biagoli, R. Reid and S. Traweek) 2(1): 151–72.

Ochs, E., Smith, R. and Taylor, C. (1989) 'Dinner narratives as detective stories'. *Cultural Dynamics*, 2: 238–57.

Ochs, E., Taylor, C., Rudolph, D. and Smith, R. (1992) 'Story-telling as a theory-building activity'. *Discourse Processes*, 15(1): 37–72.

Polanyi, L. (1989) *Telling the American Story: A Structural and Cultural Analysis of Conversational Storytelling*. Cambridge, MA: MIT Press.

Propp, V. (1986) *The Morphology of the Folktale*. Austin, TX: University of Texas Press.

Ricoeur, P. (1981) *Hermeneutics and the Human Sciences*. Cambridge: Cambridge University Press.

Ricoeur, P. (1988) *Time and Narrative*. Chicago: University of Chicago Press.

Sacks, H. (1978) 'Some technical considerations of a dirty joke'. In J. Schenkein (ed.), *Studies in the Organization of Conversational Interaction*. New York: Academic Press (edited by Gail Jefferson from four lectures delivered at the University of California, Irvine, Fall 1971). pp. 249–69.

Sacks, H. (1992) *Lectures on Conversation*. Cambridge, MA: Blackwell.

Sampson, B. (1982) 'The sick who do not speak'. In D. Parkin (ed.), *Semantic Anthropology*. New York: Academic. pp. 183–95.

Schieffelin, E.L. (1976) *The Sorrow of the Lonely and the Burning of the Dancers*. New York: St. Martin's Press.

Scollon, R. and Scollon, S. (1981) *Narrative, Literacy, and Face in Interethnic Communication*. Norwood, NJ: Ablex.

Sharff, S. (1982) *The Elements of Cinema: Toward a Theory of Cinesthetic Impact*. New York: Columbia University Press.

Shohet, M. (2007) 'Narrating Anorexia: "Full" and "Struggling" Genres of Recovery'. *Ethos*, 35(3): 344–82.

Stein, N. and Glenn, C.G. (1979) 'An analysis of story comprehension in elementary school children'. In R.O. Freedle (ed.), *New Directions in Discourse Processing*. Norwood, NJ: Ablex. pp. 53–120.

Stein, N. and Policastro, M. (1984) 'The concept of a story: a comparison between children's and teachers' viewpoints'. In H. Mandl, N. Stein and T. Trabasso (eds), *Learning and Comprehension of Text*. Hillsdale, NJ: Erlbaum.

Taylor, C. (1995) '"You think it was a fight?": co-constructing (the struggle for) meaning, face, and family in everyday narrative activity'. *Research on Language and Social Interaction*, 283: 283–317.

Todorov, T. (1984) *Mikhail Bakhtin: The Dialogical Principle*. Minneapolis: University of Minnesota Press.

Watson-Gegeo, K. and White, G. (eds) (1990) *Disentangling: Conflict Discourse in Pacific Societies*. Stanford: Stanford University Press.

White, H. (1981) 'The value of narrativity in the representation of reality'. In W.J.T. Mitchell (ed.), *On Narrative*. Chicago: University of Chicago Press.

White, M. (2007) *Maps of Narrative Practice*. New York: W.W. Norton.

Wilce, J.M. (1998) *Eloquence in Trouble: The Poetics and Politics of Complaint in Rural Bangladesh*. New York: Oxford University Press.

Williams, R. (1982) *The Sociology of Culture*. New York: Schocken.

Williams, R. (1983) *Writing in Society*. London: Verso.

FIVE

Argumentation

Frans H. van Eemeren, Sally Jackson
and Scott Jacobs

WHAT IS ARGUMENTATION?

Argumentation uses language to justify or refute a standpoint, with the aim of securing an agreement in views. The study of argumentation typically centres on one of two objects: either interactions in which two or more people conduct or have arguments such as discussions or debates; or texts such as speeches or editorials in which a person makes an argument (O'Keefe, 1977). An adequate theoretical approach to argumentation should have something to say about both the process of argumentation and the arguments produced in that process. Consider the following passage, adapted from a syndicated newspaper story (Associated Press, 1993):

(1)   A recent study found that women are more likely than men to be murdered at work. 40% of the women who died on the job in 1993 were murdered. 15% of the men who died on the job during the same period were murdered.

The first sentence is a claim made by the writer, and the other two sentences state evidence offered as a reason to accept this claim as a true. This claim-plus-support arrangement is what is most commonly referred to as an argument.

But arguments do not only occur as monologic packages; an argument may also be built in the interaction between someone who puts forward a standpoint and someone who challenges it, as in the following exchange between a young female patient and a middle-aged male therapist (from Bleiberg and Churchill, 1977; see also Jacobs, 1986). (In transcriptions of conversation, square brackets are commonly used to indicate the points at which one person's speech overlaps another's, as when the doctor begins talking before the patient ends. A period in parentheses indicates a short pause.)

(2)   1   Pt: I don't want them to have anything to do with my life, except (.) [security(?)
      2   Dr: [You live at home?
      3   Pt: Yes.
      4   Dr: They pay your bills?
      5   Pt: Yeah.
      6   Dr: How could they not have anything to do with your life?

In turn 1 the patient's statement that she does not want her parents ('them') to have anything to do with her life seems to commit her to the standpoint that it is indeed possible for her parents to have nothing to do with her life. The therapist calls out and challenges this standpoint by asking a series of questions whose answers can be seen to support a contradictory position: it is not possible for the patient's parents not to have anything to do with her life.

Examples (1) and (2) illustrate features that are central to the concept of argumentation. First, a characteristic inferential structure can be extracted from both cases: propositions put forward as claims and other propositions (reasons) put forward as a justification and/or refutation of those claims. Second, the arguments in both examples are about an issue which has two sides and which provides for two opposing communicator roles: a protagonist who puts forward a claim and an antagonist who doubts that claim, contradicts it, or otherwise withholds assent. For the newspaper story, the antagonist is a sceptical audience projected or imagined as needing proof to be convinced of the claim; for the therapy session, the antagonist is the therapist who challenges the patient's position and puts forward a contradictory standpoint. Third, these examples point to the way in which arguments are embedded in acts and activities. In the newspaper story, the writer does not openly make the claim or the argument for the claim that women are more likely than men to be murdered at work; the writer reports the claim and supporting argument made by 'a recent study', thereby avoiding any personal responsibility for the truth of what is being argued. In the therapy session, the argument for the therapist's standpoint is secured through questions that elicit concessions by the patient that commit her to an inconsistent position, forcing her to back down from her initial standpoint. The argument emerges from this collaborative activity. Moreover, the patient's initial standpoint occurs in the act of expressing a wish, and it is the therapist who seems to pin on the patient the further claim that such a wish is a realistic possibility.

These two arguments have another feature in common: both involve questionable means of building a case. In (1), the conclusion seems plausible only because of a very serious flaw in reasoning that, by its nature, is difficult to notice. Women are in fact much less likely than men to be murdered at work. While the statements contained in the support may be true, their truth does not guarantee the truth of the conclusion, for reasons we will explore shortly. The problem with the argument in (2) is not so much with the truth of what is said or with the reasoning itself as with the aggressive method by which the therapist pushes forward. The rhetorical question in turn 6 and the brusque, declarative form of the other questions amount to a 'put-down' of the patient that discourages her from advancing any serious defence of her standpoint. The analysis of such inadequacies (generally termed fallacies) is among the most long-standing concerns of the study of argumentation.

A BRIEF HISTORY OF THE STUDY OF ARGUMENTATIVE DISCOURSE

The tradition of argumentation study has a very long history that can be traced back to ancient Greek writings on logic (proof), rhetoric (persuasion), and dialectic (inquiry), especially the writings of Aristotle. Since argumentation's function is to convince others of the truth, or acceptability, of what one says, the enduring questions addressed in the theory of argumentation have had to do with matters of evaluation: what it takes for a conclusion to be well supported, which criteria should govern the acceptance of a standpoint, and so on. Historically, the study of argumentation has been motivated by an interest in the improvement of discourse or a modification of the effects of that discourse on society. Aristotle treated argumentation as a means to expose errors in thinking and to shape discourse toward a rational ideal.

Central to Aristotle's logic was a distinction between form and substance. Rather than giving a particularistic analysis of the strengths and weaknesses of individual arguments, Aristotle's logic identified argument patterns that could lead from statements that were already known to be true to other statements whose truth had yet to be established. These patterns applied universally, with the result that any contents could be substituted for any other contents with the same result. Consider the following argument:

(3) Some child molesters are teachers.
Some teachers are women.
Therefore, some child molesters are women.

In arguments of this sort (called 'categorical syllogisms'), the first two sentences (the premises) refer to three categories, with each premise stating a relationship between two of the three categories. The third sentence (the conclusion) states a relationship between the two categories that are not paired in the premises. The conclusion is likely to be accepted as true by most people, as are the two premises offered in its support. But the conclusion is not in fact justified by the two premises, as can be seen by abstracting from the argument just the formal relationships asserted to hold among the three categories mentioned. By convention, we use S to stand for the category that appears as the subject of the conclusion, P to stand for the category that appears in the predicate of the conclusion, and M to stand for the 'middle' term that connects S and P by being paired with S in one premise and with P in the other. We can eliminate the complication of substance by substituting S for 'child molesters', M for 'teachers', and P for 'women', so as to exhibit the form of the argument as follows:

(4)   Some *S* are *M*.
      Some *M* are *P*.
      Therefore, some *S* are *P*.

The flaw in this argument is that the *S* category may be completely contained in the portions of *M* that are not *P*, so that it is possible that no *S* are *P*. So, while the conclusion is possibly true, it is not necessarily true. It may be true that some child molesters are women, but this is not assured by the truth of the premises. When an argument's form guarantees that the conclusion will be true any time the premises are true, the form is said to be 'valid'. But when the conclusion may be false even though the premises are true, the form is said to be 'invalid'.

People will rarely present their arguments in the form of complete syllogisms. Nevertheless, these forms do have an intuitive grounding in everyday reasoning, as can be seen in the following exchange between an uncle and his four-year-old nephew:

(5)   ((Curtis runs into the kitchen and crashes into his uncle))

      Uncle: Curtis, what are you doing?
      Curtis: I'm a spaceman.
      Uncle: You can't be a spaceman. You're not wearing a helmet.
      Curtis: Han Solo doesn't wear a helmet.
      Uncle: Yeahhhh.
      Curtis: He's a spaceman. (.) As you can see, not all spacemen wear helmets.

             ((Curtis races off into the living room))

By filling in the suitable missing premise and paraphrasing each expression to fit a certain standard form, the uncle's argument can be made to correspond to a valid form of syllogism. The missing premise is that helmet-wearing is a necessary property of being a spaceman, ordinarily expressed as 'All spacemen wear helmets'. In standard syllogistic form, all statements express a relationship between two categories, so we can further paraphrase the premise as 'All spacemen are helmet-wearers'. To represent the uncle's argument in the standard form of a syllogism, the subjects and predicates of all statements must be treated as general categories. So 'Curtis' must be considered a category with a single member, in which the explicitly stated premise 'You are not wearing a helmet' can be rewritten as 'All Curtisses are non-helmet-wearers', or, by a relation called 'obversion', also rewritten into the logically equivalent form 'No Curtis is a helmet-wearer'. Substituting in the abstract category labels *P*, *M*, and *S* for 'spacemen', 'helmet-wearers', and 'Curtis', we can get the movement from ordinary conversational expression to the abstract categorical representation shown in Table 5.1. Notice that whether we choose this particular translation or some other similar translation (for example, allowing 'non-helmet-wearers' as a category), we will get a form in which, if the premises are true, the conclusion cannot be false; this is the defining feature of a valid form, and this property then transfers to any 'substitution instance' of the form.

Table 5.1

Conversational expression	Categorical paraphrase	Categorical abstraction
All spacemen have helmets.	All spacemen are helmet-wearers.	All P are M.
Curtis does not have a helmet.	No Curtis is a helmet-wearer.	No S are M.
Therefore, Curtis is not a spaceman.	Therefore, no Curtis is a spaceman.	No S are P.

Table 5.2

Conversational expression	Categorical paraphrase	Categorical abstraction
Han Solo does not have a helmet.	No Han Solo is a helmet-wearer.	No P are M.
Han Solo is a spaceman.	All Han Solos are spacemen.	All S are M.
Therefore, not all spacemen are helmet-wearers.	Therefore, some spacemen are not helmet-wearers.	(Assuming that there is at least one member of S) Some S are not P.

Though the argument is valid, that does not mean that the truth of the conclusion is beyond doubt; one or both premises may be false. The conclusion that Curtis is not a spaceman follows given the truth of the premises, but one may still challenge the truth of the conclusion by challenging the truth of one of the premises, and in the dialogue itself this is what occurred. Curtis inferred the syllogistic requirement that his uncle must be assuming that all spacemen wear helmets, and he concentrated on rebutting that inferred premise. In this case we substitute S for 'spacemen', P for 'helmet-wearers', and M for 'Han Solo' (again treating a specific individual as a category with just one member), as can be seen in Table 5.2. The conclusion of Curtis's syllogism contradicts the first premise of his uncle's syllogism, which was never actually stated but which is nevertheless necessary to represent the form and content of the uncle's reasoning. Given the existence of Han Solo, Curtis infers a proposition that in classical syllogistic logic is called the 'contradictory' of his uncle's proposition. One of the two propositions must be true and one must be false.

From Aristotle's logic, the study of argumentation has taken a tradition of analysing the form of argumentative inference independent of its content. The development of modern symbolic logic is a direct response to the concern for formally representing the inferential structure of seemingly acceptable or unacceptable arguments.

Classical rhetoric has to do with effective persuasion: with principles that lead to assent or consensus. Aristotle's rhetoric bears little resemblance to modern-day persuasion theories, which are heavily oriented towards the analysis of attitude formation and change but largely indifferent to the problem of the invention of persuasive messages (Eagly and Chaiken, 1993; O'Keefe, 1990). In Aristotle's rhetoric, the emphasis was on the production of effective argumentation for an audience where the subject matter did not lend itself to certain demonstration. Whereas the syllogism was the most prominent form of logical demonstration, the enthymeme was its rhetorical counterpart. Enthymemes were thought of as syllogisms whose premises could be drawn from the audience. These are usually only partially expressed, their logic being completed by the audience. The failure of the uncle's argument in (5) is an enthymematic failure by his audience (Curtis) to accept an implied premise (though Curtis does recognize the premise). The enthymematic quality of every-day ('marketplace') arguments leads to one of the enduring problems of argumentation analysis: how to represent what is left implicit in ordinary argumentative discourse.

Also important for the subsequent study of argumentation was the analysis of fallacies (what were first termed 'sophistical refutations' or 'sophisms', after the Sophists, a group of ancient theorist-practitioners who were accused of equating success in persuasion with goodness in argumentation). Among the sophisms Aristotle identified were argument forms that have a false appearance of soundness, such as the fallacy of equivocation – a reasoning error that arises from an unnoticed shift in the meaning of terms used within an argument.

The argument about on-the-job murder rates in (1) contains such a fallacy of equivocation: this lies between two possible concrete meanings for 'probability' or 'likelihood'. The conclusion refers to the probability of a woman (or man) being murdered on the job calculated by comparing the number of women (or men) who are murdered on the job in proportion to all working women (or men). The conclusion suggests that this proportion is higher for women than for men. But the grounds for the conclusion define probability quite differently, as a proportion calculated by comparing the number of women (or men) who are murdered on the job against the number who die on the job. The conclusion of the story would follow on from these grounds only if men and women had similar overall rates of death on the job. But the same article reports that men account for 93 per cent of all workplace fatalities. The difference this makes is very pronounced: based on other statistics reported in the story, one can calculate that there were 849 men murdered on the job, but only 170 women murdered, even though (as the article also reports) men and women today are fairly evenly represented in the American workforce (55 per cent and 45 per cent respectively). The grounds for the conclusion are true: comparing only men and women who die on the job, the probability that a male death is due to murder is lower than the probability that a female death is due to murder. Nevertheless, when comparing all employed men and women, the probability of a male worker being murdered is much higher than the probability of a female worker being murdered.

Over the long history of argumentation theory, one mainstay has been the cataloguing and analysis of fallacies (Hamblin, 1970). The work involved in this form of theory will apparently never be completed, as the invention of new forms of argumentation (such as probabilistic reasoning) creates new opportunities for fallacies to emerge and new opportunities to identify them and explain why they are fallacious.

To complete the overview of Aristotle's contributions to the study of argumentation, the Aristotelian concept of dialectic is best understood as the art of inquiry through critical discussion. Dialectic is a way of putting ideas to a critical test by attempting to expose and eliminate contradictions in a position: a protagonist puts forward a claim and then provides answers to a sceptical questioner (an antagonist). The exchange between the therapist and patient in (2) captures the structure of such a method, if not its cooperative spirit. While the paradigm case of dialectic is the question and answer technique of the Socratic dialogues, a pattern of assertion and assent may also be employed, as in (5). The adequacy of any particular claim is supposed to be cooperatively assessed by eliciting premises that might serve as commonly accepted starting points, and then by drawing out implications from those starting points and determining their compatibility with the claim in question. Where difficulties emerge, new claims might be put forward that will avoid such contradictions. This method of regimented opposition amounts to the pragmatic application of logic, a collaborative method of putting logic into use so as to move away from conjecture and opinion towards a more secure belief.

While Aristotle outlined duties for the roles of questioner and answerer and the types of questions and answers allowed, the dialectical conception of argumentation has, until recently, been largely ignored in the development of argumentation theory. Notions like burden of proof, presumption, or *reductio ad absurdum* proof have developed in argumentation theory without much notice being taken of their dialectical echo. The recent rediscovery of dialectical conceptions of argument marks a decisive shift in attention being given to argumentation theory and research.

CONTEMPORARY PERSPECTIVES

The turning points for a contemporary study of argumentation came with Perelman and Olbrechts-Tyteca's *La Nouvelle Rhétorique* (in English, *The New Rhetoric*), and Toulmin's *The Uses of Argument*, both published in 1958. Toulmin argued for a new, non-formal conception of rationality, tied to substantive discourse contexts ('fields') that varied in their normative organization. Perelman and Olbrechts-Tyteca's new rhetoric reintroduced the audience to argumentation and provided an inventory of effective argumentation techniques. Most important for contemporary argumentation study were the shift towards an interactional view of argument and the move away from formal logic. Both Toulmin and Perelman took judicial argument as a model for argumentation generally, focusing attention on the interchange between two opposing arguer roles. These landmark works took the first steps toward studying argumentation as a linguistic activity.

The principal contribution of the new rhetoric has been to return argumentation to a context of controversy in which some audience is to be addressed. Rhetoric has often been understood as anti-rational or as a departure from a rational ideal. But in contemporary rhetorical theory there is a striking retreat from a hard distinction between rhetoric – the study of effective techniques of persuasion – and dialectic – long associated with ideals of reasonableness, rationality, and a tendency towards truth. The distinctive theme in these modern re-examinations of rhetoric is the situated quality of argumentation and the importance of orientation towards an audience. The central theoretical questions are how opposing views come to be reconciled through the use of language and how actual audiences may be brought through rhetoric itself to more closely approximate the stance of an ideally rational audience.

This tendency towards dialectification is even more explicit in the philosophical work of Hamblin (1970). In his detailed critique of the 'standard treatment' of fallacies, Hamblin built the case for seeing argument as a dialectical process organized around disputants' efforts to convince one another of their respective standpoints. Important features of Hamblin's approach are the emphasis on rules defining speaker commitments and regulating interactional moves rather than an emphasis on logical forms as the generative mechanism for argumentation, as well as the recognition of the self-constituting and self-regulating character of argumentation. Hamblin's interest in the formal analysis of dialogue is a direct precedent for many of the most interesting current trends in argumentation theory.

Although it is possible to approach dialectic formally and non-contextually, the dialectical approach to argumentation tends to be accompanied by an interest in 'real' arguments as they arise in the back and forth of real controversies. Because of concerns with the problems of assessing the adequacy of ordinary argumentative cases, with the conditions of ordinary argument, and with the communicative and interactional means by which argumentation is conducted, dialectical approaches have tended to align themselves with pragmatic approaches to discourse and conversational interaction.

Accompanying a broad trend toward dialectification has been an equally influential trend toward functionalization and contextualization. Central to this trend has been Toulmin's work (1958; 1970). In broad outline, Toulmin theorized that, regardless of substantive context, argument could be seen as the offering of a claim together with answers to certain characteristic questions, but that standards for judging the adequacy of arguments would be variable from one argument field to another. The question of what a speaker has 'to go on' gives rise to what Toulmin called 'grounds' – roughly equivalent to the premises of classical logic. The question of what justifies the inference from these grounds to the claim gives rise to the 'warrant' or 'inference licence' – better understood as a kind of reasoning strategy or rule than as another premise. 'Backing' for the warrant might take the form of substantive information similar in kind to the 'grounds', so that the structure nowadays called 'the Toulmin model' differs from a classical description of argument in focusing not on the formal relationships among parts of an argument but on the functional relationships.

Consider how we might 'diagram' the arguments in (1) and (3). In doing so, we will often find that we must add in elements not actually stated but still necessary to represent the speaker's reasoning. In example (1), we must add in an assumption about how one computes and compares probabilities, as in Figure 5.1.

Example (3) is much more complicated, despite its apparent simplicity, because to diagram it adequately we must treat it as two arguments, one of which builds the grounds for the other. As with example (1), we must add in content that is left implicit. Specifically, we must attribute to the uncle the belief that having a helmet is a necessary feature for a spaceman, not just a property that happens to be shared by all spacemen. This implicit belief can be partitioned into a factual proposition about the various properties of the category 'spacemen'

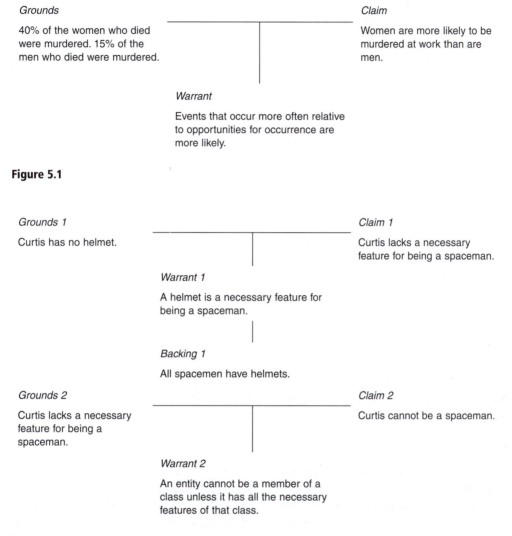

Grounds

40% of the women who died were murdered. 15% of the men who died were murdered.

Claim

Women are more likely to be murdered at work than are men.

Warrant

Events that occur more often relative to opportunities for occurrence are more likely.

Figure 5.1

Grounds 1

Curtis has no helmet.

Claim 1

Curtis lacks a necessary feature for being a spaceman.

Warrant 1

A helmet is a necessary feature for being a spaceman.

Backing 1

All spacemen have helmets.

Grounds 2

Curtis lacks a necessary feature for being a spaceman.

Claim 2

Curtis cannot be a spaceman.

Warrant 2

An entity cannot be a member of a class unless it has all the necessary features of that class.

Figure 5.2

(appearing in Figure 5.2 as backing for an assumption about category membership require-ments) and a reasoning rule that specifies the conditions under which something may be treated as a member of a class. Factual materials specific to the individual case provide the grounds for the conclusion or the backing for the warrant; reasoning rules and other similar elements serve as warrants, as shown in the diagram in Figure 5.2.

These diagrams not only help to explain how the various parts of the arguments are related; they also help to locate the problems in each argument. In the upper diagram, the problem can be easily recognized as having to do with what is considered an 'opportunity' for each event to occur; the probability of a woman's being murdered on the job is reasonably measured not as the proportion of deaths that are murders but as the proportion of all working women murdered on the job – a much lower figure. In the lower diagram, the fault is in the unstated part of the backing for the warrant: the apparently mistaken belief that all spacemen have helmets and the correspondingly faulty assumption that having a helmet is a necessary feature of being a spaceman.

The embeddedness of argumentation in substantive discourse contexts is also foreshadowed in Toulmin's work, especially in the idea that standards for the evaluation of argument are 'field-dependent' and in the still more fundamental idea that the field-independent elements of argumentation (claim, grounds, warrant, etc.) can be understood as answers to the questions of an idealized interlocutor. Although the style of analysis inspired by Toulmin's work (diagramming of arguments as completed units) may seem to focus more on argument form and content than on interactions, the argument structure is really the product of an interaction with each part of the argument defined in terms of some specified interactional function – as answers to particular questions or challenges to the initial claim.

One thread leading forward from Toulmin's work is the 'informal logic' movement (Govier, 1988; Johnson and Blair, 1983). Although the name suggests otherwise, informal logic is not a new kind of logic. Rather, it is a normative approach to argumentation in everyday language that is broader than the formal logical approach. The informal logician's objective is to develop norms, criteria and procedures for interpreting, evaluating and construing argumentation that are faithful to the complexities and uncertainties of everyday argumentation. A common theme in informal logic is that formally invalid arguments are often quite reasonable as the bases for practical decisions.

According to Blair and Johnson's (1987) programme, the cogency of argumentation is not identical to formal validity in deductive logic. They argue that the premises for a conclusion must satisfy three criteria: 1) relevance, 2) sufficiency, and 3) acceptability. With relevance, the question is whether or not there is an adequate relation between the contents of the premises and the conclusion; with sufficiency, whether or not the premises provide strong enough evidence for the conclusion in the face of objections and counterargumentation; and with acceptability, whether or not the premises are true, probable or otherwise reliable.

A step further toward a functional, interactional view of argument is taken by pragmatic argumentation theories such as the pragma-dialectical theory of van Eemeren and Grootendorst (1984; 1992; van Eemeren et al., 1993; see also Walton, 1989; 1995). The pragma-dialectical theory begins with the assumption that the purpose of argumentation is to resolve a difference of opinion, so that the opposition of argumentative roles is a characteristic feature of argumentative discourse. Argument is seen as a kind of interaction that arises in the context of other interactional business, when something said, implied, or otherwise conveyed makes plain that there is a difference of opinion between two parties. This description is necessarily abstract, since argumentation can take any form from a single, written text by an author addressing an unknown audience to a heated back-and-forth debate between two people talking face to face. But the important, defining feature of argument is that it occurs as a means of addressing – and attempting to resolve – a difference of opinion by means of exploring the relative justification for competing standpoints. The writer envisions an audience to be persuaded by means of arguments offered to support the writer's views or to refute the audience's own views. Arguers in conversation with one another will allow their respective positions to unfold in direct response to each successive move by their partners. But in both cases, the organization of the argument will depend on the existence of opposing roles and on each arguer's understanding of the issues that must be resolved to overcome the opposition.

Reflecting broad trends toward dialectification, functionalization, and the contextualization of argument, pragma-dialectical theory offers a model of argumentative discourse not in terms of form and content but in terms of discussion procedure. In place of a set of standards to be applied to individual units of proof, the pragma-dialectical model offers rules for argumentative interaction and associated preconditions having to do with such things as participant abilities, attitudes, and power.

Argumentation is seen within the pragma-dialectical view as a discourse device for the regulation of discourse itself. It falls within the class of devices known as 'repair mechanisms' and its function is to locate and resolve differences of opinion (Jackson and Jacobs, 1980). The view of argumentation as a form of repair (pre-emptive or *post hoc*) is important, because it draws attention to the embeddedness of argument within other sorts of interactional business. In other words, the analysis of any particular argument – including such arguments as those occurring in the newspaper story about murders on the job and in the spaceman conversation – is relativized, placed within some broader discourse context that guides the analysis by defining what is at stake.

To say that argumentation comes about as a form of repair is also to say that the organization of argument must be understood in terms of general interactional principles. In the pragma-dialectical view, insights from speech act theory (Searle, 1969) and Grice's (1989) theory of conversational implicature are used as a bridge between the special organization of argumentation and the general principles that organize discourse and interaction (see van Eemeren et al., 1993, especially Chapters 1 and 5).

Recently, van Eemeren and Houtlosser (2002b) extended the scope of the pragma-dialectical theory by introducing the notion of 'strategic manoeuvring' (van Eemeren, 2010). Strategic manoeuvring refers to the efforts arguers will make in argumentative discourse to combine making argumentative moves that are effective, with observing at the same time critical standards of reasonableness (or giving at least the impression they are doing so). This means that strategic manoeuvring is aimed at keeping a sound balance between the rhetorical dimension and the dialectical dimension of argumentative discourse. Strategic manoeuvring manifests itself in the discourse simultaneously via topical choices, an adaptation of the discourse to audience demands, and the exploitation of presentational devices. If rhetorical considerations gain the upper hand over maintaining dialectical norms of reasonableness, and a rule for critical discussion is violated, the strategic manoeuvring will then derail and a fallacy will have been committed (van Eemeren and Houtlosser, 2003).

CASE STUDY: CRITICAL ANALYSIS OF ADVERTORIALS

Dialectical theories of argumentation have their most transparent application in argumentative discussion, that is, to direct the exchange of views between two disputants. Many published analyses of such materials can be found (see for example, van Eemeren et al., 1993; Chapters 5–7). We have chosen for a case study a more challenging set of materials: a series of monologic texts representing just one side of a discussion. What makes our analysis 'dialectical' is not that its object is dialogue but that it places any argumentative text into the context of one party's effort to convince another of a standpoint by answering doubts and objections and by grounding conclusions in mutually acceptable starting points. The trick is to see that these short monologues reflect the image of an author as protagonist (here, RJR Tobacco) and also project an image of an addressee as antagonist or sceptical interlocutor (here, a young person considering whether or not to smoke).

The two texts presented in examples (6) and (7) originally appeared as editorial advertisements (or 'advertorials') published in American magazines during the period 1984–6 and were paid for by the R.J. Reynolds Tobacco Company. The two advertorials were ostensibly acts of advice urging young people not to smoke. They make particularly interesting cases for reconstruction because of the way in which these advertorials exploited and subverted the very standards of open and cooperative discussion they seemed to promote. The appearance of a good faith effort as reasonable argument only serves to disguise the fallacious design.

(6)	1	Some surprising advice to young people
	2	from R.J. Reynolds Tobacco.
	3	Don't smoke.
	4	For one thing, smoking has always been an adult custom. And even for adults, smoking has
	5	become very controversial. So even though we're a tobacco company, we don't think it's a good idea
	6	for young people to smoke.
	7	Now, we know that giving this kind of advice to young people can sometimes backfire.
	8	But if you take up smoking just to prove you're an adult, you're really proving just the
	9	opposite. Because deciding to smoke or not to smoke is something you should do when you don't have
	10	anything to prove.
	11	Think it over. After all, you may not be old enough to smoke. But you're old enough to think.
	12	*R.J. Reynolds Tobacco Company*

(7)	1	Some straight talk about smoking
	2	for young people.
	3	We're R.J. Reynolds Tobacco, and we're urging you not to smoke.

4   We're saying this because, throughout the world, smoking has always been an adult custom.
5   And because today, even among adults, smoking is controversial.
6   Your first reaction might be to ignore this advice. Maybe you feel we're talking to you as if
7   you were a child. And you probably don't think of yourself that way.
8   But just because you're no longer a child doesn't mean that you're already an adult. And if you
9   take up smoking just to prove you're not a kid, you're kidding yourself.
10   So please don't smoke. You'll have plenty of time as an adult to decide whether smoking is
11   right for you.
12   That's about as straight as we can put it.
13   *R.J. Reynolds Tobacco Company*

While one can readily sense that something is amiss, the problem is how to bring the argument to account for the offences committed. Argument reconstruction is an analytic tool that may serve such a critical function. What we will try to show in this section is that the arguments provided are so weak as to be virtually self-defeating. The arguments in these advertorials invite the conclusion that there are no good arguments why young people should not smoke. How this communicative effect is achieved in texts that seem to argue against young people smoking can be shown through a reconstruction of the arguments.

Considered dialectically, the advertorials must be seen as contributions to the broader public debate concerning the role of tobacco and the tobacco industry in American society. By 1984 public attitudes toward smoking had shifted dramatically, leading to unprecedented restrictions on smoking in restaurants, hotels, government buildings, trains and airlines. Congressional hearings were scheduled to consider, among other things, further restrictions on the advertising of cigarettes. Part of the call for such hearings was the argument that cigarette companies were advertising to children to replace the growing number of adult smokers who were quitting or dying. So, even though the two advertorials appear to be self-contained rhetorical acts simply directed toward young people, we should expect broader circumstances to motivate the way in which arguments are selected and fashioned. Not coincidentally, these two advertorials were followed by a third, entitled 'We don't advertise to children'. As part of the proof of this claim, the third advertorial argued: 'First of all, we don't want young people to smoke. And we're running ads aimed specifically at young people advising them that we think smoking is strictly for adults.'

At least on the surface, the arguments in (6) and (7) have the appearance of being reasonable efforts at dialectical engagement. Both begin with seemingly plain and direct justifications for why young people should not smoke (lines 4–5). First, smoking has always been an adult custom. Second, even for adults smoking is controversial. These arguments define a kind of disagreement space in which protagonist and antagonist engage not so much over the issue of whether or not smoking is a bad idea in general, but rather over an issue that might plausibly be raised by a young reader considering smoking: if (as RJR Tobacco must believe) it is okay for adults to smoke, why is it a bad idea for young people to smoke?

The reactions of a young interlocutor are then more openly anticipated and addressed in both ads. In lines 7–11 of (6) the tobacco company anticipates that giving this kind of advice might somehow backfire, provoking young people to try to prove they are adults by doing exactly what is being advised against. The nature of the problem is more explicitly anticipated in lines 6–9 of (7): this kind of advice may be rejected because it might seem condescending (by talking to the reader as if they were a child). In both cases RJR argues that rejecting the advice by taking up smoking will not prove that a young person is an adult or not a kid.

Finally, both advertorials lay claim to the special credibility of 'disinterested' argumentation. In (6), RJR implies that they are arguing against their own self-interest as a tobacco company, calling their advice 'surprising' and then asserting that they don't think it is a good idea for young people to smoke 'even though we're a tobacco company' (line 5). In (7), the advertorial opens and closes by characterizing its message as 'straight'.

So far, we have described the arguments more or less informally, restricting ourselves to the claims and reasons that closely parallel material presented in the texts. The two primary arguments for not smoking could be presented as follows:

> (8)   Claim: Young people should not smoke.
>   Reason 1:   Smoking has always been an adult custom.
> (9)   Claim: Young people should not smoke.
>   Reason 2:   Smoking is controversial even among adults.

Like most naturally occurring arguments, the texts themselves are incomplete as outlines of the underlying reasoning. This does not mean that the arguments are inferentially defective or that the reasons fail to give any adequate justification for the claim, but only that we have to fill in what has been left implicit.

Intuitively, people will understand more in these arguments than is being said explicitly. Some set of tacitly shared beliefs and meanings is taken for granted in building these arguments, and the assumption of these beliefs and representation of these meanings allow the reasons to stand in a justifying relation to the claim. This is the characteristic feature of enthymematic argument. But what are these tacit beliefs? And by what principles would a satisfactory representation be constructed? This is the problem of unexpressed premises, and can be usefully seen as a special instance of the problems of coherence and inference in discourse generally.

One way to handle the problem is to try to identify assertable propositions which, though unexpressed, could still be treated as premises to which the arguer is committed in making the argument. We presume that RJR Tobacco is attempting to make a cooperative contribution to the debate and, following Grice's (1989) theory of implicature, we should look for propositions which, though unstated, are mutually available and would be recognized by reasonable people to make the argument acceptable if they were stated. At a minimum, a reasonable arguer should be held to be committed to an inferential pattern that is valid and whose premises are true, or at least, plausible. One such pattern would be the following:

(10) Premise 1:   If smoking has always been an adult custom, then young people should not smoke.
     Premise 2:   Smoking has always been an adult custom.
     Conclusion: Young people should not smoke.
(11) Premise 1:   If smoking is controversial even among adults, then young people should not smoke.
     Premise 2:   Smoking is controversial even among adults.
     Conclusion: Young people should not smoke.

In each case, a premise has been added that fits a deductively valid pattern of inference called modus ponens. Modus ponens is a form of reasoning about propositions; its 'elements' are propositions rather than categories. Using p and q as propositional variables (symbols that can stand for any proposition), we can represent the abstract form of (10) as follows, where p is the proposition 'smoking has always been an adult custom' and q is the proposition 'young people should not smoke':

(12) If p then q
     p
     Therefore, q.

Notice that while the advertorials do not state the 'if p then q' premise, the protagonist (RJR) is nonetheless committed to its truth by virtue of offering p as a reason for accepting q. Since the argumentative functions of the 'reason' and 'claim' in (8) and (9) are more or less transparent, so is the commitment to the added premise in (10) and (11).

But explicating such a premise as a step in reconstruction is rather pointless unless it helps us to find the substantive grounds that the premise itself stands in for. Adding a premise that asserts, in effect, 'If reason then claim' can be done with any two statements that appear in an argumentative relation. This does nothing more than state that inferring the one statement from the other is permitted. While such a premise satisfies the logically minimal criteria for valid inference, it does not really answer the question of why one might think that one assertion is a good enough reason to claim the other. Where possible, one should search for unexpressed premises that are informative in this way and not substantively vacuous. Thus, in (5), the unexpressed premise in the uncle's argument is better seen as something like 'All spacemen wear helmets' than as the trivial 'If you're not wearing a helmet then you can't be a spaceman'. What is wanted, then, is a more informative alternative to premise 1 or a more informative unpacking of its basis.

Let us first consider the reasoning in (10): what does smoking being an adult custom have to do with why young people should not smoke? R.J. Reynolds builds into its arguments the assumption that whether or not to smoke is something that adults are entitled to decide for themselves ('Deciding to smoke or not to smoke is something you should do when you don't have anything to prove', (6) lines 9–10; 'You'll have plenty of time as an adult to decide whether smoking is right for you', (7) lines 10–11). This is at least part of what it means to assert that something is an adult custom.

And we can also readily extract from both advertorials the proposition that young people are not adults. In (7), it is supposed that young people probably do not think of themselves as children. And RJR answers by denying that this shows they are adults (lines 8–9). In both (6) and (7), young people are projected as trying to prove they are indeed adults – an attempt which, according to the advertorial, only proves the opposite. But so what if young people are not adults? Why is voicing this pertinent to the claim that young people should not smoke?

Because to assert that something is an adult custom means not just that adults have a right to practise it, but also that it is only adults who are entitled to do so. If someone is not an adult, they are not entitled to practise it ('smoking is strictly for adults').

Therefore, we can unpack the argument in (10) as being grounded in the following line of reasoning. Only a person who is an adult is entitled to practise an adult custom. (If a person is an adult, that person is entitled to practise an adult custom. If a person is not an adult, that person is not entitled to practise an adult custom.) Young people are not adults. It follows from this that young people are not entitled to practise an adult custom. Since smoking is an adult custom, young people are not entitled to smoke. And, since it is safe to assume that people should not do what they are not entitled to do, it can be concluded that young people should not smoke.

The substance of this reasoning is certain to be rejected by young people who are considering smoking, but it is all that the advertorials offer as grounds for their advice. And here is where we can begin to see the troublesome weakness of the arguments in these advertorials. No matter how much we wiggle around trying to find a substantive basis for connecting the stated reasons to the claims, we will consistently find a chain of reasoning that seems only to presume and reassert the adult entitlement, adult privilege, and adult authority to restrict children's choices.

RJR Tobacco is defending a position that only adults are entitled to smoke, and young people are excluded from this category. But why are young people excluded? Here, we should notice that the categories of 'adult' and 'child' are primarily moral and not biological classifications. Adults have rights that children do not have. And exercising these rights requires a capacity for mature decision making. Now, it is a widely taken-for-granted assumption that children are incapable of making wise decisions about health issues and are therefore in need of protection from their own bad choices. Indeed both ads allude to childish, immature reasoning by young people (in (6): 'But if you take up smoking just to prove you're an adult, you're really proving just the opposite'; in (7): 'If you take up smoking just to prove you're not a kid, you're kidding yourself'). But RJR pointedly blocks any assumption that this is the basis for excluding young people from adult classification. Example (6) concludes by urging young people to 'Think it over' and by asserting that they 'may not be old enough to smoke. But [they're] old enough to think.'

Actually, no real argument is ever put forward to think that young people are different in any important respect from adults. Both ads anticipate that a young reader will reject the classification as non-adult (and will attempt to prove their adult status by smoking), but neither ad substantively defends the premise. In (7), RJR does not justify withholding this adult status from young people; they only deny that the fact that the reader is not a child does not mean the reader is an adult (line 8). In (6), RJR defends the claim that young people are not adults through the kind of circular reasoning that Fogelin and Sinnott-Armstrong (1992) call a self-sealing argument: by pushing the burden of proof onto young people to prove that they are adults (and attributing a motive that a young reader is highly likely to disavow), the tobacco company guarantees that they cannot be adults because adults are persons who do not have anything to prove. In both cases, what looks like a substantive refutation and counterargument is really a refusal to mount a defence. By failing to accept the burden of justifying its classification of young people, the advertorials leave this issue at an impasse.

Also noticeably withheld is any real justification for why smoking is a restricted activity. Yet this is presumably the basis for the controversy in the first place: young people do not recognize the legitimacy of the restriction to adults. The advertorials merely yoke their claim that young people should not smoke to the presumption by custom that they are not entitled to smoke until they become adults. Invoking the force of presumption is what is done by saying that smoking has 'always' been an adult custom, and that this is the case 'throughout the world'.

The lack of genuine substantive support is particularly noticeable since the advertorials do not make use of the seemingly strongest available arguments against smoking: cigarettes are a lethal, addictive drug, and this is especially so for young people. One might think that the argument reconstructed in (11) alludes to these substantive objections to smoking; but in saying that smoking is controversial nothing more is really conveyed than that some people approve of smoking and others do not. The argument functions only to bolster the presumption of exclusion.

To see this, we must first unpack the meaning of 'controversial'. To say that something is controversial is to say that there are two sides to the issue, neither of which is clearly correct, and so that issue is contested but essentially undecided. To say that 'smoking is controversial' means that it is neither clearly right to smoke nor clearly wrong to do so. And in the absence of a decisive conclusion the position with the presumption wins – adults should be entitled to smoke if that is what they choose to do.

But there is another sense of 'controversial' that especially applies to issues where one position enjoys a presumption, namely the sense of a position being strongly challenged. To preface the reason in (9) with the qualification 'even among adults' conventionally implicates that smoking is more 'controversial' for some group other than adults. Presumably young people form this contrast group since it is the status of smoking for this group that is at issue in the advertorials. If smoking is controversial among adults, it must be more so among young people. And here the meaning is that for young people, smoking is even more questionable, more challengeable. That is, the case that smoking should not be permitted is stronger for young people than it is for adults.

But what makes the case stronger? No substantive basis for challenge or contrast is provided in either advertorial. The only difference is that adult smoking has a customary presumption – as something that does not apply to young people.

The paradoxical quality of the arguments is pernicious, working to undermine the credibility of the very advice they offer while simultaneously resisting critical examination. The advertorials appear to openly engage the doubts and challenges of young people with substantive argumentation and frank refutation, but in fact they consistently refrain from advancing any serious arguments. They also appear to provide arguments that are disinterested, balanced, and objective, yet the manner and content of these are subtly crafted to maintain a strategic consistency with the position that adults' smoking is because of a legitimate, mature, and reasonable decision. Most importantly, the advertorials offer advice but do this in a fashion that is paradoxically adapted to young people – i.e. adapted not by the selection of premises the audience is likely to accept but by the selection of premises the audience is almost sure to reject.

PRACTICAL APPLICATIONS OF ARGUMENTATION STUDY

To understand the whole field of argumentation study, it is first necessary to imagine three (or more) distinct scientific objectives. The first objective is prescriptive: to arrive at a set of principles that will direct people in how to argue well. This altogether practical interest was the first to emerge and is clearly embodied in centuries of writings on rhetoric, dialectic and logic. The second objective is descriptive: to arrive at an empirically correct model of argumentative discourse, analogous in form and compatible in substance to models of such phenomena as talking on topic, managing the floor in conversation, or negotiating social identities. Obvious examples of descriptive argumentation research can be found within conversation analysis and related streams of work (Coulter, 1990; Goodwin, 1983; Jacobs and Jackson, 1982; Schiffrin, 1984). Modem formal logic and cognitive science have also taken a recent turn towards the description of natural inferential processes, as in efforts to model such long-neglected phenomena as the use of heuristics and the structure of 'default reasoning'. In addition the experimental study of social influence offers a form of descriptive argumentation research, heavily oriented towards identifying what factors actually influence people when presented with argumentative texts (Eagly and Chaiken, 1993; O'Keefe, 1990). The third objective is critical: to develop a framework for the evaluation and improvement of actual argumentative practices, treating these both as phenomena to be explained and as opportunities for intervention – that is, in attempts to bring about social change (Goodnight, 1982).

Each of these aims has some form of practical spin-off, for the study of argumentation has from classical times been a practical business concerned with the improvement of reasoning and reason-giving discourse. Contemporary argumentation study, with its emphasis on substantive discourse practices and discourse contexts, embodies this practical component a little differently to what more traditional approaches have done. In the broad interdisciplinary domain of argumentation research, there are two principal sorts of applications, as follows.

Pedagogical applications: the cultivation of argumentative competence

The first sort of application is most obviously connected with the centuries-old rhetorical tradition: the development of critical capability. In the study of argumentation, one objective is to cultivate competence in analysis and critical inquiry. The study of fallacies is, in its best pedagogical embodiments, the cultivation of a critical sense that makes students better participants in argumentative discourse: 'better' not in the sense of being able to win in debates, but 'better' in the sense of being able to advance a discussion towards a rational resolution. So, for example, in teaching students to recognize self-interest as a potential threat to rationality, we create antagonists for views that should be opened to inspection. Case studies such as our analysis of tobacco industry advertorials, for example, serve not only as potential contributions to an ongoing discourse, but also as exemplars for critical thinking about public persuasion.

But to say that contemporary pedagogical applications have close ties to classical rhetoric is not to suggest that these contemporary applications merely recycle the achievements of the past. On the contrary: since discourse practices themselves evolve along with other social conditions, critical analysis will necessarily face new challenges related to changing practices. For example, in contemporary public discourse, the extremely pervasive use of public opinion polls as a tool for the management of public opinion creates some distinctively modern forms of fallacy that require careful theoretical analysis and systematic pedagogical attention (see for example, Harrison, 1996).

Interventions: the design of discourse processes

The second sort of application, associated conceptually with pragmatically oriented approaches such as Willard's (1982; 1989) interactionist theory and with our own pragma-dialectical theory, centres on the design of discourse processes. Human societies have always designed communication systems, but an explicit and detailed examination of the design features of particular systems is a recent development stimulated by broader social changes such as the explosion in communication and information technology. As we have pointed out elsewhere (van Eemeren et al., 1993: Chapter 8), the blending of descriptive and normative concerns supports not just the individual-level pedagogical applications long associated with argumentation study, but also social- or institutional-level applications that take the form of proposals for how to conduct discourse.

How might we think about interventions for the case study we have been examining? Probably the first lesson is that in a world of advertorials, infomercials and docudramas, where talk radio serves as a public forum, and the quality of jury decisions in murder trials is judged against the results of public opinion polls, what the public needs is not just more or better information about the content of issues but more and better information about the way in which information is being provided. What is so insidious about messages like the R.J. Reynolds Tobacco advertorials is not so much the deceptive content of their arguments, as the disarming frame within which these arguments are presented. It is unlikely that any set of regulations or procedures for critical discussion can anticipate or prevent their own subversion and exploitation. Rather, what needs to be provided for is the self-regulating capacities of the argumentation process itself. The only effective way to control fallacious argumentation is with a counter-argumentation that points out what is going on.

And this leads us on to another lesson. There is no natural argumentative forum for reasoned opposition to 'paid' editorials like those published by R.J. Reynolds. An argumentative solution to the problem presented by this case might require not only the development of text to rebut text but also the design of structures to support the activity of rebutting (such as government grant programmes for the development of anti-smoking educational campaigns).

The design features of disputation structures – whether they are adversarial or non-adversarial, how they provide for balanced competition among views, what endpoints they recognize as resolutions, and so on – are properly within the domain of argumentation study. Of special interest from a pragma-dialectical perspective is the way in which the design of disputation can correct for the obstacles to rational discussion encountered in real-life circumstances.

FURTHER READING

As guidance to further reading, we would like to refer, firstly, to a comprehensive general overview of the state of the art in argumentation theory; secondly, to some influential monographs explaining different theoretical approaches; and, third, to some recent publications relating to the integrating notion of strategic manoeuvring.

van Eemeren, F.H., Garssen, B., van Haaften, T., Krabbe, E.C.W., Snoeck Henkemans, A.F. and Wagemans, J.H.M. (2011) *Handbook of Argumentation Theory*. Dordrecht: Springer.
The *Handbook* offers an introduction to argumentation theory, an explanation of its classical and modern theoretical backgrounds, and a comprehensive overview of the most prominent current approaches.

Johnson, R.H. (2000) *Manifest Rationality. A Pragmatic Theory of Argument*. Mahwah, NJ: Lawrence Erlbaum.

van Eemeren, F.H. and Grootendorst, R. (2004) *A Systematic Theory of Argumentation: The Pragma-Dialectical Approach*. Cambridge: Cambridge University Press.

Walton, D.N. and Krabbe, E.C.W. (1995) *Commitment in Dialogue: Basic Concepts of Interpersonal Reasoning*. Albany, NY: State University of New York Press.

Each of the three monographs explains a particular theoretical approach to argumentative discourse: Johnson an informal logic approach, van Eemeren and Grootendorst the pragma-dialectical approach, and Walton and Krabbe a related dialectical approach.

Jacobs, S. (2006) 'Nonfallacious rhetorical strategies: Lyndon Johnson's daisy ad', *Argumentation*, 20: 421–42.

Tindale, C.W. (2006) 'Constrained maneuvering: rhetoric as a rational enterprise', *Argumentation*, 20: 447–66.

van Eemeren, F.H. (2010) *Strategic Maneuvering in Argumentative Discourse. Extending the Pragma-Dialectical Theory of Argumentation*. Amsterdam/Philadelphia: John Benjamins.

Zarefsky, D. (2006) 'Strategic maneuvering through persuasive definitions: implications for dialectic and rhetoric', *Argumentation*, 20: 399–416.

Van Eemeren's monograph offers a theoretical approach to strategic manoeuvring in argumentative discourse as aimed at the simultaneous pursuit of rhetorical effectiveness and maintaining dialectical reasonableness. Jacobs, Tindale, and Zarefsky present three particular views on argumentative discourse that are, each in their own way, pertinent to examining strategic manoeuvring.

ONLINE READING

The following articles are available at www.sagepub.co.uk/discoursestudies.

Eemeren, F.H. van and Houtlosser, P. (1999) 'Strategic Manoeuvring in Argumentative Discourse', *Discourse Studies*, 1(4): 479–497.

Richardson, J.E. (2001) "Now is the Time to Put an End to all this': Argumentative Discourse Theory and 'Letters to the Editor", *Discourse & Society*, 12(2): 143–168.

Rips, L.J., Brem, S.K. and Bailenson, J.N. (1999) 'Reasoning Dialogues', *Current Directions in Psychological Science*, 8(6): 172–177.

REFERENCES

Associated Press (1993) 'Women are more likely to be murdered at work than men, study finds'. *Arizona Daily Star*, 2 October: A5.

Blair, J.A. and Johnson, R. (1987) 'Argumentation as dialectical', *Argumentation*, 1: 41–56.

Bleiberg, S. and Churchill, L. (1977) 'Notes on confrontation in conversation'. *Journal of Psycholinguistic Research*, 4: 273–8.

Coulter, J. (1990) 'Elementary properties of argument sequences'. In G. Psathas (ed.), *Interaction Competence*. Washington, DC: International Institute for Ethnomethodology and Conversation Analysis, and University Press of America. pp. 181–203.

Eagly, A.H. and Chaiken, S. (1993) *The Psychology of Attitudes*. Fort Worth, TX: Harcourt Brace Jovanovich.

Fisher, A. (1988) *The Logic of Real Arguments*. Cambridge: Cambridge University Press.

Fogelin, R. and Sinnott-Armstrong, W. (1992) *Understanding Arguments: an Introduction to Informal Logic* (4th edn). San Diego, CA: Harcourt Brace Jovanovich.

Goodnight, G.T. (1982) 'The personal, technical, and public spheres of argument: a speculative inquiry into the art of public deliberation'. *Journal of the American Forensic Association*, 18: 214–27.

Goodwin, M.H. (1983) 'Aggravated correction and disagreement in children's conversations'. *Journal of Pragmatics*, 7: 657–77.

Govier, T. (1988) *A Practical Study of Argument* (2nd edn). Belmont, CA: Wadsworth.

Grice, H.P. (1989) *Studies in the Ways of Words*. Cambridge, MA: Harvard University Press.

Hamblin, C.L. (1970) *Fallacies*. London: Methuen.

Harrison, T. (1996) 'Are public opinion polls used illegitimately?: 47% say yes'. In S. Jackson (ed.), *Argument and Values: Proceedings of the Ninth SCA/AFA Summer Conference on Argumentation*. Annandale, VA: Speech Communication Association.

Jackson, S. and Jacobs, S. (1980) 'Structure of conversational argument: pragmatic bases for the enthymeme'. *Quarterly Journal of Speech*, 66: 251–65.

Jacobs, S. (1986) 'How to make an argument from example in discourse analysis'. In D.G. Ellis and W.A. Donohue (eds), *Contemporary Issues in Language and Discourse Processes*. Hillsdale, NJ: Lawrence Erlbaum. pp. 149–67.

Jacobs, S. (2006) 'Nonfallacious rhetorical strategies: Lyndon Johnson's daisy ad'. *Argumentation*, 20: 421–42.

Jacobs, S. and Jackson, S. (1982) 'Conversational argument: a discourse analytic approach'. In J.R. Cox and C.A. Willard (eds), *Advances in Argumentation Theory and Research*. Carbondale and Edwardsville, IL: Southern Illinois University Press. pp. 205–37.

Johnson, R. and Blair, J.A. (1983) *Logical Self-Defense*. Toronto: McGraw-Hill.

O'Keefe, D.J. (1977) 'Two concepts of argument'. *Journal of the American Forensic Association*, 13: 121–8.

O'Keefe, D.J. (1990) *Persuasion: Theory and Research*. Thousand Oaks, CA: Sage.

Perelman, C. and Olbrechts-Tyteca, L. (1958) *La Nouvelle Rhétorique: traité de l'argumentation*. Brussels: University of Brussels.

Perelman, C. and Olbrechts-Tyteca, L. (1969) *The New Rhetoric: a Treatise on Argumentation* (trans. J. Wilkinson and P. Weaver). Notre Dame, IN: University of Notre Dame Press.

Schiffrin, D. (1984) 'Jewish argument as sociability'. *Language in Society*, 13: 311–36.

Searle, J.R. (1969) *Speech Acts*. Cambridge: Cambridge University Press.

Tindale, C.W. (2006) 'Constrained maneuvering: rhetoric as a rational enterprise'. *Argumentation*, 20: 447–66.

Toulmin, S.E. (1958) *The Uses of Argument*. Cambridge: Cambridge University Press.

Toulmin, S.E. (1970) *An Examination of the Place of Reason in Ethics*. Cambridge: Cambridge University Press.

van Eemeren, F.H. (2010) *Strategic Maneuvering in Argumentative Discourse. Extending the Pragma-Dialectical Theory of Argumentation*. Amsterdam/Philadelphia: John Benjamins.

van Eemeren, F.H. and Grootendorst, R. (1984) *Speech Acts in Argumentative Discussions*. Dordrechts: Foris.

van Eemeren, F.H. and Grootendorst, R. (1992) *Argumentation, Communication, and Fallacies: a Pragma-Dialectical Perspective*. Hillsdale, NJ: Lawrence Erlbaum.

van Eemeren, F.H. and Grootendorst, R. (2004) *A Systematic Theory of Argumentation: the Pragma-Dialectical Approach*. Cambridge: Cambridge University Press.

van Eemeren, F.H. and Houtlosser, P. (2002a), 'Strategic manoeuvring with the burden of proof'. In F.H. van Eemeren (ed.), *Advances in Pragma-Dialectics*, pp. 13–29. Amsterdam: Sic Sat.

van Eemeren, F.H. and Houtlosser, P. (2002b) 'Strategic maneuvering: maintaining a delicate balance'. In F.H. van Eemeren and P. Houtlosser (eds.), *Dialectic and Rhetoric: the Warp and Woof of Argumentation Analysis*, pp. 131–59. Dordrecht: Kluwer Academic Publishers.

van Eemeren, F.H. and Houtlosser, P. (2003) 'More about fallacies as derailments of strategic maneuvering: the case of *tu quoque*'. In H.V. Hansen, C.W. Tindale,. J.A. Blair, R.H. Johnson and R.C. Pinto (eds), *Argumentation and its Applications: Proceedings of the Conference Organised by the Ontario Society for the Study of Argumentation in May 2001*, CD-ROM. Windsor, Ontario: Ontario Society for the Study of Argumentation.

van Eemeren, F.H. and Houtlosser, P. (2006). 'Strategic maneuvering: a synthetic recapitulation'. *Argumentation*, 20: 381–92.

van Eemeren, F.H., Grootendorst, R., Jackson, S. and Jacobs, S. (1993) *Reconstructing Argumentative Discourse*. Tuscaloosa, AL: University of Alabama Press.

van Eemeren, F.H., Grootendorst, R., Snoeck Henkemans, F., Blair, J.A., Johnson, R.H., Krabbe, E.C.W., Plantin, C., Walton, D., Willard, C.A., Woods, J. and Zarefsky, D. (1996) *Fundamentals of Argumentation Theory*. Hillsdale, NJ: Lawrence Erlbaum.

van Eemeren, F.H., Houtlosser, P. and Snoeck Henkemans, A.F. (2007) *Argumentative Indicators in Discourse: a Pragma-Dialectical Study*. Dordrecht: Springer.

Walton, D.N. (1989) *Informal Logic: a Handbook for Critical Argumentation*. Cambridge: Cambridge University Press.

Walton, D.N. (1995) *A Pragmatic Theory of Fallacy*. Tuscaloosa, AL: University of Alabama Press.

Walton, D.N. and Krabbe, E.C.W. (1995) *Commitment in Dialogue: Basic Concepts of Interpersonal Reasoning*. Albany, NY: State University of New York Press.

Willard, C.A. (1982) *Argumentation and the Social Grounds of Knowledge*. Tuscaloosa, AL: University of Alabama Press.

Willard, C.A. (1989) *A Theory of Argument*. Tuscaloosa, AL: University of Alabama Press.

Zarefsky, D. (2006) 'Strategic maneuvering through persuasive definitions: implications for dialectic and rhetoric', *Argumentation*, 20: 399–416.

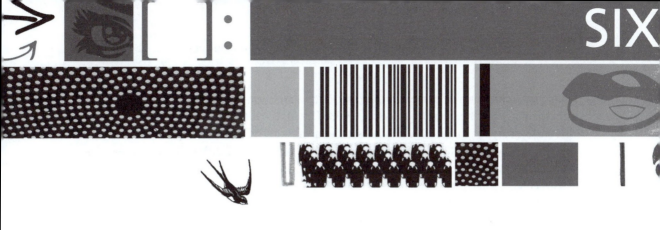

SIX

Discourse Semiotics

Theo van Leeuwen and Gunther Kress

MULTIMODAL DISCOURSE ANALYSIS

Four twentieth-century schools of linguistics have engaged with semiotic modes other than language. The first was the Prague School, which, in the 1930s and 1940s, extended linguistics into the visual arts and non-verbal aspects of the theatre, and included studies of folklore and collaborations with avant-garde artists (cf. e.g. Matejka and Titunik, 1976; Mukařovský, 1977). Second was Paris School semiotics, which used concepts and methods from structuralist linguistics and focused for the most part on an analysis of popular culture and the mass media, rather than on folklore or avant-garde art (e.g. Barthes, 1967; 1977; 1983). In roughly the same period American linguists took an interest in the multimodal analysis of spoken language and non-verbal communication. Ray Birdwhistell (e.g. 1973), for instance, developed an intricate set of transcription methods for analysing body motion, and Pittenger et al. (1960) published a highly detailed and groundbreaking multimodal analysis of the first five minutes of a psychiatric interview. The fourth school developed in the 1990s, inspired by the linguistics of M.A.K. Halliday (1979; 1985). It was this school which first adopted the term 'multimodality', and developed the tools and methods for multimodal discourse analysis (Baldry and Thibault, 2006; Hodge and Kress, 1988; van Leeuwen, 2005).

The term 'multimodality' designates a phenomenon rather than a theory or method – the phenomenon in texts and communicative events whereby a variety of 'semiotic modes' (means of expression) are integrated into a unified whole. Conversation, for example, integrates language with intonation, voice quality, facial expression, gesture and posture, and some conversation analysts have therefore begun to integrate non-verbal elements into their transcriptions (Goodwin, 2001; Ochs, 1979). Writing not only uses words and sentences, it is also a graphic form of expression, and so, once again, some linguists have begun to look at graphology and typography (Crystal, 1998; Graddol, 1996; Walker, 2000). 'Multimodal discourse analysis' therefore designates a field of study which investigates the common properties as well as the different communicative potentials of different modes, and analyses how these modes are used in multimodal texts and communicative events. In doing so it uses concepts and methods from linguistics, but also takes inspiration from other relevant disciplines, such as art and design theory and musicology.

This contemporary interest in multimodality derives from the fact that communication itself has become increasingly multimodal over the past ninety years or so. Magazines and advertising began to mix language, image and graphic communication in the 1920s, and American comic strips did the same in the 1930s. The arrival of film changed acting, enlarging subtle aspects of non-verbal communication, and so influencing how people will talk and move and smile the world over. The microphone foregrounded the nuances of voice quality and intonation, and television made non-verbal communication a decisive factor in politics, most famously in the televised election debate between Nixon and Kennedy in the early 1960s. Clearly, discourse can no longer be adequately studied without paying attention to non-verbal aspects of communication, whether in conversation, in therapeutic sessions, or in political discourse – to mention just a few examples.

Initially multimodal discourse analysis investigated the different modes of communication *separately*, using linguistic models to describe visual communication as a 'language of images', musical communication as a 'language of music', and so on. Roland Barthes was an exception here, as he not only paid attention to the general principles underlying multimodal communication, devising a conceptual framework that could be applied to all semiotic modes (1967), but also developed a theory of the ways in which text and image could integrate with multimodal texts (1977). But even in Barthes' work the 'linguistic message' and the 'visual message' were still separate and to be understood separately before they could be related to each other, before an image could be understood as 'illustrating' a text, for instance, or a text as 'anchoring' a picture (giving it a more specific and precise meaning). For many kinds of multimodal texts, this was – and still is – entirely plausible, but for other texts it is no longer adequate. Text and image are too closely integrated, too interdependent, to be understood in isolation. The photographer Matt Siber demonstrated this by photographing streetscapes and shop interiors, and then in one version eliminating the words on the billboards, signs and so on, while in another removing everything *but* the words. Without context, the words, distributed in an apparently random fashion, read like a strange concrete poem. Without words, the arrows, frames and pictorial fragments on the billboards and signs no longer made sense (Siber, 2005).

Siber's demonstration could have been equally applied to contemporary comic strips, or magazine advertisements, or web pages. A single page advertisement for cat food, for instance, showed, at the top, a fluffy grey cat with yellow eyes; below that, in flowing script, were the words 'spoilt, spoilt, spoilt, spoilt'; and below that again were four yellow tins of cat food. These elements combined into a single, multimodal proposition, something like:

'This cat is spoilt four times over, by four different tins of cat food'. The 'subject' of the proposition was visual (the picture of the cat), the 'predicate' was verbal ('spoilt, spoilt, spoilt, spoilt') and the 'passive agent' visual (the tins of cat food). The visual and the verbal were thus fused. Words and images no longer made sense in isolation, and needed each other to communicate the message. And this is the case, not only in multimodal texts, but also in the way these texts are produced. While in the past each mode required specialist equipment and specialist skills (the writer, the typesetter, the camera operator, the sound recordist), now a single person can command the whole range of modes from one and the same keyboard, and multimodal communication is no longer the province of specialist producers but accessible to all. Everyday written communication today makes use of a wide range of fonts, layouts and colours, and talks and presentations will combine the spoken and written word with the graphic resources of PowerPoint slides. Yes, language continues to play an important role, but it is now only one among a range of communicative modes. As linguists and discourse analysts we therefore need to broaden our field of study into multimodality theory and multimodal discourse analysis.

SOCIAL SEMIOTICS

The theory that underpins multimodal discourse analysis is 'social semiotics'. It can be described as the study of 1) the material resources we use in multimodal communication, and 2) the way we use these resources for purposes of communication and expression.

Semiotic resources may be physiological or technical. Physiological resources include the voice and the muscles we use to create the facial expressions, gestures and postures of non-verbal communication. Technical resources extend the potential of our physiological resources. We communicate not only with our voice, but also with musical instruments; not only through facial expression and gesture, but also through the clothes we wear and the way we groom our bodies. And in addition to all of this we have developed technologies that can extend our semiotic actions in time and space, distributing them across distances (e.g. broadcasting and telephony) and preserving them over time (e.g. writing, painting, video recording).

Social semiotics first of all studies these resources themselves – their specific, culturally produced, yet also mode-inherent communication potential. On the one hand semiotic resources have inherent characteristics that make them suitable for specific communicative purposes, whether on the basis of their material qualities or on the basis of the senses we use to perceive them. Sounds can be heard even when they are behind us, while vision is 'narrow beam'. Sound is therefore a better medium for summoning people (e.g. the school bell) or for sounding an alarm (e.g. the siren of the ambulance), while visual resources are better at displaying precise spatial relations, for instance in maps and floor plans. On the other hand, if it becomes desirable for practical or cultural reasons, cultural practices and technologies can override inherent characteristics – developing directional microphones, for instance, or replacing maps with voice-based route finders. So we must pay attention to the specific communicative potential of specific modes, but also be aware of their common properties and potentials. The same story can be spoken or written or filmed; the same phenomenon can be explained with a diagram or in writing. Of course, the result will not be quite the same, and which resources are preferred for which types of communication will vary over time for historically and culturally specific reasons. Today many things that used to be done with words are done visually, and as a result the meaning potential of visual semiotic resources changes and extends into areas which it could not cover before.

Semiotic resources have a *meaning potential* that is based on their past uses. As soon as we have identified a semiotic resource (say, visual composition), we can ask, 'In what ways has composition been drawn into meaning-making and what kind of meanings have so far been made with them?' Closely related is the term 'affordance', which stems from the work of the psychologist James Gibson (1979). According to Gibson, affordances are the potential uses of a given object. These, he says, stem directly from their observable properties. However, different observers may notice different affordances, depending on their needs and interests, and on the specifics of the situation at hand. The difference between the term 'meaning potential', which stems from Halliday (1979), and the term 'affordance', is that 'meaning potential' refers to meanings that have already been established as part of the repertoire of a given context, whereas 'affordance' also brings into play meanings that, as it were, lie latent in objects or materials. Both are of course of interest to social semioticians – the use of existing resources as well as the creation of new resources. We will return to this issue later in the chapter.

Meaning potentials are only *potentials*. They will be actualized in concrete social contexts, and our next question is, therefore, how are semiotic resources actually used in multimodal texts and communicative events? In answering this question we need to pay attention to the rules and regulations which govern the use of semiotic resources, and which are given by the interests of the social and cultural institutions in and for which the rules are produced; but we also need to remain aware that wholly or partially new ways of using these resources are always possible, and that sign-makers can choose the most apt 'signifiers' (material, perceivable resources) from the resources available to them to express the 'signifieds' (meanings) they need to express in a given situation.

Let us provide an example. In a study of the semiotics of children's toys (cf. van Leeuwen, 2005), ten mothers were filmed playing with their three- to four-month-old babies using two different pram rattles. One consisted of four identical rabbits made of shiny, rigid plastic and strung on an elastic string which could be attached to the sides of a pram or cot with plastic hooks. Pushing or kicking the string would cause them to rotate and produce a soft, tinkling rattle. The other consisted of three very different characters, looking like friendly monsters, with eyes on stilts, dragon tails, horns, etc., and were made of soft fleecy fabric in dark cyans, purples and oranges. Each character had its own distinctive sound that could be produced in different ways (one had to be squeezed, another rubbed, etc.) and they were held together by Velcro fasteners, with gold stars in between.

As it happens, there are rules for the use of this particular semiotic resource. There is a 'normative discourse' which every mother comes across, whether in parenting books, in magazines, or via the advice of experts or peers, and it tells us that mothers must encourage their babies to swipe or kick the rattles, so as to teach them 'hand-eye co-ordination'. Here is one example of this, from the magazine *New Baby* (May, 2000):

> [pram rattles] are great for teaching hand-eye co-ordination and cause and effect – if your baby bats the hanging toys with his hands or feet, they'll move and maybe make a noise. Show your baby how to swipe things then let him explore.

As a result the mothers all knew what to do with the rabbit pram rattles: they held them up and moved them around, encouraging their babies to kick. Here is a brief extract from one of the tapes:

> Mother: Oh look, put 'em by your feet.
> She holds up the rattle in front of the baby's feet and shakes it.
> Mother: Ooooh! Kick, kick, kick … Ooh, you've had a busy morning today
> The baby's feet now actually kick the rattle.
> Mother: Look … oooh … they are lovely … you like those …

With the other pram rattles they tried to do the same thing, but it did not work. Shaking these did not produce a noise and made the rattles come apart. They then gave up and tried something else, and in doing so they made creative use of the visible and tactile characteristics of the toy (the softness of the material, the 'individuality' of each character, the 'monster' iconography, etc). One caressed the baby's cheek with one of the characters; another used one of these as a doll, making it walk across the baby's tummy; a third created a little puppet show. In doing so they treated their babies, not as being pre-occupied only with 'motor control', as the normative discourse would have it, but as already interested in stories and imaginative play, even at three or four months old. Here is a brief extract:

> The mother holds the rattle close to her ear, shaking one of the characters and listening to it. One of the Velcro fasteners comes unstuck.
> Mother: Oh, they come off.
> She shakes the character that has come unstuck and discovers that pinching it makes it squeak.
> Mother: Oooh … (creating a voice for the alien) … Ho-ho-ho … It's like a dragon.

Normative discourses can be of different kinds. Some will provide highly prescriptive, authoritative rules to indicate which signifiers should be used to communicate which signifieds. Here is an example from the University of Newcastle (Australia) – an authoritative colour code in which specific colours will signify specific disciplines, such as Architecture, Medicine, etc. For all practical purposes the choice of colour is 'arbitrary', so it is hard to see why Business rather than Education should be turquoise, or why Engineering rather than Architecture should be lapis lazuli.

The academic dress for graduates of the University shall be:

Doctors of Architecture, Doctors of Education, Doctors of Engineering, Doctors of Letters, Doctors of Medicine, Doctors of Music, Doctors of Nursing, Doctors of Science, Doctors of the University – a festal gown of cardinal red cloth with a hood of garnet cloth lined with silk cloth of the appropriate colour, namely

Doctor of Architecture – deep Indian red
Doctor of Business – turqoise
Doctor of Education – jade
Doctor of Engineering – lapis lazuli

...

The normative discourse in our earlier example was an 'expert discourse'. Today's media are full of semiotic experts who will tell us what the colours or styles within fashion signify:

Dramatic, passion-inspiring purple is the season's hottest hue. To instantly make any outfit feel more 'fall 2007', just add a hint of plum.

Expert discourse of course is not quite as prescriptive as authoritative normative discourse. Fashion may be said to 'dictate', but while Doctors of Architecture must wear a deep Indian red lining on their hoods, at least during graduation, there is no requirement to wear purple when we feel passionate. The signifiers of fashion, and of many other expert discourses, are also 'motivated' rather than arbitrary – purple is an apt signifier for passion, as the reference to a 'hint of plum' already suggests.

'Role models' (movie stars, pop stars, sports people and other celebrities) can embody normative discourses as well. The meanings, values and identities associated with the roles they play, the songs they sing, or the way they are portrayed in the media then become the signified, while the way they look, talk, dress, and move becomes the signifier. Lauren Bacall recalls in her autobiography how Howard Hawks conceived of her character in *To Have and Have Not* (1944) as 'a masculine approach – insolent. Give as good as she gets, no capitulation, no helplessness' (Bacall, 1979: 87). To this end Hawks not only invented 'the look' for her – a quizzical look upwards with the head slightly bowed, suggesting feminine deference as well as insolence – but also told her to work on her voice, and to 'keep the register low'. In time that low voice would become Bacall's trademark and a new semiotic resource for the expression of a certain kind of female identity.

Today semiotic software can also incorporate normative discourses, for instance through default choices. Every time you insert a new PowerPoint slide, for instance, you will be invited to provide a title. The norm is that the page is a single textual unit with a single topic (in this, PowerPoint pages are very different from web pages). You can of course override this, but most people do not, and in this way technologies like PowerPoint are able to create a conformity of practice without the need for any rules.

Normative discourses are produced by powerful institutions. National academies, education systems and publishing houses have long produced the normative discourses that govern our use of language. Today, global semiotic industries such as the fashion industry, the media, advertising, and software producers will produce normative discourses for many key semiotic resources. They will no longer use authoritative prescription, but they nevertheless remain very effective in distributing the common understandings and practices which everyone who is at all exposed to contemporary media will come in to contact with.

DISCOURSE

In the next few sections we will discuss three layers of analysis for multimodal texts and communicative events – 'discourse', 'design' and 'production'. All of these provide their own semiotic resources for the production and interpretation of texts and communicative events, and in each case normative discourses seek to govern how they should be used in specific contexts. Although for the sake of clarity we will have to discuss them separately, in reality they will of course be perceived as a seamless whole.

We would define 'discourses' (note the plural) as 'socially constructed knowledges about some aspect of reality'. Discourses are therefore resources for constructing and interpreting the *content* of texts and communicative events. As such they have no physical existence: they are knowledges, mental resources, although we of course get to know about them through texts and communicative events. But while they are mental phenomena, they are also 'socially constructed' – developed in the context of specific social institutions, be they large (e.g. multi-national corporations) or small (e.g. a specific family), in ways that are appropriate to the interests that dominate in these contexts. In van Dijk's terminology, they are 'social cognitions' (2009: 78).

Let us look at one example. There is, for instance, a 'discourse of the innocence of childhood' in which children are a-sexual, do not know anything about sexuality, and must be protected from all knowledge of, and contact with, sexuality. Today this idea forms part of most people's mental furniture, regardless of whether they agree with it or not, but, as the historian Philippe Ariès has shown, this is not of all times and all places, and in Europe developed slowly from approximately the sixteenth century onwards, predominantly in a religious context, which increasingly saw children in an ambivalent way, as on the one hand 'comparable to the angels, and close to Christ who loved them', and on the other hand still lacking in 'reason', 'fragile creatures of God who needed to be safeguarded and reformed' to become 'thinking men and good Christians' (1973: 129).

This discourse played a role in recent events in Australia, where an exhibition of photographs by photographer Bill Henson, which contained some nude shots of adolescents, was about to be opened when police confiscated the pictures as pornographic, a charge which later had to be withdrawn. Questioned about this during one of his regular television appearances, the then Australian Prime Minister Kevin Rudd said he found the pictures 'absolutely revolting':

> Kids deserve to have the innocence of their childhood protected. I have a very deep view of this. For God's sake, let's just allow kids to be kids.

Subsequently many other politicians, the Police Commissioner and many members of the public echoed this same sentiment.

There are of course different discourses of childhood, discourses which *do* see children as sexual beings. More than a hundred years ago, Sigmund Freud wrote (1973: 243):

> First and foremost it is an untenable error to deny that children have a sexual life and to suppose that sexuality only begins at puberty and with the maturation of the genitals …

His theories were controversial at the time and have remained so ever since. As Freud said (*ibid*):

> It cannot be said that the world has shown much gratitude to psychoanalytic research for its revelation of the Oedipus complex. On the contrary, the discovery has provoked the most violent opposition among adults.

Let us note a few key characteristics of these discourses:

1) Discourses can be condensed into 'dogmas' – nuggets of essential wisdom, such as 'children are innocent', 'children are already sexual beings'. Such statements will be repeated on many different occasions and in many different formulations, and then elaborated and enhanced with reasons, examples, anecdotes, and so on, but nevertheless will always centre around that basic dogma of 'innocence' (or 'already sexual').
2) Discourses are plural. As we have already seen, there are different discourses of childhood, different views on the essential nature of 'the child', and they often are at the core of disagreement and difference, as in Freud's time, and as in the Bill Henson case in Australia.
3) Discourses legitimate specific practices and serve the interests of specific institutions. The discourse of the 'innocent child', for instance, is used in practices of censorship that seek to shield children from exposure to sexuality (but not, as has often been noted, from violence). The Bill Henson case is but one example of this. But there may be a broader issue as well. The protection of innocence usually serves to support the continued power of the 'protectors'. In many societies the repression of women is justified as the protection of their 'sexual innocence' or virginity.
4) Discourses are socially constructed and historically specific. In *Centuries of Childhood* Philippe Ariès demonstrated that in the sixteenth century 'everything was permitted in the presence of children: coarse language, scabrous actions and situations: they had heard everything and seen everything' (1973: 101), something which only gradually disappeared as the 'discourse of the innocent child' gained ascendance.
5) Discourses can be realized in different genres and different modes or combinations of modes. The discourse of the sexualized child, for instance, can be realized linguistically, as a piece of academic prose (as in the Freud quotation above) or multimodally, even in a children's book, as in *The Bear* (Briggs, 1994), in which a bear enters Tilly's bedroom through the window, after which she invites him into her bed and sighs 'Oooh Bear! You're so warm! Won't Mummy be surprised when she finds us in bed together?' The next day her father jealously asks 'What about me?', and Tilly answers 'You've got no *fur*, Daddy. But you're *quite* nice. I do still like you a *little* bit.'

DESIGN

Designs, in the way in which we use the term here, are more or less conventionalized formats or templates for texts and communicative events. As such they stand midway between content (discourse) and expression (production), the actual material realization of multimodal discourse which we will discuss in the next section. They have two key characteristics:

- They contextualize discourses by embedding them in structures which have particular communicative purposes and signify particular relationships between the participants (equal or unequal relationships, formal or informal relationships, etc.). Thus the 'discourse of the innocent child' can be embedded in a newspaper article, a television interview with a prime minister, a movie, a booklet advising parents about the sexual education of their children, and much more.
- They can be realized in different material forms. An advertisement, for instance, has a particular communicative purpose and encodes a particular relationship between the participants (salesperson/potential customer; or persuader/to-be-persuaded person), but it can still take different forms and be realized, for instance, as a radio commercial, a television commercial, a magazine ad, a poster, and so forth.

Let us illustrate these key characteristics of design with an example. In our book *Reading Images* (1996) we argued that visual composition assigns different information values to the elements of the composition according to where they are positioned – on the right or on the left, on top or below, in the centre or the margins, and so forth.

The left-right dimension, we argued, creates a dynamic contrast between a 'Given' and a 'New'. If two elements – one placed on the right, the other on the left – are 'polarized' (differing or contrasting in one way or another) then the left element will be the Given, a to-be-taken-for-granted departure point for the message which the reader or viewer is assumed to already be familiar with, while the element on the right will be the New, providing new information to which the reader or viewer is meant to pay special attention. This is a culturally specific arrangement – in cultures that write from right to left, the Given appears on the right and the New on the left.

When there is vertical polarization – polarization between an element placed in the upper and an element placed in the lower section of the picture, page or screen – the top element is the 'Ideal', the idealized or generalized essence of the message, and the bottom element the 'Real', contrasting with the Ideal in presenting factual details, or documentary evidence, or practical consequences. In single page magazine advertisements, the Ideal often depicts the 'promise' of the product, the glamour or success it will bring to consumers, or the sensual satisfaction it will give them, while the Real shows the product itself and provides factual information about it.

The Centre is another key compositional zone. Instead of polarizing the elements of the composition, the Centre unifies them, providing the elements that surround it – the Margins – with a common meaning or purpose. The cover of a brochure put out by Rank Xerox for its staff, titled 'Rewards and Recognition', had the Centre representing the silhouette of a happy Rank Xerox employee, literally jumping with joy, and the words surrounding him suggesting the attributes Rank Xerox rewards ('team focused', 'flexible', 'spontaneous', 'empowerment focus', 'effective', etc.).

Putting these dimensions of composition together results in a compositional design with four quadrants, as shown in Figure 6.1.

Figure 6.1   Visual space in Western visual semiotics

The elements of the compositional template discussed here can be combined in various ways. Or to put it another way, there is the schema (the grid) and there are the things one can do with it. A poster for Amnesty International contained three horizontal zones. The left one was reserved for the name of the organization, as a Given; the right one was empty, a zone for the viewer's future action; while the larger Centre, like a modern triptych, was the 'Mediator' connecting the two (Kress and van Leeuwen, 2006: 198–9), and contained an irregularly typed story of political persecution, with the face of the victim looming faintly behind it. This triptych then formed the 'Ideal', the essence of Amnesty's message, taking up about two-thirds of the space of the poster, while the Real provided the official version of Amnesty's objectives and methods as well as a contact address.

It is therefore the communicative purpose of composition to relate the elements of a composition both to each other and to the viewer in particular ways, e.g. to position viewers as people who are already in possession of a particular piece of information (the 'Given') but not yet aware of another piece of information (the 'New'). The Amnesty poster, for instance, positions the viewer as already having heard of Amnesty. This may not actually be the case, but even viewers who have not heard of Amnesty will realize that, in the given context, they are supposed to have already heard of it.

As we have already mentioned, design is still separate from material realization, or 'production', as we will call it. The design schema we have discussed here can apply to pictures as well as to multimodal texts which combine text, image and graphic design, as in the case of the Amnesty poster. Indeed, as we have tried to show in detail elsewhere (van Leeuwen, 2005; Kress and van Leeuwen, 2006), it can apply to any spatial configuration, whether in two or three dimensions – to images, texts, museum displays, stage design, architectural facades, and so on.

Finally, as with discourses, designs must be understood in their cultural and historical context. Let us illustrate this with another example, taken from *Cosmopolitan* magazine (November 2004):

How to Erase Your Dating Mistake

Did your bowl-him-over move backfire? Smooth things over with these three steps.

- **Apologize ASAP**. Own up to your gaffe by saying 'I was so nervous/temporarily brain-dead, I ended up doing something out of character'. Your confession shows that you recognize your boobish behaviour. Plus, you may even evoke a little empathy.
- **Make it up to him** by showing your true colors. For example, if you barked his ear off the night before with a long list of personal problems, spend the next couple of dates subtly encouraging him. Once he sees that you're not a chronic complainer or babbler, he'll realize that your faux pas was a one-time occurrence.
- **Play it cool**. Wait a week, then assess where you stand: if your union is back on track or you two are able to joke about your blunder, thumbs up. But if he seems iffy about hanging out or won't let your goof-up go the next few times you talk, you might have to concede defeat and move on.

This text is structured as a piece of instruction. It first of all indicates the 'task' which the reader will be taught ('How to Erase Your Dating Mistake'). It then positions the reader as having a problem (she has been too forward), offers a solution, a strategy for 'smoothing over' the mistake, and a three-step method for achieving this aim ('apologize', 'make it up', and 'play it cool'). The design of the text can therefore be schematized as follows:

Task
↓
Problem
↓
Solution
↓
Step 1
↓
Step 2
↓
Step 3

These elements are marked typographically. The task is in a larger font size, and black; the font of 'problem' and 'solution' is second largest in size, white, and indented; and the font of the three 'steps' is smallest, with a white bullet point, a black 'intro' (e.g. 'Apologize ASAP') and white text. The different elements are also separated by spacing, and the whole is contained in a box and printed against a lilac background.

Clearly, many different discourses can be embedded in this design – in a magazine like *Cosmopolitan* especially discourses that construct aspects of reality such as beauty, health, relationships and work. Equally clearly the design can be realized in a range of material forms – spoken or written, visual or verbal, or some multimodal combination of these. In many advertisements 'problems' and 'solutions' are visualized. The problem of 'migraine' may be visualized by a photo of a man or woman with a pained expression, the solution by a picture of the pharmaceutical product advertised.

The examples we have used also illustrate that designs exist at different levels – there are designs for textual elements and designs for texts as a whole. Clause structures, for example, are designs for linguistic text elements (which can then be realized in a spoken or written form) and the generic structures of text types (letters, reports, fairy tales, etc.) are designs for linguistic texts.

But there is something else as well. As a culturally specific approach to 'counselling' in matters of relationships, the design of a text like 'How to Erase Your Dating Mistakes' has meaning in and of itself. It reveals something about the world we live in. On the one hand it provides women with an independent source of advice in matters of relationships, so that they no longer need to be dependent on family, religion, tradition. In many countries (and *Cosmopolitan* is distributed globally and translated in 48 languages), traditions have served to maintain patriarchic systems, and a new, independent source of counsel can therefore have a liberating effect for women (although in this example the woman of course is being advised to apologize for being too forward!). On the other hand, as a form of counsel, it also positions women as being on their own, bereft of supportive networks, and left with only one option – consulting media and internet experts to search for survival strategies. As Machin and van Leeuwen have shown (2007) this design is a global one and therefore all the more important, even though the actual advice given by *Cosmopolitan* (the discourse) can vary locally.

PRODUCTION

We have seen that discourses and designs are relatively independent. In other words, texts may draw on different discourses, but use the same design (for instance newspaper editorials taking a different line on a particular issue), or draw on the same discourse, but use a different design, as when the same discourse of childhood is realized in an academic essay or a children's book.

As we have already mentioned, the third variable is 'production': the same design can be realized by different material semiotic resources or combinations of material resources; the 'same' text (same from the point of view of discourse and design) can be spoken, written on paper, carved in stone, sprayed on walls; the 'same' picture (again, same from the point of view of discourse and design) can be drawn in charcoal, painted in oils, arranged in front of a camera and then photographed either in black and white or colour, and so on.

In a still recent past it was often thought that production did not add further meaning, and this principle in fact governed the use of material semiotic resources in many of the most prestigious forms of communication and expression. Typography is a good example. If only one type of font is available, as used to be the case with typewriters, the typographic expression will be severely restricted. All it would mean is 'this is type-written', with whatever associations clinging to that. Many professional typographers still maintain that typography may at most 'to a very limited extent (...) help to express a feeling or a mood that is in harmony with the words' (McLean, 2000: 56), and that 'for the the most part "lettering and calligraphy are abstract arts"' (ibid: 54). More recently, however, the advent of the word processor has made a wealth of typographic resources available to all of us, even if not everyone knew immediately what to do with it, and typographers have begun to argue that typography is 'a fully developed medium of expression', possessing 'a complex grammar by which communication is possible' (Neuenschwander, 1993: 13, 31). Typographers everywhere are now exploring and expanding this new semiotic resource (cf. e.g. Triggs, 2003; 2005).

The voice is another example. For a time, there were uniform and institutionalized standards of educated propriety for public speech, and singular aesthetic ideals for good elocution in acting and for the *bel canto* style of classical singing. This of course never resulted in complete uniformity. On the contrary, it allowed for subtle forms of individuality and distinction, more or less in the same way that the cut of apparently almost identical grey business suits can nevertheless signal subtle degrees of sartorial elegance and finesse. Then amplification came along, allowing actors and singers to develop their own, immediately recognizable voices. In the course of less than a century, voices such as those of Lauren Bacall, Marilyn Monroe, Jimmy Stewart, Marlon Brando and others built a new semiotic resource, a new language of the voice, as did the singing voices of Ray Charles, Bob Dylan, Nina Simone and Astrud Gilberto, to name but a few.

How do such new semiotic resources develop? Let us demonstrate this through one example, the voice of Marlon Brando in *The Godfather*. It is a voice which is (1) rather high, (2) hoarse, (3) articulated with a stiff jaw and almost closed mouth, and (4) soft, almost whispering. Brando used the affordances of these vocal characteristics to express his character of the Godfather. A high voice in men signifies power and dominance. In operas the tenor is the hero, and rock singers will usually sing about at least an octave higher than their normal speaking voice (the Lauren Bacall example earlier showed that with women it is the opposite). So Brando expressed the domineering side of the Godfather's character by reference to common experience, to something everyone could observe about the pitch range in men's and women's voices. In addition, his voice was hoarse, rough, and this literal, physical roughness could then become a metaphor, expressing a more figurative roughness – the roughness, harshness and unforgivingness of the Godfather's character. Brando also did not open his mouth very much and articulated his front vowels rather far back. In other words, he held back, and this literal holding back could then become a metaphor for a figurative holding back that made it hard to tell what he was really thinking and what he was likely to do. And as a final touch, it is a common experience that people will whisper for conspirational reasons, or in intimate situations, and so Brando's whisper could endow his unforgiving and closed character with a disturbingly sensual attraction.

In short, building a meaning potential for a new semiotic resource can be done by appealing to common experiences and by means of experiential metaphors in which concrete physical qualities of the signifier come to stand for more abstract meanings, values and identities. Our account of this approach to making meaning is inspired by the metaphor theory of Lakoff and Johnson, who argue that metaphors are understood on the basis of concrete experiences: 'No metaphor can ever be comprehended or even adequately represented independently of its experiential basis' (1980: 19).

But there is another source of meaning – connotation. In connotation, as we define it here (in earlier work we also used the term 'provenance'), a signifier is imported from a particular domain where it has been well established, so to speak, into another domain where it has until then not been used. In that new domain it then comes to stand for the meanings, values and identities that people in this *new* domain would associate with the domain from which they have imported the signifier. Dialects are a good example here. In the era of semiotic uniformity, they had signalled more or less permanent, stable identities such as origin and class, and they often stigmatized speakers. To upper-middle-class city dwellers, country dialects were backward, working-class dialects were inferior, and foreign accents either suspect or funny. Dialects and accents carried the kind of connotations that Barthes (1973) had called 'myths' and referred to with terms such as 'Italian-ness', a term meant to encompass the stereotypes and values popular culture would typically associate with Italy. In Hollywood films, dialects soon became important signifiers. As one Hollywood manual of scriptwriting of the 1950s put it (Herman, 1952: 198):

> Dialect is as revelatory as make-up, as picturesque as costume, as characteristic as gestures, as identifiable as physical disabilities, and as dramatically effective as facial expressions.

Thus dialects lost their ties with specific places or social groups and became a new medium of expression, based on cultural connotation. Speaking 'broad Australian', for instance, was no longer a matter of destiny, indexing the milieu in which you happened to be born, but became an identity choice – a choice as to how much to associate yourself with 'Aussie' values and lifestyles. In the postmodern era, this principle of cultural connotation also extends to the iconic voices of key actors and singers, which now began to be understood, not on the basis of their vocal characteristics, but holistically, and on the basis of the movie roles and songs in which they had been used.

Much the same line of reasoning can be applied to our other example, typography. In the Amnesty poster, for instance, the typewriter font can be understood on the basis of a cultural connotation, of 'where it comes from' – from an old, battered typewriter, used by someone without access to a computer, somewhere in the Third World, perhaps – and this then gives the text the quality of an authentic document. But experiential metaphor also plays a role here – there is a deliberate irregularity in the way letterforms are spaced and placed on the baseline. Typographers will often use irregularity to signify an unwillingness to produce neat, regular forms, which, in context, can come to mean 'unconventionality', 'playfulness', 'rebellion', 'a lack of discipline', and so on. Metaphors like this are based on what the letterforms literally are (irregular), and on what we know about why they might have been produced (e.g. to signify unconventionality, rebellion or playfulness), or how this has happened (e.g. with leaking pens, or battered typewriters).

We can now distinguish two types of semiotic resources. 'Modes' are semiotic resources that have been regulated by normative discourses, whether explicitly or not. They provide templates for semiotic production which are not closely tied to particular modes of expression. Such templates can be schemas that leave much room for interpretation and creation (for example the chord schemas jazz musicians use to improvise) or scripts that leave less room for interpretation (for example musical scores or screenplays). However, both will still leave room for the kind of meanings that are made in production, the timbres of the musical instruments used by the jazz musicians for instance, or the different ways in which the 'same' piece of classical music might be arranged for different instruments, or interpreted by different conductors.

'Media' are semiotic resources that are less systematically organized and rely on cultural connotation and experiential metaphor to make meaning. We can therefore use the term 'medium' not just in its technical sense (television, the internet), but also in a much wider sense that also encompasses the way artists use it when they say that their medium is 'oils on canvas' or 'acrylics on board'. 'Media' are less governed by normative discourses, at least at the present time, although what needs to be part of the design and what can be left up to production will almost always be regulated by normative discourses.

Although 'media' can be used to express discourses, they seem to be particularly apt for the expression of identity, and it is not always easy to separate the two. In the Gwen Stefani song 'Bubble Pop Electric', a 1950s teenage date is evoked ('Drive-in movie. Drive in move me'). The setting, that era of 'penny loafers and poodle skirts', and the impatient anticipation of 'petting' in the backseat, is portrayed not only by the lyrics, but also by the timbre of Stefani's voice, which alternates between seduction, as she addresses her boyfriend in a low, breathy voice ('Tonight I'm falling, won't you catch me'), and teenage pop culture, as she repeats the words 'Bubble Pop Electric' in a higher, tenser voice with a somewhat artificial, 'electric' sheen. But that combination of innocence and seduction also creates a complex multi-dimensioned identity for the character the song evokes.

In our book *Multimodal Discourse* (2000) we distinguished a fourth layer, besides 'discourse', 'production' and 'design'. We called it 'distribution', and defined it as the technical 're-coding' of a semiotic production for purposes of distribution or preservation. But although there are domains in which technology does just that – recording and/or broadcasting an already complete semiotic product without adding anything new to it – in many other cases it is becoming increasingly difficult to separate 'distribution' from either design or production. The gramophone, for instance, was invented as a medium for reproduction, but it was later adopted by DJs to become a medium for 'production', a kind of musical instrument, a new semiotic resource. There are many other examples in which the material affordances of technologies designed to just distribute and reproduce have been exploited and developed as a semiotic resource.

In the case of semiotic software, normative discourses for the use of semiotic modes such as layout, typography and colour are built into the software. PowerPoint for instance provides layout designs of precisely the kind we have discussed previously in the chapter. Although it is perfectly possible on PowerPoint to create centre-margin designs, the handful of basic designs presented as the default choice in PowerPoint 2003 and 2007 favour 'polarized' structures over centre-margin structures. Thus PowerPoint builds in a normative preference for polarized structures, and this will no doubt result in more frequent use of this structure, especially since PowerPoint presentations are often put together in a hurry. The study of such 'built-in' normative discourses should become an important part of the study of semiotic resources, their meaning potentials and their actual uses.

RECAPITULATION

- **Affordance**
  Affordances (Gibson, 1979) are the potential uses of a given object, stemming from the perceivable properties of the object. Because perception is selective, depending on the needs and interests of the perceivers, different perceivers will notice different affordances. But those that remain unnoticed will continue to exist objectively, latent in the object, waiting to be discovered.
- **Arbitrary**
  The term 'arbitrary' is used of a sign which cannot be understood on the basis of some kind of motivation, so that the signifier appears to have been allotted to the signified for no particular reason.
- **Connotation**
  Connotation occurs when a semiotic resource is imported from one domain into another where it is not normally used. It then stands for the ideas and values which those who import the resource will associate with the domain from which they have imported it. Connotative signs will generally signify ideas, values and identities, rather than refer to concrete people, places and things, and are therefore a particularly important aspect of semiotic inquiry. They are also typical of the way meanings are made in the 'production' layer.
- **Design**
  A design is a format or template for embedding discourses in specific social contexts, and adds to the discourse a communicative purpose and a set of relations between the participants in the communication. Any given design can be realized by means of different semiotic resources or combinations of semiotic resources.
- **Discourse**
  A discourse is a socially constructed knowledge about some aspect of reality that can drawn upon when that aspect of reality is to be represented in texts or communicative events. There may be different, competing discourses representing the same aspect of reality, including and excluding different things, and serving different interests.
- **Distribution**
  Distribution refers to the way semiotic texts and communicative events can be technically re-coded for purposes of distribution and preservation. However, these means of distribution and preservation will also often become means for the production of meaning.

- **Experiential metaphor**
  A metaphor is understanding one thing in terms of another with which it has a relation of (partial) similarity. According to Lakoff and Johnson, our understanding of the world is based on metaphors. Experiential metaphors allow us to understand complex and abstract ideas on the basis of our concrete experiences. In social semiotics, an experiential metaphor is one of the ways in which a sign can be motivated, and is typical of the way meanings are made in the 'production' layer.

- **Interest**
  The term 'interest' denotes the reasons why a sign-maker or sign-making institution chooses particular signifiers to communicate particular signifieds. These reasons can include the immediate communication situation and its specific exigencies and the type of communication in which the sign-making takes places, as well as its broader social and cultural environment. It has thus both an immediate and specific and a broader social and cultural dimension.

- **Meaning potential**
  A meaning potential is the totality of meanings that can be expressed by and through a given semiotic resource, as based on past documented or collectively remembered uses of the resource.

- **Medium**
  A medium is a particular material or physical phenomenon that has been drawn into social communication and expression.

- **Mode**
  A mode is a semiotic resource for creating designs, for instance a language or visual composition. It is usually not tied to a specific material realization. Modes need to be defined in relation to their historical and cultural contexts. The mode of visual composition, for instance, might either be defined to include all the compositional schemas that have been developed within the last six hundred years of Western visual arts, or, more narrowly, as the compositional schemas possible with PowerPoint.

- **Motivated**
  The term 'motivated' is used of a signifier which is chosen by a sign-maker or sign-making institution as an apt signifier to signify a particular signified, for instance because it resembles the signified in some aspect, or because it can be associated with the signifier in some other way. Connotations and experiential metaphors are always motivated.

- **Multimodal discourse analysis**
  Multimodal discourse analysis is the analysis of multimodal texts or communicative events. In the approach presented in this chapter it involves three or four layers of analysis – discourse, design, production and distribution.

- **Multimodality**
  Multimodality is the phenomenon that texts and communicative events make use of a range of means of expression. Speech typically goes together with facial expressions, gestures, posture and self-presentation through dress and grooming, whereas writing goes together with layout, typography, visual illustration, etc.

- **Normative discourse**
  Normative discourses are socially constructed knowledges about the way semiotic resources should be used in specific social and cultural contexts. They take different forms in different contexts: prescriptive authoritative rules; expert advice; role modeling; and today also the preferences built into semiotic software. They can be communicated through different kinds of texts: regulations; magazine articles; training and teaching courses; or informal conversations – to mention just a few possibilities.

- **Production**
  Production refers to the way actual physical phenomena or materials are used to realize designs. The use of particular materials or physical phenomena adds further meaning to those already implicit in the discourse and design. These meanings may express the qualities of the things to be represented, including emotive aspects, as well as the identity of the communicator (in the particular context).

- **Semiosis**
  A term for the creation of new meaning potentials.

- **Semiotic resource**
  Semiotic resources are the actions, materials and artifacts we use to communicate. They have a meaning potential that is based on their past documented or collectively remembered uses, and a set of affordances that is based on their possible uses. In concrete social contexts their use is governed by normative discourses, though such discourses will allow different degrees of freedom in different contexts.

- **Signified**
  The particular meaning communicated by a signifier.
- **Signifier**
  A specific perceivable (visible, audible, tactile) physical object or event used for the purpose of communicating a particular signified.
- **Social semiotics**
  The study of semiotic resources and the way they are used in the production and interpretation of multimodal texts and communicative events.

FURTHER READING

The approach described in this chapter condenses theories and methods developed by the authors in a range of publications. Although this work draws on a variety of references, the first step in further reading would be to explore the authors' work in greater detail, through the references below. This should then be followed up by an exploration of the sources they acknowledge in their work.

Hodge, R. and Kress, G. (1988) *Social Semiotics*. Oxford: Polity.
Building on their earlier work in critical linguistics, this book introduced the social semiotic approach to multimodal discourse analysis, and placed it in the context of the 'founding fathers' of semiotics.

Kress, G. and van Leeuwen, T. (2001) *Multimodal Discourse – The Modes and Media of Contemporary Communication*. London: Arnold.
This book first developed the framework that underpins this chapter, describing multimodal communication as combining 'discourse', 'design', 'production' and 'distribution', and distinguishing between 'modes' and 'media'.

van Leeuwen, T. (2005) *Introducing Social Semiotics*. London: Routledge.
This book begins by discussing a number of key semiotic concepts, then presents a social semiotic approach to the concepts of discourse, genre, style and modality, and finally explains four different approaches to the analysis of multimodal texts.

Kress, G. (2010) *Multimodality*. London: Routledge.
In this book Kress integrates and extends more than twenty years of research in a definitive statement of his approach to multimodal discourse analysis, revisiting many of the concepts discussed in this chapter.

ONLINE READING

The following articles are available at www.sagepub.co.uk/discoursestudies.

Martinec, R. and Salway, A. (2005) 'A system for image-text relations in new (and old) media', *Visual Communication*, 4(3): 337–371.
O'Halloran, K. (2008)'Systemic functional-multimodal discourse analysis (SF-MDA): constructing ideational meaning using language and visual imagery', *Visual Communication* 7(4): 443–474.
Iedema, R. (2003)'Multimodality, resemiotization: extending the analysis of discourse as multi-semiotic practice', *Visual Communication* 2(1): 29–57.

REFERENCES

Ariès, P. (1973) *Centuries of Childhood*. Harmondsworth: Penguin.
Bacall, L. (1979) *Lauren Bacall by Myself*. London: Jonathan Cape.

Baldry, A.J. and Thibault, P. (2006) *Multimodal Transcription and Analysis*. London: Equinox.

Barthes, R. (1967) *Elements of Semiotics*. London: Jonathan Cape.

Barthes, R. (1973) *Mythologies*. London: Fontana.

Barthes, R. (1977) *Image-Music-Text*. London: Fontana.

Barthes, R. (1983) *The System of Fashion*. New York: Hill and Wang.

Birdwhistell, R. (1973) *Kinesics and Context*. Harmondsworth: Penguin.

Briggs, R. (1994) The Bear. London: Julia MacRae.

Crystal, D. (1998) 'Towards a typographical linguistics'. *Type* (1): 72–3.

Fairclough, N. (1992) *Discourse and Social Change*. Cambridge: Polity.

Foucault, M. (1972) 'The order of discourse'. In C. Kramarae and N. Thorne (eds), *Language, Gender and Society*. Rowley, MA: Newbury House.

Foucault, M. (1979a) *The Archaeology of Knowledge*. London: Tavistock.

Foucault, M. (1979b) *Discipline and Punish: The Birth of the Prison*. Harmondsworth: Penguin.

Freud, S. (1973) *Introductory Lectures on Psychoanalysis*. Harmondsworth: Penguin.

Gibson, J.J. (1979) *The Ecological Approach to Visual Perception*. Boston, MA: Houghton Mifflin.

Goodwin, C. (2001) 'Practices of seeing visual analysis: an ethnomethodological approach'. In T. van Leeuwen and C. Jewitt (eds), *Handbook of Visual Analysis*. London: Sage.

Graddol, D. (1996) 'The semiotic construction of a wine label'. In S. Goodman and D. Graddol (eds), *Redesigning English: New Texts, New Identities*. London: Routledge.

Halliday, M.A.K. (1979) *Language as Social Semiotic*. London: Arnold.

Halliday, M.A.K. (1985) *An Introduction to Functional Grammar*. London: Arnold.

Herman, L. (1952*) A Practical Manual for Screen Playwriting for Theater and Television Films*. New York: New American Library.

Hodge, R. and Kress, G. (1988*) Social Semiotics*. Oxford: Polity.

Kress, G. and van Leeuwen, T. (2000) *Multimodal Discourse – The Modes and Media of Contemporary Communication*. London: Arnold.

Kress, G. and van Leeuwen, T. (2006) *Reading Images – The Grammar of Visual Design*. London: Routledge.

Lakoff, G. and Johnson, M. (1980) *Metaphors We Live By*. Chicago: University of Chicago Press.

Machin, D. and van Leeuwen, T. (2007) *Global Media Discourse*. London: Routledge.

Matejka, L. and Titunik, I.R. (eds) (1976) *Semiotics of Art: Prague School Contributions*. Cambridge, MA: MIT Press.

McLean, R. (2000) *Manual of Typography*. London: Thames and Hudson.

Mukařovský, J. (1977) *The Word and Verbal Art*. New Haven: Yale University Press.

Neuenschwander, B. (1993) *Letterwork – Creative Letterforms in Graphic Design*. London: Phaidon.

Ochs, E. (1979) 'Transcription as theory'. In E. Ochs and B.B.Schieffelin, (eds), *Developmental Pragmatics*. New York: Academic Press.

O'Halloran, K. (2004) *Mathematical Discourse – Language, Symbolism, and Visual Images*. London: Continuum.

Pittenger, R.E., Hockett, C.F., and Danehy, J.J. (1960) *The First Five Minutes*. Ithaca, NY: Martineau.

Scollon, R. and Wong Scollon, S. (2003) *Discourses in Place – Language in the Material World*. London: Routledge.

Siber, M. (2005) 'Visual literacy in the public space'. *Visual Communication* 4(1): 5–20.

Thibault, P. (1991) *Social Semiotics as Praxis: Social Meaning Making and Nabokov's 'Ada'*. Minneapolis: University of Minnesota Press.

Triggs, T. (2003) *Type Design: Radical Experimentation and Innovation*. London: Thames and Hudson.

Triggs, T. (2005) *The New Typography*. Special issue of *Visual Communication* 4(21).

van Dijk, T.A. (2009) 'Critical discourse studies: a socio-cognitive approach'. In R. Wodak and M. Meyer (eds), *Methods of Critical Discourse Analysis*. London: Sage.

van Leeuwen, T. (2005) *Introducing Social Semiotics*: London: Routledge.

Walker, S. (2000) *Typography and Language in Everyday Life: Prescriptions and Practices*. London: Longman.

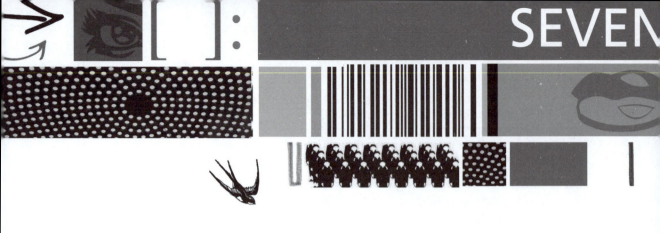

SEVEN

Discourse and Cognition

Arthur C. Graesser and Keith Millis

Discourse comprehension is a very rich, multilevel cognitive activity. Consider what it takes to read a simple news story. The words contain letters, pronunciation patterns, meanings, and sometimes emotional nuances. Sentences have syntactic composition, semantic ideas, and stylistic features. Deep comprehension requires the construction of referents of nouns, a discourse focus, presuppositions, and plausible inferences. The reader needs to distinguish old (given) versus new information in the discourse and to acknowledge implicitly what is shared knowledge among individuals in the discourse community (called the common ground). At more global levels, the reader needs to identify the category of the discourse (e.g., objective reports versus editorials), the rhetorical structure, perspectives of different people, and sometimes the attitude of the writer. The processing of all of these levels is effortlessly achieved at a rate of 150 to 400 words per minute by a proficient adult reader. It is simply astonishing that we can understand anything that we read given the many levels of language and discourse that must be mastered.

The various levels of oral conversation and printed text have been identified by discourse researchers over the years. Discourse researchers in the cognitive tradition typically include five levels (Graesser, Millis, and Zwaan, 1997; van Dijk, 2008; van Dijk and Kintsch, 1983):

1) *Surface code*   The words and syntax that are expressed verbatim.
2) *Textbase*   The semantic representation of the explicit text in a stripped down form that removes surface details with few if any semantic consequences. The core idea units are often called propositions.
3) *Situation model*   The referential content of what the discourse is about. It includes explicit and inferred people, objects, states, events, actions, processes, goals, and other types of content, as will be illustrated later.
4) *Genre and rhetorical structure*   The type of discourse and its structural composition. Example genres at a coarse-grain level are description, narration, exposition, and persuasion; a more fine-grained differentiation of narration would distinguish

folktales, romance novels, historical fiction, and many other subtypes. Each genre has its distinctive structural components, as in the case of setting+plot+moral in a folktale or claim+evidence in an argument.

5) *Pragmatic communication* The point or message that the speaker/writer wishes to convey to the listener/reader in a conversational turn, coherent message, or longer stretch of discourse in a specific social situation. This includes speech participants' intentions, attitudes, emotions, gestures, and joint action in addition to the explicit verbal expressions. The situated context includes the setting (time and place), the participants (communication roles, social status, identities, social relations), the actions being performed, and the mutual cognitions of participants.

Cognitive researchers have spent over forty years investigating these levels of representation and how they are constructed in the minds of both children and adults. They do this by adopting rigorous scientific methods that explore cognitive mechanisms during and after comprehension or production. The typical scientific experiments: a) manipulate the discourse, context, and instructions to the participant; b) collect various cognitive and behavioural measures (e.g., reading times, eye tracking, think-aloud protocols, word naming, ratings, recall, summarization, question answering); and c) measure or stimulate brain activities. The field of *discourse processes* analyses the multiple levels of discourse and investigates how the mind comprehends or produces the discourse by using the scientific method.

INFERENCES

It is important to emphasize that inferences are needed in order to construct most if not all of the five levels of discourse. Inferences are ideas that the reader generates and attaches to one of the five levels (typically levels 2 through to 5). Cognitive researchers have conducted experiments to determine which of these inferences are generated during discourse comprehension. For illustration, consider the following excerpt from the beginning of Ian Rankin's *A Good Hanging*:

It was the perfect murder.
  Perfect, that is so far as the Lothian and Borders Police were concerned. The murderer had telephoned in to confess, had then panicked and attempted to flee, only to be caught leaving the scene of the crime. End of story. (1998: 1)

The following four inferences would potentially be made at particular points in the text, and be part of level 3 (situation model)

a) *Superordinate goal*: 'The murderer wanted to turn himself into the police' is an inference when reading the clause *The murderer had telephoned in to confess.*
b) *Subordinate goal/action*: 'The murderer dialled a telephone number' is an inference when reading the clause *The murderer had telephoned in.*
c) *Causal antecedent*: 'The murderer changed his mind' is an inference when reading the clause *he then panicked.*
d) *Causal consequence*: 'The murderer tried to escape' is an inference when reading the clause *he then panicked.*

Of course, other inferences could probably be generated. For example, you probably inferred that you were reading a novel (perhaps a murder mystery) rather than a newspaper article, although this information was not given. These aspects would be part of level 4 (genre).

Cognitive researchers have investigated the classes of inferences that are routinely made during comprehension, versus those classes that are not typically made. According to the constructionist theory of Graesser, Singer and Trabasso (1994), for example, adult readers would normally generate inferences A and C, but not B and D. Inferences A and C are answers to why-questions, which are the foundational questions that guide discourse levels 3, 4, and 5. So when asked 'Why did the murderer telephone in?', a plausible answer would be 'in order to turn himself in to the police'. When asked 'Why did the murderer panic?', a plausible answer would be 'because he changed his mind and did not want to turn himself in to the police'. Inference B is an answer to a how-question ('How did the murderer telephone in?'), not a why-question. Therefore it would be mere ornamentation and not generated unless the reader had the idiosyncratic goal to monitor characters' precise actions. Inference D is an answer to a what-happened-next-question ('What happened after the murderer panicked?'), not a why-question, and would not theoretically be routinely generated.

These predictions of the constructionist theory are not universally accepted by cognitive researchers. For example, an embodied cognition framework would predict that subordinate actions (D) are constructed. According to the embodied cognition framework, the reader mentally simulates (i.e., generates, constructs) the actions of characters in the story world in rich detail (Glenberg and Kaschak, 2002). Resonance and minimalist models would predict that most of these inferences are not constructed unless there are surface and text-based features that will accurately trigger the correct memories at the right time (Lea et al., 2008; O'Brien et al., 1998). Discourse psychologists continue to hold heated debates and conduct experiments on what inferences are generated during normal comprehension.

BREAKDOWNS AND MISALIGNMENTS IN MULTILEVEL DISCOURSE

Comprehension is not always effortless, fast and satisfactory. When beginning readers struggle over individual words, reading slows down and deeper levels of comprehension are compromised. Even the most proficient adult reader will struggle with a technical expository text on an arcane topic, such as the ingredients of a prescription drug, a legal document, or installation instructions for a piece of computer software. A successful reader will be forced to enact deliberate, conscious, effortful, time-consuming strategies in order to repair or circumvent a reading component that is problematic.

Comprehension can break down at any of the five levels according to a multilevel framework (Pickering and Garrod, 2004). The cause of such a breakdown may be attributed to either deficits in the reader (i.e., a lack of knowledge or processing skill) or the discourse (e.g., incoherent text, unintelligible speech). Breakdowns can range from a temporary and minor irregularity that captures the comprehender's attention, to a full meltdown of comprehension. A breakdown at one level might negatively affect other levels. In addition, the comprehender may attempt to compensate for a breakdown at one level by using information from other discourse levels, world knowledge, or external sources (such as other people or technologies). For example, consider the scenarios below that illustrate breakdowns or minor glitches at various discourse levels, along with the resulting consequences.

- (Scenario 1) An immigrant arrives in the United States and does not understand the English language at all. A complete breakdown at discourse level 1 also blocks the deeper levels of 2–5.
- (Scenario 2) A child has trouble reading aloud a book on dinosaurs because she stumbles on all of the rare words. She has no trouble reading *The Princess and the Pea* because she has heard the story dozens of times. Memory and knowledge compensate for word deficits at level 1.
- (Scenario 3) Two homebuyers read a legal document that has lengthy sentences with embedded clauses and many logical operators (*and, or, not, if*). They have only a vague idea what the document explicitly states because of complex syntax and a dense textbase (a deficit at levels 1 and 2). However, the couple sign the contract because they understand the purpose of the document and trust the real estate agent. In this case, levels 4 and 5 circumvent the need to understand levels 1–3 completely.
- (Scenario 4) A father and son read the directions to assemble a new desk. They get into an argument on how to connect a handle to a drawer because they don't know which screw to attach to the handle. They have no problem understanding the words and textbase in the directions (levels 1 and 2). They also have no problem understanding the genre and purpose of the document (levels 4 and 5). However, they are confused about the screws in the situation model level (level 3). After a series of arguments, mental simulations, and trial and error problem solving, they manage to understand the assembly directions.
- (Scenario 5) A novelist loved reading French novels, but painfully recalls receiving a C in French literature when he was in college. Years later, while reading a book on French history, he realized in a flash what had been missing. He had a great memory and appreciation for the settings and plots of those French novels but never understood their deep meaning because he had missed the intentions and attitudes of the authors. A knowledge of French history was vital to reconstruct the authors' intent. In this case, discourse levels 1–4 were intact, but the novelist did not make it to level 5 while taking the course in college.

CONSTRAINTS AND PROCESSING STREAMS

The scenarios above illustrate how deficits in one or more discourse levels can have profound consequences on our comprehension and affiliated cognitive processes, such as attention, consciousness, memory, problem solving, and social interactions. Available cognitive research supports some generalizations about the processing order, interaction, coordination, compensatory mechanisms, and the constraints of the different levels of discourse comprehension. Here are some of these generalizations:

- **There are soft, statistical constraints rather than hard, brittle rules**. The information that accrues at the different levels gets built in and influences other levels probabilistically rather than according to hard and fast rules. In line with the construction-integration model developed by Kintsch (1998) there is a construction phase of activating code, memories, and rules to varying degrees, followed by an integration phase that probabilistically converges on a final representation through mutual constraint satisfaction.
- **There are bottom-up dependencies of meaning**. The ordering on depth is assumed to be 1 $\rightarrow$ 2 $\rightarrow$ 3 $\rightarrow$ 4 $\rightarrow$ 5. That is, the lower levels constrain the higher levels more than vice versa. However, the ordering is a tendency rather than being rigid because comprehension is a combination of bottom-up and top-down mechanisms. For example, the genre and rhetorical structure might help guide the construction of the textbase and situation model. Nevertheless, a partial analysis of levels 1–3 is needed to adequately construct the rhetorical structure.

- **Breakdowns at one level will propagate problems to deeper levels**. A breakdown at one level (L) leaves the previous levels intact but threatens the building of level L and the higher levels. As illustrated in Scenario 1, if the reader cannot construct a textbase at level 2, there will be problems constructing an adequate situation model, genre, and pragmatic communication, even though level 1 is intact. The individual in Scenario 5 made it through level 3, but had problems at level 4 and never achieved level 5 while in college. Comprehenders will normally achieve the deepest level of comprehension that is supported by the discourse, their knowledge, and their processing skill, but may get blocked at any level in the processing stream.

- **Novel information requires more processing effort than familiar and automatized components**. Novelty of information is a foundational cognitive dimension that attracts attention and effort and is salient in memory. It could be argued that rare words, the textbase level, and the situation model tend to have the highest density of novel information. In contrast, most aspects of levels 1, 4, and 5 will tend to have components that are frequently experienced and therefore well learned and automatized. Reading-time studies confirm that more processing time is allocated to rare words than high frequency words (Just and Carpenter, 1987), as well as to new information expressed in the textbase and situation model, to a greater extent than old information already mentioned (Haberlandt and Graesser, 1985; Millis, King and Kim, 2001). In contrast, levels of genre, rhetorical structure, and author characteristics are normally familiar structures that are invisible to the comprehender unless there are irregularities or breakdowns.

- **Attention, consciousness, and effort gravitate toward breakdowns and misalignment among levels**. Breakdowns at any level of analysis are likely to draw cognitive resources. Reading-time studies have shown that that extra processing time is allocated to pronouns that have unresolved or ambiguous referents (Rayner, 1998); to sentences that have breaks in cohesion (Gernsbacher, 1990); to sentences that have coherence breaks in the situation model (Zwaan and Radvansky, 1998); and to sentences that contradict ideas already established in the evolving situation model (O'Brien, Rizzella, Albrecht, and Halleran, 1998). Attention drifts toward sources of cognitive disequilibrium, such as obstacles, anomalies, discrepancies, contradictions, and cohesion gaps (Graesser, Lu, Olde, Cooper-Pye and Whitten, 2005).

- **Breakdowns may be repaired or circumvented by world knowledge, information at other discourse levels, or external sources**. The scenarios illustrate some compensatory mechanisms that will repair or circumvent the misfires. World knowledge fills in the lexical deficits in Scenario 2, whereas the syntax and textbase deficits in Scenario 3 are circumvented by the information in discourse levels 4 and 5. The gaps and misalignments in the situation model of Scenario 4 are rectified by extended conversations between father and son and by active problem solving.

The multilevel framework discussed so far provides a plausible sketch of the complexities of constructing meaning at different levels during discourse comprehension. In summary, there are multiple levels of meaning that will mutually, but asymmetrically, constrain each other. The components at each level are successfully built if the text is well composed and a reader has the prerequisite background knowledge and processing skills. However, there will be periodic problems that will range from minor misalignments and comprehension difficulties to comprehension breakdowns. These irregularities are magnets for attention which will sometimes trigger the compensatory mechanisms that can repair or circumvent the problems.

DISCOURSE COGNITION EMBRACES CORPUS ANALYSIS AND COMPUTATIONAL LINGUISTICS

Discourse is ubiquitous in the daily activities of members of a culture so there are millions of minutes to learn and to hone the relevant discourse skills. A word, syntactic structure, genre or other discourse component is assumed to be automatized and quickly processed after extensive experience. In contrast, the more novel components are time-consuming, as discussed in the previous section. In order to get a more precise handle on discourse cognition, researchers in the cognitive area have recognized that it is essential for the researcher to put together some record of the language and discourse that the community frequently experiences. This need is filled by researchers in the field of *corpus linguistics.* Corpus linguists will systematically analyse a large body of naturalistic texts or spoken discourse (called a *corpus*) along various dimensions of language and discourse. The discourse corpus is analysed by counting the frequency and distribution of discourse elements, categories, features, sequences, global patterns, or combinations of these linguistic/discourse entities. Advances in corpus linguistics are now mainstream in cognitive science and discourse processing.

The corpora analysed by researchers in discourse cognition are normally quite large, so computers are needed to systematically analyse the printed texts or transcribed oral conversations. During the last decade there have been some revolutionary advances in automating the interpretation of language, discourse, and text on computers. *Computational linguistics* is a hybrid field that integrates computer science, theoretical linguistics, and statistical analyses on discourse corpora. Computers are now able to extract information from texts with a degree of accuracy that can convince some people that computers are indeed able to understand the meaning of language, at least to some degree and along some dimensions. For example, an automated essay grader has been developed that can grade essays just as reliably as experts in English composition (Landauer, Laham and Foltz, 2003). There is a system that can classify texts into different discourse genres on the basis of 67 different linguistic and discourse features (Biber, 1988). Some of these systems have direct relevance to medicine, mental health, and quality of life. For example, Pennebaker, Booth and Francis (2007) have developed a Linguistic Inquiry and Word Count (LIWC) system that will automatically analyse the words in narratives that are written by victims of traumatic events. Interestingly, the LIWC system can predict both how well the person will cope with the trauma and the number of visits the person made to a medical doctor. The Question Understanding Aid (QUAID, www.psyc.memphis.edu/quaid.html) identifies problematic survey questions that have difficult words, a complex syntax, or will overload the working memory (Graesser, Cai, Louwerse and Daniels, 2006). The questions that QUAID identifies as problematic have been shown to influence the patterns of eye movements and also to lower the reliability of humans answering questions on surveys. It should be noted that psychologists or discourse researchers developed all of these computer systems that can automatically analyse discourse.

One computer tool called Coh-Metrix (Graesser, McNamara, Louwerse and Cai, 2004, http://cohmetrix.memphis.edu) analyses language and discourse on levels 1 through 4. There are over 60 measures of discourse on the public website, whereas the internal research version has nearly 1,000 measures at various stages of testing. The Coh-Metrix tool is easy to use and free to the public. The user simply enters text in a window, clicks a button, and then the system produces dozens of measures of the text.

The primary focus of Coh-Metrix was originally on discourse cohesion and coherence, but eventually took on a large landscape of language and discourse measures. *Cohesion* is defined as characteristics of the explicit text that play some role in helping the reader to mentally connect ideas in the text. *Coherence* is defined as a cognitive representation that reflects the interaction between linguistic/discourse characteristics and world knowledge. Coh-Metrix was designed to move beyond standard readability formulas, such as Flesch-Kincaid Grade Level (Klare, 1974–1975), that rely exclusively on word length and sentence length to define text difficulty. Some Coh-Metrix measures refer to the characteristics of individual words, but the majority will scale texts on deeper levels that will analyse syntax, referential and semantic cohesion, dimensions of the situation model, and the rhetorical composition.

As an illustration of Coh-Metrix, consider the following passage on the drug *pseudo-ephedrine*. This popular medication helps those who periodically get nasal congestions from allergies, colds, or flu. However, it was once subject to abuse by drug addicts so the drug market had to seek substitutes. The public wanted to know about the uses, warnings, and side effects of this class of drugs and the associated substitutes. The passage below comes from the container label for one of the commercial drugs containing pseudoephedrine:

> Temporarily relieves nasal congestion due to the common cold, hay fever or other upper respiratory aller-gies, and nasal congestion associated with sinusitis. Temporarily relieves sinus congestion and pressure. Do not use if you are now taking a prescription monoamine oxidase inhibitor (MAOI) (certain drugs for depression, psychiatric, or emotional conditions, or Parkinson's disease), or for 2 weeks after stopping the MAOI drug.

When we submitted the passage to Coh-Metrix and recorded the scores on a number of metrics, we discovered that the passage would prove a challenge to most of the public. The Flesch-Kincaid readability score showed a 12-grade reading level, so members of the public who did not manage to graduate from high school would allegedly have trouble reading these instructions about the use and the warnings about pseudoephedrine. The word frequency scores were low for a number of words (monoamine, oxidase, inhibitor), which would create comprehension problems. The conceptual cohesion between successive sentences in the text was intermediate for referential cohesion and low for situation model coherence, whereas there was a high density of logical operators (*and, or, if, then, not*). This profile of measures supports the conclusion that readers would need to have high reasoning and verbal skills to comprehend the passage, so the information it sought to convey would not effectively reach major segments of the public.

This Coh-Metrix example illustrates the importance of integrating corpus linguistics and computational linguistics into research projects that investigate the cognitive foundations of discourse processing. An understanding of cognition requires a systematic analysis of discourse in the real world and the computational foundations for computing meaning. Researchers are also integrating neuroscience into their research projects, which is an exciting trend but beyond the scope of these researchers to address (see Schmalhofer and Perfetti, 2007). This is yet another sign that discourse cognition has fulfilled its time-honoured, explicit mission to be interdisciplinary. Nearly every major research project in contempo-rary discourse cognition involves a serious interdisciplinary collaboration with corpus lin-guistics, computational linguistics, and/or neuroscience.

THE CHALLENGES OF COMPREHENDING TECHNICAL TEXTS

Citizens in most cultures are expected to keep up with advances in science, technology, and other technical topics that are relevant to their jobs and daily lives. However, both children and adults have trouble comprehending technical expository text at deep levels even though they are skilled readers. A deep comprehension of technical text is a difficult challenge because the reader will have minimal knowledge of the technical terms, key conceptualizations, mental models, and other forms of background knowledge. Even those with the relevant background knowledge and general reading skills can struggle.

The challenges of comprehending technical text have been documented in studies that use tests which assess our understanding of the situation model. In one particular study on Newtonian physics (VanLehn et al., 2007), college students were assigned to one of three conditions: 1) to work on physics problems with an intelligent computer tutor (called AutoTutor, which will be discussed later); 2) to read a textbook on the same content for the same amount of time as the AutoTutor condition; or 3) to read nothing. Before and after training, there was a pre-test and a post-test with multiple choice questions that tested their understanding of deep physics knowledge. There were substantial learning gains from AutoTutor, which was positive news for its developers. A more surprising outcome, however, was that the post-test scores showed no learning gains from reading the textbook. The scores in the textbook condition did not differ from reading nothing at all. A similar finding was found on the topic of computer literacy and critical thinking on the scientific method (Graesser, Jeon and Dufty, 2008).

There are many reasons why deep knowledge does not routinely emerge from reading textbooks. These cannot be attributed to the use of poor textbooks because those chosen in all of the above studies were very popular (the physics text was on its 8th edition) or had been written by accomplished scientists. The reason is more likely to be attributed to readers' taking insufficient time and effort to construct deep and accurate situation models. However, that reason raises another question: why didn't the readers take the time and effort to accurately comprehend the material? Two reasons are most likely. First, the readers are not able to calibrate their comprehension with sufficient accuracy. Second, they did not use reading strategies that facilitate deep comprehension.

The notion that the comprehension calibration in adults is faulty has been confirmed in dozens of studies in discourse cognition (Maki, 1998). Comprehension calibration is measured by computing a correlation between 1) the readers' ratings of how well they comprehend a text and 2) scores on an objective test of text comprehension. The correlation is modest ($r = .27$), indicating that many readers do not have an accurate sense of when they are comprehending versus not comprehending the material. Discourse psychologists have documented many other findings that support the general conclusion that adult readers will routinely settle for a shallow standard of comprehension (Sanford and Sturt, 2002). Readers will often miss contradictions in text, unless the premises are prominently juxtaposed in the discourse. They will get fascinated with seductive details and interesting titbits (e.g., *Isaac*

Newton's mother wanted him to be a farmer) that will then distract them from the deep situation model (e.g., *force equals mass times acceleration*). Readers will also miss faulty presuppositions that obviously clash with prior knowledge. For example, consider this exchange in a classroom.

> Teacher: How many animals of each kind did Moses put on the Ark?
> Class (children, in unison): Two.
> Teacher: Ah hah. It was Noah, not Moses, who had animals on the Ark.

This *Moses illusion* illustrates that comprehenders may deeply monitor information in the discourse focus, but will usually gloss over the presupposed information (Van Oostendorp and Kok, 1990). They will adopt the assumption that the speaker/writer is expressing only true presuppositions, so this information will not be deeply scrutinized. It is frequently those comprehenders with a high background knowledge who will admit that they do not understand. This is because it takes knowledge to know what one does not know. Researchers who investigate metacognition (i.e., what people believe about their thinking processes) have been able to document many of these paradoxes and counterintuitive results (Hacker, Dunlosky and Graesser, 2009).

Readers' comprehension strategies are not usually pitched at deep standards of comprehension when the text is technical. Therefore, they will need to learn better strategies. One of the exciting trends in discourse cognition has been to develop learning environments and interventions to help students learn better comprehension strategies (McNamara, 2007). There are now strategies designed to improve: a) the comprehension of sentences and local text excerpts; b) the bridging and connecting of text constituents; c) the grounding of the text to personal experiences and everyday activities; d) mastery of the rhetorical structure and genre of text; e) social interaction with experts, tutors, and peers; and f) the processes of question asking, question answering, reflection, and summarization. One strategy, for example, is to encourage students to generate *self-explanations* of the text while reading. This is because self-explanations are known to improve comprehension (Chi, de Leeuw, Chiu and LaVancher, 1994; McNamara, 2004). That is, as the reader comprehends the text, sentence by sentence, the individual constructs explanations that can explain why events occur, why the author has expressed something, how ideas are connected, and how the material is related to the reader's prior knowledge and personal experiences. Comprehension strategy training has traditionally occurred in the classroom or through human tutoring, but recently has shifted to computer environments.

ELECTRONIC TEXTS, DISCOURSE AND MULTIMEDIA

It seems that we are doing more and more reading on digital displays, whether these are computers, cell phones, PDAs, laptop computers, e-book readers, or video monitors. What we are reading also appears to be more varied than the genres mentioned earlier: emails, instant messages and multimedia displays, as well as surfing the World Wide Web. The popularity of such gadgets certainly speaks of our desire to keep in contact with other people in addition to completing tasks more efficiently.

Technology is indeed changing the way that we read. More of what we read is presented on a digital display. There are obvious advantages to having discourse presented on a digital device. One of these is that through e-book and other portable devices, we can have a wealth of discourse available to us 24/7. For example, the *Kindle* system sold by Amazon. com uses WiFi technology to download thousands of books. Another advantage is that the technology can aid the reader in particular levels of comprehension. We can change the font size of text or look up a word's meaning by clicking on a dictionary tab. These would correspond to levels 1 (surface) and 2 (textbase), respectively. And there is no reason to stop at these levels. In the near future, there could be short interchanges between the e-book and the reader to assess whether the latter has formed an adequate situation model.

It is still too early to tell whether all of our paper-based books will be replaced by e-books. What we do know is that the cost of books versus eBooks is changing rapidly so it is impossible to say which is most economical. Aside from the costs, there is something familiar and soothing about holding a book and flipping through its pages, especially on a cold and rainy day spent sitting beside the fire. Some people, especially those with low vision, will have difficulty reading digital displays. If the contrast between the letters and background is not exactly right, then they will have trouble focusing and their eyes will easily get tired. Fortunately, vision specialists and researchers in psychology are teaming up with private industry to help solve these problems arising from reading text that is presented on digital displays. One solution here is called *visual syntactic text formatting*. Instead of presenting text in a regular paragraph form, the text is presented this way:

> You are reading
>   this sentence
> as formatted
> by visual-syntactic text
>   formatting.

Despite its odd appearance, there is growing evidence that this type of formatting reduces eye strain and increases comprehension (Walker, Schloss, Fletcher, Vogel and Walker, 2005). It appears to increase comprehension by helping the reader syntactically parse the sentence (level 1) so they can spend their mental resources on higher levels.

There are other technological means for helping us understand the written word. One is multimedia, where information is presented via different presentation modes (verbal, pictorial) and sensory modes (visual, auditory, and perhaps touch) that use different delivery systems (video, text, simulations, pictures). Information presented through such multimedia increases memory and comprehension, provided that the process does not produce an attention overload. One why that pictures (photographs, videos) facilitate memory is by increasing the number of methods that the information can be retrieved at a later time. For example, a student who is shown a diagram of a hydrogen atom would exhibit a better memory of this than a student who had read a verbal description of it. The student who sees the diagram would encode both its image and a verbal representation of it ('the nucleus is in the centre', 'electrons circle the nucleus', etc.), whereas the student who only reads the description may not produce a mental image. Therefore, the student who sees the diagram would have a greater chance of retrieving one of the representations at a later time (a verbal description or an image).

In addition to memory, multimedia can help readers achieve a deep understanding of the material available. Pictures, graphical displays, animation, and videos all have the potential to help readers achieve a deep, complete and accurate situation model of the accompanying text. Imagine reading a text on the inner workings of a computer: the CPU, XOR gates, bits, inputs and outputs, and so on. Readers might have trouble comprehending the complex temporal, causal, spatial, logical, and semantic relations which exist in such an intricate domain. However, many of these relations can be conveyed quite easily via nifty animation, a graph, or a simulation in which the user can control some parameter (e.g., a logic gate, the size of a memory) and observe the consequences.

Mayer (2005) has extensively studied how multimedia will affect comprehension, memory, and learning. He has generated sets of principles that specify how multimedia can increase learning based on how the information is selected, organized, and integrated. Although multimedia can help with comprehension by providing a semantically rich integrated experience, multimedia displays can also interfere with comprehension. For example, a series of static images that convey important functions might actually be better than an animation because the latter might occur too quickly for a viewer to apprehend all of the information (Ainsworth, 2008). In addition, there are split attention effects. This happens in PowerPoint presentations when a speaker is talking at the same time as a word-rich slide is being shown. The viewer's attention is thus being split between the speaker and the slide and this overloads the working memory, with the result that little of the information is being comprehended. Similar processes occur in multimedia displays if any one modality is overloaded at a critical moment.

Today we are living in the time of eLearning, when much of our learning, training, and education is being delivered through electronic means. In our old educational environment, students and co-workers would meet at a specified place and time to be instructed by a human teacher or boss. In the new environment, we can be instructed through a tutorial over the web that we can view at home or even on an iPhone while riding on the bus. Advocates of eLearning point to a future when learning is more student-centred, active, and engaged; not limited to a particular space and time; multimedia-rich; individualized; contextualized in realistic situations; problem-based (versus instruction-based); social; and opportunistic of portable computing devices. The teacher will therefore become a guide on the side rather than a sage on a stage.

The 'net' generation seem to be well-suited for such a future because they have grown up with the World Wide Web, instant messaging, cell phones, and video games (Gee, 2003). Indeed, some researchers in education, psychology, discourse processing, and Artificial Intelligence are teaming up with the gaming industry in an effort to create engaging educational games. They have noticed the vast appeal of massively multi-player on-line role-playing games (MMORPGs), where thousands of players will interact virtually (being represented by 'avatars') and simultaneously over the Web. In 2008, there were some 10,000,000 subscribers to *World of Warcraft*, a fantasy-based MMORPG. To the dismay of many parents, the average teenage gamer will play video games for around 20 hours per week, far longer than they will spend on academic homework. Consider the impact of having a deeply engrossing video game that teaches in-depth biology, chemistry, algebra, or political science concepts (Ritterfeld, Cody and Vorderer, 2009). Most parents would be thrilled if their son or daughter actually looked forward to doing their homework.

ANIMATED CONVERSATIONAL AGENTS

Virtual learning environments (educational games, simulations, multi-user virtual environments) are increasingly using animated pedagogical agents. Pedagogical agents are virtual entities that come in a variety of forms (e.g., people, plants, animals, insects, common objects) that can move (e.g., walk, point, gesture), communicate (speak, listen), show personality (e.g., rude, polite), simulate different cognitive states (e.g., learn, forget) and display emotions (e.g., surprise, happiness, scepticism). Because an 'agent' might be defined as any entity with a point of view, developers of learning environments have provided animated agents with a number of pedagogical roles or functions: teacher, tutor, student, expert, friend, on-looker, and so on (Baylor and Kim, 2005). In some learning environments, there might be a single animated agent, while in others there might be two or three or even more. These animated agents can communicate with their human user by asking and answering questions, but they can also communicate with each other. For example, a 'student agent' can model a task for the human user by holding a conversation with the 'teacher agent'. As one might expect, animated pedagogical agents can be very engaging to interact with, opening up a whole new world of possibilities. Moreover, discourse psychologists have played a central role in building and testing these conversational agents (Graesser, Jeon and Dufty, 2008; McNamara, 2007; Millis et al., 2009). One powerful way of advancing our understanding of conversation is to build an agent that can successfully communicate with humans and other agents.

Animated agents in learning environments can provide a natural and engaging interface for navigating the user (student) toward acquiring a deep understanding of the topic. As mentioned earlier, most readers will not know whether or not they truly understand what they are reading. Pedagogical agents can be used to challenge a reader's understanding so that incomplete knowledge and misconceptions can then be identified, addressed, and fixed. One example of a learning environment that has been successful in this endeavour is AutoTutor (Graesser, Jeon and Dufty, 2008; VanLehn et al., 2007). AutoTutor is a computerized intelligent tutor that helps students learn by holding a conversation in natural language. The AutoTutor agent poses problems to the user, assesses the quality and completeness of the answer, and guides the user in forming a complete answer by giving short feedback (positive, negative, neutral), hints, prompt queries to elicit a specific word, and pumps ('what else?'). AutoTutor also answers some types of student questions and provides summaries at various points in the dialogue. It relies on methods in computational linguistics to 'understand' the answers given by the human user. AutoTutor has so far been developed for science and technology topics, such as physics, biology, research ethics, computer literacy, research methods, and critical scientific thinking, and has been successful in increasing students' comprehension. Based on several studies, students interacting with AutoTutor scored nearly a letter grade above various control conditions on tests for comprehension and learning (Graesser et al., 2008). This is roughly double the effect size of most of the human tutors that students will interact with in middle school through to university settings.

The framework behind AutoTutor can suit many different types of goals in various learning environments. One of these is an educational game called *Operation ARIES!*, which is currently being produced. *ARIES* is an acronym for **A**cquiring **R**esearch and **I**nvestigative and **E**valuative **S**kills (Millis et al., 2009). The learning objective of *Operation ARIES!* is for teaching students how to critically evaluate research found in the media. A central key to the storyline behind the game is that aliens from the Aries constellation are discreetly trying to confuse human beings about the scientific method by publishing flawed research. In the first level of the game, the human student needs to complete a science course by reading an online textbook about research. The human is given the opportunity to test out each chapter by taking a 'challenge' multiple-choice test, or by waiting until after the chapter has been read to be tested. At this point in the game there are two animated agents: Dr Quinn, who is the teacher, and Glass Tealman, who is a student peer also taking the course.

After the human player has answered a multiple choice question, there will be a brief conversation among the three agents: the player, Dr Quinn, and Glass. These are called *trialogs* and are orchestrated by a modified version of AutoTutor. The purpose of these trialogs is to increase student learning through discourse and to help the student regulate their own learning in a fashion that is aligned with their own level of knowledge. When performance on the test questions indicates that the student has a low knowledge of the test topic, the human will watch Dr Quinn engage Glass in a tutorial dialogue. There is evidence that low knowledge students can be helped by watching others interact (Craig, Sullins, Witherspoon and Gholson, 2006). When performance indicates a moderate depth of knowledge, Dr Quinn will then engage the human student in a brief tutorial dialogue, very similar to the original AutoTutor. Finally, when the human shows a high degree of knowledge, she will be asked to teach Glass. That is to say, one way to help good students learn even more is to have them teach other students or agents.

Table 7.1 shows an example trialog of this last condition in which the human teaches a peer agent. The topic is dependent variables, which are the measured outcomes in an experiment. Glass asks Amanda (a real psychology undergraduate) for help in defining 'dependent variable'. The system wants Amanda to say that 1) dependent variables are measured and 2) they depend on the independent variable (the variable manipulated by the experimenter). Amanda indicates that she knows 2) but not 1) in her first two contributions. Glass tries to get her to say 'measured' by supplying her with a prompt, but she fails to do so, leading Dr Quinn to interrupt with the correct answer. After a hint is supplied by Glass, Amanda finally articulates the desired idea, namely that the experimenter measures the dependent variable.

One might argue that the dialogue is not perfect, and a little clunky. However, these types of interactions encourage students to perform a number of processes that are known to

Table 7.1 Example trialog (Glass = animated student, Dr Quinn = teacher, Amanda = human student)

GLASS:	I think I'm confusing independent and dependent variables. Amanda, what is a dependent variable again?
AMANDA:	A dependent variable is the variable that is affected by the independent variable.
GLASS:	Thinking about dependent variable variables makes me think about cause and effect relationships for some reason.
AMANDA:	The manipulation of the independent variable is the cause of the dependent variable.
GLASS:	I know the dependent variable isn't the variable that's manipulated. So, that means it must be the variable that is what?
AMANDA:	Controlled.
DR. QUINN:	Measured
GLASS:	Dependent variables have something to do with the data.
AMANDA:	They are what the experimenter measures the independent variable against.
DR. QUINN:	Brilliant!
GLASS:	I've got it. A dependent variable is the outcome that gets measured. These measurements depend on the groups that make up the independent variable.

increase comprehension. These include having the student use the desired vocabulary, generate explanations, discriminate relevant from irrelevant information, and address misconceptions. These processes target the surface, textbase and situation model levels of discourse. It should also be noted that Glass needs the human player's help, which will hopefully motivate the human to do well. Here the pragmatic level becomes relevant. That is, the human should be explicit in her contribution since she would assume Glass does not have the information that she does, and hence cannot assume a common ground. Indeed, it is an interesting question as to whether humans will assume similar pragmatic stances with animated agents as they do with fellow humans.

A sceptic may object that the conversational agents will ultimately prove to be a huge problem when they do not completely understand the human. We suspect this may be true when there are high expectations of precision and common ground. However, this is not the case when the content involves verbal elaboration rather than mathematical operations and when the student has little-to-moderate knowledge about the topic. The agent also has the option of hedging on how well it understands the student (e.g., 'I can understand much of what you say but please understand that I am not perfect and cannot be a mindreader'). The fundamental test of the pedagogical value of these conversational agents does not lie in their ability to comprehend perfectly, but rather in their comparisons to humans and in their ability to facilitate learning.

CONCLUSION

This chapter has reviewed recent research on discourse processing that takes a cognitive slant. Sufficient progress has been made in the fields of discourse processes, cognitive science, corpus linguistics, and computational linguistics to build detailed models of how discourse is comprehended and produced at multiple levels: the surface code, the textbase, the situation model, genre and rhetorical structure, and pragmatic communication. These models are formulated and tested by collecting empirical data with rigorous scientific methodologies. Many of these levels are sufficiently well specified to automate them on computers. The computational models have evolved to the point of building useful computer technologies, such as essay graders, text analysers (that go well beyond readability formulae), automated conversational tutors, and multiparty interactive games. Researchers in discourse cognition have continued their interdisciplinary tradition of embracing the insights and methodologies of other fields, most recently in corpus linguistics, computational linguistics, education, multimedia, conversational agents, and neuroscience. Given the dramatic changes to the field that have occurred during the last decade, it is difficult to forecast what breakthroughs will emerge during the next ten years. However, the interdisciplinary stance of those in discourse cognition gives us every reason to remain optimistic.

NOTE

Acknowledgements go to the funders of our research on reading comprehension and discourse processing, including the National Science Foundation (ITR 0325428, ITR 0325428, REESE 0633918), the Institute for Education Sciences (IES R3056020018-02, R305H050169, R305B070349, R305A080589), and the DoD Multidisciplinary University Research Initiative (MURI) administered by ONR under grant N00014-00-1-0600. Requests for reprints should be sent to Art Graesser, Institute for Intelligent Systems, 365 Innovation Drive, University of Memphis, Memphis, TN 38152.

FURTHER READING

The following is a list of books in which the interested reader may learn more about the topics touched upon in this chapter.

Graesser, A.C., Gernsbacher, M.A. and Goldman, S.R. (eds) (2003) *Handbook of Discourse Processes*. Mahwah, NJ: Erlbaum. This work provides a nice overview of contemporary work on discourse processes, including literary, educational, spoken, written, and computer-mediated discourse. The book also presents different theories, perspectives and methodologies used by a set of interdisciplinary researchers.

Schmalhofer, P. and Perfetti, C. (eds) (2007) *Higher Level Language Processes in the Brain: Inferences and Comprehension Processes*. Mahwah, NJ: Erlbaum.
The book elaborates on the different levels of comprehension that begin this chapter, in particular the textbase and the situation model. It also emphasizes recent research on the underlying neural representations that support them.

McNamara, D.S. (ed.) (2007) *Reading Strategies*. Mahwah, NJ: Erlbaum.
In order to gain deep understanding of tough material, readers use several different types of reading strategies, such as self-explanation, reviewing, and asking questions. A reader who would like to know more about current theory, interventions and technologies regarding reading strategies will find this book useful.

Spector, J.M., Merrill, M.D., van Merriënboer, J.J.G. and Driscoll, M.P. (eds) (2008) *Handbook of Research on Educational Communications and Technology*. London: Taylor & Francis.
The handbook examines emerging information and communication technologies (ICT) that are becoming more relevant as we progress through the digital age. It contains sections on historical foundations, instructional and learning strategies, tools and technologies, models of learning, design and development, and methodological issues.

Ritterfeld, U., Cody, M. and Vorderer, P. (eds) (2009) *Serious Games: Mechanisms and Effects*. Mahwah, NJ: Routledge, Taylor and Francis.

Serious games are interactive computer games that are designed to teach skills and content. This book explores psychological and social mechanisms related to serious games, summarizes research on their effectiveness, and discusses their promises and limitations in educational settings.

ONLINE READING

The following articles are available at www.sagepub.co.uk/discoursestudies.

Graesser, A.C. (2006) 'Views from a cognitive scientist: Cognitive representations underlying discourse are sometimes social', *Discourse Studies*, 8, 59–66.

Wiley, J., Goldman, S.R., Graesser, A.C., Sanchez, C.A., Ash, I.K. and Hemmerich, J.A. (2009) 'Source evaluation, comprehension, and learning in Internet science inquiry tasks', *American Educational Research Journal*, 46, 1060–1106.

REFERENCES

Ainsworth, S. (2008) 'How do animations influence learning?' In D.H. Robinson and G. Schraw (eds), *Recent Innovations on Educational Technologies that Facilitate Student Learning*. Charlotte, NC: Information Age.

Baylor, A.L. and Kim, Y. (2005) 'Simulating instructional roles through pedagogical agents'. *International Journal of Artificial Intelligence in Education, 15*: 95–115.

Biber, D. (1988) *Variation across Speech and Writing*. Cambridge: Cambridge University Press.

Biber, D., Conrad, S. and Reppen, R. (1998) *Corpus Linguistics: Investigating Language Structure and Use*. Cambridge: Cambridge University Press.

Chi, M.T.H., de Leeuw, N., Chiu, M. and LaVancher, C. (1994) 'Eliciting self-explanation improves understanding'. *Cognitive Science, 18*: 439–77.

Conrad, F.G. and Schober, M.F. (eds) (2007) *Envisioning the Survey Interview of the Future*. New York: Wiley.

Craig, S.D., Sullins, J., Witherspoon, A. and Gholson, B. (2006) 'Deep-level reasoning questions effect: the role of dialog and deep-level reasoning questions during vicarious learning'. *Cognition and Instruction, 24*: 565–91.

de Vega, M., Glenberg, A.M. and Graesser, A.C. (eds) (2008) *Symbols and Embodiment: Debates on Meaning and Cognition*. Oxford: Oxford University Press.

Gee, J.P. (2003) *what Video Games Have to Teach Us About Learning and Literacy*. New York: Palgrave/Macmillan.

Gernsbacher, M.A. (1990) *Language Comprehension as Structure Building*. Hillsdale, NJ: Erlbaum.

Glenberg, A.M. and Kaschak, M.P. (2002) 'Grounding language in action'. *Psychonomic Bulletin and Review, 9*: 558–65.

Graesser, A.C., Cai, Z., Louwerse, M. and Daniels, F. (2006) 'Question Understanding Aid (QUAID): A web facility that helps survey methodologists improve the comprehensibility of questions'. *Public Opinion Quarterly, 70*: 3–22.

Graesser, A.C., Gernsbacher, M.A. and Goldman, S.R. (eds) (2003) *Handbook of Discourse Processes*. Mahwah, NJ: Erlbaum.

Graesser, A.C., Jeon, M. and Dufty, D. (2008) 'Agent technologies designed to facilitate interactive knowledge construction'. *Discourse Processes, 45*: 298–322.

Graesser, A.C., Lu, S., Olde, B.A., Cooper-Pye, E. and Whitten, S. (2005) 'Question asking and eye tracking during cognitive disequilibrium: comprehending illustrated texts on devices when the devices break down'. *Memory and Cognition, 33*: 1235–47.

Graesser, A.C., McNamara, D.S., Louwerse, M.M. and Cai, Z. (2004) 'Coh-Metrix: Analysis of text on cohesion and language'. *Behavioral Research Methods, Instruments, and Computers, 36*: 193–202.

Graesser, A.C., Millis, K.K. and Zwaan, R.A. (1997) 'Discourse comprehension'. *Annual Review of Psychology', 48*: 163–89.

Graesser, A.C., Singer, M. and Trabasso, T. (1994) 'Constructing inferences during narrative text comprehension'. *Psychological Review, 101*: 371–95.

Haberlandt, K.F. and Graesser, A.C. (1985) 'Component processes in text comprehension and some of their interactions'. *Journal of Experimental Psychology: General, 114:* 357–74.

Hacker, D.J., Dunlosky, J. and Graesser, A.C. (eds) (2009) *Handbook of Metacognition in Education*. Mahwah, NJ: Erlbaum/Taylor & Francis.

Jurafsky, D. and Martin, J.H. (2008) *Speech and Language Processing: An Introduction to Natural Language Processing, Computational Linguistics, and Speech Recognition*. Upper Saddle River, NJ: Prentice-Hall.

Just, M.A. and Carpenter, P.A. (1987) *The Psychology of Reading and Language Comprehension*. Boston, MA: Allyn & Bacon.

Kintsch, W. (1998) *Comprehension: A Paradigm for Cognition*. Cambridge: Cambridge University Press.

Klare, G.R. (1974–1975) 'Assessing readability'. *Reading Research Quarterly, 10*: 62–102.

Landauer, T., Laham, D. and Foltz, P.W. (2003) 'Automatic scoring and automation of essays with the Intelligent Essay Assessor'. In M.D. Shermis and J. Burstein (eds) *Automated Essay Scoring: A Cross-disciplinary Perspective* (pp. 87–112). Mahwah, NJ: Erlbaum.

Landauer, T., McNamara, D.S., Dennis, S. and Kintsch, W. (eds) (2007) *Handbook of Latent Semantic Analysis*. Mahwah, NJ: Erlbaum.

Lea, R.B., Rapp, D.N., Elfenbein, A., Mitchel, A. and Romine, R.S. (2008) 'Sweet silent thought: alliteration and resonance in poetry comprehension'. *Psychological Science, 19*: 709–15.

Maki, R.H. (1998) 'Test predictions over text material'. In D.J. Hacker, J. Dunlosky and A.C. Graesser (eds), *Metacognition in Educational Theory and Practice* (pp. 117–44). Mahwah, NJ: Erlbaum.

Mayer, R.E. (2005) *Multimedia Learning*. Cambridge: Cambridge University Press.

McNamara, D.S. (2004) 'SERT: Self-explanation reading training'. *Discourse Processes, 38*: 1–30.

McNamara, D.S. (ed.) (2007) *Reading Strategies*. Mahwah, NJ: Erlbaum.

McNamara, D.S., Levinstein, I.B. and Boonthum, C. (2004) 'iSTART: Interactive strategy trainer for active reading and thinking'. *Behavioral Research Methods, Instruments, and Computers, 36*: 222–33.

Millis et al. (2009).

Millis, K.K., King, A. and Kim, J. (2001) 'Updating situation models from descriptive texts: a test of the situational operator model'. *Discourse Processes, 30*: 201–36.

O'Brien, E.J., Rizzella, M.L., Albrecht, J.E. and Halleran, J.G. (1998) 'Updating a situation model: a memory-based text processing view'. *Journal of Experimental Psychology: Learning, Memory, & Cognition, 24*: 1200–10.

Pennebaker, J.W., Booth, R.J. and Francis, M.E. (2007) *Linguistic Inquiry and Word Count*. Austin, TX: LIWC.net (www.liwc.net).

Pickering, M. and Garrod, S. (2004) 'Toward a mechanistic psychology of dialogue'. *Behavioral and Brain Sciences, 27*: 169–226.

Rankin, I. (1998) *A Good Hanging*. London: Orion Books.

Rayner, K. (1998) 'Eye movements in reading and information processing: 20 years of research'. *Psychological Bulletin, 124*: 372–422.

Ritterfeld, U., Cody, M. and Vorderer, P. (eds) (2009) *Serious Games: Mechanisms and Effects*. Mahwah, NJ: Routledge/Taylor and Francis.

Sanford, A.J. and Sturt, P. (2002) 'Depth of processing in language comprehension: not noticing the evidence'. *Trends in Cognitive Sciences, 6*: 382–86.

Schmalhofer, P. and Perfetti, C. (eds) (2007) *Higher Level Language Processes in the Brain: Inferences and Comprehension Processes*. Mahwah, NJ: Erlbaum.

Snow, C. (2002) *Reading for Understanding: Toward an R&D Program in Reading Comprehension*. Santa Monica, CA: RAND Corporation.

Spector, J.M., Merrill, M.D., van Merriënboer, J.J.G. and Driscoll, M.P. (eds) (2008) *Handbook of Research on Educational Communications and Technology*. London: Taylor & Francis.

Spivey, M., Joanisse, M. and McRae, K. (eds) (2009) *Cambridge Handbook of Psycholinguistics*. Cambridge: Cambridge University Press.

Van Dijk, T.A. (2008) *Discourse and Context: A Socio-cognitive Approach*. New York: Cambridge University Press.

Van Dijk, T.A. and Kintsch, W. (1983) *Strategies of Discourse Comprehension*. New York: Academic.

VanLehn, K., Graesser, A.C., Jackson, G.T., Jordan, P., Olney, A. and Rose, C.P. (2007) 'When are tutorial dialogues more effective than reading?'. *Cognitive Science, 31*: 3–62.

Van Oostendorp, H. and Kok, I. (1990) 'Failing to notice errors in sentences'. *Language and Cognitive Processes, 5*: 105–13.

Walker, S., Schloss, P., Fletcher, C.R., Vogel, C.A. and Walker, R.C. (2005) 'Visual-syntactic text formatting: a new method to enhance online reading'. *Reading Online, 8(6)*. Posted May 2005: International Reading Association, Inc. ISSN 1096–1232.

Zwaan, R.A. and Radvansky, G.A. (1998) 'Situation models in language comprehension and memory'. *Psychological Bulletin, 123*: 162–85.

EIGHT

Discourse Pragmatics

Shoshana Blum-Kulka and Michal Hamo

PRAGMATIC THEORY

In the broadest sense, pragmatics is the study of linguistic communication in context: the choices users of language make and the process of meaning-making in social interaction. Language is the chief means by which people communicate, yet simply knowing the words and grammar of a language does not ensure successful communication. Words can mean more – or something other – than what they say. Their interpretation depends on a multiplicity of factors, including familiarity with the context, intonational cues and cultural assumptions. The same phrase may have different meanings on different occasions, and the same intention may be expressed by different linguistic means. Phenomena like these are the concern of pragmatics.

Historically, pragmatics originates in the school of *ordinary language philosophy* associated with the late writings of Ludwig Wittgenstein, and with John Austin, John Searle and H. Paul Grice. Work in this tradition encapsulated the key features of language as social action and offered specific analytic frameworks for understanding how language works.[1] These frameworks were later adopted by students of discourse and applied to the analysis of actual sequences of text and talk in context, rather than isolated utterances, as in classic pragmatics. Such research, subsumed here under *discourse pragmatics*, has often gone beyond the core pragmatic models and incorporated influences from other approaches.

[1]This line of thought has been continually developed by philosophers of language focusing on pragmatic theory (e.g., Kasher, 1998; Recanati, 2004).

Concurrently, interest in discourse from a gamut of other fields, such as linguistic anthropology, ethnography of communication, and interactional sociolinguistics, has been informed and inspired by the basic insights of pragmatics as a theory of language use.

In this chapter we discuss three seminal models from the core tradition of pragmatic research: Grice's theory of *implicatures*; Austin's and Searle's *speech act theory*; and Brown and Levinson's model of *politeness*. Our focus will be on the relevance of each model to *the analysis of discourse*, including the contribution of pragmatics to the study of cross-cultural communication, linguistic development and media discourse. Finally, we shall come back to issues of contact and contrast between pragmatics and other theories of language use.

GRICE'S THEORY OF MEANING

One of the basic philosophical insights about the nature of language use is offered by H. Paul Grice's (1957, 1968) definition of intentional communication. For Grice, intentional linguistic communication is the process by which a speaker, by saying X, wishes to communicate a specific communicative intent and achieves his or her goal when this intent is recognized by the hearer and becomes *mutual knowledge*. Grice's (1957, 1968) theory of meaning stresses that what the speaker says does not necessarily encode his or her communicative intent explicitly. Thus when I say 'The door is open' I may be inviting you to come in or I may be asking you to close the door. The choice between these and other pragmatic meanings in practice will be minimally a matter of pairing the words with the context in which they are uttered. Processing the words on the basis of linguistic knowledge alone will provide *sentence meaning* (providing the information that 'the door is open'); considering the *circumstances* of the utterance (along with other types of pragmatic knowledge, to be elaborated on below) will help in deciphering the *speaker meaning* (that is, deciding whether the utterance was meant as an invitation, a request or something else).[2] Pragmatic theory is concerned with explaining how interlocutors bridge the gap between sentence meanings and speaker meanings; hence its units of analysis are not sentences, which are verbal entities definable through linguistic theory, but rather *utterances*, which are units of communication in specific contexts.

The process by which interlocutors will arrive at speaker meanings necessarily involves inferencing. According to Grice (1975, 1989), communication is guided by a set of rational, universal principles and sub-principles (called *maxims*) which systematize the process of inferencing and ensure its success. All communication is based first and foremost on the general tacit assumption of cooperation: in Grice's words, in any talk exchange, interlocutors

---

[2] In early formulations Grice (1957) distinguished between sentence meaning and 'utterer's meaning'. He later introduced an intermediary level to bridge the gap between speaker meaning and sentence meaning, called 'applied timeless meaning of an utterance type', namely the usual meaning carried by the utterance independently of context (Grice, 1968). This level was labeled 'utterance meaning' in later formulations (Dascal, 1983).

will assume that all the participants will make their contribution 'such as required, at the stage at which it occurs, by the accepted purpose or direction of the talk exchange' (1975: 45). Furthermore, to ensure efficient communication, interlocutors will assume that all the participants will abide by the following four maxims: 1) the maxim of *quality*, whereby one does not say what one believes to be false, and that for which there is no adequate evidence; 2) the maxim of *quantity*, whereby conversational contributions need to be made neither more nor less informative than is required; 3) the maxim of *manner*, whereby speakers are required to avoid obscurity and ambiguity and be brief and orderly; and finally 4) the maxim of *relevance*, which Grice defines succinctly as 'make your contribution relevant' (1975: 45–6).

Grice is not suggesting that all of these principles should be strictly adhered to in all communication. His point is more subtle: these conversational norms serve as a set of inferential heuristics by which interlocutors can judge each other's contributions to the talk and make sense of what is being said. Consider the following exchange, recorded at the dinner-table of an Israeli middle-class family. Three children participate: Danny, 11.5 years old; Yuval, 9; and Yael, 7.

(1) Mother: Danny, do you have any homework?
     Danny: I've finished it already.
     Yael: Danny didn't answer Mommy's question.
     Yuval: He did, he did; and when he said that he's already done it, he saved her the next question.
     (Blum-Kulka, 1989: translated from Hebrew)

Taken literally, Danny's reply fails to answer his mother's question, and thus seems to violate the maxim of relevance. To an adult such infringements are hardly noticeable, since by social convention a parental query about having homework is bound to be interpreted as a check on performance. But to a younger child the inferencing needed is far from obvious, as evidenced by Yael's comment. Yuval, who is older, understands that a response may be relevant to what is *meant* rather than to what is *said*. Such *standard conversational implicatures*[3] are part and parcel of everyday communication. Instead of replying 'Fine' or 'Not so good' to a 'How are you?' query, one can just as easily reply 'I won the lottery' or 'I failed the test in pragmatics', and in either case the hearer will be able to infer the speaker's intention owing to his knowledge of the world and shared assumptions of cooperation and relevance.

Later *Neo-Gricean* theories have suggested different reformulations of the four maxims, either by positing one basic maxim to account for all inferences (relevance theory, Sperber and Wilson, 1986) or, more recently, by exploring the systemacity of inference that might be connected to linguistic structure (Ariel, 2008). Much theoretical work in pragmatics has continued to explore the relationship between literal meaning ('what is said') and inferred

---

[3]These types of implicatures are referred to as 'Group A' in Grice's (1975) classification of types of conversational implicatures; the label 'standard' for this group was introduced by Levinson (1983).

meaning ('what is meant') (e.g., Carston, 2002; Recanati, 2004). Some neo-Gricean theories explain why certain expressions have favoured interpretations arrived at by virtue of precedence. For example, in the case of scalar implicatures associated with the use of expressions such as *some* or *all*, an assertion of the lower ranking expression (*some*) implicates that the speaker is not in a position to assert the higher ranking one (*all*) – for if the speaker was in that position, he or she would, by the *quantity principle*, have asserted the stronger sentence, and not doing so would count as a violation (Levinson, 2000).

Grice is especially interested in *conversational implicatures* based on the intentional exploitation of the maxims: cases in which a speaker *blatantly violates* one of the maxims in order to imply something. Certain figures of speech, such as tautologies and irony (Grice's example is 'He is a good friend', said about a friend who has betrayed a secret), are extreme examples of *flouting* the maxims. A tautology like 'men are men' is a blatant violation of the maxim of quantity, and is informative only at the level of what might be implied – if it were uttered by a woman in reference to a man's behaviour, for example.

The intentional exploitation of maxims to generate meaning, and the potential risks it involves, are illustrated in the following quote from a newspaper interview with the then Israeli air force commander, Dan Halutz. Throughout the interview, Halutz fends off requests to address the moral, psychological and emotional aspects of air attacks on residential areas in the Gaza strip, while the interviewer persists through repeated questions. The interview ends with the following exchange:

(2) Q: A pilot drops a bomb and inadvertently kills children. Isn't it legitimate to ask the pilot how he feels as a result? Isn't it reasonable to expect him to ask himself that question? Isn't it reasonable to inquire if inside the air force this question was even asked?

A: No. This is a non-legitimate question and it's also not being asked. But if you still really want to know what I feel when I release a bomb, then I'll tell you: I feel a light blow to the aircraft, as a result of releasing the bomb. A second later it's gone, and that's it. This is what I feel.

(Levi-Barzilay, 23 August 2002; translated from Hebrew)

In his response, Halutz blatantly flouts two maxims: by using over-wording, repetitions and meta-comments before and after his answer, he violates the maxim of *quantity*. In his long pre-response he allows for a double reading of 'feel' as relating to both the emotional and physical dimensions ('if you really want to know what I feel'), but in the response itself he blatantly restricts his use of 'feel' to the physical dimension only, sidestepping the original question and violating the maxim of *relevance*. While it is clear from Halutz's response that it is an attempt to resolve the difficulty to answer a highly challenging question by inviting conversational implicatures (Weizman, 2008), the nature of the specific implicatures generated is ambiguous. Examining Halutz's full statement in the context of the entire sequence, one way of reading it is as a conversational implicature reiterating the explicit meta-communicative criticism that opens his reply, and as an indirect refusal to answer. In this reading, Halutz, being sarcastic, implies that a pilot's emotional state is a strictly private matter, and not a legitimate topic for public discussion, as pilots will focus on the mission they're carrying out and compartmentalize their personal thoughts. Note that Halutz generates this implicature while adhering to the *form* of a direct answer ('then I'll tell you'), perhaps as a way of avoiding the possibility of being sanctioned by the interviewer as non-responsive yet again. In this reading Halutz's response is a clear case of 'non-serious' use of language.

However, Halutz failed to realize that in light of the highly charged topic and his established public image as a detached 'analytic mind', the simpler and more readily available interpretation of his statement is that of generating a standard conversational implicature: namely, that had he any emotional reaction to report, he would not have restricted his response to physical sensations only – hence, he feels nothing. This interpretation was taken up by the newspaper, the media and the general public, leading to harsh criticism of Halutz as morally bankrupt and generating a 'talk scandal' (Ekström and Johansson, 2008), which was resumed three years later when Halutz was nominated the next IDF chief of staff. Repeated quotes of Halutz's statement were highly de-contextualized and focused solely on the single utterance 'a light blow to the aircraft', thus foreclosing the sarcastic meta-communicative dimension of his response. The phrase later became a cultural catchphrase, often evoked in discussions of military ethics and morality to this day.

As this example illustrates, the process of generating and inferencing implicatures is highly context-sensitive, and the application for Grice's maxims is *subject to contextual variation*. Expectations for the degree of informativeness, for example, will vary with the social roles of the participants and other features of the interactional setting. Furthermore, in many institutionalized asymmetrical encounters (teacher–student, therapist–patient, interviewer–interviewee) the degree of adherence to the maxims may by dictated by the party in power and ruled by institutional constraints. It is often the teacher, the therapist, or the interviewer who will pass judgment (sometimes by using metapragmatic comments) on whether the response to a question is relevant and informative enough, and failing to meet his or her expectations may carry serious implications.

The interpretation of the maxims is also *culture dependent*. Cultures may vary in their expectations of a degree of adherence to the maxims as required in different situations, as well as in the relative importance of each maxim. In the closely knit agricultural society of Madagascar, for example, all significant new information is considered a rare commodity. In this community a speaker is not necessarily required to meet the informational needs of his or her partner, and whether or not one is expected to 'be informative' at all will vary with the social situation and the type of information in question (Keenan Ochs, 1974).

SPEECH ACT THEORY

Grice's theory of meaning is concerned foremost with the ways in which interlocutors will recognize each other's communicative intentions; speech act theory is concerned with providing a systematic classification of such communicative intentions and the ways in which they are linguistically encoded in context.

The philosopher John L. Austin laid the foundations for what was to become known as standard speech act theory. In his book *How to Do Things with Words* (1962), Austin moves from a basic insight about the capacity of certain linguistic expressions to perform communicative acts to a general theory of communicative actions, namely *speech acts*. Austin first noted that certain expressions, such as 'I apologize' or 'I hereby christen this child', cannot be verified as either true or false, since their purpose is mainly to 'do' things with language. He termed such utterances *performatives*, to be distinguished from all other utterances. He further noted that to achieve their performative function as an apology or a warning, such utterances need to meet certain contextual conditions, called *felicity conditions* (or *appropriateness conditions*).

But Austin also went a step further: he realized that performing communicative acts was not limited to the given subset of utterances included under his original performatives, but was rather an inherent property of *every* utterance. Any utterance simultaneously performs at least two types of act: [4]

1) *Locutionary act*: the formulation of a sentence with a specific sense and reference. The locutionary act is what is *said*, typically containing a referring expression (such as 'John', 'the teacher', 'the government') and a predicating expression ('is getting married', 'left her job', 'will negotiate a peace treaty').
2) *Illocutionary act*: the performing of a communicative function, such as stating, questioning, commanding, promising, etc. The illocutionary act is what the speaker *does* in uttering a linguistic expression. For example, if a teacher says 'Open your books at page 20', the illocutionary act performed – the utterance's *illocutionary force* – is that of a directive (Austin, 1962).

Working from Austin's theories, John R. Searle (1969, 1975) went several steps further in classifying types of speech acts and systematizing the nature of the felicity conditions needed for their performance. Searle (1979) suggested five main types of illocutionary acts:

1) *Representatives*: utterances that describe some state of affairs by asserting, concluding, claiming, etc.
2) *Directives*: utterances used to get the hearer to do something, via acts like ordering, commanding, begging, requesting and asking (questions constituting a sub-class of directives).
3) *Commissives*: utterances that commit the hearer to doing something, and include acts like promising, vowing, and pledging alliance.
4) *Expressives*: acts used to express the psychological state of the hearer, by thanking, apologizing, congratulating and condoling.
5) *Declarations*: utterances which effect a change in some, often institutionalized, state of affairs. Paradigm examples are christening a baby, declaring peace, firing an employee, and excommunicating (the types of acts included originally in Austin's 'performatives').

Searle's classification however is far from being universally accepted. Some critics are mainly concerned with the principles of classification (Bach and Harnish, 1979), while

---

[4]Austin also posited a third type of act, called a *perlocutionary act*, which specifies the effects of the utterance on the hearer(s). Perlocutionary acts drew relatively little attention in speech act theorization, and they remain under-defined (see Gu, 1993, for a discussion).

others reject Searle's claim that speech acts operate by universal pragmatic principles, demonstrating the extent of cross-cultural variation in speech acts' conceptualization and modes of verbalization (e.g., Rosaldo, 1990).

Searle advocated that for any act of expression to be successful, it needs to meet its *specific contextual conditions*. These conditions are *constitutive* of the different illocutionary forces performable, and their realizations *vary systematically with the type of speech act performed*.

Searle proposed four such conditional parameters:

1) *Propositional content*: features of the semantic content of the utterance. For example, requests will usually contain a reference to the future, whereas apologies will typically refer to an act in the past.
2) *Preparatory conditions*: the necessary contextual features needed for the speech act to be performed, such as the ability of the hearer to perform a requested act (for directives), or the assumption that some offence has been committed (for apologies).
3) *Sincerity conditions*: the speaker's wants and beliefs, such as his wish that the hearer does the requested act (for requests), or his belief that an offence has been committed and recognized as such by the hearer (for apologies).
4) *Essential condition*: the convention by which the utterance is to count as an attempt to get the hearer to do something (for requests) or as an undertaking to remedy a social imbalance (for apologies).

These conditions demonstrate that the identification of speech acts in actual use relies on specific combinations of linguistic features (propositional content), contextual features (preparatory and sincerity conditions) and cultural conventions (essential condition). This way of thinking can be important in identifying the discursive manifestations of problematic speech acts like incitement, thus contributing to evaluating the social and moral implications of specific utterances (Kurzon, 1998).

Indirect speech acts

As Searle (1975) noted, indirectness is one of the most intriguing features of speech act performance. Whereas of course one may issue a request directly, specifying communicative intent and the nature of the act to be carried out in unambiguous terms ('Please close the door'), one may also attempt to achieve the same communicative intent indirectly by uttering any of the following:

(3) May I ask you to close the door?
(4) Could you please close the door?
(5) It seems a bit chilly in here.

Some indirect forms such as (3) and (4) are governed by language specific *conventions of use* (Morgan, 1978; Searle, 1975); thus in at least English, French, Spanish and Hebrew, a question regarding the hearer's ability to perform the act carries a requestive force, but only when phrased in a specific manner ('Can you close the window?' rather than 'Are you able to close the window?'; Blum-Kulka, 1989). Not all indirect forms are governed by such wording conventions: for instance, 'It's a bit cold in here', or 'It's very cold here', or 'It's freezing', though not equivalent semantically, all carry the same requestive pragmatic force potential. Hence we can distinguish between two types of indirectness in requests: *conventional indirectness* (as in examples (3) and (4)) and *non-conventional indirectness* (as in example (5)) (Blum-Kulka, 1989).

The interpretation of indirect speech acts seems to be closely tied to degree and type of conventionality. Thus *conventional indirectness* like that in (3) is inherently ambiguous; a requestive interpretation is part of the utterance's meaning potential, and is potentially co-present with the literal interpretation. On the other hand, in *non-conventional indirectness* as in example (5), the interpretation can be much more open-ended. An utterance such as 'I'm hungry', depending on the context, may be: coming from a beggar, a request for money; coming from a child at bed-time, a request for prolonged adult company; or, when said entering the dining room, an anticipatory statement for the gastronomic pleasures to come.

Research building on speech act theory has evolved in various directions. One major focus has been on the realization patterns of individual speech acts, including requests, apologies, complaints and compliments, in a widening range of languages (e.g., Ogiermann, 2009). An ongoing debate concerns the effectiveness of the various methods used in these studies: the 'armchair' method of analysing intuited and invented examples; the 'laboratory' method of eliciting data in controlled settings; and the 'field' method of analysing naturally occurring discourse (Jucker, 2009). A second focus, which is the subject of ongoing empirical research in psycholinguistics, is on the interpretation of indirectness, including conventional and non-conventional forms (e.g., Clark, 1992).

Another debate concerns the suitability of speech act theory to the analysis of sequences of interaction (Parret and Verschueren, 1992). Arguably, a discourse pragmatic perspective, applying speech act theory to the analysis of interaction, may contribute to the understanding of interaction, while at the same time offering important insights on speech act theory. This will be illustrated by the following example.

A discourse pragmatic perspective on speech acts: Negotiating meaning in context

(6) The following is an extract from a dinner-time conversation of an Israeli middle-class family. There are several dishes on the table. Gadi and Sara are husband and wife; also present are their two pre-adolescent sons and an observer.

44	Gadi:	What, what's the plan Sara?
45	Sara:	I don't know what this is.
46	Gadi:	No, the plan for, for food, [so I'll know if to prepare for myself
47	Sara:	[((there's)) no plan for food.
48	Gadi:	[that's the food?
49	Sara:	[I see that you're also, e:: carrying it out on your own, I can warm up for you
50	Gadi:	[no, I want to know what
51	Sara:	[or you can make for yourself.
52	Gadi:	Except for the rice, is everything else here on the table?
53	Sara:	Yes.

54 Gadi: Wonderful, great.
55 Sara: yes.
56 Gadi: So is it, is it OK if I go and prepare for myself, I mean
57 Sara: I refuse to respond to that. Especially about the the the is it OK, I refuse. ((both laugh))
   ∘is it OK.∘ Whatever I do, I'll probably still be his mother. ((in a tired tone))
(Weizman and Blum-Kulka, 1992)[5]

A full analysis of this sequence is beyond the scope of the present chapter; in the following we shall focus on several principles of discourse pragmatics it illustrates:

- **Discourse can be ambiguous and multi-layered**
  As typical of indirect speech acts, Gadi's utterance 'What's the plan?' (turn 44) is highly ambiguous: it may be meant as, at least, an information-seeking question, indirect criticism, an indirect request for food, or an indirect permission request to leave the table and prepare food. This ambiguity can be intentional, meant to balance Gadi's wishes with interpersonal considerations and avoid accountability.

  Gadi's individual goal of a permission request becomes clear in turn 56, but Sara's reaction in turn 57 indicates that the collective goal of the couple in this conversation remains fuzzy: are they negotiating a division of labour at the table, or gender and power? Accordingly, Gadi and Sara may understand, or misunderstand, each other, on any of the two levels: their individual intentions, and the collective purpose of the interaction (Weizman and Blum-Kulka, 1992). Thus, the extract illustrates the layeredness of language use, which involves the interplay of individual and collective, as well as instrumental and interactional meanings (Brown and Yule, 1983).
- **Step by step requesting: interaction and collaboration are crucial in the production and specification of speech acts**
  Gadi's request goes through several transformations throughout the extract, gradually clarifying the speech act performed. This process of gradual disambiguation and fixation of meaning is achieved in collaboration, as Sara's responses in each stage demand clarification (see turns 44–46). Thus, the sequence highlights the importance of uptake and the interlocutor's role in negotiating meaning.
- **Discourse is context embedded; context is crucially important for interpretation**
  Two spheres of context are essential for both participants and researchers to make sense of the conversation. First, the immediate setting and situation: for example, the ambiguity of turn 46 is evident against the fact that the food has already been laid out on the table. The second sphere is much more open ended, and involves ever-extending layers of personal and interpersonal history, which serve to establish the preparatory conditions for the success of the speech acts performed (i.e., Gadi's utterances can serve as requests only on the condition that Sara is assumed to be in charge of food). Additionally, in order to assess the keying of the interaction on the continuum from banter to serious conflict, the participants are presumably relying on their shared knowledge of the family's conversational norms and style.
- **Discourse is context shaping, as it does identity and power work**
  From a macro-level perspective, it seems that the extract is part of an on-going negotiation of power, gender roles and familial relationships. As such, it both builds on the history of the couple's relationship and contributes to its further development (see also De Fina, Chapter 13 this volume; Fairclough, Mulderrig and Wodak, Chapter 17 this volume; Lazar and Kramarae, Chapter 11 this volume). Note that this is particularly evident in Sara's meta-communicative comments in turn 57, indicating that reflexivity is an important part of language use and a valuable resource for understanding norms and expectations (e.g., Blum-Kulka, 1997; Weizman, 2008; see also the analysis of example 2 above).

Aspects of identity, relationships and power are taken up in pragmatics more fully in politeness theory.

---

[5]Translated from the original Hebrew. Turn numbers indicate their location in the original transcript of the full interaction. Transcription conventions: [words] – overlap; ((comment)) – transcriber's comments; wo:rd – sound stretch; ∘words∘ – low volume.

POLITENESS THEORY

The discussion of indirectness suggests that languages around the world provide their speakers with alternative modes for the achievement of communicative goals. In actual usage, speakers will often not conform to the four Gricean maxims, and will not express their intentions in the clearest and most explicit way possible. The theory of 'politeness', as developed first by Penelope Brown and Stephen Levinson (1987), builds on the assumption of cooperation, and suggests that social motivations can explain such deviations from explicitness and directness and their social implications.

In essence, research into the pragmatics of politeness aims at explaining contextual and cultural variability in linguistic actions: what social motivations are inherent in and what social meanings are attached to the choice of verbal strategies (that is, 'politeness strategies') for the accomplishment of communicative goals. For Brown and Levinson *politeness* is the intentional, strategic behaviour of an individual that is meant to satisfy self and other *face wants* in case of threat.

As Erving Goffman suggested, when individuals interact they are concerned with presenting and maintaining a public image of themselves, that is, *face*: 'the positive social value a person effectively claims for himself by the line others assume he has taken during a particular contact' (1967: 5). Following Goffman, Brown and Levinson claim that maintaining face is a basic motivation of human interaction and has two dimensions. One is *positive face*, which is the person's concern that he or she be thought well of by others. At the same time, a person wishes to preserve a certain degree of autonomy, a 'space' within which he or she has freedom of action and the right not to be imposed upon. Claiming the right for non-imposition is called *negative face*. Social interaction is based on interlocutors balancing the satisfaction of their own positive and negative face needs with the face needs of other interactants.

The need to balance face needs derives from the fact that most acts of communication are inherently imposing, or *face threatening*. For example, directives challenge the hearer's need for freedom of action (*negative face*), and may also threaten the requestor's *positive face* by displaying her as needing assistance; the speaker's positive face is threatened by the admission of guilt involved in an apology, and her *negative face* by the commitment to a future action involved in making a promise. Politeness strategies are the means by which interactants will fend off and *redress* such risks to face. Thus, in example (6) above, Gadi's extreme indirectness is arguably motivated by the need to redress the potential threat to his wife's positive face in her role as care-giver.

If the risk is minimal, or if there are overwhelmingly good reasons for ignoring face risks, speakers may go *Bald on Record* in realizing the communicative act in the most direct and efficient way possible (e.g., 'Open your books at page 20' in the classroom).

Attending to the face needs of the interlocutor, speakers can use *positive politeness strategies* such as expressing concern, stressing reciprocity, displaying a common point of view and showing optimism (e.g., 'Uncle Jim inquires about your health and would like to know if he can borrow your hammer'). Other typical positive politeness strategies include the use of in-group identity markers, slang, jokes, endearments and nicknames.

Alternatively, speakers may opt for *negative politeness strategies*, geared towards satisfying the hearer's need for freedom from imposition. These are realized by asking about (rather than assuming) cooperation; by giving options to the hearer not to do the act; by adopting a pessimistic attitude; and by various kinds of hedging. Negative politeness strategies include conventional indirectness (e.g., '*I wonder* if you know whether Bill has been around'), linguistic markers of deference, and appeals to the hearer's rationality through logical explanations.

In cases of great risks, the speaker may realize the act *Off the Record*, in a way that leaves maximal options for deniability (e.g., as non-conventional indirect requests or hints, such as Gadi's 'What's the plan?').

Finally, if the risk is considered too great, the speaker may decide to *Opt Out* and refrain from realizing the threatening act altogether.

The choice between these five strategies in context is presumably determined by the configuration of three contextual variables: the *social distance* between the speaker and the hearer; their *relative power*; and the relative *ranking of the imposition* in the given culture.

This conceptualization of politeness as the expression of autonomous, rational individuals striving to avoid conflict and preserve interactional harmony through indirectness has been strongly contested by scholars studying non-Western cultures. Theoretically, the presumption of a universal notion of face relies uncritically on Western-specific premises of individualism and rationality (e.g. Hanks, Ide and Katagiri, 2009). Furthermore, Brown and Levinson claim that the list of five strategies represents a universal scale of politeness, from directness to indirectness. Yet there is evidence to suggest that certain cultures exhibit different scales that do not conform with the equation of politeness with indirectness (Blum-Kulka, 1987). For example, in a culture that tends to minimize social distance and stress collectivism, like that of Israel, the prevalent style is that of positive politeness, and directness is not necessarily always deemed impolite (Blum-Kulka, 1997; Katriel, 1986).

Recent years have seen a flourishing of scholarly work on politeness in varied disciplines, dealing with issues ranging from gender relations to CMC. These studies are discourse-based, examining politeness in sequence and in its cultural, institutional and social contexts. Much of this work critiques Brown and Levinson as offering a theoretically-driven model that defines politeness as an abstract analytic concept. Alternatively, this new line of work focuses on the ways politeness is defined and evaluated by actual language users and communities of practice. This new interest in politeness has also broadened the scope of analysis from the intentional linguistic conduct of rational individuals who seek to mitigate face-threatening acts (FTAs) in several directions: these studies explore the entire spectrum of polite, appropriate and impolite behaviour; focus not just on speaker conduct but also on listeners' evaluations; pay attention to a wide range of linguistic and non-linguistic cues and resources; and, finally, they explore the distinctions and relations between politeness, facework and, relational and identity work more generally (Culpeper, 1996; Mills, 2003; Watts, 2003).

As the following example demonstrates, analysis of politeness phenomena in discourse shows the way in which variations in the choice of politeness strategies reflects and constructs the social world.

(7)   Two girls, Racheli (4 and 7 months) and Naomi (5 and 10 months), are dressed up as queens for the celebration of the Jewish holiday of Purim in the kindergarten. One of them is wearing a crown she has brought from home.

129	Racheli:	This? (2.9) It's mine. ((Probably in response to Naomi touching her crown))
130	Naomi:	(4.3) Ye::s?=
131	Racheli:	=it's mine↑
132	Naomi:	>it's but is it possible to wear ((it))?< Yes?
133	Racheli:	Only to try if it's your si↑ze?
134	Naomi:	Yes. Then if it's my size is it possible, to:: to wear it a bit?
135	Racheli:	Yes. ((Racheli hands her crown over to Naomi))
136	Naomi:	Good↑, it's an excellent size for me. ((Speaking in a high pitched voice, very pleased))

(Blum-Kulka, 2008)[6]

As in adult usage, this negotiation of the value of the requested goods is related to the degree of imposition involved in the request, and is directly reflected in the verbal effort invested to minimize this imposition. It also demonstrates how this is achieved in sequentially appropriate moves and in finely tuned negotiations between requester and requestee. The valued good in this case is the crown that one of the girls is wearing. Naomi, who covets the crown, exercises the utmost caution to get her friend to allow her to wear it: she first acknowledges the other's ownership declaration (129) by a non-committal 'yes' (130), before she formulates her request carefully in the polite language of mitigated conventional indirectness ('is it possible' is a highly conventionalized form in Hebrew), using several further mitigating devices (132) – the use of 'but', the questioning intonation, and specific syntactic and lexical choices (the use of an impersonal infinitive construction and of the tag 'yes?'). When her friend stalls by laying down a condition ('only to try if it's your size?', 133), Naomi uses acceptance to prepare the next move. First she concedes, and then goes on to reformulate her request (134), incorporating Racheli's condition as a syntactic mitigator for the current request, repeating the indirect impersonal construction and adding yet another downgrader ('a bit'). Once she succeeds and the crown has been handed over, she uses the

---

[6]Translated from the original Hebrew. Turn numbers indicate location in the original transcript of the full interaction. Transcription conventions: (2.9) – timed pauses, in seconds; ((comment)) – transcriber's comments; wo:rd – sound stretch; = – overlatch; wo↑rd – sharp rise in pitch; >words< – fast rhythm; word – emphasis. See Hamo, Blum-Kulka, and Hacohen, 2004, for a full discussion of data collection and transcription methods.

'only your size' restriction as a warrant for establishing her temporary ownership: 'it's an excellent size for me' (136). This example also demonstrates the function of politeness behaviour in constructing and acknowledging social roles and relationships, as both girls' behaviour positions the crown's owner in a position of momentary power.

AREAS OF INTEREST IN DISCOURSE PRAGMATIC RESEARCH[7]

Cross-Cultural and Intercultural Pragmatics

One widely researched area in cross-cultural pragmatics concerns comparisons of particular types of linguistic actions across cultures and among native and non-native speakers (e.g., Chen, 1993; Rose, 2009). For example, the study of the realization of requests and apologies in different languages shows a high degree of cultural variability, with the speakers of different languages choosing different levels of directness for requesting in a given situation (Blum-Kulka, House and Kasper, 1989).

Such cultural differences in pragmatic systems may have important implications for intercultural communication (Scollon and Scollon, 2001). In native/non-native communication, non-native speakers may rely on the pragmatic norms of their source culture, yielding miscommunication (e.g., the Japanese norm of highly indirect refusals may not be understood by non-Japanese interlocutors). Whereas grammatical deviances from target language norms are easily recognizable, lending their producers a protective 'non-native' identity, pragmatic deviances are not, and may carry the risk of being attributed to flaws in personality or ethnocultural origins (e.g., attributing rudeness to Indian English speakers in Britain; Gumperz, 1982).

Translation

Since the pragmatic meaning in a given text might be encoded through language-specific pragmalinguistic means, translators may and do sometimes fail to provide pragmatic equivalents (such as expressions that carry the same pragmatic meaning potential) in the target language. For example, the phrase 'I beg your pardon' may be used in American English to signal a lack of comprehension, to express indignation, or to give an apology. In context, the phrase may be deliberately ambiguous, as it is when used by a (married) female character in John Updike's novel *Rabbit, Run* after her offer of coffee to a (married) male character has been turned down in a way that makes clear his interpretation of her offer ('No, look … You're a doll … but I have got this wife now') (Updike, 1960: 223). The Hebrew translator of the phrase opted for the literal translation 'I'm asking for your

---

[7]Another area of growing interest in discourse pragmatics is the interfaces of grammar and pragmatics, explored using natural data (Ariel, 2008). This issue is often pursued in relation to discourse markers and has included corpus-based analyses (Bordería, 2008; see also Maschler, 2009).

forgiveness', allowing only for the apologetic meaning and thereby losing the pragmatic meaning potential of the original.

Developmental Pragmatics

The major tenet of studies in developmental pragmatics is a broad functional view of language, going beyond traditional conceptions of the field of pragmatics to consider language as inherently multi-functional and context based, and the process of language acquisition as evolving via a collaborative process of creating shared meanings. Research on the development of pragmatic competence grew as a reaction to the Chomskyan theories prevailing in the 1960s and early 1970s, tilting the balance back from a focus on formal aspects of language to language as communication (Bates, 1976). Though the scope and orientation of research in the field have much changed over the years, the foregrounding of semantic and pragmatic aspects of language and viewing communication of meaning as the central thing about language are shared by a myriad of functional approaches to language development, including developmental pragmatics in a first and second language (Kasper and Rose, 2002; Ninio and Snow, 1996), language socialization across cultures (Blum-Kulka, 1997; Duff and Hornberger, 2008), and usage-based approaches to language acquisition (Tomasello, 2003). Studies in developmental pragmatics in a first language have focused on three major domains: speech acts, conversational skills, and genres of extended discourse like narratives, explanations and definitions.

The study of language acquisition from a pragmatic perspective across these domains reveals several principles for the development of communicative competence, with important implications for linguistic communication at large. First and foremost, perhaps, is *the developmental precedence of meaning over form* and the different paces of their development: children will acquire most of the communicative speech uses – markings, games, attention direction, discussions and action negotiation – by age two and a half. Between then and age five, children will not significantly enlarge their communicative repertoire, but rather will improve the linguistic means for the expression of previously acquired communicative intents.

Second, the developmental path of pragmatic competence unveils the importance of *intersubjectivity* for linguistic communication, as well as its complexity. Thus, for example, *speech acts*, which require a complex socio-cognitive understanding that takes the hearer into account, like committing oneself to an act in the future by a promise, are not mastered until very late (Ninio and Snow, 1996). The difficulty and slow acquisition of taking the hearer into account are also evident in the development of conversational skills. Although young children will take turns appropriately from very early on, much before the onset of speech – thus revealing *sociality* as a primary driving force behind communication – their ability to participate in sustained *dialogic* conversational interactions will develop through interactions with adults and peers more slowly, indeed well into the school years, and specific skills such as performing as an active listener will be acquired relatively late (Hamo and Blum-Kulka, 2007).

Finally, developing the skills needed for the production of *extended genres*, like narratives, explanations, definitions or arguments, places specific demands on children. It requires a consideration of the reciprocity of perspectives and a fine tuning to the audience's state of mind as well as a familiarity with different genre conventions and the linguistic means needed to produce coherently structured stretches of discourse. For example, research on narrative development, that most studied of extended genres, shows a refinement of linguistic structures to achieve narrative functions such as temporality and causality with age, accompanied by a parallel development in mastering narrative macro-structures and in gaining sophistication in modes of conversational story-telling (e.g., Berman and Slobin, 1994; Blum-Kulka, 2005).

Media Discourse

In recent decades, media talk and media texts have become the focus for a growing interest on the part of discourse analysts. While some of this work is carried out within specific disciplinary traditions, the study of media discourse increasingly involves the interdisciplinary integration of varied approaches and analytic frameworks. Pragmatics has been drawn on as one strand contributing to the flexible toolkit used in the analysis of media talk, which combines pragmatically-oriented concepts – such as discourse as social action or intersubjective inference rules – with concepts drawn from Critical Discourse Analysis, Conversation Analysis, interactional sociolinguistics and linguistics, among others. This analytic toolkit is applied to the study of diverse genres, including broadcast news, celebrity interviews, talk shows and political campaigns, in their socio-cultural contexts (for a review, see Tolson, 2006).

Pragmatics has also informed the study of media discourse in two more specific paths:

- *As a theory of communication*, in Paddy Scannell's work on the phenomenology of television and radio, which in turn forms the basis for much work on media talk. Scannell views pragmatic models, particularly Grice's theory of communication and Brown and Levinson's theory of politeness, as encapsulating key presuppositions of any type of social interaction. Drawing on pragmatic models, he emphasizes the importance of intentionality and accountability in programming and production and in shaping the communicative ethos of television and radio (Scannell, 1996).
- *As an analytic framework for research on media discourse* using specific pragmatic models. Work in this tradition focused mainly on *mediated political discourse*, including, for example, the exploration of face and politeness in political contexts (e.g., Harris, 2001); the study of specific speech acts in public and political discourse (e.g., apologies; Kampf, 2009); and the application of pragmatic models of coherence and meaning-making to the analysis of political interviews (e.g., Weizman, 2008). Two key pragmatic features emerge as central to political discourse – the use of indirect and ambiguous messages, and the impact of social and self-presentational considerations on the design of discourse.

The adaptation of pragmatic models and concepts to the study of media discourse may contribute to further theoretical developments in discourse pragmatics. First, the public mediated nature of discourse on television and radio, which addresses a non-present distributed audience, highlights the need to attend to the impact of *different discursive positions and roles*, of both speakers and hearers, on discursive processes (Fetzer and Weizman, 2006; Weizman, 2008). Second, the diversity of media talk, whereby different genres and formats give rise to unique conditions, draws attention to the *context-sensitivity* of pragmatic concepts such as maxims of cooperation (Tolson, 2006). Finally, public and mediated discourse often offers examples of the *strategic uses* of pragmatic processes, such as deliberate violations of discursive norms (Tolson, 2006; Weizman, 2008), or the use of politeness as a discursive resource for aggressive, rather that deferential, behaviour (Harris, 2001; Kampf, 2009). Such uses call attention to the possible complexity and multi-layeredness of pragmatic processes.

CONCLUSION

As the above overview suggests, discourse pragmatics emerges as an interdisciplinary approach that integrates insights and analytic tools from diverse traditions, while maintaining a basic pragmatic orientation towards language use and meaning making. Such an orientation is arguably derivable from the two fundamental assumptions of pragmatic theory: first, the view of *language use as social action*; second, the view of *language use as ongoing meaning-making*. These assumptions encapsulate key features of linguistic communication and resonate to varying degrees in diverse sub-fields that are subsumed under 'Discourse Analysis' at large.

Language as social action

The view of language as social action and not as an autonomous system is a major motivating force behind contemporary discourse analysis. Thus, for example, for Critical Discourse Analysts language merits attention for its political power as a tool in manipulating social realities, whereas for Conversation Analysts language-in-interaction is the major process by which social realities are constructed and maintained (see also, Jiwani and Richardson, Chapter 12 this volume).

From the point of view of language use as social action there follows an emphasis on the motivated nature of language use, considering interlocutors as *intentional and accountable* social agents. Thus, interlocutors are seen as intentionally and unintentionally motivated by a plethora of considerations, ranging from attention to cognitive constraints on comprehension to interpersonal obligations such as face concerns (for example, in the choice of politeness strategies).[8] Interlocutors are also seen as being held accountable to a social contract of abiding by certain conditions for success, such as sincerity (Searle, 1969), and to a basic social contract of cooperation (Grice, 1975). In later pragmatic theory, this concept is extended to include moral and ethical aspects of language use (Mey, 2001).

The view of language use as social action entails recognizing its *multi-functionality*. The original insight of multi-functionality in pragmatics was linked to the observation that one utterance could fulfil different speech acts depending on its varying conditions of use, but was later extended to consider more carefully the impact of variations in context and co-text. For instance, Clark and Carlson (1982) note that the same utterance can fulfil different speech acts for different recipient roles. This is especially the case in political discourse, where speech acts can be highly equivocal, producing different effects for different target audiences (Bavelas et al., 1990).

Language use as meaning-making

The centrality of meaning-making in pragmatics derives from the insight that discourse is inherently *multi-layered*, requiring a constant bridging between what is said and what is meant. While there is a consensus that meaning-making is multi-dimensional and central, there is no agreement on the process of interpretation. For some, pragmatic theory presents a code-based, monological approach to meaning-making, by which language use and interpretation are understood as operating by a set of rigid rules for coding and decoding messages. Thus, pragmatics is criticized as focusing on the individual speaker and ignoring the role of others, as well as focusing on the individual utterance as an autonomous unit of meaning (Linell, 1998). In contrast, we would argue that a recognition of the essentially *dialogic and intersubjective* nature of human communication underlies pragmatic theories from their very inception, and certainly features strongly in their later developments. This is salient in pragmatic theories concerned with interpretation, beginning with Grice's Cooperative Principle. Cooperation is measured against 'the accepted purpose or direction of the talk exchange', which is assumed to be shared by all participants (Grice, 1975: 45). In later pragmatic theory, the idea of *shared intentionality* received sustained attention from several directions. Thus for Dascal (1992), conversations are genuine forms of collective action; participants may have different I-intentions, but all contributions necessarily need to abide by a common we-intention, ranging minimally from that of participating-in-the-conversation to more specific shared goals.

Another aspect of dialogicity in pragmatics has to do with the relation between subsequent utterances in interaction. Initial attention to the importance of *sequence* in meaning-

---

[8]In Critical Discourse Analysis, this pragmatic orientation is complemented by an understating of the messages carried by unintentional aspects of language use, including ideological implications (see van Dijk, Chapter 18 this volume).

making is implicit in Austin's (1962) concept of uptake, which acknowledges the role of the hearer. From a theoretical perspective, the sequence becomes prominent in Grice's model, where utterances are judged against the expectations set up by previous utterances in a sequence.

A basic tenet of a pragmatic orientation to discourse is the centrality of *context* to our understanding of language use. The question that remains, however, is how context can be construed theoretically and empirically.[9] Classic pragmatic theory was interested in the links between language and its immediate context (deixis and indexicality in general) and in the cognitive context, indexed by presuppositions or mental models (van Dijk, 2006; Levinson, 1983). Attention to social context within pragmatics was enhanced with the formulation of politeness theory, in which social context is identifiable via the major parameters of social distance, status and degree of imposition (Brown and Levinson, 1987). As pragmaticians became interested in natural discourse, the notion of social context gained more prominence and developed to include a plethora of parameters such as affect, social roles, gender and cultural identity (e.g., Blum-Kulka, 1997; Holmes, 1995). Furthermore, discourse pragmatics has moved away from the concept of context as given-only and determining language use, to a more dynamic, reciprocal and dialectical view of context-talk and context-text relationships. In this view, context is both assumed and construed by interactants: on the one hand, an awareness of given social roles and positions informs language use; on the other, social roles and positions are re-negotiated and constructed through the interaction (see also Jiwani and Richardson, Chapter 12 this volume). This is specifically pursued by later work on indexicality (Hanks, 1996).

The study of discursive sequences (both written and spoken) raises another aspect of context discussed above, namely, the *sequential organization* of text and talk as informing discourse structure, expectations and interpretation. The above analyses demonstrated how sequential placing and the step-by-step unfolding of interactions inform meaning-making. Another aspect, not illustrated here, is the overall macro-structure of text and talk, and its inner cohesion and coherence (Brown and Yule, 1983).

Taking all these aspects into consideration, in discourse pragmatics research, context is examined as a multi-dimensional concept, including setting, cognitive context and mutual knowledge, socio-cultural context, and discursive sequence (Hamo et al., 2004).

On a final note, the contribution of pragmatics to our understanding of language use supersedes specific models for discourse analysis. Rather, it offers a functional, multi-layered, socially-contextualized, reciprocal and emergent view of meaning-making in text and talk. As such, pragmatics is best construed as a theory of communication.

---

[9]This question has been a continuous focus of debate within Discourse Analysis, specifically between Conversation Analysis and Discursive Psychology or Critical Discourse Analysis (Billig and Schegloff, 1999). Pragmaticians have not been directly involved in this debate; yet, as our discussion shows, the pragmatic stance offers the most comprehensive notion of context.

NOTE

We would like to thank Teun van Dijk, Talia Habib, Sherna Kissilevitz, Zohar Kampf and Elda Weizman for their helpful comments and suggestions on earlier versions of this chapter.

FURTHER READING

Literature on pragmatics is vast, including canonical theoretical papers, introductory textbooks and recent empirical work. Current research in discourse pragmatics appears mainly in the *Journal of Pragmatics, Pragmatics, Discourse Studies* and the *Journal of Politeness Research: Language, Behaviour, Culture.*

Grice, H.P. (1975) 'Logic and conversation'. In P. Cole and J. Morgan (eds), *Syntax and Semantics 3: Speech Acts.* New York: Academic Press. pp. 41–58.
A canonical theoretical paper presenting Grice's model for meaning-making in conversation, and establishing some basic assumptions of pragmatic theory.

Austin, J. (1962) *How to Do Things with Words.* Oxford: Oxford University Press.
This short groundbreaking book laid the foundations for speech act theory.

Searle, J. (1969) *Speech Acts.* Cambridge: Cambridge University Press.
Building on Austin and others, Searle has developed the most detailed and well known theory of speech acts to date.

Brown, P. and Levinson, S. (1987) *Politeness: Some Universals in Language Usage.* Cambridge: Cambridge University Press.
This canonical, theoretical and empirical study served as the basis for contemporary politeness research.

Thomas, J. (1995) *Meaning in Interaction: An Introduction to Pragmatics.* London: Longman.
A comprehensive overview of pragmatics.

Ariel, M. (2008) *Pragmatics and Grammar.* Cambridge: Cambridge University Press.
A recent exploration into the intricate relationship between pragmatics and grammar.

Mills, S. (2003) *Gender and Politeness.* Cambridge: Cambridge University Press.
An example of the current re-interest in the re-conceptualization of politeness.

ONLINE READING

The following articles are available at www.sagepub.co.uk/discoursestudies.

Billig, M., & Schegloff, E.A. (1999). Critical Discourse Analysis and Conversation Analysis: An exchange between Michael Billig and Emanuel A. Schegloff. *Discourse & Society, 10*, 543–582.

Ekström, M., & Johansson, B. (2008). Talk scandals. *Media, Culture & Society, 30*, 61–79.

Harris, S. (2001). Being politically impolite: Extending politeness theory to adversarial political discourse. *Discourse & Society, 12*, 451–472.

REFERENCES

Ariel, M. (2008) *Pragmatics and Grammar*. Cambridge: Cambridge University Press.

Austin, J. (1962) *How to Do Things with Words*. Oxford: Oxford University Press.

Bach, K. and Harnish, R.M. (1979) *Linguistic Communication and Speech Acts*. Cambridge, MA: MIT Press.

Bates, E. (1976) *Language and Context: The Acquisition of Pragmatics*. New York: Academic Press.

Bavelas, J.B., Black, A., Chovil, N. and Mullett, J. (1990) *Equivocal Communication*. London: Sage

Berman, R. and Slobin, D. (eds) (1994) *Relating Events in Narrative: A Crosslinguistic Developmental Study*. Hillsdale, NJ: Lawrence Erlbaum.

Billig, M. and Schegloff, E.A. (1999) 'Critical Discourse Analysis and Conversation Analysis: an exchange between Michael Billig and Emanuel A. Schegloff'. *Discourse & Society, 10*: 543–82.

Blum-Kulka, S. (1987) 'Indirectness and politeness in requests: same or different?'. *Journal of Pragmatics, 11*: 131–46.

Blum-Kulka, S. (1989) 'Playing it safe: the role of conventionality in indirectness'. In S. Blum-Kulka, J. House and K. Kasper (eds), *Cross-cultural Pragmatics: Requests and Apologies* (pp. 37–70). Norwood, NJ: Ablex.

Blum-Kulka, S. (1997) *Dinner Talk: Cultural Patterns of Sociability and Socialization in Family Discourse*. Mahwah, NJ: Lawrence Erlbaum.

Blum-Kulka, S. (2005) 'Modes of meaning-making in children's conversational storytelling'. In J. Thornborrow and J. Coates (eds), *The Sociolinguistics of Narrative* (pp. 149–71). Amsterdam: John Benjamins.

Blum-Kulka, S. (2008) '"If it's my size, would it be possible to wear it a bit?": Israeli children's peer talk requests'. In A. Stavans and I. Kupferberg (eds), *Studies in Language and Language Education: Essays in Honor of Elite Olshtain* (pp. 23–47). Jerusalem: Magnes.

Blum-Kulka, S., House, J. and Kasper, G. (eds) (1989) *Cross-cultural Pragmatics: Requests and Apologies*. Norwood, NJ: Ablex.

Bordería, S.P. (ed.) (2008) 'Empirical data and pragmatic theory'. Special issue of *Journal of Pragmatics, 40* (8).

Brown, P. and Levinson, S. (1987) *Politeness: Some Universals in Language Usage*. Cambridge: Cambridge University Press. [First published as Brown, P. and Levinson, S. (1978) 'Universals of language: politeness phenomena'. In E. Goody (ed.), *Questions and Politeness* (pp. 56–324). Cambridge: Cambridge University Press.]

Brown, G. and Yule, G. (1983) *Discourse Analysis*. Cambridge: Cambridge University Press.

Carston, R. (2002) *Thoughts and Utterances: The Pragmatics of Explicit Communication*. Oxford: Blackwell.

Chen, R. (1993) 'Responding to compliments: a contrastive study of politeness strategies between American English and Chinese speakers'. *Journal of Pragmatics, 20*: 49–75.

Clark, H.H. (1992) *Arenas of Language Use*. Chicago: University of Chicago Press.

Clark, H.H. and Carlson, T.B. (1982) 'Hearers and speech acts'. *Language, 58*: 332–73.

Culpeper, J. (1996) 'Towards an anatomy of impoliteness'. *Journal of Pragmatics, 25*: 349–67.

Dascal, M. (1983) *Pragmatics and the Philosophy of Mind*. Amsterdam: John Benjamins.

Dascal, M. (1992) 'On the pragmatic structure of conversation'. In H. Parret and J. Verschueren (eds), *(On) Searle on Conversation* (pp. 35–56). Amsterdam: John Benjamins.

Duff, P.A. and Hornberger, N.H. (eds) (2008) '*Encyclopedia of Language and Education, Vol 8: Language Socialization*. New York: Springer.

Ekström, M. and Johansson, B. (2008) 'Talk scandals'. *Media, Culture & Society, 30*: 61–79.

Fetzer, A. and Weizman, E. (2006) 'Political discourse as mediated and public discourse'. *Journal of Pragmatics, 38*: 143–53.

Goffman, E. (1967) *Interaction Ritual: Essays on Face to Face Behavior*. New York: Doubleday.

Grice, H.P. (1957) 'Meaning'. *Philosophical Review, 66*: 377–88.

Grice, H.P. (1968) 'Utterer's meaning, sentence meaning and word meaning'. *Foundations of language, 4*: 1–18.

Grice, H.P. (1975) 'Logic and conversation'. In P. Cole and J. Morgan (eds), *Syntax and Semantics 3: Speech Acts* (pp. 41–58). New York: Academic Press.

Grice, P. (1989) *Studies in the Way of Words*. Cambridge, MA: Cambridge University Press.

Gu, Y. (1993) 'The impasse of perlocution'. *Journal of Pragmatics, 20*: 405–32.

Gumperz, J.J. (1982) *Discourse Strategies*. Cambridge: Cambridge University Press.

Hamo, M. and Blum-Kulka, S. (2007) 'Apprenticeship in conversation and culture: emerging sociability in preschool peer talk'. In J. Valsiner and A. Rosa (eds), *The Cambridge Handbook of Social-Cultural Psychology* (pp. 423–44). Cambridge: Cambridge University Press.

Hamo, M., Blum-Kulka, S. and Hacohen, G. (2004) 'From observation to transcription and back: theory, practice and interpretation in the analysis of children's naturally occurring discourse'. *Research on Language and Social Interaction, 37*: 71–92.

Hanks, W.F. (1996) *Language and Communicative Practices*. Boulder, CO: Westview Press.

Hanks, W.F., Ide, S. and Katagiri, Y. (2009) 'Towards an emancipatory pragmatics'. *Journal of Pragmatics, 41*: 1–9.

Harris, S. (2001) 'Being politically impolite: extending politeness theory to adversarial political discourse'. *Discourse and Society, 12*: 451–72.

Holmes, J. (1995) *Women, Men, and Politeness*. London: Longman.

Jucker, A.H. (2009) 'Speech act research between armchair, field and laboratory: the case of compliments'. *Journal of Pragmatics, 41*: 1611–35.

Kampf, Z. (2009) 'Public (non-) apologies: the discourse of minimizing responsibility'. *Journal of Pragmatics, 41*: 2257–70.

Kasher, A. (ed.) (1998) *Pragmatics: Critical Concepts*. London: Routledge.

Kasper, G. and Rose, K.R. (2002) *Pragmatic Development in a Second Language*. Malden, MA: Blackwell.

Katriel, T. (1986) *Talking Straight: Dugri speech in Israeli Sabra culture*. Cambridge: Cambridge University Press.

Keenan Ochs, E. (1974) 'Norm-makers and norm-breakers: uses of speech by men and women in Malagasy community'. In R. Bauman and J. Sherzer (eds), *Explorations in the Ethnography of Speaking* (pp. 125–43). New York: Cambridge University Press.

Kurzon, D. (1998) 'The speech act status of incitement: perlocutionary acts revisited'. *Journal of Pragmatics, 29*: 571–96.

Levi-Barzilay (2002, August 23) 'Bleeding hearts, you're growing old'. *Haaretz* (in Hebrew: available at http://www.haaretz. co.il/hasite/pages/PrintArticle,jhtml?itemNo=344000 last accessed 2 November 2008.)

Levinson, S. (1983) *Pragmatics*. Cambridge: Cambridge University Press.

Levinson, S. (2000) *Presumptive Meanings: The Theory of Generalized Conversational Implicatures*. Cambridge, MA: MIT Press.

Linell, P. (1998) *Approaching Dialogue: Talk, Interaction and Contexts in Dialogical Perspectives*. Amsterdam: John Benjamins.

Maschler, Y. (2009) *Metalanguage in Interaction: Hebrew Discourse Markers*. Amsterdam: John Benjamins.

Mey, J. (2001) *Pragmatics: An Introduction (2nd edn)*. Oxford: Blackwell.

Mills, S. (2003) *Gender and Politeness*. Cambridge: Cambridge University Press.

Morgan, J. (1978) 'Two types of convention in indirect speech acts'. In P. Cole and J. Morgan (eds), *Syntax and Semantics 9: Pragmatics* (pp. 261–81). New York: Academic Press.

Ninio, A. and Snow, C. (1996) *Pragmatic Development*. Boulder, CO: Westview.

Ogiermann, E. (2009) 'Politeness and in-directness across cultures: a comparison of English, German, Polish and Russian requests'. *Journal of Politeness Research: Language, Behaviour, Culture, 5*: 189–216.

Parret and J. Verschueren (eds) (1992) *(On) Searle on Conversation*. Amsterdam: John Benjamins.

Recanati, F. (2004) 'Pragmatics and semantics'. In L. Horn and G. Ward (eds), *The Handbook of Pragmatics* (pp. 442–62). Oxford: Blackwell.

Rosaldo, M. (1990) 'The things we do with words: Ilongot speech acts and speech act theory in philosophy'. In D. Carbaugh (ed.), *Cultural Communication and Intercultural Contact* (pp. 373–407). Hillsdale, NJ: Lawrence Erlbaum. [Originally published in 1982.]

Rose, K.R. (2009) 'Interlanguage pragmatic development in Hong Kong, phase 2'. *Journal of Pragmatics, 41*: 2345–64.

Scannell, P. (1996) *Radio, Television and Modern Life*. Oxford: Blackwell.

Scollon, R. and Scollon, S.W. (2001) *Intercultural Communication: A Discourse Approach (2nd edn)*. Malden, MA: Blackwell.

Searle, J. (1969) *Speech Acts*. Cambridge: Cambridge University Press.

Searle, J. (1975) 'Indirect speech acts'. In P. Cole and J. Morgan (eds), *Syntax and Semantics 3: Speech Acts* (pp. 59–82). New York: Academic Press.

Searle, J. (1979) 'The classification of illocutionary acts'. *Language in Society, 5*: 1–24.

Sperber, D. and Wilson, D. (1986) *Relevance: Communication and Cognition*. Cambridge, MA: Harvard University Press.

Tolson, A. (2006) *Media Talk: Spoken Discourse on TV and Radio*. Edinburgh: Edinburgh University Press.

Tomasello, M. (2003) *Constructing a Language: A Usage based Theory of Language Acquisition*. Cambridge, MA: Harvard University Press.

Updike, J. (1960) *Rabbit, Run*. New York: Fawcett Crest.

van Dijk, T.A. (2006) 'Ideology and discourse analysis'. *Journal of Political Ideologies, 11*(2): 115–40.

Watts, R.J. (2003) *Politeness*. Cambridge: Cambridge University Press.

Wiezman, E. (2008) *Positioning in Media Dialogue: Negotiating Roles in News Interviews*. Amsterdam: John Benjamins.

Weizman, E. and Blum-Kulka, S. (1992) 'Ordinary misunderstandings'. In M. Stamenov (ed.), *Current Advances in Semantic Theory* (pp. 417–33). Amsterdam: John Benjamins.

NINE

Conversation Analysis: An Approach to the Analysis of Social Interaction

Anita Pomerantz and B.J. Fehr

INTRODUCTION

We humans spend a considerable portion of our lives interacting with one another. As social animals we coordinate our activities together, thereby constituting the familiar interactions and social institutions of everyday life. We walk to work with a friend, discussing the day to come. We return the call of a client who is checking the progress of a project. We coordinate with other crew members to dig a hole and put up a new telephone pole. We change the baby's diaper and pause for a round of tickling. We shop for dinner at a local market, avoiding collisions with others' shopping carts, and prepare the evening meal for the family so that it is ready when everyone gets home. We chat on the phone with Mom about her trip to Yosemite.

Examined a bit more closely, these various activities can be seen to involve a progression or sequence of actions. Walking to work with a friend might begin with a greeting ('Hi Alex') and be followed by a personal state inquiry ('How are you?'). As the talk proceeds, one or the other friend might report news ('Did you hear ... ?'), seek information ('How long will that take?'), or commiserate about a heavy work load ('Gee, that's a lot!') – as both parties all the while adjust their pace so as to stay side by side. Such sequential and simultaneous coordination of talk and bodily movement with others is typical of our daily round of activities. From the perspective of Conversation Analysis (CA), these routine activities collectively constitute the social order. And it is these actions and interactions and how they are assembled that provide CA with its analytic focus.[1]

Conversation Analysis arose in the mid-1960s in the work of Harvey Sacks and his colleagues and collaborators, Emanuel A. Schegloff and Gail Jefferson. Sacks was investigating the possibility of a social science grounded in the empirical details of everyday interaction when he came upon audio-tape recordings of calls to a suicide prevention centre. Figuring that these recordings provided access to the kind of routine, mundane conduct that social science should be able to handle, Sacks set to work analyzing the interactions on the tapes. From his encounter with these materials, CA was born (Schegloff, 1992a).

The organization of human social life had long been a topic for philosophy, the humanities and social sciences, which, with few exceptions, concluded that the details of everyday conduct were without order, nearly random and ungrammatical (see, for example, Chomsky, 1965). The investigations of Sacks and his colleagues demonstrated, to the contrary, that we humans actually produce our routine conduct in methodic and orderly ways, subject to detailed analysis. CA has produced a substantial body of rigorous analyses of the organization of social interaction in the ensuing forty years.[2] Our purpose in this chapter is to provide a characterization of CA's programme of research, an elucidation of its basic analytic concepts, a set of analytic tasks, and an illustration of how to use these tasks to begin working on materials from the perspective of CA.

THE ANALYTIC PROGRAMME OF CONVERSATION ANALYSIS

CA's analytic project is to provide an empirically grounded explication of the social organization of naturally occurring human action and interaction. More specifically, CA aims to explicate the methods or practices people employ to assemble the actions and activities of everyday life. For example, greetings are a routine type of action performed in many settings. A CA analytic question about them is: in and through what conduct do society members collaboratively constitute greetings? Utterances such as 'Hello', 'Hey', 'Hi' and 'Yo' can be employed to do greetings. Hand waves, smiles and eyebrow flashes are visually available movements that can also serve as greetings, depending on the context of their production.

---

[1]Conversation Analysis (CA), as the name for the research tradition herein discussed, is something of a misnomer and can lead to confusion as to the phenomena under investigation. Both informal (e.g., conversational) and formal (e.g., institutional) interactions are of interest to conversation analysts. Talk, including paralinguistic features such as intonation and pauses, as well as visually available body positions and movements are included in CA studies. CA inquiries focus on the organization of meaningful human conduct across settings and modalities (visual, auditory) of production and understanding.

[2]Please see Further Reading (page 186) for a sample of this extensive literature.

CA assumes that action and interactions are inextricably tied to their context of production. The relation between action/interaction and context is reciprocal: the context is in part constituted by the actions/interactions performed and the actions/interactions are responsive to the context of their construction. Greeting a co-worker on first meeting at the job site in part proposes the context as one in which greetings are appropriate. The work setting and prior relationship between the parties may be reflected in producing a more informal greeting ('Hey, how's it goin?').

CA, further, gives analytic priority to the perspective of the participants. To the extent that their conduct is orderly and recognizable, it was produced as such by the participants for each other. In order to make sense, participants must attend to the inherent contingencies of any scene or setting and produce conduct that hearably, observably reveals their understanding of how the interaction is proceeding and what they are doing together.

The orderly assembled practices that constitute our everyday lives are sense-making practices. When participants employ these practices, they collaboratively produce an understanding of their own and their co-interactants' conduct. For example, a speaker can propose the importance of a topic by raising it first thing in a conversation. The speaker might introduce the topic immediately after greetings, or perhaps even dispense with greetings altogether and launch right into the topic. This practice provides a method for suggesting the importance of a topic that participants can use to both produce and understand the sense of their actions in coordination with others. As a further example, an interactant can ascertain a co-interactant's focus of attention by monitoring the latter's eye gaze, and in monitoring the other, reveal her own attentional focus.

From this perspective, culture is conceived of as the collected repertoire of such practices and actions. As Sacks put it in one of his lectures (1992, Vol. I: 226): 'A culture is an apparatus for generating recognizable actions ... '. Members of a culture share the ability to use these practices and actions in interaction with each other to produce orderly, intelligible courses of action and interaction: to make sense together.

Thus, CA takes everyday, naturally occurring instances of interaction as its analytic focus. Schegloff (2006: 70) characterizes such interactions as 'the primary, fundamental embodiment of sociality'. As people coordinate their conduct together, they constitute the social world as we know it. The living human being produces conduct through the deployment of the human body with all its capabilities and resources – thus we speak of 'embodied' action and interaction.

Talk is obviously a defining capability of human beings and talk is a central component of much human action and interaction. The origins of CA, and much subsequent work, have focused on explicating the methodic organization of talk-in-interaction. Basic orders of organization for interaction described in the CA literature were all originally formulated on instances of talk-in-interaction (see Schegloff, 1996, for action; Sacks, Schegloff and Jefferson, 1974, for turns; Schegloff and Sacks, 1973, for sequential organization; Schegloff, Jefferson and Sacks, 1977, for repair; Heritage, 2008, for epistemic claims; and Schegloff and Sacks, 1973, for the overall structure of episodes of interaction).

When parties to an interaction are co-present, the human body is visible as well as hearable, and the relevance of the contribution of eye gaze, facial expressions, gestures, body position and movement can be investigated. The pioneering work of Charles and Marjorie Goodwin (C. Goodwin, 1980, 1981; M. Goodwin, 1980) and Christian Heath (1981) is notable in this regard. More recently, evidence of an increase in the number of analyses examining both talk and visible bodily activity can be seen in a number of special editions of journals and edited collections in books (Jones and LeBaron, 2002; LeVine and Scollon, 2004; Sidnell and Stivers, 2005).

Methodologically, these considerations lead to some specific recommendations. Because conduct in interaction can be seen to be tied to the context of its production and understanding, CA investigations are conducted in the naturally occurring settings of everyday life. Recordings are made of the naturally occurring actions and interactions. These recordings serve as resources for and constraints on the analyst, who can thereby view and review the interaction in developing an analysis. The recordings also serve as a resource for those who read the analysis; it enables them to review the same materials employed by the analyst. Audio-video recordings are recommended for co-present interactants; audio recordings are acceptable for telephone calls. Thus far, synchronous interactions have been the primary focus, although one can envisage CA studies of asynchronous interactions which technological developments have made so common in the past decade.

Transcripts are routinely made of the interactions under study. These transcripts detail what and how things were said and, when relevant, provide an indication of the visual aspects of an interaction. Gail Jefferson (2004) developed a transcription system for talk-in-interaction that is used by conversation analysts. Individual researchers have worked out ways to represent visual features of the interaction they are investigating. The transcript is an important tool to use in conjunction with the recording; it enables the analyst to 'freeze' the action for closer consideration.

ANALYTIC CONCEPTS

The analytic literature in Conversation Analysis has produced detailed explications of a number of orders of organization found in interaction. Some work in CA puts greater emphasis on the structural properties of these orders of organization, and other work gives greater emphasis to the contingent, interactional enacting and managing of these orders of organization. We will briefly consider six here: activities and actions, turns, sequence, repair, epistemics, and the boundaries of episodes of interaction. In order to illustrate these routine elements of human interaction, we have provided a transcript (please see this chapter's Appendix) of a segment of a seminar meeting involving six medical students and their instructor. They were seated around a table as follows:

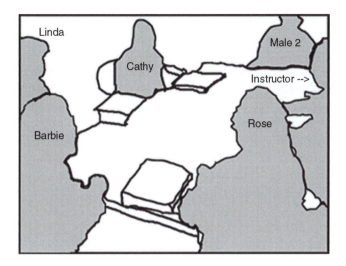

This seminar was video recorded; the camera viewed the group situated between Barbie and Rose. It was not possible for the camera, given its position and lens, to take in the entire group all at once. Therefore the camera operator panned the camera during the interaction, capturing only a subset of the group at any one time.

This seminar meeting began with a guest speaker and discussion. The group then took a break. During the break, the seminar participants discussed arrangements for a dinner party to which the instructor had previously invited the students. Just prior to where the transcript begins, the instructor was giving his home address and directions for getting there. The students are jotting this information down in their calendars and notebooks, or in one case opening a can of soda, when the instructor poses the question: 'Six thirty?' (line 1). (Please take a moment to read through the transcript in the Appendix as we will be using it for illustration throughout the remainder of the chapter.)

Activities and actions

Activities and actions are basic constitutive elements of interaction. People organize much of what they do in terms of activities, for example telephoning a friend, giving a lecture, or taking a break during a seminar. Generally within an activity there are one or more sequences of conversational actions. Actions refer to what the participants are doing inter-actionally *vis-à-vis* one another; they often are performed within turns (Schegloff, 1996). For example, inviting recipients to dinner, suggesting a time to arrive, and requesting infor-mation are all things done, or actions performed, in the interaction under study.

Actions are composed of practices that provide for their intelligible enactment. When the instructor utters 'Six thirty?' (line 1) with a rising intonation at the end, it is hearable in part as the action of 'suggesting a time for invited guests to arrive at his home'. Only one student responds vocally; Linda says 'Ka:y' (line 3), affirming the acceptability of 6:30 as a time to arrive at the instructor's house. Four of the five students visible in the video initiate writing in response to the suggestion of 6:30. This conduct can also be seen as affirming the acceptability of the time. The fifth student continued writing. This is a good illustration of the kinds of things that would be missed if one were to try to analyse this interaction with an audio recording only.

Actions may be performed in and through the enactment of other actions (Schegloff, 2007). In the seminar, Linda offers a report that indicates her eating habits in saying: 'I'm not really a meat eater' (line 14). This report is responsive to an inquiry about dietary restrictions, and can also be heard as a request for a vegetarian meal, or perhaps vegetarian options as part of the meal.

Turns

Actions often are performed in turns, which are structured via the routine practice of 'one speaker/interactant at a time'. Turn components (e.g., turn constructional units, TCUs) and rules for changing who has the floor over the course of an interaction (e.g., current speaker selects next speaker) have been described (Sacks, Schegloff and Jefferson, 1974). Turns are interactional time segments or moments that are taken by and allotted to participants. It is a time when a participant's contribution can be put forward. For many interactional formats, one person at a time is allotted a turn. Interactants, by and large, stay out of others' turns and can be sanctioned for intruding into someone else's turn. There are appropriate displays of recipiency to the turn-structured contributions of others. Examination of the transcript of the seminar group reveals that the talk of any given person is, for the most part, not overlapped by the talk of others in the room, thus providing an example of the one-at-a-time organization. There is, however, one occasion when Linda and Barbie answer a question in overlap with each other. In the immediately prior turn, Cathy asked: 'You'll eat chicken and fish °though°?' (line 30). This question can he heard as directed to both Barbie and Linda because in prior turns they both described themselves as not really meat eaters. Thus their speaking in overlap (lines 31–32) does not appear to be, nor is treated as, an interruption of each other (see Lerner, 2002).

Sequential organization

The organization of conduct over time is a central interest of CA. Interactants produce actions with an orientation to the unfolding character or sequential organization of an interaction. Participants produce actions which display an understanding of prior actions and project relevancies for which actions should or might come next, or in some cases, indicate no next actions are due (Schegloff and Sacks, 1973). For example, Cathy in her utterance 'You'll eat chicken and fish °though°' (line 30) displays an appreciation of the foregoing discussion in which Linda and Barbie report that they are both not really meat eaters. Cathy also introduces a new possibility, namely that Linda and Barbie will eat chicken and fish.

Her formulation of this possibility makes relevant a reply which confirms or disconfirms Cathy's proposal. Both Linda and Barbie confirm Cathy's proposal. Linda and Barbie's confirmations do not make relevant a particular next action. Actions such as Cathy's are understood as initiating actions, although they also display an orientation to what has come before. Actions such as Linda and Barbie's confirmations are understood as responsive actions, though they also can have implications for what can sensibly come next even if it is not particularly specified.

Repair

Interactants have ways of fixing, modifying or correcting what they and their co-participants are saying and doing as they interact. Interactants distinguish between correcting one's own talk (self-repair) and correcting the talk of a co-participant (other-repair). Repair generally occurs within three turns of the repairable item. Linda's utterance: 'Uhm I'm not- I'm not a big- I'm not really a meat eater' (line 13–14) provides an illustration of the phenomenon of self-repair within same turn. Linda begins this utterance three times before she carries it through to completion. The first two beginnings are abruptly abandoned when she finds herself speaking in overlap with the instructor. She completes the utterance on the third attempt though with some modification.

Other-correction often is treated as a delicate action. Interactants may initiate a repair sequence without doing the correction, thereby allowing the other person to correct him or herself. Alternately, they may embed a correction of the co-interactant's talk or action in the topical flow, thereby not exposing it as a correction. (See Jefferson, 1974; 1987; Schegloff, 1979; 1992b; 1997; 2000; Schegloff, Jefferson and Sacks, 1977.)

Epistemic order

Interactional participants will display an orientation towards the knowledge that they presume both they and others are entitled, required or forbidden to have. Heritage (2008) discusses such orientations as an epistemic order. For example, people are expected to know certain things about themselves and these expectations are displayed in conduct. When the instructor asks whether any of the seminar members have dietary restrictions, he presumes that the recipients are required to know about their own dietary restrictions. He does not ask whether or not they might know if they have dietary restrictions but straightforwardly asks for the information: '>Any of you have< any dietary restrictions we should know about?' (line 7).

The knowledge that participants introduce into an interaction can also propose certain relational alignments (Raymond and Heritage, 2006). For example, when Cathy claims without equivocation 'You'll eat chicken and fish °though°' (line 30) after Linda and Barbie describe themselves as not really meat eaters, she speaks as one who knows Linda and Barbie and is familiar with their eating habits. Further, Cathy makes this utterance as one entitled to speak on Linda and Barbie's behalf.

Interaction episodes

Interaction episodes are opened and closed in ways that differentiate them from other activities (Schegloff and Sacks, 1973). Interactions frequently begin with greetings and end with good-byes that serve to mark the boundaries of an interaction. Interactions such as the seminar meeting can also have sub-segments that are begun and ended in similar ways and also serve to separate different kinds of activities. In the medical seminar, the instructor proposes a termination of the dinner party-related talk and the resumption of the focus of the seminar in saying: 'Uh where- we don't have anything on this woman on the floor do we?' (line 86). Following the talk about the dinner party, the instructor shifts the focus to the patient ('this woman') to be discussed during the rest of their meeting.

ANALYTIC TOOLS: TASKS TO PERFORM WHEN STARTING ANALYSIS

An important starting place for working up a CA analysis is to make observations that are derived from a recorded interaction. Observations may be directed by various interests. The analytic interests that direct CA observations are aimed at increasing our understanding of the practices that people use and rely on when they interact, practices with which they make sense of their own and others' conduct and with which they can accomplish their actions and activities.

The tasks in Table 9.1 are intended to serve as a guide for getting started with analysis, for directing analysts' observations. They direct analysts to closely scrutinize the interactional conduct that occurs during some bounded period of time, for example, during someone's speaking turn or during a turn-transition period, and then move to examine the conduct in another bounded period of time. Our examination of the conduct during some bounded period of time includes characterizing the actions; considering how these fit within larger sequences of actions; analysing how the actions are performed; considering how these relate to prior actions and anticipate possible future actions; showing the interactional, collaborative aspects of the actions; and pointing out the role and relationship implications

Table 9.1   Sequence of analytic tasks

Task 1	Select a sequence and examine the opening and closing as achievements.
Task 2	Select a turn within the sequence for close analysis.
Task A	Characterize the actions performed in the turn. Consider how the actions fit within sequences of actions.
Task B	Describe the methods used to perform the actions. Consider the understandings provided by the use of those methods.
Task C	Describe the methods used for taking, keeping, and transitioning between turns. Consider the understandings provided by the use of those methods.
Task D	Consider the ways in which the interactants enact identities, roles and/or relationships.
Task 3	Select other turns within the sequence and do Tasks A–D for each of the turns.

of that conduct. The tasks are aimed at developing analyses of practices used for performing and recognizing actions and for the enactment of role and relationship identities.

DEMONSTRATING THE ANALYTIC TASKS

Task 1: Select a sequence and examine the opening and closing as achievements

When watching or listening to a recording, identify the activities in which the participants are engaged. Often within an activity there will be one or more sequences of conversational actions. Select a sequence of actions for close observation. You might choose a particular sequence of actions for any number of reasons: you might have noticed something of interest within it; you might have a special interest in that type of action; you might want to start early in the activity to see how it evolves; you might see the action as relatively self-contained, or you might want to start with an audibly and visibly clear segment. You might be tempted to choose sequences that are funny, novel or topically interesting. However in our experience, the quality of one's findings is unrelated to one's interest in the sequence.

Once you select a sequence, look for identifiable boundaries. For the start of the sequence, locate the turn in which one of the participants initiated an action. For the end of the sequence, follow through the interaction until you locate the place in which the participants were no longer specifically responding to that action.[3] Treat sequence openings and closings as products of negotiation. While one party may offer a possible start or finish, the start or finish is usually not fully accomplished without ratification by the co-participant.

We selected the sequence in which the instructor/host was attempting to determine whether any of the students/invited guests had dietary restrictions. The entire sequence is included in the Appendix. Identifying the beginning of the sequence was unproblematic because the instructor/host produced the opening turn of talk as disjunctive from the prior sequence.[4] The prior sequence consisted of two actions: the instructor/host's proposal of an arrival time (line 1) and the students'/invited guests' acknowledgement of it by a verbal 'Ka:y' (line 3) and/or by a written notation. There was a long gap of six seconds during which the instructor/host took a sip of soda and the students/invited guests continued to write on the papers in front of them. During the six second gap, the prior sequence had come to a potential close: no participant attempted to extend it, and no participant initiated a new sequence.

Prior to this point in the interaction the instructor had provided information regarding the party's location and its starting time, and the students/invited guests acknowledged

---

[3]When participants perform new actions and respond to prior actions, their co-participants generally can recognize that they are doing this. Inasmuch as initiating a new sequence of actions or responding to a prior action is recognizable to interactants, they also are recognizable to analysts.

[4]Sometimes identifying the start of a sequence can be problematic because there can be step-wise transitions of topics. With topical pivots, a turn can be related both to a prior topic/sequence and to a next topic/sequence. (Jefferson, 1984).

the information verbally and/or by writing. The instructor/host then performed a topic/ sequence transition – he put his soda can down and uttered line 5 ('Mhmm:: aah::okay'), indicating that he was moving on to the next activity (which in the classroom could mean the end of a break and a resumption of instructional activities). However, following his transition marker, the instructor continued with further party-related talk, this time seeking information from the students/invited guests that could be relevant for the food to be served at the dinner party. The inquiry about whether any of the students/invited guests had any dietary restrictions is the beginning of the sequence that we will closely examine.

The instructor/host initiated the close of the topic/sequence pertaining to food choices for the dinner party, and the students collaborated in closing it. The instructor moved to end the sequence about food preferences by offering a maxim or figurative expression, 'All right well this you could chalk up to a new experience then' (Drew and Holt, 1999). After uttering the figurative expression, he turned his body and looked at the chalkboard and said 'we don't have anything on this woman on the board do we?'. In short, he conveyed to the students that the previous sequence was over and that it was time to begin instructional activities again. The students collaborated in terminating the break by turning their attention to the chalkboard.

Task 2: Select a turn within the sequence for close analysis

We selected the first turn in the sequence about dietary restrictions for close examination ('>Any of you have< any dietary restrictions we should know about?'). Starting at the beginning of a sequence allows us to have a better sense of how the sequence unfolds than if we start in the middle.

```
 1   Instruc:   Six thirty?
 2              (0.6)
 3   Linda:     Ka:y
 4              (6.0)
 5   Instruc:   Mhmm:: aah::okay
 6              (1.0)
 7   Instruc:   >Any of you have< any dietary restrictions we should know about?
 8              (1.4)
 9   Barbie:    °Mht mhm°
10              (0.6)
11   Instruc:   Can't eat onions (.) 'llergic ta peanuts (.)
12              ve[getarians anything like that]
13   Linda:       [Uhm I'm not-    I'm    not] a big-
14              I'm not really a meat eater[5]
15              (0.4)
```

---

[5]In the transcript we identified the participants as 'instructor' and with pseudonyms for students for ease of reading and for making sense of the scene. However we are not claiming that the speaker we designated as 'instructor' was always speaking as an instructor. Given the discussion of the upcoming party, that speaker also had the role identity of 'host of the upcoming dinner party'. Whether one or the other or both role identities are relevant is an analytic issue.

Task A: Characterize the actions performed in the turn and consider how the actions fit within sequences of actions

There are several different actions that the speaker of the turn may be seen to be performing and different sequences in which that turn may play a part.[6] First we will describe the action as part of an information exchange sequence, then as a request for confirmation or disconfirmation. After that we discuss a larger sequence in which the information seeking action may play a part, and finally we describe a context in which this type of information seeking may be done.

One action that the speaker is performing when he says '>Any of you have< any dietary restrictions we should know about?' is a *request for information* from the recipients. The speaker's act of *requesting* party-relevant information represents a departure from his previous actions of providing information about the party to the recipients and, as discussed above, launches a new sequence of actions. While his talk initiates this, it also relates to the prior sequences and topic inasmuch as it concerns arrangements for the upcoming dinner party. Requesting information is a first, or initiating, action that provides the relevance of a specific next action. Upon hearing the speaker's request for information, the recipients would be expected to produce the sought-after information.

While the speaker's action is appropriately called requesting information, that action can be further specified. The dietary restrictions inquiry is a yes/no question, in which the information sought is whether or not the recipients have food restrictions. That is, the speaker is *requesting confirmation or disconfirmation* of their having food restrictions. While the particular form of the request for information makes relevant as next actions either confirmation or disconfirmation, these are not equivalent options sequentially. In many sequential and interactional environments, confirmations are performed relatively straightforwardly, and disconfirmations are performed more elaborately, often incorporating delays, hedges, accounts, apologies, etc. Interestingly, in the sequential environment at hand, we would expect disconfirmations of dietary restrictions to be straightforward and unelaborated, and confirmations to be more elaborate. The bases for the complexity of confirmations are tied to a shared understanding of the implications of an invited guest's indicating food restrictions.

Inasmuch as recipients routinely analyse requests for information in terms of the inferred or stated purposes for asking (Pomerantz, 1988), the recipients-as-invited guests could infer that the host's purpose in asking was to see if the party menu needed to be adjusted or planned accordingly. A confirmation in this situation, then, could be treated as creating an imposition on the host.[7]

---

[6]Novice analysts may find it difficult to characterize the actions. It is reassuring to remember that there are often several actions and not just one that can be appropriately applied to a turn. Also we need to treat initially named actions as provisional – as first attempts that we could perhaps change if and when we think of any other actions that seem to fit the turn better.

[7]Acts that create impositions have been described in the politeness literature as negative face threats (Brown and Levinson, 1987) and in the Conversation Analytic literature as dispreferred actions (Pomerantz, 1984a).

A more extended action sequence that the speaker-as-host may be seen to be initiating involves determining whether or not a change in menu is called for. In the request for confirmation/disconfirmation about dietary restrictions, the speaker-as-host may be seen to be performing a preliminary inquiry that could *lead to an offer*, that is a *pre-offer*. Asking about their dietary restrictions implies the host's willingness to adjust the menu if an invited guest reports dietary restrictions; thus it can be seen as a pre-offer. Sequentially, a confirmation from an invited guest about food restrictions would raise the question as to whether or not the host should adjust the party food accordingly, often along with negotiations in which the 'host' offers to adjust the menu and the guest indicates there is no need to do so. In contrast, a disconfirmation of food restrictions is tantamount to a report of having no problem or issues with any party menu, and it would require no extension of the sequence.

Another use of the speaker-as-host's request for confirmation/disconfirmation involves potentially *overcoming a possible hesitancy*, on the part of the invited guests, *to report* food restrictions to the host. Pomerantz (1984a) analysed how delicate actions, such as criticisms, may be withheld over the course of entire sequences, delayed from an early positioning within sequences, or withheld in one sequential environment and coaxed out in another.[8] Invited guests may be reluctant to indicate their food restrictions if they assume thereby that the host may feel obligated to adjust the menu accordingly, which is an imposition on the host. An action that the speaker-as-host performs with his inquiry is to *provide an opportunity for recipients to report food restrictions*. When the host asks the invited guests about their food restrictions, he provides a context for their reporting dietary restrictions as an answer to his question rather than as a volunteered report. If an invited guest provides a report of food restrictions as an answer to a question, he or she may be seen as simply answering the question honestly rather than indirectly making an imposing request.

Task B: Describe the methods used to perform the actions. Consider the understandings provided by the use of those methods

When examining the methods through which the participants performed the action in question, conversation analysts should pay attention to gestures, eye gaze, body position, the

---

[8]Pomerantz (1984a: 79) gave the following example of a speaker's withholding of a criticism in one sequential environment and finally being prompted or encouraged to articulate it in another. F had previously done a nail manicure for N and was asking if it had worked.

    F: .hh well how did the polish work otherwise.
    N: F-eh fi:ne, fi:ne,. In fact I didn' even touch em up this week at all
    F: You didn't
    N: No
    F: .hh Well I was afraid maybe they might uhh uh bubble a little bit y'know they [kinda
    N: [Well they di:d. Tha-tha-that one
         thing it with the artificial nail bubbled some
    F: Yeah. Well I was afraid it would
    N: ( ) the patch bubbled …

This excerpt illustrates that a participant might have a sense of the kind of information that may be withheld and may employ a number of information-seeking strategies to elicit such a report.

formulations used, the timing of the talk relative to the prior turn, and the material objects employed. The aim is to see: how these aspects of the enactment can provide for the sense or meaning that is conveyed; how they will relate to the prior conduct; and how they will shape or structure the response options for recipients. Unfortunately, the instructor/host is not on screen during his speaking turn, so nothing can be said about his gestures, gaze, or body position before, during or immediately after the turn. We will focus on the sense of the action that is, in part, shaped by the formulations employed.

Asking invited guests to a dinner party about their 'dietary restrictions' is a very different matter from asking them about their food preferences. The formulation, 'dietary restrictions', asks about the foods that invited guests are unable to eat, whereas the formulation 'food preferences' asks about those foods which the guests enjoy or dislike. 'Restrictions' suggests that the relevant dietary items asked about are not a matter of the recipients' preferences but are instead constraints to which the recipients are subject as a consequence of digestive system problems or allergies.

The inclusion of 'any' before 'dietary restrictions' ('>Any of you have< any dietary restrictions we should know about?') suggests that the speaker is aware that there are multiple types of dietary restrictions that could be reported, and that the recipients would know what counts as types of dietary restriction. The formulation seems to encourage the recipients to report any that might apply to them. However, a study of primary, acute-care medical visits suggests that 'any' might not encourage recipients to report their concerns as much as other formulations would (Heritage, Robinson, Elliott, Beckett and Wilkes, 2007: 1432).[9]

> Practitioners may be surprised that the ANY intervention, which is widely promoted in textbooks of medical interviewing, was relatively ineffective in eliciting additional concerns and in reducing unmet concerns. It appears that the negative polarity of the single word 'any,' with its subtle communication of an expectation for a 'No' response, tends to vitiate the opportunity to raise unmet concerns that the question might otherwise create.

Based on this finding, we wonder whether incorporating 'some' rather than 'any' with 'dietary restrictions' ('>Any of you have< any dietary restrictions we should know about?') might have provided a more encouraging environment for the invited guests to report on their dietary restrictions.

When the instructor-host asked the student/guests about dietary restrictions, he added '[that] we should know about?' He phrased the question in a way that asked the students/guests to make a judgment about which food restrictions might be relevant for planning the dinner menu. Asking what information the students have that the host should be given relies

---

[9]Heritage, Robinson, Elliott, Beckett, and Wilkes (2007) designed an intervention in which physicians were randomly assigned to solicit additional concerns by asking either 'Is there anything else you want to address in the visit today?' (ANY condition) or 'Is there something else you want to address in the visit today?' (SOME condition). They found that the SOME intervention eliminated 78 per cent of the unmet concerns whereas the ANY intervention could not be significantly distinguished from the control condition.

on the students' deciding what the host should know. It also suggests the host's willingness to adjust the meal to accommodate his guests' dietary restrictions. The implication is that the host cannot accommodate dietary restrictions if he does not know about them, and if he does know about them, he can plan the menu accordingly.

Task C: Describe the methods used for taking, keeping, and transitioning between turns. Consider the understandings provided by the use of those methods

The instructor/host self-selected to be the speaker in a conversational environment in which the prior sequence of actions could be seen as complete. The students/invited guests had affirmed the arrival time for the dinner either verbally or by writing on their papers, and a sizable gap emerged with no one initiating any actions. When the instructor started his inquiry about dietary restrictions, two of the students were still looking down and writing. The instructor treats his inquiry as hearable by the students while they are writing, and as non-interruptive of their writing.

In asking '>Any of you have< any dietary restrictions we should know about?' the instructor/host designates the intended recipients of his query with the formulation 'Any of you'. In that way at least, he addresses his inquiry to everyone in the room and invites any person or persons to self-select in response. It is unfortunate that we cannot see the instructor/host's gaze during his turn, as this might have revealed his intended recipients, whether or not he searched for recipients, and so forth (Goodwin, 1981; Kidwell, 2005; Lerner, 2003).

In arriving at the end of the turn constructional unit (TCU), the instructor/host provides a transition-relevance place for the students/invited guests to confirm or disconfirm their having dietary restrictions. Recipients, however, do not wait until the completion of turn constructional units to make sense of what is being said and done; they make sense during the course of speakers' turns. They have ways of showing that they are attending to the speaker's talk in progress. One way a participant shows that he or she is attending to what is being said is by gaze direction. Two of the students gaze at the instructor/host while he is producing the inquiry:

```
Instructor:    Any of you have any diet[ary re[strictions we should know about
Male 2:                           [Looks at instructor
Linda:                                  [Looks at instructor
```

Male 2 looks to the instructor/host within the word 'dietary' and continues to look at him throughout the remainder of his turn and into the turn-transition space. Linda looks at the instructor after the first syllable of 'restrictions' and also continues to look at him through his turn and into the turn-transition space. Through their gazing practices, those two participants are displaying their attention to the speaker and his talk during the turn.

After the instructor/host has completed the inquiry, a gap emerges. After 1.4 seconds, Barbie, still looking down, utters a quiet 'Mht mhm' with a little head shake. By so doing,

Barbie enacted both verbally and with a head shake a very subdued disconfirmation of having dietary restrictions.

At about the same time (about 1.5 seconds after the prior inquiry was complete) Cathy turns her head to the right and looks at Linda. Cathy's conduct, while certainly responsive to the instructor's inquiry, is not a conditionally relevant responding action to the inquiry. Rather, looking and smiling at Linda can be seen as Cathy's displaying her understanding of for whom this inquiry could be trouble. It locates Linda as the object of interest and anticipates the reporting dilemma that the inquiry poses for Linda. In this way, Cathy's look and smile respond to the prior action and anticipate an upcoming action, without changing the conditionally relevant next actions in the sequence of actions.

Task D: Consider the ways in which participants enact role and/or relationship identities

A fundamental way that knowledge is organized is in terms of category sets (Pomerantz and Mandelbaum, 2005; Sacks, 1992; Schegloff, 2006). Sacks (1992) suggested that sets of categories that describe a population are 'inference-rich'. By this he meant that 'a great deal of the knowledge that members of a society have about the society is stored in terms of these categories' (1992: 40). Part of that lay-knowledge is the recognizable association between categories of persons, on the one hand, and typical activities, actions, motives, and interests attributed to incumbents of those categories, on the other. That assumed association may be used to interpret both what people are doing as well as who they are (their identities).

An interactional role that the speaker of the query about dietary restrictions enacted was that of *orchestrating the flow of activities*. With respect to the series of activities captured on videotape, one particular participant initiated the discussion after the guest speaker left; initiated the class break from instruction; and initiated the end of the break/return to instructional activities. Inasmuch as orchestrating the flow of activities in the seminar is understood as a right and/or obligation of persons occupying the institutional role identity of instructor, that participant can be seen to be enacting the role identity of instructor. All role enactments require joint participation or ratification of some sort. The students validated the instructor's right to direct the movement of the activities by complying, with no sign of resistance, with his initiating and terminating the series of activities.

Another interactional role that the speaker enacted was that of information giver (as it pertained to the matter of the upcoming dinner party). The speaker gave his address, provided directions to his house, set the arrival time for the invited guests, and sought information about the invited guests' dietary restrictions. As such activities are linked to the category of host, by engaging in these, the instructor during that time span was enacting the role-identity of party host.[10]

---

[10]Given that the action in which he is engaged (i.e. asking about any food restrictions) is bound to the category 'host,' his use of 'we' in '[that] we should know about' is understandable as he and his wife, the menu planners.

In the turn transition space after the instructor/host completes his inquiry, Cathy enacted being in a close relationship with Linda. Upon hearing the instructor/host's inquiry, Cathy looked up and then over toward Linda, and smiled. With this conduct, she displayed that she had heard the instructor's question as particularly relevant to Linda, thereby also showing that she had knowledge of Linda's eating habits. In smiling, she displayed an expectation that Linda would likely have some trouble responding to the inquiry. In putting herself in Linda's position, she displayed a knowledge not only of Linda's eating habits but also of the way she might react to being in the difficult situation of having food restrictions but not wanting to impose them on the hosts, perhaps especially because the host was the instructor.

Task 3: Select other turns in the sequence and do Tasks A–D for each selected turn

We selected the instructor's next turn at talk as the focal turn.

Task A: Identify the actions. Consider how the actions fit within sequences of actions

One action that the instructor-host performs with 'Can't eat onions (.) ''llergic ta peanuts (.) vegetarians anything like that' is *clarifying* what he meant by dietary restrictions. He clarifies what he meant by dietary restrictions by giving examples of types of dietary restrictions. By offering examples of dietary restrictions, the instructor/host treats his previous query about dietary restrictions as needing clarification. The repair sequence is occasioned by the lack of sufficient responses by the students/invited guests. In offering a clarification, the speaker implies that the order of problem with respect to the failure to respond is one of not knowing what he meant by 'dietary restrictions'. Offering the clarification sets up the relevance in the next turn for the recipients to display whether or not the clarification solved the problem. The repair sequence would be terminated by the students/invited guests providing the information requested by the query about dietary restrictions.

Another action that the instructor/host performs in saying 'Can't eat onions (.) ''llergic ta peanuts (.) vegetarians' is *prompting* the students to respond – sequentially, prompting links back to an earlier utterance. The coherence of the items enumerated depends upon understanding these as examples of dietary restrictions, which he asked about in his previous turn. Prompting treats any responses to date as inadequate and/or unsatisfactory and proposes that an adequate and/or satisfactory response still is due. It conveys that a response is still relevant and that the prompter still is waiting for it.

Task B: Consider the methods used to perform the actions

The method that the instructor/host uses to clarify his prior utterance is listing types of dietary restrictions as examples of the type of information he was seeking. The first two instances of dietary restrictions were formulated in ways that cast the matter not as preferences or choices but rather as constraints to which a person was subject without respect to his or her wishes, preferences, or tastes. In the first example, 'can't eat onions', the formulation 'can't eat' proposes an interest in foods that the guests would be unable to eat safely. In his second example, ''llergic ta peanuts', the formulation ''llergic' suggests that he was asking the recipients if there were any foods that would cause them harm. His third example of a dietary restriction was 'vegetarian'. While vegetarianism is generally regarded as a matter of choice, it is generally a life-style choice that often carries a moral and ethical commitment which supports it. The examples retained the sense of the type of information that the instructor/host had sought with his previous formulation of 'dietary restrictions'. Following the three examples, the instructor/host adds 'anything like that' as a way to emphasize his having given examples but not an exhaustive list of the types of food restrictions being asked about. It serves as an invitation to the students/invited guests to report dietary restrictions other than the ones he specified.

Regarding the methods through which prompting is accomplished, the instructor/host names examples of dietary restrictions, delivering them one by one and with opportunities provided for the recipients to report on whether or not they have any dietary restrictions. (For a further discussion of the methods used, please see the discussion under Task C, next.)

Task C: Consider turn-taking phenomena

From the completion of his initial inquiry about dietary restrictions to the beginning of his clarifying/prompting them with examples, the instructor/host allowed 2.5 seconds to emerge for responses. In the absence of sufficient responses to his inquiry, he pursued responses by offering each item in what could be a turn constructional unit (TCU). He named the first example of a dietary restriction, 'Can't eat onions', using the intonation for an item on a list, and slightly paused at its completion. This practice (list intonation plus pause) can be seen as providing recipients with an invitation/opportunity to respond while also indicating that the speaker can say more. In this possible turn transition space, the students/invited guests did not audibly respond.

The instructor/host then names a second example of a dietary restriction, ''llergic to peanuts'. This example is also delivered with the intonation of a list item and a slight pause, providing the students/invited guests with an invitation/opportunity to respond.

After the instructor/host provides the second example of a dietary restriction, two of the students/invited guests, Cathy and Linda, do offer responses to the inquiry about dietary restrictions. While it might appear that Cathy and Linda are responding to the initial sound in 'vegetarian', we find it more plausible that they are a beat late in responding to the completion of ''llergic ta peanuts'.

```
Instruc:   [Can't [eat on[ions, (.) ['llergic ta peanuts, (.) ve[getarian anything like that
Cathy:     [Looking at Linda    [Gaze to Instruc        [head shake
Linda:              [Looks at Instruc                    [Uhm I'm not I'm not
Barbie:               [Gaze to Instruc
```

As discussed earlier, Cathy turns to look at Linda and smile after the instructor/host poses the initial query about dietary preferences. Cathy then continues to look at Linda through the instructor/host's offering the first example ('can't eat onions'). While the instructor is giving a second example of a dietary restriction, Cathy gazes at him. Just as he starts to offer a third example of a dietary restriction, Cathy shakes her head, indicating no dietary restriction. This is a conditionally relevant response to the initial inquiry, done non-verbally, to indicate that she has no dietary restrictions.

Two points seem particularly noteworthy to us. First, while Cathy may have had an interest in seeing what Linda would do with the question, the instructor/host's continuing to prompt with examples motivated or prompted her to show she was attending to his talk. She did this by directing her gaze at him. Second, before giving a response to his inquiry about dietary restrictions, she directed her gaze at him. Part of the enactment of responding to his inquiry was to gaze at him when starting to respond.

When the instructor/host completed his initial inquiry, Linda was in the course of eating. During the 2.5 seconds gap, she takes a bite and chews her food but then strikes a pose. The pose involves her dropping her hand to her lap, slightly dropping her trunk, and looking up with a closed mouth smile. The best way we can characterize the look is as 'I'm not comfortable about something that I have to say'. This pose continues through the beginning of the instructor/host's first example when she then looks at the instructor/host and holds the gaze until she starts responding to his query about dietary restrictions.

There are several points of note here. First, while we do not know where the instructor/host was gazing during the 2.5 seconds after he completed his first inquiry, we can surmise (based on Cathy's turning to Linda and smiling, and Linda's somewhat strange pose and expression) it might have been available to him that there was some sensitivity involved in responding. This sensitivity would be associated with affirming dietary restrictions. The prompting that he does may have been responsive to the lack of a satisfactory response to the initial inquiry and/or to the cues that were available that something had not yet been said that was proving uncomfortable for the concerned students/invited guests. Second, the practices of doing reluctance may involve more than delaying reports and then giving the reports with hedges, perturbations, etc. Part of the enactment of displaying reluctance (and hence doing dispreferred actions: Pomerantz, 1984a) might well include displaying specific kinds of grins or grimaces, dropping the body, etc.

Task D: Consider the enactment of role and/or relationship identities

Through his conduct, the instructor/host claims the role identity of accommodating host. He does so by first inquiring about the dietary restrictions of the invited guests and then by pursuing the matter when no response is forthcoming. The claim to that identity is even more apparent when he offers to change the menu: 'Gladys and I probly eat meat once a week at the tops (.) cause we're pretty vegetarian too (0.5) so we're perfectly willing to change to make it vegetarian'. Through their conduct, the students with dietary restrictions claim the role identity of not wanting to impose. They do so by delaying confirming that they have dietary restrictions and then reporting such restrictions with considerable hedges.

The identity claims of the host and the invited guests with dietary restrictions are in potential conflict.[11] If the host were to be accommodating about dietary restrictions, the guests with those restrictions would be imposing. After a delicate dance involving each party's positioning in ways that will display the appropriate role identities, the outcome is that the hosts would serve the beef dish which would be a 'new experience' for the students/ invited guests with dietary restrictions.

CONCLUSION

Our aim in this chapter has been to introduce the reader to some of the central premises and concepts in Conversation Analysis and to provide a set of tasks to assist them in getting started in analysing social interaction. In this section, we address two areas. First, we situate the analytic tasks we described in this chapter as one alternative among several that a person might use to begin analysis. Second we suggest how the analyst might move beyond the analytic tasks described here to develop analyses of practices.

Alternative paths to beginning analysis

Drawing on Schegloff (1996), Clayman and Gill (2004) suggest two pathways into the data: beginning with a noticing and beginning with a vernacular action. When starting with a noticing, they suggest that after an analyst has noticed something about the way a speaker says or does something at a given point within the interaction, he or she should then ask what actions are being accomplished by that way of speaking/acting and how might that way of speaking/acting contribute to the ongoing course of the interaction. When starting with a vernacular action, Clayman and Gill suggest that after the analyst has characterized an action or actions being accomplished at a point in the interaction, the analyst should explore the different ways that action can be carried out and also consider how the various alternatives could be consequential for subsequent talk.

There is a range of phenomena of potential interest to investigators of social interaction, and hence there are numerous domains about which observations can be made. Clayman and Gill (2004) indicate that interactional phenemena can be investigated at several different

---

[11]See Chen (1990/91) for an analysis of the conflicting face concerns between hosts and guests at a Chinese dinner table and the strategies the participants used to deal with those conflicting concerns.

levels, each of which may shed light on the underlying procedures through which the activities and actions are to be accomplished. The levels they list are activity frameworks, discrete sequences of actions, singular actions, specific lexical choices, intonation contours, non-vocal behaviours, and other turn components mobilized within turns at talk.

Operating with the assumptions that there are many kinds of interactional phenomena to observe and that novices will benefit by being encouraged to make focused technical observations, Lerner and Schegloff developed an approach they called 'keys' that they used during data sessions in successive years at the Conversation Analysis Advanced Study Institute. These *keys*, when used singly or in combination, are a list of analytic interests that can provide entry into 'unlocking' interactional segments. Included here are: the sequential connections in turn composition; the sequence-organization connections; the transition space practices and actions; person reference; formulations; same-turn repair initiation; overlap onset, resolution, and consequences; silence; and laughter and in-speech laughter.

Developing analyses of practices

A detailed description of what the participants say and do in an interaction is not the same as an analysis of a *practice* that participants will use to accomplish an action. One model of an analysis of a practice is that it should enable someone to competently use that practice to perform an action. This involves moving away from discussing what particular people did on the occasion, to considering what people need to know and do in order to appropriately perform the action in any new situations they encounter. Ideally this should include describing the method of performing the action; the interactional environments in which the practice is used; the options for relevantly responding; the entitlements and constraints associated with employing the practice; possible role/relationship implications; and perhaps contrasting how the practice functions in comparison with other ways of accomplishing the action.

To provide a type of consideration involved in moving beyond initial observations and toward analysing practices, we would offer some comments about two possible practices as they have emerged from the interaction sequence discussed in this chapter. One possible practice involves pursuing a response by using examples; the other possible practice involves enacting a close relationship by displayedly anticipating interactional trouble for you.

Pursuit by offering examples

Recall that when the instructor/host said 'Can't eat onions (.) ''llergic ta peanuts (.) vegetarians anything like that' he was pursuing a response by offering examples of possible responses to his prior query about dietary restrictions. He delivered the examples, one by one, thus inviting/providing opportunities for the recipients to respond.

Pomerantz (1984b) analysed practices for pursuing responses when the recipients of initial assessments did not immediately agree or disagree. In that environment, one format or action that was used to pursue agreement/disagreement was clarifying an understanding problem. In Pomerantz's data, the speakers pursued a recipient's agreement or disagreement by replacing a demonstrative pronoun used in the initial assessment with a clarifying noun in the follow-up utterance.

In the instance we examined, the instructor/host pursued a response by successively giving examples of types of dietary restrictions that the invited guests might have, that is, he suggested candidate responses to his inquiry. We wonder if that method of pursuing responses is employed when speakers have reason to believe that recipients are reluctant to give up the requested information. Here we would wish to collect more instances of pursuing responses and compare how these are performed and the environments in which they are used. We would also want to see how gaze operates with respect to pursuing responses in different types of sequential environments (Rossano, 2009).

Doing closeness by anticipating interactional trouble

Recall that when the instructor/host asked '>Any of you have< any dietary restrictions we should know about?' Cathy looked at Linda and smiled. In doing so, she displayed that she could anticipate the trouble that the inquiry might create for Linda, that she can put herself in Linda's place, and that she has some level of knowledge about Linda's eating habits and the way she deals with them interactionally. In short, this appears to be a practice for doing closeness.

Drew and Chilton (2000) studied telephone conversations between family members who regularly phoned each other just to keep in touch. They identified three types of small talk which the participants performed in first topic position: participants would report 'noticings' about the immediate local environment; they would also report, or elicit a report from the other, about the day's happening; and they would make requests for new updates about events or circumstances that were current when they last spoke. The enactment of relationships is a reciprocal process, where one person may make a bid and the second person either ratifies or rejects that bid. Pomerantz and Mandelbaum (2005) identified four verbal practices that would help constitute persons as enacting reciprocal friendships: P1 inquires about specific events in P2's life and P2 provides more details about that event; P1 discusses his/her own problems and P2 displays an interest in P1's problems; P1 makes oblique references to shared experiences and P2 forwards the talk about those experiences; and P1 uses improprieties and P2 takes up the improprieties by using additional improprieties and/or laughter.

We would suggest that in addition to the verbal relationship-implicative activities identified by previous researchers, directing one's gaze and smiling at a target person in anticipation of how that person will analyse and react to an event in progress is an additional way of claiming one has the knowledge, rights, and obligations associated with the category of 'friend'. In the case of Cathy and Linda, the latter does smile after the instructor/host has asked the question about dietary restrictions, but we are not able to say whether she sees Kathy's smiling at her when she smiles.

We will conclude this discussion by noting that analysis is a slow process of transcribing, making observations, finding more instances of potentially interesting phenomena, etc. As you continue to watch or listen to a recording of interaction and note your observations, your initial analytic thoughts will gradually take on more shape. No one, experienced

Conversation Analysts included, can produce a finished analysis the first time around. This type of work lends itself to successive revision and refinement. Indeed producing the demonstrations for this chapter involved this sort of slowly evolving work. The versions published here look quite different from our early passes through the materials, and these could be developed further. Generally it is the joy of discovering interactional phenomena, of seeing interactions in ways not previously seen, that continually brings us back to closely examining the conduct of social life.

NOTE

The authors would like to thank William Husson for his helpful commentary and suggestions on an earlier version of this chapter. We are indebted to Curtis LeBaron for granting us permission to use his data for our illustration.

FURTHER READING

Becoming a competent Conversation Analyst requires that one gain analytic skills through practice; read and understand the work of pioneers in Conversation Analysis; and know the empirical research that has been done in different interactional domains. The readings listed below will provide newcomers with an understanding of the methods of, and findings in, the field.

Sacks, H. (1992) *Lectures on Conversation*, vols I and II. Oxford: Blackwell. Edited by Gail Jefferson, with an introduction by Emanuel Schegloff.
Delivered between 1964 and 1972, Sacks' lectures were edited by Gail Jefferson and published in 1992, with an introduction by Emanuel Schegloff. Given Sacks' untimely death in 1975 and the relatively few papers he published during his life, these lectures provide an invaluable insight to his analytic thinking. Although entitled *Lectures on Conversation*, they include discussion and analysis of a much wider range of topics on 'the social organization of mind, culture and interaction'. (Schegloff, 1992)

Schegloff, E.A. (2007) *Sequence Organization in Interaction: A Primer in Conversation Analysis I*. Cambridge: Cambridge University Press.
This is the first volume in a proposed collection of books introducing and detailing the principles, practices and findings of conversation analysis. In this first volume, Schegloff provides a comprehensive overview of the relevance of sequence, basic sequential structures, and how different types of organization intersect with sequential organization. All of the transcribed interaction segments are available for viewing and/or hearing via links on the Cambridge University Press website.

Drew, P. and Heritage, J. (eds) (2006) *Conversation Analysis*. London: Sage.
Newcomers often complain that they do not know which conversation analytic papers represent high quality research across the field. This four volume edited collection provides easy access to a wide range of well-regarded conversation analytic work. It includes many papers on turn-taking, turn design, repair, action formation, sequence, interaction organization, and institutional talk.

Hutchby, I. and Wooffitt, R. (2008) *Conversation Analysis*, 2nd edn. Cambridge: Polity.
This introductory textbook to conversation analysis includes a discussion of the foundations of the field, its analytic viewpoint, and a survey of central findings across a variety of settings. In addition there are two chapters focused on the practices of analysis and a final chapter relating conversation analysis to other social science disciplines.

ONLINE READING

The following articles are available at www.sagepub.co.uk/discoursestudies.

Mondada, L. (2007) ' Multimodal resources for turn-taking: pointing and the emergence of possible next speakers'. *Discourse Studies*, 9(2): 194–225.

Craven, A. and J. Potter (2010) 'Directives: Entitlement and contingency in action'. *Discourse Studies*, 12(4): 419–442.

Jefferson, G. (2004) 'A note on laughter in "male-female" interaction'. *Discourse Studies*, 6(1): 117–133.

REFERENCES

Brown, P. and Levinson, S.C. (1987) *Politeness: Some Universals in Language Use*. Cambridge: Cambridge University Press.

Chen, V. (1990–91) '*Mien Tze* at the Chinese dinner table: a study of the interactional accomplishment of face'. *Research on Language and Social Interaction,* 24: 109–40.

Chomsky, N. (1965) *Aspects of the Theory of Syntax*. Cambridge, MA: MIT Press.

Clayman, S.E and Gill, V.T (2004) 'Conversion analysis'. In M. Hardy and A. Bryman (eds), *Handbook of Data Analysis*. London: Sage.

Drew, P. and Chilton, K. (2000) 'Calling just to keep in touch: regular and habitualised telephone calls as an environment for small talk'. In J. Coupland (ed.), *Small Talk*. Harlow: Pearson Education. pp. 137–62.

Drew, P. and Heritage, J. (eds) (2006) *Conversation Analysis*. London: Sage.

Drew, P. and Holt, E. (1999) 'Figures of speech: figurative expressions and the management of topic transition in conversation'. *Language in Society, 27*: 495–522.

Goodwin, C. (1980) 'Restarts, pauses, and the achievement of mutual gaze at turn-beginning'. *Sociological Inquiry, 50* (3–4): 272–302.

Goodwin, C. (1981) *Conversational Organization: Interaction between Speakers and Hearers*. New York: Academic.

Goodwin, M.H. (1980) 'Processes of mutual monitoring implicated in the production of description sequences'. *Sociological Inquiry, 50* (3–4): 303–17.

Heath, C. (1981) 'The opening sequence in doctor-patient interaction'. In P. Atkinson and C. Heath (eds), *Medical Work: Realities and Routines*. Farnborough: Gower. pp. 71–90.

Heritage, J. (2008) 'Conversation analysis as social theory'. In B. Turner (ed.), *The New Blackwell Companion to Social Theory*. Oxford: Blackwell. pp. 300–20.

Heritage, J., Robinson, J.D., Elliott, M., Becket,t M. and Wilkes, M. (2007) 'Reducing patients' unmet concerns: The difference one word can make'. *Journal of General Internal Medicine, 22*: 1429–1433.

Hutchby, I. and Wooffitt, R. (2008) *Conversation Analysis* (2nd edition). Cambridge: Polity.

Jefferson, G. (1974) 'Error correction as an interactional resource'. *Language in Society, 3* (2): 181–99.

Jefferson, G. (1984) 'On stepwise transition from talk about a trouble to inappropriately next-positioned matters'. In J.M. Atkinson and J. Heritage (eds.) *Structures of Social Action: Studies in Conversation Analysis*. Cambridge: Cambridge University Press. pp. 191–222.

Jefferson, G. (1987) 'On exposed and embedded correction in conversation'. In G. Button and J.R.E. Lee (eds), *Talk and Social Organization*. Clevedon: Multilingual Matters. pp. 86–100.

Jefferson, G. (2004) 'Glossary of transcript symbols with an introduction'. In G. Lerner (ed.), *Conversation Analysis: Studied From the First Generation*. Amsterdam: John Benjamins. pp. 13–31.

Jones, S.E. and LeBaron, C.D. (2002) Guest editors of a special issue of the *Journal of Communication 52* (3): 'Research on the relationship between verbal and nonverbal communication: emerging integrations'.

Kidwell, M. (2005) 'Gaze as social control: how very young children differentiate "the look" from "a mere look" from their adult caregivers'. *Research on Language and Social Interaction, 38* (4): 417–49.

Lerner, G.H. (2002) 'Turn-sharing: the choral co-production of talk-in-interaction'. In C. Ford, B. Fox and S. Thompson (eds), *The Language of Turn and Sequence*. Oxford: Oxford University Press. pp. 225–56.

Lerner, G.H. (2003) 'Selecting next speaker: the context-sensitive operation of a context-free organization'. *Language in Society, 32* (2): 177–201.

LeVine, P. and Scollon, R. (2004) *Discourse and Technology: Multimodal Discourse Analysis*. Washington, DC: Georgetown University Press.

Pomerantz, A. (1984a) 'Agreeing and disagreeing with assessments: Some features of preferred/dispreferred turn shapes'. In J.M. Atkinson and J. Heritage (eds.) *Structures of Social Action: Studies in Conversation Analysis*. Cambridge: Cambridge University Press. pp. 57–101.

Pomerantz, A. (1984b) 'Pursuing a response'. In J.M. Atkinson and J. Heritage (eds), *Structures of Social Action: Studies in Conversation Analysis*. Cambridge: Cambridge University Press. pp. 152–63.

Pomerantz, A. (1988) 'Offering a candidate answer: an information seeking strategy'. *Communication Monographs, 55*: 360–73.

Pomerantz, A. and Mandelbaum, J. (2005) 'Conversation analytic approaches to the relevance and uses of relationship categories in interaction'. In K.L. Fitch and R.E. Sanders (eds), *Handbook of Language and Social Interaction*. Mahwah, NJ: Lawrence Erlbaum. pp. 149–71.

Raymond, G. and Heritage, J. (2006) 'The epistemics of social relationships: owning grandchildren'. *Language in Society, 35* (5): 677–705.

Rossano, F. (2009) 'Using gaze to pursue responses'. *American Sociological Association Annual Meeting*, San Francisco.

Sacks, H. (1992) *Lectures on Conversation*, vols I and II. Oxford: Blackwell. (Edited by Gail Jefferson, with an introduction by Emanuel Schegloff).

Sacks, H., Schegloff, E.A. and Jefferson, G. (1974) 'A simplest systematics for the organization of turn-taking for conversation'. *Language, 50*: 696–735.

Schegloff, E.A. (1979) 'The relevance of repair for syntax-for-conversation'. In T. Givon (ed.), *Syntax and Semantics 12: Discourse and Syntax*. New York: Academic Press. pp. 261–88.

Schegloff, E.A. (1992a) 'Introduction'. In G. Jefferson (ed.), *Harvey Sacks: Lectures on Conversation*, volume 1. Oxford: Blackwell. pp: ix–lxii.

Schegloff, E.A. (1992b) 'Repair after next turn: the last structurally provided place for the defense of intersubjectivity in conversation'. *American Journal of Sociology, 95* (5): 1295–345.

Schegloff, E.A. (1996) 'Confirming allusions: toward an empirical account of action'. *American Journal of Sociology, 102* (1): 161–216.

Schegloff, E.A. (1997) 'Practices and action: boundary cases of other-initiated repair'. *Discourse Processes*, 23: 499–545.

Schegloff, E.A. (2000) 'When "others" initiate repair'. *Applied Linguistics, 21* (2): 205–43.

Schegloff, E.A. (2006) 'Interaction: the infrastructure for social institutions, the natural ecological niche for language, and the arena in which culture is enacted'. In N.J. Enfield and S.C. Levinson (eds), *Roots of Human Sociality*. Oxford: Berg. pp. 70–96.

Schegloff, E.A. (2007) *Sequence Organization in Conversation*. Cambridge: Cambridge University Press.

Schegloff, E.A. and Sacks, H. (1973) 'Opening up closings'. *Semiotica, 8*: 289–327.

Schegloff, E.A., Jefferson, G. and Sacks, H. (1977) 'The preference for self-correction in the organization of repair in conversation'. *Language, 53* (2): 361–82.

Sidnell, J. and Stivers, T. (2005) Guest editors of a special issue of *Semiotica* 156 (1/4) on multi-modal interaction.

APPENDIX

'Dietary restrictions'

```
1    Instruc:  Six thirty?
2              (0.6)
```

```
 3   Linda:    Ka:y
 4             (6.0)
 5   Instruc:  Mhmm:: aah::okay
 6             (1.0)
 7   Instruc:  >Any of you have< any dietary restrictions we should know about?
 8             (1.4)
 9   Barbie:   °Mht mhm°
10             (0.6)
11   Instruc:  Can't eat onions (.) 'llergic ta peanuts (.)
12             Ve[getarians anything like that]
13   Linda:      [Uhm  I'm   not-  I'm  not] a big-
14             I'm not really a meat eater
15             (0.4)
16   Barbie:   I'm not either
17             (0.2)
18   Barbie:   >But I-<
19             (1.8)
20   Linda:    I always feel good when Barbie's-=
21             [this happened [u(h)m before didn't it?
22   Barbie:   [.hhh          [heh heh
23   Linda:    NO:
24             (1.2)
25   Linda:    We weren't in a group together [before.
26   Barbie:                                  [°Mht mhm°
27             (1.2)
28   Linda:    I always feel better when there's someone else in the group that do(h)esn't e(h)at
29             m(h)eat t(h)oo
30   Cathy:    You'll eat chicken and fish °though°
31   Linda:    [Mm mhm
32   Barbie:   [Oh yeah!
33             (0.3)
34   Cathy:    Just not °pork and beef°
35   Instruc:  Not red meat (.) okay.
36   Linda:    °Yeah° But if (.) you wanna make that
37             [there are other things
38   Cathy:    [Pork's the other white meat
39   Linda:    like salads and stuff I can just- (0.6) my husband (2.0) he prolly (.) I don't know hhh.
40   Instruc:  I think she's planning to make what's called carbanona flamand which is a
41             Belgian dish but it's got beef in it
42             (0.6)
43   Linda:    That's fine. I mean-
44             (1.3)
45   Instruc:  It isn't a steak
46             (1.0)
47   Linda:    That's fine. I re:ally- (0.4) I mean I don't- (1.0) I don't know if you ever real- See you
48             had lamb before right
49   Barbie:   °Mm mhm°
50             (0.5)
```

51	Linda:	We're both kinna hypocritical about it
52	Instruc:	Well-
53	Cathy:	heh heh [heh heh heh
54	Instruc:	[Gladys and I probly eat meat once a week at the tops (.) cause we're
55		pretty vegetarian too.
56		(0.5)
57	Instruc:	so we're <u>perf</u>ectly willing to change to make it vegetarian
58		(1.5)
59	Linda:	O::h I don't wanna ask you to do tha:t
60		(2.2)
61	Linda:	I don't- I'm not- I don't have like a religious thing about it or anything like that I [just don't-
62	Instruc:	[Just don't like it
63		(1.0)
64	Linda:	No I don't even not (0.6) like it
65	Rose:	Hhh. N(h)ow- now that you said- if you said that you were making hot dogs or something
66		like you know then it would
67		[(change it)
68	Linda:	[Yeah I don't like [hot dogs ((laughs))
69	Rose:	[But now that you said m(h)m you're making this
70		[nice Belgian dish
71	Linda:	[Like <u>Bel</u>gian with this [<u>name</u> and I've=
72	Rose:	[Yeah yeah
73	Linda:	<u>ne</u>ver had it It so(h)unds go(h)od ((laughter))
74	Rose:	Now now the veg[etarians (doesn't care)
75	Cathy:	[Make the Belgian!
76	Rose:	Yeah.
77	Male:	((laughter))
78	Rose:	In other words
79		((Most of the group is laughing and talking at once.))
80	Rose:	(We need) carnivores
81		((More overlapping talk and laughter))
82	Linda:	(... a chance for plastic or stuff like that)
83	Cathy:	((laughs))
84	Instruc:	All right well this you could chalk up to a new experience then.
85	Cathy:	((laughs))
86	Instruc:	Uh: where- we don't have anything on this woman on the board do we?
87	Male:	mht mhm.
88	Female:	uht uh.
89	Instruc:	So we could start clean over there I guess,

TEN

Dialogue in Institutional Interactions

Paul Drew and Marja-Leena Sorjonen

INSTITUTIONAL DIALOGUE: THE FIELD OF STUDY

When we visit the doctor, hold meetings at our workplaces, appear as witnesses in court, negotiate business deals, ask for goods in convenience stores, interview for a job, call a medical or other information help line, summon the emergency services, (as faculty) meet students in office hours, or (as counsellors or clients) participate in therapeutic counselling sessions, we are talking, communicating and interacting in recognizably institutional 'contexts'. We use language to conduct the kinds of affairs involved when dealing with the variety of organizations we encounter in our daily lives, either as professional members of those organizations, or as their clients (customers, students, patients, citizens and the like). Language – in the form of talk-in-interaction – is the means by which the participants perform and pursue their respective institutional tasks and goals.

Other modes of communicating and forms of language, such as written documents, e-mail and text messaging, the internet and on-line order forms, video conferencing and other communicative technologies, also play an increasing role in institutional encounters (Arminen, 2005, ch.8; Hutchby, 2001). In many types of institutional interactions, references to and the manipulation of different kinds of documents and physical objects are central. Consequently in specific institutional interactions there may be an interplay between these various modes of communication, for instance between the talk and other forms of technologically mediated and socially relevant information; however, in this chapter we focus specifically on spoken dialogue conducted face-to-face or over the telephone. The study of *institutional* dialogue is, then, the study of how people use language to manage their practical tasks, and to perform the particular activities associated with their participation in institutional contexts – such as teaching, describing symptoms, cross-examining, making inquiries, negotiating, selling and buying, and interviewing. When investigating institutional dialogue, we are focussing on linguistic resources at various levels – lexical, syntactic, prosodic, sequential, etc. – which all are mobilized to accomplish the interactional work of institutions.

Although institutional interactions frequently occur within designated physical settings, such as hospitals and schools, social security offices and shops, it is important to emphasize that they are not restricted to such locations. Thus, places not usually considered institutional, for example, a private home, may well become the setting/arena for institutional or work-related interactions (e.g. as when home helps or health visitors come to the home to assist the elderly; or when phoning to place an order or make an appointment). Similarly, people in a workplace may engage in casual social conversations that are unconnected with their work. Thus, the *institutionality* of talk is not determined by its occurrence in a particular physical setting.

So let's consider the issue of what precisely constitutes 'institutional' interactions and therefore institutional dialogue. We can illustrate the complexities involved (for the difficulty of defining contexts in general, see e.g. Goodwin and Duranti, 1992) by considering the following extract from the beginning of an internal telephone call between personnel in a US State administrative office.[1]

(1)   [J1MORE:12:4]

```
 1   Kate:   Hey Jim?
 2   Jim:    How are you Kate Fisher
 3   Kate:   How are you doin'
 4   Jim:    Well I'm doin' all right [thank you very [much
 5   Kate:                           [We-          [Well goo:d
 6   Jim:    And a lo:vely day it is.
 7   Kate:   Oh:, isn't it gor[geous=
 8   Jim:                     [Yes
 9   Kate:   =I snuck out at lunch
10           it's [really [difficult to come [back
11   Jim:         [hhh  [You(h)oo       [.hhh that was not- good
12   Kate:   See it (was[ese-)
13   Jim:               [You're s'pose to stay in your office
14           and work work work [heh ha:h
15   Kate:                      [Well-
```

[1]The data extracts cited in this chapter have been transcribed using the conventions developed within conversation analysis by Gail Jefferson and widely adopted by researchers studying naturally occurring discourse from a variety of perspectives.

We are grateful to Brenda Danet, John Heritage, Robert Hopper and Anita Pomerantz for giving us access to some of the previously unpublished data examples cited here. Their colleagueship in this respect is much appreciated.

```
16   Kate:   Jean and I went- she- she works in our office too
17           we went together too: uh- .hhhh u:h do some shopping
18   Jim:    [Um hum
19   Kate:   [A:nd we each made each other come ba:ck,
20   Jim:    Atta girl, ye:s I know what you mean
21   Kate:   So maybe that's the ke(h)y of going [like that
22   Jim:                                        [Huh huh huh
23   Jim:    That's it
24   Jim:    pt .hhhh [What's up
25   Kate:           [Well-
26   Kate:   Well, I've had a call from Paul toda:y and after he called,
27           I checked with your- terminal over there and they said
28           our order's not awarded ...
```

We can see from lines 26–28 that Kate has called a colleague, Jim, in order to conduct some work-related business; the call is in a general sense concerned with these participants' institutional tasks. But before they come to dealing with the call's official business, they converse briefly in a way that might be considered merely being sociable (lines 1–25). Thus within a single encounter participants may engage in and move between sociable and institutional talk.

Notice, though, that the institutionality of this interaction might not be restricted to the phase in which they discuss the call's official business. For example, even in the initial, sociable pleasantries in lines 1–23, their orientation to their institutional identities (i.e. colleagues in an administrative office) is manifest through the ways in which the topics of the weather and shopping are set in the context of office routines and employees' duties (e.g. Kate's 'admission' in lines 9–10 and Jim's teasing chide in lines 11 and 13–14). It is possible also that an institutional flavour is imparted to their talk by certain linguistic and sequential features in this phase (e.g. their greetings in lines 1–4; cf. Drew, 2002; Jim's use of repetition rather than ellipsis in his response in line 4; and his somewhat unusual word order in line 6, technically, the fronted predicate nominal *a lovely day*). Moreover, they attend explicitly to their identities as co-workers in the administrative agency (e.g. lines 13, 16–17 and 19).

Thus on the one hand participants may fluctuate between different kinds of discourse – or genres (e.g. Eggins and Martin, 1997) or styles (e.g. N. Coupland, 2007) – within a single conversation; and on the other hand an apparently non-institutional phase may be suffused with the institutionality of its context. Indeed it appears that talk about social pleasantries may play an essential part in constructing an institutionally appropriate rapport with one's colleagues and clients; for instance, building a rapport through 'social' talk is emphasized in (British) JobCentre interviews with unemployed benefits claimants, and in sales interactions (Clark, Drew and Pinch, 2003). Despite these fluctuations between social and business talk, the dialogue in Example 1 can be considered generally institutional insofar as the participants engage in and accomplish institutionally relevant activities (e.g. checking that an order has been placed), and in doing so, orient to the relevance of their institutional identities for the interaction.

The fluctuation between different types of discourses and the role of what is commonly termed as small-talk, as evidenced in Example 1, has recently gained more attention in research (e.g. J. Coupland, 2000). Consequently a more analytic understanding is beginning to emerge of the ways in which casual, sociable or apparently un-business-like small-talk is deployed in systematic places in interactions, and how its placement and role in different types of institutional interactions will vary (cf. Holmes and Stubbe, 2003: 87–108; Raevaara and Sorjonen, 2006; also Raevaara's (2009) study of the accounts given in convenience stores for the purchase of goods like chocolates, and how these accounts can generate talk about customers' lives, etc.).

To summarize, the boundaries between institutional talk and conversation are not fixed. The institutionality of dialogue is constituted by participants through their orientation towards relevant institutional roles and identities, and the particular responsibilities and duties associated with those roles, and through their production and management of institutionally relevant tasks and activities. Analysing institutional dialogue involves investigating participants' orientations to and engagement in their institutional roles and identities through their use of language, as well as through the co-ordinated interplay between talk, non-vocal conduct and the spatial and technological dimensions of a setting.

DEVELOPMENT OF THE FIELD

The study of institutional dialogue has emerged as a distinctive field of research during the past thirty years from developments in a number of cognate disciplines and perspectives, notably (interactional) sociolinguistics, discourse analysis, the ethnography of speaking and linguistic anthropology, the microethnography of face-to-face interaction, and especially conversation analysis.

Traditionally, sociolinguistic studies have focussed on language variation associated with such social identities as class, ethnicity, age and gender, shifting more recently to the kinds of variation associated with the social situation of use – somewhat independent of other (speaker-related) identities and sources of variation. *Interactional sociolinguistics* has been particularly innovative in turning the sociolinguistic paradigm away from its traditional focus on explaining language variation in terms of speaker attributes, towards focussing instead on the situational/contextual accomplishment of social identity (e.g. N. Coupland, 2007; Gumperz, 1982). The key contribution of this approach is to recast speaker identities not as background 'givens', but instead as interactionally produced in those contexts that are strategic sites in contemporary bureaucratic industrial societies. This programmatic objective (see Gumperz and Cook-Gumperz, 1982) has been pursued through a series of studies in settings such as job interviews, committees, schools (Rampton, 2006), courtroom interrogations (Cotterill, 2007), counselling, industrial training and medical interactions (e.g. Cordella, 2004).

The recognition that speech events are built out of particular component actions, or *speech acts*, has been fundamental to most perspectives concerned with institutional dialogue. But the approach that built most directly on the notion of speech acts (from the philosophy of language) in the analysis of spoken interaction is *discourse analysis*, as developed by the Birmingham discourse analysis group. Their description of the standardized sequences of acts and moves which make up exchanges that are characteristic of particular settings, such as the classroom and medical interaction, represented a more dialogic approach to language in institutional settings (Coulthard and Ashby, 1976; Sinclair and Coulthard, 1975). Recognition of the characteristic sequential/structural patterns of dialogue in particular institutional settings was a significant development in this field (e.g. Mehan, 1979). Although this approach might now be regarded as being over structural and missing something of the contingent character of interactional sequences, nevertheless it represents a significant milestone in this area. What is presently termed as discourse analytic work on institutional dialogue has become diversified and comprises a range of approaches of which one of the most prominent ones is Critical Discourse Analysis (see Chapter 17 by Fairclough, Mulderrig and Wodak in this volume).

Studies associated with *linguistic anthropology and the ethnography of speaking* have emphasized that a speaker's 'identity' is bound up with her membership of a speech community (for overviews see Keating and Duranti, Chapter 16 this volume). They have shown that the distinctive cultural communication style associated with particular speech communities is one of the ethnographic factors to be taken into account when analysing talk in particular speech settings – thereby introducing a much broader sense of what constitutes the ethnographic context of a speech event. In this perspective, the analysis of communicative meanings requires a description and understanding of such socio-cultural features as speakers' social identities; their past history and other biographical details; the states of knowledge and expectations, manifest in their talk, that they bring to speech events; and the rights, duties, and other responsibilities attached to participants' roles or positions in particular institutional events. Thus research in this area is characterized by an emphasis on integrating the analysis of utterance meaning with a description of such ethnographic particulars (see e.g. Duranti, 1997; Fitch, 1998; Heath, 1983).

A similar emphasis is to be found in *microethnographic studies of face-to-face interaction* in institutional settings, e.g. Erickson and Shultz's (1982) study of academic advice/counselling interviews. Such work examines how the ethnographic particulars of an occasion – including its social and cultural context, and the knowledge which participants bring to it by virtue of their membership of speech communities – are reflected in and consequential for the fine detail of the organization of verbal and non-verbal action. One of the distinctive features of such microethnographic studies is their focus on the dynamic unfolding of particular interactions, in terms of the locally produced understandings, responses and moves – and hence the coordination of communicative sequences.

This more contingent and dynamic approach to institutional interactions has been developed principally through the work of *conversation analysis* (CA). Within sociology, other trends contributed to the emergence of the study of institutional dialogue, most notably Goffman's (1972) explorations of the interaction order in face-to-face encounters, including those in institutional settings such as mental hospitals and medical surgery, whilst developments in sociological ethnography foregrounded the closer analysis of verbal interaction in such settings as, for example, paediatric clinics (Silverman, 1987). But undoubtedly the most significant exploration of interactions in institutional settings has been provided by studies informed by the conversation analytic perspective. Sacks (1992 [1964–1972]) originated CA in the course of his investigations into telephone calls made to a suicide prevention centre, and face-to-face interactions in group therapy. Subsequent studies in CA – which now extends across a number of disciplinary boundaries – have developed that interest in showing how participants, in and through the ways in which they construct their turns and sequences of turns, will display their orientation to particular institutional identities, and thereby manage the practical tasks associated with any given institutional setting (see the further reading listed at the end of this chapter for overviews and exemplars).

Developments in the areas outlined above have converged around three principal themes: a) the expansion of the sociolinguistic notion of 'context' to include the sensitivity of language to a variety of social situations, including institutional settings; b) the emergence of analytic frameworks that recognize the nature of language as action and which handle the dynamic features of social action and interaction; and c) methodologically, the analysis of audio and video recordings of naturally occurring interactions in specific institutional and occupational settings. Across these different themes, the study of institutional dialogue coalesces around the following key analytic and empirical issues:

- Participants' orientations to their institutional roles and identities.
- Their management of institutionally-relevant activities.
- Their orientations to institutionally relevant inferences and meanings.

We shall now turn to illustrate each of these themes.

PARTICIPANTS' ORIENTATION TO THEIR INSTITUTIONAL ROLES AND IDENTITIES

Following our earlier observations about recasting the sociolinguistic notion of speaker identity, participants' institutional identities can be viewed, not as exogenous and determining variables, but as accomplished *in* interaction. Hence a key focus of research into institutional dialogue is to show how participants will orient to their institutional identities and tasks through their verbal conduct, including *turn-taking*, and their use of linguistic resources such as *person reference*, *lexical choice* and *grammatical construction*.

Turn-taking

In considering what seems to be particularly characteristic of institutional talk, or even what might be considered to make talk institutional, perhaps what first comes to mind is the relatively rigid or formal organization of the *turn-taking system* in some institutional settings. Participants' conduct in, for instance, courts of law, classrooms, city council meetings, news and job interviews, is shaped by reference to constraints on their contributions to talk. The most evident constraint lies in their adherence to turn-taking systems which depart substantially from the way in which turn-taking is managed in casual conversations. For example, interactions in courtrooms (Atkinson and Drew, 1979; Maynard, 1984), classrooms (Jones and Thornborrow, 2004; Margutti, 2006; McHoul, 1978; Seedhouse, 2004), police interrogations (Stokoe and Edwards, 2008), TV debate programmes (Emmertsen, 2007), counselling (Peräkylä, 1995; Peräkylä, Antaki, Vehviläinen and Leudar, 2008; Silverman, 1997), meetings (Asmuss and Svennevig, 2009; Ford, 2008), Presidential press conferences (Clayman, Heritage, Elliot and McDonald, 2007), and news interviews (Clayman and Heritage, 2002) exhibit systematically distinct forms of turn-taking which powerfully structure many aspects of conduct in these settings.

These turn-taking systems involve the differential allocation of turn types among the participants; notably, the interactions are in most cases organized in terms of question-answer sequences, in which questioning is allocated to the professional (e.g. attorney, interviewer, teacher), and answering to the client (e.g. witness, interviewee, pupil) (see Heritage, 1997).

However, even institutional contexts, in which there is no formal prescription governing the turn-taking system, appear to be characterized by the asymmetric distribution of questions and answers among the participants. This suggests that the question-answer structure of talk is an emergent property of the local management of interaction by participants (Frankel, 1990). Similarly, even if the turn-taking system is prescriptively pre-determined, nevertheless the task of analysis is to specify *how* it is locally managed, in ways that display participants' orientations to what they should properly be doing in a setting. Thus we can view any specialized institutional turn-taking system as the product of participants' orientations to their task-related identities and roles.

It is quite familiar that news interviews exhibit a question-answer structure. However, the following example from a British news interview begins to show how this structure is achieved through the local practices for managing the talk as asking and answering questions.

(2) [from Clayman and Heritage, 2002: 106]

```
1   IE:   er The difference is that it's the press that
2         constantly call me a Ma:rxist when I do not, (.)
3         and never have (.) er er given that description
4         myself. [.hh I-
5   IR:              [But I've heard you-
6         I've heard you'd be very happy to: to: er
7         .hhhh er describe yourself as a Marxist.
8         Could it be that with an election in the
```

```
 9         offing you're anxious to play down that you're a
10         Marx[ist.]
11   IE:        [er ] Not at all Mister Da:y.=And I:'m (.)
12         sorry to say I must disagree with you,=you have
13         never heard me describe myself .hhh er as a
14         Ma:rxist.
```

The significant points here are, first, that the interviewer (IR) constructs his turn (lines 5–10) so that, whatever else he does (see the declarative form in lines 5–7), its last element is a question (produced through an interrogative, lines 8–10) – thereby constituting his local task as one of 'asking questions'. Second, although the interviewee (IE) disagrees with the IR's statement in lines 5–7, he withholds his answer/disagreement until a question has explicitly been asked. Thus the fact that IR constructs his turn as a question and IE only speaks (answers) after a question has been asked, displays both participants' orientations to their respective tasks in the interview. It is in this sense that we mean that the turn-taking organization is an emergent product of participants' locally managed interactional practices.

There are interesting and important issues here about what constitutes a 'question'. The activity of questioning is more than a matter of grammatical form (Heritage and Roth, 1995). Empirically, there can be some evident convergence between 'asking a question' and 'challenging' an interviewee, for instance through expressing a contrary opinion. This possible convergence is of real significance to participants, as is evident in the following excerpt in which the IR is pressing the IE, to the point at which, apparently, it is no longer clear that the IR is simply 'asking questions'.

```
(3)   [US ABC This Week: Oct 1989: Savings & Loan Bailout]

 1   IR:   Isn't it a fact, Mr. Darman, that the taxpayers
 2         will pay more in interest than if they just paid
 3         it out of general revenues?
 4   IE:   No, not necessarily. That's a technical
 5         argument-
 6   IR:   It's not a- may I, sir? It's not a technical
 7         argument. Isn't it a fact?
 8   IE:   No, it's definitely not a fact. Because first
 9         of all, twenty billion of the fifty billion is
10         being handled in just the way you want-
11         through treasury financing. The remaining-
12   IR:   I'm just asking you a question. I'm not
13         expressing my personal views.
14   IE:   I understand.
```

Several features of the IR's 'questioning' in this excerpt lend it the character of an interrogation. One is the IR's use of the prefatory *Isn't it a fact …* , commonly used in courtroom cross-examinations when posing to witnesses contradictory evidence or 'facts' (e.g. *And isn't it a fact Miss (name) where you went to on this evening was at least a quarter of a mile from the main highway?*). Second is the way in which the IR presses the IE by cutting in on his talk (see the IR's turn incomings at lines 6 and 12). The IE attributes a 'position' to the IR when he says in line 10 *in just the way you want*; that is, he treats the IR as not simply asking questions but rather as expressing an opinion or position – an implied charge that the IR acknowledges and defends himself against in lines 12–13 (*I'm just asking you a question* …). On occasions the charge that an IR has overstepped the boundary between 'questioning' and 'interrogating' is made more explicitly.

(4)   [UK BBC TV *Newsnight*: 2 Nov 1993: UN Investigation]

```
1   IR:    Is that a yes or a n:o?
2          (0.5)
3   IE:    Uh: Is it a cour:t. (.) Or: a: interview.
4   IR:    So- you are: prepared to make yourself available
5          to UN investigators or no[:t.
6   IE:                              [Of course.
```

As is clear from the IR's first question in this excerpt, he is pressing the IE on the matter of whether or not he is prepared to make himself available to UN investigators (this is the third such question in a sequence). When the IE asks *Is it a court or an interview*, he is explicitly challenging the nature or neutrality of the questioning.

So when considering the specialized turn-taking system which might operate in a given institutional setting, and how that system might be associated with, or generate, asymmetries of opportunity for participants, we are also exploring ways in which the nature and character of questioning, for example, is fitted with participants' institutional tasks, and how 'questioning' can be exploited to manage other activities in certain kinds of interactions.

Person reference and lexical choice

Turning to a more local level, participants may display their incumbency of an institutional role, or as somehow representing an institution, in their selection of the *ways of referring to each other* and to third parties. They will do so, for instance, by using a *personal pronoun* which indexes their institutional rather than their personal identity. An example of this can be seen in the following, taken from a call to the emergency services in the USA:

(5)   [from Whalen et al., 1988: 344]

```
1   Desk:    Mid-city Emergency
2              .
3              .
4   Desk:    Hello? What's thuh problem?
5   Caller:  We have an unconscious, uh: diabetic
6   Desk:    Are they insiduv a building?
```

7 Caller: Yes they are:
8 Desk: What building is it?
9 Caller: It's thuh a<u>dult</u> <u>book</u>store?
10 Desk: We'll get somebody there right a<u>way</u>…

In this fragment the caller refers to himself through the first person plural pronoun *we* (line 5), thereby indexing that he is speaking not in a personal capacity (e.g. as a relative of the victim) but on behalf of the shop in which the victim happened to fall ill (line 9, *adult bookstore*). Similarly, the desk uses a third person plural pronoun in inquiring about the victim, previously referred to in the singular (cf. *an unconscious diabetic* in line 5 vs. *they* in line 6), as well as the first person plural pronoun *we* in line 10 when announcing the action he is ready to mobilize.

In the following example from a Finnish doctor-patient consultation, the person reference forms are also shaped by 'institutional' considerations, although they do not directly index an institutional role as in Example 5. In this fragment, the doctor, who has just completed the verbal and physical examination of the patient, begins to outline the treatment:

(6) [Doctor-patient 12B1: 8][2]

1 D: .mhh >Kyllä meiän täytyy ny   si̠llä tavalla tehdä
              surely we   have.to now the way   do
           .mhh >We do̠ have to do so now
2   että me alotetaan se verenpaine°lää:kitys°.=
        that we'll start   the blood pressure °medication°.=
3   =Ja koetetaan e̠delleen sitä la̠ihdutusta ja
         and try   still   the diet   and
        =And let's continue trying to di̠et and
4   °.hh° ja jos koettaisitte jättää vielä °a-°
              and if try-CON-PL2 leave   still   ?
        °.hh° and if you'd try to leave out even ° ( )-°
5   (0.4) v̠ielä tiukemmalle sen su̠ola ja (0.2)
              still stricter   the salt   and
        (0.4) even mo̠re salt and (0.2)
6   o- 0 yrittäis   olla vaikka ilman   a̠lkoholiaki
        ?be 0 try-CON.SG3 be say   without alcohol-even
        be- try to be say even without a̠lcohol
7   jos vaa #onnistuu ja#,
        if just succeeds and
        see if that #works out and#,

Here, the doctor outlines four different things that the patient should do to reduce his high blood pressure, namely take some medication (lines 1–2), diet (line 3), reduce his intake of salt (lines 4–5) and cut out all alcohol (lines 6–7). He does so by using three different

---

[2]The glossing symbols in the example are: CON = conditional; SG3 = singular third person; PL2= plural second person

devices for indicating whose responsibility it is to put this treatment into effect. In the first two utterances, the doctor uses the first person plural pronoun *me* 'we' and/or the verb form associated with it (lines 1–2, 3).[3] He thereby formulates the actions as their joint project. Then (line 4) he moves to using the second person plural verb form *koettaisitte* 'you would try', treating the next action as the responsibility of the patient. Finally, in suggesting that the patient should give up alcohol, he employs the verb in its third person singular form (*yrittäis* 'would try', line 6) without a subject pronoun, that is, with no explicit person reference form – a way of indexing, for example, the delicacy involved in raising the topic, in this case the patient's drinking habits. Thus here the doctor uses resources available for person reference to index a particular stance toward each single element of the treatment, in terms of dimensions such as who has the primary responsibility for executing the action (i.e. carrying out the treatment) and the possible delicacy of a topic (see Sorjonen, Raevaara, Haakana, Tammi and Peräkylä, 2006).

These brief examples not only illustrate how participants exhibit and orient to their institutional identities through person reference forms, but also begin to show the inseparable constitutive relationship between the linguistic devices for person reference and managing institutional activities. This is true also with respect to the more general dimension of *lexical choice* – the selection of descriptive terms and other lexical items treated by participants as appropriate to, and hence indicative of, their understandings of the situation they are in (see for example Danet, 1980). Plainly, this connects with linguistic notions of setting-specific, situationally appropriate registers, codes or styles. Speakers will orient to the institutionality of the encounter, in part through their selection of terms from the variety of alternative options for describing people, objects or events. This involves the descriptive adequacy of lexical choice with respect to the type of institutional context concerned (e.g. whether this is legal, educational, medical, etc.).

We can now begin to see how the lexical selection invokes institutional settings and tasks by using the following extract from a call by the attendance clerk in an American high school (AC is the attendance clerk; M is mother, F is father):

(7) [Medeiros 5]

```
1   AC:   Hello this is Miss Medeiros from Redondo
2         High School calling
3   M:    Uh hu:h
4   AC:   Was Charlie home from school ill today?
5         (0.3)
6   M:    .hhhh
7         (0.8)
8   M:    ((off phone)) Charlie wasn't home ill today
```

---

[3]Utterances in the first and second person need not have a separate subject pronoun since the verb form indicates person and number. The verb form regularly associated with the first person plural in colloquial language is the so-called passive form, used in lines 2 and 3.

```
 9          was he?
10          (0.4)
11   F:     ((off phone)) Not at all.
12   M:     No:.
13          (.)
14   AC:    N[o?
15   M:      [No he wasn't
16   AC:    .hhh (.) Well he wz reported absent from his
17          thir:d an' his fifth period cla:sses tihday.
18   M:     Ah ha:h,
19   AC:    .hhh A:n' we need him t'come in t'the office
20          in th'morning t'clear this up
```

Having first inquired whether her child was ill at home that day, the attendance clerk then informs the mother that her child has been *reported absent* that day (lines 16–17). Notice that the attendance clerk says that the child was *reported* absent, not simply that he *was* absent. Her use of the verb *reported* here in collocation with *absent* is cautious or equivocal – at least insofar as it avoids directly accusing the child of truancy, and instead leaves the determination of his possible truancy for subsequent investigation. Moreover, it alludes to the procedures in the school for reporting absences, the possible fallibility of these procedures, and hence their possible incompleteness. So whilst the verb *reported* is by no means restricted to institutional settings, its inclusion here is part of the proper management of the attendance clerk's task (see Drew and Heritage, 1992: 45–46; also Pomerantz, 2004). Furthermore, the selection of the complement *absent* to describe the child's non-presence at school activates a specifically institutional form of non-presence (for instance, one is 'absent' from school or the workplace, but not from a party).

The institutional relevance of lexical choice, manifested in the selection of *absent* in (7) above, is particularly transparent in those cases where participants use a terminology that is more clearly restricted in its situation-specific distribution (e.g. technical terminology). Many studies have documented the ways in which the use of technical vocabularies (e.g. in medical and legal contexts) can embody definite claims to specialized technical knowledge. Generally, such studies point to the interactional salience for participants of professionals' use of technical vocabularies. Often this is related to asymmetries of knowledge between professional and lay participants and to claims that their use of technical vocabulary is one of the ways in which professionals may variously control the information available to the clients, thereby possibly influencing what emerges as the outcome of an interaction (for a review of these issues in studies of medical interaction, see Roter and Hall, 1992).

However, research concerning professional control through technical vocabulary may turn out to rely on a rather oversimplified dichotomy between professionals' possession of technical knowledge, and clients' (e.g. patients') possession of lay knowledge. For one thing, lay participants are easily able to display a certain epistemic equality regarding knowledge about technical vocabulary, as in this example at the beginning of a primary care visit in a US hospital.

(8)　[US primary care]

```
1   Pat:   W'll- (.) I have (.) som:e shoulder pa:in
2          a:nd (0.2) a:nd (.) (from) the top of my a:rm. a:nd
3          (0.2) thuh reason I'm here is because >a couple years
4          ago< I had  frozen shoulder  in thee other a:rm, an'
5          I had to have surgery. and=( ) this is starting to
6          get stuck, and I want to stop it before it gets stuck.
7          (0.4)
8   Doc:   A[d h e : s i]ve capsuli[tis.
9   Pat       [I'm losing]        [Ri:ght.
10  Pat:   I'm losi:ng (0.4) range of motion in my a:rm.
```

When the doctor uses the more technical diagnostic *adhesive capsulitis* in place of the patient's *frozen shoulder* (compare lines 4 and 8), the patient's confirmation *Ri:ght* in line 9 displays that the doctor is correct – thereby claiming/displaying a certain epistemic authority over knowledge about (how to describe) her medical history. Moreover, lay participants may on occasions use more technical terms than the professional, as in this example from an out-of-hours call to a British general practitioner's (GP) practice.

(9)　[Out-of-hours call, British primary care]

```
1   Clr:   He's ly:ing in be:d really absolutely wre:tched. hhh
2   Doc:   And he's had thuh pain in 'is  tummy  all night (h)as ['e?
3   Clr:                                                       [Y:es,
4          in the lower part of his hh
5          (1.0)
6   Doc:    tummy.h
7          (0.3)
8   Clr:    abdome[n. Yes
9   Doc:          ['hhh Does the pain come and go:?
```

The caller, who has described her husband as suffering *the most awful stomach pains*, resists the doctor's systematic use of the more colloquial *tummy*, and instead (in a form of embedded repair) uses the more technical *abdomen* (line 8). So it appears that more complex issues may be involved in participants' uses of technical vocabulary (e.g. concerning accuracy, epistemic authority arising from previous experience, etc.), than simply that professionals will attempt to 'control' lay participants through the use of technical jargon.

The investigation of lexical selection in the design of turns at talk goes beyond person reference forms and technical vocabulary. As indicated in the discussion of the extract from a call from a high school truancy office above (example 7), the wording or phrasing used – as in *reported absent* in announcing a student's (possible) truancy – can be immensely informative about the conduct of certain institutional activities. For instance, Heritage et al. (2007) conducted a study where one group of physicians was asked to solicit – towards the end of the consultation, after a patient's main concern had been dealt with – additional concerns from their patients by asking 'Is there *anything* else you want to address in the visit today?', whereas another group was asked to use the question design 'Is there *something* else you want to address in the visit today?'. The results showed that the use of the polarity marker *something* in the question can be a powerful device for encouraging patients to voice the majority of their remaining concerns, without increasing the length of the visit. When doctors asked whether there is *anything* else, patients generally did not reveal any of their further medical concerns, but they readily did so when the doctors altered only one word of their enquiry, to ask instead whether there was *something* else.

Grammatical forms

In addition to lexical choice, participants also have a range of grammatical resources available when they are designing their turns and hence the actions they are performing. The use of particular lexico-syntactic forms, such as certain question structures, is not exclusive or restricted to institutional settings. However various grammatical forms are the resources available to participants in managing their particular institutional tasks. Insofar as those tasks are part of the interactional routine for a given setting (e.g. giving advice about treatment is part of the routine in medical consultations; attempts at undermining a witness's evidence is part of the routine of cross-examination), then particular grammatical forms are likely to have distinctive distributions in given settings. That is to say, certain grammatical forms may be prevalent in certain settings; or they may show characteristic patterns of use associated with the particular activities in which participants engage in a setting.

For example, Lindström (2005) and Heinemann (2006) discuss ways of designing requests in Swedish and Danish home help service respectively, interactions between elderly care recipients and their home help assistants. They show how, through the selection of grammatical forms in turn design, the elderly care recipient can display her understanding of the contingencies related to her request and her stance towards whether or not she is entitled to make the request. For instance, the choice between imperatives and interrogatives is closely related to issues of entitlement, whilst declaratives display that the request can be negotiated. Heinemann (ibid.) showed that whether or not a request is formed with positive or negative polarity is associated with entitlement: with a positive interrogative request (e.g. *vil du* 'will you'), the care recipient orients to her request as one she is not entitled to make, and this is underscored by other features (e.g. mitigating devices and the choice of verb). The negative interrogative (e.g. *ka'du ikk'* 'can't you'), in contrast, is a way of orienting to the request as one the speaker is entitled to make. Lindström and Heinemann show how the recipient, the home help assistant, orients to the issue of entitlement in their responses to the request and how that orientation comes up also when the request speaker provides an account for the request.

The ways in which the lexico-syntactic forms of requests display – and are oriented towards by participants as displaying – the relative contingencies in granting requests, and entitlements to ask for a service, are clearly illustrated by comparing requests made for the out-of-hours doctors' service provided by (British) GPs' practices with those to the emergency services. Callers to both out-of-hours GPs' services and to the emergency (police) services generally do not make explicit requests; usually they will just report a condition (describing the symptoms), when phoning the doctor, or will report an incident, when phoning the police emergency number. However, when callers request that the doctor visits the patient at home, they will generally use the form *I wonder if* … .

(10)   [Out-of-hours calls, UK: 1:2:4]

1	Clr:	I b- I been takin' Paracetmols for last <u>week</u>.
2		(.)
3	Doc:	Right,
4	Clr:	(I mean) get rid of the pain, it's gone away fer an hou:r,
5		(0.2) an' comin' <u>ba</u>:ck, I been tryin' ta <u>stand</u> (it) 'cause you
6		only (dropped tame) (.) every four hours didn't you. (Every
7		[four)
8	Doc:	[Yes,
9	Clr:	So what i-is that the mo- I wonder if you could (<u>not</u>) give
10		(us) some pain killers (for it <u>all</u>).
11		(0.5)
12	Clr:	(I try an' see-) (.) I know you hang on for Monday but <u>I</u> tell
13		ya the pain is really (.) <u>bad</u> y'know wh't I mea' ((sniff))
14	Doc:	<u>R</u>:ight, I mean- ˙hh Whu- i- i- so you've had it fer (.) <u>mo</u>nths. di'jou say?=

(10 lines omitted)

15	Clr:	But eh:: I tryin'a say really it may- if ya come to <u>s</u>een it oh
16		y-well, ya might know what i's about, or: (if) <u>p</u>ainkillers o:r
17		(0.5) get an X-ray on it=I don't know…

(6 lines omitted)

18	Doc:	Yeah. ˙hh A:um well I mean <u>o</u>bviously X-rays (anythin' like)
19		that. We tend to: uh: ˙hhh <u>fuh</u> things that aren't eh absolu'ly
20		a<u>c</u>ute. emergencies t- we tend tuh prefer to: fer your <u>own</u>
21		doctor to see them o- on the Mon:day, ˙hh if you understand,

The caller's use of the construction *I wonder if* … in requesting the doctor to visit to give him painkillers (line 9), combined with his conditional construction in pursuing this in line 15, clearly display his awareness of the contingency associated with his request – a contingency which he makes explicit in line 12, *I know you hang on for Monday* (by which the caller means that it's likely that the doctor will recommend that the patient visits the surgery after the weekend). That contingency is confirmed in lines 19–21, where the doctor in effect declines to visit. So *I wonder if* … conveys the speaker's understanding of a lack of entitlement to a service, given the contingencies associated with the request (Curl and Drew, 2008).

By contrast, when callers explicitly request emergency police assistance, they will generally use a modal form of the requesting verb, usually *could* … , as in this example.

(11) [Police emergency call, UK: 19]

```
 1   CT:    Police eme:rgency can I help you?
 2                   (0.5)
 3   Ca:    Yeah hi .hhh e:rm could we have uh police patrol car tuh report to: (0.8) er Old
 4          Green House in Grayling.
 5   CT:    Old Cream House.
 6   Ca:    Old Green House,
 7                   (0.8)
 8   Ca:    In Grayling.
 9                   (1.8)
10   Ca:    ((To someone off phone)) ((name)) get tuh thuh do:or. (1.1)
11          Shut this [do:or. [Shut the door don't Shut the door
12   A:                       [( ) [Please (name) don't don't don't (.) don't.
13   Ca:    Don't open thuh door (name).
14   A:     Don't op- (.) open thuh door [(name )
15   Ca:                                 [Can we have uh
16   CT:    Yeah what wa[s-
17   Ca:                [( )
18   CT:    Yea[h sorry=
19   Ca:       [Thi-
20   Ca:    =There's uh woman here thut's (0.5) claims she's
21          bin raped she's panicked. Thuh bo:yfriend's
22          outside
23   CT:    Right [okay-
24   Ca:          [This is thuh security lodge here.
```

It is quite apparent from the way in which the caller asks for police assistance in this emergency call that he does not expect there to be any contingency that might prevent the police attending the scene. The seriousness of the incident (a claim of rape, lines 20/21) is enough to warrant a police presence. Notice also that the caller is not an ordinary citizen, but has a relevant institutional identity, a security guard (line 24), an identity which is prefigured in his use of the plural first person pronoun, the institutional *we* noted earlier. Moreover the caller asks for a police car *to report to* an address (line 3), a lexical selection that is both highly institutional and somewhat 'assertive'. But the caller's expectation that the police will come to provide assistance (and that no contingency will prevent them from doing so) is particularly evident in *how* he asks for police assistance – his use of the modal verbs *could we have* ... and *can we have* ... (lines 3 and 15 respectively). In contrast to the tentativeness of the caller in (10) asking whether the doctor might make a home visit, and that caller's recognition that this action may not be something the doctor is prepared to undertake, here in (11) the caller uses request forms that plainly display no such tentativeness; instead his request is constructed to display his understanding that there is nothing to prevent the police attending the scene (for more on the expectations concerning contingency and entitlement to services that are embodied in different request forms, see Curl and Drew, 2008). In sum, in calls to the emergency number callers do not use *I wonder if* to preface their requests;

requests in emergency calls are designed to indicate that this is an emergency, and that the police (or fire or ambulance services) should attend.

PARTICIPANTS' MANAGEMENT OF INSTITUTIONALLY-RELEVANT ACTIVITIES

It is important to remember that language does not so much deliver meaning – instead it delivers action. And in the kinds of workplace, business and institutional settings we are focussing on here, language delivers certain specialized and situationally-relevant actions and activities. Or more precisely, participants will use language to conduct activities such as *cross-examining* defendants in court; *ordering* goods or services; *negotiating* a contract, or terms of employment; *instructing* a class; *coaching* clients in how to conduct business; as Health Visitors, *advising* mothers about feeding their newly born babies; calling the emergency services to *request* police assistance; *advising* unemployed benefits claimants in Job Centre interviews, and *encouraging* them to take steps towards work, and so on. Sometimes the activities associated with a certain kind of interaction in a setting will be quite narrow in range (as when phoning to place an order, or make an appointment). More usually, though, participants may conduct a broader range of activities; for example, during primary-care medical consultations, patients will *present their problems*, whilst doctors may (verbally and/or physically) *examine* the patients, *diagnose* the problem, and *recommend* appropriate *treatment*. The key to investigating institutional discourse is to explore and understand how participants will manage these often specialized activities through language in their interactions with one another.

Some of the most significant recent research into institutional discourse concerns medical interactions, especially the interactions between doctors and patients in primary care acute visits (Heritage and Maynard, 2006; Stivers, 2007). Whilst being methodologically innovative (see e.g. Mangione-Smith et al., 2003), recent research has generated important new results by focussing – as CA has always done – on the core activities in which doctors and patients engage during primary care acute visits. For instance, they have explored the different forms of doctors' opening enquiries, inviting patients to report or describe their concerns, and the consequences the different enquiry forms have for patients' responses to doctors' opening enquiries (Heritage and Robinson, 2006; Ruusuvuori, 2000, chs. 3–4). Other research has investigated how medical authority is expressed in the different ways in which doctors will announce their diagnoses to patients and discuss treatment recommendations with them, and again, the consequences those differences in format of diagnostic delivery may have for patients' responses (Peräkylä, 1998).

One aspect of the formats through which doctors will both physically examine patients, and deliver their diagnoses, which seems to make a difference to patients' response – and especially to whether or not patients will accept the results of that examination or diagnosis – is whether or not doctors will explicitly describe the evidence for what they are observing and for their conclusions. For instance, as they conduct a physical examination, doctors may either look at or touch the patient (e.g. to palpate some part of the body) without saying anything about or otherwise revealing what they are noticing or finding. Alternatively, as they conduct the examination they may tell the patient what they are doing and what they are finding. The latter is what Heritage and Stivers (1999) call 'online commentary', illustrated in lines 22, 24 and 31 in the following example.

(12) [from Heritage and Stivers, 1999]

```
 1   Doc:   How are you feeling to[day:.
 2   Pat:                        [.hhhhh Better, hh[hhhhhh
 3   Doc:                                         [And your sinuses?
 4            (.)
 5   Pat:   Well they're still: they're about the same.
 6            (.)
 7   Doc:   About the sa:me? Okay. Why don't I have you sit up here for a second.
 8            (1.1)
 9   Doc:   I gave you a lot of medicine over the la:st (0.5) (general) month or so.
10          fer your sinuses.
11            (0.4)
12   Doc:   But the heemobi::d and the vancena::se and then the antibiotic. the
13          augmentin.
14            (0.7)
15   Doc:   A::nd you should be noticing a pretty big difference.
16   Pat:   Compared to the first visit, (.) a lot.
17            (.)
18   Doc:   O:[kay.
19   Pat:      [It's still .hhh >you know< it's not a hundred percent.

          . ((Talk about medications, moving to physical examination, omitted))
          .
20   Doc:   Y:eah because that one you usually you need to take a little bit lo:nger.
21            (3.4)
22   Doc:   Well I don't see any fluid=your ears look goo:d.
23            (3.6)
24   Doc:   This one does too:.
25            (5.6)
26   Doc:   Let's see if we see any drainage
27            (.9)
28   Doc:   Say ah::,
29   Pat:   Ahh,
30            (0.2)
31   Doc:   And that looks real good too:.
32            (0.8)
33   Doc:   Are you having any real specific problems with the cou::gh, or anything
34          like that. >With your sinu[ses<
35   Pat:                             [Uh::(m) the only thing every once in a while I
36          get a- uh: a really wi:ld (0.2) extreme tickle in my throat. And I:(ve)
37          gotta cough cough cough for: (0.2) seconds.
```

```
38                          (.)
39   Doc:    O[kay::
40   Pat:    [And then I (.) clear my throat a couple of times and it goes away,
41                          (.)
42   Doc:    °°O[kay:°° ]
43   Pat:        [But it just reoccurs (0.4) >two a three< times a day.
44   Doc:    °(Well) let's check your sinuses an' see how they look today.°
45                     (1.0)
46   Doc:    That looks a lot better=I don't see any inflammation today.
47                     (0.8)
48   Doc:    G[ood.
49   Pat       [(Good.)
50                     (.)
51   Doc:    That's done the trick.
52                     (1.0)
53   Doc:    So you should be just about o:ver it. I don't- (I'm) not really (.)
54           convinced you have an ongoing infection=it seems like the
55           augmentin really kicked °it.°
56   Pat:    Good.
57   Doc:    O:kay. (.) An' what else did we need to address your EKG:?
```

This way of conducting the physical examination of a patient – by providing an online commentary of what is being observed or felt, and of the physician's evaluation – can play an immensely important role in helping to persuade patients that there is nothing seriously wrong with them. The patient in (12) has presented with continuing sinus problems, for which he has been taking medication. It is pretty clear that the patient persists with his symptomatic complaints (e.g. lines 5, 19 and 35–37), until the doctor's continued online commentary (see lines 22 on) finally convinces them that there is nothing amiss (lines 48–56), after which they turn to other matters (line 57). Heritage and Stivers (1999) found that when a patient and doctor differed in their assessments of a patient's condition – the patient believing his/her condition to be worse than does the doctor – then a doctor's use of online commentary as she examines the patient generally works to convince the patient that there is nothing really very wrong.

There is an important corollary to the use of online commentary, as illustrated in (12); by overcoming patients' resistance to 'no problem' diagnoses, they are more willing to agree to a non-antibiotic treatment plan, thereby reducing the likelihood that the physician would inappropriately prescribe antibiotics (Mangione-Smith et al., 2003). This begins to suggest how research into institutional discourse can have practical applications – a topic that we do not have space enough here to elaborate upon (but see Antaki, forthcoming).

INSTITUTIONALLY SPECIFIC INFERENCES

Participants orient to institutional settings through their recognition of and response to the particular inferences that they attribute to each other's turns at talk. 'Inference' refers to participants' understandings of the actions that each is performing and the situationally relevant meanings of their utterances; those understandings are based on normative expectations concerning the nature of the occasion and each other's roles within it.

The inferential basis for participants' recognition of what the other means or is doing in an utterance includes expectations associated with each participant's relevant institutional activities. For example, in the following extract from a visit by a health visitor (HV), the mother (M) treats HV's observation that the baby is enjoying sucking something (line 1) as implying that the baby might be hungry (line 3). In so doing she orients both to the HV's institutional task as monitoring and evaluating baby care, and to her own responsibility and accountability for that care (note that the father treats the action implicature of HV's observation very differently, line 2).

(13) [from Drew and Heritage, 1992: 33]

```
 1   HV:   He's enjoying that [isn't he.
 2   F:                       [Yes, he certainly is=
 3   M:    =He's not hungry 'cuz (h)he's ju(h)st (h)had 'iz bo:ttle .hhh
 4         (0.5)
 5   HV:   You're feeding him on (.) Cow and Gate Premium.
```

The following example further illustrates participants' orientation towards institutionally specific inferences. The extract comes from an American cross-examination by the prosecution attorney (DA) of a defendant (D) who is charged with being an accessory to a murder. Briefly, her boyfriend, Pete, shot dead a friend of theirs, after an altercation during which the friend/murder victim stabbed Pete. The charge is that she aided Pete by getting admission to the victim's apartment. Here the purpose of the cross-examination appears to be to establish her motive in aiding her boyfriend.

(14) [Murder trial: Cheek:35-A-1:136]

```
 1   DA:   And you had strong feelings over Pete at that time?
 2   D:    Yes (.) I was his girlfriend at the time.
 3   DA:   You were upset because he was stabbed?
 4   D:    I wasn't upset.
 5   DA:   You weren't upset? You were happy?
 6   D:    No.
 7   DA:   You had no feelings at all about the wound that he
 8         had.
 9   D:    I was concerned about what was going on.
10   DA:   Did you feel sad that he was wounded?
11   D:    I don't know.
12   DA:   You don't know how you felt? I mean you could have
13         been happy?
14   D:    No.
15   DA:   You know you didn't feel happy.
16   D:    I gue::ss
```

17 DA: But you don't know if you felt sad or not?
18 D: I felt ba:d some. ((voice breaks))
19 DA: You felt ba:d some. You <u>do</u> remember.
20 D: Yes, I felt bad some.
21 DA: You remember that.
22 D: Yes.
23 DA: You felt angry.
24 D: Yes.
25 DA: You felt anger towards the person who stabbed him.
26 D: <u>No</u>.
27 DA: You remember specifically that you had no anger at
28   all about the person who stabbed him?
29 D: I felt angry about ... ((confused and inaudible))
30 DA: You weren't angry at <u>him</u>.
31 D: No.

It is fairly clear here that the DA's questioning is designed to establish that the defendant's motive for assisting her boyfriend arose from her feelings about him having been stabbed by the victim. It is clear also that it is evident to the defendant that this is the line of questioning which the DA is pursuing (on witnesses' recognition of lines of questioning, see Atkinson and Drew, 1979: 112–121, 173–181). This is evident in her resistance to the DA's suggestions about how she felt, and to his attempts to cast doubt on, and undermine, her qualified versions of her feelings about the incident. In her answers she, for example, rejects the DA's suggestion that she was upset because her boyfriend had been stabbed (lines 3–4), or that she *felt anger towards the person who stabbed him* (lines 25–26); and she responds to his suggestion that she *had no feelings at all about the wound* by agreeing to a qualified version of her feelings, which was that she was *concerned about what was going on* (line 9).

In these and other respects, her orientation towards the implications of the DA's questions, and her strategic attempts to avoid those implications, are particularly transparent. Likewise, the ways in which the DA is alive to the implications of her answers, and his attempts to combat her resistance, are equally transparent. The participants therefore design their turns with respect to the inferences to be drawn from each other's descriptions, in the context of the charge and the attendant circumstances of the incident with which it is concerned. Each thereby orients to the *strategic* purpose underlying the other's descriptions, and constructs her/his descriptions with a view of their strategic goals (Drew, 1990). This association between the inferential meaning and strategy is part of what might be referred to as the 'pragmatics' of institutional dialogue.

CONCLUSION

We should highlight a point that until now has, perhaps, only been implicit. Participants in institutional encounters employ verbal and non-verbal interactional resources which they will possess as part of their linguistic and cultural competences – competences that they have acquired through socialization, and that underlie their participation in talk-in-interaction generally, that is, in ordinary mundane social interaction, as well as everyday (and sometimes less mundane) workplace and institutional interactions (a particularly interesting study involving the interplay between 'mundane' and 'institutional' forms is Maynard's (2003) account of the delivery of bad news in everyday and clinical settings). Hence the linguistic practices to be found in institutional settings are not exclusive to such settings. One of the principal objectives of research concerning institutional dialogue is, therefore, to show either that a given linguistic practice or pattern is specially *characteristic* of talk in a given (institutional) setting, or that a certain linguistic feature or practice has a characteristic use when deployed in a given setting.

This objective arises from the quite general issue which has informed our outline of this area of interactional analysis – namely, the importance of demonstrating not merely that dialogue happens to occur in a certain institutional setting, but that through their language use, participants will orient towards their respective institutional identities, roles and tasks in that setting, i.e. that participants' institutional identities and roles are *proceduraly relevant* for their talk (cf. the discussion of extract (1) above; see Schegloff, 1992, on these issues). The investigation of language use in any of the respects (levels) outlined here – lexical selection, grammatical/syntactic, sequential (including turn-taking), and pragmatic inference – can reveal aspects of how participants themselves will orient to their institutional identities and manage their institutional activities.

We have had space only to illustrate aspects of the use of language in institutional interactions, particularly turn-taking, word selection, syntactic/grammatical construction, activities, and setting-specific inferences. There is, of course, much more involved in, and to be learned from, the analysis of institutional interactions. However, we hope that this discussion has at least illustrated what we can begin to find through investigating how co-participants use language to conduct their activities when visiting the doctor, conducting a job interview, being interviewed for the radio, making a social security claim, appearing in court, and such like.

For the future, it is likely that this field of research will develop in a range of ways, including:

- by exploring in greater depth the interface between ordinary so-called social talk-in-interaction and institutional interactions, coming to a deeper understanding of both what is distinctive about institutional talk-in-interaction, and how ordinary interaction provides the analytic bedrock for understanding how we use language in more specialized settings;
- the investigation of an ever-expanding range of institutional settings, or types of interaction;
- the further development of research into medical interactions, because so much of the success of medical care depends on the communication between health care professionals and patients, and with one another;
- more genuinely applied research, which will contribute to the effectiveness of communication in institutional settings.

FURTHER READING

Clark, C., Drew, P. and Pinch, T. (2003) 'Managing prospect affiliation and rapport in business-to-business sales encounters', *Discourse Studies*, 5: 5–31.
http://dis.sagepub.com/content/5/1/5.full.pdf+html

Peräkylä, A. (1998) 'Authority and accountability: the delivery of diagnosis in primary health care', *Social Psychology Quarterly,* 61: 301–20.

Stokoe, E. and Edwards, D. (2008) '"Did you have permission to smash your neighbour's door?": Silly questions and their answers in police-suspect interrogations', *Discourse Studies,* 10: 89–111.
http://dis.sagepub.com/content/10/1/89.full.pdf+html

There are a few general texts on institutional discourse, discussing the broader theoretical and methodological issues involved, and covering a range of institutional settings. Some other monographs and edited collections focus on interactions within specific institutional settings, such as medical interactions, or courts of law. Among the key publications which would expand your knowledge of this developing and increasingly significant area, are the following.

Heritage, J. and Clayman, S. (2010) *Talk in Action: Interactions, Identities and Institutions.* Chichester: Wiley.

This is an authoritative and comprehensive overview of the entire area, including accounts of the most relevant research in a range of areas (medical, legal etc.). It is now the standard and best text on institutional dialogue.

Arminen, I. (2005) *Institutional Interaction – Studies of Talk at Work.* Aldershot: Ashgate.
This is an excellent, up-to-date overview of the area; the thematic organization of this monograph is both unusual and analytically interesting.

Atkinson, J.M. and Drew, P. (1979) *Order in Court: The Organisation of Verbal Interaction in Judicial Settings.* London: Macmillan.
This was perhaps the first study to investigate institutional interactions – here in courts and courtroom examination – using CA's perspective and methods.

Drew, P. and Heritage, J. (eds) (1992) *Talk at Work: Interaction in Institutional Settings.* Cambridge: Cambridge University Press.
Highly recommended, as the key 'textbook' in the area, with a clear theoretical and methodological introduction, and studies of a considerable range of institutional settings.

Heritage, J. and Clayman, S. (2010) *Talk in Action: Interactions, Identities, and Institutions.* London: Blackwell.
The most recent textbook in the area – a 'must have', with an excellent introductory overview of the field, and chapters focusing on medical consultations, calls to the emergency services, courts, media news interviews and political speeches.

McHoul, A. and Rapley, M. (eds) (2002) *How to Analyse Talk in Institutional Settings: A Casebook of Methods.* London: Continuum International.
A practical and methodological approach from a rather different perspective.

Sarangi, S. and Roberts, C. (eds) (1999) *Talk, Work and Institutional Order. Discourse in Medical, Mediation and Management Settings.* Berlin: Mouton de Gruyter.
An interesting and useful collection, intelligently edited, from a more eclectic methodological standpoint.

ONLINE READING

The following articles are available at www.sagepub.co.uk/discoursestudies.

Clark, C., Drew, P. and Pinch, T. (2003) 'Managing prospect affiliation and rapport in business-to-business sales encounters'. *Discourse Studies,* 5, 5–31.

Stokoe, E. and Edwards, D. (2008) '"Did you have permission to smash your neighbour's door?" Silly questions and their answers in police-suspect interrogations'. *Discourse Studies,* 10, 89–111.

REFERENCES

Antaki, C. (ed.) (forthcoming) *Applied Conversation Analysis: Changing Institutional Practices*. London: Palgrave.

Arminen, I. (2005) *Institutional Interaction – Studies of Talk at Work*. Aldershot: Ashgate.

Asmuss, B. and Svennevig, J. (eds) (2009) 'Meeting talk'. Special issue, *Journal of Business Communication*, 46 (1): 3.

Atkinson, J.M. and Drew, P. (1979) *Order in Court: The Organisation of Verbal Interaction in Judicial Settings*. London: Macmillan.

Clark, C., Drew, P. and Pinch, T. (2003) 'Managing prospect affiliation and rapport in business-to-business sales encounters'. *Discourse Studies, 5*: 5–31.

Clayman, S. and Heritage, J. (2002) *The News Interview: Journalists and Public Figures on the Air*. Cambridge: Cambridge University Press.

Clayman, S., Heritage, J., Elliot, M. and McDonald, L. (2007) 'When does the watchdog bark? Conditions of aggressive questioning in presidential news conferences'. *American Sociological Review, 72*: 23–41.

Cordella M. (2004) *The Dynamic Consultation: A Discourse Analytical Study of Doctor-Patient Communication*. Amsterdam: John Benjamins.

Cotterill, J. (ed.) (2007) *The Language of Sexual Crime*. Basingstoke: Palgrave Macmillan.

Coulthard, M. and Ashby, M.C. (1976). 'The analysis of medical interviews'. In M. Wadsworth, and D. Robinson (eds), *Understanding Everyday Medical Life* (pp. 69–88). London: Robertson.

Coupland, J. (ed.) (2000) *Small Talk*. London: Longman.

Coupland, N. (2007) *Style: Language Variation and Identity*. Cambridge: Cambridge University Press.

Curl, T.S. and Drew, P. (2008) 'Contingency and action: a comparison of two forms of requesting'. *Research on Language and Social Interaction, 41*: 129–53.

Danet, B. (1980) '"Baby" or "fetus": language and the construction of reality in a manslaughter trial'. *Semiotica, 32*: 187–219.

Drew, P. (1990) 'Strategies in the contest between lawyers and witnesses in court examinations'. In J.N. Levi and A.G. Walker (eds), *Language in the Judicial Process* (pp. 39–64). New York: Plenum.

Drew, P. (2002) 'Out of context: an intersection between domestic life and the workplace, as contexts for (business) talk'. *Language and Communication, 22*: 477–94.

Drew, P. and Heritage, J. (1992) 'Analyzing talk at work: an introduction'. In P. Drew and J. Heritage (eds), *Talk at Work* (pp. 3–65). Cambridge: Cambridge University Press.

Duranti, A. (1997). *Linguistic Anthropology*. Cambridge: Cambridge University Press.

Eggins, S. and Martin, J.R. (1997) 'Genres and registers of discourse'. In T.A. van Dijk (ed.), *Discourse as Structure and Process: Discourse studies: A Multidisciplinary Introduction. Volume 1* (pp. 230–56). London: Sage.

Emmertsen, S. (2007) 'Interviewers' challenging questions in British debate interviews'. *Journal of Pragmatics, 39*: 570–91.

Erickson, F. and Shultz, J. (1982) *The Counsellor as Gatekeeper: Social Interaction in Interviews*. New York: Academic.

Fitch, K. (1998) *Speaking Relationally: Culture, Communication, and Interpersonal Connection*. New York: Guilford.

Ford, C.E. (2008) *Women Speaking up: Getting and Using Turns in Workplace Meetings*. New York: Palgrave Macmillan.

Frankel, R. (1990) 'Talking in interviews: a dispreference for patient-initiated questions in physician-patient encounters'. In G. Psathas (ed.), *Interaction Competence* (pp. 231–62). Washington, DC: University Press of America.

Goffman, E. (1972) *Encounters: Two Studies in the Sociology of Interaction*. London: Penguin.

Goodwin, C. and Duranti, A. (1992) 'Rethinking context: an introduction'. In A. Duranti and C. Goodwin (eds), *Rethinking Context: Language as an Interactive Phenomenon* (pp. 1–42). Cambridge: Cambridge University Press.

Gumperz, J.J. (ed.) (1982) *Language and Social Identity*. Cambridge: Cambridge University Press.

Gumperz, J.J. and Cook-Gumperz, J. (1982) 'Introduction: language and the communication of social identity'. In J.J. Gumperz (ed.), *Language and Social Identity* (pp. 1–21). Cambridge: Cambridge University Press.

Heath, S.B. (1983) *Ways with Words: Language, Life and Work in Communities and Classrooms*. Cambridge: Cambridge University Press.

Heinemann, T. (2006) '"Will you or can't you?": displaying entitlement in interrogative requests'. *Journal of Pragmatics, 38*: 1081–104.

Heritage, J. (1997) 'Conversation analysis and institutional talk: analyzing data'. In D. Silverman (ed.), *Qualitative Research: Theory, Method and Practice* (pp. 161–82). London: Sage.

Heritage, J. and Maynard, D.W. (eds) (2006) *Communication in Medical Care: Interaction between Primary Care Physicians and Patients*. Cambridge: Cambridge University Press.

Heritage, J. and Robinson, J.D. (2006) 'The structure of patients' presenting concerns: physicians' opening questions'. *Health Communication, 19*: 89–102.

Heritage, J. and Roth, A.L. (1995) 'Grammar and institution: questions and questioning in the broadcast news interview'. *Research on Language and Social Interaction, 28*: 1–60.

Heritage, J. and Stivers, T. (1999) 'Online commentary in acute medical visits: a method of shaping patient expectations'. *Social Science and Medicine, 49*: 1501–17.

Heritage, J., Robinson, J., Elliott, M., Beckett, M. and Wilkes, M. (2007) 'Reducing patients' unmet concerns in primary care: the difference one word can make'. *Journal of General Internal Medicine, 22*: 1429–33.

Holmes, J. and Stubbe, M. (2003) *Power and Politeness in the Workplace: A Sociolinguistic Analysis of Talk at Work*. London: Pearson.

Hutchby, I. (2001) *Conversation and Technology: From the Telephone to the Internet*. Cambridge: Polity.

Jones, R. and Thornborrow, J. (2004) 'Floors, talk and the organisation of classroom activities'. *Language in Society, 33*: 233–423.

Levinson, S. (1992) 'Activity types and language'. In P. Drew and J. Heritage (eds), *Talk at Work: Interaction in Institutional Settings* (pp. 66–100). Cambridge: Cambridge University Press.

Lindström, A. (2005) 'Language as social action: a study of how senior citizens request assistance with practical tasks in children's speech'. In A. Hakulinen and M. Selting (eds), *Syntax and Lexis in Conversation* (pp. 209–30). Amsterdam: John Benjamins.

McHoul, A. (1978) 'The organization of turns at formal talk in the classroom'. *Language in Society, 7*: 183–213.

Mangione-Smith, R., Stivers, T., Elliott, M., McDonald, L. and Heritage, J. (2003) 'Online commentary during the physical examination: a communication tool for avoiding inappropriate prescribing?', *Social Science and Medicine, 56*: 313–20.

Margutti, P. (2006) '"Are you human beings?": order and knowledge construction through questioning in primary classroom interaction'. *Linguistics and Education, 17*: 313–46.

Maynard, D.W. (1984) *Inside Plea Bargaining: The Language of Negotiations*. New York: Plenum.

Maynard, D.W. (2003) *Good News, Bad News: Conversational Order in Everyday Talk and Clinical Settings*. Chicago: Chicago University Press.

Mehan, H. (1979) *Learning Lessons*. Cambridge, MA: Harvard University Press.

Mondada, L. (2007) 'Operating together through videoconference: members' procedures for accomplishing a common space of action'. In S. Hester and D. Francis (eds), *Orders of Ordinary Action: Respecifying Sociological Knowledge* (pp. 51–67). Aldershot: Ashgate.

Peräkylä, A. (1995) *AIDS Counselling: Institutional Interaction and Clinical Practice*. Cambridge: Cambridge University Press.

Peräkylä, A. (1998) 'Authority and accountability: the delivery of diagnosis in primary health care'. *Social Psychology Quarterly, 61*: 301–20.

Peräkylä, A., Antaki, C., Vehviläinen, S. and Leudar, I. (eds) (2008) *Conversation Analysis and Psychotherapy*. Cambridge: Cambridge University Press.

Pomerantz, A. (2004) 'Investigative reported absences: "neutrally" catching the truants'. In G. Lerner (ed.), *Conversation Analysis: Studies from the First Generation* (pp. 109–29). Amsterdam: John Benjamins.

Raevaara, L. (2011) 'Accounts at convenience stores: doing dispreference and small talk'. *Journal of Pragmatics*, 43: 556–71.

Raevaara, L. and Sorjonen, M.-L. (2006) 'Vuorovaikutuksen osanottajien toiminta ja genre: keskustelunanalyysin näkökulma'. In A. Mäntynen, S. Shore and A. Solin (eds), *Genre – tekstilaji* (pp. 122–50). Helsinki: Finnish Literature Society.

Rampton, B. (2006) *Language in Late Modernity: Interaction in an Urban School*. Cambridge: Cambridge University Press.

Roter, D.L. and Hall, J.A. (1992) *Doctors Talking to Patients/Patients Talking to Doctors*. Westport, CT: Auburn.

Ruusuvuori, J. (2000) '*Control in medical consultation: practices for giving and receiving the reason for the visit in primary health care*'. Electronic PhD dissertation, University of Tampere. Acta Electronica Universitatis Tamperensis 16. http://acta.uta.fi

Sacks, H. (1992 [1964–1972]) *Lectures on Conversation*: Volumes 1 & 2 (edited by Gail Jefferson). Oxford: Blackwell.

Schegloff, E.A. (1992) 'On talk and its institutional occasions'. In P. Drew and J. Heritage (eds), *Talk at Work: Interaction in Institutional Settings* (pp. 101–34). Cambridge: Cambridge University Press.

Seedhouse, P. (2004) *The Interactional Architecture of the Language Classroom: A Conversation Analysis Perspective*. Malden, MA: Blackwell.

Sinclair, J.M. and Coulthard, M. (1975) *Towards an Analysis of Discourse: The English used by Teachers and Pupils*. Oxford: Oxford University Press.

Silverman, D. (1987) *Communication and Medical Practice: Social Relations in the Clinic*. London: Sage.

Silverman, D. (1997) *Discourses of Counselling: HIV Counselling as Social Interaction*. London: Sage.

Sorjonen, M.-L., Raevaara, L., Haakana, M., Tammi, T. and Peräkylä, A. (2006) 'Lifestyle discussions in medical interviews'. In J. Heritage and D.W. Maynard (eds), *Communication in Medical Care* (pp. 349–78). Cambridge: Cambridge University Press.

Stivers, T. (2007) *Prescribing under Pressure: Parent-Physician Conversations and Antibiotics*. Oxford: Oxford University Press.

Stokoe, E. and Edwards, D. (2008) '"Did you have permission to smash your neighbour's door?": silly questions and their answers in police-suspect interrogations'. *Discourse Studies, 10:* 89–111.

Whalen, J., Zimmerman, D.H. and Whalen M.R. (1988) 'When words fail: a single case analysis'. *Social Problems, 35:* 335–62.

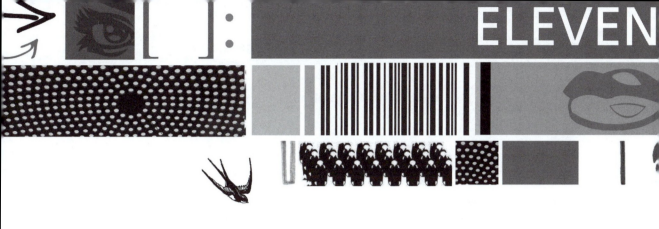

ELEVEN

Gender and Power in Discourse

Michelle M. Lazar and Cheris Kramarae

INTRODUCTION

Many of us are now familiar with at least some of the ways that hierarchical social structures and norms divide people into two classes, men and women, and how somewhat different tasks, expectations, and evaluations are assigned to those classes and to the way women and men talk. In this chapter, we shall take a deeper look at conceptions of gender and power asymmetries, and discuss some of the ways discourse analysis research is helping to change ideas about how 'gender' is constructed through various types of talk and text.

Some people think that the terms 'women' and 'gender' are synonymous, and assume that if the research is about 'gender' then it belongs primarily in Women's Studies, or in courses dealing with 'special' or 'marginal' interests. Our discussion shows that the study of gender encompasses girls and boys, women and men, and helps explain why feminist critiques of gender in discourse are of critical value to anyone interested in current and important social and political issues.

The chapter is organized around the three key words of our title: 'Discourse', 'Gender' and 'Power'. Although these three are inextricably linked – it is hard to disentangle 'gender' from 'power', and both quite crucially shape, and are shaped by, discourse – we will put the spotlight on each of these concepts in turn, in order to tease out the relevant issues that have occupied scholars in the field. In organizing the chapter thus, we draw together examples and case studies from a variety of approaches and methodologies pursued by language and gender scholars who, although committed to particular theoretical, methodological and analytical positions, all broadly orientate towards, and demonstrate, the vibrancy of these issues. Before we conclude, we provide a brief feminist discourse analysis based on excerpts from *Sex and the City: The Movie* (2008), which highlights and pulls together some of the points raised about gender and power in discourse.

GENDER AND POWER IN *DISCOURSE*

In the 1970s and early 1980s, study and criticism of 'sexist language' (as exemplified in statements such as 'Everyone will receive his chance at promotion' and in the disproportionate lists of differing terms used to describe sexually active women and men) received a lot of media attention (and, often, ridicule). Less focus was given to studies that were calling attention to the gendered dynamics of everyday interaction indicating that sexist meanings are socially (re)produced and reside in language users and contexts of use, and not in the words themselves. However, it is now more widely accepted that it is the users of the language and the uses to which the language is put that merit greater critical scrutiny.

Much current scholarship on language and gender focuses on the social constitutiveness of discourse. Instead of viewing language as merely mirroring pre-existing realities, the consensus is that our social worlds, including gender and power, are partly shaped by, and shape, our use of language. The turn towards discourse marks a shift from earlier concerns with 'sexist language' to the study of gender (and gender asymmetries) in discourse. It has been observed that even in the absence of non-sexist linguistic terms, the ways language is used routinely in stereotypical, biased ways in social interaction and through social practices and institutional structures, (re)produces a view of girls and women that demeans and disadvantages them (Cameron, 2006; Weatherall, 2002).

For example, a study of talk between adults and adolescents in the South-West of England helps us understand some of the ways that teenagers may learn about gender and embodiment. Kathryn Lovering (1995) found that partly owing to the generally accepted regulation of talk about the body and sexuality between adults and adolescents in British culture, and the lack of equality in dealing with sexuality in schools, boys and girls developed differential ways of knowing about 'growing up', which affected the way they viewed each other. The girls and boys talked in ways that assumed that the female body was shameful and extra-ordinary, whereas the male body was ordinary and not the focus of attention, ridicule or oppression to the same extent as the female body. For instance, this can be heard from the girls' responses: 'It feels like the girls go through all the changes because we are not taught anything about the boys REALLY' (p. 24); 'I just can't stand it when the boys laugh'; 'Because it puts us off and makes us hide it all inside' (p. 27).

Yet, school boys will often talk to continually establish their masculinity and heterosexuality. In another study, of the talk in small group discussions in English classes in England, the girls experienced an undercurrent of ridicule and aggression, and individual boys were often singled out as not possessing the traits of 'real' boys (Davies, 2003). One boy, who focused on the assigned task about the colours mentioned in a poem being studied, used such words as 'dazzling', 'gorgeous', 'yellow gold', and 'golden galaxy'. Throughout the discussion, he and his talk were criticized by the other boys, with such comments 'You're just stupid, you', 'Shut up', 'Listen to him/Listen to him/oh God/', 'See?/do you HAVE to speak like that and moving your hands about like a queer?' and such names as 'stupid', 'queer', and 'bum-bandit'. Masculinity, in this situation, is precarious and must be earned. Further, as Davies (2003) observed, the boys' homophobic teasing and their anti-school, anti-female culture made it more problematic for them to stay on task, as they were often victims of their own policing involving displays of what they thought of as (heteronormative) masculinity.

Depending on the historical and societal context, there can be more than one way of knowing about particular social practices and experiences. In such situations, the interplay of the different discourses in the same texts or talk, and the implications this may have for people's knowledge about themselves and others in regard to the discourses, are of interest.

For example, in a critical analysis of gender relations in a series of government advertisements promoting family life in Singapore, Michelle Lazar (2000) found the co-existence of two discourses of gender relations pertaining to parenthood in the same set of texts. One was a progressive discourse based upon (feminist) egalitarian principles; for instance, there was a preference for use of the gender-neutral term 'parents'/'parenthood', along with representations of shared parenthood. The other discourse was a conservative one, based upon culturally normative expectations of women and men; for example, whereas the advertisements repeatedly addressed women as needing to 'balance' their career with family responsibilities, and making the 'right choices' in favour of the family (p. 392), such was not the case when addressing men. The assumption was that the maternal identity was more central for women's sense of self than the paternal identity was for men. Through close analysis of the linguistic (and other semiotic) features of the discourses, tensions and points of convergences between the apparently competing discourses were documented, with the implications of power relations among women and men examined. Further, the study showed that the dual discourses of gender were embedded in a common discourse of heteronormativity, signified by heterosexual marriage. The inseparability of the discourses of gender and sexuality produced differentiated ways of knowing how to be a heterosexual wife and mother (as supportive and 'other-centred') and a heterosexual husband and father (as the 'significant other', head of household and a 'leisure father') in the given society.

In researching discourse and gender, analysts have used contextualized, naturally-occurring and spoken, scripted and print data from a wide variety of domains such as education, the media, law, medicine, workplaces, family, play groups, and informal social networks. In keeping with technological developments, data for gender analysis have extended beyond the traditional print and face-to-face interactions to include the internet and the study of various forms of computer-mediated communication (CMC). Uses of new communication technologies usually develop within existing patterns of interaction so we can see teasing, joking, and gossiping in familiar patterns even in CMC environments that seemingly operate in ways that are quite different from face-to-face settings.

There is great value in analysing the interplay of semiotic modalities in the study of gender. This is richly illustrated by Gerry Bloustien's (2001) work, based on 15 months of fieldwork as well as a study of the videos made by the participants with a loaned camera. In her analysis of the ways that Australian teenage girls, from diverse backgrounds, engaged with, perceived, and represented their world through their choice of clothing, stance, gesture, touch, and language, Bloustien notes the constant scrutiny of, and comments on, physical appearances as the girls discussed and explored space, body, and relationships. They learnt about accommodation, incorporation, and resistance to what they understood as the (impossible) task of both fitting in and yet also maintaining their individuality amid the pervasive contradictions in their culture about what girls and women should look like and how they should behave. For example, the girls talked about the difficulty of learning that their bodies were perceived by others as sexual objects and that their 'good reputation' could be quickly lost. One of the girls said 'When a boy is called a *gigolo* he is pleased. But when a girl is called a *slut* – well she cries.' Another noted, 'You can get a bad reputation in a week. But to lose it – (shrugs with a resigned laugh) well, it can take a year!' Seeing the 'body work' of the girls, as well as hearing their interpretations of the embodied practices of others, was critical in helping the researcher investigate the ways the girls enacted their sense of self.

Multimodal analysis of discourse in Language and Gender Studies is still in its infancy; however, we project that it will increase in the near future, especially with the proliferation of new technological tools and multimedia formats, with resulting new forms of discourse. Much innovative feminist scholarship moves across levels of analysis, from a close inspection of everyday interaction to looking at the context of the interaction, which includes institutions and social structures (Thorne, 2001). Multimodal analysis of discourse promises to broaden and deepen our understanding of gender and contemporary life.

GENDER AND POWER IN DISCOURSE

In the late 1960s and early 1970s, feminists distinguished between the terms 'sex' and 'gender': sex was seen to be ascribed by biology,[1] whereas gender was achieved through psychological, cultural, and social processes (West and Zimmerman, 1987). The gender socialization theories of this time assumed that sex and gender were coterminous, such that the 'only two sexes' division was mapped on to social differences between women and men, resulting in identity categories that were usually considered fixed, stable and dichotomous (viz., essentializing ways of thinking, which we elaborate on below).

Such an understanding was operative in much of the early work on language and gender, which was characterized by the common use of binary descriptors (for example, 'female

---

[1]Even those variations in verbal practice or ability, such as voice pitch and intonation, that have been assumed to be the result of biological differences, are revealed as determined, in part, by different socialization practices for girls and boys, related to sexual orientation, socioeconomic status and ethnicity (McConnell-Ginet, 1978).

and male' and 'two genders'); stereotypes regarding women's and men's speech styles;[2] expectations about appropriate ways of speaking; and (consequently) an inadequate vocabulary for ways of discussing the relationship between sexual differences and gender identities. A problem with this sort of research is that any differences searched for and found in the studies were largely, even if unintentionally, interpreted as deficits in women, since male behaviour was perceived normatively (Lakoff, 1975). In sum, a focus only on differences often supports, rather than challenges, gender stereotypes.[3]

The pervasive focus on female/male *differences* in many language and psychology studies also does not do justice to what is usually happening in most types of interaction, and such a focus may lead to downplaying similarities. In many USA school settings, for example, boys will spend time playing 'boy games' and girls will spend time playing 'girl games' but there is also cross-gender play that may not be seen or heard by researchers if attention is only paid to differences (Thorne, 1990). A focus on differences also does not tell us what speakers are trying to accomplish as they interact. For instance, if a study should discover that women use the intensive 'so' more often than men do in their talk, that does not tell us about why that may be or in what contexts (Swan, 2002: 51). Further, 'gender differences' research has overlooked the complexity of the category 'gender'.[4] For example, in the Pacific region, some males in Tongan 'act like women' and adopt the speech styles stereotypically associated with Tongan women, such as speaking with a high pitched voice, a fast tempo, and incorporating English in their linguistic repertoire. In so doing, these transgendered males (or *fakaleitī*) index femininity and distance themselves from 'masculine attributes' (Besnier, 2003).

In fact, the view in contemporary language and gender studies has radically shifted away from investigations arising from assumptions of what gender *is* and its expression in discourse, to focus on how gender emerges as an outcome of discourse in situated contexts and communities of practice. From the late 1980s and early 1990s onward, the idea that gender is something that people enact, and not something people are or possess, has gained prominence. Gender is not a pre-existing, fixed condition and is not coterminous with

---

[2]Some stereotyped characteristics of women's talk include: indirect, emotional, gossipy, and friendly, while some stereotyped characteristics of men's talk include: direct, unemotional, forceful, and having a sense of humour (Kramer, 1978; Holmes, 2006, 6). Extensions of this earlier work point out the importance of considering 'race' as well as 'sex'. In a study of the stereotypes held by Whites, Black speakers (both women and men) were rated as more direct and emotional, and less socially appropriate and playful, than when the White students rated White speakers (Popp, Donovan, Crawford, Marsh, and Peele, 2003).

[3]This is not, however, to say that research and claims about differences in language use between women and men (or between gay men and heterosexuals or any of the other linked identity 'groups') aren't sometimes useful. As Baker (2005) suggests, we need to acknowledge the existence of these categories and the stereotypes associated with them since they are pervasive in our cultures; we can use them not to reinforce the existence of the categories but to reveal how they are constructed as oppositions and are changeable (pp. 14–18).

[4]The 'two genders' view has been robustly challenged by queer and transgender theorists. Judith Halberstam (1998), for instance, has documented what she terms 'female masculinity', which covers a range of forms of masculinity *without* men.

sex[5]; rather, gender is constantly worked out in behaviour and discourse. Gender is a routine and recurring activity that is accomplished interactionally in a variety of institutional contexts. 'Doing gender' creates hierarchical differences between women and men, which are used to reinforce the 'essentialness' of gender and justify discrimination (West and Zimmerman, 1987). Judith Butler (1990: 25) posits that gender is the 'repeated stylization of the body, a set of repeated acts within a highly rigid regulatory frame that congeal over time to produce the appearance of substance, of a natural sort of being'. Applying Butler's ideas to language use more particularly, language and gender scholars have come to see discursive acts as sites where people produce their gender identity (not the other way around), and that, in performing gender, people also reproduce the culture's regulatory norms. If gender is something that is accomplished or performed, it follows that gender can also be 'undone' (Deutsch, 2007) or 'de-constructed' (Butler, 1990).

The performance of gender identity through talk is illustrated in a study about the conversational styles adopted by fantasy-line operators in San Francisco. Kira Hall (1995: 200) found that in order to cater to their (heterosexual) male clients, the phone-sex operators in the study consistently produced a type of language that adhered to hegemonic male perceptions of the 'ideal woman' – language that was characterized by the frequent use of intensifiers; female lexical items (e.g. 'curly', 'snuggery'); supportive questions and comments (e.g. 'oh do you like that?'); and a dynamic intonation pattern ('a feminine, lilting quality'). As Hall notes, these are all linguistic features that early studies in language and gender had identified as powerless 'women's language', which the operators used to perform a kind of femininity that 'sold' to a (heterosexual) male market. Based on this basic conversational style, the fantasy-line operators could then go on to perform a variety of other feminine identities intertwined with race and age indicators as well. For example, among the repertoires performed by one operator was a girl with a high-pitched eighteen-year old voice, a woman with a demure Asian accent, and a dominating 'older woman' with an Eastern European accent. Men, too, can perform a (heterosexual) feminine identity, as illustrated in the study, as a (bisexual) male operator projected a 'soft and quiet' voice and adopted the attentive discourse style stereotypically associated with women (1995: 201–203). This study is striking for its illustration of the conscious performance of gender identity. However, what is less remarkable and yet no less a performance is the often unconscious ways that people will routinely and repeatedly behave and talk, that get perceived within the culture as 'belonging' to a particular gender.

In sum, gender study in discourse analysis illuminates the ways that interactions can produce and change gender identity categories. At the same time, contemporary feminist theories insist that in order to avoid making simplistic and universalizing claims, 'gender' needs

---

[5]No categorization system (e.g. women/men) is solid or 'natural'. Some people have gender identifications that do not correspond with the way others might label them biologically; some people are physically altered in a surgical effort to change 'sex' or to conform to the 'only two sexes' division. Sexual orientations do not always match neatly the ways the dominant sex division is enforced in social and legal practices. People wanting to identify with a certain category will often adopt speech characteristics that are conventionally associated with that group.

to be viewed as interconnected with other categories and hierarchies of social identity such as race/ethnicity, social class and position, sexuality, (dis)ability, age, culture and nationality. This means that women and men participate in a wide variety of interactions as they move through their days and years, speaking in a wide variety of ways that defy generalizations. Because of the 'double consciousness' of Blacks and other people of colour in the USA, and of minority people in other places, they may be especially skilled in several language styles, switching as this seems necessary or desirable (Bucholtz, 1996; Scott, 2002). Boys, like girls, can be heard to construct their gender identity through complex references to sexuality, class, ethnicity, and age (Frosh et al., 2002). We need to pay attention to these 'differences', recognizing that gender, for instance, is racialized and classist, even as we guard against the danger of slipping back into stereotyping (Kroløkke and Sørensen, 2006). In the process, it becomes imperative to recognize that gender identity is not homogeneous or singular; rather, femininities and masculinities are heterogeneous and plural.

At a time of technologically-aided rapid cultural globalization, the relationship between the 'global' and the 'local' provides another dimension to the study of gender that is situated within a web of social identities. An illustration of the intersections of gender, sexuality, and transnational/global identities comes from the ways that some Chinese netizens are constructing their identities through innovations and adaptations of Chinese writing systems (Gao and Yuan, 2005; Yang, 2007). In recent years, a playful innovative use of '同志' (comrade), which draws on local linguistic uses, has been widely used as an alternative for '同性恋' (homosexual), a change that may be connected to the desires of gays and lesbians in creating their national identities. From Chinese online communities for lesbians, an even newer term solely for lesbians – '拉拉' (pronounced as [la: la:]), an adaptation of the Chinese writing system for the English initial of 'lesbian' – has emerged and become well accepted. Creatively working together with national and international linguistic resources, therefore, some Chinese lesbians have created a unique identity, which suggests a desire to connect to the world and yet remain local (see Zhang and Kramarae, 2008).

GENDER AND *POWER* IN DISCOURSE

The work on gender in discourse studies has been critical in helping to document the somewhat *changing* relations of power, over the last decade, in various countries and subcultures, arising from important social changes. For example, more women can now make greater decisions about sexual reproduction, have access to education and paid employment, and a few seem to have broken through the proverbial glass ceiling. Blatant gender discrimination is not as widespread in some education systems, workplaces, and the media, and more women and men declare themselves supportive of gender equality.[6]

---

[6]In some societies, however, young women especially will distance themselves from the identity label 'feminist', even as they support the principles of gender equality.

Yet it is not clear how lasting, or deep, the changes have been. Most women throughout the world are still bunched together in the same types of jobs, earn less than men, have more difficulty obtaining leadership positions, and do most of the household work and care for children and the elderly. Some women have it harder than other women – in the USA, for example, African American and Latina women are at a particular disadvantage in the labour market (Browne, 1999). Even in societies where there is legislation against blatant sexism, sexual harassment and physical violence against women still persist. Where cyberspace was once considered a potentially democratic 'neutral' frontier for women with access to participate on an equal footing with men, it quickly became evident that gender asymmetries in face-to-face interactions had carried over into virtual encounters. Women particularly have been targets for cyber-bullying, tactics which include humiliation, destructive messaging, gossip, slander and other 'virtual taunts' communicated through e-mail, text-messaging, instant messaging, chatrooms, blogs and other online social networks.

Even in a women-friendly academic electronic discussion list women are sometimes bullied, according to a (1998) study by Susan Herring, Deborah Johnson and Tamra DiBenedetto. Although women's overall contributions comprised only 30 per cent of the total postings on a list they studied, on one occasion when the women's contributions on a feminist topic exceeded men's, the discussion was disrupted by complaints from some men, who threatened to unsubscribe from the list, claiming that they were being 'silenced', and that the women's tones were 'vituperative' and 'unreasonable'. The researchers found that contrary to the complaints, the only message that was indisputably negative in tone was one posted by a man, who 'accused women on the list of "posting without thinking through carefully first", and in general, of "bashing", "guilt-tripping", and "bullying" men who didn't toe the strict feminist line'(p. 202).

Some theorists suggest that although major power imbalances continue to exist, people may be less willing or able to articulate the reasons for these imbalances, often suggesting that gender is irrelevant to them, and that reasons other than sexism account for injustices and continued gender inequality (Wetterer, 2003). Increasingly, in many settings being either a perpetrator or a victim of sexism is now becoming socially undesirable and something that is to be denied. The study of women's and men's discourse can give us an insight into how conflicting perceptions of gender justice operate and also point to mechanisms of subtle sexism. For example, in studying the responses of Swiss information communication technology workers when asked to explain the scarcity of women in this work area, Elisabeth Kelan (2007) found that, while male workers denied that the company discriminated against women, they used many 'I don't knows' along with often conflicting and complicated reasons for the scarcity of women in the field.

Gender stereotypes will often form part of the taken-for-granted assumptions about the way power relations are constructed in workplace interactions. In a (2005) study of New Zealand workplaces, Janet Holmes found that people's expectations about gendered discourse patterns that associate power-talk with men and supportive-talk with women contribute to ways in which it is considered appropriate, indeed 'normal', for men and women to behave within workplace cultures. When women managers transgressed the boundaries of appropriate gender behaviour, by adopting 'masculine' discourse styles in 'doing power' overtly, they or others would often react in ways that signalled their awareness of these boundaries. For instance, a woman manager who uncompromisingly vetoed a team proposal later asked her colleagues, 'did people feel disempowered by that decision [?]' (p. 51), which demonstrated her self-consciousness about such a blatant discourse style being inappropriately unfeminine. The study illustrates that gender is always present below the surface in social interactions, ready to emerge and reinstate the limits of acceptable behaviour for women at work in a way that is absent for male managers.

Recent studies of gender in discourse highlight the complexity of social power relations, as gender interacts with other hierarchies such as race, class, sexuality and place. Studies also now emphasize the relationality (rather than the absoluteness) of power, in which the agency and resistance of women are considered within the constraints of given social structures. For example, global discussions about sex work by lobbying groups and government workers often portray the women involved as 'slaves' or 'victims', and as helpless, ignorant, and duped. Yet in her talks with sex workers in Cambodia, Larissa Sandy (2007) found that many of their narratives showed that larger economic structures had interacted with family experiences to shape their actions: the women were often driven to this work as a practical, if unwanted, response to their situation. The women's choices were constrained 'by hierarchal structures such as gender, class and socio-cultural obligations and poor employment opportunities' (see Abstract, http://www.aas.asn.au/TAJA/Contents_18_2.html). They were not merely victims, they were also actors making decisions, albeit with very limited resources, about how to survive. Moralistic or paternalistic analyses and remedies could not resolve their problems. Social welfare programmes and other major social changes based on understandings of the many social institutions involved would be a start. As Victoria DeFrancisco (1997) states, discourse analysis that carefully considers links among individuals *and* social institutions and hierarchies can play a role in change – locally and globally.

Another study shows how, in spite of their subordinate position at home and their exploitation in their factory workplace, a group of young working-class Javanese women created a protest discourse against their factory oppressors (Berman, 1994). Repetition, adopted as a discursive resource in their oral narratives, was used to fulfil two functions. By directly quoting their oppressors in the Indonesian language used by the factory management to silence the workers' concerns, the women distinguished themselves from the immoral and unjust authority. At the same time, a repetition of each other's words within the cohort, uttered in their native Javanese tongue, indexed the women's solidarity and shared oppression. They were doubly oppressed and silenced through gender and poverty, yet they attempted to resist the dominant ideologies that disempowered them. Unlike earlier studies that focused solely on the dominance of men over women, Berman's research emphasized the empowerment and solidarity discursively enacted among the women (even though the protest itself failed in this case).

Another aspect of the complexity of power relations that has been documented is how social issues of gender and power have been appropriated and neutralized by actors in institutional settings. Michelle Lazar (2006, 2007) demonstrates this in the formation of what she terms 'power femininity' in the global media. Power femininity is an identity associated with a neo-liberal postfeminist discourse, which incorporates feminist values of emancipation and empowerment, while circulating popular postfeminist assumptions that feminism and sexism are passé, that full equality for (all) women has been achieved, and that power relations are shifting in favour of women. Media language and visual images are of women as powerful agents, who are autonomous, in control, and active. Advertisements for beauty products, for example, verbally urge consumers to 'discover the alpha female in you' and 'defy conventions and take the lead' or represent women's voices as self-determined: 'It's my body. I'll call the shots'. Visually – through a direct gaze, stance, and sometimes 'kick ass' fighting poses – women are presented as assertive and confident. From a critical perspective, Lazar argues that the neo-liberal postfeminist discourse is problematic for its striking absence of social struggle, community, and social justice. Instead, it promotes a commodified empowerment that is individualistic and narcissistic and that coexists with the goals and practices of traditional (non-feminist) femininity without apparent contradiction.

ANALYSING GENDER AND POWER IN DISCOURSE: EXCERPTS FROM *SEX AND THE CITY*

In this section, we provide a sample analysis of discourse to illustrate how gender is performed in a contemporary text. The chosen text is excerpted from *Sex and the City: The Movie* (2008), which followed from the popular, award-wining HBO television series of the same title (from 1997 to 2005), involving four female friends – Carrie, Charlotte, Miranda and Samantha. Like others of its ilk (e.g. *Bridget Jones's Diary* and *Lipstick Jungle*), *Sex and the City* (both the television series and the movie) belongs to the genre of 'chick lit' (or 'chick flick') which, although largely produced for a target female audience in the West, is distributed and consumed more globally. Productions like it both reflect and contribute to the formation of a 'postfeminist ethos' within popular culture. As mentioned earlier, based upon the assumption that feminism is passé, and taking women's emancipation and empowerment as as 'given', well as embracing anew normative femininity as an entitlement, the postfeminist ethos is characteristically contradictory and ambivalent, in that it meshes feminist, non-feminist and anti-feminist elements (see Lazar, 2009), the complex sum of which muddies questions of social and political power/empowerment and stalls feminist critique, which is why we regard it to be especially of interest to a contemporary critical feminist analysis of discourse. Furthermore, chick flicks like *Sex and the City* have enormous popular appeal, offering young women a source of viewing pleasure which cannot be overlooked or underestimated and which also, thus, makes a feminist critique of texts like this all the more imperative.

The text we analyse is an extended excerpt from the movie that comprises three successive segments (see the transcript in this chapter's Appendix). Before the first segment, Carrie and her 'manfriend' Big have looked at apartments in Manhattan with a plan to move in together. Carrie is entranced by a penthouse far above their price range (although she thinks the closet for her clothes and shoes is not big enough). Big, as a surprise for Carrie, closes the deal on the apartment, and promises to build her a bigger closet. The first segment shows Carrie excitedly sharing news about the apartment with Charlotte and Miranda as the three walk together down a fashionable New York street. The segment then closes with them meeting Samantha. In the second segment, the four friends go into an auction house, where Samantha unsuccessfully bids on a flower ring upon which she had her heart set. The third segment returns to a scene involving Big and Carrie. Following cautionary discussion with her friends, Carrie worries that if the apartment is solely purchased in Big's name, she would then have no legal rights to it should they separate. Big then suggests that they get married.

The excerpt, of course, is only an interactional 'snapshot' and is embedded in the wider context of the whole movie, as well as being associated intertextually with the television series. The analysis of the excerpt we undertake, therefore, cannot be expected to be self-contained. Nor do we intend our sample analysis to be exhaustive. Rather, our aim is to use the text as an example to show how gender gets performed in discourse, and to highlight, with an eye on power relations, some of the contradictions and ambivalences in this performance that are undergirded by a postfeminist ethos. In providing an analysis of gender, we have organized this section in terms of constructions of gender *relations* and gender *identity*. One aspect of gender relations involves the construction of relationships among women – the four friends – another, between women and men, notably, Carrie and Big.

The relationship among the four women is one of close friendship and solidarity. Like gender, friendship is also socially constructed through meanings and practices that are continually performed. Throughout the movie and the series the women exchange opinions and offer criticism and support for one another in long-term relationships. In the first segment of the excerpt, we see Carrie animatedly sharing her news about the penthouse with Charlotte and Miranda, and the rapport demonstrated by Charlotte and Miranda. Charlotte shows interest and involvement both verbally ('It sounds perfect') and through laughter at Carrie's remark that she currently has to keep her sweaters in the stove. Miranda's involvement is expressed through concern, as she says 'So he bought it and you'll live there with him', and again later 'But he'll own the place, so you're keeping your own place, right?' Against the carried-away excitement of Carrie, Miranda represents the voice of reason. Miranda's use of 'so' in the two instances and the adversative 'but' function to re-state (in order to clarify) for Carrie the reality of the situation – that it is Big alone who owns the apartment. Miranda makes her concern for Carrie explicit when she says 'I just wanna be sure that you're being smart here', which Carrie understands and appreciates – 'And I love you for that'. Although Miranda is cautious for Carrie, she is also able to participate in her joy as well. Carrie obviously needs a different kind of support from Miranda at this point, which Carrie makes known and to which Miranda complies smilingly (see the excerpt below). Miranda's re-alignment with Carrie is seen in her echoing Carrie's word 'jealous', which she then elaborates in her own words in the next conversational turn.

Carrie:	But for now, can't you stop worrying for me and just go ahead and feel what I want you to feel, jealous? Oh, jealous of me living in this gorgeous penthouse in Manhattan.
Miranda:	All right, I'm jealous.
Carrie:	Oh thanks.
Miranda:	You live in real-estate heaven and I live in Brooklyn.

The friendship bond is also performed in the act of the New York friends being present to accompany Samantha, who had flown in to bid on an elegant ring at an auction. The greeting scene is testimony of their unity – they greet each other with enthusiastic noises, kisses and hugs, and their voices blend, making it difficult to distinguish between speakers. In a following scene, Carrie's and Samantha's closeness is enacted:

Samantha:	[...] This flower ring is the essence of me. One of a kind, filled with fire.
Carrie:	And a little too much.
Samantha:	Exactly. [...]

Out of context, Carrie's quip could be construed as a face threatening act, as her remark about the ring implicates Samantha as well, who had described the ring as 'the essence' of herself. However, in the context of their friendship, Carrie's continuation of Samantha's description in those terms expresses intimacy. In fact, in response, Samantha affirms Carrie's observation as spot on. In a later scene, too, the closeness of the friendship continues to be 'done' when Carrie consolingly squeezes Samantha's hand when the latter fails to secure the ring at the auction.

The solidarity and support among the friends harken a 'sisterhood' – indeed, we do not see or hear about the women's own family members, if they exist – which feminists can appreciate. The women are individuals, but also a 'collective force' (Southard, 2008: 153). This is visually evident in the street scene where Carrie places her arms around Charlotte and Miranda, and all three walk down the street side by side and physically linked. At the auction house, also, Carrie, Charlotte and Miranda gather around Samantha and together they inspect the ring on display, and later sitting in a row during the auction. Notwithstanding the women's solidarity for each other, it is noteworthy that much of their interaction both in the movie and the series centre around shopping, men and relationships (Gerdes, 2008). Little is said about wider social concerns or attempting to link the personal with the political. Further, their friendship is marked in part by its exclusion from other women, such as when Charlotte calls another woman bidding against Samantha 'Bitch'.

Turning to the aspect of gender relations between women and men, in this excerpt, we see the negotiation of power between Carrie and Big. In one instance, Carrie's later decision to sell her apartment in order to contribute to the purchase of the penthouse signifies her desire for equality and partnership in the relationship: 'I want it to be ours'. In a sense, the decision attempts to rectify the earlier power asymmetry of their interaction:

Carrie: Can … ? Can we afford this?
Big: I got it. [to realtors:] Okay, let's sign some contracts.

Carrie is doubtful that they can afford the penthouse, and invites some discussion on it. In response, Big makes a unilateral decision and states matter-of-factly 'I got it'. The 'let's' in the following utterance refers to the realtors and himself, and does not include Carrie. However, at this point Carrie does not experience the situation as disempowering. In fact, getting over the surprise of the purchase, Carrie is shown looking smilingly in the direction of Big and in the next scene is excitedly re-telling the episode to her friends. Clearly, from the exchange, we know that Big can afford the penthouse on his own. Carrie's offer later on to co-finance the property, therefore, renders it a symbolic gesture, rather than contributing towards a financial necessity. Further, interestingly, at the end of our transcript there is an expectation by Carrie that Big would (and should) still build her a bigger closet – 'Just get me a really big closet'. The expense and responsibility of building the closet, which is entirely for Carrie's use, fall to Big.

In the discussion about marriage, again we find some of the earlier asymmetry at play.

Big: Did you wanna get married?
Carrie: Well, I didn't … I didn't think that was an option.
Big: What if it was an option?
Carrie: Why? What, do you wanna get married?
Big: I wouldn't mind being married to you. Would you mind being married to me?
Carrie: No. no, not if … not if that's what you wanted … I mean, is … is that what you want?
Big: I want you. So … okay.
Carrie: So … ? Really? We're … we're getting married?
Big: We're getting married.

Carrie's responses above are marked by hesitation, pauses and false starts showing her as fumbling, unsure and in need of affirmation. In fact, each of her turns is phrased as a question. Visually, too, her bodily stance and facial expression show how unsure she is; she shrugs her shoulders, and does not maintain an even gaze as she speaks. By contrast, Big is decisive and self-confident, and his gaze is direct and pointed. Finally, it is his pronouncement 'We're getting married' that ends the discussion. They are getting married. Period. (As a general point, elsewhere in our transcript also, we find that Carrie's speech style when talking to Big is characteristically marked by false starts (e.g. 'Can … Can we afford this?'), whereas this is not the case with Big's speech style. When talking among her women friends, the false starts are remarkably absent.)

Having examined how gender relations are interactionally enacted, we now turn our attention to the construction of a postfeminist feminine identity. We organized this section first by considering how emancipation and autonomy are performed in the excerpt and the ambivalence surrounding it, followed by a discussion on how gender identity interacts with other salient social identities that are present also.

Samantha's utterances 'Let's go spend some of my hard-earned Hollywood money' and 'I work hard, I deserve this' index the financial independence of the modern professional woman as well as an attitude of being entitled to a hedonistic pleasure because she's earned it. The ability to spend money of her own on expensive jewelry for herself evinces a consumer-based source of enablement. Liberation and independence, in other words, are interpreted rather narrowly as being able to fulfil personal desires through consumption. The flower ring, which Samantha describes as capturing the essence of herself, as well as the act of spending on herself become a symbol of personal autonomy. Notwithstanding the individualistic and materialistic interpretation of autonomy, the signification of the ring, however, changes when we later learn that it is Smith, Samantha's partner, who buys the ring for her in celebration of their anniversary as a couple. Re-signified as a symbol of a (heterosexual) relationship, even after their break-up, the latter meaning of the ring remains as Samantha promises to think of him whenever she would look at it.

To be bought for (rather than to buy for onself) apparently is a heterosexual privilege, which is evinced elsewhere in the excerpt as well. Note that the flower ring that originally belonged to the Blair Elkenn character was bought for by her then boyfriend; Big asks Carrie whether they (read: he) should buy her a diamond (engagement) ring; and Big offers and Carrie expects him to build her a bigger closet. What we see from the discussion, therefore, is a tension between personal autonomy and being in a heterosexual relationship, which shrouds the notions of liberation and independence of the 'modern' woman in ambivalence.

Repeated references to being 'smart' and a 'smart girl' also signify an emancipated feminine identity. In context, smartness in a woman means being rational and also mindful of her legal rights. Its use as a buzz word four times in the excerpt, either self-referentially or of another woman, presupposes, in fact, that women stereotypically are emotional and naïve. Blair Elkenn apparently stopped being 'smart' when she gave in to her emotions: 'She was a smart girl till she fell in love'. Miranda's advice to Carrie, 'I just wanna make sure that you're being smart', and Carrie's utterances (to Miranda) 'I haven't figured out the details, but I'm a smart girl' and (to Big) 'Come on, I have to be smart here. We're not married; I'd have no legal rights, you know, to … to this home that I built with you', are assertions of reason over emotion. The examples all suggest an implied tension and polarization between emotion and reason with which women struggle, and must resolve in favour of the latter, which represents empowerment. Furthermore, the phrase 'smart girl' exhibits an interesting tension too. Although smartness is a valued attribute associated with the savvy emancipated woman, the lexical choice of 'girl' invites one not to be taken too seriously, for the word semantically cues youth and a lack of maturity. As a point of comparison, in the movie, Big objects to being called Carrie's '*boy*friend' because, as someone in his forties, he does not identify with the semantics of the term, and so Carrie good-humouredly offers an alternative word 'manfriend'. However, Carrie, also in her forties, embraces the term 'girl'

('I'm a smart girl') as a self-description. Viewed more widely, within postfeminist popular culture, there has been a celebration of girlhood with media portrayals of young female superheroes (e.g. the Power Puff Girls and Buffy the Vampire Slayer). As such, it is likely that the use of 'girl' in the *Sex and the City* excerpt represents a reclamation of the term (to refer to empowerment) for adult women also. Indeed, *Sex and the City* (the movie and series) has been described as belonging to a 'New Girl Order' (Hymowitz, 2007). While this may be the case, however, the privileging of perpetual youthfulness in women as a marker of empowerment remains unquestioned.

The formation of a postfeminist feminine identity in *Sex and the City* depends upon the co-presence of several other relevant social categories. Here we will focus on the salient ones pertaining to class, regionalism, and heterosexuality. However, before we do so there are a couple of brief remarks that can be made about whiteness and age also.

Although New York is a multicultural and cosmopolitan city, the primary focus of *Sex and the City* is on the lives of white women. Whiteness, although not overtly marked in the language in our excerpt, is significant visually in the embodiment of the four female friends. Some have also noted the uniformity of their 'WASP surnames': Hobbes, Bradshaw, York, and Jones (Negra, 2004: 12). Age is not a salient category in our excerpt, although it is a point of focus elsewhere in the movie (about Carrie getting married in her forties, and Samantha reaching fifty). In relation to our excerpt, we have already mentioned the problematic attribution of perpetual girlhood to mature women. On the one hand, terms like 'girl' and 'baby' (which Big calls Carrie) undermines such women as not having attained full adulthood (Negra, 2004: 12). On the other hand, girlhood for adult women is celebrated as a state of empowerment by an ageist culture; even as women age, they must be forever young.

Middle-class identity is fundamental to the construction of a postfeminist feminine identity of the women in the show, who can afford to consume. That consumption and material acquisition are key to the identity of these women is evident from Samantha flying into New York to bid on a costly ring, and Carrie wanting a bigger closet space. High fashion and luxury living play a significant role in the plot and in the women's talk with one another, with all of the four wearing designer clothing and shoes, acquiring expensive accessories, and living comfortably. Such practices normalize the actions and thoughts of white middle-class women who seldom question their jobs and privilege, and thus marginalize the poor.

Regionalism and urbanism contribute to the middle-class lifestyle displayed by Carrie and her friends. New York (specifically MANhattan) is presented as a 'happening' place for affluent women. The setting for the women's walk, in the excerpt, includes Times Square, Tiffany's, and Christie's, all iconic places of success and glamour (although not typical of the places that many New York working women could afford). During their walk, there are no homeless people appearing, speaking or spoken to, any of which might limit the street expansion of the beauty (artistic, colourful store windows) of their walk or the pleasures of the women as they talk about their plans and desires.

There is reference made to three relationships in our excerpt, all of which are heterosexual: Carrie's relationship with Big; Blair Elkenn's failed relationship; and Samantha's brief mention of Smith. Heterosexuality for the women is a 'given' in the excerpt and throughout the movie (and series), normalized through their frank discussions about men, sex and relationships that occupy much of their talk.[7] Heterosexual marriage is not assumed as an expected outcome in the modern woman's relationship with men.[8] In the exchange quoted earlier between Big and Carrie (partly reproduced below), we can see that Carrie is taken off guard by Big's question to her about getting married (which, three turns later, she poses back to him); they both describe marriage in terms of options; and Big raises its possibility as a hypothetical question:

Big: Did you wanna get married?
Carrie: Well, I didn't … I didn't think it was an option.
Big: What if it was an option?
Carrie: Why? What, do you wanna get married?

Ironically, however, marriage is still ultimately seen as offering women some economic security, especially if it breaks down and they can claim their legal rights. In the story of Blair Elkenn her friends had advised her to get married, and her failure to do so had left her vulnerable – 'she came home one night, and he had locked her out. She didn't even have anywhere to live'. In Carrie's case the topic of marriage arises from an issue of financial insecurity – that she would have no legal right to the apartment if they separated. Underlying the two scenarios is the view of marriage as women's surety, needed to maintain their middle-class consumerist lifestyle.

One can learn a lot from looking closely at this very popular, fashionable fantasy world of work (although we do not see much evidence of actual work) and play. We have only included a couple of excerpts from the movie. Yet even here, as we observe the kinds of individualistic, consumerist 'demands' or 'rights' expressed in these segments (e.g., financial security for oneself, a big closet, an expensive ring), we can note what is said *and* what isn't said in the larger context of the concerns of the women's liberation movement. This includes equal pay and education for all; social as well as personal choices; legal and financial independence; and freedom from violence or sexual coercion, and from exploitation and discrimination based on such classifications as race, class, age, and sexual orientation. In the excerpts, midde-class affluence and aggressive individual acquisition (rather than an assertion of women's agency in general) are what is stressed. The analysis shows how postfeminism not only engages feminism selectively and partially, it also generates a set of contradictions that suggest, illogically, that the feminist movement is dead, victorious and ultimately a failure (Walters, 1991: 106). Readers can further determine the relationship of the rest of the talk and other actions in this movie to the gender identity practices and power connections we have mentioned throughout this chapter.

---

[7] We thank Erin Kevin for pointing out that in one of the seasons, in the TV series, Samantha dates a woman for a while. This represents a brief foray into lesbianism in an otherwise predominantly heteronormative gender order inhabited by the four friends.

[8] Yet, note that the movie's central plot rests on Carrie and Big's wedding, and culminates in a 'happily ever after' fairy-tale ending.

CONCLUSION

This chapter provided examples of discourse study that analysed some of the many ways that people construct, resist, and subvert traditional gender norms. As anthropologists and linguists have argued for years, meaning is always situated and never only based on linguistic structures. While generalized, decontextualized 'sex difference' studies can provide us with guides about some of the relationships of gender and language, such studies do not take us much closer to understanding how gender and gender asymmetries are structured and reproduced in everyday life. Context, and the impact of context, are not reducible to any set of independent variables (such as, for example: sex, classroom, and a response to questions). Language use develops from the social practices, and thus power relationships, of individuals, groups, and communities.

Throughout this chapter, we have indicated that social categories, including 'women' and 'men' are not fixed, but are instead socially constructed and variable. Yet in the worlds we live in, those categories are often treated as fixed and self-evident, with women as a class subordinate to men as a class – a situation, remarkably, shared by communities across time and place. So as we are problematizing all social categories, we also need to recognize and analyse the conditions that enable these categories to prevail. We, therefore, require a collaboration among discourse analysts and social researchers from many other disciplines, such as sociology, economics, anthropology, political science, and law. Working together we can reveal injustices and help figure out considered interventions.

This chapter has focused on some of the ways that discourses shape and are shaped by power relationships in social institutions and societies, and has suggested that major social changes are unlikely to take place without paying close attention to language and other forms of semiosis. Discourse analysis helps reveal the subtle as well as the blatant ways that sexism, racism, class status and other inequalities are simultaneously furthered in everyday life. An underlying assumption of this discussion is that if we can inform ourselves about the ways powerful participants control and constrain the contributions of people in groups with lesser power, we can then move towards more equitable opportunities for all participants to choose from and practise speech acts.

Yet some researchers and theorists have argued that power is inherent in *all* verbal interactions – just often more overtly in institutional settings than in casual conversations in 'personal' groups such as family and intimate friendship networks. It would be unrealistic, therefore, to assume that there can be true equality, which would include taking turns and developing topics in an ideal ongoing dialogue, complete with continuous reconsideration and without coercion (see Wang, 2006). However, even if such symmetry of interaction is not a possibility, it still seems critical, in any society that comes to a shared aspiration of democratic ideals, that we both inspect the ways that discourses reproduce and challenge social inequalities and power relationships and work toward more egalitarian practices.

A developing feminist approach to communication called 'invitational rhetoric' (Zhang and Kramarae, 2008), which includes more respectful, fluid, and flexible collaborations, may be useful in generating new insights about communication possibilities, and options of framing discussions and of reaching decisions through listening, offering, reflecting, and changing perhaps not others but ourselves, as we generate new insights in the process of more respectful and rounded dialogues and multilogues.

APPENDIX

Setting	Language	Images
Carrie and Big looking at a large penthouse in Manhattan, NY, with realtors.	*Big*: I can build you a better closet. Welcome home, baby.	Big looks at Carrie and grins.
	Carrie: Can … ? Can we afford this?	Carrie looks incredulously at Big.
	Big: I got it.	Big gives Carrie a 'look', and a quick nod.
	[Big to realtors]: Okay, let's sign some contracts.	Camera is on Carrie looking at Big with a slow smile.
Carrie, Charlotte and Miranda are walking down a fashionable New York street. Carrie is in the middle.	*Carrie*: 'I got it.' Just like that. 'I got it.' Like he was picking up a check for coffee or something.	
	Charlotte: It sounds perfect.	
	Carrie: Except for the closet, which Big says he can redo. And he says the kitchen needs work. Of course, I don't know about that because I keep sweaters in my stove.	
	Charlotte: [Laughter]	
	Miranda: So he bought it and you'll live there with him.	
	Carrie: Yes, together. That's right.	
	Miranda: But he'll own it, so you're keeping your own place, right?	
	Carrie: [Oh Miranda,] I haven't figured out the details, but I'm a smart girl. I'll figure out something that I'm comfortable with.	
	Miranda: I just wanna be sure that you're being smart here.	
	Carrie: And I love you for that. But for now, can't you stop worrying for me and just go ahead and feel what I want you to feel, jealous? Oh, jealous of me living in this gorgeous penthouse in Manhattan.	Carrie faces Miranda and puts her hands on Miranda's arms. Carrie puts her arms around both women. Miranda nodding.

Setting	Language	Images
	Miranda: All right, I'm jealous.	Carrie still has her arms around her two friends; all three are walking together in unison.
	Carrie: Oh thanks.	
	Miranda: You live in real-estate heaven and I live in Brooklyn.	
	Carrie: Well	
	Miranda: New York magazine said Brooklyn **is** the new Manhattan.	
	Carrie: Ah	
	Miranda: Whoever wrote that lives in Brooklyn. [Laughter]	
The four women are in front of Christie's, the elegant auction house.	*Carrie* [seeing Samantha]: Hey, there she is. Hey, Hollywood.	Shot of Samantha smiling broadly, with arms outstretched.
	Hey.	
	[?] Oh, lady. Hi.	Samantha is greeted with hugs and kisses.
	Charlotte: How was your flight?	
The women enter Christie's, the auction house. Piano music in background.	*Samantha*: Fabulous.	
	[?] Oh, good. – Good.	
	[?] Let's go in. I'm so excited.	
	[?]Show us.	In the background are large photos of Elkenn, and in the foreground are display cases with jewelry. The four women, along with others present, are browsing through the exhibits.
	[Voice-over by Carrie]: It was a rare occasion that brought all types of New York women together. Blair Elkenn was a waitress turned model turned actress, turned billionaire's girlfriend who came home one night to find herself unceremoniously turned out on the street. And now she was getting the ultimate breakup revenge: an embarrassing and very public auction of all the jewelry he had given her when they were happy.	
	Samantha: There it is. My baby.	Samantha peering through a display case at a flower ring.
	Charlotte: Oh, she's a beauty.	All four women standing around the case peering at the ring.
	Sam: When I saw it in the catalogue, I said to Smith [the man she lives with]: 'This flower ring is the essence of me. One of a kind, filled with fire.'	
	Carrie: And a little too much.	
Piano music stops. The four women sit in a row, along with other people at the auction. Samantha has a paddle with a number with which to make her bid.	*Sam*: Exactly … Let's go spend some of my hard-earned … Hollywood money.	
	[The women laugh.]	
	Woman auctioneer: And now Lot 39, the flower ring. We'd like to start the bidding on this at $10,000, please. At ten-thousand doll … Thank you, madam. [Directed to Samantha] At 10,000. Fifteen thousand. At $15,000.	Samantha signals her bid.
		All four women look at a competitor bidder further down the row.

(Continued)

(Continued)

Setting	Language	Images
	Charlotte: Hey, she's bidding for somebody on the phone.	
	[?] That's not fair.	
	Charlotte: Bitch.	Competitor signals bid.
	Carrie: Umm. The gloves are off.	
	Auctioneer: At $30,000. Now it's against you. Thirty-five thousand.	Samantha bids.
	Samantha [in whisper to Carrie]: I work hard, I deserve this.	Competitor bids.
	Auctioneer: At 40,000 now. At 40? Forty thousand? Forty thousand, thank you. Forty-five thousand. At $45,000. Now 50,000?	
	Samantha [in loud voice]: Fifty fucking thousand.	
	[Laughter in the room]	
After the bidding, the friends are in the washroom facing the mirrors, along with other women.	*Auctioneer*: At 50,000. Fifty-five thousand? At $55,000 against you. [To Samantha] Would you like to say 60? Sixty to our colourful bidder? At 60,000?	Carrie squeezes Samantha's hand.
	Samantha [to Carrie next to her]: I draw the line at 50.	
	Charlotte: I thought this auction would be more fun, but it's kind of sad.	
	A woman in a blue dress: Isn't it. I thought it was just sad for me because I know her. But it really is sad, huh? And it's funny because they were so happy.	
	Samantha: Yeah, till they weren't.	
	Woman in blue: I know, right? We all told her to get married but she didn't wanna listen. He'd been married three times before, so she let it ride and then she came home one night and he had locked her out. She didn't even have anywhere to live. Such a shame. After 10 years. She was a smart girl till she fell in love.	The woman in blue exits. The friends are quiet. Miranda looks at Carrie who briefly returns her gaze.
Big and Carrie are in Big's kitchen, preparing a meal. Big is standing chopping ingredients, and Carrie is seated, shucking ears of corn. Piano music plays in the background.	*Carrie*: I'm thinking ... I'm going to sell my apartment and put the money towards heaven on 5th.	He is grinning.
	Big: Why? You love your apartment.	Continues to grin with an eyebrow lifted.
	Carrie: I know, but there's plenty of room in the new place and, and besides, I ... I want to make us a life there. You know, I ... I want it to be ours.	

Setting	Language	Images
	Big: It is ours. I bought it for us.	
	Carrie: And that's so amazing, but **you** bought it. So really it's your place and if anything were to happen …	Carrie shrugs.
	Big: What's going to happen?	Lightly shrugs shoulders again.
	Carrie: Come on, I have to be smart here. We're not married; I'd have no legal rights, you know, to … to this home that I built … with you.	Big looks straight at her.
	Big: Did you wanna get married?	Looks at her again.
	Carrie: Well, I didn't … I didn't think that was an option.	Carrie's eyes are darting up and down.
	Big: What if it was an option?	Looks intently at her.
	Carrie: Why? What, do you wanna get married?	He shrugs.
	Big: I wouldn't mind being married to you. Would you mind being married to me?	
	Carrie: No. No, not if … not if that's what you wanted … I mean, is … is that what you want?	She shakes her head. Then extends her arms forward to gesture size. Both smile and Carrie laughs.
	Big: I want you. So … okay.	
	Carrie: So … ? Really? We're … we're getting married?	
	Big: We're getting married. Should we get you a diamond?	
	Carrie: No, no. Just get me a really big closet.	

FURTHER READING

Our ideas about gender influence the constructions of our institutions, discourse and other actions. While some scholarship still supports existing assumptions without reflecting on or questioning common beliefs about gender, now there is a great deal of thoughtful and careful research regarding the relationship of gender and language. This research comes from scholars in many disciplines including linguistics, communication, anthropology, and sociology, as well as from feminist thinkers, activists and analysts. Below are just a few sources that offer clear discussions of some of the many topics regarding gender that can be informed by linguistic analysis.

Cameron, Deborah (2006) *On language and sexual politics*. London, N.Y.: Routledge.
This collection of essays about the gender and language debates illustrates the ways that our everyday communication choices are political choices with many social and political consequences. Cameron deals with a variety of linguistic approaches including critical discourse, textual, and semantic analyses.

Eckert, Penelope and McConell-Ginet, Sally (2003) *Language and gender*. Cambridge: Cambridge University Press. This book re-evaluates several decades of language and gender research, from several countries, offering new ways of studying what we are doing with language, and the kinds of resources we use to present ourselves as certain kinds of women and men.

Holmes, Janet and Meyerhoff, Miriam (eds.) (2003) *The handbook of language and gender*. Malden, MA: Blackwell. This volume offers a wide spectrum of approaches and topics in the study of language and gender. It raises ideas and questions of current interest, as well as re-visits long-standing concerns in language and gender research.

Lazar, Michelle (ed.) (2005) *Feminist critical discourse analysis: Gender, power and ideology in discourse*. Basingstoke: Palgrave Macmillan.
The volume brings together research in critical discourse analysis and contemporary feminist theory to investigate how questions of gender, power and ideology are imbricated in discourse in a variety of cultural and international contexts.

ONLINE READING

The following articles are available at www.sagepub.co.uk/discoursestudies.

Lazar, Michelle M. (2009) 'Entitled to consume: postfeminist femininity and a culture of post-critique', *Discourse and Communication*, 3(4): 371–400.

Weatherall, Ann (2000) 'Gender relevance in talk-in-interaction and discourse', *Discourse & Society*, 11: 290–292.

West, Candace and Don Zimmerman (1987) 'Doing gender', *Gender & Society*, 1: 125–51.

REFERENCES

Baker, Paul (2005) *Public discourses of gay men*. London: Routledge.
Berman, Laine (1994) 'Empowering the powerless: The repetition of experience in Javanese women's narratives'. In Mary Bucholtz et al. (eds), *Cultural performances: proceedings of the third Berkeley women and language conference*. Berkeley, California: University of Berkeley. pp. 28–36.
Besnier, Niko (2003) 'Crossing genders, mixing languages: The linguistic construction of transgenderism in Tonga'. In Janet Holmes and Miriam Meyerhoff (eds), *Handbook of Language and Gender*. Oxford: Blackwell. pp. 279–301.
Bloustien, Gerry (2001) 'Far from sugar and spice: Teenage girls, embodiment and representation'. In Bettina Baron and Helga Kotthoff (eds), *Gender in interaction: Perspectives on femininity and masculinity in ethnography and discourse*. Amsterdam/Philadelphia: John Benjamins. pp. 99–136.
Browne, Irene (ed.) (1999) *Latinas and African American women at work: Race, gender, and economic inequality*. New York: Russell Sage Foundation.
Bucholtz, Mary (1996) 'Black feminist theory and African American women's linguistic practice'. In Victoria L. Bergvall, Janet M. Bing and Alice F. Freed (eds), *Rethinking language and gender research: Theory and practice*. London/New York: Longman. pp. 267–90.
Butler, Judith (1990) *Gender trouble: Feminism and subversion of identity*. New York: Routledge.
Cameron, Deborah (2006) *On language and sexual politics*. London & New York: Routledge.
Coates, Jennifer (2004) *Women, men and language: A sociolinguistic account of gender differences in language* (third edition). London: Pearson Longman.

Davies, Julia (2003) 'Expression of gender: An analysis of pupil's gendered discourse styles in small group classroom discussions'. *Discourse & Society*, 14(2): 115–32.

DeFrancisco, Victoria (1997) 'Gender, power and practice: Or, putting your money [and your research] where your mouth is'. In Ruth Wodak (ed.), *Gender and discourse*. London and Thousand Oaks, CA: Sage. pp. 37–56.

Deutsch, Francine (2007) 'Undoing gender'. *Gender & Society*, 21: 106–27.

Frosh, Stephen, Anne Phoenix and Rob Pattman (2002) *Young masculinities: Understanding boys in contemporary society*. Hampshire, NY: Palgrave.

Gao, Liwei and Rong Yuan (2005) 'Linguistic construction of modernity in computer-mediated communication'. In Qian Gao (ed.), *Proceedings of the seventeenth North American conference on Chinese linguistics (NACCL-17)*: 66–83.

Gerdes, Lindsay (2008) 'Carrie Bradshaw's feminism is a sham'. *Business Week*, 25 March.

Goodwin, Marjorie Harness (2007) 'Occasioned knowledge exploration in family interaction'. *Discourse & Society*, 18(1): 93–110.

Hague, Gill, Audrey Mullender, and Rosemary Aris (2003) *Is anyone listening? Accountability and women survivors of domestic violence*. London & New York: Routledge.

Halberstam, Judith (1998) *Female masculinity*. Durham, NC: Duke University Press.

Hall, Kira (1995) 'Lip service on the fantasy lines'. In Kira Hall and Mary Bucholtz (eds), *Gender Articulated: Language and the socially constructed self*. London & New York: Routledge. pp. 183–216.

Herring, Susan C., Deborah A., Johnson, and Tamra DiBenedetto (1998) *Language and Gender: A reader*. Oxford: Blackwell. pp. 197–210.

Holmes, Janet (2005) 'Power and discourse at work: is gender relevant?'. In Michelle Lazar (ed.), *Feminist critical discourse analysis: Gender, power and ideology in discourse*. Basingstoke: Palgrave. pp. 31–60.

Holmes, Janet (2006) *Gendered talk at work*. Oxford: Blackwell.

Hymowitz, Kay S. (2007) 'The New Girl Order'. *City Journal*. Autumn 2007. Retrieved 17 June 2008 at http://www.city-journal.org/html/17_4_new_girl_order.html

Jones, Rodney H. (2004) 'The problem of context in computer-mediated communication'. In Phillip LeVine and Ron Scollon (eds), *Discourse and technology: Multimodal discourse analysis*. Washington, DC: Georgetown University Press. pp. 20–33.

Kelan, Elizabeth K. (2007) '"I don't know why": Accounting for the scarcity of women in ICT work'. *Women's Studies International Forum*, 30: 499–511.

Kramer, Cheris (1978) 'Women's and men's ratings of their own and ideal speech'. *Communication Quarterly*, 26(2): 2–11.

Krołøkke, Charlotte and Anne Scott Sørensen (2006) *Gender communication theories & analyses: From silence to performance*. Thousand Oaks and London: Sage.

Lakoff, Robin (1975) *Language and woman's place*. New York: Harper and Row.

Lazar, Michelle M. (2000) 'Gender, discourse and semiotics: The politics of parenthood representations'. *Discourse & Society*, 11(3): 373–400.

Lazar, Michelle M. (2006) 'Discover the power of femininity! Analyzing global "power femininity" in local advertising'. *Feminist Media Studies*, 6(4): 505–17.

Lazar, Michelle M. (2007) 'Feminist critical discourse analysis: articulating a feminist discourse praxis'. *Critical Discourse Studies*, 4(2): 141–64.

Lazar, Michelle M. (2009) 'Entitled to consume: postfeminist femininity and a culture of post-critique'. *Discourse and Communication*, 3(4): 371–400.

Lovering, Kathryn (1995) 'The bleeding body: adolescents talk about menstruation'. In Sue Wilkinson and Celia Kitzinger (eds), *Feminism and discourse: Psychological perspectives*. London: Sage.

Negra, Diane (2004) '"Quality postfeminism?": Sex and the single girl on HBO'. *Genders OnLine Journal*, 39: 1–16.

McConnell-Ginet, Sally (1978) 'Intonation in a man's world'. *Signs*, 3(3): 541–59.

Pascale, Celine-Marie (2007) *Making sense of race, class, and gender*. New York and London: Routledge.

Popp, Danielle, Roxanne A. Donovan, Mary Crawford, Kerry L. Marsh, and Melanie Peele (2003) 'Gender, race, and speech style stereotypes'. *Sex Roles*, 48(7/8): 317–25.

Sandy, Larissa (2007) 'Just choices: Representations of choice and coercion in sex work in Cambodia'. *Australian Journal of Anthropology*, 18(2): 194–206.

Scott, Karla (2002) 'Conceiving the language of Black women's everyday talk'. In Marsha Houston and Olga Idriss Davis (eds), *Centering ourselves: African American feminist and womanist studies of discourse*. Cresskill, NJ: Hampton Press. pp. 53–76.

Southard, Belinda A. Stillion (2008) 'Beyond the backlash: *Sex and the City* and three feminist struggles'. *Communication Quarterly*, 562: 149–67.

Swan, J. (2002) '"Yes, but is it gender?"'. In Lia Litosseliti and Jane Sunderland (eds), *Gender identity and discourse analysis*. Amsterdam: John Benjamins. pp. 43–67.

Tannen, Deborah (1991) *You just don't understand: Women and men in conversation*. London: Virago.

Thorne, Barrie (1990) 'Children and gender: construction of difference'. In Deborah Rhode (ed.), *Theoretical perspectives in sexual differences*. New Haven, CT: Yale University Press. pp. 100–13.

Thorne, Barrie (2001) 'Gender and interaction: widening the conceptual scope'. In Bettina Baron and Helga Kotthoff (eds), *Gender in interaction: Perspectives on femininity and masculinity in ethnography and discourse*. Amsterdam/ Philadelphia: John Benjamins. pp. 3–18.

Trinch, Shonna (2003) *Latinas' narratives of domestic abuse: Discrepant versions of violence*. Amsterdam: John Benjamins.

Walters, Suzanne Danuta (1991) 'Premature postmortems: "postfeminism and popular culture"'. *New Politics*, 3(2): 103–12.

Wang, Jinjun (2006) 'Questions and the exercise of power'. *Discourse & Society*, 17(4): 529–48.

Weatherall, Ann (2000) 'Gender relevance in talk-in-interaction and discourse'. *Discourse & Society*, 11: 290–292.

Weatherall, Ann (2002) *Gender, language, and discourse*. New York: Routledge.

West, Candace and Don Zimmerman (1987) 'Doing gender'. *Gender & Society*, 1: 125–51.

Wetterer, Angelika (2003) 'Rhetorische Modernisierung: Das Verschwinden der Ungleichheit aus dem zeitgenössischen Differenzwissen'. In Gudrun-Axeli Knapp and Angelika Wetterer (eds), *Achsen der Differenz – Gesellschaftstheorie and feministische Kritik Vol. 2*. Münster: Westfälisches Dampfboot. pp. 286–319.

Yang, Chunsheng (2007) 'Chinese internet language: A sociolinguistic analysis of adaptations of the Chinese writing system'. *Language@Internet, 4*. Retrieved 20 January 2008, from http://www.languageatinternet.de/articles/2007/1142

Zhang, Wei and Cheris Kramarae (2008) 'Feminist invitational collaboration in a digital age: Looking over disciplinary and national borders'. *Women and Language*, Fall. (This article is also published as a (collaborative, changing) wiki at http://en.wikibooks.org/wiki/Gender,_Communication,_and_Technology)

TWELVE

Discourse, Ethnicity and Racism

Yasmin Jiwani and John E. Richardson

INTRODUCTION

The power of discourse in defining and shaping the realities of minoritized groups in society cannot be underestimated. Racist talk and thought are most evident in the everyday conversations and texts that the dominant society produces about minority groups. Yet in contemporary Western cultures, openly racist talk and similarly explicitly coded racist texts are taboo, often legally outlawed and socially censured. Nevertheless, borrowing a concept from Liz Kelly's (1987) work on sexual violence, it can be argued that racist talk and thought span a continuum of discursive violence, wherein subtle racism occupies one end of the continuum while the overt, far right discourse of racism inhabits the other. In this chapter, we use the tools of discourse analysis to examine more overt examples of racist discourse, both in everyday conversations and in mass-mediated texts, in part to demonstrate that such explicit racism does still exist. These texts, we argue, are politically promiscuous – absorbing, recasting and refracting issues of race and racism, and thereby reproducing dominant definitions about minority groups and perpetuating unequal relations of power.

We begin the chapter by outlining some of the tools of discourse analysis that have been used to analyse racist talk and texts. Thereafter, we discuss the phenomenon of uncensored racist talk, demonstrating the discursive strategies that are used to describe and define others. Racist discourse is also encoded in mass-mediated texts such as books used in schools and universities, popular media formats such as films and television programming, and news and current affairs. The mass media have the power to amplify and legitimate racist discourse and, hence, offer us a lens through which to interrogate popular assumptions and premises regarding race and racism. However, the analysis of mediated texts involves a consideration of wider societal structures and historical contexts.

The mass media are also strategic sites through which racist political groups and parties may disseminate their propaganda. Thus in the latter sections of the chapter we discuss the British National Party, paying particular attention to visual discourse through an analysis of the party's leaflets. In closing, we emphasize the spectrum of racist discourse that operates to perpetuate unequal relations of power and maintain hierarchies of privilege in contemporary Western societies.

TOOLS OF DISCOURSE ANALYSIS

Explicitly racist derogatory terms are used far less regularly in the contemporary discourse than a century or even fifty years ago. Nevertheless, the last few decades have witnessed increasing racism, in form and frequency, recontextualizing and recycling older forms of racism to target new(ly) racialized groups (Richardson and Wodak, 2009). To explain how such messages can be advanced – often only implicitly – we need to utilize a wide range of tools for analysis.

Like many of the contributors to this volume, we assume that language use is a social practice that is dialectically related to the context of its use: both created by and creating social understandings, and hence contributing to social realities – including racist inequalities. To examine how discourse can do this, our analysis needs to be focused on three levels: on texts; on the discursive practices of production and consumption; and on the wider socio-cultural practices which discourse helps (re)produce. If racism is reproduced through discourse, then it will be in evidence at all three 'levels' of discursive communication – social practices, discursive practices and the texts themselves – in ways which are integrated and mutually self-supporting (van Dijk, 2005). The analysis of texts involves looking at the form, content and function of the text, starting with an 'analysis of vocabulary and semantics, the grammar of sentences and smaller units, [...the] analysis of textual organisation above the sentence' and so on (Fairclough, 1995: 57). Recently, multi-modal analysts of the grammar of visual design (Kress and van Leeuwen, 2001) have introduced a new dimension to this level of analysis. A multimodal approach requires analysts to examine the ways that *visual* discursive elements 'can create moods and attitudes, convey ideas, create flow across the composition, in the same way that there are linguistic devices for doing the same in texts' (Machin, 2007: xi).

We also need to consider the discursive practices of the communicative event, which usually involves an examination of 'various aspects of the processes of text production and text consumption. Some of these have a more institutional character whereas others are discourse processes in a narrower sense' (Fairclough, 1995: 58). A key assumption of this level of analysis is that textual meaning cannot be divorced from the contexts of production and consumption. Further, given 'the meaning of an utterance rests in its usage in a specific situation' (Wodak, 1996: 20), a fully rounded examination should involve an analysis of the discourse's sociocultural practices. This level of analysis 'may be at different levels of abstraction from the particular event: it may involve its more immediate situational context, the wider context of institutional practices the event is embedded within, or the yet wider frame of the society and the culture' (Fairclough, 1995: 62).

Hence, discourse should be analysed at various levels and by focusing on different linguistic dimensions, each of which 'may be involved directly or indirectly in discriminatory interaction against minority group members' (van Dijk, 1999: 4). In a series of studies, van Dijk (1987; 1992; 1993a) developed a conceptual tool called 'the ideological square' which he argues dominates racist talk and text on and about 'racial' and ethnic others. This ideological square is characterized by a Positive Self-Presentation and a simultaneous Negative Other-Presentation and is observable across all linguistic dimensions of a text. Following Reisigl and Wodak (2001: 44) we find it useful to focus on five questions in taking discourse apart and operationalizing our examination of the ideological square:

- *Referential Strategies*: How are people named and referred to semiotically?
- *Predicational Strategies*: How are these people described? What qualities or characteristics are attributed to them?
- *Argumentation*: What arguments (explicit and/or implicit) are used to support these characterizations, and/or justify exploiting and discriminating against others?
- *Perspectivization*: From whose perspective are such namings, descriptions and arguments expressed?
- And are these utterances stated explicitly or implicitly? Are they intensified or mitigated?

Reisigl and Wodak (2001: 45) show that in the act of naming people

> one constructs and represents social actors: for example, ingroups and outgroups. This is done is a number of ways, such as membership categorisation devices, including reference by tropes, biological, naturalising and depersonalising metaphors and metonymies, as well as by synecdoches in the form of a part standing for a whole (*pars pro toto*) or a whole standing for the part (*totum pro parte*).

Of course, the open use of explicitly racist terms is now likely to be received with at least public scorn and sometimes contempt. Modern racist discourse tends to use either 'negative words to describe the properties or actions of immigrants or minorities (for instance, "illegal")' or else will adopt special code words such as 'welfare mothers' or 'inner city youths' in negative contexts (van Dijk, 1991). The riots in several British cities during the 1980s provided one such negative context, where familiar negative labels for 'racial' and ethnic minorities were used frequently and repeatedly by all newspapers. Some of these labels, and the referential strategies they enacted, were as follows:

- *The Sun*: headline '*BARBARIANS*' (primitivization)
- *The Daily Mail*: 'the worst elements of society' (superlative problematization)
- *The Times*: 'mindless yobs [who] can set out and in one night destroy a community' (negative mental somatization; criminalization)
- *The Guardian*: 'Drug Fraternity' (criminalization)

As Reisigl and Wodak (2001: 46) argue, examining the ways that people are named is 'of great help for us in accurately describing some of the more subtle forms of discriminatorily [...] constructing, identifying or hiding social actors'.

Clearly referential strategies bear the imprint of *predication* – defined by Reisigl and Wodak (2001: 54) as 'the very basic process and result of linguistically assigning qualities to persons, animals, objects, events, actions and social phenomena'. However, it is through predicational *strategies* that people 'are specified and characterised with respect to quality, quantity, space, time and so on' (ibid.). Sometimes, such predication is achieved through reference to a 'space' (political, cultural, social, mental, physical or metaphorical) rhetorically made separate from 'Our own' space, thereby placing a (negative) social value on this space and, by extension, its occupants. For example, in 2000 there was the tragic case of the 10-year-old Nigerian schoolboy Damilola Taylor, who was killed in London while he walked home from school; in 2006, two brothers were eventually were convicted of his manslaughter. Across five articles in one issue of *The Sunday Times* (3 December 2000) the paper referred to:

- 'a community used to violent crime' (Woods and Gadher, p. 1);
- a '*violent ghetto culture that claimed Damilola*' (Woods et al., pp. 14–15), and 'a moral, spiritual and emotional vacuum' arising 'from rage, rooted in emotional chaos and neglect' which existed amongst 'the squalor of the area where the Taylor family was living' (*Children learn to kill in a moral dead zone*, Phillips, p. 19).

Note that none of these quotes explicitly states that the 'blackness' of the children was the cause of their criminal behaviour, or that black people are more criminal than whites. However, these and other articles reporting the crime were forthright in asserting that criminality, immorality (cf. 'moral vacuum'), degradation, violence, etc. are typically experienced qualities of this Afro-Caribbean community, since they are 'used to' them. It is then only a small inferential step to concluding that the 'blackness' of the residents in this 'violent ghetto' played a role in the tragedy. Thus, the choice of words used in naming and describing people and places is of particular significance in analysing the positive self-presentation and negative other-presentation integral to the 'ideological square'.

Third, there are argumentation strategies and a fund of *topoi* through which positive and negative attributions are justified. Reisigl and Wodak (2001) define *topoi* as content-related warrants or 'conclusion rules' which connect the argument or arguments with the conclusion or standpoint. Less formally, *topoi* can be described as reservoirs of generalized key ideas from which specific statements or arguments can be generated (Ivie, 1980, cited in Richardson, 2004: 230). Frequently, these are used to justify the exclusion of migrants through quasi-rational arguments ('they are a burden for the society', 'they are dangerous, a threat', 'they cost too much', 'their culture is too different', and so forth). In this way, migrants are constructed as scapegoats; they are blamed for unemployment, for crime, for abusing social welfare systems, or they are more generally perceived as a threat to 'our' culture (Richardson and Wodak, 2009). Arguments, about Them and Us, can also be advanced through using less direct, or pseudo-argumentative (Kleiner, 1998), strategies such as *disclaimers*. These disclaimers are semantic manoeuvres that combine an overall strategy of positive self-presentation and negative other-presentation, and include moves such as:

- Apparent denial: 'I have nothing against immigrants, but … '
- Apparent concession: 'Of course *some* Muslims are tolerant, but generally …'
- Apparent empathy: 'Of course asylum seekers endure hardships, but …'
- Apparent ignorance: 'Now, I don't know all the facts, but …'
- Reversal: '*we* are the real victims in all this … '
- Transfer: 'of course *I* have nothing against them, but my customers … ' (adapted from van Dijk et al., 1997)

These manoeuvres are labelled 'apparent' disclaimers because the structure of their discourse is such that the ostensible function of an utterance – conceding a point, emoting empathy, and so on – 'is immediately flouted by the following clauses' (van Dijk et al., 1997: 170). Reflecting 'common-place' values of the wider community (Billig, 1991), such disclaimers are used by participants 'in an effort to forestall negative inferences by others, and to project an image of rationality, objectivity and fairness' (Kleiner, 1998: 206).

The 'transfer disclaimer' leads us onto the fourth discursive strategy involved in positive self-presentation and negative other-presentation: Reisigl and Wodak (2001) suggest analysis can benefit from focusing on perspectivization. By this they mean the ways that speakers will express – or conceal – their involvement in discourse, and so position their point of view in the description, narration or quotation of relevant events or utterances (cf. Richardson and Wodak, 2009). Fifth, and finally, analysis should examine strategies of intensification and mitigation. In spoken discourse these can be enacted through emphasizing particular words, as well as the pitch (and change of pitch), volume (and change of volume) and speed of delivery. Aside from these forms of expression, intensification may be signalled by repetitions as well as by gestures and facial expressions (Reisigl and Wodak, 2001: 83). Textually, involvement may be 'expressed by intensity markers such as emphasising particles ("really", "very", "absolutely", "only")' (ibid.) or, on the other hand, by mitigating and attenuating particles ('doubtfully', 'questionably', 'trivial', 'insufficient'). These strategies can be an important aspect of the discourse inasmuch as they either sharpen or tone down its ideational content and, in so doing, help construct a particular (perhaps 'non-racist') identity for the speaker or writer.

If we now take a look at some examples, the utility of these tools of analysis may become clearer.

RACISM IN EVERYDAY TALK

Analysing naturally occurring talk is a hard thing to do, given the difficulties inherent in recording such data. This is especially true of talk on and about race, racism and minority communities, because some people find talking about race, etc. particularly tough. This, and the social taboos against the free expression of racist sentiments, mean that talk on such topics is 'often regarded as somewhat elusive in terms of their "capturability" for research and analysis' (Stokoe and Edwards, 2007: 341). Indeed, the increasing 'social taboos during the past 50 years against openly expressing racist sentiments have led to the development of discursive strategies that present negative views of out-groups as reasonable and justified while at the same time protecting the speaker from charges of racism and prejudice' (Augoustinos and Every, 2007: 124). Nevertheless, the prejudiced views of out-groups *are* still present in everyday talk, through the discursive repertoires we referred to in the previous section, as well as through stories, jokes and arguments; social convention now requires that these prejudices are re-cast as reasonable. Van Dijk (1987: 58–9) shows that, thematically, prejudiced 'talk about ethnic groups […] focuses on a few central notions, such as difference, deviance and threat'. In particular, the 'origins' of ethnic minorities stand as a 'major category of the structure of ethnic prejudice' (van Dijk 1987: 52). With first-generation migrants, this topic manifests itself in quasi-rational arguments such as 'they have outstayed their welcome', 'immigration policies should be stricter' and, in extreme formulations, that 'they should be sent back'. In relation to second- and third-generation racialized groups, the topic is expressed in the question 'Where [that is: *what country*] are you from?' – a question that similarly presupposes 'they are immigrants' (Jiwani, 2006). Faced with the 'capturability problem' of such discourse, researchers have tended to adopt one of two strategies to examine 'race talk' – conducting interviews or gathering 'naturalistic data'.

Interview studies have focused on the variety of features of talk in interaction, including ways that speakers 'may take joint responsibility for policing conversation and for correcting and suppressing the articulation of prejudiced talk' (Condor et al., 2006: 441). These draw on stereotypical accounts of people, and employ a range of discursive strategies to deflect potential charges of prejudice (Billig et al., 1988; van Dijk, 1987; see also several chapters in van den Berg et al., 2003a). However, some academics argue that such data are a poor substitute 'for the observation of actual behaviour' (Heritage and Atkinson, 1984: 2). As Stokoe and Edwards (2007: 342) put it, interview studies teach us 'little about how talk about ethnicity or racism *occurs* in everyday life because interactions are inevitably guided by the researcher's topics and agenda, and by the nature and context of interviewing itself, as a form of social interaction'. We would agree with such an argument, up to a point. However, we would also suggest that interviews on or referring to 'race' retain an interest as a 'research topic in their own right because they constitute a specific category of institutional talk' (van den Berg et al., 2003b: 4). To explore the kinds of questions that Stoke and Edwards raise, naturalistic data are required – recorded either without the participants fearing censure or without their being aware that they are being recorded.

Given that racist prejudice is widely associated with irrationality and poor reasoning (Billig, 1991), in order to appear *non*-prejudiced 'it is important to present one's views as reasonable, rational and thoughtfully arrived at. […] To justify their views, speakers often appeal to observable and thus purported "factual" claims about minority out-group behaviour that is represented as negative, anti-social or transgressing the dominant group's social norms'

(Augoustinos and Every, 2007: 127). Stories about undesirable out-group behaviour present one way in which speakers can ground their own (prejudicial) views in an external world. In other words, they can position their negative opinion of racialized others as an inevitable outcome of social contact with 'them' and, in a classic argumentative reversal, that 'they' only have themselves to blame for the racism they experience. The following extract was recorded without the participants' knowledge during an election rally of the Austrian far-right political party the Freiheitliche Partei Österreich (FPÖ), held on 11 November 1991 (Wodak et al., 1990; Wodak, 1997). The FPÖ's party policy and politics are conspicuously anti-foreigner, anti-European Union and widely populist (Wodak and Pelinka 2002), and so their rallies attract people sympathetic to such views. Here, three participants (Y and E are male, F is female) share a story about 'The Jews'; any inaudible material is indicated by (…):

Y: Yeah, he inherited from his Uncle, from a Jew, yeah, well, and where did the Jew come by it?
F: They work just like we do
[…]
Y: I've seen the Jews first-hand, I've seen it first-hand, it was like this
Y: but they used us again and again, and I'll tell you something, I grew up in the country. This Jew came, we didn't have anything to eat, nothing to wear, my parents had to go into debt to buy clothes for me and food. Jew came at harvest time and took everything, in summer, and this then we we once again didn't have anything left to eat, that's the way it was, the way the Jew is, my dear lady, well, I ask you now
F: well, I worked for Jews as a young
Y: I lived through it myself. I lived through it myself, didn't I? Boy
F: girl (…)
Y: did they have it good. What I heard about what happened to
F: (…)
Y: the Jews, I have a lot of friends, and they told me that they used them
F: (…)
Y: again and again too, used them again and again. Good, there was a good one, look, there are good and bad everywhere, but I can, but, but
F: exactly. Most Jews, they are really honest (…)
Y: but but there were in fact many bad ones and this Jew he he let them that, didn't he? He didn't didn't till it himself there and that (…) he skimmed it off from somewhere, didn't he? Well, then, you the Jews.
F: they work hard
Y: the Jew is a businessman, he doesn't work himself, he lets others work for him.
F: well, all right, he just
E: The Jew has it here, my dear lady [pointing to his head]

This exchange took place as part of a longer exchange in which the problems of, and caused by, foreigners – principally Turks, labelled with the pejorative *Tschuschen* – were discussed. The story functions to implicitly cast (Austrian) Jews as foreign, as Other, given that it is provided as another example of Austrians' bad experiences with foreigners in general. At the very start of this extract, the male speaker Y uses the generalizing predication 'the Jew' – '*der Jude*' in the original. This predicate, used in the singular, is an eternalizing strategy typical of antisemitic discourse. Here, using a 'part for whole' argumentative synecdoche, the strategy serves to generalize and essentialize 'in a levelling manner to a whole group of persons' (Reisigl and Wodak, 2001: 57).

Following this essentialization, the second function of the story is to characterize these Jews as bad. Of course, an archetypal antisemitic characterization of 'The Jew' is the money-man – a tricky, fraudulent, prototypical, capitalist exploiter (Reisigl and Wodak, 2001: 56). Drawing on this enduring antisemitic stereotype, speaker Y presents his apocryphal story of 'The Jew' as an economic parasite, getting others to work instead of himself and taking the property of destitute (Gentile) farmers. In this sense, the story is based on a reversal: an inversion of victim and perpetrator given the mass appropriation of Austrian Jews' property and belongings following the *Anschluss* of Austria and Nazi Germany in 1938. Wodak (1997) comments that this story 'is very similar in structure and content to many other stories we found in 1986 and 1987', during the 'Waldheim Affair', when details of Kurt Waldheim's Nazi war record were revealed during his campaign for the Austrian Presidency (for details see Wodak et al., 1990; Reisigl and Wodak, 2001). This generalization arises from the single empirical example recounted in the story, reflecting and perpetuating the antisemitic stereotype of 'The Jew' as exploiter. And, although Y acknowledges that 'there are good and bad everywhere', this is only an apparent concession, since he then follows this with an immediate restatement of what '*der Jude*', in fact, is. The story finally ends with a further generalization, from man E, when he points to his head and says 'The Jew has it here'. We can assume that he was suggesting 'The Jew' is intelligent, perhaps cleverer than Gentiles. The local semantics, specifically the way this follows Y's story, are such that this further generalization is put to work augmenting the central prejudiced claims of the story – 'namely, because Jews are intelligent, they do not have to work themselves' (Wodak, 1997: 85).

The remarks of the female participant are intended to counteract the stereotypical generalization of the man Y; however, she also positions 'The Jews' as part of 'them': they are talked about in the third person and positioned as an out-group. This discursive construction is not benign or without potential material consequences. The histories of racist politics across Europe, and particularly in Central Europe, show us that once Jews have been seen as 'them', 'then the dynamics of ethnic politics often meant that the "rational", even "modern" answer was to target the Jewish "out group" as the source of compensation for the "compact majority"' (Beller, 2007: 70).

While this interpersonal interaction is local and confined to a small number of participants who are articulating shared sentiments, the power of racist discourse is substantially amplified when it is magnified through the mass media (Hall et al., 1978).

MASS-MEDIATED RACIST DISCOURSE

Mediated communication involves the 'technologically and institutionally based mass production and distribution' of discourse (Gerbner, 1972 [1967]: 51), including textual, graphic and audio-visual media. From school textbooks and children's literature to adult-oriented news and entertainment media, the reproduction of racism through these various discourses is multiplicative and intertextual. Yet despite the difference in genres and media formats, these mediated discourses encode an ideological square that revolves around a superior construction of 'us' and an inferiorization of 'them' (Henry et al., 1995).

In his (2003) analysis of the representation of Aboriginal peoples in 77 sociology textbooks in Canada, John Steckley draws on the work of Michel Foucault to describe the strategic ways in which knowledge about others is either buried or disqualified. The most common strategy within these school texts was to adopt a discourse of erasure such that the contribution of minorities to the building of the nation, or in the case of white settler societies (like Australia and Canada), the conquest of Aboriginal peoples is evacuated altogether. Instead, minority contributions are framed as either non-existent, or are minimized, or are rendered as actions that are self-advantageous. In other words, 'they' have come to improve their lot and seek refuge from their war-torn, poverty-stricken countries. Such accounts elide the histories of conquest, colonization and neocolonization that have shaped these societies as dependent on Western economic power and largesse. Steckley argues that, 'So much of what is wrong with Canadian introductory sociology textbooks in their discussion of Aboriginal peoples involves what they don't say, the questions they don't ask, the answers they never think of, the sources they don't cite, and the voices they do not listen to or allow to speak' (2003: 14). This echoes the five points we raised earlier regarding how people are named, perceived, described and characterized, as well as the various argumentative strategies that are used to justify actions (as in native genocide) or inaction (as in ignoring their plight).

Referential strategies that seek to conceal the power of dominant groups are not just confined to textbooks, but are also utilized strategically in other media formats. For instance, television crime dramas such as the American *24* and its Canadian counterpart *The Border* have ideological purchase through their exploitation of fears generated by news and current affairs programming. Both of these popular crime dramas trade on our fear of terrorism. *The Border*, which was launched in Canada in 2008 and has since been syndicated to France, focuses on the 'longest undefended border' which separates Canada from the United States. The programme features a multiracial cast who work as a team under the leadership of a white male ex-army officer. This team manages a fictional government-run agency – Immigration and Customs Security (ICS) – that not only patrols the border but also legitimizes the increasing use of surveillance technologies. Most of the episodes in the first season focused on illegal arms and people moving across the border, their seizure, and in the case of people, their subsequent deportation or conditional acceptance as legitimate asylum-seekers (see Jiwani, 2010).

The sole black male on the team is the character of Acting Inspector Darnell Williams. An assimilated African-Canadian, Williams exemplifies the non-threatening, domesticated Other. In their analysis of five North American police dramas aired on television between 1985 and 1986, Deroche and Deroche found that 'black men are modelled for us as more bourgeois than their white counterparts, more self-directed and effectively well-managed, and more tasteful' (1991: 86). They argued that the currency of these representations rested on the need for 'comforting images' that would evacuate notions of structural racism and affirm the ethos of liberalism. As they put it, 'The straight, upstanding image of the black man resonates well with white audiences that are tired of guilt and also with a black middle class constituency that is anxious to lay claim to a socio-economic rather than a racial master-status' (1991: 87; see also hooks, 1992; Gray, 1986). Darnell Williams' representation can be construed as a sign of 'enlightened racism' (Jhally and Lewis, 1992) or modern racism (Entman, 1990) – a racism that seeks to evacuate notions of racial inequality and emphasize upward mobility through progress while normalizing middle-class values and behaviours.

One especially interesting episode (#8) of *The Border* revolved around the interrogation of a Muslim woman, Sorraya, who had synthesized Anthrax that was to be released onto Toronto's underground subway system. (Note how, once again, it is the Muslim who is the terrorist.) Within this episode, Darnell Williams was portrayed in a manner that carefully erased the historical exploitation of Canada's minorities by using a discourse of equivalence – thereby flattening out the differences:

Sorraya:	Don't you find it ironic that you, an African man, are interrogating me, a Muslim woman, while white men are watching us through a one-way mirror? [note the referential strategies]
Williams:	Actually I am a Canadian man.
Sorraya:	Your ancestors were African.
Williams:	Everybody's ancestors were something.
Sorraya:	They were dragged here in chains.
Williams:	To America. They came to Canada to be free.
Sorraya:	They were treated like shit here!
Williams:	Everybody was treated like shit. Read your Canadian history. The Natives, the Chinese; hell even the Irish. That's what history is. People treating each other like shit.
Sorraya:	In Afghanistan the past is all we have. Even in the most primitive villages. *We* know our history. Thousand years back.
Williams:	Picking at it like a sore that never gets to heal. Who can live like that? Who can sustain being that pissed off every single day? Why are you so angry? What do we do to you?

Again, one can see a discursive move here which denies history, levels all oppressions, and concludes with a portrayal of Sorraya (and by proxy, all Afghans) as being driven by their obsession, unwilling to let go of the past, and being overcome by an unresolved and unspent anger. This exchange centres on the contestation of referential strategies used as part of the participants' narratives of a colonial past/present. Sorraya first refers to Darnell as 'an African man', a despatializing and implicitly racialized referential strategy; in her next response she attempts an originalization, through using the origonym 'ancestors'. He responds with a specific spatializing referential strategy – he is 'a Canadian man'. This directly counters Sorraya's implication that he has (or should have) a supra-national affiliation, based on a racial identity that is different from – or potentially in conflict with – the racial identities of his fellow (white, Canadian) officers.

The whole exchange affords one a tangible sense of the assimilation ethic – all of us have been treated 'like shit' so why complain? The argumentative strategy of equivalence between the Natives, Chinese and Irish is revealing insofar as it levels the differences between those who were directly colonized and those who were used as agents of coloniz-ation. It also evacuates the history of Black settlement in Nova Scotia, Canada, which, as Sorraya rightly notes, demonstrates how the Blacks were treated 'like shit'. Not all of those who migrated to Canada were loyalists like Darnell Williams and nor do all Blacks in Canada identify as Canadian (Hay, 1996). Nonetheless, Darnell has the last word in the interrogation. Here, he utilizes a predicational strategy which emphasizes the anger and persistent resentment of Afghan peoples, thus reproducing the notion of 'them' as barbaric and primitive, and 'us' as progressive, liberal and democratic. Through the discursive strategies used in this exchange, the hierarchies of power and inequality are concealed. White dominance is exnominated. It remains in the background, unseeing but observing all (Fiske, 1996).

Hegemony, as Hall (1997) argues, is never stable, never completely achieved. It is always in a state of flux. The labour involved in obtaining consent is perpetual. To maintain this, *The Border* reflects a Canadian self-image that is tempered with compassion, with humanity – and this is why other episodes make a pointed attempt to 'rescue' illegal immigrants and to provide shelter for those who are wrongfully accused or deported. Interestingly, in the epi-sode described above, Sorraya reveals herself to be an American woman who has converted to Islam – in other words, one of 'us' gone native!

'Race' and racism in the news

Journalism is an activity deeply entrenched in national discourses. As Richard Kaplan eloquently notes, 'the news is a tale of the nation, which commemorates and commiser-ates in the nation's tragedies as well as its triumphs' (2003: 212). Examining the ways in which journalistic accounts of minority groups are played out in the nation's dai-lies provides us with a view as to how the news reproduces inequality and relations of domination (Henry and Tator, 2002; van Dijk, 1991). A recent analysis of a corpus of 190 stories in *The Globe and Mail* (a major Canadian daily) published over a seven-year period shows a marked erasure of the structural violence perpetrated on Canadian Aboriginal women (see Carter, 1997; Smith, 2005, for an account of historical and con-temporary violence against Aboriginal women). Instead, these stories emphasize the cul-pability of Aboriginal women who are largely portrayed as abject victims of poverty, their lives marked by alcohol and drug addictions, homelessness, high infant mortality and morbidity rates, a greater incidence of HIV, hepatitis infections and gynaecological cancers. In effect, they are represented as one of the most hopeless segments of society (Jiwani, 2009b).

In contrast, *The Globe and Mail*'s coverage of Afghan women over this same period is noticeably different. While the Afghan women are also portrayed as victims of the Taliban regime, they are not cast as complete and abject victims, culpable for their own fate. Rather, Afghan women are individualized – they are named more often than the Aboriginal women – and their acts of resistance are emphasized and celebrated (Jiwani, 2009a). The binary between 'good' and 'bad' women in this comparative analysis rests on the kind of woman who can be 'saved' and thus made useful for Western imperial interests. Aboriginal women do not fit this bill, but Afghan women do, given the lucrative tasks of reconstruction that have played out in Afghanistan.

A comparison of some of the headlines of the stories concerning Afghan and Aboriginal women in *The Globe and Mail* offers an insight into the ways in which language is used to discursively reproduce particular constructions for these women.

Table 12.1

Aboriginal Women	Afghan Women
Natives face more violence, study says (Sallot, 9 August 2001)	National News Female Afghan athletes want to live with dignity (Dareini, 30 October 2001)
Natives shed tears for 'stolen sisters'. Six young women have gone missing on remote B.C. road. (Lunman, 11 March 2003)	Waiting in the shadows for some justice in Kabul; women hope new Afghan constitution clarifies their rights, but old law's victims still languish in jail. (Ghafour, 22 December 2003)
Remains of more women found; police task force finds evidence of nine more victims discovered during B.C. pig-farm probe. (Armstrong, 28 January 2004)	Beauticians without borders teach basics to Afghan women. (Ghafour, 24 February 2004)

A cursory analysis of these headlines demonstrates how one group of women (Afghan) can be extolled for their heroism, resistance to the Taliban and assertion of women's rights. In contrast, the Aboriginal women's stories emphasize their encounters with the law, as victims and perpetrators, and their having a high-risk statistical profile. Government is shown to be benevolent, inclusive, concerned and apologetic. The referential and predicational strategies that are at work in these accounts complicate the ideological square in that those who are positively valued and represented are women 'out there' as opposed to women who are 'over here'. Such differential valuations and the argumentative strategies utilized in these accounts suggest a 'concealment of dominance' (van Dijk, 1993b), wherein the motivations underpinning such valuations lie in the material interests that are at play and in the advantages accrued by the elite from deflecting the national attention to a situation 'out there' so as to occlude the condition of women 'over here' (Khan, 2001). Yet, it is important to bear in mind that a hierarchy of power prevails which defines Aboriginal women as occupying a lower status *vis-à-vis* their white counterparts.

Veiling the issue – the 'imperilled Muslim woman'

The attacks on the World Trade Center and the Pentagon on September 11, 2001 (a.k.a. 9/11) signaled a heightened potency to the already prevailing discriminatory attitude levelled against Muslims and Arabs within the United States and elsewhere. Razack (2008) observes that within the resulting mediated landscape the Muslim terrorist, the imperilled Muslim woman, and the heroic, white male figure, have come to dominate the cast of characters. Much has been written, from a critical discourse analytical framework and a discourse-historical approach, about the events of and following these attacks (e.g., Graham, Keenan and Dowd, 2004; Stenvall, 2003). In the section below, we focus on the *hijab*.

From the French Republic's refusal to allow Muslim women to wear the *hijab*, to similar legislation passed in other European countries, this has become a much disparaged and reviled piece of clothing. The subject itself has generated a vast and extensive literature (e.g. Alvi, Hoodfar and McDonough, 2003; Klaus and Kassel, 2005; Macdonald, 2006; Scott, 2007; Sreberny, 2002; Tévanian, 2005; Vivian, 1999; Yeğenoğlu, 1998) and we would be remiss in not mentioning how this symbol has become an iconic representation of an oppressive and tradition-bound Islam. Notwithstanding its strategic uses both in accessing information about the Taliban and in legitimizing rescue operations to liberate Afghan women (Russo, 2006), the *hijab* and *burka* have become freighted with meanings which mark Muslim women as inferior and sexualized others in the West. The media's reporting and framing of the *hijab* have accomplished much of this. Witness, for instance, this interview conducted by a radio talk-show host with a Muslim woman political candidate running for local office that was subsequently reported in Canada in the *Montreal Gazette*:

> The host, Benoît Dutrizac, invited [Samira Laouni] for a frank chat Wednesday …
>
> 'It's very cute, your veil, the Islamic veil – it's very sexy,' Dutrizac began.
>
> 'It's my headscarf,' Laouni corrected him.
>
> 'No, but it's beginning to become sexy for us. Men in the West, miscreants like me, we're starting to find that sexy – be careful!'
>
> [.....]
>
> After the break, Dutrizac went on the attack again. Can a 'good Muslim woman' have sex with different men? Can she drink wine?
>
> She's free to make her own choices, Laouni replied. 'It's not up to me to judge anyone.'
>
> Did she know that under Muslim sharia law, 'if I were to rape you here today, you'd need witnesses to testify that you weren't consenting?' Dutrizac asked.
>
> (Heinrich, 2008: A15)

The very tone of this exchange implies that the radio-talk show host was intent on shocking the candidate by making extreme declarative statements about Islam. The argumentative strategy he utilized was intensified by his repeated reference to sex, rape and sexiness. Heinrich, the journalist who recounted this, clearly underlines Dutrizac's extreme behaviour by using words such as 'went on the attack again'. Nonetheless, the interview demonstrates how 'banal' racist statements have become such that they can be articulated on talk-shows without eliciting widespread censure. The interview invokes a range of discursive moves and apparent concessions and reveals the discursive violence that is being enacted. There is also a reversal strategy at work here as the women themselves are held accountable for the sexual violence that may be inflicted upon them. That this interview was reprinted in Quebec's largest English language daily demonstrates how elite dissension – in this case between the French and English dominant (or 'Charter') groups – plays itself out in a competition over who is more racist and, conversely, who is more tolerant (Jiwani, 2006), both of which require a certain degree of power (Hage, 1998).

The iconic symbolism of the veil is also apparent in political discourse in the form of party rhetoric and publicity materials, as we discuss in the section below.

'RACE', RACISM AND POLITICAL DISCOURSE

Given the discursive and material power of political discourse, it should come as no surprise that it has attracted a great deal of analysis (see Blommaert and Verschueren, 1998; Mehan, 1997; Reeves, 1983; and especially the chapters in Wodak and van Dijk, 2000). Here, too, a general pattern of positive self-presentation and negative other-presentation dominates, with political debate on and about 'ethnic affairs' 'premised on humanitarian values of tolerance, equality and hospitality', yet simultaneously advancing 'more subtle forms of elite racism when they present immigration and minority relations as essentially problematic' (van Dijk, 1997: 31). Accordingly, political elites 'use a variety of discursive formulations such as civil rights slogans, nationalist rhetoric and populism to represent themselves as tolerant, hospitable and rational, whereas minorities are portrayed in ways that problematise and marginalise them' (Augoustinos and Every, 2007: 129).

That said, we can still find instances of overt racism. British political discourse has frequently, and particularly since the 1950s, constructed immigration as a *problem* that politicians need to *solve*. The racist propaganda used by the Conservative Party in the Smethwick constituency of Birmingham during the six years prior to the 1964 General Election represented a watershed for the place and prominence of 'race' in electioneering. Prior to this election, the Conservative candidate Peter Griffiths wrote the following to his local newspaper:

> Apparently the plight of English children held back by the presence of non-English speaking children in a class doesn't bother the immigrant leaders. Well, it bothers the Smethwick Tories and our kids are going to get a square deal in spite of the combined opposition of the Socialists and their immigrant friends.
> (Letter to the *Smethwick Telephone*, 17 January 1964, cited in Foot, 1965: 46)

During the election itself, the same Peter Griffiths campaigned against the incumbent Labour MP Patrick Gordon-Walker, using the slogan 'If you want a nigger neighbour, vote Labour'. Although the campaign received a lot of publicity, very little of it was critical.

When the Labour MP protested, even announcing that 'gangs of children had been organised to chant' the slogan, Griffiths told *The Times* 'I would not condemn anyone who said that. I regard it as a manifestation of popular feeling' (Foot, 1965: 44). When Griffiths won, and took a seat in the House of Commons, it was, in the words of Layton-Henry (1984: 57) 'a shattering result and a disaster for race relations as it appeared to show that racial prejudices could be effectively exploited for electoral advantage'. As Dummett has argued, since then British political discourse has assumed two things: first that 'the British masses are racist'; and second, 'that in comparison with the masses all political leaders and 'Establishment' people are [...] liberal and must bend their efforts to restraining or quietening down any popular signs of racism, brushing it under the carpet where they don't succeed in cleaning it away' (1973: 244). These assumptions open up an argumentative space in which it is possible for elites 'to adopt positions defending racist measures while criticising certain people for acting in a more racist manner than them' (ibid.). Such strategies are observable in other democratic states, for example Australia (Hage, 1998), Austria (Reisigl and Wodak, 2001), Canada (Thobani, 2007), France (van der Valk, 2003), Germany (Jäger, 1992), the Netherlands (van der Valk, 2002) and the USA (Mehan, 1997).

A further dimension to political discourse on racialized others is the presence and influence of far-right political parties on mainstream debate. In certain circumstances, far-right parties can capitalize on the 'legitimacy granted to anti-immigration discourse via their popularisation by mainstream politicians and journalists' (Richardson, 2008: 322). Conversely, in certain circumstances the success of a far-right party in attracting votes and members can be undermined by mainstream parties shifting to the right and aping the language or even the policies of the far right. For example, before winning the General Election as Conservative Leader in 1979, Margaret Thatcher received particular attention – in the form of praise from the right and criticism from the left – for stating the following opinion in a TV interview:

> I am the first to admit it is not easy to get clear figures from the Home Office about immigration, but there was a committee which looked at it and said that if we went on as we are then by the end of the century there would be four million people of the new Commonwealth or Pakistan here. Now, that is an awful lot and I think it means that people are really rather afraid that this country might be rather swamped by people with a different culture and, you know, the British character has done so much for democracy, for law and done so much throughout the world that if there is any fear that it might be swamped people are going to react and be rather hostile to those coming in.[1]

Subsequently, in the early 1980s, Thatcher's authoritarian, New Right government caused a collapse in support for the National Front during a time that saw an escalation in violent attacks on British Black and Jewish communities (Troyna, 1982). Clearly there are dialectic relations between different elements in the political field, where effects can become causes and vice versa. Dummett and Dummett (1982: 100) have also discussed this, calling it an

---

[1]Margaret Thatcher (1978) TV Interview for Granada's *World in Action*, Margaret Thatcher Foundation, http://www.margaretthatcher.org/speeches/displaydocument.asp?docid=103485 (accessed 15 December 2009).

'interplay' in which 'the activities of politicians have not merely mirrored, but have been the primary cause of, the grave inflammation of racialist [*sic*] attitudes' that took place in the UK during the 1960s. With this interplay in mind, we present an example of far-right propaganda, produced by the British National Party (BNP).

To set the scene, the BNP are Britain's largest far-right political party and are currently achieving a level of electoral success that has so far been unparalleled in the history of the British far-right. In the 2010 General Election the BNP polled 563,743 votes in total, for the 338 candidates it fielded, well over double the 193,000 votes amassed in the 2005 General Election and up significantly from 2001 when it attracted only 47,000 votes. This success relates, directly, to the prominence of prejudiced ideas and arguments about racial and ethnic others in mainstream political discourse. Thus, it was 'widely noted that when the BNP were elected in Tower Hamlets in 1993 immigration had been an important issue nationally. Similarly, the issues of immigration and asylum have been a national concern in the last few years' (Rhodes, 2005: 9) and so the BNP have again gained local councillors. A racist anti-immigrant policy, based on a nativist ideology, remains openly at the heart of the party: their Constitution states they are 'committed to stemming and reversing the tide of non-white immigration and to restoring, by legal changes, negotiation and consent, the overwhelmingly white make-up of the British population that existed in Britain prior to 1948'.

The party has a highly developed propaganda network, producing a newspaper, a magazine, two regularly updated websites, a wide variety of leaflets on national and local issues and, most recently, a record label. In 2008, the BNP produced a glossy, four-page A4 leaflet as part of their electoral campaign for seats on the Greater London Authority (GLA). The front page of this leaflet has been reproduced (see Richardson and Wodak, 2009, for a detailed analysis).

Here, 'The Changing Face of London' is used both metaphorically, to refer to the ways that the character, persona or disposition of London has (apparently) changed, as well as literally, referring to the actual faces of London's inhabitants who metonymically represent the city. The first of the two images shows happy, smiling, white families – the vast majority of whom are women and children – who are out socializing on a terraced street. The Union Flags place the street in the United Kingdom. The arrow on the left – headed 'From this ... ' – directs the viewer's attention towards a woman with a broad, open smile, thus providing a welcoming entry point into the image. The women in the second image are far less friendly. It is immediately apparently that they are Muslims; wearing the *niqab* means that you can only see their eyes, which look out at the reader in an expressionless way. Their attention is again directed by use of the arrow on the left, this time pointing to a women putting up two fingers – a peculiarly British gesture which broadly means 'get lost' (or a more abusive message!).

Using these two images in opposition to each other enabled the BNP to project issues of race and religion onto this claimed loss of 'community values'. In an interesting melding together of racism and sexism, the leaflet uses these images of women to represent this loss of innocence and the threat to 'our values': in short, London has changed to the extent that

Figure 12.1

'we' can no longer look at friendly, smiling, attractive (white) women; all there are are abusive, veiled (Muslim) women. This is a relatively new direction for the BNP, and speaks to the male gaze that is endemic in their propaganda (Miller, 1999).

The choice to depict Muslim women in the *niqab*, the selection of this particular point in time (of someone making an abusive gesture), and the production decision to frame them in an enlarged close-up, thereby denying them a sense of place and context, make it difficult to construct any interpretation of the image other than one that emphasizes their Muslimness. So, from this contrast, we can construe that London has changed:

'From this [white women and children] to this [Muslim women]'

And it is this change that has brought with it the loss of a variety of positive social characteristics. However, the fact that the linguistic content of the leaflet doesn't refer to race ('white') or religion ('Muslim'), provides the BNP with a degree of 'plausible denial'. In other words, to the uncritical eye, the leaflet could be proposing a return to 'community values and social inclusiveness' – a proposition that many people would have difficulty opposing. However, in concert with the images, the racialized assumptions of the proposition cannot be overlooked: it is, in effect, an argument for the racial or religious purification of a city. From this, it is possible to reconstruct a standpoint and its arguments.

London used to be like this [white].
When it was [white] like this, London was at ease with itself, friendly, happy and secure.
The BNP wants London to be at ease with itself, friendly, happy and secure.
Being at ease, friendly, happy and secure means being [white] like this.
Therefore, the BNP will make London [white] like this again.

It is the repeated use of the vague indexical '*this*' that allows for a rhetorical cross-fertilization between visual and verbal components of the argument – and also enables the BNP a rhetorical get-out about what, exactly, 'this' can be taken to mean.

CONCLUSION

As this chapter demonstrates, racist discourses are pervasive. A critical discourse analysis reveals how language can be used to reproduce existing social inequalities, and in the process, to legitimize racism. Through various strategies of argumentation, rhetorical figures, lexical styles, story-telling, propositions, and a reliance on elites as authorized sources of knowledge, everyday talk and mediated texts communicate a valuation of the self that is positive while negatively valuing the other. By problematizing, marginalizing and inferiorizing others, such talk and texts affirm 'our' sense of ourselves as rational, civilized, and progressive, and ultimately as justified in how 'we' treat others. Yet, therein lies the danger of such talk and texts. For, as suggested in this chapter, these responses are in effect reversals.

They displace the issue onto an emotive level – that of feeling – by eliding the structural frameworks that necessitate the presence of others, as for example, the histories of colonization and imperialism that have served to displace and exploit so many. These reversals also obfuscate the class inequalities that are perpetuated by and in the interest of elites so as to consolidate power and privilege. They are, in other words, strategic moves that blame the victim and thereby conceal the power of the dominant.

FURTHER READING

There are a great many texts examining racism in/and discourse, so we have selected four books which examine the themes introduced in this chapter in greater depth.

On discourse and race/racism

Reisigl, M. and Wodak, R. (2001) *Discourse and Discrimination. Rhetorics of Racism and Antisemitism.* London: Routledge.
Using the discourse historic approach to critical discourse analysis, and analyzing a range of genres including political speeches, legal documents, newspaper articles and everyday speech, Reisigl and Wodak's book examines how racism, antisemitism and ethnic prejudice are reflected, constructed and recreated in discourse.

On interpersonal discourse

van den Berg, H., Wetherell, M. and Houtkoop-Steenstra, H. (eds) (2003a) *Analysing Race Talk: Multidisciplinary Approaches to the Interview.* Cambridge: Cambridge University Press.
An edited collection in which the contributors, all discourse analysts, analysed the same data: three interviews conducted by Margaret Wetherell, collected as part of a large scale project on racist discourse. The chapters employ a variety of different discourse analytic approaches (including conversation analysis, discursive psychology and frame analysis), and highlight a range of phenomena in the data.

On mass media discourse

Hall, S. (ed.) (1997) *Representation, Cultural Representation and Signifying Practices.* London: Sage in association with the Open University.
Hall provides a succinct introduction and opening chapter to the study of representations from a semiotic and cultural studies perspective. The book is intended for students and explains complex concepts in a clear manner.

On political discourse

Wodak, R. and van Dijk, T.A. (eds) (2000) *Racism at the Top.* Klagenfurt: Drava.
An edited collection examining discourse on race, ethnicity and 'difference' in European parliaments. The chapters from the contributors demonstrate the significant role that political elites can play in the production and reproduction of racism.

ONLINE READING

The following articles are available at www.sagepub.co.uk/discoursestudies.

Augoustinos, M. and Every, D. (2007) 'The language of "race" and prejudice: a discourse of denial, reason, and liberal-practical politics', *Journal of Language and Social Psychology*, 26(2): 123–41.

Klaus, E. and Kassel, S. (2005) 'The veil as a means of legitimization: an analysis of the interconnectedness of gender, media and war', *Journalism* 6(3): 335–55.

van der Valk, I. (2003) 'Right-wing parliamentary discourse on immigration in France', *Discourse & Society*, 14(3): 309–348.

REFERENCES

Alvi, S.S., Hoodfar, H. and McDonough, S. (eds) (2003) *The Muslim Veil in North America: Issues and Debates*. Toronto: Women's Press.

Augoustinos, M. and Every, D. (2007) 'The language of 'race' and prejudice: a discourse of denial, reason, and liberal-practical politics'. *Journal of Language and Social Psychology*, 26(2): 123–41.

Beller, S. (2007) *Antisemitism: A Very Short Introduction*. Oxford: Oxford University Press.

Billig, M. (1991) *Ideology and Opinions: Studies in Rhetorical Psychology*. London: Sage.

Billig, M., Condor, S., Edwards, D., Gane, M., Middleton, D.J. and Radley, A.R. (1988) *Ideological Dilemmas: A Social Psychology of Everyday Thinking*. London: Sage.

Blommaert, J. and Verschueren, J. (1998) *Debating Diversity: Analysing the Discourse of Tolerance*. London: Routledge.

Carter, S. (1997) *Capturing Women: The Manipulation of Cultural Imagery in Canada's Prairie West*. Montreal: McGill-Queens.

Condor, S., Figgou, L., Abell, J., Gibson, S. and Stevenson, C. (2006) '"They're not racist": prejudice mitigation and suppression in dialogue'. *British Journal of Social Psychology*, 45: 441–62.

Deroche, C. and Deroche, J. (1991) 'Black and white: racial construction in television police dramas'. *Canadian Ethnic Studies*, 23(3): 69–92.

Dummett, A. (1973) *A Portrait of English Racism*. London: Penguin.

Dummett, M. and Dummett, A. (1982) 'The role of government in Britain's racial crisis'. In C. Husband (ed.), *'Race' in Britain: Continuity and Change*, pp. 97–127. London: Hutchinson.

Entman, R.M. (1990) 'Modern racism and the image of blacks in local television news'. *Critical Studies in Mass Communication*, 7: 332–45.

Fairclough, N. (1995) *Media Discourse*. London: Arnold.

Fiske, J. (1996) *Media Matters: Race and Gender in US Politics* (revised edn). Minneapolis/London: University of Minnesota Press.

Foot, P. (1965) *Immigration and Race in British Politics*. Harmondsworth: Penguin.

Gerbner, G. (1972 [1967]) 'Mass media and human communication theory'. In D. McQuail (ed.), *Sociology of Mass Communications*, pp. 35–58. Harmondsworth: Penguin.

Graham, P., Keenan, T. and Dowd, A.M. (2004) 'A call to arms at the end of history: a discourse-historical analysis of George W. Bush's declaration of war on terror'. *Discourse & Society*, 15(2–3): 199–221.

Gray, H. (1986) 'Television and the new black man: black male images in prime-time situation comedy'. *Media, Culture & Society*, 8: 223–42.

Hage, G. (1998) *White Nation: Fantasies of White Supremacy in a Multicultural Society*. Annandale, Australia: Pluto.

Hall, S. (1990) 'The whites of their eyes, racist ideologies and the media'. In M. Alvarado and J.O. Thompson (eds), *The Media Reader*, pp. 9–23. London: British Film Institute.

Hall, S. (ed.) (1997) *Representation, Cultural Representation and Signifying Practices*. London: Sage, in association with the Open University.

Hall, S., Critcher, C., Jefferson, T. and Roberts, B. (1978) *Policing the Crisis: Mugging, the State, Law and Order*. London: Macmillan.

Hartley, J. (1982) *Understanding News*. London and New York: Methuen.

Hay, S. (1996) 'Blacks in Canada, the invisible minority'. *Canadian Dimension*, 30(6): 14–17.

Heinrich, J. (2008) 'Politics 101: the art of staying calm in the event of obnoxious questioning'. *The Montreal Gazette*, 13 September, p. A15.

Henry, F. and Tator, C. (2002) *Discourses of Domination: Racial Bias in the Canadian English-Language Press*. Toronto, London, Buffalo: University of Toronto Press.

Henry, F., Tator, C., Mattis, W. and Rees, T. (1995) *The Colour of Democracy: Racism in Canadian Society*. Toronto, ON: Harcourt Brace Canada.

Heritage, J. and Atkinson, P. (1984) *Structures of Social Action: Studies in Conversational Analysis*. Cambridge: Cambridge University Press.

hooks, b. (1992) *Black Looks: Race and Representation*. Toronto: Between the Lines.

Jäger, S. (1992) *BrandSätze: Rassismus im Alltag* (DISS-Studien). Duisburg: Duisburger Institut für Sprach- und Sozialforschung.

Jhally, S. and Lewis, J. (1992) *Enlightened Racism: The Cosby Show, Audiences, and the Myth of the American Dream*. San Francisco, CA: Westview.

Jiwani, Y. (2006) *Discourses of Denial: Mediations of Race, Gender, and Violence*. Vancouver: University of British Columbia Press.

Jiwani, Y. (2009a) 'Helpless maidens and chivalrous knights: Afghan women in the Canadian press'. *Toronto Quarterly*, *78*(2): 728–44.

Jiwani, Y. (2009b) 'Symbolic and discursive violence in Canadian media representations of Aboriginal women'. In D. Weir and M. Guggisberg (eds), *Violence in Hostile Contexts*. Oxford: Inter-Disciplinary Press. Available at http://www.inter-disciplinary.net/publishing/id-press/ebooks/understanding-violence-contexts-and-portrayals/, 2009

Jiwani, Y. (2010) 'Soft power – policing the border through Canadian TV crime drama'. In J. Klaehn (ed.), *The Political Economy of Media and Power*, pp. 275–93. New York: Peter Lang.

Kaplan, R.L. (2003) 'American journalism goes to war, 1898–2001: a manifesto on media and empire'. *Media History*, *9*(3): 209–19.

Karim, K.H. (2000) *Islamic Peril*. Montreal, Quebec: Black Rose.

Kelly, L. (1987) 'The continuum of sexual violence'. In J. Hanmer and M. Maynard (eds), *Women, Violence and Social Control*, pp. 46–60. London: Macmillan.

Khan, S. (2001) 'Between here and there: feminist solidarity and Afghan women'. *Genders*, 33. Available at http://www.genders.org/g33/g33_kahn.html

Klaus, E. and Kassel, S. (2005) 'The veil as a means of legitimization: an analysis of the interconnectedness of gender, media and war'. *Journalism*, *6*(3): 335–55.

Kleiner, B. (1998) 'The modern racist ideology and its reproduction in "pseudo-argument"'. *Discourse and Society*, *9*(2): 187–216.

Kress, G. and van Leeuwen, T. (2001) *Reading Images*. London: Routledge.

Layton-Henry, Z. (1984) *The Politics of Race in Britain*. London: Allen & Unwin.

Macdonald, M. (2006) 'Muslim women and the veil: problems of image and voice in media representations'. *Feminist Media Studies*, *6*(1): 7–23.

Machin, D. (2007) *Introduction to Multimodal Analysis*. London: Hodder Arnold.

Mehan, H. (1997) 'The discourse of the illegal immigration debate: a case study in the politics of representation'. *Discourse and Society*, *8*(2): 249–70.

Miller, L. (1999) 'Ideological themes of eugenics and gender in contemporary British fascism: a discursive analysis'. Unpublished PhD Thesis, Loughborough University.

Razack, S. (2008) *Casting Out: the Eviction of Muslims from Western Law and Politics*. Toronto: University of Toronto Press.

Reeves, F. (1983) *British Racial Discourse: A Study of British Political Discourse About Race and Race-related Matters*. Cambridge: Cambridge University Press.

Reisigl, M. and Wodak, R. (2001) *Discourse and Discrimination: Rhetorics of Racism and Antisemitism*. London: Routledge.

Rhodes, J. (2005) 'The "local" politics of the British National Party'. *SAGE Race Relations Abstracts*, *31*(4): 5–20.

Richardson, J.E. (2004) *(Mis)Representing Islam: the Racism and Rhetoric of British Broadsheet Newspapers*. Amsterdam: John Benjamins.

Richardson, J.E. (2008) '"Our England": discourses of "race" and class in party election leaflets'. *Social Semiotics*, *18*(3).

Richardson, J.E. and Wodak, R. (2009) 'The impact of visual racism: visual arguments in political leaflets of Austrian and British far-right parties'. *Controversia*, *6*(2): 45–77.

Russo, A. (2006) 'The Feminist Majority Foundation's campaign to stop gender apartheid'. *International Feminist Journal of Politics, 8*(4): 557–80.

Scott, J.W. (2007) *The Politics of the Veil*. Princeton: Princeton University Press.

Shohat, E. and Stam, R. (1994) *Unthinking Eurocentrism, Multiculturalism and the Media*. London and New York: Routledge.

Smith, A. (2005) *Conquest, Sexual Violence and American Indian Genocide*. Cambridge, MA: South End.

Sreberny, A. (2002) 'The power of the veil: Reviews Editors' Introduction'. *Feminist Media Studies, 2*(2): 267–72.

Steckley, J.L. (2003) *Aboriginal Voices and the Politics of Representation in Canadian Introductory Sociology Textbooks*. Toronto: Canadian Scholar's Press.

Stenvall, M. (2003) 'An actor or an undefined threat? The role of "terrorist" in the discourse of international news agencies'. *Journal of Language and Politics, 2*(2): 361–404.

Stokoe, E. and Edwards, D. (2007) '"Black this, black that": Racial insults and reported speech in neighbour complaints and police interrogations'. *Discourse & Society, 18*(3), 337–72.

Tévanian, P. (2005) *Le Voile Médiatique: Un Faux Débat, L'affaire du Foulard Islamique*. Paris: Raisons d'agir éditions.

Thobani, S. (2007) *Exalted Subjects: Studies in the Making of Race and Nation in Canada*. Toronto: University of Toronto Press.

Troyna, B. (1982) 'Reported racism: the "British way of life" observed'. In C. Husband (ed.), *'Race' in Britain: Continuity and Change*, pp. 275–91. London: Hutchinson.

van den Berg, H., Wetherell, M. and Houtkoop-Streenstra, H. (eds) (2003a) *Analysing Race Talk: Multidisciplinary Approaches to the Interview*. Cambridge: Cambridge University Press.

van den Berg, H., Wetherell, M. and Houtkoop-Streenstra, H. (2003b) 'Introduction'. In H. van den Berg, M. Wetherell and H. Houtkoop-Streenstra (eds), *Analysing Race Talk: Multidisciplinary Approaches to the Interview*, pp. 1–10. Cambridge: Cambridge University Press.

van der Valk, I. (2002) *Difference, Deviance, Threat? Mainstream and Right-Extremist Political Discourse on Ethnic Issues in the Netherlands and France (1990–1997)*. Amsterdam: Aksant.

van der Valk, I. (2003) 'Right-wing parliamentary discourse on immigration in France'. *Discourse & Society, 14*(3): 309–48.

van Dijk, T.A. (1987) *Communicating Racism: Ethnic Prejudice in Thought and Talk*. Newbury Park, CA: Sage.

van Dijk, T.A. (1991) *Racism and the Press*. London: Routledge.

van Dijk, T.A. (1992) 'Discourse and the denial of racism'. *Discourse and Society, 3*(1): 87–118.

van Dijk, T.A. (1993a) *Elite Discourse and Racism, Vol. 6: Race and Ethnic Relations*. Newbury Park, CA: Sage.

van Dijk, T.A. (1993b) 'Principles of critical discourse analysis'. *Discourse & Society, 4*(2): 249–83.

van Dijk, T.A. (1997) 'Political discourse and racism: describing others in Western parliaments'. In S.H. Riggins (ed.), *The Language and Politics of Exclusion: Others in Discourse*, pp. 31–64. Thousand Oaks, CA: Sage.

van Dijk, T.A. (2005) *Racism and Discourse in Spain and Latin America*. Amsterdam: John Benjamins.

van Dijk, T.A., Ting-Toomey, S., Smitherman, G. and Troutman, D. (1997) 'Discourse, ethnicity, culture and racism'. In T.A. van Dijk (ed.), *Discourse Studies: A Multidisciplinary Introduction, Vol. 2*, pp. 144–80. London: Sage.

Vivian, B. (1999) 'The Veil and the visible'. *Western Journal of Communication, 63*(2): 115–39.

West, C. (2002) 'A genealogy of modern racism'. In P. Essed and D.T. Goldberg (eds), *Race Critical Theories*, pp. 90–111. Malden & Oxford: Blackwell.

Wodak, R. (1996) *Disorders of Discourse*. London: Longman.

Wodak, R. (1997) '*Das Ausland* and anti-Semitic discourse: the discursive construction of the other'. In S.H. Riggins (ed.), *The Language and Politics of Exclusion: Others in Discourse*, pp. 65–88. Thousand Oaks, CA: Sage.

Wodak, R. and Pelinka, A. (eds) (2002) *The Haider Phenomenon*. New Brunswick: Transaction.

Wodak, R. and van Dijk, T.A. (eds) (2000) *Racism at the Top*. Klagenfurt: Drava.

Wodak, R., Nowak, P., Pelikan, J. Gruber, H., de Cillia, R. and Mitten, R. (1990) *Wir sind alle unschuldige Taeter! Diskurshistorische Studien zum nachkriegsantisemitismus*. Frankfurt/Main: Suhrkamp.

Yeğenoğlu, M. (1998) *Colonial Fantasies: Towards a Feminist Reading of Orientalism*. Cambridge and Melbourne: Cambridge University Press.

THIRTEEN

Discourse and Identity

Anna De Fina

INTRODUCTION

Human communication is about exchanging information, getting things done, expressing feelings and emotions – but it is also, crucially, about conveying to one another what kind of people we are; which geographical, ethnic, social communities we belong to; where we stand in relation to ethical and moral questions; or where our loyalties are in political terms. While we use language to convey images of ourselves we also use it to identify others, to classify and judge people, to align ourselves with them, signalling our similarities, or to distance ourselves from them, underlining our differences. In these and many other ways language and discourse are central to the construction and negotiation of identities.

The closeness of this connection has often been recognized in the past, but it is only in relatively recent times that identity has become a well-accepted and independent field of inquiry in discourse analysis as well as in many other disciplines in the social sciences. An exhaustive discussion of identity as a concept or of the many existing approaches to its study would be a monumental task. And even a more modest state of the art description would require far more space than is allowed in this volume. Thus, the following introduction to discourse and identity will necessarily be selective. My aim will be to present a recapitulation of theoretical developments in the field with a particular stress on the recent shift towards a social constructionist, interactionist paradigm. In particular, in the first part of the chapter I will describe how developments in different disciplines have shaped the field's evolution in recent years. In the second part I will discuss different kinds of identities and analyse some of the discursive processes that have been identified as central to the construction of identity within the interactionist paradigm: *indexicality*, *local occasioning*, *positioning* and *dialogism*. Taking *categorization* as a starting point I will also discuss the problem of the interplay of micro and macro identities in discourse, and advocate for an approach that stresses the interactionist perspective without losing sight of the impact of the wider social context on local interaction. In the closing section I will present some concluding remarks.

IDENTITY, SELF, INTERACTION AND DISCOURSE

Recent trends in the study of identity within discourse bring together theorizations on the self, the role of interaction in the creation of personal and social worlds, and the contribution of language to socio-cultural processes. The incorporation of these different trends speaks to the interdisciplinary nature of this recent effort at redefining the field. The result of twenty years of reflection and debate about identity and language has been the emergence of a new paradigm that can be characterized as social constructionist and oriented towards practice and interaction (see De Fina, Schiffrin and Bamberg, 2006, on this point). This shift in perspective can be attributed not only to developments within discourse studies, but also to the growing influence of trends of thought and movements that come from other disciplines: among these the most significant are reflections about the post-modern self within social theory (Bauman, 2005; Giddens, 1991), feminist theorizing about identity (Butler, 1990), social constructionism (Berger and Luckman, 1967), symbolic interactionism (Mead, 1934), and ethnomethodology (Garfinkel, 1967). I will illustrate below how each of these theoretical frameworks has contributed to recent developments in discourse analysis, but first I want to look at three areas in which shifts in perspective have taken place, thus leading to a general change in the way discourse analysts approach the study of identity.

The first area is the reflection on the nature of the self. Here there has been a shift towards anti-essentialism via a critique of the traditional view of the self as an isolated, self-contained entity. A second area involves conceptions about the role of interpersonal communication in the constitution, enactment and negotiation of identities. In that respect, the focus has shifted away from a view of identity as individual expression towards a recognition of the centrality of human interaction as the site for the production of identities. A third domain in which there has been change is the theorization of the relationships between identity and language. In particular, the recent past has seen a growing dissatisfaction with a tendency in traditional sociolinguistic studies to reduce the connection between language and identity to a one-to-one relationship between social categories and linguistic phenomena. This orientation has brought to the fore a new focus on discourse practices as opposed to isolated language items, and on variability as opposed to homogeneity. Let us turn to the analysis of each of these areas.

Identity and the self

Notwithstanding the growing interest in identity in the social sciences and the surge in the number of articles and books devoted to this field, definitions of identity are surprisingly hard to find and those that exist present a dazzling variety and diversity in terminology and foci. Identity can been seen and defined as a property of the individual or as something that emerges through social interaction; it can be regarded as residing in the mind or in concrete social behaviour; it can be anchored to the individual or to the group. Furthermore, it can be conceived of as substantially personal or as relational. Therefore, conceptualizations of identity and the methods for studying its concrete manifestations in language have been profoundly influenced by the choices made by researchers in terms of these alternative views. However, there is no doubt that, historically, identity has been persistently associated with the concept of the self. Such a connection has been particularly strong in psychology where theories of identity have been consistently linked with theories about the persona and the self. A definition by the psychologist Erik Erikson, author of important studies on the development of personality, provides an example here. Erikson states that identity 'connotes both a persistent sameness within oneself (selfsameness) and a persistent sharing of some kind of essential character with others' (1980: 109). The language of essences and conti-nuities adopted in this definition reveals the influence of a paradigm, particularly strong in modern psychological theories in the United States, within which the self is seen as a prop-erty of the individual, firmly located in the mind. In her review of psychological theories of the person, Vivien Burr (2002: 4–5) notes that the modern conception of the individual regards it as defined by a fixed set of traits constituting his/her personality, as a Cartesian being whose actions are the result of rational deliberation, as someone who strives for moral integrity and is well separated from her/his group.

This dualism between individual and social, and the tendency to essentialize and abstract the self from its social environment, have been fiercely opposed in the past by symbolic inter-actionists such as George H. Mead (1934), who believed in the social nature of the self. However, the criticism against these conceptions has become particularly widespread only in the last twenty years, giving way to a more nuanced, historically sensitive view. Observers of contemporary societies like Anthony Giddens (1991) and Zygmut Bauman (2005) have noted that post-modern life is characterized by uncertainty, fracture, and physical and social dis-placement, as well as by the experience of flow and disunity. Modern men and women have become much more aware of the lack of continuity and permanence both in their personal life and in the environment. Thus the idea that the self is essentially unitary, continuous and rational is seen as a product of history rather than as a necessary and characteristic condition.

Identity as a social construction

Feminist thinkers such as Judith Butler have also contributed to this movement towards a non-essentialist view of the self. Butler (1990), whose reflections on gender resonated among scholars of identity across various disciplines, noted that gender identity cannot be defined in terms of a core of fixed common characteristics, but is a much more flexible construct. She also emphasized that identity is not something that one 'has', but rather something that one 'does', or 'performs' and recreates through concrete exchanges, discourses and interactions between human beings. Hence what it means to be a man or a woman, or a member of any social category, is not only contextually variable and open to continuous redefinitions, but is also related to actions and behaviours as much as to feelings and thoughts (on this point see also Chapter 11 by Lazar and Kramarae in this volume). The notion of performance has become very popular in identity studies thanks to its ability to evoke the concrete and communicative aspects of the construction and communication of identity. The connection between identity and performance implies that projecting an identity is regarded as acting and speaking in certain ways in concrete social encounters or communicative situations.

Let us look at an example of how identities may be performed. The conversation reproduced below took place between two young men in their twenties. The two had been friends since they were children, but had gone separate ways after high school. They kept in regular communication by phone and e-mail. The transcript reproduces the beginning of a face-to-face encounter between them. Ed had been away from Washington DC to pursue his studies. He had been back for a brief time and met Alex, who still lived there.

(1)

Ed: Alex what's up guy? How you doin' man?
Alex: Chillin' yo chillin' man.
Ed: Long time no see guy.
Alex: It's been a minute son I should be sayin'.
Ed: What's thrashing the DC scene man?
Alex: Ahh ufff I mean everything's pretty much the same man, you know man how it is!

This verbal exchange represents a typical instance of small talk as language is used to create a rapport and to break the ice between two people who have not seen each other for a while. The linguistic details of the conversation, however, also reveal that the two men are 'doing' identity work. Through their linguistic choices Alex and Ed are performing a 'young person' identity, while at the same time projecting their own closeness to each other as people who 'speak the same language'. The language choices they make function as cues to signal these identities. Both of them employ a language variety that corresponds to the definition of slang as 'a colloquial departure from standard usage' which is at the same time 'imaginative and vivid' (Crystal, 1997: 53). Slang is made up of words, expressions and ways of pronouncing sounds and its main function is to signal group membership. In this case, the salient cues are the word 'chill' to signify 'take it easy'; the frequent interjection of the expressions 'man' or 'guy' as terms of address; and the use of metaphoric expressions such as 'What's thrashing the DC scene?' to mean 'What is going on in DC?'. Other significant linguistic cues are the deletion of the 'g' sound in -ing verb endings (as in 'doin', 'chillin' and 'sayin'), a feature that is typically associated with informal speech, and the deletion of the verb copula ('How you doing man?'), normally related to African American vernacular speech (a non-standard variety). The choice of this slang shows how identity can be performed in that the two men are not saying, but acting out, through linguistic cues, their membership of the category of young people and their closeness to each other insofar as they can speak the same kind of language and understand each other.

The focus on identity as 'doing' rather than 'being' and the de-essentialization of the self are two central pieces of social constructionism, an approach to the study of socio-cultural phenomena that has become particularly influential in discourse studies as well an in many other fields of the social sciences. The basic idea proposed within this movement is that social reality does not exist as an independent entity but is socially constructed. Social constructionist thinkers (see Hall, 2000) argue that one should look at identity as a process (identification) rather than as an attribute or a series of attributes, and that focusing on the process allows for a consideration of the concrete ways in which people will assume identities, attribute to each other the membership of various categories, or resist such attributions. In other words, they point to 'constructing identities' as a kind of social and 'discursive work' (Zimmerman and Wieder, 1970).

Interaction and discourse

We have seen that critics of a Cartesian conception of the self emphasize the social nature of identity. Among social processes, interaction is seen by many as the most important and as a privileged locus for the production of identities since it represents the main playing field for everyday life. People acquire most of their knowledge about life and society and then share it in interactions with others. Symbolic interactionists such as George H. Mead (1934) and Herbert Blumer (1969), sociologists such as Erving Goffman (1967 and 1981), and ethnomethodologists such as Harold Garfinkel (1967) emphasized that interaction is also the domain of social life where rules of conduct and moral values become apparent, as they constitute the basis for the smooth conduct of social affairs.

If interaction is ubiquitous and central to the enactment and negotiation of identity, so is language. Although it is true that people can convey their identities through many symbols, such as clothing, demeanour, or the use of certain objects, the single most important system of symbols for expressing and negotiating identities is language. The relations between language and identity have been at the centre of sociolinguistic research since the 1960s. In his classic studies of English as it was spoken in New York City, William Labov (1966 and 1972a), for example, illustrated how categories such as class, gender and age determined the way people pronounced its sounds. He showed, for instance, that the habit of dropping the 'r' sound in words like 'fourth' or 'floor' correlated with social class, so that people belonging to the lower classes were far more likely to drop their 'r's than people who belonged to upper classes. After Labov much of the effort in sociolinguistics was focused on detailing how language changed according to these variables. This body of work has greatly contributed to advancing our knowledge about language variation in society. However, as Coupland

(2008: 268) argues, within this tradition, there has also been a tendency to see correlations between language and identity choices in too simplistic terms. For this reason, more recent studies have proposed a nuanced view of the connection between linguistic behaviour and identity, arguing that using a particular language variety does not automatically imply identifying with the group who speaks that language. People will put on accents and imitate language styles for a variety of reasons which may include mocking or rejecting the identities associated with them. On the other hand, they may 'cross' (Rampton, 1995) into out-group languages and styles to express solidarity with them. So, for example, a white American youngster may adopt features of African American speech in order to convey an affiliation with his school's youth urban culture (Bucholtz, 1999), while a group of German adolescents may choose a speaking style that is typical of Turkish immigrants as a fun in-group code (Depperman, 2007). These considerations have led to a greater attention to the linguistic practices of communities and the study of discourse rather than isolated speech elements.

Let us now turn to some important distinctions between types of identities and then to some of the processes that can be used in their discursive construction and communication.

TYPES OF IDENTITIES

We have already talked about identities being plural and complex. Such complexity is also shown in the fact that the production of identities may involve different kinds of agents and processes of communication. For example, there is a difference between individual and collective identities. When we engage in conversation with a friend or talk to a psychologist in a therapy session, we will, in most cases, be negotiating our own identity as individuals (for example, presenting ourselves as depressed or care-free persons) and we will be uniquely responsible for the kinds of image we project. On the other hand, in a public meeting or an institutional encounter we may be talking as members of a group, such as a political party or a firm, and at least part of our discursive constructions will involve the identity of the community we represent. In addition, while some identities will have personal and concrete referents (John Brown), others such as those related to national or religious communities may be very abstract and not be associated with particular people (Americans). In addition to these distinctions between *individual* and *collective identities*, we must also consider the differences between personal and social identities. *Social identities* are large categories of belonging such as those pertaining to race, gender, and political affiliation (Latinos, Catholics, etc.), while *personal identities* are constructs that may include not only sets of membership categories, but also moral and physical characteristics that distinguish one person from another (a courageous person or a coward). Finally, *situational identities* may be seen as roles related to the specific context of interaction such as those of teacher/student or doctor/patient (see Zimmerman, 1998, on this point).

All of these distinctions may however become quite blurred in actual discourse since, for example, personal identities are built on the basis of social identity categories, while collective identities may be personalized (as shown in the famous declaration, '*L'État c'est moi*' ['I am the State'], attributed to Louis XIV, King of France). Also, social identities do not always correspond with well defined macro-social categories such as gender or age, since new identities are being continuously created. At the same time, some identities such as those attached to nations or religious communities may emerge throughout complex historical processes and become rather fixed and stable, while others (for example identities related to new online communities) may be more fleeting and negotiable. Nonetheless, all of these identities will be appropriated and negotiated in everyday processes of communication and usually it is through those that they will become available to people. In this chapter I will focus more on social identities and on the everyday processes of communication, but as I hope to show, different kinds of identities and micro and macro processes are intricately interconnected.

IDENTITY PROCESSES

Indexicality

Identities are communicated in different ways. They may be openly discussed and focused upon, or indirectly and symbolically conveyed. When a person claims to be a 'good mother', or 'an American', or a 'fan of Manchester United', that person is openly embracing an identity. People in a political panel may self-describe as 'true conservatives' or 'pacifists' and lay out and negotiate the criteria for membership of those categories. However, as we saw in Example (1), a great deal of identity work is done indirectly through meaning associations. Sounds, words, expressions of a language and styles are continuously associated with qualities, ideas, situations, social representations, and entire ideological systems (on this point, see van Dijk Chapter 18 this volume). These, in turn, are related to social groups and categories that can be seen as sharing or representing them in a process of meaning creation that rests on accepted social meanings while continuously modifying them. This process has been called *indexicality*, based on the idea that symbols (and not only linguistic ones) will 'index' (Silverstein, 1976) or point to elements of the social context. For example, the use of an expression such as 'mate' by one person to address another may index the existence of a close relationship between them. However, words, accents and expressions may also become associated with aspects of the larger context as when they evoke specific traits, ideas, activities and properties that may be seen as typical of certain social identities. Because these associations are continuously repeated and circulated, they become part of socially shared representations about groups and categories, but they are also open to constant contestation and revisiting thanks to the processes of meaning creation.

Indexicality is at work when, for example, associations are created between a type of accent or the use of specific words and expressions and a certain kind of persona. For example, in Italy the uvular pronunciation of the *r* sound is associated with a snobbish and stiff persona. These stereotypical associations are exploited in political discourse as politicians will often manipulate their language in order to project specific identities. A recent case in point has been the use of language by the Republican vice-presidential candidate in the 2008 US presidential election, Sarah Palin, at the time, governor of Alaska. Essential to her introduction to the political scene was her depiction as an outsider to Washington politics, a 'regular hockey mom', and an unpretentious, down-to-earth woman who was just like any average American. Central to the creation of this persona was her language, characterized by a careful choice of words and aimed at creating a 'folksy rhetoric' (Goyette, 2008) that could promote this populist image. The connection between language and identity is openly discussed in the following political commentary, published in *The Washington Post* after the first vice-presidential debate between Sarah Palin and the Democrat Joe Biden, a debate in which the Republican nominee tried to emphasize her populist persona through language and gestures.

(2)

Well, *darnit all*, if that *dadgum girl* (wink wink) didn't beat the tarnation out of Joe Biden. Maverick Sarah Palin *fersure* surpassed expectations and said everything under the sun, also. Palin is a populist pro. She hit all the notes that resonate with non-elite Americans: family (*Hi, Mom and Dad*), *'Can I call ya Joe?'* personal responsibility, Wall Street greed, children with special need. Her most effective technique was speaking directly to the American people and letting Joe know that's what she *was gonna do, doggonit.* (Parker, 2008: author emphasis)

As we can see, the reporter presents Sarah Palin as a populist and as someone who wants to appeal to 'non-elite Americans', focusing on how her language indexes the characteristics and qualities associated with those groups: family values, personal responsibility, and antagonism toward the rich and powerful. The association with a non-elite American social identity is seen as being communicated basically through the use of informal expressions such as 'darnit all' or 'doggonit', and the choice of informal language, such as calling the opponent by his first name ('Can I call ya Joe?'), that index simplicity and 'down to earthedness'. The reporter also imitates in writing the accent used by Palin to pronounce certain words ('fersure' instead of 'for sure' and 'ya' instead of 'you') to convey the idea that such pronunciation would index her identification with simple everyday Americans. This example shows the importance of indexicality as a process for the construction and communication of identities and for the network of shared assumptions and knowledge on which this process is based. In fact, Sarah Palin's language could not have communicated such a 'folksy' persona if the words and expressions that she used had not been conventionally associated with popular language.

Local occasioning

Researchers who look upon identity as a communicative process that takes place within concrete social contexts and practices underscore the importance of paying close attention to the details of local talk in order to understand how identities are brought about and negotiated. Antaki and Widdicombe borrow from conversation analysis the principle of *local occasioning* as a way to attend to these local understandings. They argue that 'for a person to "have an identity" is to be cast into a category with associated characteristics or features' (1998: 3) and that such casting is indexical and locally occasioned. The concept of local occasioning captures the idea that the way people present their identity or ascribe identities to others not only crucially depends on the context in which the discourse is taking place but also shapes that context, making identities relevant and consequential for subsequent talk. That the communicative context makes specific kinds of identities relevant is rather uncontroversial. Social roles and the identities associated with them may be pertinent to certain social occasions and practices but not to others. Thus, in introducing myself at a meeting at my university I will most likely choose to describe myself as a member of the Italian department, while in doing the same at a parents' reunion at my children's school I will find it adequate to say that I am 'Silvio's mother'.

But the notion of local occasioning goes beyond the recognition of a mutual relationship between identities, contexts and practices, and taps into the dynamic nature of identity claims by pointing to the fact that, while identities and roles are context dependent, the very meaning of categories is indexical as well and may vary depending on circumstances and participants. Therefore, the same social identity category may be used to identify someone, but this category will have different meanings according to different aspects of the context.

Indexicality and local occasioning are processes that can help us understand how identities are enacted and communicated through linguistic behaviour in contextualized ways and how people go about understanding and negotiating them.

Relational processes: positioning and dialogism

We have talked about identity being a socially grounded process that involves a continuous confrontation of the self with others. This social nature of the definition of who we and others are is reflected in a view of identity as a fundamentally relational and dialogical process. Individuals and collectivities express and negotiate their identities by occupying social and verbal spaces that are charted in oppositions or complementarities with others. Who we are is often defined in terms of who we are not, or who we are similar to. These oppositions and compatibilities often characterize identity construction even in monological talk. For example, research on political discourse converges in indicating the construction of 'us' versus 'them' as one of the central mechanisms for the expression of political identities (see, among others, Wilson, 1990; De Fina; 1995; Van Dijk, 2010). This same opposition is recreated in the discourse construction of identity in a great many different contexts since differentiation is a fundamental process of self-affirmation.

This dynamism and relationality in identity work is well captured in the concept of *positioning*. Positioning has been used by some social theorists to describe the process through which discourse constrains identities (Fairclough, 1992). However, the construct has been recently reframed in more dynamic terms by Davies and Harré, who defined it as 'the discursive production of a diversity of selves' (1990: 47), proposing it as an antidote to the static notion of role. The definition stresses the fact that identities are plural since they relate to the kinds of social situations and discursive practices in which people are involved, but also that they are relational since people continuously position themselves, are positioned by others, and position others.

The concept of positioning has found an application mainly in narrative studies of identity (see, among others, Bamberg, 1997; Bamberg and Georgakopoulou, 2008; Moita Lopes, 2006) as it has been used to analyse how tellers juggle between their identities as narrators, as characters in story-worlds, and as persons in actual communications with others. However, its significance is not limited to the narrative mode since any kind of discourse involves a dynamic placing of the self and others into social or moral positions. Positioning processes are evident in debates and conflict talk but are also at work in more mundane, everyday and non-confrontational activities. Let us look at an example taken from data I collected while conducting ethnographic research on identity constructions among members of an Italian American card-playing club in the Washington area (see De Fina, 2007a and b). The fragment discussed below starts at the point when two friends meet and greet each other in my presence:

(3)

1. *J:*   Louis!
2. *L:*   I was late tonight.
3. *J:*   How are you doing?
4. *L:*   Good how are you?
5. *J:*   You gained some weight.
6. *L:*   ((talking to the researcher)) Now see he looks good, he looks like
7.   the skiing one who just got off the slope.
8. *J:*   I don't, I don't do that.
9. *L:*   You don't do that any more?
10. *J:*   In my time we didn't go to the ski slope.
11. *L:*   @@@
12. *J:*   You know ((…)) my own time.
13. *L:*   That's right.
14. *J:*   We didn't go, we had no automobile.

At the beginning of the transcript Joe and Louis greet each other in a friendly manner. Then Joe points to the fact that Louis has gained some weight (line 5) and Louis responds by stating that in contrast to him Joe looks good and calls him 'the skiing one' (line 7), a freshly coined identity category. Joe is implying that Louis goes skiing in order to keep his figure and therefore positions him as privileged since skiing is an expensive sport and an activity often connected with the wealthy. We can see that Joe immediately reacts by saying 'I don't do that' (line 8), i.e. trying to reposition himself by rejecting his inclusion in the category of skiers. Louis' response is to position him again into the same category by asking him if he does not do that 'any more' (line 9), and thus implying that he used to before. We can see that Joe again denies that he had a habit of skiing in the past (line 10) and then emphasizes that his family did not have an automobile (14). With this last line Joe repositions himself as not wealthy (and not snobbish).

The example shows how identities can be ascribed, rejected and assumed by people in a constant negotiation with one another. However, not all identities can be easily negotiated, as social agents are involved in power relations that may allow some to have a voice while denying this basic right to others. Thus, often people and groups will be positioned into roles that they cannot easily refute. This is the case for example with media stories in which depictions of individuals take on a life of their own and the persons affected will then have a difficult time changing them. Such processes are particularly hard on the weakest members of society (see Briggs, 2007). Therefore positioning has to be interpreted as a construct that can capture both the flexibility and the inflexibility of identity ascriptions.

Identity's relationality is clear in its dialogic nature as well. Not only do language users express their identities within linguistic activities that involve a concrete or virtual interaction with others, but also discourses can be seen as polyphonic and including a multi-layering of voices representing different identities. The sociologist Ervin Goffman captured this multi-vocality in his concept of 'footing', or 'the alignment we take up to ourselves and the others present as expressed in the way we manage the production or reception of an utterance' (1981: 128). He proposed to de-construct the notion of speaker into:

- *the animator*: the person who physically produces an utterance;
- *the author*: the person responsible for putting together the utterance, the originator of the utterance;
- *the principal*: the person 'whose position is established by the words that are spoken' (1981: 144), i.e. the person responsible for and committed to the content of the utterance.

These notions of animator, author and principal are useful for understanding how speakers can produce different identities in their discourse by assuming different degrees of authorship and responsibility for what they are saying. Even though the speaker is normally both the author and animator of the words uttered, the circumstances or intent may make those differentiations manifest. For instance, it is tacitly accepted that a spokesperson will normally only take the role of animator and sometimes of the author of a speech, and therefore will separate their identity from that of the person or groups whose positions they represent. But speakers may exploit those distinctions in a variety of ways. Thus they may erase their identity and become the principal of a group (see De Fina, 1995). On the other hand, they may choose to mock someone else's voice as a way to deflect authorship and responsibility from the content of an utterance.

Sociolinguists (see Eckert and Rickford, 2001; and chapters in Auer, 2007) have underscored that *style* and *stylization* play a fundamental role in identity processes insofar as they provide strategies for the presentation of different selves and voices in discourse. As we saw when we analysed the case of Sarah Palin's linguistic choices, styles are created through consistent associations between ways of speaking, social categories and contexts. By exploiting such associations, people may present different voices and therefore different identities in discourse. While style may be used as an affiliative or disaffiliative strategy, stylization more often communicates the otherness of someone's voice. Coupland notes that

> Single utterances can be stylized when speakers are being studiedly 'artificial' or 'putting on a voice.' Stylized utterances have a performed character and index a speaker's identity switch of some kind, in the sense that he/she makes clear to other interactants that the identity taken up is not the one that would be expected of him/her in that context. (2001: 346)

Again, in Example (2) the stylized utterances communicate the author's distancing from the character he is depicting. Positioning, footing, style and stylization are all important mechanisms for conveying a speaker's constructions of who they and others are. They demonstrate the centrality of dialogism and relationality in identity processes.

Categorization

Let us now turn to the discussion of another discursive process which is central to identity construction and communication: *categorization*. Identity categories used in discourse reflect not only the inventory of identities available in the situation at hand, but also the kinds of identities more generally in use in a given society and historic moment. In the USA for example, ethnic categorization into whites, blacks, Hispanics, Asians, etc. is a formidable mechanism for identifying people, and constructions of these categories are continuously found in discourse. The study of categorization allows researchers to tap into the broad labels used for identification, the criteria used for membership of those categories, and the attributes, the actions and situations that are typically associated with them. It is for this reason that this area of investigation has become one of the most significant fields for identity studies. But another reason for discussing it here is that, as I have argued elsewhere (De Fina, 2006), categorization processes are central to understanding how the local identities expressed in interaction are both reflective and constitutive of wide social processes, including representations, beliefs and ideologies, and social relations between individuals and groups.

The relation between local and global identities in discourse is at the centre of a debate about different ways of conceiving and analysing identity that divides researchers into different camps. One question that is debated revolves around the acceptance or rejection of a cognitive component to social categories and categorization processes. Critical discourse analysts such as van Dijk (1998; 2010) argue for a view of social identities not only as social but also as cognitive structures that are rather fixed and stable and which to some extent presuppose and precede their enactment in social interaction. Such structures are mental models that include social identities, social knowledge, ideologies, norms and values. Within this view, when people make claims about identities, they instantiate and continuously modify their mental representations. At the opposite end of the spectrum there are the conversation analysts, particularly proponents of the Membership Categorization Analysis (henceforth MCA) movement (see for example Hester and Eglin, 1997; Antaki and Widdicombe, 1998). The latter have worked around ideas on categorization first developed by Sacks (1972 and 1995) to explain the underlying assumptions according to which inter-actants will create and use 'membership categories' and routinely link certain activities to them. Proponents of MCA have been vocal opponents of 'cognitivist' explanations of how categorization works (Edwards, 1998: 18) and have invited analysts to stick to a discussion of the local context and the local orientations of participants in their analysis of how identities are discursively constructed.

In my view, categorization cannot be seen solely as an emergent discursive process, first of all because it rests on knowledge, beliefs, ideologies, presuppositions, roles, etc. that interactants share. To argue that all this knowledge and all the processes that surround and contextualize people's identity claims can be captured exclusively through a close analysis of interactional moves is to ignore the immense complexity of the social and historical contextualization of discourse. In addition, there is no doubt that social identity categories are related to situations, roles, characteristics, and ideologies that are often stereotypical, and that these associations become part of the shared knowledge and representations of groups which in turn feed into wider ideologies and beliefs. In that sense, it is difficult to argue that identities are just created in talk and have no independent life outside of it. However, the problem that discourse analysts face is how to find a balance between a view of identities as simple reflections of pre-existing social and mental categories and a vision of identities as creative and locally contextualized productions. The focus on emergence and interaction in the discourse study of identities tries to address the importance of a close analysis of linguistic behaviour and of social practices, as opposed to a top-down process in which analysts 'find' a confirmation of their hypotheses in this analysis. Thus many interactionists, i.e. researchers who focus on interaction as an important site to study socio-linguistic phenomena, are addressing the importance of finding out which categories people use for identification, in which contexts, how these are negotiated, and what they mean to people, more than they are rejecting a cognitive basis whose exact nature is in any case far from clear.

Let us now look at an example of how categorization may be used to index and discuss identities in narrative. Narratives are seen by many (e.g. Schiffrin, 1996; De Fina, 2003; Georgakopoulou, 2007) as an important locus for the articulation of identities because they afford tellers an occasion to present themselves as actors in social worlds while at the same time negotiating their present self with other interactants. In this case the narrative told by Alberto, a Mexican immigrant to the United States, during a sociolinguistic interview allows him to present both an interpretation of a troubling experience that he had at work, and, implicitly, his views about racial identity. The function of utterances in the narrative is categorized following Labov (1972b), who distinguishes between *orientation*, *complicating action* and *evaluation* clauses. Through orientation the narrator provides details about the time, place and characters within the events. The complicating action represents the main events in the narrative, while evaluation conveys the point of view of the narrator externally (through open comments) or internally (via a character's voice).

This narrative was collected as part of a study of immigrant discourse and identity (see De Fina, 2003). It was told after Alberto had been asked whether he had seen any differences between the USA and Mexico. He had answered that the difference with his village was that one could go undisturbed by night there while in the USA things were dangerous. At the point where the transcript begins, he had been prompted to explain if he had any dangerous experiences (line 01). Participants in the interview included Alberto (A, a pseudonym for his real name), the researcher (R), and another Mexican immigrant, Ismael (I).

(4)

```
01   R:   A usted le ha pasado algo aquí?
02   A:   Nada más una vez (.)
03        nos asaltaron trabajando en un apartamento,
04   R:   Uhu.
05   A:   Remodelando un apartamento, entraron y nos asaltaron ahí mismo,
06        a mí y a un patrón,
07        mhm,
08        y con pistola y se imagina qué hacíamos,
09        a mí me quitaron veinte dólares que traía nada más,
10        a mi patrón su reloj y su dinero,
11        y toda la herramienta se la llevaron,
12        y y fueron morenos verdad? morenos,
13        y todavía cuando fuimos a poner la demanda,
14        nos dice el policía, 'Y cuántos hispanos eran?'
15   R:   @@[@@@@
16   I:      [@@@
17   A:   A ver.
18   R:   Directamente.
19   A:   Uhu.
20        y, y, y se enojó porque, el policía era moreno,
21        le digo 'No, eran puros morenos,
22        puros negros,'
23        verdad? (.)
24        ahora por ejemplo aquí ya no se puede salir ya ni en paz-,
25        ya no se vive en paz aquí,
26        por tanta droga que hay,
27        tanta, tanta drogadicción, tanta cosa.
```

Translation

```
01   R:   Did anything happen to you here?
02   A:   Only once (.)
03        they attacked us while working in an apartment,
04   R:   Uhu.
05   A:   While remodelling an apartment they came in and attacked us there,
06        me and an employer,
07        uh,
```

```
08        and with a pistol and can you imagine what could we do,
09        they took from me twenty dollars that I had nothing else,
10        from my employer his watch and his money,
11        and all the tools they took,
12        and and they were dark skinned you see? Dark skinned,
13        and on top of it when we went to notify the police,
14        the policeman says to us, 'How many Hispanics were they?'
15   R:   @@[@@@@
16   I:      [@@@
17   A:   Let's see.
18   R:   Directly.
19   A:   Uhu.
20        and, and, and the policeman got mad because he was dark skinned,
21        I tell him, 'No they were all dark skinned,
22        only blacks.'
23        right? (.)
24        now for example here one cannot go out in peace any more-
25        one does not live in peace any more,
26        because of so much drug that there is
27        so much drug addiction, so many things.
```

In response to the question contained in line 01 Alberto describes an attack to which he was exposed at work. At the time, he was working for a constructor and remodelling an apartment. Notice that Alberto does not describe the assailants at the beginning of the story. He refers to them as 'they' (lines 03 and 09) without qualifications. His first evaluation (line 08) underscores his and his employer's sense of impotence when facing the robbers since the latter were armed. He then goes on to describe the things that were taken from him (twenty dollars) and his employer (his watch and some money plus all the tools). Up to line 11 there is not much evaluation of the events and the robbers have not been identified. But in line 12, almost as if adding a detail, Antonio provides a further orientation and specifies that the robbers were 'dark skinned'. Such a category was used by the Mexicans interviewed in the study as a more 'politically correct' label for 'black'. It is interesting to notice that this orientation has an evaluative function, signalled by the repetition of the qualifier at the end of the line. Alberto starts building on the relevance of this description of his assailants in racial terms when he recounts that the police officer when notified of the assault asked 'how many Hispanics' there were (line 14).

Although nothing explicit is said here about relations between the ethnic groups, Alberto is implicitly conveying the idea that policemen are prejudiced against Hispanics. That this implication is understood is clear from the reaction of the researcher, who first laughs and then comments, 'Directly' (line 18), thus indexing her surprise at the fact that the policeman had so openly voiced his prejudice against Hispanics. Also the preceding laughter by the researcher and Ismael (lines 15–16) shows an awareness of such an interpretation and an alignment with Alberto's implicit rejection of it. At this point Alberto has signalled, and his interlocutors have accepted, the relevance of the identification of the assailants as black.

He has also signalled the relevance of the opposition black/Hispanic through both an external evaluation (his comment that his assailants are black) and an internal evaluation, since the characters themselves voice their own understanding of how being black or Hispanic can affect the interpretation of events. In particular, the policeman is presented as presupposing that the actions have been carried out by Hispanics (line 20), while Alberto is presented as contesting that interpretation (lines 21–22). The relationship between being black or Hispanic and the action in the story world is also emphasized by the fact that the policeman's anger is explained by his being black (notice the use of the connective *because* in line 20: 'the policeman got mad *because* he was dark skinned'). Through this management of evaluation, Alberto portrays the policeman as prejudiced.

Other storytelling strategies allow Alberto to convey his stance not only towards the particular events and characters, but also towards interracial relationships more in general. The narrator stresses the ethnicity of the assailants through repetitions at different points (lines 12, 21, 22), thereby emphasizing the opposition between the facts and the policeman's interpretation. However, the repetition also has the effect of emphasizing the importance of ethnicity as a construct to interpret some of the further implications of the story. In fact, in the evaluation lines after the end of the story (24–27) Alberto speaks of the difficulty of living in peace in his neighbourhood. Thus the story is recast as an illustration of the kinds of things that have happened in the neighbourhood based on the experience of the narrator as the victim of a robbery. Since, in this case, the narrator underlines the ethnicity of the robbers, the discourse function of the story changes: it is not just a robbery, but a robbery carried out by blacks. This information creates a relevance space not only with respect to the action in the story world, but also with respect to a more general evaluation of the story: since it deals with black people acting in a criminal way, drug consumption and violence in the neighbourhood can also be more easily attributed to them.

We can see how in this narrative Alberto uses categorization to talk about identities. The narrative is built around an (implicit) opposition between Hispanics and blacks. While Hispanics are presented as victims of aggression and prejudice, blacks are depicted as the aggressors and as prejudiced in the story world, and as potentially responsible for the spread of drugs and violence in the neighbourhood. These characterizations intertextually echo a mainstream discourse about blacks being criminals and respond to similar mainstream conceptions about Hispanics as is voiced in the story through the figure of the policeman. Although this is not done openly as in argumentative stories, the narrative works as an exemplary case because the actions are attributed to characters not as individuals but as members of a group. However, in this narrative the relevance of the relationships between ethnic categories and story actions is not explicitly proposed in discourse, but instead is built exclusively through connections between identities and actions in the story world.

Narratives such as the one we have analysed illustrate the multiple contexualizations of storytelling and of identity claims. On one level, membership categories are made relevant and negotiated locally. In this case, the participants index their roles as interviewed and interviewer through turn-taking and in the way they speak to each other. At another level, however, their use of racial categories in this particular discourse cannot be divorced from the wider world of ideologies, beliefs and group relations as they are shaped and reshaped in social and discursive practices at large. In this case, categories such as 'black' and 'Hispanic' are historically and socially constituted in certain ways and their use is enforced in innumerable social practices. From the compilation of statistical comparisons among different sections of the US population, to the setting of categories in public documents, to the presentation of information by the press, the imposition of these social categories as real is socially orchestrated. The stereotypical associations of categories with qualities and actions are also continuously reproduced.

This does not mean that the storytellers and participants in narrative events do not negotiate new meanings and challenge presuppositions about what it means to be part of a social category. On the contrary, a close analysis of what people mean when they invoke social identity categories and how they use them is a central task for discourse analysis. But it also means that, contrary to what some proponents of MCA would argue (see Edwards, 1998), the analyst cannot cast a narrow glance onto the interaction at hand without considering the wider implications of what is being recounted in specific social encounters.

CONCLUSIONS

In this chapter I have offered a general view of the development of the field of discourse-oriented identity studies in recent years. I have described the varied influences that have contributed to the formation of a social constructionist paradigm and of an approach to identity that advocates for a clear focus on social practices, interaction and the study of participant orientations. I have focused on the processes that allow for a deep understanding of identities as the product of discursive practices: indexicality, local occasioning, positioning, dialogism and categorization. I have also used the discussion of categorization to propose a view of identity as emerging from multiple contextualizations, both local and global, and the need to find a compromise between an exclusive reliance on the details of the interaction at hand and the tendency to apply ready-made categories to the analysis of discursively constructed identities.

FURTHER AND ONLINE READING

For a conversation analysis and ethnomethodology oriented introduction to discourse and identity, see Benwell, B. & Stokoe, E. (2006) *Discourse and Identity*. Edinburgh: Edinburgh University Press. Also important from a theoretical perspective is Buchóltz, M. and Hall, K. (2005) 'Identity and interaction: a sociocultural linguistic Approach'. Discourse Studies, 7(4–5): 585–614. Available at www.sagepub.co.uk/discoursestudies. These authors make a general proposal for a socio-interactional framework for the study of identity.

On identity and gender see Bucholtz, M., Liang, A.C. and Sutton, L. (eds) (1999) *Reiventing identities. The gendered self in discourse*. Oxford: Oxford University Press. For perspectives on identity and style the papers collected in Auer, P. (ed.) (2007) *Style and social identities: Alternative approaches to linguistic heterogeneity*. Berlin: Mouton de Gruyter, are a must.

To become acquainted with critical discursive approaches, see the study of political identities in van Dijk (2010) and of national identities in De Cillia, R., Reisigl, M. & Wodak, R. (1999) 'The discursive construction of national identities'. *Discourse & Society*, 10(2): 149–173. Available at www.sagepub.co.uk/discoursestudies.

For earlier work on identity and discourse, an important reference is LePage, R. and Tabouret-Keller, A. (1985) *Acts of identity: Creole-based approaches to language and ethnicity*. New York: Cambridge University Press, and for cross-disciplinary work on identity from disciplines such as philosophy, psychology and sociology see Du Gay, P., Evans, J. & Redman, P. (2000). *Identity: A reader*. London: Sage and the Open University.

REFERENCES

Antaki, C. and Widdicombe, S. (eds) (1998) *Identities in Talk*. London: Sage.

Auer, P. (ed.) (2007) *Style and Social Identities: Alternative Approaches to Linguistic Heterogeneity*. Berlin: Mouton de Gruyter.

Bamberg, M. (1997) 'Positioning between structure and performance'. *Journal of Narrative and Life History*, 7: 335–42.

Bamberg, M. and Georgakopoulou, A. (2008) 'Small stories as a new perspective in narrative and identity analysis'. In A. De Fina and A. Georgakopoulou (eds), 'Narrative analysis in the shift from text to practices'. Special Issue, *Text & Talk*, 28 (3): 377–96.

Bamberg, M., De Fina, A. and Schiffrin, D. (eds) (2007) *Selves and Identities in Narrative and Discourse*. Amsterdam: John Benjamins.

Bauman, Z. (2005) *Work, Consumerism and the New Poor*. London: Open University Press.

Benwell, B. and Stokoe, E. (2006) *Discourse and Identity*. Edinburgh: Edinburgh University Press.

Berger, P. and Luckmann, T. (1967) *The Social Construction of Reality*. Harmondsworth: Penguin.

Blumer, H. (1969) *Symbolic Interactionism: Perspective and Method*. Englewood Cliffs, NJ: Prentice-Hall.

Briggs, C. (2007) 'Mediating infanticide: theorizing relations between narrative and violence'. *Cultural Anthropology*, 22 (3): 315–56.

Bucholtz, M. (1999) '"You da man": narrating the racial other in the production of white masculinity'. *Journal of Sociolinguistics*, 3 (4): 443–60.

Bucholtz, M. and Hall, K. (2005) 'Identity and interaction: a sociocultural linguistic approach'. *Discourse Studies*, 7(4–5): 585–614.

Bucholtz, M., Liang, A.C. and Sutton, L. (eds) (1999) *Reiventing Identities: The Gendered Self in Discourse*. Oxford: Oxford University Press.

Burr, V. (2002) *The Person in Social Psychology*. Hove, East Sussex: Psychology Press.

Butler, J. (1990) *Gender Trouble: Feminism and the Subversion of Identity*. New York: Routledge.

Coupland, N. (2001) 'Dialect stylization in radio talk'. *Language in Society*, 30 (3): 345–75.

Coupland, N. (2008) 'The delicate constitution of identity in face-to-face accommodation: a response to Trudgill'. *Language in Society*, 37 (2): 267–70

Crystal, D. (1997) *The Cambridge Encyclopedia of Language*. Cambridge: Cambridge University Press.

Davies, B. and Harré, R. (1990) 'Positioning: the discursive construction of selves'. *Journal for the Theory of Social Behaviour*, 20: 43–63.

De Fina, A. (1995) 'Pronominal choice, identity, and solidarity in political discourse'. *Text*, 15 (3): 379–410.

De Fina, A. (2003) *Identity in Narrative. A Study of Immigrant Discourse*. Amsterdam: John Benjamins.

De Fina, A. (2006) 'Group identity, narrative and self representations'. In A. De Fina, D. Schiffrin and M. Bamberg (eds), *Discourse and Identity* (pp. 351–75). Cambridge: Cambridge University Press.

De Fina, A. (2007a) 'Style and stylization in the construction of identities in a card-playing club'. In P. Auer (ed.), *Style and Social Identities: Alternative Approaches to Linguistic Heterogeneity* (pp. 57–84). Berlin: Mouton de Gruyter.

De Fina, A. (2007b) 'Code switching and ethnicity in a community of practice'. *Language in Society*, 36 (3): 371–92.

De Fina, A., Schiffrin, D. and Bamberg, M. (eds) (2006) *Discourse and Identity*. Cambridge: Cambridge University Press.

Depperman, A. (2007) 'Playing with the voice of the other: Stylized *Kanaksprach* in conversations among German adolescents'. In P. Auer (ed.), *Style and Social Identities: Alternative Approaches to Linguistic Heterogeneity* (pp. 325–60). Berlin: Mouton de Gruyter.

Du Gay, P., Evans, J. and Redman, P. (2000) *Identity: A Reader*. London: Sage and the Open University.

Eckert, P. and Rickford, J.R. (eds) (2001) *Style and Sociolinguistic Variation*. Cambridge: Cambridge University Press.

Edwards, D. (1998) 'The relevant thing about her: social identity categories in use'. In C. Antaki and S. Widdicombe (eds), *Identities in Talk*. London: Sage. 15–33.

Erikson, E. (1980) *Identity and the Life Cycle*. New York/London: Norton.

Fairclough, N. (1992) *Discourse and Social Change*. Cambridge: Polity.

Garfinkel, H. (1967) *Studies in Ethnomethodology*. Englewood Cliffs, NJ: Prentice Hall.

Georgakopoulou, A. (2007) *Small Stories, Interaction, and Identities*. Amsterdam: John Benjamins.

Giddens, A. (1991) *Modernity and Self-Identity: Self and Society in the Late Modern age*. Stanford: Stanford University Press.

Goffman, E. (1967) *Interactional Ritual: Essays on Face to Face Behavior*. Garden City, NY: Anchor.

Goffman, E. (1981) *Forms of Talk*. Philadelphia: University of Pennsylvania Press.

Goyette, B. (2008) 'Comment: On Sarah Palin's use of language'. *The McGill Daily*, 30 October, retrieved 3 Nov 2008, from http://www.mcgilldaily.com/article/5536–comment-on-sarah-palin-s-use

Hall, S. (2000) 'Who needs identity?' In P. Du Gay, G. Evans and P. Redman (eds), *Identity: A Reader* (pp. 15–30). London: Sage and the Open University.

Hester, S. and Eglin, P. (1997) *Culture in Action: Studies in Membership Categorization Analysis*. Washington, DC: International Institute of Studies in Ethnomethodology and Conversation Analysis/University Press of America.

Labov, W. (1966) *The Social Stratification of English in New York City*. Washington, DC: Center for Applied Linguistics.

Labov, W. (1972a) *Sociolinguistic Patterns*. Philadelphia: University of Pennsylvania Press.

Labov, W. (1972b) 'The transformation of experience in narrative syntax'. In W. Labov (ed.), *Language in the Inner City: Studies in the Black English Vernacular* (pp. 354–96). Philadelphia: University of Pennsylvania Press.

LePage, R. and Tabouret-Keller, A. (1985) *Acts of Identity: Creole-based Approaches to Language and Ethnicity*. New York: Cambridge University Press.

Mead, George, H. (1934) *Mind, Self, and Society* (edited by C.W. Morris). Chicago: University of Chicago Press.

Moita Lopes, L. (2006) 'On being white, heterosexual and male in a Brazilian school: multiple positionings in oral narrative'. In A. De Fina, M. Bamberg and D. Schiffrin (eds), *Discourse and Identity* (pp. 288–313). Cambridge: Cambridge University Press.

Norris, S. (2007) 'The micropolitics of personal national and ethnicity identity'. *Discourse and Society*, *18* (5): 653–74.

Parker, K. (2008) 'Views from *Post* pundits'. *The Washington Post*, 4 October, A17.

Rampton, B. (1995) *Crossing: Language and Ethnicity among Adolescents*. London: Longman.

Sacks, H. (1972) 'On the analyzability of stories by children'. In J. Gumperz and D. Hymes (eds), *Directions in Sociolinguistics: The Ethnography of Communication* (pp. 325–45). New York: Rinehart and Winston.

Sacks, H. (1995) *Lectures on Conversation* (edited by G. Jefferson). London: Blackwell.

Schiffrin, D. (1996) 'Narrative as self-portrait: sociolinguistic construction of identity'. *Language in Society*, *25* (2): 167–203.

Silverstein, M. (1976) 'Shifters, linguistic categories, and cultural description'. In K.A. Basso and H.A. Selby (eds), *Meaning and Anthropology*. New York: Harper and Row.

van Dijk, T.A. (1998) *Ideology: A Multidisciplinary Approach*. London: Sage.

van Dijk, T.A. (2010) 'Political identities in parliamentary debates'. In C. Ilie (ed.), *European Parliaments under Scrutiny: Discourse Strategies and Interaction Practices* (pp. 29–56). Amsterdam: John Benjamins.

Wilson, J. (1990) *Politically Speaking: The Pragmatic Analysis of Political Language*. Oxford: Blackwell.

Wodak, R., de Cillia, R., Reisigl, M. and Liebhart, K. (1999) *The Discursive Construction of National Identity*. Edinburgh: EUP.

Zimmerman, D.H. (1998) 'Identity, context and interaction'. In C. Antaki and S. Widdicombe (eds), *Identities in Talk* (pp. 87–106). London: Sage.

Zimmerman, D.H. and Wieder, D.L. (1970) 'Ethnomethodology and the problem of order: comment on Denzin'. In J.D. Douglas (ed.), *Understanding Everyday Life: Toward the Reconstruction of Sociological Knowledge* (pp. 285–98). Chicago: Aldine.

APPENDIX

Transcription conventions

((smiling))	Non-linguistic actions
(…)	Inaudible
(.)	Noticeable pause
.	Falling intonation followed by noticeable pause (as at end of declarative sentence)
?	Rising intonation followed by noticeable pause (as at end of interrogative sentence)
,	Continuing intonation: may be a slight rise or fall in contour (less than "." or – "?"); may not be followed by a pause (shorter than "." or "?")
-	Self interruption
=	Latched utterances by the same speaker or by different speakers
::	Vowel or consonant lengthening
[	Overlap between utterances
→ (line)	Highlights key phenomena
@	Laughter (the amount of @ roughly indicates its duration)

FOURTEEN

Organizational Discourse

Dennis K. Mumby and Jennifer Mease

The study of organizational discourse allows us to understand and explore the ways in which the most mundane aspects of organizing – employee conversations, meetings, documents, daily rituals, and so forth – are actually the very 'stuff' of organizations. While we often tend to think of these as large, imposing, and stable structures that exist independently from the people who work 'in' them, research from a discourse perspective suggests that organizations are surprisingly precarious structures that only exist through members' everyday discursive practices. This process-oriented perspective suggests that discourse is *constitutive* of organizing (Deetz, 2003; Pacanowsky and O'Donnell-Trujillo, 1982; Putnam, 1983); thus, it is impossible to separate the everyday discursive practices of members from the organization itself. This approach is 'meaning-centred' in its efforts to explore the complex ways that members collectively construct social realities and institutional structures. The goal of meaning-centred research, then, is to examine organizations 'from the native's point of view' (Geertz, 1983) through qualitative research methods (interviews, ethnographies, etc.) that can provide insight into the assumptions that underlie the creation of organizational realities.

The idea of organizations as 'discursive constructions' (Fairhurst and Putnam, 2004) has been taken up with great enthusiasm by scholars of organizations in North and South America, Europe, and Australasia. This proliferation of scholarship has been accompanied by conferences, special issues of journals, debates about definitions and the scope of terms and concepts and, perhaps most significantly, the publication of the *Handbook of Organizational Discourse*, which brings together voluminous research in this interdisciplinary field of study (Grant, Hardy, Oswick, Phillips, and Putnam, 2004).

However, this explosion of research is actually characterized by a number of different issues and perspectives. First, scholars differ in how they frame the relationship between 'discourse' and 'organization'. Second, the study of organizational discourse is approached from multiple theoretical perspectives, including critical, postmodern, and feminist, among others. In the next section we briefly address the 'discourse-organization' relationship. We then examine some of the theoretical approaches to organizational discourse that have developed over the last two decades.

FRAMING THE DISCOURSE-ORGANIZATION RELATIONSHIP

One of the issues that has occupied organizational discourse scholars in the last few years concerns the appropriate way to conceptualize the relationship between discourse and organization (Alvesson and Karreman, 2000a, 2000b; Chia, 2000; Fairhurst and Putnam, 2004; Keenoy, Marchak, Oswick and Grant, 2000; Reed, 2000). While this may seem like a purely academic debate, it speaks to important questions about how we can understand the ways that organizational practices and processes construct real people's lives.

Drawing on the work of Alvesson and Karreman (2000a, 2000b), Fairhurst and Putnam (2004) argue that in the study of organizations researchers use the notion of 'discourse' in two ways. First, at the 'macro'-level, 'Discourse' (with a capital 'D') functions to frame the broad social context within which everyday organizing processes occur. For example, an organization may operate via a Discourse of diversity, whereby organizational behaviour and decision making are premised on increasing the presence of under-represented groups in the organization. Of course, this Discourse may be in competition with other Discourses that frame organizational behaviour in terms of efficiency, profitability, accountability to stockholders, and so forth, each of which can effect the ways that 'diversity' as an organizational Discourse is interpreted by organization members. At the micro-level, organizational discourse (with a lower-case 'd') refers to the ways that, at an everyday level, an organization's members will interact, have meetings, create documents, gossip, tell stories and jokes, and so forth; in other words, 'd'iscourse in this sense consists of the very 'stuff' of organizing – the everyday, meaning-making activities that give organizations substance.

For many researchers, then, the study of organizational discourse requires a careful examination of the relationship between the micro- and macro-levels of discourse. Understanding organizations involves exploring how Discourses frame and can provide both a context and the resources for everyday organizational behaviour and meaning construction; at the same time, researchers can examine how everyday organizational discourse can both affirm and resist the macro-level, institutionalized Discourses of organizing. In this sense, discourses and Discourses function in a reciprocal, dialectical manner. We will examine several applied examples of this relationship later in the chapter.

In addition to the distinction between micro- and macro-level discourses, Fairhurst and Putnam argue that discourse studies can be classified by three different orientations toward the discourse-organization relationship: 1) the object orientation; 2) the becoming orientation; and 3) the grounded in action orientation. In the object orientation, organizations are conceived as objective, stable structures that exist relatively separate from, and prior to, discourse. In this perspective, the organizational structure is reified and relatively detached from members' actions. The becoming orientation reverses this relationship, arguing that discourse creates the very possibility of organizing, and that the organization itself is an ongoing product of members' talk. Here, the agency of members is emphasized over the limiting structure of organizational forms. Finally, while the first approach emphasizes structure and the second agency, the grounded in action orientation focuses on the mutually constitutive relationship between the two. Hence, discourse can be seen both as a resource that knowledgeable actors draw on to produce social realities, and as a sedimented structure (e.g., rules and institutional texts and artifacts) that shapes and constrains what is considered legitimate action (Giddens, 1979).

These three perspectives adopt competing positions regarding how humans – as discourse-producing social actors – are determined by, or function relatively autonomously to, the social structures that they inhabit. If one adopts a more 'realist' perspective, then one will tend to privilege the role of social structures over individual agency; if one gives primacy to discourse as constituting organizations as social structures, then the role of the human agent and his or her possibilities for action will take centre stage. As we will see below, different research traditions have taken up this relationship in different ways.

In the next section we move from ways to think about the discourse-organization more broadly, to a discussion of three research traditions that examine the relationships among power, discourse, and organizing. Implicit in both readings of the discourse-organization relationship discussed above is the idea that organizations are, by definition, sites of power where different stakeholders with varying resources struggle to exercise agency and control over organizational meanings and structures. Depending on your perspective, conceptions of organization members range from relatively unwitting dupes of organizational structures of control, to active and self-knowing agents with the ability to resist and subvert organizational control efforts. Below, we unpack the discourse-power-organization connections.

DISCOURSE, POWER AND ORGANIZING

While space prohibits an extensive overview, the general trajectory of research on power has been from a behavioural view of power as a personal possession or material resource that can be expended (Bachrach and Baratz, 1962; Dahl, 1957; Pfeffer, 1981), to a more recent view in which power is linked directly to the ability to shape and fix meanings and social realities (Clegg, 1989; Foucault, 1979; Lukes, 1974; Mumby, 2001). In the latter conception, discourse and power are both directly linked and dialectically related; that is, power relations both provide the larger context within which discourse and meanings unfold, and are constituted discursively (van Dijk, 1993). We will unpack this dialectical relationship below.

The study of the relationships among power, discourse, and organizing has resulted in a large body of research that examines power as enacted and contested through various discursive forms. These include: organizational storytelling (Boje, 1991; Brown, 1998; Helmer, 1993; Mumby, 1987, 1993; Witten, 1993); workplace rituals (Collinson, 1988; Rosen, 1985, 1988); organizational metaphors (Deetz and Mumby, 1985; Smith and Keyton, 2001; Smith and Eisenberg, 1987); humour (Collinson, 1988; Holmes, 2000; Rhodes and Westwood, 2007); everyday workplace talk (Holmes, 2006; Holmes and Stubbe, 2003); and irony and cynicism (Fleming and Spicer, 2003; Hatch, 1997; Taylor and Bain, 2003), amongst others. Much of this research is concerned with exploring how these various discursive forms enable competing stakeholder groups to shape the organizational meanings and interpretations that will legitimate their own interests and 'stake' in the organization.

Because power lies in the shaping of routine sense-making practices, the study of everyday discourse is key to understanding how this dynamic occurs. However, the study of the relationships among discourse, power, and organizing is further complicated by the development of multiple perspectives, each of which emphasizes different aspects of this relationship. Below we discuss three of these perspectives: 1) critical studies; 2) postmodern studies; and 3) feminist studies.

Critical studies of organizational discourse

Research from a critical perspective has grown out of a neo-Marxist tradition with a focus on issues of ideology and hegemony (Althusser, 1971; Gramsci, 1971; Marx, 1967). From this perspective, discourse studies focus on the ways that capitalist organizations are able to produce and reproduce relations of domination in the workplace. While Marx saw these relations as largely coercive, the contemporary critical tradition focuses more on how, under modern work conditions that are ostensibly more humane and participatory, workers will still consent to systems of power that will not necessarily work in their best interests. In this context, the concepts of ideology and hegemony play a central explanatory role.

The term 'ideology' refers less to a simple system of ideas and more to a whole lived relation to the world that is shaped through various discursive and non-discursive practices. Ideology provides an interpretive frame through which social actors make sense of their relationship to the world. However, ideology does not frame the world in a neutral manner but rather simultaneously embodies and obscures underlying relations of power. As Marx explained, ideology works to obscure the origins of the ruling ideas in a society, such that they are presented not as the particular product of a specific, historically-located ruling class, but as a set of universal, generally accepted 'truisms'. That such ruling ideas are historically specific rather than universal is easily demonstrated by thinking about now archaic but previously universal beliefs such as, for example, a belief in kings being divinely chosen or, much more recently, the idea that women are not qualified to vote or hold high office.

In both instances, such 'universal truths' serve the interests of certain groups (the aristocracy and men, respectively) and disenfranchize others (peasants and women, respectively). The important point about ideology is that it functions to maintain the status quo while at the same time obscuring the fact that this same status quo is both historically contingent and in the interests of certain groups over others.

The concept of hegemony (Gramsci, 1971) is related to ideology, but refers to a particular kind of power relation among competing interest groups. For power to be exercised most effectively, the ruling group must not coerce subordinate groups but instead create the conditions whereby the latter will consent to and, indeed, actively support the ideas and meaning systems – the ideology – of the ruling group. When a group is 'hegemonic', then, its ideas and worldview will be 'spontaneously' accepted as 'the way things are' by members of other groups.

In the context of critical organization studies, researchers have explored how organizational discourse functions ideologically to structure workplace power relations. Perhaps the best-known early example of this work is Burawoy's (1979) ethnographic study of workers at a machine parts factory. In this study, he showed how these workers were driven to work harder for the company, not by coercive management practices, but by a shopfloor game called 'making out', in which they would compete amongst themselves and against the machines to figure out how productivity bonuses were most achievable. Burawoy argued that the game of 'making out' – discursively constructed and collectively practised by the workers – functioned ideologically to maintain and reproduce the hegemonic relations between management and workers. Framed in neo-Marxist terms, Burawoy claimed that the game ideologically reproduced capitalist relations of production by getting the workers to focus on the game itself and their desire to beat the machines rather than on the fundamentally antagonistic relations between management as the agents of capitalism and the workers themselves. As Burawoy argued, the game secured 'surplus value' for the capitalists while obscuring the origins of this value in the exploitation of the workers themselves.

In the thirty years since Burawoy's study critical organizational scholars have explored the ideological functions of numerous forms of discourse, including stories (Helmer, 1993; Mumby, 1987; Witten, 1993), rituals (Rosen, 1985, 1988), humour (Collinson, 1988; Linstead, 1985) metaphors (Deetz and Mumby, 1985), and everyday talk (Huspek and Kendall, 1991; Mumby and Stohl, 1992). While many of these studies explore how hegemony is produced and reproduced at the level of everyday discourse, a significant body of research has examined how forms of struggle and resistance to dominant meanings and ideologies frequently emerge in the workplace. As this work shows, power, by definition, is very much a contested phenomenon. One of the most useful and insightful aspects here is the ability to demonstrate how the everyday, mundane (little 'd') discourse of organization members can have significant implications for broader issues of organizational power and resistance.

An excellent example of a critical study of organizational power and resistance is Collinson's (1988) study of everyday workplace humour on the shopfloor of a truck factory.

In this study he showed that not only is humour a pervasive and defining feature of the culture of this all-male shopfloor, but that it also figures heavily in struggles around competing definitions of work and appropriate manager-worker relations. Thus, humour is used both to stave off workplace boredom and to parody and resist managerial efforts to co-opt workers into a new corporate culture that emphasizes management-labour cooperation. In a shopfloor culture that is rooted in a strong sense of working-class masculinity and a deep suspicion of managerial motives, humour is a powerful means by which to legitimate and reproduce that masculinity while simultaneously resisting managerial efforts to shape the organizational reality. As one of the workers pithily stated, 'Fellas on the shop-floor are genuine. They're the salt of the earth, but they're all twats and nancy boys in th' offices' (1988: 186). Collinson demonstrated how 'having a laff' and being able to give and take insults was not only seen as integral to a masculine working-class identity, but also negated white-collar workers as less than masculine ('nancy boys'). As homophobic and sexist as this comment is, it speaks to how the shopfloor workers connected their masculine identity to 'real work' (hard, physical labour) while negating clerical work as feminized. As one worker said to Collinson on observing him washing his hands in the bathroom, 'Have you fallen down, then?' The implication here, of course, is that as a 'knowledge worker' he couldn't possibly have gotten his hands dirty doing real work.

Collinson's study is a useful example of critical discursive analysis because it effectively illustrates how organization members' everyday discursive practices are closely tied to the dynamics of power and resistance. Furthermore, his study stands at the intersection of discourse/Discourse studies in that he framed the analysis of everyday discourse within an understanding of macro-level Discourses of working-class masculinity and capitalist relations of production. Each level of discourse analysis effectively informs the other.

In general, then, critical studies of organizational discourse have provided important insights into how power and meaning intersect at the level of everyday organizational life. Much of this scholarship is interested in the possibilities for workplace agency; that is, the extent to which employees are able to 'act otherwise' (Giddens, 1979) and construct alternative organizational realities to those articulated by managerial interests.

Postmodern studies of organizational discourse

Starting roughly in the early 1990s, postmodern studies of organizational power and discourse reflect a somewhat different set of conceptual and empirical concerns than those of critical studies (see Alvesson and Deetz, 1996, for a useful comparative analysis of these two approaches). First, postmodern studies reflect and attempt to capture the changing character of work and organizations. While critical, neo-Marxist studies typically focused on traditional Fordist organizational forms characterized by centralized power, strong hierarchies, clearly demarcated stakeholder groups (managers, workers, etc.), formal bureaucratic structures, and so forth, postmodern studies have usually examined forms of organizing (often called 'post-Fordist') that reflect the 'new workplace' – that is, organizations characterized by flatter hierarchies, decentralized and/or team-based decision structures, knowledge-intensive work processes, 'just-in-time' production systems, and so on.

Second, and drawing heavily on the work of French philosopher Michel Foucault, postmodern organizational discourse studies frame power not in terms of processes of ideology and hegemony, but rather as a disciplinary mechanism that constructs employee subjectivity. In Foucault's (1979) sense, then, power is 'productive' rather than negative. Thus, postmodern scholars attempt to account for the ways that organizational discourses construct identities that are then subject to the mechanisms of disciplinary control embedded in the new workplace. This new workplace structure functions 'panoptically' in that employees are constantly aware of the possibility of surveillance even at those times when they are not being directly observed by their superiors, or even by fellow workers. Whether observed or not, workers engage in a form of 'self-surveillance' whereby they internalize a workplace subjectivity that is premised on, and beholden to, the work ethic as it is articulated and monitored by the whole group.

Postmodern studies, then, reflect a sense that a new form of power characterizes the (post)modern organization. Rather than thinking of power as centralized with an élite group (usually owners/managers), a postmodern view sees this as dispersed throughout the organization in a decentralized manner. While at first glance such a diffuse system of power seems more egalitarian and democratic, postmodern researchers would argue that, paradoxically, such dispersed structures of power work to create organizational forms that are more oppressive than the older type of Fordist organization. Let us illustrate this rather counter-intuitive argument with an example.

Barker (1993, 1999) provided a fascinating case study of how a high tech company's shift from a traditional bureaucratic organizational structure to a flatter, decentralized form of decision making simultaneously gave employees a much greater level of participation in the organization's daily functioning and introduced a system of power and control that was far more pervasive and insidious than the previous bureaucratic system. How did this occur? Barker showed how the company literally switched overnight from its traditional, bureaucratic decision-making system to a decentralized system in which employees were organized into autonomous work teams with complete control over all decisions about the work process. Faced with this new structure, employees were at first unsure how to behave. What if they did something wrong? The company president assured them that there were no 'wrong' decisions, and that while he was available for advice, he would not intervene in their discussions about how to organize their work. Barker illustrated how, over time, this apparent freedom in decision making evolved into a system of self-generated 'concertive control' that underpinned everything that the team members said and did.

Barker (following Tompkins and Cheney, 1985), argued that under this concertive control the locus of authority would shift from the impersonal bureaucratic system of rules to the 'value consensus of its members and its socially created generative rules system' (1993: 412). In other words, while in a bureaucratic structure an employee might come to work on time because the rules say they must and they'll get into trouble if they don't, under a system of concertive control an employee will arrive on time because the team members have collectively generated a 'value premise' within which timeliness is seen as integral to both the successful performance of work and to the team's own definition of excellence. In this sense, employees are then unable to argue that the system of rules was simply imposed on them. Furthermore, employees operate according to a self-generated set of values rather than a set of bureaucratic rules, the reasons for which may not even be apparent.

In Barker's study, then, he described how this system of concertive control would emerge from the employee teams, creating a level of oversight and surveillance that would be far more extensive than anything that had occurred under the old bureaucratic model. As one team member stated, 'I don't have to sit there and look for the boss to be around; and if the boss is not around, I can sit there and talk to my neighbor or do what I want. Now the whole team is around me and the whole team is observing what I'm doing' (1993: 408).

Barker's study made clear that in the post-Fordist workplace one of the principal struggles for power and control occurs around the construction of workplace identities and subjectivities. Again building on the work of Foucault, scholars have explored how employees have become particular 'objects of knowledge' who are 'disciplined' to behave as 'good employees' (lest they be revealed as a bad employee!). This move also includes employees' view of *themselves* as objects of self-knowledge; that is, by virtue of the panoptical effect of disciplinary discourses, employees will routinely scrutinize their own behaviours and attitudes to see if these match up to the espoused organizational standards. Such a system routinely produces insecurities and instabilities around identity issues, as employees consistently find themselves to be lacking in what it takes to be successful, at least as organizationally defined – a definition that regularly shifts (Collinson, 2003).

An excellent example of how this intersection of power, discourse, and subjectivity operates in the workplace is provided by Holmer Nadesan (1997) in her analysis of the widespread use of employee personality tests in modern organizations. Many readers of this chapter will probably have taken one or more of these tests. Frequently companies will administer them to prospective or current employees as a way of 'objectively' measuring their suitability for certain kinds of employment. Holmer Nadesan argues that 'the widespread use of personality exams should be understood as a discursive practice' (1997: 190) that constructs a particular model of personhood by means of which companies can discipline and objectify employees. Using a Foucauldian framework, she analyses personality tests as a 'confessional technology' through which the employee reveals to him or herself and others 'objective' features of their personality. In this sense, the employee is then constructed as a certain 'personality type' and as both a (manageable) object of knowledge to the organization and a subject of self-knowledge to the employee. As Holmer Nadesan shows, such tests do not 'discover' personality traits that already exist in employees so much as they create a particular subject, defined in a very specific (though claimed as objective) manner, who can in turn be employed as a 'human resource' in a way that best serves the company.

Nadesan's study is a perfect example of how, from a postmodern perspective, power works discursively to create objects of control that did not exist prior to the construction of the discourse itself. It is also an excellent example of how organizational discourse researchers are interested not only in the everyday talk of organization members, but also in the 'Big D' Discourses that shape the very idea of what it means to be a member of an organization. In this instance, Nadesan illustrates how an apparently neutral system of evaluation of (potential) employees serves to actually *construct* the ideal employee as an object of knowledge (both to her/himself and the organization).

A final example of how power-as-discourse produces subjects is Boris Brummans' brilliant and moving (2007) discussion of his own father's signed euthanasia declaration. While Brummans would probably not agree with our categorization of his essay as postmodern, it is nevertheless a powerful example of how discourse – in this case a single document – constructs the identities and actions of those people who interact with it. Coming out of the 'Montréal School' of organizational communication studies (Cooren, 2000; Cooren and Taylor, 1997; J.R. Taylor, Cooren, Giroux and Robichaud, 1996; J.R. Taylor and Van Every, 2000), this essay examines how a document (in this case a euthanasia declaration) is not just a neutral means of conveying information, but rather also has its own agency that creates the conditions of possibility for those who interact with that document. This essay is unusual because much of it is a poem that is written from the perspective of the document itself, hence further emphasizing the agency that the document takes on in the lives of those who engage with it (Brummans' father and the members of his family). Thus, the 'article' begins in the following manner:

> not alive
> like you
> or the man
> i will help to kill
> i do not breathe nor remove
> a textual agent
> defined by sign and signature
> a euthanasia declaration
> acting for
> hub brummans
> whose death near
> his life's connected to mine
> acting for others too
> boris (his son)
> josine (his daughter)
> tea (his wife)
> today the day i was born
> my actions are in effect
> not long before
> they will be known
>
> (Brummans, 2007: 712)

Brummans argues that the euthanasia declaration inscribed a set of conditions that shaped in important ways how he and his family subsequently behaved. For example, in speaking about the agency of the declaration he states:

> In a sense, decisions were no longer only up to the persons we were in the last week before my dad's death. They were also up to the people we used to be, which we had formalized in textual form. Curiously, the text we had signed to ascertain that my dad's will would be carried out also seemed to act with a will of its own. It spoke *for* people we were not and re-presented ... people we were no longer. Why was it so difficult to break with those we had said to be? Why did this simple piece of paper have such force? (2007: 724)

Brummans illustrates how we not only use texts (to make declarations, assertions, create laws, etc.), but are also at their mercy in an important manner. When humans create texts, those texts can act back upon humans in a way that will significantly shape our perceptions of the world and those around us. Thus, in analysing the euthanasia declaration, Brummans asserts that: 'As a nonhuman agent among human agents, the text projected the end of my dad's life from the past, creating a field of action that was demarcated by whom we had thought to be and were – a space that felt surreal, but was real' (p. 723).

For Brummans, then, the euthanasia declaration that ultimately ended his father's life was a profoundly personal example of how, as humans in a meaning-laden world, we are both enabled and constrained by the agency of the myriad texts we create. Texts, in this sense, are interconnected webs of significance that, while having multiple potential meanings, nevertheless inscribe social reality in ways that will profoundly shape human identities and the manner in which they engage with the world and others.

Thus, organizational forms of 'power-knowledge' (of which texts such as euthanasia declarations are a part) do not simply prohibit or approve certain kinds of behaviour, but rather then 'systematically form the object of which they speak' (Foucault, 1979: 49); power is *productive* of certain subjectivities, which then become objects of knowledge and discipline in the workplace. Foucault's (1979, 1980) work has been applied extensively in organizational discourse studies as researchers have attempted to examine critically the complex processes through which particular forms of workplace subjectivity are constructed (Brewis, 2001; Clegg, 1998; Knights and Vurdubakis, 1994; McKinlay and Starkey, 1998).

Lest we leave the impression that postmodern organization studies focus exclusively on disciplinary practices, many researchers have also extensively examined various kinds of worker resistance, including discursive forms such as humour, irony and cynicism (Fleming and Sewell, 2002; Fleming and Spicer, 2003, 2007; Hatch, 1997; Sotirin and Gottfried, 1999; Taylor and Bain, 2003). This research is particularly interesting from a discourse perspective because it examines how organization employees contest and resist dominant organizational meanings through a discursive repertoire that does not directly oppose dominant discourses, but rather appropriates them in subversive ways. Taylor and Bain (2003), for example, illustrate how workers at a call centre (the archetypal and extensively studied post-Fordist organizational form) utilized both humour and cynicism to undermine management authority. For example, one flyer surreptitiously circulated amongst employees stated:

Are you lonely? Hate having to make decisions? Rather talk about it than do it? Then why not hold a meeting? You can:

Get to see other people
Sleep in peace
Offload decisions
Learn to write volumes of meaningless notes
Feel important
Impress (or bore) colleagues
And all in work time!

'Meetings': The practical alternative to work!

Another flyer depicts a bathroom stall that has been set up as a work-station – complete with computer and phone – thus parodying management's efforts to appropriate employees' every waking moment.

Studies like Taylor and Bain's are significant in two ways. First, they indicate the importance of paying attention to apparently trivial, unofficial organizational texts, which will frequently reveal hidden, marginalized, or alternative discursive constructions of organizational life – constructions that reveal a very different reality from the one sanctioned by management. Second, they illustrate how resistance does not have to involve direct confrontation, nor does it require collective action; rather, it can involve subtle (and not so subtle!) efforts to reframe dominant meanings and discursively articulate alternative – and often subversive – worldviews. Such studies depict employees not as passive subjects of disciplinary power, but as active agents who construct alternative workplace identities for themselves.

Feminist studies of organizational discourse

The last area of organizational discourse scholarship that we will discuss is feminist studies. We examine this area of study not because it is distinct from critical or postmodern studies (indeed it is often influenced by and overlaps with these areas), but as a body of scholarship marked by a growing recognition that organizations as sites of discourse, power, and identity are strongly 'gendered' (Acker, 1990); that is, organizations are fundamentally structured around, and generate meanings through, conceptions and relations of masculinity and femininity. In this sense, research moves beyond the idea that men and women act in certain ways and exhibit particular communication styles, and instead attempts to understand how everyday power relations are played out through gendered organizational processes and structures (see Ashcraft, 2004, for a useful overview of this research). Simply put, this area of research is rooted in the basic assumption that gender, power, and discourse are intimately connected.

Researchers have examined gender as both macro-level 'Discourse' and micro-level 'discourse'. From a macro-level perspective, scholars are interested in understanding how both men and women are positioned within societal-level discourses that will both enable and constrain the performance of gender identities. From a micro-level point of view, researchers view gender as a situated and provisional accomplishment that belies the apparent stability of gender identities. In this sense, gender is an ongoing performance that is constantly account-able regarding its fidelity to gendered norms (West and Zimmerman, 1987).

While in some ways analytically distinct, these two perspectives come together in inter-esting ways in the study of organizations, as researchers explore how, at the level of every-day talk and behaviour, men and women take up these larger discourses, both reproducing and resisting them in various ways (Ashcraft and Mumby, 2004a, 2004b; Holmer Nadesan, 1996; Holmes, 2006; Holmes and Stubbe, 2003; Murphy, 1998, 2003; Trethewey, 1997, 2001). For example, Trethewey's (2001) interview study of middle-aged professional women's talk about their bodies revealed complex sense-making efforts to come to terms with a macro-level societal discourse that positions older women as 'in decline' physically and hence less valuable professionally. Trethewey showed how some of her interviewees reproduced this discourse, claiming that they did everything in their power to remain young, fit, and attractive and thus also remain professionally competitive. Others rejected this dominant discourse of decline and embraced both their maturity and their wrinkles. These interviewees argued that as older women they were no longer objectified and subject to the male gaze as they were when they were younger; hence, they felt a certain sense of lib-eration and lack of accountability to others. Trethewey's study shows that women's prof-essional identities are more conspicuously gendered and in a way that men's professional identities are not; the dominant discourse dictates that while women age (and sometimes not very gracefully) men merely become more distinguished. The point here is that because of the way in which this discourse of decline differentially constructs men and women, the latter are positioned in a way that holds them continuously accountable for their gendered performance of aging.

A number of feminist studies have explored how gender and power get played out through everyday discourse. Bell and Forbes (1994), for example, illustrate how female clerical staff used 'office graffiti' (photocopied cartoons) in an ironic way that parodied gender stereotypes ('I have PMS and a handgun. Any questions?') in order to subtly chal-lenge the formal bureaucratic system in which they worked (note the connection to Taylor and Bain's study, discussed above). Murphy (1998) used ethnographic methods to examine how female flight attendants engaged in everyday practices of resistance to subvert the airline's efforts to construct them as a specific kind of feminine identity in terms of their weight, appearance, and deferential demeanour.

While not adopting an explicitly feminist perspective, sociolinguist Janet Holmes has developed a body of research that adopts a micro-level approach to the relationships among gender, power, and the workplace (Holmes, 2000, 2006; Holmes and Stubbe, 2003). Adopting a 'community of practice' perspective, her focus is on the ways in which language contributes to the construction of gender identity in the workplace. Holmes argues that in order to understand members of a community or group, the focus must be on what they do – 'the practice or activities which indicate that they belong to the group' (2006: 13).

In examining the practice of gender, including talk, Holmes argues that this focus should not be on the gender differences between men and women, but rather on the differences that gender creates; that is, how do men and women exploit gendered resources, including language, to create structures of inclusion and exclusion? In this context, the use of language in face-to-face interaction is particularly significant for our understanding of how important social boundaries are constructed. As such, Holmes argues that, 'the culture of the workplace is constantly being instantiated in ongoing talk and action; it develops and is gradually modified by large and small acts in regular social interaction within ongoing exchanges' (2006: 15).

Holmes's research differs from most studies of gender, power, and organization in that her analysis involves a careful examination of workplace interaction at the level of conversational turn-taking. She carefully transcribes everyday conversations (e.g., during meetings), and then subjects these transcripts to an analysis that illustrates how talk functions to create meaning communities that will include and exclude social actors. For example, the exchange below between two female colleagues (Penelope and Hettie) is used to illustrate how a sense of both collegiality and a sense of power is conversationally constructed:

1. **Pen**: /and yes and and\ stood our ground
2. **Het**: /mm yeah yeah\
3. **Pen**: [inhales] strode up the street/[laughs]
4.   letting fly a number of expletives\…
5. **Het**: /[laughs]: I'm sure that you get the general gist:\
6.   [others laugh]
7. **Pen**: and she felt exactly the/same we'd both been feeling like this\
8. **Het**: /yep [laughs]\
9. **Pen**: I mean that's of course what happens when people abuse you
10.   That's what you do feel angry and and uncooperative
11.   and all of the things that we were feeling

(Holmes, 2006: 16)

Notice here how there is no attempt by the researcher to edit the dialogue for repetition and grammar, and the places where simultaneous talk occurs (signified by [ ]) are carefully documented, thus conveying a strong sense of the energy in the conversation. Holmes's purpose in analysing this conversational fragment is two-fold. First, she illustrates how two female colleagues (who have just come from a meeting at another company where they felt they were treated dismissively) can take the floor at a meeting and together discursively construct a view of themselves as assertive and strong ('strode up the street … letting fly … expletives'), hence repairing their sense of self in the wake of the earlier meeting. Note that both women work collaboratively and are clearly on the same wavelength when sharing this experience. Holmes's second purpose is to show how at the end of the segment Penelope (who is the organization's CEO) changes her communication style and adopts a much more assertive, distancing, masculine tone, 'constructing herself as a leader, someone with the right to evaluate the significance of the interaction' (2006: 17).

Of course, interactions such as these take place hundreds, perhaps thousands of time a day in organizations. Holmes's point is that 'larger patterns are established through the accumulation of repeated individual instances, and each instance gains its significance against the backdrop of the established norms' (2006: 15). Thus, in isolation, Penelope and Hettie's interaction is relatively insignificant but it illustrates how gendered talk both draws on sedimented norms and conventions as well as simultaneously reproducing those norms (e.g., women have to act collaboratively to maintain positive identities; women leaders must sometimes draw on masculine modes of discourse to reassert their status as leaders).

As one final example of a gendered analysis of organizational discourse, we will briefly discuss Karen Ashcraft's work on male airline pilots (Ashcraft, 2005; Ashcraft and Mumby, 2004a, 2004b). This research provides a useful contrast to Holmes's analyses in that Ashcraft adopts a more macro-level approach to the ways that gendered identities are constructed. Her research consists both of archival studies that examine how historically the airlines have constructed the identity of the male airline pilot, and of interview studies in which male airline pilots talk about what it means to them to be pilots. Archival research is particularly important in Ashcraft's work because it shows how the airlines deliberately and strategically constructed a Discourse that was heavily gendered in creating a pilot identity that is masculine (professional, rational, cool, fatherly, assertive, etc.) and a complementary flight attendant identity that is feminine (sexy, nurturing, emotional, caring, etc.). Ashcraft's point is that this Discourse did not develop accidentally, but was a consequence of the airline industry's need to convince a skeptical public that flying was safe; such safety could be conveyed partly by constructing two very different yet complementary gendered identities – one employee group to fly the plane in a professional manner, the other to take care of passengers and take their minds off where they were and how fast they were travelling!

Interestingly, Ashcraft shows that despite recent changes in a profession that historically has been predominantly white and male, many airline pilots still derive their identity and sense of professionalism from this gendered Discourse and have a hard time making sense of recent changes in the demographics of the airline pilot profession (though in many respects this demographic shift – that admitted more women and minority pilots – has been relatively small). In interviews with airline pilots this sense of threat to a previously secure identity becomes clear:

Pilot: You'd like to think of this job as something that's real, like you say, it kind of becomes something that take a lot of skill ... And then you see this, some little slight gal, you know, flying away, flying this big airplane ... You kind of think, shit! ... in fact, when I see these, sometimes when I see some of these gals ... I've thought, well, boy, you know, now if she can be a captain and do the job, hey, what do I do, what's the big, what have I been sweating all the time, you know?

Interviewer: And what do you mean, 'Boy is she's a captain what have I been sweating?' What do you mean?

Pilot:	Well it's just – that's the male-female thing for you. It's like, it's just like if you were going into combat, you know, and it's a big thing for you. You gotta well up the courage and determination to go fight that enemy, and you're thinking this could only be done by some hard, prepared guy. And then all of a sudden you see some woman walking out of the fray of the battle, holding a machine gun on her shoulder. And you realize, hey, how in the hell did you do that?
Interviewer:	And it hurts a little bit?
Pilot:	It does. It does hurt a tad. It pricks something.

(Ashcraft and Mumby, 2004a: 36)

In this interview fragment the male pilot makes a direct connection between a certain kind of dominant, virile masculinity and his professional identity. The dominant, gendered Discourse of the airline industry has functioned as a resource through which he has been able to construct a secure sense of (professional) self – a supremely competent, rational, father-figure who is responsible for the safety of hundreds of people. Women's entrance into this once exclusive domain challenges that (gendered) sense of security and leads him to question his very sense of professional worth. From a discourse perspective, what is particularly interesting about this example is that it illustrates not only how gendered identities draw on specific Discourses, but also – and perhaps more significantly – how fragile these identities are once alternative Discourses begin to challenge them. There is perhaps no better example of how identities are discursively constructed and contingent on specific historical conditions.

CONCLUSION

Let us end this chapter with some practical recommendations for readers who might be interested in doing their own research on organizational discourse. This is not intended to be a 'how to' account, but rather will hopefully provide a few 'sensitizing' suggestions that may help orient readers towards what to think about in examining organizational life from a discourse perspective.

1   Organizational discourse studies attempt to capture the complexities of the collective sense-making processes of organization members; how is it that people engage in organizing, and in the process make meaning? As such, discourse research needs to be sensitive to how members will make sense of organizational life in their own terms. In Clifford Geertz's famous (1983) phrase, what do organizations mean 'from the native's point of view?' The researcher's goal is not to impose his or her own predetermined meanings on organizations, but to explicate, through an analysis of members' discourse, what organizations – and the everyday behaviour that constitutes them – mean to their members.

2   At the same time (and this one of the difficult parts of analysing organizational discourse), explicating members' meanings does *not* mean simply accepting what organization members say. The best kind of discourse studies tread a fine line between respecting members' sense-making efforts and providing a critical analysis of the underlying assumptions upon which sense making is based. People are only able to make partial sense of the web of meanings that they inhabit (think about how, for example, as native speakers of a language we only have insight into a small

percentage of the rules we use to speak that language). The airline pilot in Ashcraft's study, for example, would probably not describe himself as sexist, but nevertheless was probably largely unaware of the gendered discourses that he routinely drew on to construct his identity; it was Ashcraft's task as a researcher to explicate the larger Discourses that enabled the pilot to construct his identity in a particular manner. The task of organizational discourse researchers, then, is to respect the sense-making practices of organization members, while simultaneously attempting to explicate the 'deep structures' of meaning that often elude those who work 'in the trenches' of organizational life.

3   There's no such thing as an 'objective', value-free analysis of organizations. Every analysis is a 'construction of a construction' – an effort to make sense out of other people's everyday sense-making efforts. Researchers approach organizations with various theoretical and methodological tools that enable a highlighting of certain organizational features but obscure others. Neo-Marxist analyses are attuned to class issues, but often neglect gender issues; feminist analyses privilege gender issues but sometimes forget about race and class issues. Furthermore, the methodological tools employed will shape the kind of data that will emerge. Holmes's approach, for example, is to carefully transcribe naturally occurring talk and submit it to an almost turn-by-turn analysis in order to capture the ways in which the conversational 'minutiae' of organizational life can provide insights into the larger processes of inclusion and exclusion. Ashcraft, on the other hand, transcribes talk that is gathered through interviews in order to gain access to how organization members make sense of themselves and their organization or profession when placed in a position of reflection by the interviewer. Both approaches are equally valid, but they unearth quite different aspects of the organizing process. In thinking about what kinds of methodological tools or theoretical perspectives to use, then, it is important to know what kinds of research questions you are interested in answering.

4   The most interesting organizational discourse research makes a concerted effort to connect the micro- and macro-levels of organizational life. That is, what do the everyday discursive efforts of organization members tell us about the larger, institutional structures of meaning and power? Similarly, how can discourse at the micro-level be analysed as drawing on and/or resisting those larger, institutional forms? The important point here is that discourse analyses should do more than simply remain at the 'local' level; interpreting social actors' talk and text involves situating it within the broader Discourses and institutions that provide the very 'conditions of possibility' within which discourse 'on the ground' makes sense. Organizations are everyday places of work and social activity, but they are also important sites of social stratification; research that loses sight of this connection also loses much of its analytic power.

5   Finally, really good organizational discourse studies are, we would argue, the enemies of commonsense views of the world. That is, while organizations are incredibly complex and often-contradictory systems of multiple meanings, they are usually treated as stable structures that exist independent from the people who inhabit them. Insightful discourse studies go beyond taken-for-granted, commonsense understandings and explore how apparently stable realities are social constructions that are often relatively precarious, and must be reproduced in the moment to moment of everyday life. Interesting discourse studies, then, contain an 'aha' moment in which they bring to light the complex workings of this social construction process, subtly altering our view of the world.

FURTHER READING

The following short list of further reading will provide you with both conceptual and empirical studies that will aid you in better understanding how scholars go about trying to understand how organizational reality is constructed discursively.

Alvesson, M. and Karreman, D. (2000b) 'Varieties of discourse: On the study of organizations through discourse analysis', *Human Relations,* 53: 1125–1149.
An excellent discussion of the distinction between 'Discourse' and 'dicourse' that we discuss in the chapter.

Collinson, D. (1988) '"Engineering humor": Masculinity, joking and conflict in shop-floor relations', *Organization Studies,* 9: 181–199.
A great example of how gendered workplace identities are constructed through workers' everyday discourses.

Grant, D., Hardy, C., Oswick, C., Phillips, N. and Putnam, L.L. (eds) (2004) *Handbook of Organizational Discourse.* London: Sage.
A 'state of the art' overview of theory and research in the study of organizational discourse; brings together scholars from the fields of management and organizational communication.

Holmes, J. (2006) *Gendered Talk at Work: Constructing Gender Identity Through Workplace Discourse.* Oxford: Blackwell.
Provides a close, micro-level, 'communities of practice' approach to everyday workplace talk, examining how gendered structures of inclusion and exclusion are created.

Mumby, D.K. (1987) 'The political function of narrative in organizations', *Communication Monographs,* 54: 113–127.
An early example of how organizational storytelling can be analyzed from a discourse approach.

ONLINE READING

The following articles are available at www.sagepub.co.uk/discoursestudies.

Ashcraft, K.L. (2005) 'Resistance through consent? Occupational identity, organizational form, and the maintenance of masculinity among commercial airline pilots'. *Management Communication Quarterly,* 19: 67–90.

Holmes, J. (2000) 'Politeness, power and provocation: how humour functions in the workplace'. *Discourse Studies,* 2: 159–185.

van Dijk, T.A. (1993) 'Principles of critical discourse analysis', *Discourse and Society,* 4: 249–283.

REFERENCES

Acker, J. (1990) 'Hierarchies, jobs, bodies: a theory of gendered organizations'. *Gender and Society, 4*: 139–58.
Althusser, L. (1971) *Lenin and Philosophy.* New York: Monthly Review.
Alvesson, M. and Deetz, S. (1996) 'Critical theory and postmodernism approaches to organizational studies'. In S. Clegg, C. Hardy and W. Nord (eds), *The Handbook of Organization Studies* (pp. 191–217). Thousand Oaks, CA: Sage.
Alvesson, M. and Karreman, D. (2000a) 'Taking the linguistic turn in organizational research: challenges, responses, consequences'. *Journal of Applied Behavioral Science,* 36: 136–58.
Alvesson, M. and Karreman, D. (2000b) 'Varieties of discourse: on the study of organizations through discourse analysis'. *Human Relations, 53*: 1125–49.
Ashcraft, K.L. (2004) 'Gender, discourse, and organizations: framing a shifting relationship'. In D. Grant, C. Hardy, C. Oswick, N. Phillips and L.L. Putnam (eds), *Handbook of Organizational Discourse.* Thousand Oaks, CA: Sage. pp. 275–98.
Ashcraft, K.L. (2005) 'Resistance through consent? Occupational identity, organizational form, and the maintenance of masculinity among commercial airline pilots'. *Management Communication Quarterly,* 19: 67–90.
Ashcraft, K.L. and Mumby, D.K. (2004a) 'Organizing a critical communicology of gender and work'. *International Journal of the Sociology of Language, 166*: 19–43.

Ashcraft, K.L. and Mumby, D.K. (2004b) *Reworking Gender: A Feminist Communicology of Organization*. Thousand Oaks, CA: Sage.

Bachrach, P. and Baratz, M. (1962) 'Two faces of power'. *American Political Science Review, 56*: 947–52.

Barker, J.R. (1993) 'Tightening the iron cage: concertive control in self-managing teams'. *Administrative Science Quarterly, 38*: 408–37.

Barker, J.R. (1999) *The Discipline of Teamwork: Participation and Concertive Control*. Thousand Oaks, CA: Sage.

Bell, E.L. and Forbes, L.C. (1994) 'Office folklore in the academic paperwork empire: the interstitial space of gendered (con) texts'. *Text and Performance Quarterly, 14*: 181–96.

Boje, D. (1991) 'The storytelling organization: a study of story performance in an office-supply firm'. *Administrative Science Quarterly, 36*: 106–26.

Brewis, J. (2001) 'Foucault, politics and organizations: (re)-constructing sexual harassment'. *Gender, Work and Organization, 8*: 37–60.

Brown, A.D. (1998) 'Narrative, politics and legitimacy in an IT implementation'. *Journal of Management Studies, 35*: 35–58.

Brummans, B. (2007) 'Death by document: tracing the agency of a text'. *Qualitative Inquiry, 13*: 711–27.

Burawoy, M. (1979) *Manufacturing Consent: Changes in the Labor Process under Monopoly Capitalism*. Chicago: University of Chicago Press.

Chia, R. (2000) 'Discourse analysis as organizational analysis'. *Organization, 7*: 513–18.

Clegg, S. (1989) *Frameworks of Power*. Newbury Park, CA: Sage.

Clegg, S. (1998) 'Foucault, power and organizations'. In A. McKinley and K. Starkey (eds), *Foucault, Management and Organization Theory: From Panopticon to Technologies of the Self* (pp. 29–48). London: Sage.

Collinson, D. (1988) '"Engineering humor": masculinity, joking and conflict in shop-floor relations'. *Organization Studies, 9*: 181–99.

Collinson, D. (2003) 'Identities and insecurities: selves at work'. *Organization, 10*: 527–47.

Cooren, F. (2000) *The Organizing Property of Communication*. Amsterdam: John Benjamins.

Cooren, F. and Taylor, J.R. (1997) 'Organization as an effect of mediation: redefining the link between organization and communication'. *Communication Theory, 7*: 219–60.

Dahl, R. (1957) 'The concept of power'. *Behavioral Science, 2*: 201–15.

Deetz, S. (2003) 'Reclaiming the legacy of the linguistic turn'. *Organization, 10*: 421–29.

Deetz, S. and Mumby, D.K. (1985). 'Metaphors, information, and power'. In B. Ruben (ed.), *Information and Behavior*, Vol. 1 (pp. 369–86). New Brunswick, NJ: Transaction.

Fairhurst, G. and Putnam, L.L. (2004) 'Organizations as discursive constructions'. *Communication Theory, 14*: 5–26.

Fleming, P. and Sewell, G. (2002) 'Looking for the good soldier, Svejk: alternative modalities of resistance in the contemporary workplace'. *Sociology, 36*: 857–73.

Fleming, P. and Spicer, A. (2003) 'Working at a cynical distance: implications for power, subjectivity, and resistance'. *Organization, 10*: 157–79.

Fleming, P. and Spicer, A. (2007) *Contesting the Corporation: Struggle, Power and Resistance in Organizations*. Cambridge: Cambridge University Press.

Foucault, M (1979) *Discipline and Punish: The Birth of the Prison* (A. Sheridan, Trans.). New York: Vintage.

Foucault, M. (1980) *The History of Sexuality: An Introduction* (R. Hurley, Trans. Vol. 1). New York: Vintage.

Geertz, C. (1983) *Local Knowledge: Further Essays in Interpretive Anthropology*. New York: Basic.

Giddens, A. (1979) *Central Problems in Social Theory: Action, Structure and Contradiction in Social Analysis*. Berkeley: University of California Press.

Gramsci, A. (1971) *Selections from the Prison Notebooks* (Q. Hoare and G.N. Smith, Trans.). New York: International.

Grant, D., Hardy, C., Oswick, C., Phillips, N. and Putnam, L.L. (eds) (2004) *Handbook of Organizational Discourse*. London: Sage.

Hatch, M.J. (1997) 'Irony and the social construction of contradiction in the humor of a management team'. *Organization Science, 8*: 275–88.

Helmer, J. (1993) 'Storytelling in the creation and maintenance of organizational tension and stratification'. *Southern Communication Journal, 59*: 34–44.

Holmer Nadesan, M. (1996) 'Organizational identity and space of action'. *Organization Studies, 17*: 49–81.

Holmer Nadesan, M. (1997) 'Constructing paper dolls: the discourse of personality testing in organizational practice'. *Communication Theory, 7*: 189–218.

Holmes, J. (2000) 'Politeness, power and provocation: how humour functions in the workplace'. *Discourse Studies, 2*: 159–85.

Holmes, J. (2006) *Gendered Talk at Work: Constructing Gender Identity Through Workplace Discourse*. Oxford: Blackwell.

Holmes, J. and Stubbe, M. (2003) *Power and Politeness in the Workplace: A Sociolinguistic Analysis of Talk at Work*. London: Longman.

Huspek, M. and Kendall, K. (1991) 'On withholding political voice: an analysis of the political vocabulary of a "nonpolitical" speech community'. *Quarterly Journal of Speech, 77*: 1–19.

Keenoy, T., Marchak, R.J., Oswick, C. and Grant, D. (2000) 'The discourses of organizing'. *Journal of Applied Behavioral Science, 36*: 133–35.

Knights, D. and Vurdubakis, T. (1994) 'Foucault, power, resistance and all that'. In J.M. Jermier, D. Knights and W.R. Nord (eds), *Resistance and Power in Organizations* (pp. 167–98). London: Routledge.

Linstead, S. (1985) 'Jokers wild: The importance of humour in the maintenance of organizational culture'. *Sociological Review, 33*: 741–67.

Lukes, S. (1974) *Power: A Radical View*. London: Macmillan.

Marx, K. (1967) *Capital* (S. Moore and E. Aveling, Trans.). New York: International.

McKinlay, A. and Starkey, K. (eds) (1998) *Foucault, Management, and Organization Theory: From Panopticon to Technologies of Self*. London: Sage.

Mumby, D.K. (1987) 'The political function of narrative in organizations'. *Communication Monographs, 54*: 113–27.

Mumby, D.K. (ed.) (1993) *Narrative and Social Control: Critical Perspectives*. Newbury Park, CA: Sage.

Mumby, D.K. (2001) 'Power and politics'. In F. Jablin and L.L. Putnam (eds), *The New Handbook of Organizational Communication: Advances in Theory, Research, and Methods* (pp. 585–623). Thousand Oaks, CA: Sage.

Mumby, D.K. and Stohl, C. (1992) 'Power and discourse in organization studies: absence and the dialectic of control'. *Discourse & Society, 2*: 313–32.

Murphy, A.G. (1998) 'Hidden transcripts of flight attendant resistance'. *Management Communication Quarterly, 11*: 499–535.

Murphy, A.G. (2003) 'The dialectical gaze: exploring the subject-object tension in the performances of women who strip'. *Journal of Contemporary Ethnography, 32*: 305–35.

Pacanowsky, M. and O'Donnell-Trujillo, N. (1982) 'Communication and organizational cultures'. *Western Journal of Speech Communication, 46*: 115–30.

Pfeffer, J. (1981) *Power in Organizations*. Cambridge, MA: Ballinger.

Putnam, L.L. (1983) 'The interpretive perspective: an alternative to functionalism'. In L.L. Putnam and M. Pacanowsky (eds), *Communication and Organizations: An Interpretive Approach* (pp. 31–54). Beverly Hills, CA: Sage.

Reed, M.I. (2000) 'The limits of discourse analysis in organizational analysis'. *Organization, 7*: 524–30.

Rhodes, C. and Westwood, R. (eds) (2007) *Humour, Organization, and Work*. London: Routledge.

Rosen, M. (1985) '"Breakfast at Spiro's": dramaturgy and dominance'. *Journal of Management, 11*(2): 31–48.

Rosen, M. (1988) '"You asked for it": Christmas at the bosses' expense'. *Journal of Management Studies, 25*: 463–480.

Smith, F.L. and Keyton, J. (2001) 'Organizational storytelling: metaphors for relational power and identity struggles'. *Management Communication Quarterly, 15*: 149–82.

Smith, R. and Eisenberg, E. (1987) 'Conflict at Disneyland: a root metaphor analysis'. *Communication Monographs, 54*: 367–80.

Sotirin, P. and Gottfried, H. (1999) 'The ambivalent dynamics of secretarial, "bitching": control, resistance, and the construction of identity'. *Organization, 6*: 57–80.

Taylor, J.R., Cooren, F., Giroux, N. and Robichaud, D. (1996) 'The communicational basis of organization: between the conversation and the text'. *Communication Theory, 6*: 1–39.

Taylor, J.R. and Van Every, E.J. (2000) *The Emergent Organization: Communication as its Site and Surface*. Mahwah, NJ: Lawrence Erlbaum.

Taylor, P. and Bain, P. (2003) '"Subterranean worksick blues": humour as subversion in two call centres'. *Organization Studies*, *24*: 1487–509.

Tompkins, P.K. and Cheney, G. (1985). 'Communication and unobtrusive control in contemporary organizations'. In R.D. McPhee and P.K. Tompkins (eds), *Organizational Communication: Traditional Themes and New Directions* (pp. 179–210). Beverly Hills, CA: Sage.

Trethewey, A. (1997) 'Resistance, identity, and empowerment: a postmodern feminist analysis of clients in a human service organization'. *Communication Monographs*, *64*: 281–301.

Trethewey, A. (2001) 'Reproducing and resisting the master narrative of decline: midlife professional women's experiences of aging'. *Management Communication Quarterly*, *15*: 183–226.

van Dijk, T.A. (1993) 'Principles of critical discourse analysis'. *Discourse and Society*, *4*: 249–83.

West, C. and Zimmerman, D. (1987) 'Doing gender'. *Gender and Society*, *1*: 125–51.

Witten, M. (1993) 'Narrative and the culture of obedience at the workplace'. In D.K. Mumby (ed.), *Narrative and Social Control: Critical Perspectives* (pp. 97–118). Newbury Park, CA: Sage.

FIFTEEN

Discourse and Politics

Paul Chilton and Christina Schäffner

INTRODUCTION

Some philosophers – and here Descartes is the best known – have defined humans as essentially linguistic animals. Aristotle, on the other hand, famously defined humans as political animals. No doubt both definitions contain a germ of truth. What political discourse analysts would probably claim, if they were to think philosophically, would be that the one definition necessarily involves the other. It is surely the case that politics cannot be conducted without language, and it is also probably the case that the use of language in the constitution of social groups leads to what we would call 'politics' in a broad sense.

Although the study of language has never been central to the academic disciplines concerned with politics, some political philosophers have from time to time made clear their awareness of the question. In the disciplines concerned with language, it is worth noting that the study of rhetoric – i.e., the art of verbal persuasion – was thought of by Greek and Roman writers as a sort of 'political science'. In the Greek polis and in the Roman empire the rhetorical tradition played a part in the training of orators who fulfilled various important public functions, including political functions, and to a certain extent provided an apparatus for the critical observation of verbal political behaviour.

In the twenty-first century the massive expansion of print and electronic media has meant that people are now exposed to verbal messages of many kinds, a large proportion of which can be thought of as political in nature, though as we shall note below, what exactly is 'political' is a matter for interpretation. The increased mediation of political messages has important implications. One is that the opportunities for the reception, interpretation and critique of political texts and talk have vastly increased, and are growing even more as a result of the Internet expansion (for example, the opportunities offered by blogs and Twitter). Another is that the need for awareness and critical evaluations has correspondingly increased. It might be argued that the ability to deal critically with political discourse is natural and need not be studied in depth by academics or anyone else. Against such a view two arguments can be made. The first applies to all criticism of in-depth studies of human behaviour. Human learning, for instance, is natural in some sense of the term, but this does not preclude the interest and utility of psychological studies of cognition or the education process. Similarly, political discourse is a complex form of human activity which deserves to be studied in its own right. The second kind of argument is of an ethical nature. Many commentators, and indeed many ordinary people in everyday life, have the feeling that politicians and political institutions are sustained by 'persuasive' or 'manipulative' uses of language of which the public are only half-aware. Such a view was in fact upheld by some of the early rhetors – Isocrates, Plato, Cicero, for example – who suspected that public speakers were able to hoodwink citizens by adopting specious talk. In the twentieth century the notion of total linguistic manipulation was developed into the nightmare political discourse that was fictionalized in Orwell's novel *Nineteen Eighty-Four* (Orwell, 1949). Together, these two rationales for Political Discourse Analysis (PDA) contribute not only to intellectual curiosity but also to the concerns of all political animals.

POLITICS AND POLITICAL DISCOURSE

Political science and the philosophy of language

In political philosophy the meaning of words has traditionally raised problems and caused anxieties. For instance, questions about the meaning of 'democracy', 'equality', 'freedom', and the like, have been recurrent subjects of debate. Earlier studies assumed that there were 'true' meanings for such terms (Sir George Lewis, 1898), and this tendency has been strong throughout most of the twentieth century. Many 'political scientists', influenced by logical positivism and the Vienna Circle, desired to rid political language of confusion and ambiguity. Interestingly, a similar view was held also in the seventeenth century by Thomas Hobbes, who can be viewed as the founder of modern political science. In the last third of the twentieth century a more relativistic approach emerged. Sartori (1984) has a more flexible approach, while the notion that political concepts may be relative to the 'language' of the polity, and thus 'contestable', comes into clear focus in Gallie (1956), Connolly (1974), Lukes (1975), and Ball et al. (1989). This development was also influenced by the later Wittgenstein (1953) and the work of Austin (1962) and Searle (1969), as well as with an increasing recognition that language was in fact a form of action.

Post-structuralism and deconstruction

In the 1980s Anglo-Saxon departments of politics and international relations were influenced by 'continental' philosophy. A key figure then was the French social philosopher, Michel Foucault, who worked with a notion of 'discourse', which, though it included language practices, did not provide precise linguistic descriptions. The work of Jacques Derrida fostered a notion of 'deconstruction', which pushed relativist interpretations still further. While 'text' was crucial to Derrida, he did not use the theoretical framework of linguistics. There are many books and articles in the deconstructionist vein, but Shapiro (1981; 1984) and der Derian and Shapiro (1989) illustrate the evolution of approaches. What is important is that many political 'scientists' have moved towards the view that both the terms of political debate and political processes themselves are constituted and communicated through text and talk, a development which is also referred to as the 'linguistic turn' in political sciences.

Social-psychological approaches

Not entirely incompatible with the above developments, approaches deriving from social psychology have included both qualitative and quantitative methods that aimed to demonstrate the non-rational and non-explicit aspects of political behaviour. Harold Lasswell, influenced by Sapir's anthropological linguistics, held a view of language, which, together with the view that the 'science' of politics was the 'science of power', led him to quantitative investigations of the political 'functions' of language. He also distinguished analytically between *syntax*, *style* and *semantics*, concentrating on the latter, which he defined in terms of political slogans and symbols (Lasswell et al., 1949). Another important approach has been the study of political myths, and the symbolic and ritual dimension of political institutions (Edelman, 1964; 1971).

In the 1960s and 1970s some political scientists sought quantifiable empirical accounts of political verbal behaviours. They thought of communication as a simple encoding-decoding process (see, for example, Graber, 1976). A quantitative semantic approach has also been attempted in the case of political ideologies and international conflict (Leites, 1963; Osgood, 1971; Tetlock, 1985). Though such studies use the psychologist's rather than the linguist's methods, they do seek a descriptive precision that is absent in approaches influenced by the philosophical perspective.

LINGUISTICS AND POLITICAL DISCOURSE

Linguists have shared some of the above perspectives – for instance, the critical perspective and the general epistemological stance according to which political realities are constructed in and through discourse. Some, however, would insist on political objectivity (Wilson, 1990).

Where linguists most obviously differ from their colleagues in departments of politics is in the way their research is informed by theories and methods derived from linguistics. The variety of approaches they have utilized may indeed appear quite bewildering. Furthermore, they have been interested in an extraordinary variety of political issues and phenomena. In order to convey some of this variety, we consider three broad 'literatures' in PDA, which are discourses in their own right and are related, in part at least, to the historical specificities of particular countries and cultures.

Country- and region-based approaches

French approaches

What is noteworthy about the 'French school' is its combination of political scientists, political philosophers (principally *marxisants*), and a characteristically French brand of linguistics. Two main methodological tendencies are apparent.

The first is 'political lexicometry', a computer-aided statistical approach to the political lexicon, developed by the 'Laboratoire Lexicométrie et textes politiques', founded in 1967 and based at the Ecole Normale Superieure at Saint-Cloud. The method establishes a corpus (e.g. texts produced by the French Communist Party) consisting of separate texts and makes comparisons on the basis of relative frequencies. Broadly speaking, such a methodology can only be related to macro-sociological and historical questions of political discourse. For example, one study shows how the relative frequency of the words *travailleur* and *salarié* varies significantly between French trades unions, reflecting different political ideologies, and also how the frequency changes over time (the early 1970s to the late 1980s), and also reflecting chronological shifts in political ideologies (Groupe de Saint-Cloud 1982; Bonnafous and Tournier, 1995). As the Saint-Cloud group themselves acknowledge, quantitative studies provide only the raw data for interpretive political analysis.

The second methodological tendency amongst political discourse analysts, overlapping with the Saint-Cloud group, is diverse. One strand was influenced by Althusser's (1970) Marxist analysis of society emphasizing the notion of the 'state apparatus' (Pêcheux, 1975; 1990). This is congenial to a discourse approach that sees the political phenomenon of the state as involving a complex set of discourses creating political 'subjects'. Another guiding notion was 'discourse formation', which was taken from Foucault (1971). These abstract notions, however, mesh with methods of detailed linguistic analysis. Some researchers investigate detailed rhetorical patterns, for example in the presidential campaigns of 1988 and 1995 (Groupe de Saint-Cloud, 1995). The influence of Anglo-Saxon pragmatics (speech acts, conversational implicature, relevance) is also prominent, alongside that of the French linguist Benveniste (1966/1974), whose work on *énonciation* (utterance or discourse) focused on deictic phenomena. This framework enables a sophisticated analyst like Achard, who retains some of the general Althusserian framework, to produce detailed accounts of the political functioning of a very wide range of text-types (Achard, 1995).

The lexicometric approach has established itself among researchers into political discourse, drawing on and developing corpus-linguistics. There is a network (known as Céditec) of collaborating political discourse analysts, using quantitative methods, in the Paris universities in Lyon, Franche-Comté, Nice and elsewhere. A number of studies that have emerged from this strand have focused on lexical frequency distributions as an index of political cleavages, while others have examined the lexical idiosyncracies of political leaders and social issues such as racism (amongst other scholars, see Mayaffre, 2000; 2004). An on-line database known as Textopol is maintained under the direction of Pierre Fiala, who has long contributed quantitative and qualitative research to political discourse studies (see for example, Fiala and Ebel, 1983; Fiala, 1994).

More qualitative approaches have fruitfully drawn on rhetoric, recontextualizing the classical tradition within contemporary human sciences, and focusing on techniques of persuasion, with especially useful perspectives on *ethos*, the self-presentation of political speakers and *pathos*, the appeal to the public's emotions (Amossy, 2000; Chareaudeau, 2005). There are also works seeking to understand political discourse as a general human phenomenon, such as that by Le Bart (1998), which draw on an array of research into discourse, including lexicometric approaches, and distinguish between invariant or at least persistent structures and contingent strategic discursive practices. The journal *Mots: Les langages du politique* has made available a wide range of methodological approaches relating to an equally wide range of political domains, both general and conjunctural. A characteristic of the French approach is an element of activist intervention in the political process in France, a feature it shares with some scholars associated with anglophone CDA (Critical Discourse Analysis).

German approaches

Analysis of political language, political texts and political vocabulary in Germany has largely been motivated by specifically German political interests and issues, particularly the historical past of fascism and the subsequent political division into two German states. The language of fascism and neo-Nazi discourse have also been analysed by Austrian researchers, and some of their work will therefore be included in this section as well.

In studies of the language of fascism, the focus was originally on words, i.e. on specific meanings that they had developed and their use or misuse (see, for example, Klemperer, 1975). More recently, it has been argued that the language of the Third Reich cannot be defined by the linguistic forms but only by their functions. National-socialist language is treated as a social phenomenon, characterized by specific discursive practices (see, for example, Ehlich, 1989; for a comprehensive survey of the variety of approaches, cf. Sauer, 1995). Within the framework of a discursive-historical analysis, persistent argumentation patterns (e.g., allusions, denial, mitigation) can be seen, for instance, in the discourse of Austrian politicians speaking about the Nazi past (for example, Wodak, 1989; Wodak and Menz, 1990).

The development from a word-centred linguistic-semantic analysis to a text- and action-oriented communicative analysis is also evident in studies on the language (use) of the two

German states. In order to compare the semantic structure of the political vocabulary in East and West Germany, the concepts of *Ideologiegebundenheit* (the phenomenon of being ideology-bound)' and *ideologische Polysemie* (ideological polysemy) were introduced (Dieckmann, 1969; 1981; Schmidt, 1969) and dominated much of the research in the 1960s and 1970s.

One focus of research has been a critical reflection on the strategic use of political keywords for achieving specific political aims. Under the headings of 'semantic battles' and 'annexation of concepts', strategic operations with words have been analysed: for instance, 'hijacking' terms from political opponents in order to give them a new meaning or linking a basic value (such as 'solidarity', 'freedom') to a political party in such a way that ultimately the party will be identified with that value (cf. Burkhardt et al., 1989; Klein, 1989; Liedtke et al., 1991).

Some researchers, influenced by Anglo-Saxon pragmatics, conversation analysis, and media studies, have studied the organizational principles of linguistic actions (such as turn-taking strategies, schema-orientation, speech acts, conversational implicatures) occurring, for example, in interviews with politicians, political speeches and TV debates (Sucharowski, 1985; Holly, 1990; Grewenig, 1993; Schäffner and Porsch, 1993). Heringer (1990) and Krebs (1993) link the structures of political speech to the effects this had on audiences.

The process of political transformation in East Germany in 1989–1990 and the subsequent German unification offered vast scope for political discourse analysis. A wide spectrum of (mainly pragmatic, sociolinguistic, cognitive linguistic) approaches were applied to study, for example, the changing political lexicon, ritualistic discourse in the former German Democratic Republic, changes in text types and discursive strategies, and the discursive interaction between East and West Germans (see, for example, Burkhardt and Fritzsche, 1992; Lerchner, 1992; Reiher and Läzer, 1993; Roth and Wienen, 2008).

From the mid-1990s onwards, research into language and politics in both Germany and Austria has focused on the wider socio-historical, ideological and institutional contexts in which text and talk are being produced and received. Among the topics addressed are the historical changes in political communication (Jarren et al., 1998; Diekmannshenke and Meißner, 2001), features of parliamentary discourse (Dörner and Vogt, 1995; Burkhardt and Pape, 2000), the language and oratory of politicians (Patzelt, 1995; Holly, 1996), and the discursive construction of identities (Distelberger et al., 2009). Foucault's concept of discourse is often the basis for research which aims to reveal and/or reconstruct the power dimensions in texts related to racism, right-wing extremism, xenophobia, and migration (Matouschek et al., 1995; Pörksen, 2000; Jaeger and Halm, 2007; Krzyzanowski and Wodak, 2008; Wodak and Krzyżanowski, 2008). Methodologically, the various strands of critical discourse analysis dominate (i.e., socio-cognitive, discursive-historical, socio-semiotic, systemic-functional approaches), and are increasingly accompanied by corpus linguistics (Musolff, 2004). Another characteristic feature of recent research is the growing engagement of discourse analysts in public debates, as evidenced in the topics of the conferences of the German Association for the Study of the Language in Politics (*Arbeitsgemeinschaft*

Sprache in der Politik e.V.) which include 'Language and Credibility: The Linguistics of Political Affairs', 'Immigration and Otherness in Public Discourse', 'Globalisation: Media, Language, Politics', and 'Language in the Electioneering Campaigns' (see also Dörner and Vogt, 2002; Burkhardt and Pape, 2003).

Anglophone approaches

In this section we include not only British, American and Australian work, but also other work that has been disseminated in English, especially that which originates from the Netherlands and Belgium.

Orwell's informal critical stance toward political discourse was recognized by some British linguists (Fowler, Kress, Hodge, Fairclough), who sought to apply insights from modern linguistics. Following the linguistic trends of the times, transformational-generative models were influential and provided means of describing certain syntactic forms that had politically pragmatic implications (Fowler et al., 1979). More important, however, in the British and Australian approaches was the 'functional' linguistics of Halliday (1973). This framework made it possible to link linguistic form to social, and hence also to political, activity. But the tools of Anglophone political discourse analysis have been essentially eclectic, drawing particularly on pragmatics, especially the theory of speech acts, the implicit meaning of various types (Richardson, 1985; Wilson, 1990; 1991; Blommaert and Verschueren, 1991; 1993), cognitive linguistics (Chilton, 1985a), Brown and Levinson's (1987) 'politeness phenomena' (Chilton, 1990), conversation analysis (Atkinson, 1984), and European text analysis as developed by van Dijk (1980; 1985). Van Dijk himself applies a range of analytic methods, including textual, pragmatic, ethnomethodological and cognitive approaches, to political discourse and to the critique of racist discourse in the media and other domains (see van Dijk 1987; 1989; 1994; 1995; 1997; 2002; 2005). Fairclough's most recent research analyses the interrelationship between social structures, social events, social practices and discourse. Discourse is identified as an element of both social events and social practices, and changes in discourse as part of social change involve a recontextualization of discourses. He analyses such processes for example, with reference to political parties and to globalization (Fairclough, 2000; 2006; 2007).

In the United States Chomsky's critique of American foreign policy has been trenchant and controversial. Although he has referred to what are essentially discourse processes, such as 'the manufacture of consent' and 'propaganda', he has not sought to apply linguistic theory in order to analyse them (see, for example, Chomsky, 1988a; 1988b). Chomsky's revolutionary contribution to the discipline of linguistics has no *direct* application to the study of discourse or politics. Those American scholars who have sought to apply linguistic analysis to political discourse have lacked the Marxist perspective of some of the more radical European researchers, and their work often appears to be predicated on a form of linguistic idealism. Bolinger (1980) examines a range of linguistic devices from the point of view of their potential distorting or manipulative effects, a standpoint shared by American rhetorical criticism. Developments in semantic theory have provided insights into an aspect of political discourse from the time of Hobbes onwards – namely the disturbing role played by metaphor. Deploying Conceptual Metaphor Theory, Chilton and Lakoff (1995), for example, examine foreign policy discourse, while Lakoff (1996) examines the metaphorical basis of the different systems of 'morality' assumed by 'conservatives' and 'liberals' in American political culture. In this vein, a number of articles and books have also followed (Lakoff, 2004; 2008). Some of these have entered the campaigning arena, in response to contemporary events, such as presidential campaigns, the events of 11 September 2001, and the 2003 invasion of Iraq. More wide-ranging applications of metaphor theory in the realm of politics are to be found in Goatly (2007) and the emerging group of 'critical metaphor' analysts.

Chilton (2004), while still within a cognitive framework, introduces several analytical perspectives, on several domains of political discourse, including broadcast political interviews, parliamentary debates, elite influence on criminal racist talk, the phenomenon of religion-politics interdiscursivity, and the like. The study of parliamentary discourse has become a focus of interest (Bayley, 2004), as has analysis of the formal rhetoric of political speeches (see Schäffner, 1997; Ensink and Sauer, 2003)

It has, however, become clear that the language of politics involves dimensions not generally apparent or noticed in its public face. Wodak (2009) represents a landmark in this respect, extending the analytical perspectives for future researchers. On the one hand, these new perspectives focus on the everyday linguistic and non-linguistic discourse of both the 'backstage' and the 'frontstage' activities of politicians within their institutional environment. On the other hand, the new perspectives bring to the fore the notion of 'performance' in understanding politics, including the mediatization and indeed fictionalization of political life.

Since the first version of this chapter was published in 1997, the developments in the analysis of political discourse can be summarized as follows. 1) There is an increased focus on the topic as reflected in a growth of publications. Particularly noteworthy are new book series such as *Discourse Approaches to Politics, Society and Culture*, *Sprache-Politik-Gesellschaft* (Language–Politics–Society) and the new *Journal of Language and Politics*. 2) There are various conferences devoted primarily to the analysis of political discourse, such as the Political Linguistics conferences in Poland, and also conferences such as the Critical Approaches to Discourse Analysis Across Disciplines series (CADAAD) which include a significant amount of papers devoted to political discourse. 3) We can also notice a widening of the research perspectives as well as the analytical methods applied. We have already mentioned the application of Corpus Linguistics to political discourse, especially in combination with metaphor analysis (Musolff, 2004; Charteris-Black, 2004; 2005; Semino, 2008). 4) There is also increasing interest in political discourse in disciplines such as media studies and journalism (Bhatia, 2006; Fetzer and Lauerbach, 2007) and in translation studies (Inghilleri, 2005; Schäffner, 2004; 2007). 5) Researchers are more and more widespread geographically (to mention only the work of Cap in Poland, 2002; 2006; or Lu, 1999, in China), with their analyses not limited to just their own national contexts but also including comparative aspects and/or the analysis of supra-national politics (for the European Union, see for example Muntigl et al., 2000; Kryzyzanowski and Oberhuber, 2007; Millar and Wilson, 2007).

THE LINGUISTIC ANALYSIS OF POLITICAL DISCOURSE

There are many ways to study political discourse, ranging from classical rhetoric and its successors to the various approaches briefly outlined above in the previous section. The approach we offer in this chapter is by no means the only one that can be used and developed.

Political texts and strategic functions

The task of political discourse analysis is to relate the fine grain of linguistic behaviour to what we understand by 'politics' or 'political behaviour'. There are two problems here that might strike the reader immediately: 1) what is 'political' depends on the standpoint of the commentator; 2) the multiplicity of acts that are performed through language (that is, discourse), can be interpreted as serving many different purposes – not only political, but also heuristic, ludic, informative, etc. Both these problems could be the subject of a lengthy discussion, but here we have to limit ourselves to the following points.

With regard to the first problem, we will define as potentially 'political' those actions (linguistic or other) which involve power, or its inverse, resistance. Of course 'power' is a concept that has no accepted definition amongst political theorists, and we shall not attempt to resolve the matter here.

With regard to the second problem, we would link political situations and processes to discourse types and levels of discourse organization by way of an intermediate level, which we call strategic functions. The notion of *strategic functions* enables analysts of text and talk to focus on details that contribute to the phenomena which people intuitively understand as 'political', rather than on other functions such as the informational, the ludic, etc.

The following strategic functions[1] are proposed for discussion, and are certainly not definitive:

- *Coercion and resistance* Clear examples are speech acts backed by sanctions (legal and physical): commands, laws, edicts, etc. Less obvious forms of coerced behaviour consist of speech roles which people will find difficult to evade or may not even notice, such as spontaneously giving answers to questions, responding to requests, etc. Political actors will also often act coercively through discourse in setting agendas, selecting topics in conversation, positioning the self and others in specific relationships, and making assumptions about realities that hearers are obliged to at least temporarily accept in order to process the text or talk. Power can also be exercised through controlling others' use of language – that is, through various kinds and degrees of censorship and access control.

---

[1]In the first version of this chapter (Chilton and Schäffner, 1997) we distinguished four strategic functions. Chilton (2004) reduces these to three and this is the proposal followed here. For functions cf. Jakobson (1960), Halliday (1973); for 'strategic' cf. Habermas (1979; 1981). It is important to emphasize that we are not suggesting that 'legitimization' and the other 'functions' are built into a universal linguistic structure (cf. Chilton, 2004: 45).

Many of the discourse strategies used by the powerful for coercion may be counter-deployed by those who regard themselves as opposing power. However, there may be specific forms of discourse characteristic of the relatively powerless. Such forms include media (*samizdat* under the Soviet empire, *graffiti* amongst marginalized ethnic groups, posters, etc.) and specific linguistic structures (such as slogans, chants, petitions, appeals, rallies, etc.).

- *Legitimization and delegitimization*   Political actors, whether individuals or groups, cannot act by physical force alone – except in the extreme case, where it is questionable that one is still in the realm of what is understood by 'politics'. This legitimization function is closely linked to *coercion*, because it establishes the right to be obeyed, that is, 'legitimacy'. Why do people obey regimes that are very different in their policies? Reasons for being obeyed have to be communicated linguistically, whether by overt statement or by implication. The techniques used include arguments about voters' wants, general ideological principles, charismatic leadership projection, boasting about performance, and positive self-presentation.

  Delegitimization is the essential counterpart: others (foreigners, 'enemies within', institutional opposition, unofficial opposition) have to be presented negatively, and techniques here include the use of ideas of difference and boundaries, and speech acts of blaming, accusing, insulting, etc.

- *Representation and misrepresentation*   Political control involves the control of information, which is by definition a matter of discourse control. It may be quantitative or qualitative. Secrecy is the strategy of preventing people receiving information; it is the inverse of censorship, which is preventing people *giving* information. In another mode of misrepresentation, information may be given, but be quantitatively inadequate to the needs or interests of hearers ('being economical with the truth', as one British politician once put it). Qualitative misrepresentation is simply lying, in its most extreme manifestation, but includes various kinds of verbal evasion and denial ('I am not opposed to benefits, but ...'), or the omission of a reference to actors. Euphemism has the cognitive effect of conceptually 'blurring' or 'defocusing' unwanted referents, be they objects or actions. Implicit meanings of various types also constitute a means of diverting attention from troublesome referents.

The three strategic functions listed above are closely related to functions found throughout social life and not simply in 'politics'. However, to look at linguistic behaviour and other kinds of communicative behaviour in terms of the three strategic functions is to view those behaviours politically, to politicize them. Diverse areas of social life have been rendered political in this fashion. For example, for people in many societies up until relatively recently it had appeared natural (not political) to assume that 'foreigners', women, homosexuals, disabled people were inferior or sick as the case may be. Such groups, however, have come to view themselves and to be viewed by others politically. Such politicization has eroded the boundaries between institutional and non-institutional politics.

The three functions can be viewed as interpretive or productive, and in different ways. That is, they can be treated as strategies of political interpretation – in the sense that they can be so used by an analyst, or in the sense that an analyst can attribute such functions, as a hypothesis, to the (unconscious) interpretive strategies of hearers. Alternatively, they can be regarded as productive, in the sense that the analyst can attribute them, again as a hypothesis, to the strategies used by speakers in the production of coherent discourse in a given society.

How are the strategies enacted by choice of language? Such a question can only be answered by a close participatory analysis of the linguistic detail. It is important to remember that we are not concerned with text structure, syntax and lexis for their own sake, but only in so far as they are the means by which speakers and hearers will interactively produce complex and diverse meanings. This implies that we are interested in wordings and phrasings because they can be given meanings that are consistent with our background knowledges and values, given the Anglophone political culture that we as authors and you as reader inhabit. It also means that political discourse analysis, despite the importance of precise and rigorous linguistic description, is an activity in which the analyst is engaged.

Granted that what is 'political' depends on the participants, societies generally will have institutionalized discourses communicated through a cluster of different types of texts and forms of talk. Such a cluster can be seen from two perspectives: a first group comprises texts that discuss the political ideas, beliefs, and practices of a society or some part of it (text producers need not be politicians only). Strictly speaking, this is 'metapolitical discourse'. And a second group consists of texts that are crucial in giving rise to – or, to use the political term, constituting – a (more or less coherent) political or ideological community or group, or party. Such texts may function to constitute and maintain the institutions of an entire polity, or they may operate (also) in some part of the whole, say a political party, or indeed at an individual level. Within this second group one may draw finer distinctions: inner-state (domestic) discourse and inter-state (foreign policy and diplomacy) discourse; internal-political discourse (politicians talking, planning, deciding, etc. among themselves) and external-political (politicians communicating with the public). Different forms of text and talk correspond to these different discourse distinctions.

Linguistic levels

In linking the strategic functions to the linguistic analysis of texts and talk, all levels and aspects of language need to be borne in mind. An analyst of political discourse needs to refer to:

- *pragmatics* (interaction amongst speakers and hearers);
- *semantics* (meaning, structure of lexicon);
- *syntax* (the internal organization of sentences).[2]

The task that political discourse analysis sets itself is to relate the detailed linguistic choices at these levels to the three categories of political interpretation which we have referred to as 'strategic functions'.

There are two paths for investigating the political functioning of linguistic choices. First, one can work from the general linguistic levels, asking the general question of what strategic functions are typically fulfilled by, for example, falling intonation, passive syntax, lexical antonyms, or presupposed meanings in discourse? Such a question draws on one's knowledge of the language (and political culture), but can also be the goal of empirical

---

[2]Phonetics and phonology are excluded for reasons of space, although in political discourse analysis it is important in general to consider a) the phonetic resources for oratorical delivery (pauses, stress, volume, pitch) and b) the regional and class associations of particular accents, reproducing social and geographical structures of the polity.

investigation (informed of course by knowledge of the language and culture) of instances of texts and talk.

Second, one may work from texts and transcriptions, using one's understanding of the language and political culture to make clear the links between linguistic choices and strategic functions. This corresponds simply to the question that any citizen under ideal conditions of time and reflective capability might ask: 'Why has X chosen (or why is X obliged) to use such-and-such a pronunciation/intonation/wording/phrasing/text-type rather than some other possible one?'

ANALYSING POLITICAL TEXT AND TALK: AN EXAMPLE

In this section we illustrate some selected aspects of the analysis of a transcribed text, namely a speech by the former British Prime Minister John Major. In analysing this text we work from the fine linguistic detail, and ask: 'In which ways can the linguistic choices of the speaker be interpreted as functioning in a politically strategic manner, given the wider political culture and the narrower political context?' Not all relevant phenomena can be commented on directly here, and in particular the important phenomenon of indirectness in meaning is referred to only in passing.

The speech was delivered at the 11th Conservative Party Conference in Bournemouth, England, on 14 October 1994.[3] These annual party conferences are internal events, their main addressees thus UK nationals, and specifically loyal party members. The Conservative conference took place shortly after that of the Labour Party under Labour's new reforming leader, Tony Blair. The Labour Party had moved ideologically towards the political right during the preceding decade, in terms of its economic and social policy, as evidenced in such measures as their acceptance of the privatization of public industries and the restriction of the trade unions within the Labour Party conference itself. The ideological convergence of western political parties had become marked following the collapse of communist regimes and socialist ideologies in the late 1980s and early 1990s. The Tory conference here can be seen as a reaction to this changed wider context, and in the narrower context as a turn in the ongoing 'macroconversation' of domestic politics.

Pragmatics

Language as action
Conversation Analysis (CA) has shown the subtlety of the management of talk. Participants have turns and variable rights to speak and intervene, depending on the genre and their own status. Such rights or duties to speak or to listen, and the way these are assigned, imposed or claimed in face-to-face interaction, suggest a political dimension in everyday linguistic

---

[3]The transcription used here is the offical text issued by the Conservative Party News Department of the Conservative Central Office (the speech is available at http://www.totalpolitics.com/speeches/speech.php?id=254).

encounters. And what is more usually thought of as 'political' can be understood in such terms also – that is, as the distribution of rights and duties to speak or listen, give orders or obey, make laws or be law-abiding, make broadcasts or be an audience, etc. More generally, democracies and totalitarian regimes can be thought of in terms of their characteristic means of the control of discourse. From city states to large modern states the organization of the political 'conversation' defines the nature of the polity.

The linguistic details of talk can be seen to be far from accidental, but rather delicately structured and functional in the management of social, and thus potentially political, relationships. Given a particular setting or purpose, one turn will have an unmarked and marked, or 'preferred' and 'dispreferred', response. Speech acts (offers, orders, admissions, etc.), capable of being understood as threatening to one or the other of the participants ('face-threatening acts'), will be mitigated or disguised in various linguistic ways, including euphemisms, justifications ('accounts'), an appeal to common interests, to authority, and so forth. Even when a stretch of talk or text is apparently monologic, it will usually involve an implicit dialogic organization, reflecting oppositional discourses in the surrounding political culture.[4]

The notion of speech acts is central to political discourse analysis, because it dissolves the everyday notion that language and action are separate. Among many attempts at classifying speech acts, Searle usefully distinguished the following, which can be seen to have direct relevance to political discourse: *representatives* (truth claims), *directives* (commands, requests), *commissives* (promises, threats), *expressives* (praising, blaming), and *declaratives* (proclaiming a constitution, announcing an election, declaring war). Speech acts can only be performed under certain conditions, what Austin (1962) and Searle (1969) called 'felicity conditions'. In fact, such 'conditions' emerge from institutional arrangements and are open-ended. Politically relevant speech acts may include complex conditions such as the power or status of the speaker, the institutional location, the holding of an election, and the style of language used, as well as many other factors.

Neither conversational dialogue nor speech acts will occur without the participants being assigned particular speaking and hearing roles, which may involve a social and political 'role', or 'place', or 'position', in a broader sense. You may be 'positioned' as someone who speaks, gives orders, gives advice, or gives the 'facts'; or you may be 'positioned' as someone who listens, takes orders, takes advice, or accepts the 'facts'. Analysts of political discourse frequently find that pronouns, and the meanings associated with them, give a kind of map of the socio-political relationships implicit in a discourse.[5]

The leader and other subjects

The speaker in our sample text, John Major, engages in (and reproduces) a genre which constitutes very particular relationships that are not only linguistic but also social and political. This works in two ways: on the one hand, there is the set of relationships between

[4]This point was made by Volosinov (1973).

[5]Cf. Althusser's (1970) notion of 'interpellation of the subject'.

addresser, addressees, and third-party 'overhearers' or observers; and on the other hand, there is the set of political actors in his political universe, and their inter-relationships, referred to or presupposed by the speaker, though not necessarily addressed. These relationships are most obviously mediated by pronouns, which delineate a social or political 'space' in which people and groups will have a 'position'.

Amongst the resources of English it is the pronouns *I, you, we, they* (and their variants) that have a special function in producing a social and political 'space' in which the speaker, the audience, and others are 'positioned'. Simple frequency of occurrence of the pronouns *I* (*me, my*) and *we* (*our*) can be indicative: 112 occurrences of *I*, 35 of *my/me*, 125 of *we*, 45 of *our*.

The primary addressees are the delegates present at the conference: 'I can tell the Conference this', 'I'll tell you why'. What is the function of such apparently redundant formulae? Apart from simply preparing hearers to focus on a particular stretch of talk, they simultaneously define the speaker as an authoritative source of information or knowledge and define the (potentially critical) audiences as subordinate, uninformed and unknowledgeable ('I wonder how many of you know exactly how many ... hospital projects have been built ... I have the latest bulletin', 'I know', 'I understand'). They *coerce* the hearers into certain communication roles and political roles, and they *legitimate*, or rather, presuppose the legitimacy of, the speaker. Of course, there are also addressees, members of the Party, who would be critical (especially with regard to the debate on Europe), and who would need to be persuaded and convinced of the firmness of the leader. Hence the need for prefatory expressions, and the aggressive perlocutory effect these may have.

In establishing the leader-led, speaker-spoken to, and teacher-taught relationships, Major's text presents him in certain roles, by making 'I' the subject of particular verbs. These verbs belong to semantic fields associated with speaking, feeling, and action. That is, they position Major in the discourse as truthful narrator or messenger on the one hand, and man of action on the other. Thus, there are 25 references to acts of speaking, e.g. 'I just want to say', 'I'll tell you', 'My message to you'. The role of the politician is almost oracular; he is a guardian of truth, seer of the future, and bringer of good tidings: 'Let me give you some good news'. The acts of speaking include the right to criticize and condemn kinds of speaking allegedly indulged in by others: 'Take care not to confuse travesty with truth'. They also include the power to utter certain kinds of speech acts, as we will see below.

Above all, and partly in response to criticisms of 'dithering', there are 44 expressions of decision taking, order giving, and action: e.g. 'I have asked Gillian Shepherd to ... ', 'I asked for a fresh look at', 'I will not tarry ... But I will take it in my own time'. Some actions, positioning Major on a geopolitical map, are related to movement and travel to places of historic danger, and are embedded in mini-narratives: 'I was in Warsaw – where the first bombs fell in 1939 ... I flew to Berlin ... I was in South Africa ... I spoke to [the South African] Parliament ... I flew from South Africa to Chequers ... Boris Yeltsin was my guest'.

In order to demarcate the Conservatives as a party that was distinct from other parties, the speaker has to assume or manufacture an internal consensus – a collective understanding that certain concepts, actions, and relationships are true or correct. The corollary is the assuming or manufacturing of external dissensus, here *vis-à-vis* Labour. In addition, for any party, but especially for the Conservatives, it is important also (though contradictorily, since national dissensus is also necessary to their position) to claim that the consensus extends to the nation as a whole. This is a *legitimizing function* in the narrow as well as in the broader context. One of the principal ways in which politicians will position themselves and others in relation to their parties, their government, their potential electors, and their nation is through the use of the pronoun *we/us/our/ours*. In ordinary conversation *we* would usually include the speaker and the hearer(s); in Major's speech, and in political discourse generally, *we* (and its related forms) is often open to several different understandings of its intended referents.

Thus, 'we' may include the speaker, the audience in the hall, and conceivably other hearers who would consider themselves to be either members of the party or its supporters. It is given sentence-initial position, or syntactic focus, and/or (phonetic) stress. Contextually it excludes Labour ('they', 'them'), and the associated verbs come from lexical fields concerned with belief, conflict, moral rectitude, and provision (giving the good life to others). It is also striking, and consistent with other ideological elements of this discourse, that property and ownership concepts are involved in the use of the possessive form ('our', etc.). The following is a sample (underlining as in the original):

> how wrong they have been ... and how right we have been ... it is we who have ... We have won ... we've beaten ... we are the Party of the Union ... they are our issues ... This is our ground [not Labour's] ... let me tell them what we stand for ... our philosophy ... our opponents

However, the referents of 'we' can overlap or coincide with at least two other groups. The first is the government, which, in the context, may be conceived as having opponents or dissenters within the party, from whence the exclusive meanings of *we* that apparently refer to the government as distinct from the Conservative hearers as a whole come: e.g. 'we've listened ... we've changed our minds'. The second group that 'we' can designate is the entire country: 'we are now doing well as a country'. The *we* forms following this sentence then have an indeterminate meaning that could refer just to Conservatives or to the country, or, in some cases to the government, or some combination of any of these. It is unclear what category hearers will conceptualize in these instances, but one possibility is a vague category in which 'the country' and 'the Conservatives' are in some way conflated. Thus Major goes on: 'We have a recovery built to last'. But the pronoun then shifts to a mixture of plausible referents – the Conservatives, the country as a whole, or some indefinite equivalent of the pronoun 'one', as in the following:

> We [one? the Conservatives? the British?] were told unemployment would go on rising ... We [Conservatives? government? British?] were told we [Conservatives? government?] wouldn't get interest rates down. We have.

The pronoun's role in blending the references to Conservatives, government and country as a whole is particularly clear in the area of foreign policy, where there are indirect implications that the Labour Party's aims do *not* coincide with the national interest. For example:

That's Britain today. So let's [the audience, all British?] recognise what we [British] are ... put our own distinctive British mark [on the world] ... there were appeasers and accommodators [during the Cold War]. But not in <u>our</u> [Conservatives'] Party. We [Conservatives] can say with pride. We never heard their voices in this hall [invites inference: unlike the Labour Party conference where some people argued for unilateral nuclear disarmament].

Such utterances are obviously not simply statements of policy. The main function of the speech was to achieve unity within the party at a time of decreasing public support for the Conservatives and decreasing internal party support for the leader John Major. Positioning of this kind can be seen as serving not only a *legitimizing function* with respect to the leader's authority within the party, but also a *delegitimizing function*, since it drew boundaries between groups, one of which was claimed to be right and the other wrong.

Speech acts

The 'positioning' of the speaker as an authoritative narrator and messenger, and as a decisive actor, is crucial.[6] Certain kinds of speech act, for example orders, requests, advisings, warnings, promises, commitments, etc., can only be performed 'felicitously' on the basis of recognized powers. Others, such as explicit or implicit claims to truthfulness, knowledge, or an accurate assessment, depend partly on being empirically refutable in the light of events, but many bald assertions can appear to be 'felicitous' on no other basis than the authority of the speaker. Let us consider the role of just three of the five types of speech act mentioned above, namely representatives, directives, and commissives.

1   *Representatives*   The policy of the British Conservative Party is presented here by simple statements and claims, often claims to the truth. These are by far the most numerous types of speech acts, and their typical form is: 'We *are* now doing well ... Britain is making more, selling more, exporting more'. No evidence is given and the references, especially for 'making' and 'more,' are undecidable for those listening. This seems prima facie like a flouting of Grice's maxims, but in practice the audience in such situations will conventionally tolerate lower levels of information and evidence: challenges or questions are not in the rules of the current game, and the authority of the speaker is paramount. Assertions are in many cases 'boasts' – problematic though essential acts of political rhetoric which have to be hedged or mitigated by politeness devices, and which often also serve the function of obscuring the grounds of exaggerated or over-general claims. A further important point is the following: the assertions only have relevance, in Grice's sense, in relation to the background propositions that Major and his audience mutually know have been made in Labour's discourse.

2   *Directives*   Orders are probably the most power-dependent, and the most obvious linguistic realization of the coercion function. It would of course be very odd, given the genre, if explicit orders were instantiated in Major's speech. There are only three marginal examples of the basic imperative form, one being Major's 'order' to 'whisper it gently', mitigating with irony the boast that 'we *are* now doing well as a country', and the imperative 'hang on a minute'. The latter is an order to the audience to delay its response to a boast about hospital provision – an example of the speaker's right to control turn-taking but which may also be perceived as friendly interaction with the audience. And it is followed almost immediately in the speech by its counterpart – a pseudo-order to the Labour health spokesman (absent of course): 'Junk it, Blunkett!' This is intended primarily for the immediate audience: a virtual play-acting of the tough guy standing up to

---

[6]Such authority is of course also established by virtue of his different concurrent roles defined by the particular speech situation (not just the man John Major, but also the Prime Minister, Conservative Party Leader, Conference speaker).

his opponent. The purpose here can be understood not merely as refuting criticisms of Conservative health policy, but as expressing the opposition and difference between the parties.

Although there are no genuine orders enacted during the speech there are certainly constative mentions of orders being given to ministers. There are also perhaps examples of indirect speech acts which might be taken by the immediate hearers as requiring some action or change of behaviour on their part: 'it's time to put the marker down', 'it's time for this country to set its sights high again', 'it's time to accelerate this trend'. This may or may not be true for more distant hearers: 'Schools ... must open up their facilities', 'I don't want councils selling off school playing fields'.

Closely related to these examples are numerous speech acts in Major's discourse using the phrase 'let's' (not 'let us', which is open to interpretation as a request for permission, as in 'let me', which he does use quite frequently): 'So let's have the courage to look forward', 'So let's recognize what we are. Look with confidence at the new world.' The negative form here is: 'Don't let us fool ourselves'. The processes referred to here are mental, and not susceptible to being ordered in any case. The speech act in question here might be called an 'urging,' and this is characteristically performed by leaders.

3   *Commissives*   Explicit commissives (promises, threats, offerings) will be typically made with great caution, though politicians will certainly want to *appear* to be making them. Such promises are recognized idiomatically as 'empty'. Various forms of pragmatic hedging or semantic vagueness will accompany the most explicitly signalled promise performatives (*misrepresentation function*). For example:

> Since we are making a lasting change to pre-school opportunities, we will have to phase in the introduction
> of this extra provision. But what I am doing today is giving you a cast-iron commitment that it *will* happen.
> And I'm giving you that commitment now, so that Gill Shepherd can start consulting on it next week.

'A cast-iron commitment' is presumably intended to reassure, although, since the phrase is a cliché, audience members may not be convinced. Moreover, the speaker does not indicate what the precise nature of the 'provision' would be, nor does the stressed 'will' in fact specify a precise time in the future, nor is it said that Shepherd will do any more than 'consult on it'.[7]

Promises are the inverse of threats (which are close to warnings), and in political discourse the boundary is fragile, since the future action referred to in both acts may be something that is desirable to some hearers and something undesirable to others. Now Major is addressing, as we have noted, not just the gathered throng but other mediated hearers, and specifically the then bitterly divided community of Northern Ireland. So what would the different potential hearers make of the following, a speech act which Major, as elsewhere, signals before he performs it?

> But let me give this assurance. For as long as is necessary, as many policemen and troops as are necessary will
> stay on duty in Northern Ireland to protect all the people of Northern Ireland.

Readers will by now have spotted the hedge 'as are necessary'. One can also note the ambiguity of 'assurance' (something that 'reassures' and also some kind of commitment). But the commitment to the presence of troops in Northern Ireland was not something desirable to 'all the people', but to some an undesirable thing. Thus, this 'assurance' is a promise to the 'Loyalists' and a threat or warning to the 'Unionists' and some moderates.

Semantics

Words and worlds

The vocabularies of languages are commonly taken as neutral 'reflections' of the real world. They may be more accurately regarded, however, as constructions of the real that will reflect the interests of a speech community – or perhaps the interests of dominant groups in

---

[7]As it turned out, in summer 1995 the Conservative government announced a controversial 'voucher' scheme for pre-school education.

a community. As national languages become elaborated in their functions,[8] different fields of activity (government, religion, judiciary, education, bureaucracy ...) will elaborate their vocabularies. These vocabularies can often be described in terms of structured 'lexical fields'. Such fields are related to cognitive 'schemata' or 'scripts', which are knowledge bases about objects and activities (e.g. scripts for social activities such as 'making a purchase', 'voting'). Languages are historically constituted out of discourses, and are not simply a socially or politically neutral resource. Political discourse is one such discourse, not separate from the others but rather drawing on, corroborating, or modifying them. Meanings in and across fields are related in various ways (semantic relations). Sometimes the same word will have different meanings ('polysemy'), depending on the discourse differentiation (e.g. 'the source of power' in technological discourse *vs* 'the source of power' in political discourse). Antonymy is an important relation in political discourse, enabling speakers to communicate their opposition and draw boundaries (*legitimizing, delegitimizing functions*).

A crucial conceptual and semantic mechanism in the production of political meanings is metaphor. It is important to note that metaphors are not merely one-off 'rhetorical flourishes', but cognitive devices for forming and communicating conceptualizations of reality which may be in some way problematic. From the interactive perspective, metaphors can enable speakers to avoid direct (face-threatening and over-revealing) references. Recurrent metaphors are embedded in languages and cultures and depend both on the human conceptual system and on cultural systems. Selections from these systems may be used to structure particular discourses, and to reproduce those systems symbolically. In political discourse, one may cite two common metaphors: *argument is war* (for example, 'The opposition's claims were shot down in flames'), a metaphor which constitutes adversarial debate as a quasi-natural state of affairs; and *states are containers* (for example, 'The minister for external affairs was concerned about foreign penetration of the security cordon'), which constitutes the geographically and culturally bounded 'sovereign' state as the natural unit of international relations.[9]

Marketing metaphors: the real thing

The lexical fields appearing in John Major's speech are selections from the larger fields available in the language. As one would expect, politics and administration are well instantiated. Equally, the conventional *argument is war* metaphor appears: 'We have won the battle of ideas – it is an astonishing triumph'. Metaphor works by applying one taken-for-granted field of knowledge and applying it to another. One frequently used field in Major's speech is the highly lexicalized field of the market economy: this field is projected

---

[8]Cf. Haugen (1966).

[9]For research on metaphors in political discourse see, for example, Chilton (1985a; 1996), Chilton and Lakoff (1995), Lakoff and Johnson (1980), Schäffner (1991), and from the perspective of a political scientist, Opp de Hipt (1987).

metaphorically onto other domains, and this metaphorical projection has several ramifications. The following extract is evidence of this:

> What the Labour Party has done is to study our instincts and attitudes, and then go away and **market test** them ... But it is one thing for the Labour Party to commit grand larceny[10] on our language. It is one thing for them to say what **market research** has told them people would like to hear. But it is quite another to **deliver** it ...

> **Buying** Tory policy from Labour is like **buying a Rolex on the street corner**. It may bear the name. But you know it's **not real**. Our task is to **promote** the **real thing** and expose the **counterfeit** ... As for this **new, biologically improved** Labour Party. It may well **wash blander**. But I'd give it a **shelf life** of under three years. [bold added]

The bold words belong to the semantic field of the market, and in fact correspond to a structured script (*market → research → promotion → sell → delivery*). Further, the phrases 'a Rolex' and 'on the street corner' are dependent on background knowledge concerning economic value, what is 'real' and what is 'counterfeit'. Understanding the metaphor requires the audience to know and share certain values. Certain consequences will follow. If politics is marketing, then policies are saleable commodities, and commodities are by definition a form of property.

This cluster of concepts is linked to another chain of metaphors that are responsible for the coherence of the above passage. Because policies are ideas, and ideas are conceived of as the same thing as language, 'policies are commodities' entails 'language is a commodity' – hence Major speaks of 'our language', the language that 'belongs to' the Conservatives. This makes it possible to construct an argument against the Labour Party that has the following form:

1   Labour's language is Conservative language.
2   Language is a commodity.
3   Commodities are exclusively owned by someone.
4   To use a commodity owned by someone else is to steal that commodity.
5   Therefore, to use Conservative language is to steal that language.

All of this is not 'mere' metaphor. First, it is possible that the commodification of policies really is taken to be a 'fact' of political life in Conservative discourse, or that the metaphor leads people to talk, write and act as if it is. Second, whether that is the case or not, the ontology (and deontology) of the market, its concepts and potential inferences, are taken for granted as a familiar and natural reality to the hearers, a 'ground' on the basis of which metaphors can be developed without being challenged. Granted the free market model as a premise, an argument can be constructed that represents the Labour Party as performing illicit acts, or as being in some sense 'not for real'. Not only does this metaphorical strategy confirm a particular world view based on the supposed naturalness of the 'market' (*legitimizing function*), it also discredits the opponent (*delegitimizing function*).

---

[10]'Grand larceny' is defined by the *OED* as the theft of 'property ... of more than 12 pence in value'.

Table 15.1 Discourse and Politics: Paul Chilton and Christina Schäffner

	Subject	Verb	Object	Prepositional phrases
(1)	the government	sent	troops	to the Balkans
	agent	*cause, motion*	*theme*	*goal*
(2)	troops	were sent		by the government
				agent
	theme	*cause, motion*		to the Balkans
				goal
(3)	troops	were sent		to the Balkans
	theme	*cause, motion*		*goal*
(4)	troops	went		to the Balkans
	author (*or agent*)	*motion*		*goal*

Syntax

Agency and focus

Much of syntactic organization has to do with concepts and communicative functions that are not directly encoded in the content words of a language's vocabulary, and it is therefore less easy to bring to awareness.

It is often relevant to the analyst to investigate two aspects of sentence organization in political discourse: 'thematic roles' and 'topicalization'. The first have to do with, for example, who (*agent*) is doing what (*processes* of moving, affecting, causing, etc.) to whom (*patient*), where (*location*), why (*cause, purpose*), and by what means (*instrument*). The way a speaker assigns such roles can be interpretively linked with particular representations of the political universe, or to claims concerning causation, agency, and responsibility.[11] Consider the examples in Table 15.1, which are simple, hypothetical and context-less, but which indicate some of the potential implications of semantic roles. In the table, *theme* is the term used for an entity that is caused to move by an agent, and *author* is an entity that appears like an agent but is not the direct cause of the act.

Sentence structure and the semantics of lexical items combine in such a way that they cannot be made sense of without knowing or postulating knowledge of the powers of the

---

[11]Cf. Hodge and Kress (1993), Kress and Trew (1978), van Dijk (1995).

governments of sovereign states. Consider, for example, flipping the grammatical subject and object. One can just as well say 'Alf sent Bert to the Balkans' as 'Bert sent Alf to the Balkans', but what about 'troops sent the government to the Balkans'? Some might say that the latter is in some way 'ungrammatical'. Or one might say that it is still grammatical, but that the semantic roles are anomalously assigned, given the 'real world' in which the sovereignty of states includes the power of governments to order troops. This relationship, although essential for understanding the sentence, may be made in varying degrees implicit (*misrepresentation function*). Sentence (1) in Table 15.1 seems to make the relationship clearest in the most syntactically neutral form. The passive sentences (2) and (3) may be felt to express the same relationship less directly (although the end position may, in context, give special emphasis). But in English the passive construction can omit an overt reference to the agent completely, as in (3). In (4) 'troops' may be implicitly understood as the agent of their own actions, contrary to background knowledge, and though both causality and agency may be understood, neither is *overtly* expressed. Thus an event can be syntactically encoded in various ways.

The second dimension of sentence structure has to do with what the speaker wishes to indicate as the 'topic' in the ongoing universe of discourse, and with what he or she wishes to present as 'new information'. 'Topics' tend to be the first element in English sentences; 'new information' tends to be phonologically stressed or in an end position. The word order of sentences interacts with intonation and stress, and enables speakers to focus selectively on elements of the political universe, and in this fashion to constrain the real-time processing of the hearers.

The political functions of such choices will vary according to context, but it is clear, for instance, that sentence (1) might be used when claiming credit, or apportioning blame, according to whether the speaker is or is not the government itself (*legitimizing, delegitimizing function*).

Agents of change

Concepts of temporal stability are coded into the basic grammatical categories: nouns will tend to refer to more static, atemporal, and discrete phenomena; verbs to the fleeting, the temporal, and the dynamic. Speakers of English have certain choices as to the encoding of the involvement of agents in acts of causation.

Traditional Conservative ideology in general gravitates around the concept of *change*. It is opposed to planned attempts to alter the status quo and impose preconceived models. However, more recent forms of conservatism have not opposed certain forms of change and have represented themselves as dynamic. A discourse problem for a Conservative speaker is to reconcile the opposites of change and tradition, movement and stability.

Let us consider the use of the verb *change* in Major's speech, comparing its intransitive uses (no agency), its transitive use (with a causing agent), and the use of its derived nominal form (not *explicitly* expressing either, at least in this particular context):

Intransitive (no agency)

The political landscape has **changed** in the last few years and it's **changed** again in the last few months ... Britain has **changed**.
Foreign affairs: the world **has changed** ...
Hope had flowered and the world **had changed** ...[12]
Things **are changing** [with reference to Northern Ireland] ...

Transitive (agency asserted)

... it is we who have **changed** the whole thrust of politics and moved it in our direction ...
if we are to **change** the climate against crime ...
we have to **change** attitudes ...
Lech Walesa, a shipyard worker who helped **change** history ...

Derived nominal

That's what **our changes** are all about ...
after the **curriculum changes** of recent years, teachers deserve stability ...
The **changes** taking place are truly awesome ...
Harold Macmillan spoke of **the wind of change** ...
Four **snapshots of change** ...
I will just say 'no' to **change** which would harm Britain ...
Change for the sake of **change** would never appeal to any Conservative ...
In a world of **bewildering change**, this Party must stand for continuity and stability, for home and health ...

What is the significance of such patterns of occurrence? A full analysis shows that the transitive expressions of agency are significantly less frequent than the other two groups. Also, they are qualified in various ways (cf. the use of 'if' above). One refers, interestingly in quasi-Marxist terms, to the Polish leader, and another refers to changes in Conservative education policy. What explains this? Although it is important for Major to claim intention, responsibility and action, it is equally important for him to avoid charges of being 'interventionist'. It is also important for a Conservative leader to maintain a Conservative ideological premise: that planned social and political change in general is not desirable. There is another premise that explains the prevalence of intransitivity and the use of the derived nominal: that there is a 'natural' order of things and a 'natural' course of events. Thus, intransitive constructions encode the notion that the universe changes independently, and also makes it possible to avoid complex controversial issues of blame and responsibility. The derived nominal, as the reader can verify, either performs similar functions (changes just 'take place') or makes Conservative agency indirect or non-specific, while claiming credit ('our changes'). The functions served by such grammatical choices may be interpreted as self-legitimating, combining with misrepresentation. We should not, however, exaggerate the importance of the use of derived nominals. In most instances, although an agent is not explicitly referred to in the clause, it is quite possible for readers or hearers to infer the referent from the co-text and context, and there is no reasonably arguable ideological motivation.

---

[12]The formulation 'the world has/had changed' is actually used three times in the section on foreign affairs.

CONCLUSION

By showing some of the pragmatic, semantic and syntactic choices made in the text, analyses such as those above bring to our conscious consideration the conceptual world constructed in the text, as well as the relationships between the speaker and others that are established during the actual utterance of the text. On the conceptual level, though, such analyses are capable of indicating the current preoccupations of a political actor (whether an individual or a group) in terms of the issues and ideological assumptions that have been selected for expression at a particular historical moment. On the interactive level, the analysis shows what the text is *doing* – which social and political positions and relationships it is assuming or producing between actors such as the leader and the conference, the party and the public, the party and the opposition, the country and other countries.

To sum up, the analysis of the sample text illustrates the procedure for interpretively linking linguistic details on the levels of pragmatics, semantics and syntax to the strategic political functions coercion and resistance, legitimization and delegitimization, representation and misrepresentation. We propose the notion of 'strategic functions', and the particular three 'functions' we have labelled, purely by way of hypothesis. Our claim is that these strategies are enacted by the speaker – as a social actor in the political and cultural context – through linguistic choices. It is for the reader to evaluate the hypothesis in the light of their own social and political experience.

FURTHER READING

Charaudeau, P. (2005) *Le Discours politique*. Paris: Vuibert.
This work represents an important current of the very rich research on political discourse carried out by French scholars in the past few decades. Based on an approach to discourse that draws on traditional rhetoric it focuses on 'discursive strategies' utilized within the democratic public space. It also introduces a critical element in relation to modern political discourse and stresses the need for a new discursive ethic in public communication.

Chilton, P. (2004) *Analysing Political Discourse. Theory and Practice*. London and New York: Routledge.
This book offers a new theoretical perspective on the study of language and politics. Using the theoretical framework of linguistics, the author presents a methodological framework for political discourse analysis which is illustrated with a variety of discourse types from international politics (interviews, speeches, parliamentary language). The book provides insights into the cognitive and behavioural effects of political discourse.

Klein, J. (ed) (1989) *Politische Semantik. Beiträge zur politischen Sprachverwendung*. Opladen: Westdeutscher Verlag.
The book illustrates the role of language in political debates, predominantly in Germany. It is argued that ideologically loaded words are instruments of political influence, functioning as weapons in political disputes, and therefore fiercely contested. Political concepts are shown to contain (concealed) structures of argumentation. Using concepts of (lexical) semantics and argumentation theory, the book also presents types of 'fighting for words'.

Lakoff, G. (2008) *The Political Mind: Why You Can't Understand 21st-Century American Politics with an 18th-Century Brain*. New York: Viking/Penguin.

This work reflects some popular theorizing adapted by Lakoff from cognitive science, linguistics and sociology and applied to contemporary political culture in the United States. Making some strong and controversial claims, this book seeks to understand political behaviour in terms of the brain sciences, looking at what the European tradition more usually calls 'discourses' or 'ideologies'.

ONLINE READING

The following articles are available at www.sagepub.co.uk/discoursestudies.

Bhatia, A. (2006) 'Critical discourse analysis of political press conferences', *Discourse & Society*, 17: 173–203.

Chilton, P. (1990) 'Politeness, politics and democracy', *Discourse & Society*, 1(2): 201–24.

Lu, X. (1999) 'An ideological/cultural analysis of political slogans in Communist China', *Discourse & Society*, 10: 487–508.

Schäffner, C. and Porsch, P. (1993) Meeting the challenge on the path to democracy: discursive strategies in governmental declarations', *Discourse & Society*, 4: 33–55.

van Dijk, T.A. (1994) 'Discourse analysis and social analysis', *Discourse & Society*, 5: 163–64.

van Dijk, T.A. (1995) 'Discourse semantics and ideology', *Discourse & Society*, 6: 243–89.

Wilson, J. (1991) 'The linguistic pragmatics of terrorist acts', *Discourse & Society*, 1: 29–45.

REFERENCES

Achard, P. (1995) 'Formation discursive, diologisme et sociologie'. *Languages, 117*: 82–95.

Althusser, L. (1970) *Essays on Ideology*. London: Verso.

Amossy, R. (2000) *L'argumentation dans le discours. Discours politique, littérature d'idées, fiction*. Paris: Nathan.

Atkinson, M. (1984) *Our Masters' Voices*. London: Methuen.

Austin, J. (1962) *How To Do Things with Words* (The William James Lectures, 1955). Oxford: Clarendon.

Ball, T., Farr, J. and Hanson, R.L. (1989) *Political Innovation and Conceptual Change*. Cambridge: Cambridge University Press.

Bayley, P. (ed.) (2004) *Cross-Cultural Perspectives on Parliamentary Discourse*. Amsterdam and Philadelphia: John Benjamins.

Benveniste, E. (1966/1974) *Problèmes de linguistique générale* (2 vols). Paris: Gallimard.

Bhatia, A. (2006) 'Critical discourse analysis of political press conferences'. *Discourse & Society, 17*(2): 173–203.

Blommaert, J. and Verschueren, J. (1991) 'The pragmatics of minority politics in Belgium'. *Language in Society, 20*: 503–31.

Blommaert, J. and Verschueren, J. (1993) 'The rhetoric of tolerance, or what police officers are taught about migrants'. *Journal of Intercultural Studies, 14*(1): 49–63.

Bolinger, D. (1980) *Language – The Loaded Weapon: The Use and Abuse of Language Today*. London and New York: Longman.

Bonnafous, S. and Tournier, M. (1995) 'Analyse du discours, lexicométrie, communication et politique'. *Languages*, 117: 67–81.

Brown, P. and Levinson, S. (1987) *Politeness: Some Universals in Language Usage*. Cambridge: Cambridge University Press.

Burkhardt, A. and Fritzsche, K.P. (eds) (1992) *Sprache im Umbruch: Politischer Sprachwandel im Zeichen von 'Wende' und 'Vereinigung'*. Berlin: de Gruyter.

Burkhardt, A. and Pape, K. (eds) (2000) *Sprache des deutschen Parlamentarismus* (Studien zu 150 Jahren parlamentarischer Kommunikation). Wiesbaden: Westdeutscher Verlag.

Burkhardt, A. and Pape, K. (eds) (2003) *Politik, Sprache und Glaubwürdigkeit*. Wiesbaden: Westdeutscher Verlag.

Burkhardt, A., Hebel, F. and Hoberg, R. (eds) (1989) *Sprache zwischen Militär und Frieden: Aufrüstung der Begriffe?* Tübingen: Narr.

Cap, P. (2002) *Explorations in Political Discourse: Methodological and Critical Perspectives*. Frankfurt am Main: Peter Lang Verlag.

Cap, P. (2006) *Legitimisation in Political Discourse: A Cross-Disciplinary Perspective on the Modern US War Rhetoric*. Newcastle: Cambridge Scholars.

Céditec http://www.univ-paris12.fr/www/labos/ceditec/

Chareaudeau, 2005; Charaudeau, P. (2005) *Le discours politique. Les masques du pouvoir*. Paris: Vuibert.

Charteris-Black, J. (2004) *Corpus Approaches to Critical Metaphor Analysis*. Basingstoke: Palgrave.

Charteris-Black, J. (2005) *Politicians and Rhetoric: The Persuasive Power of Metaphor*. Basingstoke: Palgrave.

Chilton, P. (1985a) 'Words, discourse and metaphors: the meanings of *deter, deterrent* and *deterrence*'. In P. Chilton (ed.), *Language and the Nuclear Arms Debate* (pp. 103–27). London: Pinter.

Chilton, P. (ed.) (1985b) *Language and the Nuclear Arms Debate: Nukespeak Today*. London: Pinter.

Chilton, P. (1990) 'Politeness and politics'. *Discourse and Society, 1*(2): 201–24.

Chilton, P. (1996) *Security Metaphors: Cold War Discourse from Containment to Common House*. New York: Peter Lang.

Chilton, P. (2004) *Analysing Political Discourse: Theory and Practice*. London and New York. Routledge.

Chilton, P. and Lakoff, G. (1995) 'Foreign policy by metaphor'. In C. Schäffner and A. Wenden (eds), *Language and Peace* (pp. 37–59). Aldershot: Dartmouth.

Chilton, P. and Schäffner, C. (1997) 'Discourse and politics'. In van Dijk, T. (ed.), *Discourse Studies: A Multidisciplinary Introduction, vol. 2: Discourse as Social Interaction* (pp. 206–30). London: Sage.

Chomsky, N. (1988a) 'Political discourse and the propaganda system'. In N. Chomsky (ed.), *Language and Politics* (pp. 662–97). Montreal: Black Rose.

Chomsky, N. (1988b) 'Politics and language'. In N. Chomsky (ed.), *Language and Politics* (pp. 610–31). Montreal: Black Rose.

Connolly, W. (1974) *The Terms of Political Discourse*. Lexington, MA: D.C. Heath.

Der Derian, J. and Shapiro, M.J. (1989) *International/Intertextual Relations*. Lexington, MA: Lexington Books.

Dieckmann, W. (1969) *Sprache in der Politik: Einführung in die Pragmatik und Semantik der politischen Sprache*. Heidelberg: Sprachwissenschaftliche Studienbücher.

Dieckmann, W. (1981) *Politische Sprache: Politische Kommunikation*. Heidelberg: Carl Winter Universitätsverlag.

Diekmannshenke, H.J. and Meissner, I. (2001) *Politische Kommunikation im historischen Wandel*. Tübingen: Stauffenburg.

Distelberger, T., De Cillia, R. and Wodak, R. (2009) 'Österreichische Identitaten in politischen Gedenkreden des Jubilaumsjahres 2005'. In *Gedenken im 'Gedankenjahr': zur diskursiven Konstruktion österreichischer Identitäten im Jubiläumsjahr 2005* (pp. 29–78). Innsbruck: Studien Verlag.

Dörner, A. and Vogt, L. (eds) (1995) *Sprache des Parlaments und Semiotik der Demokratie (Studien zur politischen Kommunikation in der Moderne)*. Berlin and New York: de Gruyter.

Dörner, A. and Vogt, L. (eds) (2002) *Wahl-Kämpfe: Betrachtungen über ein Demokratisches Ritual*. Frankfurt am Main: Peter Lang.

Edelman, M. (1964) *The Symbolic Uses of Politics*. Chicago: Chicago University Press.

Edelman, M. (1971) *Politics as Symbolic Action*. New York: Academic.

Ehlich, K. (ed.) (1989) *Sprache im Faschismus*. Frankfurt: Suhrkamp.

Ensink, T. and Sauer, C. (eds) (2003) *The Art of Commemoration (Discourse Approaches to Politics, Society and Culture, 7)*. Amsterdam: John Benjamins.

Fairclough, N. (1989) *Language and Power*. London: Longman.

Fairclough, N. (2000) *New Labour: New Language?* London: Routledge.

Fairclough, N. (2006) *Language and Globalization*. London: Routledge.

Fairclough, N. (2007) 'The contribution of discourse analysis to research on social change'. In *Discourse in Contemporary Social Change'*. London: Peter Lang.

Fetzer, A. and Lauerbach, G. (2007) *Political Discourse in the Media: Cross-cultural Perspectives*. Amsterdam and Philadelphia: John Benjamins.

Fiala, P. (1994) 'L'interprétation en lexicométrie'. *Langue française, 103*: 113–22.

Fiala, P. and Ebel, M. (1983) 'Sous le consensus, la xénophobie'. *Paroles, arguments, contextes (1971–1981)*. Lausanne: ISP.

Foucault, M. (1971) *L'ordre du discours*. Paris: Gallimard.

Fowler, R., Hodge, B., Kress, G. and Trew T. (1979) *Language and Control*. London: Routledge and Kegan Paul.

Gallie, W.B. (1956) *Essentially Contested Concepts. (Proceedings of the Aristotelian Society)*. New Series, *56* (1955–6), 167–198.

Goatly, A. (2007) *Washing the Brain: Metaphor and Hidden Ideology*. Amsterdam: John Benjamins.

Graber, D.A. (1976) *Verbal Behaviour and Politics*. Urbana: University of Illinois Press.

Grewenig, A. (ed.) (1993) *Inszenierte Information. Politik und Strategische Kommunikation in den Medien*. Opladen: Westdeutscher Verlag.

Groupe de Saint-Cloud (1982) *La parole syndicale: Etude du vocabulaire confédéral des centrales ouvrières françaises (1971–1976)*. Paris: Presses Universitaires de France.

Groupe de Saint-Cloud (1995) *Présidentielle: Regards sur les discours télévisés*. Paris: INA-Nathan.

Habermas, J. (1979) *Communication and the Evolution of Society*. London: Heinemann.

Habermas, J. (1981) *Theorie des kommunikativen Handelns*. Frankfurt: Suhrkamp.

Halliday, M.A.K. (1973) *Explorations in the Functions of Language*. London: Edward Arnold.

Haugen, E. (1966) 'Dialect, language, nation'. *American Anthropologist, 68*: 922–35.

Heringer, H.J. (1990) *'Ich gebe Ihnen mein Ehrenwort': Politik, Sprache, Moral*. (Beck'sche Reihe BSR 425). München: Beck'sche Verlagsbuchhandlung.

Hodge, R. and Kress, G. (1993) *Language as Ideology* (2nd edition). London and New York: Routledge.

Holly, W. (1990) *Politikersprache: Inszenierung und Rollenkonflikte im informellen Sprachhandeln eines Bundestagsabgeordneten*. Berlin: de Gruyter.

Holly, W. (1996) 'Die sozialdemokratischen Bundeskanzler an das Volk. Die Ansprachen von Brandt und Schmidt zum Jahreswechsel'. In K. Böke, M. Jung and M. Wengeler, (eds), *Öffentlicher Sprachgebrauch* (pp. 315–29). Wiesbaden: Westdeutscher Verlag.

Ilie, C. (1994) *What Else Can I Tell You? A Pragmatic Study of English Rhetorical Questions as Discursive and Argumentative Acts*. Stockholm: Almqvist and Wiksell.

Ilie, C. (ed.) (2010) *European Parliaments Under Scrutiny. Discourse Strategies and Interaction Practices*. Amsterdam and Philadelphia: John Benjamins.

Inghilleri, M. (2005) 'Mediating zones of uncertainty: interpreter agency, the interpreting habitus and political asylum adjudication. *The Translator, 11*(1): 69–85.

Jaeger, S. and Halm, D. (eds) (2007) *Mediale Barrieren? Rassismus als Integrationshindernis*. Münster: Unrast.

Jakobson, R. (1960) 'Closing statement: linguistics and poetics'. In T.A. Sebeok (ed.), *Style in Language* (pp. 350–77). Cambridge, MA and New York: MIT Press and Wiley.

Jarren, O., Sarcinelli, U. and Saxer, U. (eds.) (1998) *Politische Kommunikation in der demokratischen Gesellschaf: Ein Handbuch*. Opladen: Westdeutscher Verlag.

Klein, J. (ed.) (1989) *Politische Semantik: Beiträge zur Politischen Sprachverwendung*. Opladen: Westdeutscher Verlag.

Klemperer, V. (1975) *LTI: Notizbuch eine Philologen*. Leipzig: Reclam.

Krebs, B.-N. (1993) *Sprachhandlung und Sprachwirkung: Untersuchungen zur Rhetorik, Sprachkritik und zum Fall Jenninger*. Berlin: Erich Schmidt Verlag.

Kress, G.R. and Trew, A.A. (1978) 'Ideological transformation of discourse; or how the *Sunday Times* got its message across'. *Journal of Pragmatics, 2*(4): 311–29.

Krzyzanowski, M. and Oberhuber, F. (2007) *(Un)doing Europe: Discourses and Practices of Negotiating the EU Constitution*. London: Peter Lang.

Krzyzanowski, M. and Wodak, R. (2008) *The Politics of Exclusion: Debating Migration in Austria*. New Brunswick, NJ: Transaction.

Lakoff, G. (1996) *Moral Politics: What Conservatives Know That Liberals Don't*. Chicago: Chicago University Press.

Lakoff, G. (2004) *Don't Think of an Elephant: Know Your Values and Frame the Debate – The Essential Guide for Progressives*. White River Junction, VT: Chelsea Green.

Lakoff, G. (2008) *The Political Mind: Why You Can't Understand 21st-Century American Politics with an 18th-Century Brain*. New York: Viking/Penguin.

Lakoff, G. and Johnson, M. (1980) *Metaphors We Live By*. Chicago: University of Chicago Press.

Lasswell, H.D., Leites, N., et al. (1949) *Language of Politics*. Cambridge, MA: MIT Press.

Le Bart, C. (1998) *Le discours politique*. Paris: Presses Universitaires de France.

Leites, N. (1963) *A Study of Bolshevism*. Glencoe, IL: Free.

Lerchner, G. (ed.) (1992) *Sprachgebrauch im Wandel. Anmerkungen zur Kommunikationskultur in der DDR vor und nach der Wende*. Frankfurt am Main: Peter Lang.

Lewis, Sir G. (1898) *Remarks on the Use and Abuse of Political Terms*. Oxford: Clarendon.

Liedtke, F., Wengeler, M. and Böke, K. (eds) (1991) *Begriffe Besetzen: Strategien des Sprachgebrauchs in der Politik*. Opladen: Westdeutscher Verlag.

Lu, X. (1999) 'An ideological/cultural analysis of political slogans in Communist China'. *Discourse & Society ,10*(4): 487–508.

Lukes, S. (1975) *Power: A Radical View*. Atlantic Highlands, NJ: Humanities.

Matouschek, B., Januschek, F. and Wodak, R. (1995) *Notwendige Maßnahmen gegen Fremde? Genese und Formen von rassistischen Diskursen der Differenz*. Wiesbaden: Westdeutscher Verlag.

Mayaffre, D. (2000) *Le poids des mots: Le discours de gauche et de droite dans l'entre-deux-guerres. Maurice Thorez, Léon Blum, Pierre-Etienne Flandin et André Tardieu (1928–1939)*. Paris: Honoré Champion.

Mayaffre, D. (2004) *Paroles de président. Jacques Chirac (1995–2003) et le discours presidential sous la Veme République*. Paris: Honoré Champion.

Millar, S. and Wilson, J. (eds) (2007) 'The discourse of Europe: talk and text in everyday life'. *Discourse Approaches to Politics, Society and Culture, 26*. Amsterdam: John Benjamins.

Muntigl, P., Weiss, G. and Wodak, R. (2000) *European Union Discourses on Un/employment: An Interdisciplinary Approach to Employment Policy-making and Organizational Change*. Amsterdam: John Benjamins.

Musolff, A. (2004) *Metaphor and Political Discourse: Analogical Reasoning in Debates about Europe*. Basingstoke: Palgrave.

Opp de Hipt, M. (1987) *Denkbilder in der Politik: Der Staat in der Sprache von CDU und SPD*. Westdeutscher Verlag: Opladen.

Orwell, G. (1949) *Nineteen Eighty-Four*. New York: Signet.

Osgood, Ch. E. (1971) 'Conservative words and radical sentences in the semantics of international politics'. In G. Abcarian and J.W. Soule (eds), *Social Psychology and Political Behaviour: Problems and Prospects*. Columbus, OH: Merrill.

Patzelt, W.J. (1995) 'Politiker und ihre Sprache'. In A. Dörner and L. Vogt (eds), *Sprache des Parlaments und Semiotik der Demokratie. Studien zur politischen Kommunikation in der Moderne* (pp. 17–53). Berlin and New York: de Gruyter.

Pêcheux, M. (1975) *Les vérités de la Palice: linguistique, sémantique, philosophie*. Paris: Maspéro.

Pêcheux, M. (1990) *L'inquiétude du discours: Textes choisis et présentés par Denise Maldidier*. Paris: Editions des Cendres.

Pörksen, B. (2000) *Die Konstruktion von Feindbildern: Zum Sprachgebrauch in neonazistischenMedien*. Wiesbaden: Westdeutscher Verlag.

Reiher, R. and Läzer, R. (eds) (1993) *Wer spricht das wahre Deutsch? Erkundungen zur Sprache im vereinigten Deutschland*. Berlin: Aufbau.

Richardson, K. (1985) 'Pragmatics of speeches against the peace movement in Britain: a case study'. In P. Chilton (ed.), *Language and the Nuclear Arms Debate: Nukespeak Today* (pp. 23–44). London: Pinter.

Roth, K.S. and Wienen, M. (eds) (2008) *Diskursmauern Aktuelle Aspekte der sprachlichen Verhältnisse zwischen Ost und West Diskursmauern*.

Sartori, G. (1984) *Social Science Concepts: A Systematic Analysis*. Beverly Hills, CA: Sage.

Sauer, C. (1995) 'Sprachwissenschaft und NS-Faschismus. Lehren aus der sprachwissenschaftlichen Erforschung des Sprachgebrauchs deutscher Nationalsozialisten und Propagandisten für den mittel- und osteuropäischen Umbruch?' In K. Steinke (ed.), *Die Sprache der Diktaturen und Diktatoren* (pp. 9–96). Heidelberg: Carl Winter Universitätsverlag.

Schäffner, C. (1991) 'Zur rolle von metaphern für die interpretation der außersprachlichen wirklichkeit'. *Folia Linguistica, 25*(1–2): 75–90.

Schäffner, C (ed.) (1997) *Analysing Political Speeches*. Clevedon: Multilingual Matters.

Schäffner, C. (2004) 'Political discourse analysis from the point of view of translation studies'. *Journal of Language and Politics, 3*(1): 117–50.

Schäffner, C. (2007) 'Politics and translation'. In P. Kuhiwczak and K. Littau (eds), *A Companion to Translation Studies* (pp. 134–47). Clevedon: Multilingual Matters.

Schäffner, C. and Porsch, P. (1993) 'Meeting the challenge on the path to democracy: discursive strategies in governmental declarations'. *Discourse & Society, 4*(1): 33–55.

Schmidt, W. (1969) 'Zur Ideologiegebundenheit der politischen Lexik'. *Zeitschrift für Phonetik, Sprachwissenschaft und Kommunikationsforschung, 22*(3): 255–71.

Searle, J. (1969) *Speech Acts*. Cambridge: Cambridge University Press.

Semino, E. (2008) *Metaphor in Discourse*. Cambridge: Cambridge University Press.

Shapiro, M.J. (1981) *Language and Political Understanding: The Politics of Discursive Practices*. New Haven and London: Yale University Press.

Shapiro, M.J. (ed.) (1984) *Language and Politics*. Oxford: Blackwell.

Sucharowski, W. (ed.) (1985) *Gesprächsforschung im Vergleich: Analysen zur Bonner Runde nach der Hessenwahl*. Tübingen: Niemeyer.

Tetlock, P. (1985) 'Integrative complexity and soviet foreign policy rhetoric: a time-series analysis'. *Journal of Personality and Social Psychology, 49*(6): 156–85.

TEXTOPOL–available at http://textopol.free.fr/

van Dijk, T.A. (1980) *Macrostructures: An Interdisciplinary Study of Global Structures in Discourse, Interaction and Cognition*. Hillsdale, NJ: Erlbaum.

van Dijk, T.A. (1985) *Discourse and Communication*. Berlin: de Gruyter.

van Dijk, T.A. (1987) *News Analysis*. Hillsdale, NJ: Erlbaum.

van Dijk, T.A. (1989) 'Structures of discourse and structures of power'. In J.A. Anderson (ed.), *Communication Yearbook 12* (pp. 18–59). Newbury Park, CA: Sage.

van Dijk, T.A. (1994) 'Discourse analysis and social analysis'. *Discourse & Society, 5*(2): 163–64.

van Dijk, T.A. (1995) 'Discourse semantics and ideology'. *Discourse & Society, 6*(2): 243–89.

van Dijk, T.A. (1997) 'Political discourse and racism: Describing others in Western parliaments'. In S.H. Riggins (ed.), *The Language and Politics of Exclusion: Others in Discourse* (pp. 31–64). Thousand Oaks, CA: Sage.

van Dijk, T.A. (2002) 'Political discourse and political cognition'. In P.A. Chilton and C. Schäffner (eds), *Politics as Text and Talk: Analytical Approaches to Political Discourse* (pp. 204–36). Amsterdam: Benjamins.

van Dijk, T.A. (2005) 'War rhetoric of a little ally: political implicatures of Aznar's legitimization of the war in Iraq'. *Journal of Language and Politics, 4*(1): 65–92. (Special issue 'The Soft Power of War: Legitimacy and community in Iraq war discourses', edited by Lilie Chouliaraki.)

Volosinov, V.N. (1973) *Marxism and the Philosophy of Language*. Cambridge, MA: Harvard University Press.

Wilson, J. (1990) *Politically Speaking: The Pragmatic Analysis of Political Language*. Oxford: Blackwell.

Wilson, J. (1991) 'The linguistic pragmatics of terrorist acts'. *Discourse and Society, 1*(2): 29–45.

Wittgenstein, L. (1953) *Philosophical Investigations* (transl. G.E.M. Anscombe). Oxford: Blackwell.

Wodak, R. (ed.) (1989) *Language, Power and Ideology: Studies in Political Discourse*. Amsterdam: John Benjamins.

Wodak, R. (2009) *The Discourse of Politics in Action: Politics as Usual*. Basingstoke: Palgrave Macmillan.

Wodak, R. and Menz, F. (eds) (1990) *Sprache in der Politik – Politik in der Sprache: Analysen zum öffentlichen Sprachgebrauch*. Klagenfurt: Drava.

Wodak, R. and Krzyzanowski, M. (2008) 'Migration und rassismus in Österreich'. In *Rassismus: Beiträge zu einem vielgesichtigen Phänomen* (pp. 257–79). Wien: Mandelbaum.

SIXTEEN

Discourse and Culture

Elizabeth Keating and Alessandro Duranti

In this chapter, we start from the assumption that human discourse is a resource for language users to work out who they are, what they are up against, and what is worth pursuing in life. Discourse, in other words, is what makes human cultures possible and unique. The fact that we use 'discourse' and 'culture' does not mean that we are not aware that each term is ambiguous and potentially contentious, as shown by their respective histories. The study of 'discourse' became popular in the 1970s as a reaction to the narrowing in scope of 'language' done by formal linguists and as a way of examining meaning in linguistic units that were larger and more complex than individual sentences. At around the same time, in the social sciences, 'discourse' became a cover term for phenomena that went beyond language and sometimes meant general concepts such as 'way of thinking' or 'way of doing things'. The term 'culture' is also ambiguous and was criticized in the 1980s by anthropologists and others who saw it as being narrowly or exclusively applied to non-western ways of being in the world. Culture was revealed to be like the 'accent' that we are ready to recognize in outsiders' speech but not in our own. Despite this line of criticism, originally inspired by anti-colonialist and anti-essentialist positions, most anthropologists and social scientists have continued to use the term 'culture' (or at least the adjective 'cultural') because it is difficult to find substitutes for what 'culture' can be used to describe. Together with our peers, we have also gained from a critical discussion of the meaning of discourse and of culture, including a more nuanced understanding of the ideological implications of our ways of writing about other people's ways of being and doing. In what follows, we will do our best to be as clear as possible about how we are using these terms. For a fuller discussion of these and related terms, we would advise the reader to consult our references.

While anthropologists in an earlier century were primarily concerned with carefully and exhaustively recording the diversity of human behaviours, recently anthropologists are being looked to for guidance about the complexities, conflicts, and puzzling failures in cross-cultural communication. This interest is being fed by the realization that people are working in increasingly diverse natural and cultural environments and that the discourse that sustains and explains these environments needs to be carefully documented and analysed.

A major shift in our understanding of language within anthropology over the last fifty years has been that it is not only a system of symbols for expressing thoughts and representing human activities and goals, but also a cultural practice, that is, a form of action that both presupposes and at the same time brings about unique ways of being in the world. It is in this respect that the term 'discourse' can at times be more useful than 'language'. Through discourse, as realized, for example, in conversational narrative activity, collective and personal pasts are connected with the present and future, and speakers have access to worlds they have never directly experienced. The analysis of discourse shows that what we call 'language' is a way of performing our identities as well as of making judgments about one another's moral character, intelligence, social class, personality, expertise, and even intentions. These language-mediated and language-constituted activities are so habitual that speakers and hearers are often unable to see their ideological underpinnings. After having studied a new language in school, when we visit the community in which that language is used, we often find that our grammar books and classroom exercises have left out some crucial components of what it means to be a competent and fluent speaker. As we operationalize our new linguistic skills, we discover many aspects of language *use* that we did not learn and whose absence in our speech can undermine how others perceive our social competence in serious ways.

By being exposed to conversation, political speeches, ceremonies, historical narratives, poetry and media such as print, television, and movies we are continually experiencing correlations between ways of speaking and ways of being someone who fits into a given cultural environment. We will show some examples of this while we provide some models for understanding the relationship between discourse and culture. We will also focus on the dynamic ways whereby categories of persons are discursively created, the various ways ways that language can be changed or suited for certain activities and goals, and reflections on the means of representation.

Here we will use data we have collected during ethnographic fieldwork in several locations – Samoa, Pohnpei, the USA, Germany, and Eastern Europe – in contexts that include such activities as speechmaking, online gaming, joking during political campaigning, gossip, metacommentaries about proper address forms, and communications via webcameras by users of sign languages. Discourse data provide an ideal means for examining how people create, maintain, and test culture moment-by-moment, and also how they can display to each other and build together shared understandings about who they are and what their activities are supposed to be about. In these activities, language can be shown to be a key resource for establishing cultural meanings, that is, meanings that can vary considerably throughout the world in terms of relationships, ideas, structures, and coherence. These are usually not directly stated, but instead are arrived at through such subtle means as alignment, agreements, disagreements, style, the amount and type of talk, paying attention to audience, and so forth. In discussing how discourse and culture constitute one another, we are continuing a longstanding tradition within anthropology that started with Franz Boas's documentation of American Indian languages and continues up until the present landscape of linguistic anthropology, which includes a wide range of issues, topics, and theoretical and methodological approaches (Duranti, 2010).

Before going very much further with giving a sense of these contemporary trends through our own work, we need to return to what we mean by culture.

WHAT IS CULTURE?

There are several ideas about what culture 'is' which are useful in understanding relations between discourse and culture (see Duranti, 1997: Chapter 2). A common view of culture is that it is made up of practices and knowledge passed down from one generation to the next, the learned and shared behaviour patterns characteristic of a group. We learn how to be a member of a group through observation, imitation, and trial and error. Some anthropologists have described this knowledge-based view of culture as a *cognitive* view, because of its focus on a principally mental organization of reality: 'culture is not a material phenomenon ... it is the forms of things that people have in mind, their models for perceiving, relating, and otherwise interpreting them (Goodenough, 1964: 36). Both propositional knowledge and procedural knowledge provide guides to understand relationships and models for how to accomplish tasks both in terms of work and in using language. How we view knowledge necessarily influences how we analyse culture. For example, it matters whether or not we include knowledge that is solely in the mind of an individual, or knowledge that emerges with others or is distributed across people and things in the environment and emerges out of collaborative endeavours.

Another view of culture is the view that culture *is* communication, or a system of signs. This *semiotic* theory of culture regards it as a representation system existing through myths, rituals, and classification. This approach focuses on interpretation processes and meaning. It does not try to provide general laws or models of behaviour, rather a system of negotiating and producing particular worldviews. The theory of culture as communication is a different way to link people with objects in their environments. Communicative elements presuppose or establish contextual features (namely point to aspects of the immediate and past contexts) as part of their message, relations that are not explicit but are nevertheless well understood.

Culture can also be looked at as a system of mediation, or as a way whereby humans can learn to use instruments and tools, including language. The linguist Edward Sapir saw languages as 'invisible garments that drape themselves about our spirit and give a predetermined form to all its symbolic expressions' (1921: 221). Whether or not we choose to follow the relativistic and deterministic view of language espoused by Sapir and his student Benjamin Lee Whorf, we can nevertheless recognize that in discourse or as discourse language mediates between the past and present, potential and actual, invisible and visible, immediately given and imagined. To the extent to which culture is something that both needs and entails others – as doers, partners, witnesses, etc. – it is a system of *participation* (Goodwin and Goodwin, 2004), where accessibility to a common code has a high value because it means being able to connect with others. Through interactions with many others over our lifetime we will build and share culture while at the same time using our knowledge of culture to organize and make sense of our social interactions. Our pasts will influence present acts, interpretations and choices (Bourdieu, 1977: 82).

All these views of culture emphasize diversity and complexity in the way we come to share with members of our group a system of habits and dispositions we hardly think about – that is until some event causes us to reflect and analyse a misunderstanding or a breakdown in communication, as sometimes happens when we find ourselves in the presence of visitors from another group or in a new environment that presupposes a different kind of expertise from that which we are familiar with.

In all of these theories of culture, discourse – as a potential resource and activity – is a primary, primordial force.

One way to imagine the close link between discourse and culture is to examine the emergence of the phrase 'Deaf culture'. This phrase was introduced as a deliberate attempt to emphasize the fact that deaf people's different experience of language has led to a unique cultural experience. Deafness, and particularly the use of a visual code, has been redefined by deaf scholars in cultural terms to resist the hegemonic privileging of the hearing experience, and to highlight instead the unique experience of deaf children who, for the most part, will grow up in hearing families who do not know sign language. This means deaf children grow up without key cultural information supplied through the use of language in their environment. The term 'culture' in this context is also an attempt to correct the perception of deafness as a disability. Deaf language communities are uniquely organized according to the properties of an individual's perceptive system (the necessity of using a visual system rather than an auditory-based language). They must rely daily, however, on hearing interpreters who mediate and can influence attitudes and understanding. Language and culture are thus highly interrelated. Attempts to understand the specifics of this relationship have resulted in many interesting studies.

In contrast with the past, most anthropologists now work with the premise that culture is public and does not only exist in people's heads or in ancient texts or objects kept in museums. Culture can be actively studied as a product of the many interactions we have, which in turn will develop our attunement to different types of contextual conditions. As culture emerges in spheres of action and participation, its study requires the immersion of the anthropologist in everyday life, a type of study known as ethnographic research. This entails participant observation, which implies a 'neutral' stance towards the many complex routine and spontaneous acts performed by members in the accomplishment of society and culture. Through acts of speaking and performing with others, members of cultures take a position 'in a social world in which all positions are moving and are defined relative to one another' (Hanks, 1996: 201). Together we build a 'socially structured universe' (Ochs, 1988: 14). This endeavour is a process that is heavily dependent on language, with many different and fascinating forms.

SOME HISTORICAL ANTECEDENTS IN THE STUDY OF DISCOURSE AND CULTURE

In Boas's early vision of anthropology or the study of culture, indigenous languages played a key role. In collecting native texts and writing descriptions of North American languages and their cultures, Boas became interested in how each language classified its speakers' experience and used his knowledge of the grammar and lexicon of a number of American Indian languages to argue against the then prevalent view of European intellectual and moral superiority (Boas, 1911). Echoing statements made by other German scholars who had come before him (e.g. Johann Herder and Wilhelm von Humboldt), but in some respects differing from them (Bauman and Briggs, 2003: Chapter 8), Boas pointed out that each language selects some concepts over others and in so doing offers different perspectives on the same aspect of reality. He was particularly concerned with what each language *must* encode. In the English example *the man is sick* (Boas, 1911: 39), certain grammatical categories must be expressed, such as definiteness (*the*), number (*the man* vs. *the men*), and tense (*is* vs. *was*). As Boas described, the English sentence could be paraphrased as 'a single man that I believe you can identify is at present sick'. However, in Kwak'wala, a Native language of British Columbia, different categories like visibility and deixis must be expressed grammatically, so that the English sentence would be something like 'definite man near him invisible sick near him invisible' or 'that invisible man lies sick on his back on the floor of the absent house' (Foley, 1997: 194). In English, visibility or non-visibility is not part of the regular grammatical expression. In many languages it is the status of speakers and referents that must be expressed. For example, when addressing another speaker, French speakers must choose between *tu* and *vous* and German speakers must choose between *du* and *Sie*, whereas present-day (but not Old) English offers only one option, *you*. Boas's student Edward Sapir (1927) further explored the idea that grammatical categories have an impact on how speakers reflect and construct diverse ways of thinking about the world.

Problems with translation between diverse meaning systems make the investigation of discourse and culture challenging but also stimulate us to think in new ways. An example is the Polynesian term *tapu*, which was borrowed into English as the word *taboo*. This term in a Polynesian universe means something considered inviolable or untouchable due to its sacredness. However, in English *taboo* is taken to mean a very strong social prohibition or ban against something that is considered undesirable or offensive. The Polynesian notion that something could at the same time be both sacred and forbidden was not a familiar notion that could be mapped onto a single term in English (see e.g. Shore, 1989). Some scholars of culture consider this type of translation incommensurability to be insurmountable and discouraging, while others see it as a tool to expand our imaginations and welcome novel ideas. Contact between cultures and the emergence of new concepts based on newly circulating influences also provide us with the opportunity to theorize social change. A well-known anthropological example of culture contact and the complexities of translatability is the term *cargo cult*, given to a practice first observed in some areas of the Pacific Islands, around the time of the Second World War. During this time extensive amounts of goods (cargo) were airdropped to soldiers occupying the islands. Indigenous groups began to theorize about how to continue the supply of goods (from the sky) and obtain the same material wealth the European cultures evidenced. They built representations of the modeled practices (simulated airstrips and control towers) and appealed to the deities and ancestors that they believed were responsible for the foreigners' unfair achievement of great wealth. The term 'cargo cult' is sometimes now used pejoratively in English, an example being the use made of it by the Nobel Prize-winning physicist Richard Feynman to refer to those who adopted the form but not the proper rigour of scientific inquiry.

Whether or not a language accepts loan words – that is, lexical borrowings – is a good indication of how closed or how open a given group of people is to foreign influences. For the Native American group the Tewa of Arizona, the discourse of religious ceremony must be free from foreign expressions or loan words (Kroskrity, 1998). In Pohnpei, Micronesia, on the other hand, words describing Christian practices were borrowed from the Spanish, the first Western colonizers, while terms for the sport of baseball, for sandals, and for underwear were borrowed from the Japanese colonizers, and words and concepts such as 'win' and 'lose' from the Americans.

The French anthropologist Claude Lévi-Strauss attempted to describe the vast differences in meaning systems and to translate discursive systems in understandable terms, by focusing on the semantic oppositions he found in myths. He used narratives about the supernatural as data to understand local systems of thought and action, eventually proposing underlying distinctions (e.g. cooked, raw, rotten) that were shared across cultures. He was partly inspired by the Russian linguist Roman Jakobson, a member of the Prague school of linguistics, which was concerned with a range of language phenomena from sound system to poetics (Jakobson, 1960). An important contribution of these types of analysis is their proposal to think of meaning in relational terms. In this view, the elements of a meaning system can best be understood by looking at the properties of each element in relationship to other elements within a given whole. The power of this approach is that by building on such comparison and contrast it can deal with minimal units like sound differences (e.g. /f/ vs. /v/) as well as with character types in a story (e.g. the hero vs. the villain).

Expanding on the work of Boas and other anthropologists and linguists, John Gumperz and Dell Hymes (1964) also recognized the important relationship between discourse and culture and set out to combine the description and analysis of culture with the description and analysis of language by using as their unit of analysis the *speech event* – a bounded activity defined by rules or norms for the use of speech (e.g. lecture, interview, telephone conversation, greeting exchange, story, news on the radio). Hymes had observed that there were no books devoted to the cross-cultural study of speaking 'to put beside those on comparative religion, comparative politics and the like' (Hymes, 1972: 50). Gumperz and Hymes's *ethnography of communication* was in part a response to the study of language advocated in the 1960s by Noam Chomsky, who had championed an analysis of language that was independent of culture or context (see Chomsky, 1975). The ethnographic descriptions of how language is culturally organized and, in turn, organizes culture, led to greater emphasis on particular contexts of language use. More recent methodological and theoretical innovations in studying discourse and culture include critical discourse analysis, the analysis of conversation, descriptions of multimodal expression, and the role of language in creating and sustaining social institutions.

A CULTURAL UNDERSTANDING OF DISCOURSE

The central theme of these scholars we have mentioned was that discourse could not be understood if it were excised from the context in which it emerged. Context is thus a central focus of investigation for all scholars of discourse. Cultural features such as the organization of space, the display, control, and interpretation of the human body, the use of tools and other artifacts are studied as relations that invite and are constrained by discourse. The conduct of a body in a culturally organized space (e.g. a kitchen, a stage, a public plaza, a dining room), for example, is developmentally shared by all humans who must learn about how to manipulate objects and how materials behave. Yet through particular interactions in particular spaces, language and cultural forms are made relevant, both through a use of forms which link relations between people and things and through the activities that happen in space. Courtrooms, men's and women's houses, churches, and homes all influence our speaking practices and give them meaning. Within these spaces speakers' identities may be defined by where they sit or stand, or by whether they sit or stand. Language can be used to mediate these dimensions such as when the voice is lowered to give the sense that what one is saying should be interpreted as for everyone or as relevant to the central focus of interaction (Goffman, 1963). Humans have a long history of using natural environments and the built environment to give meaning to interactions and to establish roles and relationships (Lawrence and Low, 1990). Space is made culturally meaningful through everyday discursive practices including pathfinding and navigation (e.g. Brown and Levinson, 1993). The creation of pictorial representations, such as graphs and navigational charts, manipulates the terrain in ways that influence cognition and imagination (Hutchins, 1995). Pacific island houses and Berber houses are places for 'writing' and 'reading' status differentiation, as we conduct the body through manners of entrance and activity (Duranti, 1992). A new form of space and architecture, cyberspace, has recently influenced relations between discourse and space and has also emerged as a productive context for work and play. Interacting in web visualization environments can require new habits of spatial reasoning and spatial under-standing (Fisher, Agelidis, Dill, Tan, Collaud, and Jones, 1997), which in turn present inter-esting challenges for humans coordinating their collaborative action across real and virtual spatial domains.

Prosody, linguistic items, embodied action, bodily orientation, gesture, facial expression, gaze, material objects, tools and instruments, and structures in the environment have cul-tural values attached to them, for example, whether it is appropriate to gaze directly at another or gesture (e.g. point) for certain purposes and in certain contexts. Through lan-guage, these ways of manipulating the body are defined as appropriate or inappropriate to the gender, age and social status of the participants in the speech event.

Understanding discourse and culture includes our learning not only how to communi-cate and what can be said but also what cannot be said. Through language we can be very particular or very ambiguous, a result of how our experience with others culturally shapes us to be. In some societies if you say 'yes' you might mean 'not at this time,' since it is impolite to directly refuse a request, while the listener must rely on the context to inter-pret how the response will affect his or her next actions. In the USA arguments in court regarding episodes of alleged date rape have been centred around the issue of how men have interpreted a woman's 'no' (Kulick, 2003). In the American deaf community, blunt-ness is highly valued and its discursive style is believed to be more open and trustworthy than that of hearing people with their comparatively indirect style. In Pohnpei and other Pacific Islands, it is impossible for brothers and sisters to speak about certain topics together. Thus being someone's brother or sister influences what can and cannot be said, and what cannot be said in turn partially creates the roles of brother and sister. These practices then support the attitudes and perceptions that become associated with these roles. In some languages, a special vocabulary is used precisely to handle those situations when one is speaking in the presence of relatives toward whom one must show respect and avoid certain topics. These 'avoidance' registers, variously called 'brother-in-law language' or 'mother-in-law language', are common in Australian Aboriginal languages and are designed to signal that the speaker is sensitive to the presence of certain types of relatives (Haviland, 1979).

In the following sections we look at some examples of how discourse establishes and maintains certain *relationships, ideas, and coherence*. Many 'micro' interactions and activ-ities throughout the day reinforce cultural practices even as participants contest and negoti-ate shared meanings, and even though there is diversity in behaviour. As Bakhtin has noted, our present actions are deeply embedded, and in dialogue with, past actions and voices. We will be using examples from widely different contexts and participants to show how discourse makes possible our unique human communities.

DISCOURSE ESTABLISHES AND MAINTAINS RELATIONSHIPS, IDEAS, AND THE COHERENCE OF THE SELF

Coherence is a cultural product. Individuals' perspectives on their own experiences, even their emotional stance and the awareness of this, are expressed and worked out through discourse with others. In Samoa, for example, village life is experienced and talked about as an intermittent but steady flow of *fa'alavelave* ('troubles' or 'accidents') that interfere with the ideal easy everyday life and require extraordinary cognitive, emotional, physical, and economic involvement. *Fa'alavelave* include weddings, funerals, ceremonies of installation of new chiefs, as well as unexpected visits by friends or relatives.

By looking at relationships between discourse and culture, anthropologists have problematized the notion of 'experience' as a natural processing of sense data and replaced it with the study of experience as a practical accomplishment mediated by discourse (Bauman, 1986; Mattingly, 1998; Throop, 2003). They have shown how discourses make public personal experiences and convey structures of experience to our respective audiences as meta-culture (Urban, 2001). Discourses about the nature of emotion, for example, can be quite different cross-culturally.

We present below three basic ways whereby discourse and culture can be examined: categories and attributes of people; categories of language; and systems of reproduction and representation. We discuss several diverse examples in detail, showing the role of context and the many levels of analysis possible in understanding culture as it is expressed and recreated through innovative language use. The examples provided are taken from our own research projects and are meant to show how people collaboratively create and coordinate a set of flexible and changing relationships while engaged in the construction of individual identities, activities, and values.

CATEGORIES AND ATTRIBUTES OF PEOPLE

It is through discourse that social categories and identities are created, defined and negotiated. In every society, for example, gender is a key social category, yet exactly how and when this category is relevant can vary. In some societies age is an important quality of a person, influencing how language is used, in other societies this is not necessarily a relevant aspect of a person's identity or ways of speaking. A graduate student research assistant helping Keating study the use of communication technologies in geographically distributed engineering firms was asked by one of the engineers: 'What does your husband say about you getting up so early to come to Houston [400 kilometres from Austin]?' The student noted that this 'friendly conversation' reflected not only the speaker's noticing of the wedding ring on her hand, but also the speaker's views on marital status, on gender, work, and the expected roles for husbands and wives in US culture.

Members of different communities can have quite different notions of the self and strategies of interpretation and these become available for analysis through acts of representation.

The construction of personhood can also vary according to what kind of identity a person is thought to have apart from his or her group. In some communities birth order is an essential quality of the person – some cultures privilege heritage matrilineally, others patrilineally. Certainly it is a cultural universal that gender identity is overdetermined in multiple modalities, through dress, adornment, hair arrangement, roles, and behaviour, a selfhood that develops as a process of the embodied subject over time and in conversations with others.

The nature of identity and which social relationships can be put into play can vary significantly. Indeed the very idea of what constitutes an individual varies. We are used to reading about Eurocentric assumptions about the person. When an individual from Ifaluk atoll (Micronesia) says 'We are not feeling well' (Lutz, 1988) in a context where a European would say 'I am not feeling well', the European and the Micronesian are invited to imagine a very different notion of what constitutes a person, illness, and the planning of a curing or adaptive process.

Politicians are constantly monitoring the coherence of their own person. For example, they consider whether what they say on one occasion may contradict what they have already said, as voters and their opponents will be evaluating them mostly in terms of the kind of person they are revealing through their talk. Because identity is perceived in the USA to be something about a person that persists over time and through interactions, a lack of coherence or consistency will be evaluated negatively in terms of honesty and trust. Political candidates not only build identities but build differences among themselves according to whether or not they identify with the local community in narratives of belonging that link them to the communities they want to serve. In public speaking contexts, they narrate their present goals and aspirations as a natural extension of their past choices and experiences. As shown below, for example, Walter Capps, a Democratic candidate, presented his decision to run for Congress in 1995–96 as an extension of his teaching at the University of California at Santa Barbara, especially of his very large and popular course on the Vietnam War (Duranti, 2006).

(1) (August 15, 1996, San Luis Obispo, California; public debate among candidates for US House of Representatives)

Capps: [...] I got into the politics as a kind of extension of the ...
teaching that I'd been doing. ... uh the- the courses that I teach. [...] I got into politics as an extension ... of the work that I've done on- the- ... impact of the Vietnam War, the class that I teach ... that's been featured three times on [the television programme] *Sixty Minutes*, ...I have- testified before congressional committees on three occasions.

As is apparent from this excerpt, his teaching experience was conceived and presented as one of the past experiences that better qualified Capps for the position he hoped to be elected to. Having testified before congressional committees was another item on Capps' list to build his case. Through discourse Capps identified himself as a recognized expert on important national issues and histories. He linked himself to being influential and interested in the future through his past engagement with students at the university and his participation in an influential national TV programme. His audience listened as he orchestrated an understanding of his character and choices. Later on, others would be able to concur, correct, object or redirect the meaning of what had been said for particular audiences.

This point is eloquently and explicitly made in a 1979 speech in the village council of the Samoan village of Falefâ, where one of the two senior orators, Moe'ono Kolio, who has decided to run for parliament, criticizes the incumbent MP from the same district for not having been an active member of his community. The negative characterization of this MP is accomplished by defining him as someone who was successful at school but did not possess good judgment about everyday experiences in the village.

> (2) (Free English translation of segment of a speech delivered at a meeting of the village council of Falefâ on January 25, 1979)
>
> *Moe'ono*: When he won his seat, he rushed to do things for his- his wife,
> everything. I had instead already advised him to build his own
> residence in the village and stay for good. … A prophet is (not)
> sacred in his own village by living in it.
> *Others*: Nicely said!
> *Moe'ono*: But apparently these days because of his childish way of trying to
> be smart … probably because he thinks that he won a scholarship …
> The Lord cannot abandon those who stick to Him.
> *Others*: Nicely said!
> *Moe'ono*: Because each one of us has a brain, with due respect to you Chiefs and (my colleague) the
> Senior Orator here and the people of the King of Atua (i.e. the other orators). No matter how
> many degrees a person gets from school, even a person who didn't go to school, but the
> Lord granted him one hundred percent of good judgment, that (person) is the best.
> *Others*: Nicely said!

Here the senior orator's speech is interpreted as signifying that even though the incumbent MP may have succeeded at school, he lacks good judgment, an essential quality for a leader. He is also described as childish in his way of trying to be smart.

Once elected, in all societies, political leaders, through everyday terms of reference and address, are continually made distinctive members of society. In Pohnpei, this distinctive social identity is created through a choice of language forms which represent the action, position, and possessions of the chief as separate from and more 'sacred' than others. In the example below, while one participant's action is indicated with a low status verb, a few moments later, the action of the secondary chief (his speaking) is indicated with a high status verb (Keating, 1998: 58).

> (3) (Preparation of kava at the feasthouse of the secondary chief, Pohnpei, 1992)
>
> *Menindei*: *patohwansang ahmw sehten koh patohdala*
> take[LOW STATUS] off your shirt you go[LOW STATUS] up there (…)
> *ohlen nek masanihonguhk*
> that man (the chief) could tell[HIGH STATUS] you
> *dahme pwungen ahmw pahn mwohd*
> the correct way for you to sit

The verb *mahsanih* can only be used for a very high status person. A paramount chief's talk can also be noted in an even higher status category through the verb *poahngok*. Studying conversations when a Pohnpeian chief or chieftess is interacting with community members shows the crucial role *lower* status speakers play in 'politely' choosing lower status forms for themselves and others, while choosing high status forms for the chiefs, thus discursively reproducing the very hierarchies which undervalue them through this choice of appropriate and authorized language forms. Pohnpeian chiefs never use status marking in their own speech except in reference to God. In other words, they never lower the status of others. It is the lower status members of the community who lower their own and others' status, and continually reconstitute the hierarchy. A single phrase in Pohnpeian can indicate two separate levels of status aimed at two separate individuals, and one participant's status can be differently constructed by two different speakers in the same interaction, showing the dynamism of this resource. Even when grammatical forms for expressing social status are not present in a language, there are utterances and embodied acts designed to signal deference and hierarchy or categories of persons.

European languages such as German, French, Russian, Italian, and Spanish also have the means to indicate categories of relationships that are contrastive, in these cases along axes of superordinate and subordinate or intimacy and distance. As in Pohnpei the process is dynamic. In the following excerpts two German high school students in a study by Keating discuss how, while there are prescriptive rules for use of the address pronouns *du* (informal, intimate 'you') or *Sie* (formal, distant 'you'), in certain contexts it can be difficult to commit oneself publicly to one or the other. This difficulty can be seen as a problem with managing the categories and attributes of a person. The students discuss conflicts they have experienced in choosing the *socially* correct form, since both forms are grammatically correct. For them a good example of the conflicts encountered is in the case of changes in social status that happen with age. As one of the students says 'a more or less unwritten law indicates that students should be addressed with *Sie* from the beginning of the eleventh grade' (*eine mehr oder weniger unge-schriebene Regel besagte, dass, ab der elften Klasse, sollten die Schüler gesiezt werden*). But in fact changes in status from a subordinate to a peer status with, in this case, teachers, are far from automatic and also subject to negotiation. In the following excerpt Andrea relates an interaction with a teacher about changing forms of address from *du* to *Sie*.

(4)

Andrea:	Also ein Lehrer hat uns gefragt: 'Soll ich euch jetzt duzen –aeh, soll ich euch jetzt siezen?' Und wir so: 'Aeh, nein, danke, sie duzen uns jetzt schon seit drei Jahren, warum sollten sie uns jetzt siezen?'
	(One teacher asked us: 'Should I address you with du, uh, am I to address you with Sie now?' And we responded: 'No, thanks, you addressed us with du for three years, why should you change that now?')

The teacher's offer to change status (where the offer to change must come from the higher status person) is rejected, and the students express their desire to remain in a '*du* relationship'.

Another student relates a similar difficulty in recalibrating her status identity in relationship to her teacher. Along with the change to *du*, she had been asked to address her teacher by his first name. She says, 'I simply couldn't do it (*aber ich konnte es einfach nicht*)':

(5)

Anna:	Ja, das kommt...da erinner ich mich dran, also zum Beispiel in der sechsten Klasse, kurz bevor ich ins Gym– ich ins Gymnasium, andere auf die Realschule oder was anderes kamen- sagte mein Lehrer: 'Also, wenn ihr dann den Abschluss macht, dann könnt ihr mich duzen. Also dann bin ich für euch der Daniel.' (*Yes, I remember that in sixth grade before I attended the Gymnasium my teacher said: 'Well, after you have graduated, you can address me with du then. I will be Daniel to you'.*)
Andrea:	Sagen viele Lehrer, ja. (*A lot of teachers say this, yes.*)
Anna:	Aber ich konnte es einfach nicht, weil irgendwie, ich weiss nicht, es ist einfach so die Beziehung, es ist einfach, dass die Lehrerbeziehung auf einmal ʼne mehr familiaere Beziehung wird, ʼne engere Beziehung, das fand ich total komisch irgendwie. Das hab ich dann auch nie gemacht. Es ging nicht darum, dass ich irgendwie unbedingt da, weisst du, so überhöflich sein wollte oder so, aber es war einfach, Gewohnheit. (*But I couldn't do it because somehow, I don't know, it is simply the relationship with the teacher, and if this is suddenly more on a familiar base, a closer relationship, then it feels weird. That's why I never addressed him with du. I was not about to be extremely friendly, I was simply used to it.*)
Andrea:	Es ist schwer sich umzugestellen, es ist sehr schwer sich umzustellen. (*It's hard to reorient; it's very hard to reorient.*)
Anna:	Auf jeden Fall. (*Definitely.*)

In addition to this discomfort in suddenly changing categories in relationships of this type, where Andrea says, 'It's hard to reorient, it's very hard to reorient' (*Es ist schwer sich umzugestellen, es ist sehr schwer sich umzustellen*), there are social consequences for making an inappropriate choice of address forms, since this choice of form shows social knowledge. A particular choice can offend the addressee by seeming too familiar or not familiar enough, and can also indicate social incompetence. Andrea faced this difficulty when she met the mother of a friend after many years (the family had moved away).

(6)

Andrea:	I was already considerably older and *Sie* played a much bigger role. It was not easy for me to address this woman with *du* again. I simply wanted to use *Sie*, I had to. And she said: 'Tell me, why are you addressing me with *Sie* now, you always said *du*?' And I was like: 'I'm so sorry, it's not my fault, I didn't mean to.'

In this case, real distance (in time and space) correlates with a perceived change in the intimacy of this relationship or relationship category.

In the American Deaf community, hierarchies are explicitly de-valued. This is partly achieved through the practice of directness in speech, where respect for the other is not conditional on the choice of language form, deference, avoidance or ambiguity. Hinting and being vague to American deaf people is 'inappropriate and even offensive' (Lane, 1992: 16).

In computer-mediated contexts, such as online gaming, players are also hard at work negotiating categories of persons and can manipulate entirely new types of identities and attributes (Keating and Sunakawa, 2010). The gamers in the example we show below had spent many hours developing their avatars or onscreen self-presentations and honing the skills that give these avatars and the players status among their peers. In the excerpt below they are preparing to play, trading 'powers,' which are attributes or, as the game manual describes, 'elements that constitute a personality'. One can 'become a distance specialist … [one can] become the 'knock out' artist' (www.cityofheroes.com/game_info/rewards/enhancements.html). The players construct their characters' powers collaboratively, building group coherence and the potentials for working together on a common goal. Player Brian offers to the other three players an endurance, accuracy or hold. Two players respond to the offer, and thus the trade is accomplished.

(7)   (Austin, Texas 2007)

Brian:	I need uh:: (.) does anyone want an endurance or
	an accuracy [or a hold?
Greg:	[uh:::]
	(1.5)
David:	Endurance? (.) [Accuracy? Uh:: never mind]
Caitlin:	[What level is the accuracy?]
Brian:	[Endurance] or accuracy or any of those
	(....)
Brian:	(?) 25 percent accuracy cause I don't wanna throw it away
	I don't really care ((David looks at Brian))
David:	= I- I'll trade it for your awaken
Brian:	Okay. So which one do you want?
David:	The accuracy.

Online, with newly created forms of sociality (Turkle, 1995), we recruit conventions from other contexts as well as exploit technologically innovative attributes and relationships. Boundaries between the real and virtual (or what in Goffman's terms reality really is) are constantly shifting with the aid of discourse, including symbolic forms provided by the game creators (Keating, 2008).

Moving on from the categories and attributes of persons, our second focus turns to the ways in which language itself can be organized into recognizable categories. There are speech acts associated with and which create certain forms of speech events and texts, for example, politics, art, curing, magic, and gossip.

CATEGORIES OF LANGUAGE: GENRE, ART, INTERTEXTUALITY

Another way to illustrate relationships between discourse and culture is by looking at the ways whereby language can be changed or suited to certain activities and goals, as well as artful or playful uses. Ways of speaking in every speech community can be organized into genres or categories which can be easily identified by native speakers. Some examples are greetings, lectures, ceremonies, songs, word play, prayer, and conversation. Culturally defined categories or native taxonomies order social life and practices, and even young speakers can master not only grammatical competence but also social competence while participating in a range of different communication events in their homes and community, and while interacting with a range of people. They can learn how to distinguish between individuals in forms of address and talk (as described in the previous section), when it is appropriate to talk and to whom, and different styles of speaking.

In Samoa, as previously discussed, the way social life is organized and conceived lends itself to the continuous production and evaluation of a particular genre, the *lâuga*, a kind of formal speech usually performed by community leaders called *matai*. Being a *matai* carries with it a duty to perform in this genre whenever the occasion arises. The knowledge and skills necessary to engage in this genre are achieved via direct observation and practice (see Duranti, 1984; 1994). In the following excerpt from Duranti's fieldnotes, the chief Savea (S) describes the importance of context in the processes of acquiring the knowledge necessary to be a competent *matai*.

(8) (Falefâ, 1979; Western Samoa, A. Duranti's fieldnotes)

AD: How do you learn all these things about the traditions and about the history of the village and [chiefly] titles?

S: From listening to what other *matai* [titled people] say. In Samoa it goes from ear to ear.

AD: Did the introduction of writing influence this process of learning?

S: Some people write down these things. But we say that if you love your son you will not let him look at your notebook [where you keep notes on the tradition], otherwise when he will be grown up and maybe get a *matai* title he will be *valea* ['stupid']. If my son comes to me and asks me 'Who was so-and-so?' If I love him I will not tell him. But instead I will say to him 'Go to the house where the *matai* are getting together. Go where the *matai* are having [the ceremonial drink] *kava* and serve'. That's what I will tell him. That's the way you learn. Remember about [the high chief] Leuga? He was a very wise man. When he died, his son would sit there and say nothing. [We all thought:] 'He must have read Leuga's notebook'.

Acquiring this knowledge of specialized ways and styles of speaking is seen as being directly connected to participating in the social organization of village life. Savea says that his son must learn by attending those events where *kava* is served, and therefore a link between serving, learning, and speaking in a particular genre is made. Since *kava* is served on important occasions, this means that a young person must be present when the elders get together for these affairs. In order to learn, one must carry out the orders of the more senior members of the community. Learning this particular highly valued speaking style is thus part of the process of positioning oneself within the existing hierarchical social order and participating in its situated discursive reproduction. Any individual who thinks that he can learn how to be an effective orator simply by reading books or going to school (see example 2 above) instead of participating and serving the elders is likely to make a fool of himself because his knowledge of the genre and style will not be adequate.

In many studies of genre the importance of the immediate audience is described as significant but is often overlooked in analysis. Similarly, the role of improvization is underplayed or ignored altogether. But in fact those who deliver public speeches are often required to adapt their delivery to the occasion in unforeseen ways. Expert public speakers are in fact evaluated precisely by their ability to change whatever plan they had made to fit new circumstances, including the composition of the audience and the unexpected presence of certain parties. This is true in Samoa as well as in the USA. The difference has to do with features such as the 'key' in which the speech is being delivered. Samoan *lâuga* tend to be delivered in a serious key (humour is usually reserved for introductory remarks or comments made after a speech has been delivered). However, in US campaign speeches, with some exceptions, humour is quite pervasive. For example, in speeches recorded by Duranti during the 1995–96 campaign for the US Congress in California's 22nd district, the political candidate who ended up winning showed on the first day of the campaign the ability to adapt his humorous punchlines according to whichever audience he was addressing. When he listed the many California communities he had already visited or was about to visit on that day – showing his commitment to communicate across the entire district – he would end the list in a different way according to the types of listeners he was facing. In the first example, he was in front of a group of mostly retired people.

(9) (Nov. 14, 1995, Paso Robles, California)

Capps: (well) we're gonna get in the car here in a minute
              because- uh because we're gonna go now to uh-
              we're gonna go to: San Luis Obispo, …
              then we're goin' to Santa Maria, …
              then we go to Santa Barbara, …
              then we go to Lompoc, …
              then we go to Buelton, …
              then we go to:- Solvang. …
              and then I think- uh after ((faster ->)) we'll probably go to bed.
Audience: ((loud laughter)) HA!! HEHEHE!

The punchline ('and then I think- uh after we'll probably go to bed') is produced in order to be understood and approved by an audience that is mostly made up of senior citizens. The poetics of the oratorical genre (form-content relationships) can be further analysed by looking at the skilful organization of the joke. Breaking the frame of the list of places is accomplished by mentioning an activity ('going to bed') that keeps the same syntactic and semantic frame of the last four clauses ('go to NOUN') but inserts a noun ('the bed') that is not a location like the other ones. In addition, the punchline describes an ordinary as opposed to a special activity, introduces a private as opposed to a public space, and implies resting, sleeping, and even more intimate acts. The resounding laughter that the joke receives suggests that the audience got pleasure out of the 'go to bed' punchline and could sympathize with the fact that one might be tired after having to visit all the places mentioned by Capps. It was also important here that for this group of people the connotation of intimate contact, if perceived, would not be felt to be problematic. At the second stop, in San Luis Obispo, when Capps had his written speech in front of him, the itinerary-narrative showed up again, but this time it was placed at the very beginning of the speech and did not have a humorous resolution, suggesting that the ending in example (9) might have been improvised. A humorous punch-line returned, however, at the third and fourth stops, both of which had mostly students as members of the audience. The fact that the punchline changed each time showed that the speaker was being quite careful in his discursive formulations. At the first stop, Hancock College near Santa Maria, Capps had been invited to speak in a political science course and he knew that the audience would include members of the media and some supporters who were not students.

(10) (Nov. 14, 1995, Hancock College, Santa Maria)

Capps:	we're in the middle of a::- ... a: very very full day. ... uhm
	we started the day at- San Miguel Mission. ... uh,
	we did that for uh ... spiritual. liturgical reasons
	to become ... °(you know) rightly .. rooted and oriented ...
	uhm in ... this life. which is:: sacred life to me.
	and then we went ... from there. to Paso Robles and met some
	people...um- on the street corner and-...talked with them for a while
	and uh- we've just come from San Luis Obispo
	and we'll go next ... back to our own campus, UCSB,
	then on to .. Lompoc
	and- .. Buelton
	and .. Solvang,
	and then -hh it will probably be time for dinner. // uhm.
Audience:	((sparse laughter)) he-he-he.

The final line about going to dinner instead of going to bed made sense here because students and young people in general are known to go to bed late, and the potential sexual connotation of going to bed might not have been seen as appropriate in this context. At the next venue, on the campus of the University of California at Santa Barbara, where Capps was professor of religious studies and a popular instructor, the list of places ended with a mention of a bar downtown which was a favorite hangout for undergraduate students but an unlikely place for Capps and his wife to go.

(11) (Nov. 14, 1995, campus of the University of California, Santa Barbara)

Capps: you know- we-we-we <u>sta</u>rted the day in San Miguel. uh,
north of here. uh-
we went all the way to the- to the Monterey County line. ...
we started the day there=.
=we went to Paso Robles next. ...
we've been to San Luis Obispo=
=we've been to Santa Maria. ...
we- we- we're here now of course.
I'm standing here.
we go //next to uh I mean it's clear.
Audience: ((sparse laughter)) haha- haha
Capps: //it's clear that I'm standing here.
Audience: ((laughter)) haha- hahaha- hahah
Capps: ((clears throat))
uh, and we go next to:- .. to Lompoc, ...
and then we go to Buelton, ...
and then we go to Solvang,=
=and then uh- ... if-
if my wife agrees we're gonna go to Matty's Tavern //after that.
Audience: ((Laughter, cheers)) hehehe-heheheheheh

The use of humour, joking and laughter can be powerful forms of creating and also resisting expectations. In these cases it also displays the speaker's knowledge of his genre and audience, a key quality of a politician.

In addition to formal speaking styles, such as oratory, anthropologists recognize informal speaking as equally important for understanding how language is suited for certain goals and activities. Gossip, for example, is an activity of reporting which is widely recognized cross-culturally as a particular kind of named speech activity. It is often delegitimized as being outside of authorized contexts of power, but is an important and valued context where people tell stories, discuss and negotiate power relations, cultural rules and community sanctions, as well as build social relationships (Brenneis, 1984; Haviland, 1977) and coherence. Assessments (Goodwin and Goodwin, 1992) are frequently made and ratified, and reported speech is used to organize common interpretations, including what is ethical (e.g. Besnier, 1990). Gossip sessions make the act of interpreting of behavior an interactional event.

In example (12) the speakers are gossiping about scandalous new forms of female dress, the result of culture contact between Pohnpei and the USA, that are perceived to threaten the traditional Pohnpeian presentation of the female body. One of the speakers, a woman, remarks self-reflexively that gossiping is not considered a valued activity – in fact it is highly sanctioned (nevertheless gossiping remains everywhere a popular pastime!).

(12) (Pohnpei, 1991)

A: *ah R ((her husband)) inda dene kilang pwe ke pahn riahla*
but R ((her husband)) says 'careful because you will be cursed' (for gossiping)

((A animates his voice)) *'kowe mwahuki kawe aramas'*
((A animates his voice)) 'you're always criticizing people
menda remw kin pil indinda songen style in emen'
never mind your habitual talking about some people's style'

The speaker criticizes the dress of another woman, M. Although M wears a culturally appropriate skirt, she chooses a fabric judged to be so sheer by the speaker A, that people can see through it, showing the outline of the woman's thighs. In Pohnpei a woman must not reveal in public the outline of her body between the waist and the knee.

(13) (Pohnpei, 1991)

A: *i pirekek kilang a likou tangete wasahn*
I turned around and saw her clothes were like this
((voice changes pitch)) 'M ((name)), ke urohs?'
((voice changes pitch)) 'M, are you even wearing a skirt?
eri mwahu men re aramas kileng weite dahngemwen
you think it's good if people can see your thighs?
dah ke kin koasongosongih ohlakan'
what are you doing always enticing men?'

Through discourses such as these, people not only express and reproduce local ideas about gender, conformity, and legitimate relations between the individual, others and the group, but also test ideas about the durability of these cultural forms (Keating, 2002).

Publicly shared representations and graphic reproductions of another kind will be discussed below, as we turn to a third basic way that discourse and culture can be examined – systems of reproduction and representation.

SYSTEMS OF REPRODUCTION AND REPRESENTATION

It has been traditional within academic discourses on culture to describe differences between literate and non-literate or preliterate societies. This historically-based model assumed the superiority of print technologies, and tended to underspecify the importance of oral narrative and memory as forms of historical and cultural documentation. This dichotomy between literate and non-literate populations has been extensively critiqued for its assumptions about the effects of literacy. It is now recognized that the integration and utilization of technologies and tools of representation can vary widely, even within what is considered as the same culture. For example, among American jazz musicians there is both admiration and contempt for literacy, and jazz musicians can be highly critical of the use of literacy (Duranti, 2008). Jazz musicians are expected to constantly invent new melodic lines that are different from the melody in the original composition. This creative part of playing forms an important part of the identity of such musicians for whom it is important to clarify that playing without reading a score is an aesthetic choice and not a lack of knowledge or training. As we saw above in example (8), Samoans consider a reliance on writing an impediment to true knowledge of the tradition, including the ability to deliver formal speeches. A person who learns from books alone is expected to have inferior knowledge. The fact that this belief exists in a community where everyone reads the Bible, and speech making often borrows expressions from the Bible, shows that cultural attitudes are crucial in determining the kind of discourse that is favoured or allowed.

The fact that for some groups (e.g. jazz musicians in the USA, Samoan speechmakers) literacy is suspect should not surprise us given that we know that literacy comes with a set of cultural values about what kind of knowledge is important. When outsiders introduce literacy to a community it can be used to delegitimize local traditional knowledge (Schieffelin, 2000) and traditional forms of discourse.

New forms of representation are being incorporated across widely different culture groups and types of work. Computer tools, for example, are changing the nature of collaboration in engineering design work (Monteiro and Keating, 2009). Now that it is easy to transmit complex engineering plans and representations, teams can be assembled virtually from dispersed locations. In the past, engineers shared a physical workspace while accomplishing design tasks. Now, due to a desire to 'stay competitive' in international economies of labour, the shortage of engineers in the USA, and the ability to share designs and communicate instantly across vast differences in culture and time, engineers are being asked by their employers to work with others in lower 'cost centres' or with engineers located in countries where the cost of living and engineering cost per hour are considerably less. In one such group, documents representing the construction plans of a processing plant and documents listing finished and unfinished work tasks form an important part of weekly conference calls to coordinate team work. In these meetings, the engineers must build a shared understanding of the state of work and information as represented by the documents in front of them, and how to translate 'needs' or 'action lists' into future distributed work. The meaning of lists is not a simple interpretive accomplishment. In the example below, as they proceed through a printed agenda, which by virtue of its conventional, abstract, decontextualized form leaves out important information that is required in order to accomplish the actions, problems emerge in understanding.

Engineers' habits of working have traditionally taken place within the same physical setting, where oral narratives and oral engineering culture prevail, and knowledge is rarely written down in the exhaustive detail required by the job at hand. As the excerpt begins the engineers are working on the weekly needs list. Almost immediately it is discovered that the list does not in fact represent the state of the shared knowledge and basis for planning. It takes several turns to reach an understanding about, and to begin to deal with, the implication of having misrepresented a key engineering feature – the number and type of sumps. This important correction, known only to some, including the Eastern Europe office, is treated as 'news' in a setting where news of this type can signify poor team communications and a lack of competence. This lack of competence then often becomes part of a list of prototypical failure events in doing cross-cultural work of this type.

(14) (12:06, April 7 2008)

E.European Mgr:	I propose to concentrate- to look on our need list.
US Engineer R:	I don't I don't see it, oh, need list, the other one now.
E.European Mgr:	Yes.
US Engineer R:	Alright. So the action list is, done.
US side (?):	Yuh.
E.European Mgr:	The action list regarding of stress.
US Engineer R:	The stress. Now we go to the action list in general.
E.European Mgr:	Yes.
US Engineer R:	Ok. (.) Go ahead.
E.European Mgr:	Item nine.
US Engineer R:	Uh, the dimension of a sump
E.European Mgr:	Hydrogen plant underground piping connection with the with the hydrogen plant. I have now one other designer which was assigned to my team for working on these areas.
US Engineer R:	Who can re- say anything about- as far as I know the sump- is ((discussion on Eastern European side))
US Engineer R:	Okay. But I'm trying to tell you about the sump first. The number nine, ok? We don't have-
E.European Mgr:	It is not number nine, I'm talking about these two sumps. One is oil and sewage, one is oil and water.
US Engineer R:	Oh, we have two sumps?
US Proj.Manager:	Yes
	(…)
US Engineer R:	Who knows about it?
US Engineer Andy:	Three sumps total

Situations such as this become source narratives for engineers to question the value of offshoring work, and to have their belief system about the superiority of the traditional way of doing engineering validated – by informal, informational, oral exchange channels within the same office with people one has long-term, daily interactions with. In what might seem at first a trivial display of problems with the coordination of printed materials and the representation of plans in documents, one discussion concerned the sequence of numbers in representing months and days, which is different in North America and Europe.

The important relation between forms of textual representation and cultural practices can be seen in a different environment when a deaf person recounts her first experience of using the TTY, a technology to transfer text over telephone lines (now made obsolete by superior visual representation potentials of the internet), which increased her autonomy and range of discursive settings.

(15) (Austin, Texas, 2000. Note: we follow the convention of using glosses in capital letters for signs)

TO: YES. ONE OF MY MOST THRILLING, BECAUSE I FINALLY CAN HAVE TTY TO TALK WITH MY FRIEND FAR. NOT MUST DRIVE, I ASK MOM, 'PLEASE DRIVE SEE MY FRIEND'. NOT MUST, COOL.
Yes. It really was one of my most thrilling experiences [using the TTY for the first time], because I could finally talk to my friend who lived far away. I didn't have to get in the car and drive, or ask Mom, 'Please drive me to see my friend'. I didn't have to do that. It was cool.

TO: NOW I USE INTERNET, BETTER INTERNET. ME TTY, FORGET IT.
      BETTER THROUGH INTERNET. AMAZING.
      Now I use the internet, the internet is better. For me, the TTY,
      forget it. It's better through the internet. It's amazing.

New systems for the representation and reproduction of human messages far beyond one's immediate space and for creating and engaging in new interactional frameworks are now taken for granted in many places. The 'amazing' internet this deaf person describes is superior to the TTY or typed text, which depended on turn-taking that must be organized through the use of GA, or 'go ahead', shown below.

(16) (A typed text or TTY exchange between E. Keating and G. Mirus, researchers)

G: HI GA
E: HI THIS IS ELIZABETH, IS ALL FINE WITH GENE THER4
      AND THE COMPUTER GA
G: UV THIS IS GENE ANDI JUST DOWNLOADED NETMEETING AND
      AM GETTING READY TO HAVE IT INSTALLED GA

Contrast this with the rich medium for representing and sending visual language forms, as shown in the image below which shows a signed conversation. Keating's image is the small square in the bottom right-hand corner. The view shown here is Keating's in Texas, while research collaborator Mirus (who is signing) is in Washington DC.

Figure 16.1

Computer-mediated signing space has resulted in some interesting impacts on signed discourse. Because signers don't share the same space, pointing or deictic references have had to be worked out (as in the case of whether pointing the forefinger means 'here' in my space or 'there' in your space) (Keating and Mirus, 2003), with new ways to create effective understanding across different properties of real and virtual space. Signers and others, however, show skilful adaptation to properties of reproduction and representation media and to new discursive fields, and they influence how these technologies of representation are used. They also show flexibility in the kinds of resources to employ to achieve coherence, and to do identity work, to maintain relationships, and to understand reciprocal perspectives.

CONCLUSION

In this chapter we have shown how discourse and culture mutually constitute one another. Drawing from our own research in Pohnpei, Samoa, the USA, Germany, and Eastern Europe, we identified a number of contexts in which social identities are produced and managed through speaking and other semiotic resources. We have also shown that different languages offer a number of specific resources for establishing and interpreting attitudes, negotiating social status, and dealing with changes in the context of interaction. Cross-cultural research makes it evident that discourse plays a key role in expressing and guiding our individual and collective experiences.

Our way of analysing discourse has deep anthropological roots in the sense that it always starts from an ethnographic experience (i.e. through participant-observation within a given community) and from the effort to reach an ethnographic understanding of a situation, that is, an understanding that is informed by the participants' point of view. We focused on the discursive constitution of categories and attributes of people because we found that much of the work done by speakers through language and other symbolic forms was directed toward identity issues. We would even go as far as saying that human existential dilemmas are to a large extent defined by a need to communicate in ways that are socially constrained and socially meaningful. In this sense, language, broadly defined, provides both the instruments for achieving our goals and the limits to what can be said and done on any given occasion. The apparent 'naturalness' with which people communicate with one another on a daily basis hides the fact that we are held responsible for every expression we produce. This is so because our cultural preferences, values, and attitudes emerge through discourse.

Linguistic anthropologists believe that this recurring, misleadingly ordinary, and yet complex process of expression and negotiation of meaning in social life can be subjected to rigorous analysis. The brief exchanges we discussed in this chapter are meant to provide a glimpse of the ways in which culture is to a great extent a discursive project.

FURTHER READING

The following are suggested for readers wishing to broaden their understanding of discourse and culture:

Gumperz, J. (1982) *Discourse Strategies*. Cambridge: Cambridge University Press.
This book shows many ways that speakers and hearers use properties of language, such as intonation and prosody as well as style shifts and code shifts, to communicate. It discusses both problems of communication between members of different cultures and ethnic groups, and analyses of social meanings expressed through language.

Duranti, A. and Goodwin, C. (1992) *Rethinking Context*. New York: Cambridge University Press.
This book explores language and context as interactively defined phenomena. It is a collection of essays on the role of context in activities such as face-to-face interaction, radio talk, medical diagnosis, political encounters and socialization practices.

Silverstein, M. and Urban, G. (1996) *The Natural History of Discourse*. Chicago: University of Chicago Press.
This book discusses the notion of culture as text, particularly the processes of 'entextualization' and 'contextualization' of discourse, in essays covering a wide range of cultural practices, from the poetry of insult among Wolof griots to law school classrooms in the USA.

Hill, J. (2008) *The Everyday Language of White Racism*. Malden, MA: Blackwell.
This book analyses how racism is produced through everyday language practices which serve to keep racist stereotypes in circulation, with a focus on American culture.

ONLINE READING

The following articles are available at www.sagepub.co.uk/discoursestudies.

Monteiro, M. and Keating, E. (2009) 'Managing misunderstandings: the role of language in interdisciplinary scientific collaboration'. *Science Communication*, Vol. 31, No. 1, 6–28.

Duranti, A. (2010) 'Husserl, intersubjectivity and anthropology'. *Anthropological Theory*, 10(1):1–20.

REFERENCES

Bauman, R. (1986) *Story, Performance, and Event*. Cambridge: Cambridge University Press.
Bauman, R. and Briggs, C. (2003) *Voices of Modernity: Language Ideologies and the Politics of Inequality*. New York: Cambridge University Press.
Besnier, N. (1990) 'Conflict management, gossip and affective meaning on Nukulaelae'. In K. Watson-Gegeo and G. White (eds), *Disentangling: Conflict Discourse in the Pacific*. Stanford, CA: Stanford University Press. pp. 290–334.
Boas, F. (ed.) (1911) *Handbook of American Indian Languages*. Washington, DC: Smithsonian Institution, Bureau of American Ethnology, Bulletin 40. Reprinted New York: Humanities Press, 1969. [Introduction reprinted with J.W. Powell, *Indian Linguistic Families of America North of Mexico*. Lincoln: University of Nebraska Press, 1966].
Bourdieu, P. (1977) *Outline of a Theory of Practice*. Cambridge: Cambridge University Press.
Brenneis, D. (1984) 'Grog and gossip in Bhatgaon: style and substance in Fiji Indian conversation'. *American Ethnologist* 11:3.
Brown, P. and S. Levinson (1993) '"Uphill" and "downhill" in Tzeltal'. *Journal of Linguistic Anthropology* 3 (1): 46–74.
Chomsky, N. (1975) *The Logical Structure of Linguistic Theory*. New York: Plenum Press.
Duranti, A. (1984) 'Lauga and Talanoaga: two speech genres in a Samoan political event'. In D.L. Brenneis and F.R. Meyers (eds), *Dangerous Words: Language and Politics in the Pacific*. New York and London: New York University Press.

Duranti, A. (1992) 'Language in context and language as context: the Samoan respect vocabulary'. In A. Duranti and C. Goodwin (eds), *Rethinking Context* . Cambridge: Cambridge University Press. pp. 77–99.

Duranti, A. (1994) *From Grammar to Politics*. Berkeley: University of California Press.

Duranti, A. (1997) *Linguistic Anthropology*. Cambridge: Cambridge University Press.

Duranti, A. (2006) 'Narrating the political self in a campaign for US Congress'. *Language in Society* 35: 467–97.

Duranti, A. (2008) 'Orality with attitude: Ambivalent views of literacy among Samoan speechmakers and jazz musicians'. *L'Homme* (printed with the title 'L'oralité avec impertinence: Ambivalence vis-à-vis de l'écrit chez les orateurs samoans et les musiciens de jazz américains'), 189: 23–47.

Duranti, A. (2010) 'Husserl, intersubjectivity and anthropology'. *Anthropological Theory*, 10(1): 1–20. ant.sagepub.com/cgi/content/abstract/10/1-2/16

Fisher, B.D., Agelidis, M., Dill, J., Tan, P., Collaud, G. and Jones, C. (1997) 'CZWeb: Fish-eye views for visualizing the world wide web'. In M.J. Smith, G. Salvendy and R.J. Koubed (eds), *Design of Computing Systems: Social and Ergonomic Considerations: Advances in Human Factors/Ergonomics*, Vol. 2. Amsterdam: Elsevier. pp. 21b, 719–722.

Foley, W. (1997) *Anthropological Linguistics: An Introduction*. Oxford: Basil Blackwell.

Goffman, E. (1963) *Behavior in Public Places: Notes on the Social Organization of Gathering*. New York: Free Press.

Goodenough, W.H. (1964) 'Cultural anthropology and linguistics'. In D. Hymes (ed.), *Language in Culture and Society. A Reader in Linguistics and Anthropology*. New York: Harper & Row.

Goodwin, C. and Goodwin, M.H. (1992) 'Assessments and the Construction of Context'. In A. Duranti and C. Goodwin (eds), *Rethinking Context: Language as an Interactive Phenomenon*. Cambridge: Cambridge University Press. pp. 147–89.

Goodwin, C. and Goodwin, M.H. (2004) 'Participation'. In A. Duranti (ed.), *A Companion to Linguistic Anthropology.* Malden, MA: Blackwell. pp. 222–244.

Gumperz, J. and Hymes, D. (eds) (1964) 'The ethnography of communication'. Special issue *American Anthropologist* 66 (6), part II.

Hanks, W.F. (1996) *Language and Communicative Practices*. Boulder, CO: Westview Press.

Haviland, J. (1977) *Gossip, Reputation, and Knowledge in Zinacantan*. Chicago: University of Chicago Press.

Haviland, J. (1979) 'How to talk to your brother-in-law in Guugu Yimidhirr'. In T. Shopen (ed.), *Languages and their Speakers*. Cambridge, MA: Winthrop.

Hutchins, E. (1995) *Cognition in the Wild*. Cambridge, MA: MIT Press.

Hymes, D. (1972) 'Models of the interaction of language and social life'. In J. Gumperz and D. Hymes (eds), *Directions in Sociolinguistics: The Ethnography of Communication*. New York: Basil Blackwell.

Jakobson, R. (1960) 'Closing statement: linguistics and poetics'. In T.A. Sebeok (ed.), *Style in Language.* Cambridge, MA: MIT Press. pp. 398–429.

Keating, E. (1998) *Power Sharing: Language, Rank, Gender and Social Space in Pohnpei, Micronesia*. Oxford: Oxford University Press.

Keating, E. (2002) 'Everyday interactions and the domestication of social inequality'. *IPRA Pragmatics* 12, 3: 347–359.

Keating, E. (2008) 'Space shifting: New technologies, new opportunities'. *Texas Linguistic Forum*, 52: 70–79.

Keating, E. and Mirus, G. (2003) 'American Sign Language in virtual space: interactions between deaf users of computer-mediated video communication and the impact of technology on language practices'. *Language in Society* 32: 693–714.

Keating, E. and Sunakawa, C. (2010) 'Participation cues: Coordinating activity and collaboration in complex online gaming worlds'. *Language in Society*, 39: 331–356.

Kroskrity, P. (1998) 'Arizona Tewa Kiva speech as manifestation of a dominant language ideology'. In B. Schieffelin, K. Woolard and P.V. Kroskrity (eds), *Language Ideologies, Practice and Theory.* New York: Oxford University Press. pp. 103–22.

Kulick, D. (2003) 'No'. *Language and Communication* 1: 139–51.

Lane, H. (1992) *The Mask of Benevolence*. New York: Vintage Books.

Lawrence, D. and Low, S. (1990) 'The built environment and spatial form'. *Annual Review of Anthropology* 19: 453–505.

Lutz, C. (1988) *Unnatural Emotions*. Chicago: University of Chicago Press.

Mattingly, C. (1998) *Healing Dramas and Clinical Plots: The Narrative Structure of Experience*. Cambridge: Cambridge University Press.

Monteiro, M. and Keating, E. (2009) 'Managing misunderstandings: The role of language in interdisciplinary scientific collaboration'. *Science Communication*, 31 (1): 6–28. ant.sagepub.com/cgi/content/short/3/2/219

Ochs, E. (1988) *Culture and Language Development: Language Acquisition and Language Socialization in a Samoan Village*. Cambridge: Cambridge University Press.

Sapir, E. (1921) *Language: An Introduction to the Study of Speech*. New York: Harcourt, Brace, Janovich.

Sapir, E. (1927) 'The unconscious patterning of behavior in society'. In E.S. Dummer (ed.), *The Unconscious: A Symposium*. New York: Knopf. pp. 114–142 [reprinted in D.G. Mandelbaum (ed.), *Selected Writings of Edward Sapir in Language, Culture and Personality*. Berkeley: University of California Press. pp. 544–59].

Schieffelin, B. (2000) 'Introducing Kaluli literacy'. In P. Kroskrity (ed.), *Regimes of Language: Ideologies, Polities, and Identities*. Santa Fe: School of American Research.

Shore, B. (1989) 'Mana and Tapu'. In A. Howard and R. Borofsky (eds), *Development in Polynesian Ethnology*. Honolulu: University of Hawaii Press. pp. 137–73.

Throop, C.J. (2003) 'Articulating experience'. *Anthropological Theory* 3: 219–41. ant.sagepub.com/cgi/content/short/3/2/219

Turkle, S. (1995) *Life on the Screen: Identity in the Age of the Internet*. New York: Simon and Schuster.

Urban, G. (2001) *Metaculture: How Culture Moves Through the World*. Minneapolis: University of Minnesota Press.

SEVENTEEN

Critical Discourse Analysis

Norman Fairclough, Jane Mulderrig and Ruth Wodak

WHAT IS CRITICAL DISCOURSE ANALYSIS?

In recent decades critical discourse analysis (CDA) has become a well-established field in the social sciences. However, in contrast with some branches of linguistics, CDA is not a discrete academic discipline with a relatively fixed set of research methods. Instead, we might best see CDA as a problem-oriented interdisciplinary research movement, subsuming a variety of approaches, each with different theoretical models, research methods and agenda. What unites them is a shared interest in the semiotic dimensions of power, injustice, abuse, and political-economic or cultural change in society. CDA is distinctive in a) its view of the relationship between language and society, and b) its critical approach to methodology. Let us take these in turn by first exploring the notions of 'discourse' and 'critical'.

The term 'discourse' is used in various ways across the social sciences and within the field of CDA. In the most abstract sense, 'discourse' is an analytical category describing the vast array of meaning-making resources available to us. At this level we can use the alternative term 'semiosis' (encompassing words, pictures, symbols, design, colour, gesture, and so forth), in order to distinguish it from the other common sense of 'discourse' as a category for identifying particular ways of representing some aspect of social life (for example Republican versus Democrat discourses on immigration). CDA sees discourse (or semiosis) as a form of social practice. This implies a dialectical relationship between a particular discursive event and all the diverse elements of the situation(s), institutions(s), and social structure(s) which frame it. A dialectical relationship is a two-way relationship: the discursive event is shaped by situations, institutions and social structures, but it also shapes them. To put it a different way, discourse is socially *constitutive* as well as socially shaped: it constitutes situations, objects of knowledge, and the social identities of and relationships between people and groups of people. It is constitutive both in the sense that it helps to sustain and reproduce the social status quo, and in the sense that it contributes to transforming it. Since discourse is so socially influential, it gives rise to important issues of power. In a dialectical understanding, a particular configuration of the social world (e.g. relations of domination and difference) is implicated in a particular linguistic conceptualization of the world; in language, we do not simply name things but conceptualize things. Thus discursive practices may have major ideological effects: that is, they can help produce and reproduce unequal power relations between (for instance) social classes, women and men, and ethnic groups, through the ways in which they represent things and position people. So discourse may, for example, be racist, or sexist, and try to pass off assumptions (often falsifying ones) about any aspect of social life as mere common sense. Both the ideological loading of particular ways of using language and the relations of power which underlie them are often unclear to people. CDA aims to make more visible these opaque aspects of discourse as social practice.

The term 'critical' is one that has been largely taken as self-evident in much CDA scholarship to date, and yet it can have quite contrasting interpretations and meanings in different cultural contexts. The notion of critique in the West has had a long tradition dating back to ancient Greece, through the Enlightenment philosophers to the modern day. The word is adopted in everyday language to mean the use of rational thinking to question arguments or prevailing ideas. Use of this term in CDA can be traced to the influence of Marxist and later Frankfurt School critical theory, in which critique is the mechanism for both explaining social phenomena and for changing them. This emancipatory agenda has important implications for CDA as a scientific practice.

CDA sees itself not as a dispassionate and objective social science, but as engaged and committed; a form of intervention in social practice and social relationships. What is distinctive about CDA compared with other approaches to research is that without compromising its social scientific objectivity and rigour, it openly and explicitly positions itself on the side of dominated and oppressed groups and against dominating groups. The political interests and uses of social scientific research are often less explicit. This certainly does not imply that CDA is less scholarly than other research: standards of careful, rigorous and systematic analysis apply with equal force to CDA as to other approaches.

This problem-oriented, critical approach to research implies a particular view of methodology. Unlike some forms of discourse-based research, CDA does not begin with a fixed theoretical and methodological stance. Instead, the CDA research process begins with a research topic; for example, racism, democratic participation, Middle East politics, globalization, workplace literacy, consumer cultures, and so forth. Methodology is the process during which, informed through theory, this topic is further refined so as to construct the objects of research (pinpointing specific foci and research questions).[1] The choice of

---

[1] For a fuller account of this view of methodology see Fairclough, 2003a; 2005.

appropriate methods (data collection and mode of analysis) depends on what one is investigating. Thus, for example, it is likely that a different set of analytical and theoretical tools will be required to investigate neoliberal ideology in welfare policy, from those needed to explore workplace sectarianism in Northern Ireland. This entails a diversity of approaches to CDA research, drawing on various linguistic analytic techniques and theories, although all will involve some form of close textual (and/or multi-modal) analysis.

CDA IN CONTEXT

The recent growth of critical discourse analysis as a field corresponds to, contributes to, but also draws upon an upsurge of critical interest in language in contemporary society. There is for instance a widespread cynicism about the rhetoric of commodity advertising, the simulated personalness used in impersonal service encounters, and the growing use of 'spin' by politicians to sell their ideas to the public. And in a different direction there is a high level of popular consciousness about sexist and racist ways of using language. Similarly, political activism and the public critique of the so-called 'War on Terror' have highlighted not only the military but also the linguistic strategies through which the war has been prosecuted and legitimated. This critical consciousness about the language practices people encounter in their everyday lives is a response to important shifts in the function of language in social life, of which some are longer term and characterize modern societies, while others are more recent and characterize 'late modernity' (Giddens, 1991).

In broad terms, language continues to be more salient and more important in a range of social processes. The increased economic importance of language is striking. In the context of 'post-Fordism', the balance of economic life has shifted increasingly from manufacturing industries to service, culture and leisure industries. The profitability and success of such industries rely heavily on the (semiotically mediated) 'face' they present to the public, which explains their preoccupation with design, presentation, and communication techniques. The marketization of public services, requiring them to operate on a competitive market basis, has entailed a large-scale extension of these design concerns (in education, see Fairclough, 1993; Mulderrig, 2003).

At the same time, key areas of social life are becoming increasingly centred on the media, especially television. This is notably the case with politics. Politicians now have unprecedented access to huge audiences on a regular basis, providing both better opportunities for them to shape opinion and win support, and greater risks of public exposure and discredit. The calculated design of political language is one crucial factor for success in political struggle, and has led to an escalation in recent years of politicians' use of publicity agents or 'spindoctors' to manicure their public image and manage the dissemination of their ideas (Chilton, 2004; Wodak, 2009). The last UK government was renowned for its use of such quasi-commercial practices, including 'rebranding' itself as 'New' Labour (Fairclough, 2000b; on its strategic presentation of policy discourse see Mulderrig, 2007; 2009; 2011a).

As these examples suggest, the increased importance of language in social life has led to a greater level of conscious intervention to control and shape language practices in accordance with economic, political and institutional objectives. This systematic integration of 'communication design' into institutional settings has been referred to as the 'technologization of discourse' (Fairclough, 1992), and is a distinctive characteristic of the contemporary linguistic and discursive order. In fact this is one aspect of a more general characteristic of late modern social life overall: a peculiarly modern form of 'reflexivity'. As Giddens (1991) puts it, contemporary life is reflexive in the sense that people will radically alter the ways in which they live their lives on the basis of ('expert') knowledge and information about those practices. The rising popularity of 'life-style' gurus in the media is one expression of this trend. A technologization of discourse is the 'top-down', institutional side of modern reflexivity, but there is also a 'bottom-up' side appertaining to the everyday practices of ordinary people. We might characterize this as a general critical awareness of discursive practices and an orientation towards transforming them as part of social struggles. This reflexive construction and reconstruction of the self is a normal feature of everyday life, and is continually taking on new forms. For example, the currently popular trend of 'social networking' creates reflexive discourse practices (e.g. Facebook, MySpace, Twitter), constructing social identities, relationships, political protest, social struggle, consumption, and entertainment. The 'critical instinct' and its application to discourse is therefore firstly a feature of contemporary social life, and only secondly an area of academic work. And critical discourse analysis as an academic pursuit is firmly rooted in the properties of contemporary life.

THEORETICAL ORIGINS OF CDA

CDA, in its various forms, has its academic origins in 'Western Marxism'. In broad terms, Western Marxism places a particular emphasis on the role of cultural dimensions in reproducing capitalist social relations. This necessarily implies a focus on meaning (semiosis) and ideology as key mechanisms in this process. Western Marxism includes key figures and movements in twentieth-century social and political thought – Antonio Gramsci, the Frankfurt School, Louis Althusser. Critical discourse analysts do not always explicitly place themselves within this legacy, but it frames their work nevertheless (for an accessible treatment of these key theorists in relation to CDA, see van Dijk, 1998). Gramsci's observation that the maintenance of contemporary power rests not only on coercive force but also on 'hegemony' (winning the consent of the majority) has been particularly influential in CDA. The emphasis on hegemony entails an emphasis on ideology, and on how the structures and practices of ordinary life routinely normalize capitalist social relations. Althusser (1971) made a major contribution to the theory of ideology, demonstrating how these are linked to material practices embedded in social institutions (e.g. school teaching). He also showed their capacity to position people as social 'subjects', although he tended toward an overly deterministic (structuralist) version of this process which left little room for action by subjects. Directed against such structuralist accounts of ideology, Foucault's work on discourse has generated immense interest in discourse analysis, but also analysis of a rather abstract sort that is not anchored in a close analysis of particular texts. For Foucault (e.g. 1971; 1979) discourses are *knowledge systems* of the human sciences (medicine, economics, linguistics, etc.) that inform the social and governmental 'technologies' which constitute power in modern society (see also Jäeger and Maier, 2009). A further influential figure has been the French sociologist Pierre Bourdieu, in particular his (1991) work on the relationship between language, social position and symbolic value in the dynamics of power relations. From within linguistics and literary studies the work of Mikhail Bakhtin (1986) has also been important in discourse analysis. Closely related, Volosinov's (1973) work is the first linguistic theory of ideology. It claims that linguistic signs are the material of ideology, and that all language use is ideological. As well as developing a theory of genre, Bakhtin's work emphasizes the dialogical properties of texts, introducing the idea of 'intertextuality' (see Kristeva, 1986). This is the idea that any text is a link in a chain of texts, reacting to, drawing on, and transforming other texts.

The term 'critical' can be particularly associated with the Frankfurt School of Philosophy. The Frankfurt School re-examines the foundations of Marxist thought. Kantian 'critique' entails the use of rational analysis to question the limits of human knowledge and understanding of, for example, the physical world. The Frankfurt School extends this to an analysis of cultural forms of various kinds, which are seen as central to the reproduction of capitalist social relations. According to Jürgen Habermas, a critical science has to be self-reflexive (reflecting on the interests that underlie it) and it must also consider the historical context in which linguistic and social interactions take place.

CURRENT APPROACHES AND DEVELOPMENTS IN CDA

In the following we give a short overview of some of the most important theoretical approaches to CDA research. For a more comprehensive treatment readers are referred to a number of book-length overviews and introductions to CDA (see 'Further reading' at the end of this chapter).

Critical linguistics and social semiotics

The foundations for CDA as an established field of linguistic research were to some degree laid by the 'critical linguistics' (CL) which developed in Britain in the 1970s (e.g., Fowler et al., 1979). This was closely associated with 'systemic' linguistic theory (Halliday, 1978), which accounts for its emphasis upon practical ways of analysing texts, and the attention it gives to the role of grammar in its ideological analysis. In general terms, CL drew attention to the ideological potency of certain grammatical forms like passive structures and nominalizations. Such linguistic forms (and others like certain metaphors, argumentative fallacies, rhetorical devices, presuppositions, etc.) have subsequently proven to be fruitful points of entry for a critical semiotic analysis of social inequality or injustice. However, it is important to state that one cannot simply 'read off' ideological analysis from such forms; while they facilitate a description of the object of research, any critical interpretation must per force relate to the social *context*.

Some of the major figures in critical linguistics later developed 'social semiotics' (van Leeuwen, 2005a; van Leeuwen and Kress, 2006). This highlights the multi-semiotic and potentially ideological character of most texts in contemporary society, and explores ways of analysing the intersection of language, images, design, colour, spatial arrangement and so forth. Recent work has focused on the semiotics of typography (van Leeuwen, 2005b) and new media, for example their kinetic design (van Leeuwen and Caldas-Coulthard, 2004). Jay Lemke's recent (2006) work explores multimedia semiotics and its implications for critical research and pedagogy. For example, he emphasizes implicit value systems and their connections to institutional and personal identity in new multimodal genres (2005b). Moreover, building on the spatiotemporal transformations involved in navigating 'hyper-texts', Lemke (2002) has argued that we increasingly experience life through a series of 'traversals' through multiple timescales (for example, those of the internet and its diverse material settings). This work extends to the analysis of 'transmedia' (2005a), namely the various forms of media related through economic and cultural ties (for example, books, films, and games associated with a franchise). Clearly the links between these media are at once semiotic, ideological, material, and economic. As such they play a key role in the political economy of so-called 'hypercapitalism', helping to transmit and embed particular social values across a global terrain (Graham, 2006).

Fairclough's approach

Fairclough's work has developed a dialectical theory of discourse and a transdisciplinary approach to social change (1992; 2003a; 2004; 2005b; 2006). Fairclough's approach has explored the discursive aspect of contemporary processes of social transformation. This commitment to transdisciplinarity – whereby the logic and categories of different disciplines are brought into dialogue with one another – similarly informs his collaborative work.[2] His recent work examines neoliberalism (in UK Labour politics, 2000a; 2000b; in relation to New Capitalism, 2004); the notion of 'community' in international security (2005a); and the politically powerful concepts of 'globalization' (2006) and the 'knowledge based economy' (Jessop, Fairclough and Wodak, 2008). In each case CDA is brought into dialogue with other sociological and social scientific research in order to investigate to what extent and in what ways these changes are changes in discourse, as well as to explore the socially transformative effects of discursive change.

---

[2]For example, Chiapello and Fairclough, 2002; Chouliaraki and Fairclough, 1999; Fairclough et al., 2007.

Discursive change is analysed in terms of the creative mixing of discourses and genres in texts, which over time leads to the restructuring of relationships between different discursive practices within and across institutions, and the shifting of boundaries within and between 'orders of discourse' (structured sets of discursive practices associated with particular social domains). For example, a major change in discursive practices affecting many public institutions in contemporary society has been the 'conversationalization' of public discourse; the simulation of conversational practices in public domains, shifting the boundary between the orders of discourse of public life and ordinary life. The purpose of selecting trends such as conversationalization or marketization as objects of research has been to draw CDA closer to contemporary sociological and other social scientific research on social and cultural change (for example, see Fairclough, 1994 on conversationalization). As a natural progression of this transdisciplinary approach to contemporary social issues, Fairclough's most recent work allies itself explicitly with the Cultural Political Economy research agenda which, among other things, incorporates a theory of discourse in analysing prevailing concepts in capitalist society like the 'information society' and 'knowledge economy'.[3]

Socio-cognitive studies

A leading figure in cognitive approaches to critical discourse studies is Teun van Dijk, whose work has highlighted the cognitive dimensions of how discourse operates in racism, ideology and knowledge (e.g. van Dijk, 1993; 1998). van Dijk's (1993) work on the role of the media and of elite public figures in the reproduction of racism has highlighted the congruence between (racist) public representations and commonly held ethnic prejudices: immigration as invasion, immigrants and refugees as spongers, criminals, and the perpetrators of violence. Further strands to his research programme include a systematic study of the relations between knowledge and discourse, developing a typology of knowledge and a contextually grounded definition of knowledge as a shared consensus of beliefs among social groups (van Dijk, 2008b). Related to this is a project developing a theory of context as something ongoingly constructed through the interpretations of the participants (van Dijk, 2008a; 2008c).

Recent developments combining cognitive perspectives and CDA include Koller's (2004; 2005) work on cognitive metaphor theory, particularly in the area of corporate discourse. Her (2008b) work also includes analyses of lesbian communities, and the use of politically resonant metaphors in corporate and public branding (2007; 2008b). Paul Chilton's cognitive linguistic approach has made important contributions to the analysis of political discourse (Chilton, 2002; 2003; 2004), as well as to the development of the CDA research agenda (Wodak and Chilton, 2005). For example, he has recently argued that in the context of an increasingly globalized research community, one of the key challenges facing CDA is to address its tendency toward culture-centrism. Specifically, he has argued that CDA frequently fails to address the fact that freedoms to engage in critical practice, as well

---

[3]Jessop et al., 2008; Sum and Jessop, forthcoming.

as understandings of 'critique', will vary considerably from one culture to the next. His latest work draws on evolutionary psychology to probe the possibility of a 'critical instinct' in human evolution, and the extent to which cultures provide the conditions to facilitate its development (Chilton, forthcoming).

Discourse-historical approach

This approach was developed by Ruth Wodak and other scholars in Vienna working in the traditions of Bernsteinian sociolinguistics and the Frankfurt School. The approach is particularly associated with large programmes of research in interdisciplinary research teams focusing on sexism, antisemitism and racism. One of the major aims of this kind of critical research has been its practical application.

The 'discourse-historical approach' (DHA) (Reisigl and Wodak, 2001; Reisigl and Wodak, 2009) was specifically devised for an interdisciplinary study of post-war antisemitism in Austria (e.g., Wodak et al., 2009). The distinctive feature of this approach is its attempt to integrate systematically all available background information in the analysis and interpretation of the many layers of a written or spoken text, specifically taking into account four layers of context (Wodak, 2001). The study for which the DHA was developed attempted to trace in detail the constitution of an antisemitic stereotyped image as it emerged in public discourse in the 1986 Austrian presidential campaign of Kurt Waldheim.

Several other studies on prejudice and racism followed this first attempt and have led the group in Vienna to more general and theoretical considerations on the nature of racist discourse (most recently Krzyzanowski and Wodak, 2008a; Wodak, 2008). The DHA is designed to enable the analysis of implicit prejudiced utterances, as well as to identify and expose the codes and allusions contained in prejudiced discourse. It has variously been applied to identity-construction in European politics (Wodak, 2007), and to right-wing politics in Austria (Wodak and Pelinka, 2002). Similarly, Richardson has investigated anti-Islamic and other forms of racism in the British press (2004) and among right-wing political parties (2009), in the process developing a systematic model for applying CDA to news media (2007).

More recently the DHA has been combined with ethnographic methods to investigate identity politics and patterns of decision making in EU organizations, offering insights into the 'backstage' of politics,[4] as well as the exploration of social change in EU countries (Krzyzanowski and Wodak, 2008a; 2008b). In its work on EU institutions, the Vienna group has also extensively explored the discursive construction of social identity, both national and gender-based.[5]

---

[4]Krzyzanowski and Oberhuber, 2007; Muntigl et al. 2000; Wodak; 2009; Wodak and Weiss, 2004; Wodak et al., 2009.

[5]Wodak, 2003; Wodak and Weiss, 2004; Wodak et al., 2009; on approaches to identity using CDA see also Caldas-Coulthard and Iedema, forthcoming.

Argumentation and rhetoric

Given CDA's traditional orientation to questions of power inequality, it is unsurprising that an important strand of theoretical and applied critical discourse research should be devoted to the language of persuasion and justification. Such a form of analysis is commonly associated with research on political discourse, although by no means exclusively. Chilton's work on the language of politics draws variously on cognitive linguistics, pragmatics, and metaphor theory (2003; 2004). Based on his sociosemantic approach to discourse strategies, van Leeuwen (1995) postulates a grammar of legitimation (2007). This approach is used to uncover the many subtle and tacitly racist ideologies underpinning immigration policy (van Leeuwen and Wodak, 1999). Similarly, Richardson (2004) identifies a range of discourse strategies used to legitimate anti-Islamic rhetoric in the UK press, while Mulderrig (2011a) shows how certain modes of self-representation can serve as legitimation strategies in New Labour discourse. Legitimation strategies (loosely, providing justifications/reasons, whether explicit or tacit) can be seen as fitting into the broader analysis of argumentation in discourse.

Numerous studies in this field have developed and applied argumentation theory[6] to a diversity of contexts ranging from newspapers' Letters to the Editor (Atkin and Richardson, 2007; Richardson, 2001), to management discourse (Clarke et al., forthcoming), to populist, nationalist, and discriminatory discourses,[7] and to political discourse more generally (Muntigl et al., 2000; Wodak, 2008). Reisigl and Wodak (2001) identify a range of common fallacies used as argumentative devices, many of which are typically found in rightwing populist discourse (Wodak, 2007). They also identify '*topoi*' (or generalized sets of ideas used as grounds for arguments) as key elements in argumentation strategies. Similarly, Richardson and Wodak (2009) apply tools from the discourse-historical approach to the analysis of visual argumentation. Ieţcu-Fairclough's work combines CDA with the Amsterdam school of pragma-dialectics (Ieţcu, 2006b) in her analyses of how a neoliberal version of transition to a free market economy was argumentatively defended in Romania throughout the nineties (Ieţcu, 2006a; 2006c). More recently, she has applied this to the study of political strategies of legitimation involving forms of moral-practical reasoning that draw on publicly justifiable norms and values (Ieţcu-Fairclough 2008).

Corpus-based approaches

A relatively recent development in CDA has been its incorporation of computer-based methods of analysis. In the British context the origins of this methodological alliance can

---

[6]In the cases cited here, the primary theoretical model is the pragma-dialectics or so-called 'Amsterdam school' of argumentation theory developed by van Eemeren and Grootendorst, 2004; and van Eemeren and Houtlosser, 2002.

[7]For example, Ieţcu, 2006a; Ieţcu-Fairclough, 2007; Reisigl, 2007a; 2007b; Wodak and van Dijk, 2000.

be traced to the long-standing research traditions at Lancaster University in both CDA (Fairclough, 1992; 2003; 2005b) and corpus linguistics (McEnery and Wilson, 2001). Mulderrig's study of UK political discourse (2003; 2007; 2009) brings these distinct modes of research into dialogue with political economy,[8] while Mautner (2005; 2009) similarly explores the role of corpus-based CDA in sociolinguistic research. Mulderrig's work analyses historical change in UK political discourse. Methodologically, it develops novel ways of using corpus tools in CDA, demonstrating their heuristic value in directing the analyst's gaze in unexpected and often fruitful directions. For example, 'keywords analysis' is linked to social theory in order to investigate the historical rise and fall of the most prominent political discourses under different British Prime Ministers (Mulderrig, 2008). This combined method also offers a systematic and thus replicable approach to CDA.[9] Specific themes explored using this method include the increasingly prominent role of the pronoun 'we' in legitimizing government action and deflecting its public accountability (Mulderrig, 2011a; forthcoming). The heuristic value of the corpus-based approach is also illustrated in its contribution to preliminary work towards the formulation of a 'grammar of governance'. Specifically, Mulderrig (2011b) postulates a new sociosemantic category of 'Managing Action', which plays a key role in the enactment of 'soft power' in contemporary governance by constructing more oblique lines of agency and subtle forms of coercion. Mautner's work explores the possible applications of this combined methodological approach in CDA (2009; see also Koller and Mautner, 2004) and points to the internet as a valuable and relatively under-used data resource for this type of research (2005). Similarly Baker et al., (2008) utilize corpus methods to critically analyse the discourse of racism in the news.

CDA IN ACTION

Our aim in this section is to give a brief example of CDA, highlighting a number of key principles that typically inform the practice of CDA through an analysis of the following extract from a radio interview with Margaret Thatcher, the former British Prime Minister.[10] Some of the principles represent a common ground for all approaches within CDA, while others are more controversial.

---

[8]See Sum and Jessop, forthcoming.

[9]For a full account of this approach see Mulderrig, 2009.

[10]The interview was conducted by Michael Charlton, and broadcast on BBC Radio 3 on 17 December 1985. For a fuller analysis, see Chapter 7 of Fairclough, 1989.

1	MC:	Prime Minister you were at Oxford in the nineteen forties and after the war Britain would
		embark on a period of relative prosperity for all the like of which it had hardly known but
5		today there are three and a quarter million unemployed and e:m
		Britain's economic performance by one measurement has fallen to the rank of that of Italy
10		now can you imagine yourself back at the University today what must seem to be the
		chances in Britain and the prospects for all now
15	MT:	they are very different worlds you're talking about because the first thing that struck me
		very forcibly as you were speaking of those days was that now we do enjoy a standard of
		living which was undreamed of then and I can remember Rab Butler saying after we
20		returned to power in about 1951-52 that if we played our cards right the standard of
		living within twenty five years would be twice as high as it was then and em he was just
		about right and it was remarkable because it was something that we had never thought
25		of now I don't think now one would necessarily think wholly in material terms because
		really the kind of country you want is made up by the strength of its people and I think
		we're returning to my vision of Britain as a younger person and I was always brought up
30		with the idea look Britain is a country whose people think for themselves act for
		themselves can act on their own initiative they don't have to be told don't like to be
		pushed around are self-reliant and then over and above that they're always responsible for
35		their families and something else it was a kind of em I think it was Barrie who said do as
		you would be done by e: you act to others as you'd like them to act towards you and so
		you do something for the community now I think if you were looking at another country
40		you would say what makes a country strong is its people do they run their industries well
		are their human relations good e: do they respect law and order are their families strong
		all of those kind of things
	MC:	[and you know it's just way beyond economics
		[but you know people still people still ask
		though e: where is she going now General de Gaulle had a vision of France e: a certain
45		idea of France as he put it e: you have fought three major battles in this country the
		Falkland Islands e:m against the miners and local councils and against public expenditure
50		and people I think would like to hear what this vision you have of Britain is it must be a
		powerful one what is it that inspires your action
	MT:	I wonder if I perhaps I can answer best by saying how I see what government should
		do and if government really believes in people what people should do I believe that
55		government should be very strong to do those things which only government can do
		it has to be strong to have defence because the kind of Britain I see would always
		defend its freedom and always be a reliable ally so you've got to be strong to your
60		own people and other countries have got to know that you stand by your word then
		you turn to internal security and yes you HAVE got to be strong on law and order
		and do the things that only governments can do but there it's part government and
65		part people because you CAN'T have law and order observed unless it's in
		partnership with people then you have to be strong to uphold the value of the
		currency and only governments can do that by sound finance and then you have to
70		create the framework for a good education system and social security and at that
		point you have to say over to people people are inventive creative and so you expect
		PEOPLE to create thriving industries thriving services yes you expect people each and
75		every one from whatever their background to have a chance to rise to whatever level
		their own abilities can take them yes you expect people of all sorts of background
		and almost whatever their income level to be able to have a chance of owning some
80		property tremendously important the ownership of property of a house gives you
		some independence gives you a stake in the future you're concerned about your
		children

        MC: but could [you sum this vision up
        MT: [( ) you said my vision
                please let me just go on and then that isn't enough if you're interested in the future yes
                you will probably save you'll probably want a little bit of independent income of your own
                and so constantly thinking about the future so it's very much a Britain whose people are
                independent of government but aware that the government has to be strong to do those
                things which only governments can do
        MC: but can you sum it up in a in a in a phrase or two the aim is to achieve what or restore
                what in Britain when clearly risking a lot and winning in a place like the Falkland Islands is
                just as important in your philosophy [for Britain as as
        MT: [I think
100   MC: restoring sound money reducing the money supply in the Bank of England
        MT: but of course it showed that we were reliable in the defence of freedom and when part of
                Britain we: was invaded of course we went we believed in defence of freedom we were
105   reliable I think if I could try to sum it up in a phrase and that's always I suppose most
                difficult of all I would say really restoring the very best of the British character to its former
                pre-eminence.
110   MC: but this has meant something called Thatcherism now is that a description you accept as
                something quite distinct from traditional conservatism in this country
        MT: no it is traditional conservatism
115   MC: but it's radical and populist and therefore not conservative
        MT: it is radical because at the time when I took over we needed to be radical e: it is populist I
                wouldn't call it populist I would say that many of the things which I've said strike a chord
120   in the hearts of ordinary people why because they're British because their character IS
                independent because they DON'T like to be shoved around coz they ARE prepared to take
                responsibility because they DO expect to be loyal to their friends and loyal allies that's why
125   you call it populist. I say it strikes a chord in the hearts of people I know because it struck a
                chord in my heart many many years ago

CDA addresses social problems

CDA is the analysis of linguistic and semiotic aspects of social processes and problems. In the remaining sections we present a critical discourse analysis of the extract above. Such an analysis might be seen as a contribution to the analysis of Thatcherism as a key foundational element of the New Right in politics. It also illustrates the importance of exploring the historical context of one's object of investigation. While Thatcherism might potentially be regarded as an outdated subject for investigation, it continues to be relevant to an understanding of both ideological (in particular neoliberalism and neoconservativism) and rhetorical (broadly, the rise of 'personality politics') aspects of contemporary Western politics.

    Seen in this context, the key claim of CDA is that major social and political processes and movements such as Thatcherism or neoliberalism have a partly linguistic-discursive character. This follows on from the fact that social and political changes in contemporary society will generally include a substantive element of cultural and ideological change.

Thatcherism as an ideological project for building a new hegemony can be seen as an attempt to restructure political discourse by combining diverse existing discourses together in a new way. This is evident in the extract above. There is a characteristic combination of elements of traditional conservative discourse (the focus on law and order, the family, and strong government, for example *do they respect law and order are their families strong*); elements of a liberal political discourse and economic discourse (the focus on the independence of the individual, for example *because their character IS independent because they DON'T like to be shoved around coz they ARE prepared to take responsibility*); and on the individual entrepreneur as the dynamo of the economy, for example *you expect PEOPLE to create thriving industries thriving services*).

These are mixed with elements from the discourses of ordinary life and ordinary experience which give Thatcher's discourse the populist quality referred to by the interviewer – for example, the expressions *stand by your word*, *shoved around*, and *strikes a chord in [people's] hearts*. This novel combination of discourses is associated with distinctive representations of social reality (including social and political relations and identities). It achieved a dominant position in the field of political discourse, though it is arguable to what extent it was hegemonic in the sense of actually winning widespread acceptance.

Power relations are discursive

CDA highlights the substantively discursive nature of power relations in contemporary societies. This is partly a matter of how power relationships (e.g., between media and politics) are exercised and negotiated in discourse, for instance in broadcast political interviews: On the face of it, interviewers can exercise a lot of power over politicians in interviews: deciding the beginnings and endings, the time allowed, the topics covered and the angles from which these are tackled, and so forth. In the case of the Thatcher interview, Michael Charlton's questions did set and attempt to police an agenda (e.g., lines 83, 93–4). However, politicians will not always comply with such attempts at 'policing', and there will often be a struggle for control. Charlton, for instance in line 83, tries to bring Thatcher back to the question he asked in lines 49–51, but she interrupts him and carries on with what is effectively a short political speech. Her speech-making points to another dimension of power relations in discourse. Thatcher tries to exercise what we might call rhetorical power, a form of 'cultural capital' which according to Bourdieu (1991) is the prerogative of professional politicians in contemporary societies. This power – in so far as it is effective – is primarily power over the audience, although it also limits Charlton's power as an interviewer. Thatcher's rhetorical power is realized for instance in the large-scale linguistic devices which organize her contributions, such as the triple parallel structure of lines 56–67 (*it has to be strong to have defence*, 56–7; *you*

HAVE got to be strong on law and order, 62; you have to be strong to uphold the value of the currency, 66–7).[11]

Discourse constitutes society and culture

We can only make sense of the salience of discourse in contemporary social processes by recognizing that discourse and society/culture are mutually constitutive. This entails that every instance of language use makes it own small contribution to reproducing and/or transforming society and culture, including power relations. That is the power of discourse; that is why it is worth struggling over.

It is useful to distinguish three broad domains of social life that may be discursively constituted: *representations* of the world, social *relations* between people, and people's social and personal *identities*. In terms of representations, for instance, lines 11–21 incorporate a narrative which gives a very different representation of history to the one in the interviewer's question: the latter's contrast between a prosperous past and a depressed present is restructured as a past Conservative government creating the present prosperity.

The extract constitutes social relations between Thatcher herself and the public in a contradictory way, partly as relations of solidarity and partly as relations of authority. Thatcher's use of the familiar indefinite pronoun *you* (in contrast to *one*), implicitly claims that she is just an ordinary person, like her voters (this is the populist element in her discourse). So too does some of her vocabulary: notice for instance how she avoids the interviewer's term *populist* and the interviewer's technical use of *radical* as a specialist political term in lines 113–20, perhaps because their intellectualism would compromise her claims to solidarity. Thatcher's use of political rhetoric referred to above is by contrast authoritative, as are the passages (including 27–36 and 119–23) in which she characterizes the British, claiming the authority to articulate their self-perceptions on their behalf.

These passages are also interesting in terms of the constitution of identities: a major feature of this discourse is how it constitutes 'the people' as a political community (note Thatcher's explicit foregrounding of the project of engineering collective identity – *restoring the very best of the British character to its former pre-eminence*), and the listing of characteristics in these examples is a striking discourse strategy, weaving together different discourses (conservative, liberal etc.), while leaving the listeners to infer the connections between them. Notice also the vague and shifting meanings of the pronoun *we* (lines 13–25, 101–4) in Thatcher's talk. *We* is sometimes what is traditionally called 'inclusive' (it includes the audience and the general population, for example *we do enjoy a standard of living which was undreamed of then*, 13–14), and sometimes 'exclusive' (for example, *after*

---

[11]Of course, in addition to the question of power in discourse, there is the question of power over discourse, which is partly a matter of access. Clearly Thatcher's power permitted her access to a much wider range of discursive opportunities than less powerful people. Discursive aspects of power relations are not, however, fixed and monolithic. It is thus fruitful to look at both 'power in discourse' and 'power over discourse' in dynamic terms.

we returned to power, 15–16, where *we* refers just to the Conservative Party). In other cases, it could be taken as either (e.g., *if we played our cards right*, 16–17). Even if we take this as exclusive, it is still unclear who the *we* identifies: is it the Conservative Party, or the government? Also, calling *we* 'inclusive' is rather misleading, for while *we* in for instance *we do enjoy a standard of living ...* does identify the whole community, it also constructs the community in a way which excludes those who have not achieved prosperity. The pronoun *you* is used in a similarly strategic and manipulative way on lines 59–88. We are not suggesting that Thatcher or her aides were consciously planning to use *we* and *you* in these ways, though a reflexive awareness of language is increasing among politicians.[12] Rather, there are broader strategic objectives for political discourse (e.g. mobilizing popular support) which are realized in ways of using language that are themselves likely to be unintended.

Finally, the discourse also constitutes an identity for Thatcher herself as a woman political leader who has political authority without ceasing to be feminine. Notice for example the modality features of lines 52–92. On the one hand, there are a great many strong obligational modalities (note the modal verbs *should, have to, have got to*) and epistemic ('probability') modalities (note the categorical present tense verbs of for instance lines 80–2), which powerfully claim political authority. On the other hand, this section opens with a very tentative and hedged expression (*I wonder if I perhaps I can answer best by saying how I see ...*) which might stereotypically be construed – in conjunction with her delivery at this point, along with her dress and appearance – as 'feminine'.

Discourse does ideological work

Ideologies are particular ways of representing and constructing society which reproduce unequal relations of power, relations of domination and exploitation. To determine whether a particular (type of) discursive event does ideological work, it is not enough to analyse texts; one also needs to consider how texts are interpreted and received and what social effects they have.

In our example, the political and economic strategies of Thatcherism are an explicit topic, and are clearly formulated, notably in lines 52–92, including the central idea of strong government intervention to create the conditions in which markets can operate freely. But Thatcher's formulation is actually built around a contrast between government and people which we see as ideological: it hides the fact that the 'people' who dominate the creation of 'thriving industries' and so forth are mainly the transnational corporations, and it can help to legitimize existing relations of economic and political domination. Ideologies are typically quite implicit – her attaching to key words which evoke, but leave implicit, ideological sets of assumptions – such as *freedom, law and order* or *sound finance*. Notice also *thriving industries thriving*

---

[12]For historical analyses of pronoun usage in political discourse, see Mulderrig, 2009; 2011a; forthcoming.

services. This is another instance of the list structure discussed above. *Thriving industries* is a common collocation, but *thriving services* is an innovation of an ideologically potent sort: to achieve a coherent meaning for the list one needs to assume that services can be evaluated on the same basis as industries, a truly Thatcherite assumption which the listener is left to infer. Note that not all common-sense assumptions in discourse are ideological, given our view of ideology.

Ideology is not just a matter of representing social reality. It is also useful to think of ideology as a process which articulates together particular representations of reality, and particular constructions of identity. In this case, the ideological work that is going on is an attempt to articulate Thatcherite representations of the economy and politics with a particular construction of 'the people' as a political community.

Discourse is historical

Discourse is not produced without context and cannot be understood without taking the context into consideration (van Dijk, 2008c). Discourses are always connected to other discourses which were produced earlier, as well as those which are produced synchronically and subsequently. In this respect, we can include intertextuality as well as sociocultural knowledge within our concept of context. Let us consider allusions which occur in the text and which presuppose certain worlds of knowledge, and particular intertextual experience, on the part of listeners. For example, to be able to understand and analyse Thatcher's responses in depth, we would have to know what the situation in Britain in the *nineteen forties* (1–2) was like, who Rab Butler (15) or Barrie (33) were, what kind of *vision* de Gaulle had (44–5), why the war in the Falkland Islands was important and what kind of symbolic meaning it connotes (58). Similarly when Thatcher alludes to *traditional conservatism* (111) we need to know what is meant by this term within the Thatcherite tradition in contrast to other meanings.

Discourse analysis is interpretative and explanatory

Discourse can be interpreted in very different ways, depending on the context and audience. Interpretation and understanding occur through the lens of feelings, beliefs, values and knowledge. The Thatcher interview is particularly complex, involving historical and synchronic intertextuality, the hybridization of genres and a considerable degree of assumed knowledge and, importantly, values. Our critical analysis must therefore decide how much contextual knowledge we need to bring to the interpretation. Does our critical reading illuminate opaque meanings in plausible and rational ways? Consider the following: *you have to say over to people people are inventive creative and so you expect PEOPLE to create thriving industries thriving services yes you expect* (lines 72–3). Here we might ask who are meant by *people*? Conservative voters? Entrepreneurs? Public service employees? All British citizens (if so, is the government also included in this creation of thriving industries and services?), or human beings in general? The group is not clearly defined, which potentially allows each listener to include themselves in its reference. However, these *people* have to be able to influence the growth of industries and services in a positive way (*thriving*). In fact it is likely only a powerful subset will be in a position to do this – elites, managers and politicians – while the remainder may instead experience the imposition of new modes of organizational management, job cuts, increased working hours, greater levels of accountability and audit, increased competition for funding, and other measures deemed necessary to achieve *thriving industries* and *services*. Thus the use of *people* is misleadingly vague: it simultaneously masks the reality of unequal social power and includes a very wide group in those who are *expected* to take responsibility for creating *thriving industries* and *services*. This short example illustrates the hegemonic potential of language which is both referentially vague and hortatory, when it used by those in a position of power (Mulderrig, 2011b), which a critical analysis can deconstruct by revealing the social implications of different readings. This implies not only a detailed analysis of the linguistic features of texts, but also of the ways in which it is embedded in its social conditions and linked to other texts and social practices, to ideologies and power relations.

Discourse is a form of social action

We stated at the beginning of our chapter that the principal aim of CDA was to uncover opaqueness and power relationships. CDA is a socially committed scientific paradigm. In contrast to many scholars, critical linguists make explicit their (political) interests.

The Thatcher example we have analysed may, for instance, form part of a wider critique of the New Right ideology in politics, linked to social campaigns against welfare retrenchment. But there exist also other examples of important applications of CDA. For example, CDA has been used as the basis for expert opinions in court, and to raise awareness about the racism of rightwing populist political figures (Wodak and Pelinka, 2002).

Non-discriminatory language use is widely promoted in different domains. One important area is sexist language use (see Lazar, 2005, on feminist CDA). CDA has also had much success in changing discourse and the power patterns in institutions, for example in doctor-patient communication (Lalouschek et al., 1990). The same is true for other institutional, educational, legal and bureaucratic settings.

CONCLUSION

We suggested earlier that late modern society is characterized by enhanced reflexivity, and that a critical orientation towards discourse in ordinary life is one manifestation of modern reflexivity. A key issue for critical discourse analysts is how the analyses which they produce in academic institutions can relate to this critical activity in ordinary life. There is no absolute divide between the two: critical discourse analysts necessarily draw upon everyday critical activities (associated for instance with gender relations, patriarchy and feminism) including analysts' own involvement in and experience of them, and these activities may be informed by academic analysis. Yet critical discourse analysis is obviously not just a replication of everyday critique: it can draw upon social theories and theories of language, and methodologies for language analysis, which are not generally available, and has resources for systematic and in-depth investigations which go beyond ordinary experience. We think it is useful to see the relationship between an everyday discourse critique and academic CDA in terms of Gramscian perspectives on intellectuals in contemporary life. From this viewpoint, critical discourse analysts ought to aspire to be 'organic intellectuals' in a range of social struggles (feminist, socialist, anti-racist, green, and so forth), but should at the same time be aware that their work is constantly at risk of appropriation by the state and capital.

FURTHER READING

The following list is for readers who wish to find out more about CDA. It includes relatively accessible books that can be used as text books or as an introduction to the some of the most well-established approaches to CDA.

Fairclough, N. (2003) *Analysing Discourse: Text Analysis for Social Research*. London: Routledge.
This book is designed for use by social scientists who have an interest in matters of discourse, but who do not necessarily have a background in Linguistics. It guides the reader through the practice of critical discourse analysis at varying levels of abstraction. It contains a glossary of concepts at the back and sample analyses of texts.

van Dijk, T. (2008a) *Discourse and Context: A Sociocognitive Approach*. Cambridge: C.U.P.
This book presents a version of critical discourse analysis that offers a rich approach to context, which is understood as being a construct of subjects themselves rather than an external 'object'. The concept of 'context models' is developed and used as a lens through which to analyse how discourse reflects people's interaction with their social environments.

Wodak, R. and Meyer, M. (eds) (2009) *Methods of Critical Discourse Analysis* (second edition). Sage: London.
This book presents an overview of the various theories and methods associated with CDA, introducing the reader to some of the main figures in the field and the methods they typically employ. The differences between these methods is discussed in order that readers may select the approach most suited to their own area of research.

van Leeuwen, T. and Kress, G. (2006) *Reading Images – The Grammar of Visual Design* (second edition). Routledge, London.
This book introduces readers to the concept of social semiotics, presenting a critical theory of multiple forms of being beyond the spoken or written word. It will be of particular interest to researchers interested in multiple forms of meaning-making (images, sound, language) and the interplay between them.

ONLINE READING

The following articles are available at www.sagepub.co.uk/discoursestudies.

Fairclough, N. (1993) 'Critical discourse analysis and the marketization of public discourse: the universities', *Discourse and Society*, 4 (2): 133–68.

Pearce, M. (2005) 'Informalization in UK party election broadcasts 1966–97', *Language and Literature*, 14(1): 65–90.

Wodak, R. (2006) 'Mediation between discourse and society: assessing cognitive approaches in CDA', *Discourse Studies* 8 (1) 179–190.

REFERENCES

Althusser, L. (1971) 'Ideology and ideological state apparatus'. In *Lenin and Philosophy and Other Essays*. London: New Left Books.

Atkin, A. and Richardson, J. (2007) 'Arguing about Muslims: (un)reasonable argument in Letters to the Editor'. *Text & Talk*, 27: 1–25.

Baker, P., Gabrielatos, C., KhosraviNik, M., Krzyzanowski, M., McEnery, T. and Wodak, R. (2008) 'A useful methodological synergy? Combining critical discourse analysis and corpus linguistics to examine discourses of refugees and asylum seekers in the UK press'. *Discourse & Society*, *19* (3): 273–306.

Bakhtin, M. (1986) *Speech Genres and Other Late Essays*. Austin, TX: University of Texas Press.

Bourdieu, P. (1991) *Language and Symbolic Power*. Cambridge: Polity.

Caldas-Coulthard, C. and Iedema, R. (eds) (forthcoming) *Identity Trouble: Critical Discourse and Contested Identities*. London: Palgrave.

Chiapello, E. and Fairclough, N. (2002) 'Understanding the new management ideology: a transdisciplinary contribution from critical discourse analysis and the new sociology of capitalism'. *Discourse & Society*, *13* (2): 185–208.

Chilton, P. (2002) 'Do something! Conceptualising responses to the attacks of 11 September 2001'. *Journal of Language and Politics*, *1* (1): 181–95.

Chilton, P. (2003) 'Deixis and distance: President Clinton's justification of intervention in Kosovo'. In M.N. Dedaic and D.N. Nelson (eds), *At War with Words*. Berlin: Mouton de Gruyter.

Chilton, P. (2004) *Analysing Political Discourse: Theory and Practice*. London: Routledge.

Chilton, P. (forthcoming) *Language and Critique: Understanding CDA*.

Chouliaraki, L. and Fairclough, N. (1999) *Discourse in Late Modernity: Rethinking Critical Discourse Analysis*. Edinburgh: Edinburgh University Press.

Clarke, I., Kwon, W. and Wodak, R. (forthcoming) 'Organisational decision-making, discourse, and power: integrating across contexts and scales'. Submitted to *Journal of Management Studies*.

Fairclough, N. (1989) *Language and Power*. London: Longman.

Fairclough, N. (1992) *Discourse and Social Change*. Cambridge: Polity.

Fairclough, N. (1993) 'Critical discourse analysis and the marketization of public discourse: the universities'. *Discourse and Society*, *4* (2): 133–68.

Fairclough, N. (1994) 'Conversationalization of public discourse and the authority of the consumer'. In R. Keat, N. Whiteley and N. Abercrombie (eds), *The Authority of the Consumer*. London: Routledge.

Fairclough, N. (2000a) 'Discourse, social theory and social research: the discourse of welfare reform'. *Journal of Sociolinguistics*, *4* (2): 163–95.

Fairclough, N. (2000b) *New Labour, New Language*. London: Routledge.

Fairclough, N. (2003) *Analysing Discourse: Text Analysis for Social Research*. London: Routledge

Fairclough, N. (2004) 'Critical discourse analysis in researching language in the new capitalism: overdetermination, trans-disciplinarity and textual analysis'. In C. Harrison and L. Young (eds), *Systemic Linguistics and Critical Discourse Analysis*. London: Continuum.

Fairclough, N. (2005a) 'Blair's contribution to elaborating a new doctrine of "international community"'. *Journal of Language and Politics, 4* (1): 41–63.

Fairclough, N. (2005b) 'Critical discourse analysis'. *Marges Linguistiques, 9*: 76–94.

Fairclough, N. (2006) *Language and Globalization*. London: Routledge.

Fairclough, N. and Wodak, R. (2008) 'The Bologna Process and the knowledge–based economy: a critical discourse analysis approach'. In R. Jessop, N. Fairclough and R. Wodak (eds), *Higher Education and the Knowledge-Based Economy in Europe*. Rotterdam: Sense. pp. 109–126.

Fairclough, N., Cortese, P. and Ardizzone, P. (eds) (2007) *Discourse in Contemporary Social Change*. Berne: Peter Lang.

Foucault, M. (1971) *L'Ordre du discours*. Paris: Gallimard.

Foucault, M. (1979) *Discipline and Punish: the Birth of the Prison*. Harmondsworth: Penguin.

Fowler, R., Kress, G., Hodge, R. and Trew, T. (eds) (1979) *Language and Control*. London: Routledge.

Giddens, A. (1991) *Modernity and Self-Identity*. Cambridge: Polity.

Graham, P. (2006) *Hypercapitalism: Language, New Media and Social Perception of Value*. Berne: Peter Lang.

Hall, S. and Jacques, M. (1983) *The Politics of Thatcherism*. London: Lawrence and Wishart.

Halliday, M.A.K. (1978) *Language as Social Semiotic*. London: Edward Arnold.

Iețcu, I. (2006a) *Argumentation, Dialogue and Ethical Perspective in the Essays of H.-R. Patapievici*, Editura Universității din București.

Iețcu, I. (2006b) *Discourse Analysis and Argumentation Theory: Analytical Framework and Applications*. Editura Universității din București

Iețcu, I. (2006c) 'Argumentation, dialogue and conflicting moral economies in post-1989 Romania. An argument against the trade union movement'. *Discourse & Society, 17* (5): 627–50.

Iețcu-Fairclough, I. (2007) 'Populism and the Romanian "Orange Revolution": a discourse-analytical perspective on the presidential election of 2004'. In *Studies in Language and Capitalism*, 2: S. 31–74. (http://www.languageandcapitalism.info/)

Iețcu-Fairclough, I. (2008) 'Legitimation and strategic maneuvering in the political field'. *Argumentation, 22*: 399–417.

Jäger, S. and Maier, F. (2009) 'Theoretical and methodological aspects of Foucauldian critical discourse analysis and dispositive analysis'. In R. Wodak and M. Meyer (eds) *Methods of Critical Discourse Analysis* (2nd edn). London: Sage. pp. 34–61.

Jessop, B., Fairclough, N., and Wodak, R. (eds) (2008) *Education and the Knowledge-Based Economy in Europe*. Rotterdam: Sense. pp. 149–70.

Koller, V. (2004) *Metaphor and Gender in Business Media Discourse: a Critical Cognitive Study*. Basingstoke and New York: Palgrave.

Koller, V. (2005) 'Critical discourse analysis and social cognition: evidence from business media discourse'. *Discourse & Society, 16* (2): 199–224.

Koller, V. (2007) '"The world's local bank": glocalisation as a strategy in corporate branding discourse'. *Social Semiotics, 17* (1): 111–30.

Koller, V. (2008a) *Lesbian Discourses: Images of a Community*. New York and London: Routledge.

Koller, V. (2008b) '"The world in one city": semiotic and cognitive aspects of city branding'. Special issue of *Journal of Language and Politics, 7* (3): 431–50.

Koller, V. and Mautner, G. (2004) 'Computer applications in critical discourse analysis'. In A. Hewings, C. Coffin and K. O'Halloran (eds), *Applying English Grammar*. London: Arnold. pp. 216–28.

Kristeva, J. (1986) 'Word, dialogue and novel'. In T. Moi (ed.), *The Kristeva Reader*. Oxford: Blackwell.

Krzyzanowski, M. and Oberhuber, F. (2007) *(Un)Doing Europe: Discourses and Practices of Negotiating the EU Constitution*. Bern: Peter Lang.

Krzyzanowski, M. and Wodak, R. (2008a) *The Politics of Exclusion: Debating Migration in Austria*. New Brunswick, NJ: Transaction.

Krzyzanowski, M. and Wodak, R. (2008b) 'Theorising and analysing social change in central and eastern Europe: the contribution of critical discourse analysis'. In A. Galasinska and M. Krzyzanowski (eds), *Discourse and Transformation in Central and Eastern Europe*. Basingstoke: Palgrave Macmillan. pp. 17–40.

Lalouschek, J., Menz, F. and Wodak, R. (1990) *Alltag in der Ambulanz*. Tübingen: Narr.

Lazar, M. (ed.) (2005) *Feminist Critical Discourse Analysis*. London: Palgrave. pp. 90–114.

Lemke, J. (2002) 'Travels in hypermodality'. *Visual Communication, 1* (3): 299–325.

Lemke, J. (2005a) 'Critical analysis across media: games, franchises, and the new cultural order'. In M. Labarta Postigo (ed), *Approaches to Critical Discourse Analysis*. Valencia: University of Valencia.

Lemke, J. (2005b) 'Multimedia genres and traversals'. In E. Ventola, P. Muntigl and H. Gruber (eds), 'Approaches to Genre', special issue of *Folia Linguistica, 39* (1–2): 45–56.

Lemke, J. (2006) 'Towards critical multimedia literacy: technology, research, and politics'. In M. McKenna, D. Reinking, L. Labbo and R. Kieffer (eds), *International Handbook of Literacy & Technology*, v 2.0. Mahwah, NJ: Erlbaum. pp. 3–14.

Mautner, G. (2005) 'Time to get wired: using web-based corpora in critical discourse analysis'. *Discourse & Society, 16* (6): 809–28.

Mautner, G. (2009) 'Checks and balances: how corpus linguistics can contribute to CDA'. In R. Wodak and M. Meyer (eds), *Methods of Critical Discourse Analysis*. London: Sage.

McEnery, T. and Wilson, A. (2001) *Corpus Linguistics: An Introduction*, 2nd edn. Edinburgh: Edinburgh University Press.

Mulderrig, J. (2003) 'Consuming education: a corpus-based critical discourse analysis of social actors in New Labour's education policy': *Journal of Critical Education Policy Studies, 1* [http://www.jceps.com/index.php?pageID=article&articleID=2]

Mulderrig, J. (2007) 'Textual strategies of representation and legitimation in New Labour policy discourse'. In A. Green, G. Rikowski and H. Raduntz (eds), *Renewing Dialogues in Marxism and Education*. Basingstoke: Palgrave Macmillan. pp. 135–50.

Mulderrig, J. (2008) 'Using keywords analysis in CDA: evolving discourses of the knowledge economy in education'. in B. Jessop, N. Fairclough and R. Wodak (eds), *Education and the Knowledge-Based Economy in Europe*. Rotterdam: Sense. pp. 149–70.

Mulderrig, J. (2009) *The Language of Education Policy: From Thatcher to Blair.* Saarbucken: VDM Dr Muller Verlag.

Mulderrig, J. (2011a) 'Manufacturing consent: a corpus-based critical discourse analysis of New Labour's educational governance'. *Journal of Educational Philosophy and Theory*, 43(6).

Mulderrig, J. (2011b) 'The grammar of governance', *Critical Discourse Studies, 8* (1): 45–68.

Mulderrig, J. (forthcoming) 'The hegemony of inclusion: constructing the subjects of Third Way politics', *Discourse and Society.*

Muntigl, P., Weiss, G. and Wodak, R. (2000) *European Union Discourses on Un/employment: An Interdisciplinary Approach to Employment Policy-making and Organizational Change*. Amsterdam: John Benjamins.

Reisigl, M. (2007a) *Nationale Rhetorik in Fest- und Gedenkreden. Eine diskursanalytische Studie zum 'österreichischen Millennium' in den Jahren 1946 und 1996*. Tübingen: Stauffenburg.

Reisigl, M. (2007b) 'Discrimination in discourses'. In H. Kotthoff and H. Spencer-Oatey (eds), *Handbook of Intercultural Communication*. Berlin/New York: Mouton de Gruyter. pp. 365–94.

Reisigl, M. and Wodak, R. (2001) *Discourse and Discrimination: Rhetorics of Racism and Antisemitism*. London: Routledge.

Reisigl, M., and Wodak, R. (2009) 'The discourse-historical approach in CDA'. In R. Wodak and M. Meyer (eds), *Methods of Critical Discourse Analysis* (2nd revised edition). London: Sage.

Richardson, J.E. (2001) '"Now is the time to put an end to all this". Argumentative Discourse Theory and Letters to the Editor'. *Discourse & Society, 12* (2): 143–68.

Richardson, J.E. (2004) *(Mis)Representing Islam: the Racism and Rhetoric of British Broadsheet Newspapers*. Amsterdam: John Benjamins.

Richardson, J.E. (2007) *Analysing Newspapers: An Approach from Critical Discourse Analysis*. London: Palgrave.

Richardson, J.E. (forthcoming) '"Get shot of the lot of 'em": election reporting of Muslims in British newspapers', *Patterns of Prejudice.*

Richardson, J. & Wodak, R. (2009) 'The impact of visual racism: visual arguments in political leaflets of Austrian and British far-right parties'. *Controversia*, 6/2: 45–77.

Rose, N. (1999) *Powers of Freedom: Reframing Political Thought*. Cambridge: Cambridge University Press.

Sum, N.L. and Jessop, B. (forthcoming) *Cultural Political Economy*. Cheltenham: Edward Elgar.

van Dijk, T. (1993) *Elite Discourse and Racism*. Newbury Park, CA: Sage.

van Dijk, T. (1998) *Ideology*. London: Sage.

van Dijk, T. (2008a) *Discourse and Context: A Sociocognitive Approach*. Cambridge: Cambridge University Press.

van Dijk, T. (2008b) *Discourse Power*. Houndsmills: PM.

van Dijk, T. (2008c) *Society in Discourse: How Context Controls Text and Talk*. Cambridge: Cambridge University Press.

van Dijk, T.A. and Kintsch, W. (1983) *Strategies of Discourse Comprehension*. New York: Academic.

van Eemeren, F. and Houtlosser, P. (eds) (2002) *Dialectic and Rhetoric: The Warp and Woof of Argumentation Analysis*. Amsterdam: Kluwer.

van Eemeren, F. and Grootendorst, R. (2004) *A Systematic Theory of Argumentation: The Pragma-Dialectical Approach*. Cambridge: Cambridge University Press.

van Leeuwen, T. (1995) 'Representing social action'. *Discourse & Society, 4* (2): 193–223.

van Leeuwen, T. (2005a) *Introducing Social Semiotics*. London: Routledge.

van Leeuwen, T. (2005b) 'Typographic meaning', *Visual Communication, 4* (2): 137–42.

van Leeuwen, T. (2007) 'Legitimation in discourse and communication'. *Discourse & Communication, 1* (1): 91–112.

van Leeuwen, T. (1999) 'Discourses of unemployment in New Labour Britain'. In R. Wodak and L. Christoph (eds), *Challenges in a Changing World: Issues in Critical Discourse Analysis*. Wien: Passagen-Verlag. pp. 87–100.

van Leeuwen, T. and Caldas-Coulthard, C.R. (2004) 'The semiotics of kinetic design'. In D. Banks (ed.), *Text and Texture – Systemic Functional Viewpoints on the Nature and Structure of Text*. Paris: L'Harmattan. pp. 356–81.

van Leeuwen, T. and Kress, G. (2006) *Reading Images – The Grammar of Visual Design* (2nd edn). London: Routledge.

van Leeuwen, T.J. and Wodak, R. (1999) 'Legitimizing immigration control: a discourse-historical analysis'. *Discourse Studies, 1* (1): 83–119.

Volosinov, V.I. (1973 [1928]) *Marxism and the Philosophy of Language*. New York: Seminar.

Wodak, R. (2001) 'The discourse-historical approach'. In R. Wodak and M. Meyer (eds), *Methods of Critical Discourse Analysis*. London: Sage. pp. 63–94.

Wodak, R. (2003) 'Multiple identities: the roles of female parliamentarians in the EU parliament'. In J. Holmes and M. Meyerhoff (eds), *Handbook of Discourse and Gender*. Oxford: OUP. pp. 71–98.

Wodak, R. (2007) '"Doing Europe": the discursive construction of European identities'. In R. Mole (ed.), *Discursive Constructions of Identity in European Politics*. Basingstoke: Palgrave. pp. 70–95.

Wodak, R. (2008) '"Us" and "Them": inclusion/exclusion – discrimination via discourse'. In G. Delanty, P. Jones and R. Wodak (eds), *Migration, Identity, and Belonging*. Liverpool: Liverpool Univ. Press. pp. 54–78.

Wodak, R. (2009) *The Discourse of Politics in Action: Politics as Usual*. London: Palgrave.

Wodak, R. and Chilton, P. (eds) (2005) *A New Research Agenda in Critical Discourse Analysis: Theory and Interdisciplinarity*. Amsterdam: John Benjamins.

Wodak. R. and Meyer, M. (eds) (2009) *Methods of Critical Discourse Analysis* (2nd edn). London: Sage.

Wodak, R. and Pelinka, A. (2002) 'From Waldheim to Haider: an introduction'. In R. Wodak and A. Pelinka (eds), *The Haider Phenomenon in Austria*. New Brunswick:Transaction. pp. vii–xxvii.

Wodak, R. and van Dijk, T. (eds) (2000) *Racism at the Top*. Klagenfurt: Drava.

Wodak, R. and Weiss, G. (2004) 'Visions, ideologies and utopias in the discursive construction of European identities: organizing, representing and legitimizing Europe'. In M. Pütz, A. Van Neff, G. Aerstselaer and T.A. van Dijk (eds), *Communicating Ideologies: Language, Discourse and Social Practice*. Frankfurt: Peter Lang. pp. 225–52.

Wodak, R., de Cillia, R., Reisigl, M. and Liebhart, K. (2009) *The Discursive Construction of National Identity* (2nd edn). Edinburgh: EUP.

EIGHTEEN

Discourse and Ideology

Teun A. van Dijk

INTRODUCTION

Consider the following fragment from a typical newspaper editorial:

> We have a spiralling population fuelled by uncontrolled immigration for which no provision has been made. This is a failure of public policy on a quite staggering scale.
>
> We are finally witnessing the full, malign impact of Labour's failure to control our borders.
>
> This Government has never actually had an immigration policy worthy of the name, simply a series of ad hoc measures with no intellectual coherence that has done nothing to curb – or even monitor – the influx of immigrants.
>
> The best estimate is that immigration has trebled over the past decade and that there are half a million illegal immigrants in this country. And an overloaded social infrastructure is not the only price we will pay.
> (*Daily Telegraph*, 7 January 2009)

Whatever the many other properties this editorial may have, most readers will agree that it expresses a negative opinion about the Labour Party and its immigration policy. For those readers who know the *Daily Telegraph*, this opinion is hardly surprising, given the conservative outlook of this British newspaper. Indeed, later in the same editorial the newspaper predictably praises the immigration policy of the Conservative Party.

What we characterized as the conservative 'outlook' of this newspaper is commonly also described as an *ideology*. This chapter aims to analyse this notion of ideology and especially the ways ideologies are expressed in, and reproduced by, discourse.

The first thing to observe about the notion of ideology is that in much of our everyday discourse it is used in a derogatory way when characterizing the ideas or policies of *others*:

whereas *we* have the truth, *they* have an ideology. Interestingly, such a derogatory use of the notion of ideology may itself be ideological when it expresses a polarization between an in-group and an out-group, between *Us* and *Them*. A well-known historical example is the widespread qualification of communism as an ideology in traditional anti-communist rheto-ric of those who defended capitalism and the free market and who would hardly describe their own ideas as ideological.

This chapter presents a *theory* and *systematic analysis* of ideology that goes beyond such informal, everyday uses of the term and that does not necessarily imply a negative evalua-tion of ideologies or the people that share them. Under specific social, political, economic and historical conditions any group may develop its own ideology in order to defend its interests and to guarantee the loyalty, cohesion, interaction and cooperation of its members, especially in relation to other social groups or classes. This may mean that ideologies, as we define them, may be used not only to dominate or to oppress others, but also in order to resist and struggle against such domination, as we know of racist *vs.* anti-racist or of sexist *vs.* feminist ideologies. In the same way, group power may be abused or be used to resist such an abuse – depending on the sociopolitical circumstances.

Indeed, what may have been a liberating ideology yesterday may be an oppressive one today. For instance, whereas classical liberalism was once an ideology that advocated indi-vidual freedom and motivated the struggle against feudalism, today it may be adhered to by those who are against the freedom of racial or ethnic Others who want to migrate to 'our' country, as we can see in the editorial from the *Daily Telegraph*. Similarly, neo-liberalism may advocate the 'freedom' (and hence the power) of the market and oppose the kind of state intervention favoured by social democrats and socialists – who traditionally defended the interests and the rights of the workers, i.e., *their* freedom *from* exploitation. Hence the stance of the same newspaper against the British Labour party, in general, and against Labour's immigration policies, in particular – even when these policies today can hardly be called generous.

Ideologies, thus informally defined, are general systems of basic ideas shared by the members of a social group, ideas that will influence their interpretation of social events and situations and control their discourse and other social practices as group members. Thus, in order to persuasively formulate and propagate its anti-Labour and anti-immigration opin-ions based on its conservative ideology, the *Daily Telegraph* uses rhetorical hyperboles such as *uncontrolled*, *failure*, *staggering*, or *malign*, and metaphors such as *spiralling* and *fuelled* to attack Labour's immigration policies. At the same time it emphasizes the alleged danger of the arrival and presence of those it calls *illegal immigrants* in order to associate these with breaking the law and thus derogating (at least many of) Them as criminals, and hence as a threat to Us, English people.

From the informal observations of this example we may conclude also that an anti-immigration stance may not only be based on a racist ideology – if the Others are ethnically or racially different from Us – but also on a nationalist or xenophobic ideology that aims to defend 'our' nation (and its language, customs and culture) against the arrival and large-scale settlement of *any* strangers. It is precisely through such public discourses as editorials that these kinds of ideologies are expressed and persuasively propagated among readers and hence reproduced in everyday life. Besides defining what ideologies are, this chapter will show how these are expressed and reproduced by socially and politically situated text and talk.

A NOTE ON THE HISTORY OF 'IDEOLOGY'

Although there is no space in this chapter to examine the history of the notion of ideology (dealt with in the several monographs referred to below), it should briefly be recalled that the first use of this notion, introduced by French philosopher Destutt de Tracy, more than 200 years ago, referred to a new discipline: *the science of ideas*. It was only later, especially with Marx and Engels, and more generally in Marxist approaches, that the notion acquired its negative connotation as a 'false consciousness', thereby referring to the misguided ideas of the working class about its material conditions of existence, an ideology inculcated by the ruling class as a means of exploitation and domination. Ideology was thus defined on the basis of underlying socio-economic structures of society and usually contrasted with *scientific knowledge*, for instance as proposed by Historical Materialism, as well as many other approaches in the social sciences until today. It was Gramsci especially who later emphasized the fundamental role of ideology as the *hegemony* of common sense, when bourgeois norms and values are adopted throughout society and domination need no longer be maintained by force.

Contrary to the still prevailing negative conception of ideology as false consciousness and as a means of domination we propose a more general, multidisciplinary theory that accounts for various kinds of ideology, including those of resistance. And instead of a materialist, economic basis for such ideologies, we would emphasize the sociocognitive nature of ideologies as the basis of the shared mental representations of social groups which in turn will control the social practices of members. We do agree, however, with the classic view that ideologies may be inculcated by specific groups in society, such as the *symbolic elites* that control the access to public discourse and hence have the means to manipulate the public at large.

Bibliographical Note

For the **history** and **introduction** to the concept of ideology, see the following books:
Billig (1982); Eagleton (1991); Larrain (1979); Thompson (1990). For **Marxism** and ideology: Abercrombie, Hill & Turner (1990); Althusser (2008); Carlsnaes (1981); Eagleton (1991); Laclau (1979); Larrain (1983); Parekh (1982); Rossi-Landi (1990); Sutton (1990).

ELEMENTS OF A THEORY OF IDEOLOGY

Before we examine the ways ideologies are expressed and reproduced by discourse, we need to analyse the concept of ideology in more explicit terms than the informal ones mentioned above, such as 'ideas' and 'false consciousness'.

In order not to depart too far from the informal uses of the notion, however, also the theoretical notion will retain that ideologies consist of 'ideas', or rather of what philosophers and psychologists call *beliefs*. That is, ideologies are, first of all, *belief systems*. This may be trivial, but it is still important because some authors will confuse ideologies as belief systems with *ideologically based practices* such as *discourse*. In the same way as we can distinguish between knowledge of a language (such as grammar, rules of discourse, etc.) and the actual use of that language in communication and interaction, we can distinguish between ideologies and their *uses* or *manifestations* in ideological practices.

Bibliographical Note

For the relations between ideology and **language**, see Blommaert (1999); Dirven (2001); Gee (1990); Hodge & Kress (1993); Malrieu (1999); Pêcheux (1982); Wodak (1989).

For ideology and **communication**, see Asperen (2005); Ballaster (1991); Fowler (1991); Garzone & Sarangi (2008); Mumby (1988). On ideology and **semiotics**: Larsen, Strunck & Vestergaard (2006); Reis (1993); Threadgold (1986); Zima (1981).

Secondly, such belief systems are not individual, personal beliefs, but social beliefs *shared* by members of *social groups*. In that sense, they are comparable to socio-cultural knowledge as it is shared by (epistemic) communities, as is also the case for languages shared by linguistic communities (see below for the differences between ideology and knowledge). This means that ideologies are a form of *social cognition*, that is, beliefs *shared* by and *distributed* over (the minds of) group members.

More specifically, for such beliefs to be shared by groups and their members, these must be beliefs that are *socially relevant* for them, for instance relevant for their interpretation of, and participation in, major events and actions of social life and the relations to other social groups. Thus, groups will develop different ideologies about their existence and history, about birth and death, gender, nature, organization, power, work, sex, competition, war, and so on. In order for ideologies to serve to defend the *interests* of a group, they will tend to articulate especially the relationships to other – dominant, dominated or competing – groups, for instance with respect to the scarce resources that are the basis of their power. In the example of the ideology of the *Daily Telegraph*, we have already observed the polarized nature of ideologies, such as those between Conservatives and Labour or between *Us* English and *Them* immigrants. Similarly, anti-racists will oppose racist practices, pacifists will oppose militarists and their wars, and feminists will oppose sexist men (and women) and their beliefs and conduct.

Socially shared belief systems such as ideologies are more useful when they apply to many different events, actions and situations. This means that they need to be fairly *general* and *abstract*. Thus feminists may advocate equal rights and opportunities for women and men, and such a basic norm may be applied to situations in the home, at work, in politics and many other domains of everyday life. More *specific* beliefs, such as to favour a specific candidate in the elections or to participate in a demonstration, would in that case be ideological only when they are based on, or derived from, the more basic beliefs that form the ideology of a group.

Bibliographical Note

For ideology, **political theory** and **politics**, see Adams (1993); Ball & Dagger (1990); Bastow & Martin (2003); Freeden (1996); Leach (2002); Rosenberg (1988); Seliger (1976); Talshir, Humphrey & Freeden (2006); van Dijk (2008b); Wodak (1989); Wodak, de Cillia, Reisigl & Liebhart (1999).

Although all ideologically based beliefs may be called part of an ideology, we shall limit the notion of ideology to the *fundamental, 'axiomatic' beliefs shared by a group*, that is, *general* beliefs that control – and are often originally derived from – more specific beliefs about concrete events, actions and situations with which group members may be confronted. Again, comparing ideologies with natural languages one may say that the 'application' of general ideologies in specific situations may be compared to situated language use – as we know from the classical distinction between competence and performance or between *langue* and *parole*.

The idea of a shared or distributed ideology among the members of a group does not mean that all members will have exactly the same 'copy' of an ideology, nor that they will apply such an ideology in the same way. As is the case for language, ideologies may also be better known by ideological 'experts', the *ideologues*, than by lay members. Many ideological groups, especially those that have been institutionalized, may have special teachers (priests, gurus, party leaders, etc.) and special communicative events (schooling, catechism, manuals, leaflets, etc.) to teach or indoctrinate new members. It is also in this way that ideologies are acquired more generally, for instance through textbooks and the mass media.

Bibliographical Note

For ideology and **social movements**, see Andrain & Apter (1995); Garner (1996); Laraña, Johnston & Gusfield (1994); Jones (1984); Oberschall (1993); Rudé (1980); Wuthnow (1989).

Since people are member of different social groups, each person may 'participate' in various ideologies: one may be a feminist, socialist, pacifist, journalist, etc. and one's activities and discourses may then be influenced by (fragments of) several ideologies at the same time, even when on each occasion one or a few of such ideologies will be dominant – as is more generally the case for identities (see Chapter 13 by Anna De Fina).

Ideologies are not *acquired* or *changed* by group members overnight. They may take years to 'learn', for instance on the basis of personal experiences as well as public discourse and interactions with other group members. They may be slowly developed and adapted in many debates, manifests and other forms of in-group discourse, as was the case for liberalism, socialism, feminism, pacifism and environmentalism. Also, in this respect, ideologies are more like language systems than (sets of) variable personal opinions about concrete events. They are *defined for groups*, and not for individual members who will 'use', 'apply' or 'perform' ideologies in their everyday lives, for which we must account in a different way, namely in terms of *mental models* (see below).

Ideologies may control many kinds of social practice, and not just discourse. A sexist ideology may give rise to sexist talk, but also to (non-verbal) sexual harassment, gender discrimination or violence. *As emphasized above, it is inadequate to reduce ideologies to their discursive manifestations*. Ideologies, as such, are forms of socially shared and distributed social cognition *at the level of groups*. They are shared mental representations that are used or applied as a basis for the specific ideological conduct of group members – of which discourse is crucial, but still just one practice among many.

Bibliographical Note

For general **theories of ideology**, see Billig (1982); CCCS (1978); Thompson (1984); van Dijk (1998); Žižek (1994). For ideology and **social theory**, see, e.g., Agger (1992); Bailey (1994); Gane (1989); Kinloch (1981); Smith (1990); Zeitlin (1994).

Ideology and knowledge

Ideologies are different from other forms of social cognition, such as *knowledge*. We have seen that historically there has been a long tradition of conflict between what was (negatively) qualified as (mere) ideology, on the one hand, and (real, scientific, etc.) knowledge, on the other hand. Unfortunately, there is no space in this chapter to develop the complex relation between ideology and knowledge. We shall simply say that an ideology is shared by the members of a specific *group* and that the ideology generally is in the *interest* of a *group* – often featuring evaluative propositions.

Knowledge, on the other hand, as defined here, is shared by a whole *community*; it is presupposed in all public discourse of the community, and also by speakers of different ideological groups, and hence is a form of Common Ground. Crucially, knowledge is belief that has been 'certified' by the (epistemic) criteria of an (epistemic) community – criteria that may vary culturally, historically and socially. Scholars will have other certification criteria or 'methods' to lay people, and we will have different ones today than existed five hundred years ago. In that sense, knowledge is always relative and contextual. However, *within* an epistemic community it is *not* relative, but assumed as a 'true' belief. That is, the relativism of knowledge is relative as well, as it should be.

Bibliographical Note

For ideology and **science**, see Aronowitz (1988); Diesing (1982).

According to this account, knowledge is more fundamental than ideologies, because ideologies, and an ideologically-based knowledge of groups, presuppose the shared knowledge of a whole community – that is, of *all* ideological groups. It is this feature of an epistemic Common Ground that enables mutual understanding and debate, even among ideological opponents, who may disagree about everything else.

Note that the relativity of knowledge also implies that what is knowledge for one community may be a mere belief, superstition or, indeed, a mere ideology, for others. As soon as there are significant social groups or institutions that will challenge general knowledge in a society, such knowledge may turn into debatable group knowledge or (counter) ideology – as was the case for the existence of God, the geocentric universe, the alleged intellectual inferiority of women or blacks, and so on. In other words, our theory of knowledge and ideology implies that beliefs which are generally accepted, shared and applied *as knowledge* in a community are by definition only 'ideological' from the perspective of another community, or at a later historical stage of the same community. In other words, beliefs count as knowledge in a community when the social practices, and hence all public discourse, of the members of the community presuppose these beliefs as being true-for-them.

Bibliographical Note

For the relations between ideology and **knowledge**, see Bailey (1994); Mannheim (1936); Dant (1991); van Dijk (1998). For ideology and **cultural studies**: Hall, Hobson, Lowe & Willis (1980); Morley & Chen (1996); Simons & Billig (1994).

The structure of ideologies

Although there has been a long tradition of philosophical and political thought about the nature of ideologies, little attention has been paid to the precise nature, the socio-cognitive structures, as well as the discursive reproduction, of ideologies. Indeed, a general, multidisciplinary theory of ideology and ideological discourse and other practices is still in its infancy.

- **Identity** (Who are we? Who belong to us? Where do we come from?)

- **Activities** (What do we usually do? What is our task?)

- **Goals** (What do we want to obtain?)

- **Norms and values** (What is good/bad, permitted/prohibited for us?)

- **Group relations** (Who are our allies and opponents?)

- **Resources** (What is the basis of our power, or our lack of power?)

Figure 18.1   Schematic categories of the structure of ideologies

As part of such a new theory, we must first characterize ideologies as forms of social cognition, that is, in psychological terms. In contemporary cognitive science, the vague notion of 'ideas' is generally analysed in terms of beliefs and belief systems, stored in 'semantic' Long-Term Memory, namely as specific *mental representations*. But what do such representations look like? What exactly is the *structure* of ideologies such as pacifism, socialism or neo-liberalism?

The easiest would be to represent ideologies as *lists* of ideological *propositions*, such as 'Women and men are equal', or 'War is wrong', and so on. However, lists are not very efficient to learn and use in concrete situations. Indeed, there are multiple mutual relationships between such propositions, and we should therefore rather think of ideologies in terms of specific *networks* (which might be related to the neurological networks of the brain – a topic we shall not deal with here) or other forms of *belief organization*.

Although as yet we do not know much about the mental organization of ideologies, analysis of ideological discourse and other practices suggests that ideologies will typically feature categories of propositions about the basic properties of groups, as in Figure 18.1.

These fundamental categories of the organization of ideologies form a general *schema* that reflects how groups will gradually develop a self-concept that is the result of their collective, shared *experiences* in society.

Ideologies as social cognition

Although ideologies are themselves belief systems and hence *cognitive constructs*, this does not mean that they are not *social* at the same time. On the contrary, as is the case for language, they are socially *shared* among the members of a *collectivity* and they are based on, and developed as a consequence of, *social interaction* in *social situations* that are part of *social structures*. This is how ideologies are developed *historically* for the group as a whole.

Once an ideology has been developed and has already spread among a group, new *individual group members* will learn it largely by inferences from the interpretation of the practices and especially of the *discourses* of parents, friends or colleagues, as well as the mass media. Some ideologies are acquired through specially designed educational discourse, that is, through the *teachings* of special group members (gurus, leaders, writers, priests, teachers: the *ideologues*). Indeed, people's personal experiences – as interpretations of events we shall call 'mental models' below – may be influenced by the ideologies they have acquired through discourse in the first place. For instance, workers do not spontaneously become socialists because of their miserable working conditions. They will only become socialists as a result of a complex process of 'learning' socialist ideas, consciousness raising, and ideological discourse, communication and interaction with (other) socialists.

Bibliographical Note

For ideology and **education**, see Apple (1979); Apple & Weiss (1983); Ward (1994).

Ideology vs. discourse

Since ideological discourse is by definition based on underlying ideologies, such discourse often shows some of the structures of these ideologies. We shall see below that this is indeed one of the ways by which we may analyse ideological discourse. Few data are better to study ideologies than text and talk, because it is largely through discourse and other semiotic messages, rather than by other ideological practices, that the contents of ideologies can be explicitly *articulated, justified* or *explained*, e.g., by argumentation, narration or exposition.

This does *not* mean that, methodologically speaking, we may circularly derive ideologies from discourse and discourse from ideologies, because – as we argued above – ideologies will also influence many other social practices, such as forms of oppression and discrimination or the struggle against them. Hence, the structures and contents of ideologies are different – for instance more general and abstract – from the ways they are used or expressed in discourse and other social practices. Indeed, we shall see below that discourse structures and ideological structures are only indirectly related through several intermediate cognitive levels. Thus one cannot always simply 'read off' the underlying ideologies of a discourse. We can *explain* ideological discourse structures (as well as other ideological practices) only *partly* in terms of underlying ideologies and only when taking into account intermediate levels of discourse production. Ideological discourses are also controlled by many other, non-ideological, constraints, such as the current goals, knowledge and conception of the current context of the participants.

This may mean that in specific communicative situations ideologies may not be expressed in discourse at all, or expressed in an indirect and transformed way. As we shall see below, relating discourse to ideology takes place at several levels of analysis, and hence is far from circular: even ideological discourse is in many ways autonomous, and is always ultimately shaped by the *whole* context, of which the ideology of the participants is only *one* dimension.

An example: a schema of a professional ideology

As an example of the ideology schema mentioned above, consider the ideology of many journalists. Such a *professional* ideology first features the *identity* of a journalist as a professional (who in a given community is seen, accepted, hired, etc. as a journalist?); their typical professional *activities* (e.g., gather and report the news); their overall *goals* (to inform the public, to 'serve as a watchdog of society'); their *norms* (objectivity, fairness, impartiality, etc.); their *relations to other groups* (sources, readers, government, corporate business, etc.); and the main *resource* that defines their power in society (information). Note that the propositions organized by this ideological schema do not describe what journalists actually think and do, but how they *positively represent* themselves: they are *ideological* propositions. In other words, an ideology is like a basic *self-image* of a group, including the interests and relationships (power, resistance, competition) to other social groups.

Ideologies, norms and values

Note that ideologies as belief systems not only represent the (possibly biased, misguided) *knowledge* of a group, but also its shared *evaluations*, according to the basic community *norms* and *values* applied in its own activities as well as those of reference groups. Indeed, professional journalists will also have criteria that will allow them to recognize 'good' or 'bad' reporting – as is also reflected in professional codes of conduct. In other words, ideologies not only tell members of an ideological group what is 'true' or 'false', but also what is 'good' or 'bad', 'permitted' or 'prohibited', and so on.

Thus, one widespread value in many communities is *Freedom*. But depending on the interests of ideological groups this value may be differently construed in their ideologies, for instance as *Freedom of the Market* in neoliberal ideologies and as *Freedom of the Press* in the professional ideology of journalists. Evaluations of actions and events that are relevant for the members of an ideological group are thus evaluated on the basis of these ideologically applied general community norms and values. Although many ideologies are transcultural, this may also mean that if the basic values of a community are different the ideologies (such as liberalism, socialism or feminism) in that community may also be different from those in other communities.

Bibliographical Note

For ideology and the **bureaucracy**, see Burton & Carlen (1979); Hwang (1998).

ATTITUDES

We have defined ideologies as *shared*, *general* and *abstract* mental representations that should be applicable to the many situations in which ideological group members may find themselves. However, it is likely that ideologies control – and are originally derived from – shared beliefs about more *specific* issues that are relevant in the everyday lives of group members. In traditional social psychology such specific representations are called *attitudes*, a notion we shall here adopt (and adapt) because of its practical use and usefulness in ideological discourse analysis. As is the case for knowledge and ideologies, attitudes are also forms of *socially shared and distributed cognition*, and hence still fairly general and abstract and *not* ad hoc personal opinions (although these are also called 'attitudes' in much of social psychology).

Attitudes are ideologically-based belief clusters about *specific social issues*, such as abortion, euthanasia, immigration, pollution, freedom of speech and the press, the vote, and so on. While focused on relevant social issues, attitudes – as we would define them here – are more directly applicable in the ideological control of discourse and other social practices than the abstract ideologies on which they are based.

Indeed, members may barely be aware of the general ideologies influencing their concrete opinions and conduct. They are usually more conscious of group attitudes about concrete issues and will orient their personal opinions accordingly. For instance, under the influence of a dominant anti-feminist discourse, many young girls may even reject the general ideological label of being feminists, but still actually subscribe to many feminist attitudes, such as equal pay, freedom of choice in questions of abortion, and so on. The same may be true for workers who may not see themselves as socialists, but would agree with many socialist-based attitudes about hiring, firing and the rights of workers in general. And conversely, quite typically, people may be against immigration and the rights of immigrants but would emphatically deny propagating a racist ideology – as would be typically the case for the journalist(s) who wrote the editorial on immigration in the *Daily Telegraph*.

We can see that in the theory of ideology, attitudes – as defined – play a crucial *intermediary* role in our minds, namely to link very general ideologies to more specific social domains, issues and practices, and ultimately to discourse. And conversely, ideologies are not usually directly acquired by generalizing from discourse and other social practices, but as further generalizations and abstractions of specific attitudes: one gradually learns to be a feminist, socialist or pacifist by learning about specific feminist, socialist or pacifist issues.

Bibliographical Note

There are few book-length studies on the cognitive or social psychology of ideology. See, for example, Billig (1982); Aebischer, Deconchy & Lipiansky (1992); Fraser & Gaskell (1990); van Dijk (1998).

IDEOLOGICAL MENTAL MODELS

In order to relate ideologies and ideologically based attitudes to concrete discourse and other social practices of individual members in specific situations, we finally need another level of socio-cognitive analysis, namely that of *personal experiences*. Such experiences are represented as *mental models*, stored in our (autobiographical) Episodic Memory, part of Long-Term Memory. Unlike underlying ideologies and attitudes, models are *subjective*, *personal* representations of *specific* events, actions and situations – that is, how people personally interpret, live and remember the events in their daily lives. Besides personal knowledge, such models may also feature personal evaluative beliefs – *opinions* – as well as the *emotions* associated with such events.

Mental models formed by individual members of a social group may be ideologically controlled by socially shared group attitudes about a specific issue. Thus, feminists will typically have a feminist opinion about a specific case of sexual harassment. This is the social dimension of the mental models they share with other feminists, and explains why members of the same group will often have similar opinions about an event.

However, models are also representations of *personal* experiences, and hence are also influenced by current goals and earlier experiences that may be at variance with the socially shared attitude. This explains why in interviews, and other forms of ideological discourse, members of the same group may at the same time show considerable variations in their personal opinions, so much so that scholars have often doubted about the very existence of underlying attitudes and ideologies that may be generally shared.

A comprehensive theory of ideology that is analytically and empirically adequate should describe and explain **both** *the personal variation of ideological discourse and conduct,* **and** *the ideologically based opinions people have in common as group members.* Since mental models – as the interface between the social and the personal – feature both dimensions, they are ideal as a basis for the explanation of personally variable, but yet socially based, ideological opinions and discourse.

Since only group members as persons – and not groups – have bodies, this also allows ideologies and attitudes to be lived, expressed and 'embodied' in the mental models of personal experiences, as is typically the case for *emotions*. Thus, sexual harassment is not just lived as an instantiation of a feminist-based ideology against gender inequality or male oppression, but also felt as a deeply *personal* and *emotional* experience – even when later *accounts* of such an experience in storytelling may combine personal feelings with ideologically-based instantiations of general attitudes about sexual harassment.

Bibliographical Note

For ideology, **gender** and **feminism**, see Afshar (1987); Ballaster (1991); Charles & Hintjens (1998); Lazar (2005); Ryan (1992); Smith (1990); Wodak (1997).

Mental models are crucial in the account of discourse and other social practices and define how we will personally plan, understand, interpret, experience and later remember all the events and actions we are involved in. Ideologically 'biased' mental models control all our ideological practices and hence also our ideological text and talk. Mental models of discourse represent what the discourse is about, or refers to, and hence account for the semantics of discourse. We may therefore also call them 'semantic models' of discourse. In other words, to interpret the meaning of a discourse, language users will construe a subjective mental model for that discourse, possibly including their opinions and emotions about the actions or events that discourse is about. We can see that mental models play a central role both in discourse production as well as in discourse comprehension. It is through *personally variable but socially similar mental models* that members of an ideological group will interpret and represent all the social events that are relevant for a group and hence the discourses about such events.

Bibliographical Note

In this chapter ideologies are primarily defined and analyzed as socially shared mental representations of groups. Their individual dimension are accounted for in terms of the 'uses' of such ideologies and attitudes by group members, and in terms of evaluative and emotional aspects of subjective mental models representing the people's personal experiences. Such an approach is different from the traditional 'psycho-dynamic' approach to ideologies in terms of people's personality, as in the 'authoritarian personality' of Adorno (1950). This latter approach, combined with a more 'top down' collective approach, has recently found new advocates and generated new empirical research, for instance in the work of John Jost and associates (among many studies, see, for example, the review article by Jost, Federico & Napier (2009)). This work stresses that, in addition to situational conditions that create fear (as is the case for terrorist attacks), specific 'bottom up' personality properties, such as 'being open to new experiences' predispose people to leftists, liberal ideologies, whereas a preference for order, stability and loyalty tend to predispose people to 'elect' conservative ideologies.

Ideological context models

Special mental models, namely *context models*, are formed from the current, ongoing *experience of interaction and communication* defining the *context* of text and talk. For instance, journalistic practices are controlled by context models that will subjectively represent the writer's own identity, roles, goals, norms and resources as journalist, combined with previous, personal experiences during news gathering and news writing. Similarly, someone may typically speak *as a feminist* when participating in a debate on sexual harassment. This means that in her (or his) current, ongoing context model the speaker will represent her- or himself as a feminist, and such a context model will influence all the levels of discourse production or comprehension.

Context models are *subjective definitions* of the communicative situation. They control how discourse is adapted to the communicative situation, and hence define its *appropriateness*.

Besides representing the current identities of, and relations between, the participants such context models will also feature information about the Setting (Time, Place), identities and relations of participants, the ongoing social activity (e.g., news writing, a conversation, a parliamentary debate, etc.), as well as the goals, the knowledge and – indeed – the currently relevant ideologies of the participants.

Context models are the basis of the *pragmatics* of discourse. This may also require that the 'semantic' mental models about some experience (what we talk *about*) are adapted to the current communicative situation. It is not always appropriate (polite, relevant, etc.) to express what one knows, believes or feels. Thus, 'pragmatic' context models will control *what* we say and especially *how* we say it (style, register) in a specific communicative situation. And, crucial for our discussion, like 'semantic' mental models, context models may be ideologically biased. Thus men (and women) may not just express sexist opinions when talking *about* women, but also when talking *to* them – that is, represent themselves and their (relation to the) interlocutor in their context model in a sexist way.

This pragmatic account of discourse and ideology is crucial, because it shows more clearly what we have said above about the sometimes indirect relations between discourse and ideology. It is true that the discourse of group members may typically be influenced by the ideology of the group, but this always depends on the context as the participants define it. Depending on current aims and interests and the opinions or ideologies of one's interlocutors, one may conceal or only indirectly express one's ideologies. Indeed, in many situations such an ideology may not even be relevant, and one need not speak *as a group member* in that case. Feminists or pacifists do not always speak as feminists or pacifists in all situations. In other words, context models are always the ultimate 'filter' for underlying ideologies, even when the ideologies in that case may subtly 'leak' through such a filter of self-control, and be detected by sophisticated discourse analysis, as we know from such formulas as *I am not a racist, but ...*

Bibliographical Note

On ideology and semantic **situation models** and **pragmatic (context) models** and ideology, see van Dijk (1998, 2008a).

IDEOLOGY AND DISCOURSE

Having sketched the nature of ideologies and the way these are related to concrete ideological practices, we now also know the socio-cognitive aspects of how ideologies are related to discourse, how they can be expressed or performed in discourse, and how they can be acquired and changed by discourse.

We have stressed that *ideologies are seldom expressed directly in discourse*, possibly with the exception of explicit ideological texts such as bibles, catechisms, party programmes, and so on. More often than not, only fragments of ideologies will be expressed, for instance in the form of attitudes about specific issues, say in a debate about immigration or government policy, as we have seen in the editorial from the *Daily Telegraph*. And even then, such a shared attitude may be combined with personal experiences and opinions in the mental models of specific group members as language users.

In other words, it must be assumed, as we did above, that there are several layers of representation between general, abstract group ideologies on the one hand (as some kind of ideological 'deep structure') and concrete ideological text and talk (as ideological 'surface structure') on the other hand. We have argued that this may also mean that ideologies are not always directly visible or detectable in discourse, especially when context models block direct ideological expression as being inappropriate of otherwise a 'bad idea' in a specific situation. In that case, an analysis of the context may be necessary in order to show that the use of specific expressions (e.g., code words) in specific situations should be interpreted as ideological – as we know from the propaganda posters of racist parties in Europe.

Bibliographical Note

For ideological discourse analysis, see De Saussure & Schulz (2005); Fowler (1991); Fox & Fox (2004); Garzone & Sarangi (2008); Gee (1990); Larsen, Strunck & Vestergaard (2006); Lazar (2005); Pêcheux (1982); Pütz, Neff-van Aertselaer & van Dijk (2004); Schäffner & Kelly-Holmes (1996), van Dijk (1998, 2008b); Wodak (1989); Wodak, de Cillia, Reisigl & Liebhart (1999).

Constraints on ideological discourse analysis

For theoretical and methodological reasons, ideological discourse analysis should be guided by three fundamental constraints: 1) *discursive*, 2) *socio-cognitive*, and 3) *social* in a broad sense (including interactional, political, historical and cultural).

This means, first of all, that *any* discourse analysis, and hence also ideological analysis, should take into account the general properties of text and talk, and hence the relation between any expression or meaning with respect other structures in discourse. For instance, as is often the case, one may interpret a passive construction as an expression of an ideological strategy for mitigating the negative role of a dominant group. However, it should not be forgotten that passive sentence constructions may also be used in discourse for several other reasons, e.g., because the agent is unknown, or because the agent has already been identified and need not be repeated, but the focus needs to be on the victims of negative actions, and so on. In other words, there may be other than ideological constraints on the structures of discourse, and one should always take into account, first of all, the 'co-textual' function of any expression or meaning within the very discourse itself.

Secondly, ideological discourse analysis is obviously about discourse structures that are influenced – even if only very indirectly – by underlying ideologies as they are shared by the members of a group. In other words, only those structures of discourse should be called ideological that can be shown to be expressions of the underlying socio-cognitive representations (such as mental models and attitudes) that are controlled by the structures of the ideology of a group. This means that those ideological structures of discourse should be focused on that express or reproduce the identity, actions, goals, norms and values, group relations and resources of a group – if we assume that these are the general categories of the structures of ideologies. Language users may engage in a positive self-presentation and negative other-presentation for personal reasons alone, and not because they wish to speak or write *as a member of a group*. In that case, the mental model that underlies discourse is not influenced by socially shared ideologies or attitudes, but features personal opinions and experiences only, or opinions based on non-ideological attitudes shared by a group. For instance, not every negative discourse by a group of students about their professors is necessarily ideologically inspired.

Thirdly, besides these discursive and socio-cognitive constraints, all social practices and hence all text and talk are conditioned by the social environment, that is, by ongoing interaction, as well as by the identity, interests, goals, relationships and other properties of the communicative situation as the participants define it, that is, by the *context*. This means, as we have seen above, that speakers may well *not* express an ideologically-based perspective or opinion for contextual reasons, for instance because of politeness, fear of ridicule, and so on.

The expression or 'performance' of ideologically-based structures always needs to be analysed with regard to the ongoing, and possibly dynamically changing, *functions of discourse in the current context*. For instance, the *Daily Telegraph* typically expresses its anti-immigration attitude in a public editorial addressed to a Labour government. It may do so because, for several other ideological reasons, it is opposed to such a government, and hence hopes its editorial will have a significant political impact, for instance on readers/voters. In other words, its ideological editorial has ideological functions in the current communicative situation (knowing the kind of readers the newspaper has, knowing the current political situation, etc.). Now, if the Conservatives were to gain power, the context would be totally different, and although the negative attitude about immigration would remain the same, an editorial about immigration policies directed at a Conservative government would most likely be quite different.

In sum, ideological discourse analysis – that is, the identification and interpretation of discursive structures and strategies as the expression and reproduction of group ideologies – must always take into account the textual, cognitive and social (contextual) constraints on all discourse. Indeed, rather trivially, not all the structures of every discourse are always ideological! It is in light of these constraints that we shall finally examine some structures of text and talk that often – but not always – have ideological functions.

In the remainder of this chapter, we shall focus on the ways ideologies are being expressed, performed and (re) produced by text and talk. The theoretical basis of that analysis, as we have outlined it above, is that ideological discourse is always controlled by the following fundamental underlying representations:

1 SOCIAL COGNITION

   a) Socially shared representations of the whole community: socio-cultural **knowledge** or **Common Ground**.
   b) Socially shared representations of a specific social group: specific **group knowledge** and **ideology** and ideological **attitudes**.

2 PERSONAL COGNITION

   a) Subjective mental **event models** of the events talked or written *about* – defining the *semantic reference, truth, etc.* of discourse.
   b) Subjective mental models – **context models** – of the current communicative situation *in which participants are currently involved,* defining the *pragmatic appropriateness* of discourse.

This means that, first of all, we may examine the ways *ideologies and their structures* will influence attitudes, mental models and finally discourse structures, though always under the control of context models, such as the current goals of the speaker or writer. This means that if ideologies are indeed organized according to the schema we proposed above, we may engage in a systematic and theoretically-based analysis of ideologies by examining how their categories show up in discourse.

The expression of ideological schemas in discourse

Following the ideology schema proposed above, we may assume that the following types of *meanings* tend to become manifest in ideological discourse:

- **Group identity and identification** Topics about who we are; who are (not) typical members of our group; what the typical properties are for our group; who can or should (not) be admitted to the group; where we come from; what our history is; what our foundational texts are; who are our group heroes; what our symbols are, or other symbolic markers (flags, etc.); and, quite crucially, what our 'own' domain is where we are autonomous. In sum, this ideological category influences a vast number of possible discourse topics and local meanings related to the *history, properties* and *boundaries* of the group. Characteristic examples of ideologies that are largely based on this category are nationalism, Euro-centrism and racism.
- **Activity** This category influences the way group members will define their typical role in society, what they will do, what is expected of them as group members. This category is especially important in professional ideologies, but also in some political and religious ones. Indeed, Christianity is not just self-defined in terms of its beliefs, but also in how Christians are supposed (not) to act towards their 'neighbours' – as laid down in the Ten Commandments. Hence, all topics of discourse that are about what *we as a group* do, or should (not) do, may be expressions of such an ideology, as are the social practices that are themselves controlled by the ideology.
- **Norms and values** Ideologies, attitudes and the practices based on them are permanently controlled by norms and values. Thus, most opinions in the ideological discourse of group members may be based on the norms and values specifically selected and combined in each ideology, such as freedom, autonomy, justice, and so on – though redefined in terms of the interest of the group (e.g., freedom of the market, freedom of speech, freedom from discrimination, etc.). Thus, all references to what is good or bad, and what is permitted and prohibited, who are good and bad people, what

are good and bad actions, etc., are expressions that are typically influenced by this category of the ideology. This category is especially important in political and religious ideologies.

- **Group relations**   Central to most ideologies is the representation of the relation between our own (in-) group and other (out-) groups, between *Us* and *Them*. Given the positive bias in ideological self-schemas, we may thus expect a generally positive representation of Us, and a negative representation of Them, at all levels of discourse. This *ideological polarization* is so pervasive in discourse that we shall pay special attention to it below. Although relevant for most ideologies, this category is quite typical for racist, nationalist and political-economic ideologies (such as socialism and neo-liberalism), as well as most ideologies of resistance, such as feminism and pacifism, but less prominent in professional ideologies.

- **Resources**   Groups need resources to be able to exist and reproduce as a group. Journalists without information, professors without knowledge, etc. would not be able to exercise their power in society. Hence, ideological discourse may be geared to the (sometimes violent) defence of our resources, privileges or power, or precisely by our lack of them. Such ideologies and their discourses are typical for most ideologies, but quite explicit for resistance ideologies (feminism, socialism) and socio-economic ideologies (neo-liberalism, etc.).

We have now outlined the general influence of ideologies and their basic categories on discourse, for instance on the kind of overall topics and local meanings of ideological discourse. However, such an analysis is still quite general, and we need to go down to more specific ways in which ideologies will shape text and talk. Theoretically ideologies may influence any part of a discourse that may vary with the ideologies of the speaker. In other words, ideologies may in principle affect all discourse structures except those following the general rules of grammar and discourse. General rules hold for all speakers and hence for all groups in a language community, and hence must be ideologically rather neutral. An exception here are those rules that have been developed as a consequence of group control, as is the case for masculine plural pronouns in Spanish, that are also used to denote collectivities of men and women, or the – grammatically masculine – names of many professions. Hence, since there are a large number of discourse structures that can be ideologically controlled, we shall only focus on some characteristic ones, and refer to the general ideological schema above to find and analyse other ideologically-based structures and strategies.

The ideological square

One of the main overall strategies of ideological discourse control in discourse is a manifestation of the *Group Relations* category of the ideology schema, that is, the way in-groups

Emphasize *Our* good things	Emphasize *Their* bad things
De-emphasize *Our* bad things	De-emphasize *Their* good things

Figure 18.2   The Ideological Square

and out-groups are represented in text and talk, prototypically represented by the ideological pronouns *Us* and *Them*. Since the underlying ideological structure of that category is largely *polarized*, we may expect the same to be the case in ideological discourse. This happens in the following way, which we have called the *Ideological Square* because of its four complementary overall strategies.

The general meta-strategies of (de-) emphasizing, as we also know it from classical rhetoric (for instance in hyperboles and euphemisms) can be applied at all levels of multimodal text and talk, as we shall see in more detail below: at the level of sound and visual structures, of syntax and the lexicon, of local and global semantics, of pragmatics, of rhetoric, and of the schematic (organizational) structures of discourse. In the editorial from the *Daily Telegraph* we have already observed several hyperboles, that is, moves to lexically emphasize the 'bad' properties attributed to Labour and its immigration policy. Below we shall show in more detail how this was done in other examples of ideological discourse.

Positive self-presentation and negative other-presentation

The complex meta-strategy of the ideological square tells us that group members will tend to speak or write positively about their own group, and negatively about those out-groups they define as opponents, competitors or enemies, if only because the Others are different.

This basic property of groups and group relations, often observed in social psychological and sociological studies on intergroup perception and interaction, requires sophisticated discourse analysis in order to examine how it is deployed at all levels of text and talk. That is, discourse analysis goes beyond a superficial content analysis of positive or negative terms describing attributed in-group or out-group characteristics.

Discourse may affect the formation or change of mental models, and hence realize persuasive goals, in many more ways, from the sound structures of intonation and the visual structures of images, via the formal structures of syntax, style and rhetoric, to the complex semantic manipulation of local and global meanings and the pragmatic dimensions of speech acts and more generally the strategies of interaction.

Thus, emphasizing the negative characteristics of out-groups may be accomplished by such diverse structures and strategies as the following.

SEMANTIC STRUCTURES: MEANING AND REFERENCE

- **Negative topics** (semantic macrostructures) – any overall discourse topic describing *Them* as breaching our norms and values: deviance, threat, insecurity, criminality, inability, etc.
- **Level of description** (generality *vs.* specificity) – *Their* negative properties or actions tend to be described in more specific (lower level) detail than *Ours*.
- **Degree of completeness** (at each level of description) – More details will be mentioned, at each level of description, about *Their* negative properties or actions.
- **Granularity** (preciseness *vs.* vagueness) – *Their* negative properties or actions tend to be described with more precise terms than *Ours*.

- **Implications** (propositions implied by propositions explicitly expressed in discourse) – propositions may be used that have (many) negative implications about *Them*.
- **Presuppositions** (propositions that must be true/known for any proposition to be meaningful) – presupposing propositions (negative about Them) that are not known to be true.
- **Denomination** (of propositions: participant description) – *They* tend to be named or identified as different from *Us* (precisely as *Them*) – strangers, immigrants, Others, opponents, enemies, etc.
- **Predication** (of propositions: meanings of sentences) – any predicate of a proposition attributing negative characteristics to Them.
- **Modality** (modal expressions modifying propositions: necessity, probability, possibility) – negative properties of *Them* may be attributed as inherent, and hence as 'necessarily' applying to *Them*.
- **Agency** (role of the arguments/participants of a proposition) – emphasizing *Their* (and de-emphasizing *Our*) agency or active responsibility of negative actions.
- **Topic *vs.* comment organization** (distribution of given/known *vs.* new information in sentences) – as with presuppositions at the propositional level, negative participants may be assumed to be known, etc.
- **Focus** Any participant, property or action may receive special focus, e.g., by special stress, volume, size, colour, etc. (see below), in order to draw attention of the recipients – e.g. in order to emphasize negative agency of Them.

FORMAL STRUCTURES

- **Superstructures** (general 'formats', 'schemas' or overall 'organization' of discourse such as those of argumentation or narration). Specific semantic categories – e.g. with negative meanings about *Them* – may be **foregrounded** when placed in an irregular (first, earlier) position, e.g. in headlines or leads. Negative properties of *Them* may be emphasized by persuasive arguments and fallacies or by captivating forms of storytelling that also promote the later memorizing of such alleged negative properties.
- **Visual structures** that emphasize negative meanings: foregrounding negative acts or events in images; type, size, colour of letters and headlines; prominent position on page or medium (e.g. front page of newspaper); photographs representing *Them* as actors of negative actions; derogatory cartoons; preciseness, granularity, close-ups, etc. of negative representations in images or film.
- **Sound structures** that emphasize negative words: volume, pitch, etc. of phonemes; intonation of sentences (e.g. expressing irony, distance, scepticism, accusations, etc.); music associated with negative emotions (e.g. signifying threat, danger, violence, etc.).
- **Syntactic structures of sentences** (word order, order of clauses, hierarchical relations between clauses, etc.) – active sentences to emphasize negative agency (*vs.* passive sentences or nominalizations that de-emphasize agency); initial dependent *that*-clauses may express unknown or false presuppositions about *Them*.
- **Definite expressions** May express unknown or false presuppositions about *Them*.
- **Pronouns** May signal in-group and out-group membership, as in *Us* vs. Them, and in general different degrees of power, solidarity, intimacy, etc. when speaking to *Us* vs. *Them*.
- **Demonstratives** May signal closeness or distance to people being described, e.g. *those people*.
- **Rhetorical moves** Repetitions, enumerations, rhymes, alliterations to emphasize and hence draw attention to emphasize negative meanings about *Them*.

We can see from this (incomplete) list that there are many ways whereby language users may emphasize negative meanings/information about Others, and thus engage in the discursive reproduction of out-group derogation that is typical of ideological text and talk. They may do so by using (semantic) structures and strategies of meaning itself, such as selecting or emphasizing negative topics or person and action descriptions, but also by many formal (visual, phonological, structural) means that may be conventionally used to emphasize these meanings and hence draw special attention to them.

Obviously the *same* semantic and formal strategies may be used for a positive self-description of in-groups and their members. In other words, and as stressed above, the general structures and strategies of discourse must themselves be ideologically neutral, since these may be used by any ideological group in the same community – they are linguistic and communicative resources that can be adopted by anyone. However, *what* is being (de-) emphasized by these discursive means is of course ideologically relevant. This also means that ideological analysis can never consist of only a *formal* analysis of text and talk: we always need to consider the *meanings* that express underlying ideological beliefs, as well as the *context*: who is speaking/writing about what, to whom, when, and with what goal.

SAMPLE ANALYSIS

Let us finally examine in some more detail another characteristic example of ideological discourse and show how its structures express and reproduce underlying ideologies. Although we could have selected a discourse exemplifying what we would call positive ideologies – e.g. those advocating justice, equality, equity, autonomy, etc. – we shall again use a discourse that exemplifies ideologies that are often deemed to be negative in democratic contexts. Such an analysis is more typical for Critical Discourse Studies, that is, a scholarly activity and movement that opposes power abuse and domination, such as racism, sexism, and so on.

As our example, we shall examine the intervention of a member of the Partido Popular (PP) in Spain, Ángel Acebes Paniagua, in the Spanish *Cortes* (Cámara de Diputados: Spanish Parliament), on 24 May 2006, addressing the Minister (Secretary) of Work and Social Affairs, Caldera, a member of the government led by PSOE (socialist) Prime Minister Zapatero, on the topic of immigration (see the Appendix for the Spanish original):

1   Mister Minister, your first decision, nearly the only one your Government
2   has taken, was to change the policy we had agreed with the European
3   Union, and to realize a massive regularization process when already
4   nobody was doing so in the European Union. Despite the warnings of this
5   parliamentary group, of France, Germany, the United Kingdom and the
6   European Commission, that this would produce a most serious call effect
7   (Commotion), you ignored this policy. The Prime Minister continued with his
8   well-known policy of letting nobody spoil him a good headline, although it
9   creates a problem for all the citizens.
10 The consequences soon followed and all Spanish citizens see them
11 every day: large groups assaulting our borders in Ceuta and Melilla –
12 there were 15 dead, Mister Minister; avalanches of people in the Canary
13 Islands – 2000 immigrants in one week, and each day 600 people enter
14 at La Junquera and through the mountain passes in the North, and many
15 more through the airports. The end result of your policy: one million more

16 irregular immigrants in one single year. You have broken all records of
17 incompetence (Commotion). You know what is most serious of all? These
18 avalanches have turned our borders into places where anybody can enter
19 as they please, and criminal gangs have taken advantage of that to enter
20 Spain. Crime taking place at our homes is due to criminal gangs that traffic
21 with human beings, engage in violent robberies, express kidnappings,
22 homicides. Of course one things leads to another, hence we insist on
23 efficient policies that resolve this problem, a problem that increasingly
24 worries the citizens. (Commotion). In the meantime, this Government, totally
25 overwhelmed, acts ridiculously, as you do when you say that all of Europe is
26 going to copy your policy … (Applause).

In order to show the international relations and coherence of widespread ideologies, we also chose this example because it deals with the same topic as the editorial of the *Daily Telegraph*, namely immigration; is also formulated by a member of a conservative institution, a political party; and is also critically directed at a 'Labour' government.

The ideological polarization here is articulated along two axes, the first one opposing the Conservative party and opposition for the Partido Popular to the socialist government, and the second opposing the autochthonous Spanish people to immigrants. Let us now compare how such underlying ideological structures have been expressed in this fragment.

The analysis of the positive self-presentation moves yields the usual ones for an in-group presentation of political parties in opposition when attacking the government. Although they are at the moment (2010) the political minority in Spain, their legitimization is sought first of all by claiming to be part of a European consensus (actually, the 2009 elections of the EU parliament showed that conservative ideologies, also on immigration, were dominant in Europe). Higher level political organizations may thus be used in ideological discourse as a warrant in an implicit argument sustaining the point of view that *Our* policies are good. Secondly, when issuing a warning that is also presented as being in line with the

Table 18.1   Positive self-presentation moves in the discourse of a conservative politician in the Spanish Parliament when talking about immigration

A. Conservatives (Partido Popular, 'Us')	Positive self-presentation
1 we had agreed with the European Union	• We are part of the international consensus
2 when already nobody was doing so in the European Union.	• Our policy is in line with EU policy
	• 'We told you so' → We know about politics
3 Despite the warnings of this parliamentary group, of France, Germany, the United Kingdom and the European Commission, that this would produce a most serious call effect	• We agree with the policy of the large EU countries
	• We foresaw problems → We are competent politicians
4 (…) although it creates a problem for all the citizens.	• We care for the citizens → We take our role as representatives seriously → We are democratic
5 Of course one things leads to another	
6 hence we insist on efficient policies that resolve this problem,	• We understand the causality of the events
	• We take political action against a problem
7 a problem that increasingly worries the citizen	

Table 18.2   Negative You/Other-presentation moves in the discourse of a conservative politician in the Spanish Parliament when addressing the socialist government about immigration

B. Socialists (Government, 'You')	Negative Other/You-presentation
1 Mister Minister, your first decision, nearly the only one your Government has taken,	• → You (minister, government, PSOE) are lazy • You deviated from a good, consensus policy; you are an exception in the EU
2 was to change the policy (…)	
3 and to realize a massive regularization process	• You admitted a vast number of immigrants (hyperbole)
4 you ignored this policy.	
5 You have broken all records for incompetence	• You are incompetent (hyperbole)
6 The Prime Minister continued with his well-known policy of letting nobody spoil him a good headline,	• You (PSOE, government) are only concerned about your image → You are superficial → You are bad politicians
7 although it creates a problem for all the citizens.	• You do not care about the citizens → You are undemocratic
8 The consequences soon followed	• Your policy has (bad) consequences → Your policy is bad
9 there were 15 dead, Mister Minister;	
10 The end result of your policy: one million more irregular immigrants in one single year.	• Your policy causes death → Your policy is lethal → Your policy is bad
11 You know what is most serious of all?	• Your ignore the seriousness of the question → You are frivolous → You are bad politicians
12 In the meantime, this Government, totally overwhelmed, acts ridiculously, as you do when you say that all of Europe is going to copy your policy …	• Your government is unable to solve this problem • Your government is ridiculous • No one follows your policy → Your policy is bad

EU consensus, the speaker also implies that they had foreseen the current problems, and thus also implies that they are good politicians. Next, the speaker seeks the legitimatization of the policies of the opposition party by repeatedly referring to the will and attitudes of the (autochthonous) citizens, and hence further implies that his party is (more) democratic because it cares for the people. We can see that positive self-presentation moves in a political discourse such as this are all geared towards one major goal: legitimatization.

In Table 18.2 we can see the complementary moves of the overall strategy of negative other-presentation. While directly addressing the Minister, first of all, opposition moves may be personal, e.g. when accusing the minister of being lazy and incompetent. Secondly, and more explicitly, the speaker derogates the Prime Minister and the government as frivolous and ridiculous, and hence delegitimizes them as bad politicians. Thirdly, by accusing the current government as going against EU policy, he implies that they are politically deviant, and hence bad. And since the government is accused of ignoring the wishes of the people, they are not only neglecting their job as representatives and current leaders of the people, but also losing all democratic legitimacy. In other words, a negative other-presentation is articulated along the criterion of international consensus (by accusing that this has been broken by the current government) and a lack of democratic support. Hence, both nationally, as well as internationally, the current socialist government is also accused of lacking legitimacy. In this case, the strategy represents an ideological opposition against a socialist government, and hence implies a positive representation of a conservative policy.

Table 18.3 Representation of immigrants in the discourse of a conservative Spanish politician

Representation of immigrants	Moves of negative Other-presentation
1 (...) a massive regularization process 2 (...) a most serious call effect 3 (...) a problem for all the citizens. 4 (...) large groups assaulting our borders in Ceuta and Mellilla 5 (...) there were 15 dead 6 avalanches of people in the Canary Islands 7 2000 immigrants in one week, 8 and each day 600 people enter at La Junquera and through the mountain passes in the North, 9 and many more through the airports. 10 one million more irregular immigrants in one single year. 11 (...) most serious of all? 12 These avalanches have turned our borders into places where anybody can enter as they please, 13 and criminal gangs have taken advantage of that to enter Spain. 14 Crimes taking place in our homes is due to criminal gangs 15 that traffic with human beings, 16 engage in violent robberies, 17 express kidnappings, homicides. 18 Of course one things leads to another, 19 a problem that increasingly worries the citizens.	• Immigrants come massively → They are a threat. • They come because they are 'called' by permissive immigration policies → They do not come because they have serious economic or political problems. • They are a problems for Us (Spanish) • They are violent ('assaulting') • They threaten our borders → They threaten Our country. • They are responsible for dead people • *Suggestion:* Our dead people and not their own dead people. • *Metaphor:* avalanches → threat of nature • *Number game:* 2000, 600, one million, etc. • *Temporal Hyperbole:* one week, one year • *Accumulation, Climax:* many more ... • Irregular → against our rules → deviants • *Metaphor:* Spanish borders described as 'coladero' = sieve • *Identification, denomination, criminalization:* Immigrants described as, identified as, criminal gangs • *Overgeneralization:* All crimes attributed to them • *Personal Threat:* They threaten us at home • They lack humanity, violate human rights: traffic in human beings • They are violent (violent robberies) • They engage in very serious crimes (assassination, kidnapping) • There is a logical relation between their arrival and these crimes • They are a problem for Us (our citizens) → Our citizens are victims.

Although in a parliamentary debate a double-sided polarization by opposition politicians will of course be primarily addressed at the current government, speakers may also express ideological attitudes about other out-groups – in this debate obviously the illegal immigrants, although implicitly and sometimes explicitly, the strategy appears to be directed against all immigrants, especially those from the 'South' and 'East' and thus those who are ethnically different – and hence appears a manifestation of a racist ideology. Table 18.3 shows the moves used to negatively represent the immigrants.

Table 18.3 hardly leaves any doubt about the ideological control of Mr. Acebes' speech by an underlying racist ideology. His representation of immigrants features all the usual racist prejudices, mainly associating (all) immigrants with threats in general, and crime in particular. In order to make sure ordinary people also get his message, he links the criminal threat especially to alleged assaults in private homes, and emphasizes that the massive numbers of threatening immigrants arriving worry all citizens. Discursively, the threat is specifically formulated with the usual metaphors of the threatening forces of nature (*avalanches*), the number game emphasizing the 'masses' of immigrants, and the accumulation of predicates implying death and violence. By recalling, in terms of an 'assault', a border incident in the Spanish enclaves in Northern Africa, Ceuta and Melilla, he at the same time represents immigrants as a threat to the whole nation, and hence as a security issue – thereby also showing elements of an underlying nationalist ideology.

Note that this is not a discourse merely referring to specific events, and hence inviting the formation of isolated mental models of incidents. Its repeated (over) generalizations directly express and intend to form or confirm the more general underlying ethnic prejudices based on a racist ideology: Immigrants are violent criminals and a threat to Our citizens. This means that the speaker at the same time contributes to the formation of the ideological polarization between Us Spanish and Them immigrants. Except in the passage on Ceuta and Melilla, it is not made explicit that the alleged threat comes from Africa, Eastern Europe and Latin America, but this is implied by the reference to the Northern borders and the airport – the speaker knows that the citizens know to whom he is referring.

Bibliographical note

For ideology and **racism**, see Barker (1981); Guillaumin (1995); Römer (1985); van Dijk (1993, 1996, 1998); Wetherell & Potter (1992).

CONCLUDING REMARK

We can see that an analysis of the assumed underlying structures of ideologies allows us to proceed in a systematic and explicit way when analysing ideological discourse. Thus, at each level of discourse, we may find traces of the underlying identity, actions, goals, norms and values, group relations, and interests of the ideological group(s) language that belong to and identify with in the current context. Most obvious here is the general polarization between a positive self-presentation and negative other-presentation, and the ways in which positive and negative attributes tend to be emphasized or minimized by the expressions and meanings of text and talk. But we have also seen that other than polarized attitudes can be expressed in ideological discourse, e.g., when the identity, actions, goals, norms and values, and resources of the group are being imposed or discussed, for instance in order to inspire, motivate, propagate cohesion and unity, and hence to strengthen the societal power of a group. The legitimatization of the control of scarce resources and other discursive forms of domination are an especially characteristic way of applying ideological control in the public sphere, typically so in terms of alleged 'higher' powers, such as those of Nature, God, Science, Reason or the People.

We have also recalled that whatever such typical 'ideological structures' of discourse may be, one always needs to analyse them in the current text, context and cognition. That is, *discourse structures do not have ideological functions in isolation*, but only when they are controlled by the underlying ideological structures shared by a social group, and within ideologically-defined texts and contexts, for instance as part of the practices that contribute to the interests of the in-group.

FURTHER READING

There is a vast literature on ideology, comprising thousands of books, especially in the humanities and social sciences. Some of these books have been referred to above in some *Bibliographical notes*. Among the many books on ideology we especially recommend the following ones. We also recommend some articles (for downloading) with concrete ideological analysis.

Billig, M. (1982). *Ideology and social psychology. Extremism, moderation, and contradiction*. New York: St. Martin's Press.
This book is a representative study within the field of discursive psychology by an author who has a long and eminent track record in social psychology, who has written extensively about ideology (e.g., about nationalism) and formulates a 'rhetorical' approach to the 'dilemmas' posed by ideologies.

Eagleton, T. (1991). *Ideology. An introduction*. London: Verso Eds.
For years the classical introduction to the study of ideology. *Very well informed about history and strategies of ideology.*

Fowler, R. (1991). *Language in the news. Discourse and ideology in the British press*. London: Routledge.
A classic collection of studies of ideology in news discourse by the late professor Fowler, the founder, at the end of the 1970s, with Gunther Kress, Tony Trew, and Bob Hodge of 'critical linguistics' — which is at the origin of Critical Discourse Studies. This book is still relevant for hands-on critical news analysis.

Fraser, C., & Gaskell, G. (Eds.). (1990). *The social psychological study of widespread beliefs*. Oxford Oxford New York: Clarendon Press Oxford University Press.
An excellent collection of papers in social psychology dealing with various kinds of social beliefs and that will be relevant to place ideologies among other forms of socially shared representations.

van Dijk, T. A. (1998). *Ideology: A multidisciplinary approach*. London, England UK: Sage Publications.
The only multidisciplinary study of ideology defined as the basis of the socially shared beliefs of a group, and with special interest in the application in the field of racist ideologies. This book elaborated the theory of ideology presented in this chapter.

ONLINE READING

The following articles published in *Discourse & Society* are available at www/sagepub.co.uk/discoursestudies and are recommended as examples of detailed ideological analysis.

Billig, M. (1990). Stacking the cars of ideology: The history of the "Sun Souvenir Royal Album". *Discourse & Society*, 1(1), 17–38.

Bonilla-Silva, E., & Forman, T. A. (2000). "I am not a racist…": mapping White college students' racial ideology in the USA. *Discourse & Society*, 11(1), 50–85.

Chiapello, E., & Fairclough, N. (2002). Understanding the new management ideology: a transdisciplinary contribution from critical discourse analysis and new sociology of capitalism. *Discourse & Society*, 13(2), 185–208.

De Goede, M. (1996). Ideology in the US welfare debate: neo-liberal representations of poverty. *Discourse & Society* 7(3), 317–357.

Van Dijk, T. A. (1995). Discourse Semantics and Ideology. *Discourse & Society*, 6(2), 243–289.

REFERENCES

Abercrombie, N., Hill, S., & Turner, B. S. (Eds.) (1990). *Dominant ideologies*. London: Unwin Hyman.

Adorno, T. W. (1950). *The Authoritarian personality*. New York: Harper.

Adams, I. (1993). *Political ideology today*. Manchester: Manchester University Press.

Aebischer, V., Deconchy, J. P., & Lipiansky (1992). *Idéologies et représentations sociales*. Cousset: Delval.

Afshar, H. (Ed.). (1987). *Women, state and ideology: studies from Africa and Asia*. New York: Macmillan.

Agger, B. (1992). *Cultural studies as critical theory*. London: Falmer Press.

Althusser, L. (2008). *On ideology*. London New York: Verso.

Andrain, C. F., & Apter, D. E. (1995). *Political protest and social change. Analyzing politics*. Washington Square, N.Y.: New York University Press.

Apple, M. W. (1979). *Ideology and curriculum*. London Boston: Routledge & K. Paul.

Apple, M. W., & Weis, L. (Eds.). (1983). *Ideology and practice in schooling*. Philadelphia: Temple University Press.

Aronowitz, S. (1988). *Science as power. Discourse and ideology in modern society*. Minneapolis: University of Minnesota Press.

Asperen, E. (2005). *Intercultural communication & ideology*. Utrecht: Pharos.

Bailey, L. (1994). *Critical theory and the sociology of knowledge. A comparative study in the theory of ideology*. New York: P. Lang.

Ball, T., & Dagger, R. (1990). *Political ideologies and the democratic ideal*. New York, NY: HarperCollins.

Ballaster, R. (1991). *Women's worlds. Ideology, femininity and the woman's magazine*. New York: Macmillan Pubs.

Bastow, S., & Martin, J. (2003). *Third way discourse. European ideologies in the twentieth century*. Edinburgh: Edinburgh University Press.

Billig, M. (1982). *Ideology and social psychology. Extremism, moderation, and contradiction*. New York: St. Martin's Press.

Blommaert, J. (Ed.). (1999). *Language ideological debates*. Berlin New York: Mouton de Gruyter.

Burton, F., & Carlen, P. (1979). *Official discourse. On discourse analysis, government publications, ideology and the state*. London Boston: Routledge & Kegan Paul.

Carlsnaes, W. (1981). *The concept of ideology and political analysis: A critical examination of its usage by Marx, Lenin, and Mannheim*. Westport, Conn.: Greenwood Press.

CCCS (Centre for Contemporary Cultural Studies), (1978). On ideology. London: Hutchinson.

Charles, N., & Hintjens, H. M. (Eds.). (1998). *Gender, ethnicity, and political ideologies*. London New York: Routledge.

Dant, T. (1991). *Knowledge, ideology & discourse. A sociological perspective*. London: Routledge.

De Saussure, L., & Schulz, P. (Eds.). (2005). *Manipulation and ideologies in the twentieth century. Discourse, language, mind*. Amsterdam Philadelphia: J. Benjamins Pub. Co.

Diesing, P. (1982). *Science & ideology in the policy sciences*. New York: Aldine Co.

Dirven, R. (Ed.). (2001). *Language and ideology*. Amsterdam Philadelphia: J. Benjamins Co.

Eagleton, T. (1991). *Ideology. An introduction*. London: Verso Eds.

Festenstein, M., & Kenny, M. (Eds.). (2005). *Political ideologies. A reader and guide*. Oxford New York: Oxford University Press.

Fowler, R. (1991). *Language in the news. Discourse and ideology in the British press*. London: Routledge.

Fox, R., & Fox, J. (2004). *Organizational discourse: a language-ideology-power perspective*. Westport, Conn.: Praeger.

Fraser, C., & Gaskell, G. (Eds.). (1990). *The social psychological study of widespread beliefs*. Oxford Oxford New York: Clarendon Press Oxford University Press.

Freeden, M. (1996). *Ideologies and political theory. A conceptual approach*. Oxford New York: Clarendon Press Oxford University Press.

Gane, M. (Ed.). (1989). *Ideological representation and power in social relations: Literary and social theory*. London New York: Routledge.

Garner, R. (1996). *Contemporary movements and ideologies*. New York: McGraw Hill.

Garzone, G., & Sarangi, S. (2008). *Discourse, ideology and specialized communication*. Bern New York: Peter Lang.

Gee, J. P. (1990). *Social linguistics and literacies. Ideology in discourses*. London England New York: Falmer Press.

Guillaumin, C. (1995). *Racism, sexism, power, and ideology*. London New York: Routledge.

Hodge, R., & Kress, G. R. (1993). *Language as ideology*. London: Routledge.

Hall, S., Hobson, D., Lowe, A., & Willis, P. (Eds.). (1980). *Culture, Media, Language*. London: Hutchinson.

Hwang, S. D. (1998). *Bureaucracy vs. democracy in the minds of bureaucrats: To what extent are these ideologies compatable with one another*. New York: P. Lang.

Jones, R. K. (1984). *Ideological groups: Similarities of structure and organisation*. Aldershot, Hampshire, England Brookfield, Vt., U.S.A.: Gower.

Jost, J. T., Federico, C. M., & Napier, J. L.(2009). *Political ideology: Its structure, functions, and elective affinities. Annual Review of Psychology*, 60 (), 307–337.

Kinloch, G. C. (1981). *Ideology and contemporary sociological theory*. Englewood Cliffs, N.J.: Prentice-Hall.

Laclau, E. (1979). *Politics and ideology in Marxist theory: capitalism; fascism; populism*. London: Verso.

Laraña, E., Johnston, H., & Gusfield, J. R. (Eds.). (1994). *New social movements. From ideology to identity*. Philadelphia: Temple University Press.

Larraín, J. (1979). *The concept of ideology*. London: Hutchinson.

Larsen, I., Strunck, J., Vestergaard, T. (Eds.). (2006). *Mediating ideology in text and image*. Amsterdam: Benjamins.

Lazar, M. M. (Ed.). (2005). *Feminist critical discourse analysis. Gender, power, and ideology in discourse*. Houndmills, Basingstoke, Hampshire New York: Palgrave Macmillan.

Leach, R. (2002). *Political ideology in Britain*. New York: Palgrave.

Malrieu, J. P. (1999). *Evaluative semantics: Cognition, language, and ideology*. London New York: Routledge.

Mannheim, K. (1936). *Ideology and utopia: An introduction to the sociology of knowledge*. London New York: K. Paul, Trench, Trubner & co., ltd. Harcourt, Brace and company.

Morley, D., & Chen, K. H. (Eds.). (1996). Stuart Hall. *Critical dialogues in cultural studies*. London: Routledge.

Mumby, D. K. (1988). *Communication and power in organizations. Discourse, ideology, and domination*. Norwood, N.J.: Ablex Pub. Corp.

Oberschall, A. (1993). *Social movements. Ideologies, interests, and identities*. New Brunswick, NJ: Transaction.

Parekh, B. C. (1982). *Marx's theory of ideology*. Baltimore: Johns Hopkins University Press.

Pêcheux, M. (1982). *Language, semantics, and ideology*. New York: St. Martin's Press.

Pütz, M., Neff-van Aertselaer, J. and van Dijk, T. A. (Eds.). (2004). *Communicating ideologies. Multidisciplinary Perspectives on Language, Discourse and Social Practice*. Frankfurt: Lang.

Reis, C. A. A. (1993). *Towards a semiotics of ideology*. Berlin: Mouton de Gruyter.

Reis, E. M. (1993). *Developing writing skills for students with bilingual special education needs. Journal of Instructional Psychology*, 20(4), 298-301.

Römer, R. (1985). *Sprachwissenschaft und Rassenideologie in Deutschland*. München: W. Fink.

Rosenberg, S. W. (1988). *Reason, ideology, and politics*. Princeton, N.J.: Princeton University Press.

Rossi-Landi, F. (1990). *Marxism and ideology*. Oxford New York: Clarendon Press Oxford University Press.

Rudé, G. F. E. (1980). *Ideology and popular protest*. New York: Pantheon Books.

Ryan, B. (1992). *Feminism and the women's movement. Dynamics of change in social movement ideology, and activism*. London: Routledge.

Schäffner, C., & Kelly-Holmes, H. (Eds.). (1996). *Discourse and ideologies*. Clevedon Philadelphia: Multilingual Matters.

Seliger, M. (1976). *Ideology and politics*. London: Allen & Unwin.

Simons, H. W., & Billig, M. (Eds.). (1994). *After postmodernism: Reconstructing ideology critique*. Thousand Oaks, CA: Sage Publications, Inc.

Smith, D. E. (1990). *The conceptual practices of power. A feminist sociology of knowledge*. Boston, Mass.: Northeastern University Press.

Sutton, F. X. (1990). *Ideology and social structure: A study of radical Marxism*. New York: Garland.

Talshir, G., Humphrey, M., & Freeden, M. (Eds.). (2006). *Taking ideology seriously. 21st century reconfigurations*. London New York: Routledge.

Thompson, J. B. (1984). *Studies in the theory of ideology*. Berkeley: University of California Press.

Thompson, J. B. (1990). *Ideology and modern culture: Critical social theory in the era of mass communication*. Stanford, Calif.: Stanford University Press.

Threadgold, T., et al. (Eds.). (1986). *Semiotics, ideology, language*. Sydney: Sydney University.

Van Dijk, T. A. (1993). *Elite discourse and racism*. Newbury Park, Calif.: Sage Publications.

Van Dijk, T. A. (1998). *Ideology: A multidisciplinary approach*. London, England UK: Sage Publications.

Van Dijk, T. A. (2008a). *Discourse and Context. A sociocognitive approach*. Cambridge: Cambridge University Press.

Van Dijk, T. A. (2008b). *Discourse and power*. Houndmills, Basingstoke, Hampshire New York: Palgrave Macmillan.

Ward, I. (1994). *Literacy, ideology, and dialogue: Towards a dialogic pedagogy*. Albany: State University of New York Press.

Wodak, R. (Ed.). (1989). *Language, power, and ideology. Studies in political discourse*. Amsterdam Philadelphia: J. Benjamins Co.

Wodak, R. (Ed.). (1997). *Gender and discourse*. London Thousand Oaks, Calif.: Sage Publications.

Wodak, R., de Cillia, R., Reisigl, M., & Liebhart, K. (1999). *The discursive construction of national identity*. Edinburgh: Edinburgh University Press.

Wuthnow, R. (1989). *Communities of discourse: Ideology and social structure in the Reformation, the Enlightenment, and European socialism*. Cambridge, Mass.: Harvard University Press.

Zeitlin, I. M. (1994). *Ideology and the development of sociological theory*. Englewood Cliffs, NJ: Prentice Hall.

Zima, P. V. (1981). *Semiotics and dialectics: Ideology and the text*. Amsterdam: J. Benjamins.

Žižek, S. (Ed.). (1994). *Mapping ideology*. London New York: Verso.

Index

aboriginal peoples and languages, 249–52, 338
aboutness, 48, 50
abstract structures in discourse, 5
accessibility of referents, 45–6
Acebes Paniagua, Ángel, 399–403
Achard, P., 306
active, *semi-active* and *inactive* concepts in discourse, 45
adverbial clauses, 27–8
affect displayed in conversation, 26
affordance, 110, 122
agoraphobia, 75–6
airline pilots, 296–8
'Alberto', 275–8
Althusser, Louis, 306, 360–1
Amazon (online retailer), 135
Amnesty International, 116, 120
anaphora, 45–7
animated agents, 137
Antaki, C., 271
anthropology, linguistic, 1, 4, 195, 332–6, 339, 353
antonymy, 320
arbitrary signs, 122
argument structure and argument reconstruction, 22–5, 97
argumentation, 85–104, 365
    Aristotelian, 87, 89–91
    contemporary perspectives on, 91–6, 102–3
    defining features of, 95
    field-dependent standards for, 94
    history of, 87–91
    practical applications of theory of, 102–4
    pragma-dialectical theory of, 94–5, 103–4
    valid and *invalid*, 88–9
Ariel, M., 45–6
Ariès, Philippe, 113–14

'Aristotelian' categories of grammar, 12–15
Aristotle, 64, 71, 73–4, 87, 89–91, 303
artficial intelligence, 2, 42
Ashcraft, Karen, 296–8
attention, cognitive processes of, 55–6
attention model of episode structure, 47
attitudes, definition of, 389
audience involvement in story-telling, 77
audio recordings, use of, 12, 168, 170
Augoustinos, M., 246–7, 254
Austin, John, 143–4, 148, 159–60, 315
AutoTutor, 137–8
'avoidance' registers of language, 338

Bacall, Lauren, 112, 119
backbone information, 52
background information, 51–2
Bain, P., 292–3
Baker, P., 366
Bakhtin, Mikhail, 77, 338, 361
Barker, J.R., 289
Barthes, Roland, 108, 120
Bauman, Zygmunt, 265
belief systems, 381–2, 389
Bell, E.L., 294
Beller, S., 248
Benveniste, E., 306
Berman, Laine, 225
biclausal constructions, 28–9
Biden, Joe, 270
Birdwhistell, Ray, 107
Black, J.B., 46
Blair, J.A., 94
Blair, Tony, 6, 314

Bloustien, Gerry, 219–20
blueprint metaphor of discourse, 38
Blumer, Herbert, 267
Boas, Franz, 333, 335, 337
Bolinger, Dwight, 9, 309
Booth, R.J., 131
The Border (television series), 249–51
Bourdieu, Pierre, 361, 369
Bower, G.H., 46
Brando, Marlon, 119–20
British National Party (BNP), 242, 256–8
Brown, Penelope, 144, 147, 152–3
Brummans, Boris, 291–2
Bruner, J., 72, 74
Burawoy, M., 287
bureaucratic structures, 289
Büring, D., 55
Burke, K., 65, 67–8, 71
Burr, Vivien, 265
Butler, Judith, 222, 265–6

CADAAD conferences, 310
call centres, 292–3
Capps, L., 75–6
Capps, Walter, 340–1, 346–8
'cargo cults', 336
Carlson, T.B., 159
categoriality, 16
categorical syllogisms, 87
categorization processes, 274–9
category overlap, 30
category sets of knowledge, 179
Céditec network, 307
Chafe, W., 18–19, 45, 54–6
Charlton, Michael, 366–9
'chick lit', 226
childhood
    discourses of, 113–14
    language acquisition in, 156–7
Chilton, K., 185

Chilton, P., 310, 363–5
Chomsky, Noam, 156, 309, 337
Clark, H.H., 45, 159
Clayman, S.E., 183–4
cleffs, 54
coerced behaviour, 311–12
cognition, 126–40
    embodied, 128
    see also discourse cognition
cognitive approaches to discourse
    semantics, 55–6
cognitive science, 1–2, 4, 10,
    102, 131
Coh-Metrix tool, 131–2
coherence and *cohesion* in text, 131–2
Collinson, D., 287–8
commissives, 319
communication
    intentional, 144
    mediated, 248–9
    non-verbal, 108–9
    pragmatic, 127
    written, 109
communication studies, 1–2, 4
comprehension, 128–39
    breakdown of, 128–30
    calibration of, 133
    increases in, 139
    of technical texts, 133–4
computational linguistics, 131–2, 138
computer applications, 350–3
conceptual representations in
    discourse, 39–40, 56–7
'concertive control', 289–90
Condor, S., 246
conduit metaphor of discourse, 38
connotation, 120, 122
constituent order, 21–2
construction-integration model
    of knowledge, 41, 56
constructionist theory of inference, 128
context models, 391–95
conversation, 26, 68, 70, 107,
    156–9, 222
    collaborative nature of, 30
    therapeutic, 74
    use of examples of, 184
conversation analysis (CA), 10,
    165–86, 195–6, 207, 271,
    274–5, 295, 314
    analytic concepts of, 168–72
    analytic programme of, 166–8
    analytic tasks and tools for, 172–83

conversational agents, 137–9
conversational implicatures, 146
conversational storytelling, 74–5
conversationalization of
    discourse, 363
corpus linguistics, 2, 131–2,
    307–10, 365–6
Cosmopolitan magazine, 117–18
Coulthard, R.M., 42
Coupland, N., 267–8, 274
critical discourse analysis
    (CDA), 158, 195, 274,
    307, 357–74
    in action, 366–73
    in context, 359–60
    current approaches and
        developments in, 361–6
    definition of, 357–9
    distinctiveness of, 357–8
    methodological diversity of,
        358–9, 374
    and social problems, 368–9
    theoretical origins of, 360–1
critical linguistics (CL), 361–2
critique, concept of, 358, 361
cultural difference, 155
culture
    definitions of, 333–5
    semiotic theory of, 333
    use of term, 331
cyber-bullying, 224

Daily Telegraph, 379–82, 389–97
Dascal, M., 159
databases of everyday talk, 30
Davies, B., 272
Davies, Julia, 219
deafness, 334, 338, 344, 351–3
declaratives, 42
deep knowledge and deep
    comprehension, 133
DeFrancisco, Victoria, 225
demonstratives, 24
Deroche, C. and J., 249–50
Derrida, Jacques, 305
Descartes, René, 303
design, 114–18, 122
Destutt de Tracy, Antoine-Louis-
    Claude, 381
developmental pragmatics, 156–7
dialectic, 90–2, 96
dialectical relationships, 357–8
dialectification, 92

dialects, 120
dialogue, institutional, 191–212
DiBenedetto, Tamra, 224
digital displays, 134–5
digitized data, 12
Dik, S., 54
disclaimers, 244–5
discourse
    and cognition, 126–40
    constraints on, 394
    and context, 11, 337
    conversationalization of, 363
    and culture, 331–53
    definition of, 4
    genres of, 5
    and ideology, 371–2, 395–6, 403
    and interaction, 267–8
    levels of, 126–31
    multi-layered nature of, 159
    and organization, 284–5
    and power relations, 285–6, 358,
        369–70
    properties of, 3–4
    sequential organization of, 160
    and social life, 370, 373
    'technologies' of, 360
    use of term, 331, 357
discourse analysis, 195, 233
    ideological, 393–5
    interpretative and *explanatory*
        nature of, 372–3
    recent developments in, 264
    see also critical discourse
        analysis
discourse cognition, 130–4, 140
discourse data, 332
discourse-functional linguistics,
    8–12, 15–19, 30–1
    explanatory themes in, 17–18
    goals of, 8–9
discourse-historical approach
    (DHA), 364
discourse management, 39–40
discourse pragmatics, 143–60
    research on, 155–6
discourse processes and processing,
    127, 132
discourse semiotics, 107–24
discourse studies
    cross-disciplines related to, 2–3
    development of, 1–2
    limitations of, 7
discourse transitivity, 13–14

discourses
  characteristics of, 114
  definition of, 113
distance model, 47–8
dominance and domination, 3–4, 56
Drew, P., 185
Du Bois, J.W., 11, 17, 22–3, 45
Dummett, A. and M., 255–6
Duranti, A., 25, 346
dynamic conception of discourse,
  5, 56

Edwards, D., 246
Eemeren, F.H., 94–5
eLearning, 136
embodied cognition, 128
emergency services, 204–7
empathy towards the referent, 23
Engels, Friedrich, 381
engineering design work, 350–1
Englebretson, R., 16–17
enthymemes and enthymematic
  argument, 89–90, 98
episodes as semantic units, 46–7
epistemic communities, 384–5
epistemic order, 171–2
equivocation, 90
ergative pattern, 23
Erikson, Erik, 265
Erteschik-Shir, N., 56
ethnographic studies, 195–6, 287,
  294, 332–7, 353
European Union (EU), 364
euthanasia declarations, 291–2
event lines, 52
Every, D., 246–7, 254
everyday life
  categories of talk in, 16–17
  conversation analysis of, 168
  databases of talk from, 30
  discursive practices in, 288
  narrative in, 64–80
  racist talk in, 245–8
evoked referents, 45
expert discourse, 112

face, maintenance of, 152–3
face-threatening acts (FTAs), 153
Fairclough, N., 242–3, 309, 360–3
Fairhurst, G., 284–5
fallacies, 87, 90, 95–6, 103–4
family members, talk amongst,
  77, 80, 185

Feld, S., 65
felicity conditions for speech acts,
  148, 315, 318
femininity, 222–3, 229–30; *see also*
  'power femininity'
feminism and feminist scholarship,
  217, 220–3, 226–7, 234, 265,
  293–7, 390–92
Feynman, Richard, 336
Fiala, Pierre, 307
field-dependent and *field-
  independent* elements of
  argumentation, 94
figures of speech, 146
film acting, 108
Finnish language, 24, 30
Flesch-Kincaid scores, 132
flight attendants, 294, 296
focus in linguistics, 40, 51–6
Fogelin, R., 101
footing concept (Goffman), 273
Forbes, L.C., 294
Ford, C.E., 26–7
foreground information, 51–2
Foucault, Michel, 249, 289–9, 292,
  305–8, 361
Fox, B.A., 47
Francis, M.E., 131
Frankfurt school of critical theory,
  358–61
French school of political discourse
  analyis, 306–7
Freud, Sigmund, 114
functional linguistics, 309

Garfinkel, Harold, 267
Geertz, Clifford, 283, 297
Geluykens, R., 27
gender identity, 222–3, 229–30,
  294–5, 339–40
gender relations, 218–33, 293–8
  and power, 220–33
genre, 5, 64, 126–30, 345–8
Gerbner, G., 248
German approaches to political
  discourse, 307–9
Gernsbacher, M.A., 41, 56
Gibson, James, 110
Giddens, Anthony, 265, 360
Gill, V.T., 183–4
given information in discourse,
  43–6
Givón, T., 13, 21, 45, 47–8

Glenn, C.G., 73
'global themes', 51
The Globe and Mail (Canadian
  newspaper), 251–2
Goatly, A., 310
Goffman, Erving, 71, 77, 152, 195,
  267, 273, 344
Goodwin, Charles 168
Goodwin, M., 66, 77, 168
Gordon, M., 55
Gordon-Walker, Patrick, 254
gossip, 66, 348
Graesser, A.C., 128
grammar, 8–17, 204–7, 335
grammatical constituents of
  stories, 73–4
grammaticalization, 9
Gramsci, Antonio, 360, 374, 381
Greenberg, J., 10
greetings, 166–7
Grice, H. Paul, 95, 98, 143–7,
  157–60, 318
Griffiths, Peter, 254–5
Grimes, J., 42
Grootendorst, R., 94
Grosz, B., 42
group relations, 395–7
Guindon, R., 46
Gumperz, John, 337
Gundel, J., 50

Habermas, Jürgen, 361
Hall, Kira, 222
Hall, S., 251
Halliday, M.A.K., 9, 44, 53–4,
  107, 110, 309, 361
Halutz, Dan, 146–7
Hamblin, C.L., 92
Harré, R., 272
Havel, V., 76
Haviland, S.E., 45
Hawks, Howard, 112
Heath, Christian, 168
Heath, S., 80
Hebrew language, 52
hegemony, concept of, 287, 360
Heidegger, Martin, 70
Heinemann, T., 204
Heinrich, J., 253
Henson, Bill, 113–14
Heringer, H.J., 308
Heritage, J., 171, 203, 208–9
Herring, Susan, 224

'He-said-she-said' narrative, 66, 70, 77
hierarchies of text and talk, 5
Hinds, J., 42, 47
historical approach to discourse, 4
Hobbes, Thomas, 304
Holmes, Janet, 224, 294–6, 298
Hopper, P., 13–17, 52
Houtlosser, P., 95
humour, role of, 288, 346–8
Hymes, Dell, 337

iconicity principle, 48
identities
    individual and *collective*, 268–9
    local and *global*, 274
    new types of, 344
    personal and *social*, 268–71, 274–5
    professional, 294
    situational, 268
identity, 263–79
    changing views of, 264
    definitions of, 265
    institutional, 200–1, 212
    and language, 264, 267–8
    and narrative, 275–8
    nature of, 340
    performance of, 266–7
    and the self, 265
    as a social construction, 265–7
    and style, 273–4
    see also gender identity;
        middle-class identity
identity processes, 269–79
'ideological square' tool, 243, 396–7
ideology, 286–7, 379–404
    and context, 394, 398
    and discourse, 371–2, 387–8, 395, 398, 403
    and group membership, 395
    history of, 381
    and knowledge, 384–5
    and mental models, 390–92
    professional, 388
    in relation to norms and values, 388, 395–6
    and resources, 396
    as social cognition, 386–7
    structure of, 385–6
    theory of, 381–7
Ieţcu-Fairclough, I., 365
imperatives, 42

implicatures, theory of, 41, 95, 98, 144–7
increment, 28
indexicality, 269–71
indirect speech acts, 149–52
Indonesian language, 225
inferable referents, 45
inferences, 41, 127–8, 145–6
    institutionally-specific, 209–11
'informal logic' movement, 94
information flow, 17–23, 26
information management in
    discourse, 38–40, 55–7
'information structure' (Halliday), 53–4
in-groups, 398
institutional interactions, 191–6, 211–12
institutional roles and identities, 196–207, 212
institutionally-relevant activities, 207–9
institutionally-specific inferences, 209–11
interaction and discourse, 267–8
interaction episodes, 172
interactional linguistics, 10, 17–18, 26–30, 194
interactionism, 275; *see also*
    symbolic interactionism
interrogation and interrogatives, 42, 198–9
intersubjectivity, 23, 156–9
intertextuality, 361
'invitational rhetoric', 234
Iraq War (2003), 310
Israel, 153

Jakobson, Roman, 336
James, W., 64
Japanese language, 16, 23–4, 30, 42, 48, 155
jargon, 203
jazz musicians, 349–50
Jefferson, Gail, 166, 168
Jews and antisemitism, 247–8
Johnson, Deborah, 224
Johnson, M., 120
Johnson, N.S., 73, 75
Johnson, R., 94
journalism, 251

Kaluli people, 65
Kantianism, 361

Kaplan, Richard, 251
Keating, E., 341–2, 352–3
Keenan, E., 27
Kelan, Elisabeth, 224
Kelly, Liz, 241
Kennedy, John F., 108
keys to interactional segments
    (Lerner and Schegloff), 184
keywords, 308
Kim, M.H., 51
Kindle system, 135
Kintsch, W., 40–1, 46, 56, 129
Kleiner, B., 245
knowledge, nature of, 384–5
knowledge integration, 38–41, 56–7
    and referential management, 46–8
known information in discourse, 44
Koller, V., 363
Korean language, 51
Krebs, B.-N., 308
Kundera, M., 64
Kwon, W., 366

labelling, 243
Labov, William, 69, 73, 267, 275
Lakoff, G., 120, 310
Lambrecht, K., 54
language, categories of, 345
language acquisition, 156–7
language conventions, 149–50
language use
    as cultural practice, 332
    and identity, 264, 267–8
    as social practice, 158–60, 242
    study of, 1–4
Lasswell, Harold, 305
Layton-Henry, Z., 255
Lazar, Michelle, 219, 226
learning environments, 138
Le Bart, C., 307
Lee, C., 55
left-dislocation, 27
legitimization and *delegitimization*
    of political regimes, 312, 318
Lemke, Jay, 362
Lerner, G.H., 184
Levinson, Stephen, 144, 147, 152–3
Lévi-Strauss, Claude, 336
Levy, D.M., 42
lexical choice, 201–3, 206
lexical classes, 15–16
lexical fields, 320
lexicalised clauses, 25–6

Lindström, A., 204
Linguistic Inquiry and Word Count
    (LIWC) system, 131
linguistic levels, 313–14
'linguistic turn' in political
    sciences, 305
linguistics,
    and political discourse, 305–11
    research on, 12
    'systemic' theory of, 361
    typological school of, 10
    see also corpus linguistics;
        critical linguistics;
        functional linguistics
literate and *non-literate* societies,
    349–50
local occasioning, 270–1
locutionary and *illocutionary*
    acts, 148–9
logic
    formal and *informal*, 94, 102
    symbolic, 89
    use of, 91
Longacre, R.E., 52
Lovering, Kathryn, 218

Machin, D., 118, 242
McLean, R., 119
macrostructures and
    macropropositions, 46–7
Madagascar, 147
Major, John, 314–24
Malay language, 22
Mandelbaum, J., 77, 185
Mandler, J., 73, 75
Mann, W.C., 42
Marslen-Wilson, W., 47
Marx, Karl, 286, 381
Marxism, 358–61, 381
masculinity, 218–25, 288
massively multi-player on-line
    role-playing games
    (MMORPGs), 137
Mathesius, V., 44
Mautner, G., 366
maxims of communication,
    144–7, 152
Mayan language, 24
Mayer, R.E., 136
Mayes, P., 23–4
Maynard, D.W., 212
Mead, George H., 265, 267
meaning

problem of, 37–8
sources of, 120
theory of, 144–7
meaning-making, 159–60,
    283–4, 297
meaning potential, 110, 123
media discourse, 157–8
media as semiotic resources, 121
Mehan, H., 42
membership categorization analysis
    (MCA), 274–5, 279
memorial activation, 45, 55
mental representations and mental
    models, 384–93, 397
metacognition, 134
metaphor, 38, 120–3, 310, 320–1
middle-class identity, 231
middle term (*M*) between subject
    and predicate, 87–9
minimalist art, 65
Mithun, M., 22
modelling of language, 31
modes, 121, 123
modus ponens reading, 99
Moe'ono Kolio, 341
moral messages, 79
morphosyntax, 31, 40–1, 56
Moses illusion, 134
motivated signifiers, 123
Mots: Les langages du politique
    (journal), 307
'moves' (Swales), 42–3
Mulderrig, J., 365–6
multi-clausal constructions, 28
multimedia, 135–6
multimodality, 30–1, 107–9,
    123, 220
multivocality, 273
Murphy, A.G., 294
music, 65
Muslim dress, 253, 257–8

Nadesan, Holmer, 290–1
narrative, 64–80, 157
    building of, 72–6
    co-authorship of, 68, 78–80
    collaborative problem-solving
        by means of, 76
    functions of, 70, 80
    and identity, 272, 275–8
    moral messages in, 79
    scope of, 64–8
    and time, 68–71

narrative identities, 77–8
National Front, 255
native languages, 335–6
neo-liberalism, 380
Neuenschwander, B., 119
neuroscience, 2–3, 132
new concepts and propositions, 53
new information in discourse, 43–4,
    130, 323
'new rhetoric', 91
New York City, 231
'newsworthiness', 22
Nixon, Richard, 108
'nominative-accusative' pattern in
    case-making, 23
normative discourses, 111–14, 121–3
noun phrase form, 19–24
    definite and *indefinite*, 20–1
nouns, use of, 15–16, 323
novels, 74

Ochs, E., 75–7, 80, 335
Olbrechts-Tyteca, L., 91
'online commentary', 208–9
Ono, T., 16, 23–4
Operation ARIES! (game), 138
opinions as distinct from facts, 389
oral narratives, 73
organizational discourse, 283–98
    critical studies of, 286–8
    feminist studies of, 293–7
    macro- and *micro*-level, 284,
        294, 298
    postmodern studies of, 288–93
Orwell, George, 304, 309
out-groups, 396–9

Palin, Sarah, 270, 273
panoptical views, 289–90
participant observation, 334–5, 353
Pennebaker, J.W., 131
Perelman, C., 91
performative utterances, 148
personal pronouns, use of,
    199–201, 317
personality tests, 290
personhood, construction of, 339–40
Pittenger, R.E., 107
plots of stories, 71–3
Pohnpeian language, 341–2
Polanyi, L., 69
Policastro, M., 73
politeness theory, 144, 147, 152–5, 160

political discourse, 157, 159,
    270–1, 303–25, 359, 365–6,
    370–1
  French approaches to, 306–7
  as a general human phenomenon,
    307
  German approaches to, 307–9
  and linguistics, 305–14
  and racism, 254–8
political discourse analysis (PDA),
    304–8, 311–24
  example of, 314–24
political lexicometry, 306–7
Polynesia, 335–6
polysemy, 320
Pomerantz, A., 176, 184–5
positioning, concept of, 271–3
post-feminism, 231
post-Fordism, 288–9, 292
postmodern studies, 288–93
potential inference, 21
'power femininity' (Lazar), 226
'power-knowledge', 292
power relations, 219–34, 287–93
  and discourse, 3–4, 285–6, 358,
    369–70
  gendered, 219–23, 226–33
PowerPoint, 112, 122, 136
pragma-dialectical theory of
    argument, 94–5, 103–4
pragmatic theory, 2–4, 143–6,
    155–60
  assumptions of, 158
  cross-cultural, 155
  see also developmental
    pragmatics; discourse
    pragmatics
Prague school of linguistics, 21, 44,
    50, 53, 107, 336
predicate of a conclusion (*P*), 87–9
predication, 244
Prince, E.F., 45, 54–5
production as a semiotic resource,
    121–3
professional identities, 294
professional ideology, 388
projective devices, 29
pronouns, use of, 21; *see also*
    personal pronouns
Propp, V., 42
pseudo-ephedrine, 132
psychological subject and
    psychological predicate, 50

public opinion polls, 103
Putnam, L.L., 284–5

Question Understanding Aid
    (QUAID), 131
questions, asking of, 197–9

racism, 241–59
  in everyday talk, 245–8
  mass-mediated discourse of,
    248–54
  and political discourse, 254–8
radio, 147–8, 253
Rank Xerox, 115
Rankin, Ian, 127
Razack, S., 253
reciprocal friendships, 185
referential distance, 47
referential management of discourse,
    40, 43–8, 55
  and knowledge integration, 46–8
referring to other people, 199–200
reflexivity, 360, 373
Reisigl, M., 243–4, 248, 365, 369
relevance theory, 145
'repair mechanisms', 95, 171
representation and
    misrepresentation, political, 312
rhetoric, 4, 89, 303, 307; *see also*
    'invitational rhetoric'; 'new
    rhetoric'
rhetorical goals for discourse
    production, 39–40, 43
rhetorical management of discourse,
    39, 42–3
rhetorical structure theory (RST),
    42–3, 126, 129–30
Rhodes, J., 256
Richardson, J., 245, 255, 364–5
Ricoeur, P., 68–9
R.J. Reynolds (RJR) Tobacco
    Company, 96–104
role models, 112
Rosch, E., 13
Rudd, Kevin, 113–14

Sacks, Harvey, 166–7, 170, 196, 275
Samoa, 339, 345–6, 350
Sampson, B., 77
Sandy, Larissa, 225
Sapir, Edward, 333–5
Sartori, G., 304
Scannell, Paddy, 157

Schegloff, Emanuel A., 166–7,
    183–4
Schieffelin, B., 27
scientific narratives, 69, 72, 79
Searle, John, 143–4, 148–9, 315
self, concepts of, 265
self-explanations of text, 134
self-sealing arguments, 101
self-surveillance, 289
semantics, 37–9, 319–20
semiosis, 357
semiotic resources, 109–13, 119–23
  types of, 121–2
semiotic software, 112, 122
semiotics, 2, 123, 362; *see also*
    discourse semiotics; social
    semiotics,
sentence structure, 322–3
September 11th 2001 attacks,
    253, 310
sequential organisation
  of conduct, 170
  of discourse, 5, 160
settings for narrative events, 74
Sex and the City: The Movie,
    217–18, 226–33
sexism and sexist language, 218,
    224, 226
sexual harassment, 391–2
sexuality, 113–14
Shohet, M., 79
short-term memory, 47
Siber, Matt, 108
side-shadowing, 79
signifiers and *signifieds*, 110,
    120, 123–4
Sinclair, J.M., 42
Singer, M., 128
Sinnott-Armstrong, W., 101
situation models, 126, 133
smoking, 96–104
social constructionism, 233, 264–7
social identity, 268–71, 274–5
social interaction, 3, 152
social networking, 360
social psychology, 1, 305
social semiotics, 4, 109–13, 124, 362
socialism, 387, 389
socialization, 72, 80
socio-cognitive studies, 363–4
sociolinguistics, 4, 194
sociology, 1–2
Socratic dialogue, 91

'soft power', 366
sophisms and the Sophists, 90
speech acts, 42, 95, 144, 147–51,
 159, 194–5, 315, 318–19, 344
 armchair, laboratory and *field*
  methods of analysis of, 150
 see also indirect speech acts
speech communities, 195
speech events, 337–8
stakeholder groups, 286
stance-taking in discourse, 23–7
standpoint theory, 85–6
starting-point of an utterance, 48, 50
status of referents, 54
Steckley, John, 249
Stefani, Gwen, 121
Stein, N., 73
Stivers, T., 208–9
Stokoe, E., 246
stories
 construction of, 72–6
 function of, 76
 goal-oriented, 73–5
 key problematic events in, 75–6
 teller-driven and *recipient-driven*,
  77
story grammars, 73–4
story prefaces, 72
story-telling, 69, 71–80
'strategic functions', concept of,
 311–14, 325
'strategic manoeuvering', 95–6
stress on certain words, 53
structure-building model of
 knowledge integration, 41, 56
stylistics, 4
stylized utterances, 273–4
subject of a conclusion (*S*), 87–9
subject–verb combinations, 25
subjectivity, 23
 of employees, 289
The Sunday Times, 244
surface code, 126

Suzuki, R., 24
Swales, J., 42–3
syllogisms, 87–90
symbolic interactionism, 265, 267
symbolic logic, 89
syntax, 26–7, 322–3

taboos, 335–6
'talk-in-interaction', 12, 167–8, 191,
 211–12
Tao, H., 17
tautology, 146
Taylor, C., 77, 80
Taylor, Damilola, 244
Taylor, P., 292–3
technical texts, comprehension of,
 133–4
technical vocabularies, 202–3
telephone conversations, 185
television, 147–8, 249–51
text representations, 39–40
textbase, 126
Textopol, 307
Thatcher, Margaret, 255, 366–73
Thatcherism, 368–72
theatrical drama, 66
thematic management of discourse,
 40, 48–52, 55
themes, 55
 clause-level, 48–51
 lower-level and *higher-level*, 51
Thompson, S.A., 13–16, 42
Tomlin, R.S., 47, 52, 55
topics, 54–6, 323
 clause-level, 48–50
topoi, definition of, 244
Toulmin, S.E., 91–4
Trabasso, T., 128
tragedy, 73–4
transcripts, use of, 12, 168
transitive and intransitive verbs,
 13–15, 22–3, 323–4
translation, 155–6, 335–6

traumatic events, coping with, 131
Trethewey, A., 294
turn-taking, 26, 156, 170, 196–9
typography, 119–21

unexpressed premises, 98–9
unknown information in discourse,
 44–5
unused referents, 45
Updike, John, 155
uptake, concept of, 159–60
utterances, 144, 148, 159–60
 stylized, 273–4

van den Berg, H., 246
van Dijk, T.A., 40, 113, 243, 246,
 254, 274, 309, 363
van der Gabelenz, G., 50
van Leeuwen, T., 118, 365
VanLehn, K., 133
verbs, use of, 15–16, 323
video recordings, use of, 12,
 168, 170
visual discourse, 242
visual syntactic text formatting, 135
vocabularies, 202–3, 320, 338
voice, 119
Volosinov, V.I., 361

Waldheim, Kurt, 248, 364
Waletsky, J., 69
Weil, H., 53
Whorf, Benjamin Lee, 334
Widdicombe, S., 271
Willard, C.A., 103
Wittgenstein, Ludwig, 143
Wodak, Ruth, 243–5, 248, 310,
 364–5, 369
women's professional identities, 294
word order, 22, 323
World of Warcraft (game), 137

Yagua language, 54